Handbook of Research on IoT, Digital Transformation, and the Future of Global Marketing

Hatem El-Gohary
College of Business and Economics, Qatar University, Qatar

David Edwards
Birmingham City University, UK

Mohamed Slim Ben Mimoun
Qatar University, Qatar

IGI Global
PUBLISHER of TIMELY KNOWLEDGE

A volume in the Advances in Marketing, Customer Relationship Management, and E-Services (AMCRMES) Book Series

Published in the United States of America by
IGI Global
Business Science Reference (an imprint of IGI Global)
701 E. Chocolate Avenue
Hershey PA, USA 17033
Tel: 717-533-8845
Fax: 717-533-8661
E-mail: cust@igi-global.com
Web site: http://www.igi-global.com

Library of Congress Cataloging-in-Publication Data

Names: El-Gohary, Hatem, 1970- editor. | Edwards, David, 1968- editor. | Ben Mimoun, Mohamed Slim, 1974- editor.
Title: Handbook of research on IoT, digital transformation, and the future of global marketing / Hatem El-Gohary, David Edwards, and Mohamed Slim Ben Mimoun, editors.
Description: Hershey, PA : Business Science Reference, [2021] | Includes bibliographical references and index. | Summary: "This book offers an understanding of the different current digital age marketing trends with an aim to link industry with academia by providing useful insights on how to improve businesses ability in creating and maximizing customers' value and loyalty"-- Provided by publisher.
Identifiers: LCCN 2020050315 (print) | LCCN 2020050316 (ebook) | ISBN 9781799871927 (hardcover) | ISBN 9781799871941 (ebook)
Subjects: LCSH: Internet marketing. | Marketing. | Customer relations. | Electronic commerce. | Internet of things.
Classification: LCC HF5415.1265 .H3567 2021 (print) | LCC HF5415.1265 (ebook) | DDC 658.8/72--dc23
LC record available at https://lccn.loc.gov/2020050315
LC ebook record available at https://lccn.loc.gov/2020050316

This book is published in the IGI Global book series Advances in Marketing, Customer Relationship Management, and E-Services (AMCRMES) (ISSN: 2327-5502; eISSN: 2327-5529)

British Cataloguing in Publication Data
A Cataloguing in Publication record for this book is available from the British Library.

Advances in Marketing, Customer Relationship Management, and E-Services (AMCRMES) Book Series

Eldon Y. Li
National Chengchi University, Taiwan & California Polytechnic State University, USA

ISSN:2327-5502
EISSN:2327-5529

Mission

Business processes, services, and communications are important factors in the management of good customer relationship, which is the foundation of any well organized business. Technology continues to play a vital role in the organization and automation of business processes for marketing, sales, and customer service. These features aid in the attraction of new clients and maintaining existing relationships.

The Advances in Marketing, Customer Relationship Management, and E-Services (AMCRMES) Book Series

addresses success factors for customer relationship management, marketing, and electronic services and its performance outcomes. This collection of reference source covers aspects of consumer behavior and marketing business strategies aiming towards researchers, scholars, and practitioners in the fields of marketing management.

Coverage

- CRM in financial services
- CRM strategies
- Relationship Marketing
- E-Service Innovation
- Cases on Electronic Services
- Telemarketing
- Ethical Considerations in E-Marketing
- Web Mining and Marketing
- Data mining and marketing
- Online Community Management and Behavior

IGI Global is currently accepting manuscripts for publication within this series. To submit a proposal for a volume in this series, please contact our Acquisition Editors at Acquisitions@igi-global.com or visit: http://www.igi-global.com/publish/.

The Advances in Marketing, Customer Relationship Management, and E-Services (AMCRMES) Book Series (ISSN 2327-5502) is published by IGI Global, 701 E. Chocolate Avenue, Hershey, PA 17033-1240, USA, www.igi-global.com. This series is composed of titles available for purchase individually; each title is edited to be contextually exclusive from any other title within the series. For pricing and ordering information please visit http://www.igi-global.com/book-series/advances-marketing-customer-relationship-management/37150. Postmaster: Send all address changes to above address.

Titles in this Series

For a list of additional titles in this series, please visit: www.igi-global.com/book-series/advances-marketing-customer-relationship-management/37150

Management and Marketing for Improved Competitiveness and Performance in the Healthcare Sector
José Duarte Santos (Polytechnic Institute of Gaya, Portugal) and Inês Pereira (ISCAP, Polytechnic Institute of Porto, Portugal)
Business Science Reference • © 2021 • 315pp • H/C (ISBN: 9781799872634) • US $225.00

Advanced Digital Marketing Strategies in a Data-Driven Era
Jose Ramon Saura (Rey Juan Carlos University, Spain)
Business Science Reference • © 2021 • 342pp • H/C (ISBN: 9781799880035) • US $225.00

Blockchain Technology and Applications for Digital Marketing
Rohit Bansal (Department of Management Studies, Vaish College of Engineering, India) Pacha Malyadri (ICSSR, Center for Economic and Social Studies, India) Amandeep Singh (Chitkara Business School, Chitkara University, Punjab, India) and Asif Pervez (Jamia Millia Islamia University, India)
Business Science Reference • © 2021 • 329pp • H/C (ISBN: 9781799880813) • US $225.00

Big Data Analytics for Improved Accuracy, Efficiency, and Decision Making in Digital Marketing
Amandeep Singh (Chitkara Business School, Chitkara University, Punjab, India)
Business Science Reference • © 2021 • 310pp • H/C (ISBN: 9781799872313) • US $215.00

Handbook of Research on Future Policies and Strategies for Nation Branding
Victoria Pistikou (Democritus University of Thrace, Greece) Andreas Masouras (Neapolis University, Cyprus) and Marcos Komodromos (University of Nicosia, Cyprus)
Business Science Reference • © 2021 • 383pp • H/C (ISBN: 9781799875338) • US $295.00

Developing Successful Global Strategies for Marketing Luxury Brands
Fabrizio Mosca (University of Turin, Italy) Cecilia Casalegno (University of Turin, Italy) and Rosalia Gallo (Universitat Autònoma de Barcelona, Spain)
Business Science Reference • © 2021 • 351pp • H/C (ISBN: 9781799858829) • US $225.00

Insights, Innovation, and Analytics for Optimal Customer Engagement
Samala Nagaraj (Woxsen University, India)
Business Science Reference • © 2021 • 334pp • H/C (ISBN: 9781799839194) • US $195.00

IGI Global
PUBLISHER of TIMELY KNOWLEDGE

701 East Chocolate Avenue, Hershey, PA 17033, USA
Tel: 717-533-8845 x100 • Fax: 717-533-8661
E-Mail: cust@igi-global.com • www.igi-global.com

Editorial Advisory Board

List of Contributors

Table of Contents

Section 5
Specialised Research Areas

Detailed Table of Contents

adapt to this digital transformation. This study aimed to draw a framework for their omnichannel strategies and implementations considering the characteristics of luxury brands and customers.

In recent years, digital transformation has begun to significantly affect the business landscape, disrupting existing business models. In the midst of this revolution, oil and gas retail companies are experiencing a strong transformation of the whole industry, which is also driving the transformation of their processes, assets, and people. In this chapter, the authors explore how oil and gas retail companies are trying to redefine their business models by providing end-users with a wide range of smart and connected solutions. The main purpose of this work is to analyse, in the face of the digital transformation era, the potential that new technologies can unleash in mature and commoditized industries such as the one of oil and gas retail. In particular, the present work focuses on the digital transformation strategy of fuel retail companies based on the improvement of customer experience.

Contemporary marketing strategies have shifted from unidirectional to bidirectional logic, according to which the rise of digitization and of social networks are changing the concept of marketing itself. The most impactful digital technologies have been digital platforms and brand communities, which have exposed companies and consumers alike to new challenges, such as online purchasing experiences. As a result, luxury retailers, who have traditionally resisted rapid adoption of market trends, have begun embracing digitization as part of their marketing strategies. This chapter highlights how understanding this topic is crucial amid changing global economics that are reshaping how luxury consumers interact with retailers. Through a qualitative approach based on semi-structured one-to-one interviews with experts from a leading digital marketing company, this chapter intends to illustrate the critical factors (and related opportunities) that luxury brands will look to exploit in the near future. The results highlight the pervading separation between digital technology and luxury brands.

Information technology has advanced by delivering an exponential increase in computing power. Telecommunication technology has likewise advanced communicating capabilities. Convergence of these two technologies has become possible due to the rapid advancements made in the respective

The purpose of this chapter is to explore the media use and preferences of Generation Z as a foundation for destination media planning. This chapter used a quantitative method with a questionnaire used as primary data source with a sample of 299 respondents. Data were analysed using descriptive statistic method. The results showed that the majority of Generation Z uses and prefers online media while at the same time offline media shouldn't be ignored. This chapter provides recommendations for the destination marketing organizations (DMOs) and media planners to better understand the media habits of Generation Z to use them as a valuable input for destination media planning.

The aim of this chapter is to better understand the gap that exists between the literature dealing with multiple channels shopping behavior and the actual shoppers' behavior. Adopting a critical analysis of a large literature of research articles dealing with consumer behavior and retailing in a multiple channel context, covering the period from 2002 to 2020, this chapter identifies an important gap in the literature: generally the authors define the different situations of multiple channels retailing (e.g., multichannel, crosschannel, and omni-channel) from the company point of view, and the main distribution channels presented in the literature review do not reproduce the richness of variety of channels available to the shoppers. Implications for future research related to multiple channel retailing and shopping behavior are discussed.

Several research studies have focused on the conceptualization, measurement, and management of service quality and their effects in electronic environments. Most of them are based on a classic paradigm, which consists in relating the quality of e-service to customer satisfaction and loyalty. The prescribing intent of the e-service as a plausible consequence of the quality of the e-service has not received enough interest from the researchers. Along these lines, this chapter examined the direct effect of the quality of the e-service on the prescribing intention of the e-service by the consumer as well as the indirect effect through a mediating variable, which is the perceived online value of the consumer.

With the changing and transforming world, the relationship between consumers and brands began to change and transform. Nowadays, it is not enough for brands to produce quality products or provide quality service for consumers. Now, consumers expect brands to be sensitive to social, ecological, economic, or health problems. This situation has enabled the two concepts to become important and popular today: brand purpose and purpose-driven marketing. Brand purpose is the "why" the brand exists. And purpose-driven marketing is a marketing trend that aims to connect brands with their consumers through common social goals. It seems that the concepts of brand purpose and purpose-driven marketing will be more common in marketing communication. The notion of purpose will change the commercial dynamics of brands in the same way that digitalization transformed the way people buy and sell stuff. This is exactly why purpose is the new digital.

UK advertising agency managers' perspectives on the impact of digital media (threats and opportunities) on their roles and models of managing are explored in this chapter. In the context of digital creative strategy, and the advertising industry specifically, there is far less published work, much of which has been in the context of larger, often global agencies rather than on independent SMEs. This interpretive research reviews the literature then employs semi-structured in-depth interviews with creative managers within a range of UK SME advertising agencies to analyse their views and responses to digital media. The study finds four key themes which illustrate how managers in SME advertising agencies have responded: 1) digital media as a pre-test laboratory, 2) unclear boundaries among the actors within the nodes of the agency social network, 3) fewer financial resources but more dedication to creative concepts, and 4) reduction in customer information processing costs. Relationships with larger agencies are being redeveloped as opportunity, but SMEs also represent a threat to agencies through innovation.

The conceptual and technological transformation of word of mouth (WOM) is one of the most effective and old factors in customers' purchasing decisions. Although digital WOM is expressed as e-WOM, it is similar to traditional WOM, but it differs in the perception of trust, as well as in speed and scope. It affects the fate of companies both positively and negatively. For this reason, it is essential for marketers to inactively and proactively develop e-WOM strategies that are as personalized as possible to ensure that a positive mark is left on the customers. This study demonstrates the e-WOM strategies and tactics that are relevant today to provide guidance to marketers.

Preface

It is a great pleasure and honour to introduce the *Handbook of Research on IoT, Digital Transformation, and the Future of Global Marketing* book to academic societies and scholars in the field of marketing. The business world today is changing enormously due to many factors that affect every element of the business cycle worldwide. From globalisation to recession, in addition to other environmental forces, companies today face numerous challenges that have a great impact on business. Among the factors that are affecting the current way business is conducted are the emergence of marketing tools including the internet, internet of things (IoT), virtual reality, mobile applications, social media, electronic word of mouth (eWoM), artificial intelligence, digital marketing, and more that have a great impact not only on customers but also on companies. It is imperative for businesses to embrace the utilization of these tools in order to expand their customer base and provide unique, successful consumer experiences.

The *Handbook of Research on IoT, Digital Transformation, and the Future of Global Marketing* provides comprehensive coverage of current global marketing trends related to the use of technology. The book links the industry with academia by providing useful insights on how to improve businesses' ability to create and customise customer value and loyalty. Covering topics including e-commerce, mobile marketing, website development, and phygital customer experiences, this book is essential for marketers, brand managers, advertisers, IT consultants and specialists, customer relations officers, managers, practitioners, business owners, marketing and business associations, students, researchers, and academicians interested in incorporating the latest technologies and marketing strategies into their businesses and studies.

The book is divided into five sections, which are "Digital Transformation," "IoT," "E-Commerce," "Social Media," and "Specialised Research Areas."

Section 1 (Digital Transformation) start with Yuce chapter on the impact of digital transformation and virtual reality in tourism marketing. Within the chapter, Yuce build and present a body of knowledge about the relationship between growing digital transformation and the tourism industry from the marketing perspective. Yuce chapter strives to expand current understanding by exploring the functionalities and unique features of VR technology for productivity growth, consumer engagement, and creating alternative digitalised tourism opportunities.

Chapter 2 of Bolzan, Ventura and Fernandes investigate the future through QR code and present a case of its potential on a digital service. Then Chapter 3 of Ali and Fidha provide insight on the Digital Transformation of companies. They also look at the opportunity to co-create value with the consumer through Digital Transformation. Afterward, Iuga chapter (Chapter 4) investigate the degree of SMEs digitalisation in the context of European digital united market through providing a SMEs level of digitalisation analysis.

Chapter 5 of Polat provide an insight on the digital transformation of luxury brands. The author provided good illustration of omnichannel strategies and implementations.

While Chapter 6 of Sola, D'Angelo and Capo examined digital transformation in the energy industry offering insights on different digital transformation strategies for fuel retail companies, Chapter 7 of Colella and Amatulli investigated critical factors and opportunities of digital marketing and digital retail strategies in the luxury sector. Through a qualitative approach based on semi-structured one-to-one interviews with experts from a leading digital marketing company, Sola, D'Angelo and Capo illustrated the critical factors (and related opportunities) that luxury brands will look to exploit in the near future. The results highlight the pervading separation between digital technology and luxury brands.

In Section 2 of the book (IoT), Chapter 8 of Rao examined IOTs and its role as an enabler for human and business activities. Rao provided a brief over view of the concepts such cloud computing, ubiquitous, and pervasive computing in the context of Internet of Things. Further, Rao chapter discusses five case illustrations with the relevance of Internet of Things.

Section 3 (E-Commerce) contained two chapters investigating E-Commerce. The first one (Chapter 9) of Alavi and Ahuja examined the impact of consumers internet self-efficacy and user friendliness of websites on E-Commerce adoption. Within the same line of thoughts, the following chapter (Chapter 10) of Bhat and Dhar examined the role of E-Commerce in the development of India's indigenous product base.

Afterward, Section 4 of the book dealt with Social Media through three chapters. The first chapter (Chapter 11) of Ladwein and Ben Mimoun investigated the impact of social capital and time spent on Facebook on social recognition and attachment. Meanwhile, Chapter 12 of Nicolaou examined the development of business through the internet and social media. Within this chapter, the author examined the professional use of audio-visual media technologies through strategic tactics and practices. Finally, the last chapter within this part of the book (Chapter 13) of Ali Akbar and El-Gohary examined brand humour advertisements on a social network platform and its impact on online consumer engagement. The authors used the case of Instagram. The authors' analysed the influence of comic wit and satire on product involvement, brand familiarity and gender, and their impact on online consumer engagement on the social network platform. Their results provide evidence that both humour techniques have a significant impact on consumer engagement when product involvement is mediating their relationship.

Within Section 5 of the book, eight chapters discussed specialised research areas that is related to the topics covered in this book. The first chapter (Chapter 14) of Ammari and El Hassoumi examined phygital customer experience mixed approach of augmented reality and customer experience (DCX) in the context of heritage tourism. Within this chapter, the authors focused on heritage tourism. The authors argue that it is necessary to study how modern technology can be developed and implemented in a meaningful way to improve tourists' experience.

In Chapter 15 of Gam and Ammari, the authors investigated intelligent customer experience in a connected commerce environment. Moreover, in Chapter 16 of Kavran and Herman, generation z's media use and preferences as a foundation for a destination media planning process was investigated. While Chapter 17 of Ladwein, Ben Achma and Ben Mimoun provided a critical view on multiple channels retailing, Chapter 18 of Ben M'Rad examined the effect of the quality of the e-service on the prescription intent of the e-service (Integration of the perceived online value). Ben M'Rad examined the dimensions of e-service quality, and customer's perceived online value.

In Chapter 19, Gülmez provided insights on brand purpose and purpose-driven marketing from a digital viewpoint. Raghubansie and Samaradivakara in Chapter 20 investigated advertising agency creative managers' perspectives on the impact of digital threats and opportunities in UK SMEs. The study found four key themes, which illustrate how managers in SME advertising agencies have responded: 1) digital media as a pre-test laboratory, 2) unclear boundaries among the actors within the nodes of the agency social network, 3) fewer financial resources but more dedication to creative concepts and, 4) reduction in customer information processing costs. Relationships with larger agencies are being re-developed as opportunity but SMEs also represent a threat to agencies through innovation.

The last chapter (Chapter 21) of Şehirli investigated the transformation of WOM (word of mouth) from traditional to digital. The author also provided current recommendations for e-WOM usage.

Finally, the editors would like to thank all the authors for submitting their high quality research chapters to the this book and very much appreciate the editorial board support and commitment as the editors endeavour to make this book one of the most valued books in the field of E-Marketing.

Hatem El-Gohary
College of Business and Economics, Qatar University, Qatar

David Edwards
Birmingham City University, UK

Mohamed Slim Ben Mimoun
Qatar University, Qatar

Section 1
Digital Transformation

Chapter 1
The Impact of Digital Transformation and Virtual Reality in Tourism Marketing:
A Conceptualized Exploration

Ali Yuce
https://orcid.org/0000-0003-4700-2006
Independent Researcher, Turkey

ABSTRACT

The study is trying to build and present a body of knowledge about the relationship between growing digital transformation and the tourism industry from the marketing perspective. As information communication technologies became more sophisticated and affordable with their size, price, and functionalities, more innovative marketing approaches are emerged to influence the consumers' behaviours and perceptions that ultimately influence intention to visit a tourism product or service. Integration of smartphones with virtual reality has revolutionized digital marketing and the tourism industry by influencing consumers' attitudes and behaviours more than other technologies. Moreover, discovering the crucial features of VR technology can help to increase customer satisfaction and improve business growth in the tourism industry. Therefore, this chapter strives to expand our understanding by exploring the functionalities and unique features of VR technology for productivity growth, consumer engagement, and creating alternative digitalized tourism opportunities.

INTRODUCTION

Digital transformation oriented the industrial revolution 4.0, fourth Industrial revolution, influencing every aspect of our individual lives and our professional environment (Ghobakhloo, 2020; Silvestri, Forcina, Introna, Santolamazza, & Cesarotti, 2020). Industry 4.0 demands companies of all sizes in every industry and public organizations, including manufacturing, health, and education institutes. Furthermore, it also suggests that even ordinary individuals can change their classical mentalities, habits, behaviours, and

DOI: 10.4018/978-1-7998-7192-7.ch001

methods to ease the adaptation process and achieve sustainable business growth (Ghobakhloo, 2020; Stentoft, Adsbøll Wickstrøm, Philipsen, & Haug, 2020). The era of industrial revolution 4.0 phenomena offers sustainability profitability, comprising physical and sophisticated digital technologies such as artificial intelligence, cloud technology, intelligent robots, big data, autonomous vehicles, and immersive technologies (Ghobakhloo, 2020; Silvestri et al., 2020). These technologies aim to develop more applicable and sustainable business models, human resource management, improve the employees' competence, increase productivity, quality, and enhance the new customers' acquisition in rapidly changing personal and professional work environments (Ringberg, Reihlen, & Rydén, 2019; Silvestri et al., 2020).

How can organizations and individuals respond to these paradigm shifts (Sharma, Sharma, & Chaudhary, 2020) from a classical business environment to a more digitalized environment to promote their products and services in the tourism sector? First of all, the development, adaptation, and diffusion of technological innovations require businesses to develop innovative-based mindsets and competence to integrate and engage with sophisticated technologies (Buhalis, 2003; Buhalis & Law, 2008; Ringberg et al., 2019). Second, analyzing the relationships between the prospective technology's functionalities and the marketplace is another vital dimension to get the most optimal results. Lastly, obtaining the best technology to improve overall productivity and increase sales depends on its unique features. The quality, size, and cost of the hardware; functionality of software such as user-friendliness, engagement aspect is some but not all the essential concepts of a VR that influence users' perceptions and stimulate their purchasing intention. Hence, regardless of their size, organizations need to consider this selection process with great detail to produce the most effective marketing strategies that focus on human behaviour, attitude, and motivation that leads to purchase intentions (Buhalis & Sinarta, 2019; Yuce, Arasli, Ozturen, & Daskin, 2020).

Technology-driven marketing strategies broke the barriers and challenges that the classical approach suffered from instant accessibility and worldwide distribution of the products and services. Although suppliers and consumers tend to challenge innovative technologies or show resilience to accept them (Seyyedamiri & Tajrobehkar, 2019), digitalization continues to impact our lives with even more sophisticated technologies (Lahiri, Ding, & Chinzara, 2018). Adaptation of the most suitable innovative technologies in the marketing field has taken businesses to the next level that elicited a remarkable transformation in every aspect of the marketplace (Buhalis & Sinarta, 2019; Lahiri et al., 2018; Seyyedamiri & Tajrobehkar, 2019). Since the beginning of advancements in technologies, tourism has been evolved significantly (Sharma et al., 2020). Metaphorically, digitalization and tourism can be seen as two souls in a single body that improve the tourism industry's overall achievement and enhance consumers' experiences with the tourism products and services. Integrating the novel technology with the marketing field also greatly fueled business performance, operations, and growth in the tourism and marketing sectors (Katsikeas, Leonidou, & Zeriti, 2019; Taiminen & Karjaluoto, 2015). Digitalization also allowed companies and marketers to distribute the products and services globally at a light speed. Digital marketing allows marketers to develop strategies to achieve all the benefits mentioned above and customer acquisition and retention, challenging to accomplish the companies' and organizations' long-term objectives. All in all, digitalization presents numerous benefits for both suppliers and consumers because it presents more reliable, attractive, accessible, and cost-effective strategies (Taiminen & Karjaluoto, 2015).

BACKGROUND

Tourism and Technology

Tourism has been a catalyst for economic growth globally. Tourism and travel are a wide-ranging industry with significant direct, indirect, and induced impacts on developed or developing countries' economies from accommodation to tour operators besides many subsectors, but is not limited to construction and agriculture. Tourism has a remarkable impact on providing economic growth, creating employment opportunities, generating revenue, planning infrastructure improvements, and promoting economic activity at the local, national, and international levels. Tourism has been a savior for many countries to generate foreign exchange that acts as a cash flow to the liquidity pool to stimulate investments and international commerce. Furthermore, foreign exchange optimizes gross domestic product (GDP) that has a remarkable impact on developing countries economic growth and overall development. According to the World Tourism Organization (World Tourism Organization [WTO], 2019), tourism is the third-largest industry in which international tourist arrivals reached 1.5 billion around the globe after oil and chemistry industries globally. Tourism contributed an average of 10.3% to the world GDP that equals US$8.9 trillion; for some countries, GDP's contribution to the economies goes up to 20%. GDP indicates the value of the products and services produced by the tourism industry.

Moreover, according to the WTTC (2020), travel and tourism account for about 1 in 10 jobs, about 330 million jobs globally, and generated 6.8% of total exports in global trade in 2019. All these charming statistical information shows how the tourism and travel sector became a leading global economic industry. However, the supply side, particularly tourism destinations, strives to develop, adopt, and adapt newer approaches to influence consumers' perceptions. At the same time, they conserve their resources' value in its original form and strengthen their competitiveness status to survive in the highly challenging tourism industry (Crouch, 2011).

Tourism is a very vulnerable and unpredictable industry due to national or international related issues such as war, economic turnovers, and health issues such as Covid-19 that have dramatically affected the entire world. The global Covid-19 epidemic had a dramatic negative impact on each layer of the national or international commerce of all sizes worldwide. Due to the Coronavirus lockdowns, many companies are looking for ways to attain new customers to sustain their existence and be more efficient and productive in the tourism sector, which has been suffering more than any other sectors globally. However, the digital transformation era reshapes the marketing industry at a breakneck speed, and it changes how we work, travel, and even how we study. From the business perspective, the Covid-19 has also accelerated to adapt newer technology-driven solutions that help organizations, at least, to maintain their productivity as well as minimizing the business operational costs.

On the other hand, understanding the relationship between the desired technology for productivity and marketing purposes and consumers' purchase intention has been critical for achieving the business objectives. Therefore, business owners have been striving to understand how to influence customers' preferences, behavior, attitudes, and purchasing intentions. Moreover, the digital marketing era allows marketers to design, develop, and present more efficient and user-centric marketing solutions based on customers' preferences, behaviours, needs, and market trends (Taiminen & Karjaluoto, 2015). One of the most effective digital channels is the Internet that enabled numerous benefits for businesses, such as real-time interactive communication between consumers and suppliers and promoting the products and services worldwide (Agag & El-Masry, 2017; Eid & El-Gohary, 2013; El-Gohary, 2010; Lee &

Chung, 2008; Standing, Tang-Taye, & Boyer, 2014). The integration of a tremendous amount of data with advanced technology allows the companies to keep the customers besides developing the most efficient business improvement strategies that create a successful and sustainable business environment (Shah & Murthi, 2021; Taiminen & Karjaluoto, 2015). Digitalization helps organizations to access the necessary data to create more effective consumer-centered approaches gradually but increasingly. Immersive technologies, among many other digitalized technologies, have been a core and mainstream innovative technology. Immersive technologies' unique features also significantly impact consumers because they offer an interactive and engaging environment in which users engage with the immersive contents. Therefore, immersive technologies have been in the center of spotlights over the past few years in multi sectors, including marketing, tourism, health, and construction.

How and when the companies, organizations, and sites will adapt the virtual environments to break the accessibility barriers for their products and services, particularly in the face of hard times like the Covid-19 pandemic? Furthermore, most companies are worried about whether their investment in technology will maximize their business operation and help them achieve objectives. In other words, to what extent Return on Investment (ROI) into the digitalized platform will improve their efficiency and profitability? Most importantly, to what extent can VR technology transform the marketplace and influence potential customers' decision-making progress towards a touristic product or service during these unpredictable days? With the advent and availability of innovational technologies, companies and marketers could analyze the different aspects of consumer and supplier relationships by creating consumer-centric marketing strategies.

The tourism market consists of various direct and indirect subsectors that are interconnected together by digital technology, which needs to contribute the economic benefits with its novel characteristics rather than creating a negative impact on business and consumers with its disruption (Schweer & Sahl, 2017; Talwar, Talwar, Kaur, & Dhir, 2020). Therefore, the need to design, develop, deploy, and adapt the right and effective technology has not been as crucial for the companies, organizations, and destinations as it has been. Each business has a target population to sell its products. However, one of the most challenging steps for a business is forming a broad customer group that will buy them. Technology as the most crucial promotional tool helps organizations to create innovative based strategies and solutions to resolve customer acquisition issues (Law, Buhalis, & Cobanoglu, 2014; Yuce et al., 2020). Investing and implementing the right technology can help them develop customer acquisition and retention policies. VR innovative technology provides new insights and opportunities for marketers to create alternative, affordable, user-friendly, and convenient environments to minimize their pain and lower their marketing costs (Yuce et al., 2020). VR technology also allows customers to 'try before you buy' opportunity to purchase the touristic products and services remotely and virtually from their homes.

Digitalization and Transformation of Marketing

Regardless of the type of the economy, including whether they are private or public organizations, they are all involved with marketing activity. Marketing aims to help companies to achieve their business goals, objectives and enhance their business growth. Marketing's task is arduous since they are responsible for satisfying both suppliers and consumers. Companies and organizations strive to develop and produce goods and services that will be recognized, acknowledged, and valued by a broader population. If the consumers do not consider or find a product valuable (Shah & Murthi, 2021), all marketing efforts and the entire production process will also be wasted, even though it is developed and presented with the most effective marketing strategies. Furthermore, while the supply side expects the marketers to develop strategies to stimulate the selling process and increase volume extensively, customers are expected to be satisfied with the goods, ideas, or services in which people find value. Therefore, businesses heavily rely on effective marketing strategies that present the product's or service's quality dimension in a reliable way to impact the people significantly.

Yet, promoting goods or services is a significant but challenging task for marketers to create superior performance than their competitors. Regardless of what type of marketing strategy will be chosen, understanding and developing newer product awareness solutions and product visibility are essential marketing concepts. Companies should promptly create awareness in society or promptly target the client population to promote the products, ideas, and services they produce for potential consumers or clients. Hence, marketers compose specialized marketing strategies to make these products and services visible to the public by stimulating their awareness with the correct information using suitable materials. Creating product awareness and improving product visibility will help the companies and organizations to get the most optimal results, such as increasing the companies' profitability, achieving the return on investment objectives, and acquiring new customers whereas retaining the customers.

Moreover, a destination's reputation or image is regarded as a substantial and decisive factor influencing the consumers' decision-making process for a touristic organization, destination, or product (González-Rodríguez, Martínez-Torres, & Toral, 2016). Because there is a strong association between the image of a product, goods, and service with customer perception, creating such reliable or trustworthy image is crucial to surviving highly competitive even in a digitalized global e-commerce (Abubakar, Ilkan, & Sahin, 2016; González-Rodríguez et al., 2016). Marketers help organizations and companies to create positive images and minimize the negative images by focusing on the quality aspect of their goods, services, or ideas. Hence, creating a desirable destination image is closely related to the destination loyalty concept to increase the repurchase intentions and influence the loyal consumers' for their volunteer-based participation to promote the tourism products.

In this context, implementing a sophisticated marketing technology is a crucial factor that helps to understand marketing trends and consumers' behaviour to maximizing business growth, creating productive and efficient marketing strategies to gain competitive advantages. Despite all the significant impact of the tourism industry on local economies, however, destinations, sites, and other tourism sources are looking for ways to attract more people to their attractions through using all possible digital tools (Abubakar et al., 2016; Marasco, Buonincontri, van Niekerk, Orlowski, & Okumus, 2018). When an effective marketing strategy is planned and performed professionally with sophisticated technology, it can also present remarkable opportunities for all destination shareholders. Effective marketing will allow destinations, organizations, and companies to take and keep more visitors to their places. Advanced and practical technology will not only help to improve the acquisition number but also will increase the retention rates of the customers.

Furthermore, since marketers guide the companies, they should plan how and when a product should be promoted. Determining the right time and the most suitable digital platform can be performed after analyzing the market's needs and the relationship between the product and consumers with digital but effective technologies and scientific methods. Despite all financial, adaptation, and technical challenges, companies and organizations need to adopt the most valuable technologies to gain competitive advantages versus rivals.

Despite the digital market phenomena date back to the early 20th century. However, its impact on the marketing and ultimately tourism industry has been improved profoundly in recent years more than ever before. The advancement of the latest technologies, as mentioned earlier, played a role like a game-changer in producing highly efficient digital-driven promotional and advertisement strategies in addition to digital distributions around the world (Theodoridis & Gkikas, 2019). Artificial intelligence (AI) catalyzed digital marketing transformation even further in understanding the consumer decision-making process. AI allowed the marketers to change the data-based-driven approach to data and knowledge-based decision-making (Theodoridis & Gkikas, 2019). The data-based driven decision enables the marketers to assess the advantages and disadvantages of the current marketing approach on consumers' decision-making process.

Organizations and marketers spend a significant amount of time, budget, and effort to reach newer customers by taking their attention, boosting motivation, and increasing satisfaction toward selling products or services. Businesses' long-term success depends on whether they have the vision, mindset, and desire to integrate modern technologies into their business operations. Innovative technology transformation provides opportunities and newer insights for those who plan for sustainable business growth in the marketplace (Ringberg et al., 2019; Taiminen & Karjaluoto, 2015).

Digitalization is the cornerstone of the marketing field that allowed businesses to promote their products and services to broader people by conquering barriers such as timely accessibility issues and high business operational costs (Ringberg et al., 2019). The classical marketing approach has been undergone a significant shift since information and communication technologies dynamically reshaped the industry with the advent of new technologies such as big data artificial intelligence, immersive and cloud technologies, the Internet, websites, email, and social media (Eid & El-Gohary, 2013; Theodoridis & Gkikas, 2019). These technologies even had more impact on how we live and businesses are made or performed. For example, big data allows marketers to analyze the findings from a complicated data pool and then understand what factors drive customers' ultimate purchase intention by examining the relationship between buyer and product. On the other hand, the Internet had an unmeasurable and remarkable impact on both providers and consumers from performing business operations, destination promotions and influencing the consumers' behaviour in the tourism industry over the last three decades (Agag & El-Masry, 2017; Buhalis & Law, 2008; Eid & El-Gohary, 2013; El-Gohary, 2010; Law et al., 2014; Standing et al., 2014).

Development and deployment of innovative technologies throughout the world also flatten all the borders, whether they are visible or not. This remarkable momentum resulted in building global digital commerce, or so-called e-commerce, around the clock. This convenience lets a notable shift in widening the target population and allowed companies to expand their marketplace worldwide. This transition also created a more accessible, user-friendly, and easy-to-use digital market environment that provided instant communication, easy payment transaction, and the ability to sell the services through digital channels. Digitalization-driven international commerce expansion also allowed the companies to save a considerable amount of their budget by minimizing their operational costs such as marketing and intermediaries due to using the technology efficiently. Furthermore, this global expansion enabled them to attract and acquire a diverse group of customers globally, boosting their business potential, maximizing profitability, and enhancing products' value at local and international levels.

Digitalization has numerous benefits for both companies and consumers. Nevertheless, besides the positive impact of technologies on businesses of all sizes, there is considerable technology adoption resistance due to companies' limited budgets and consumers' unwillingness to use innovative technologies. (Talwar et al., 2020). The lack of an efficient budget to deploy and willingness to use these innovative technologies are the significant reasons for technology failure and business failure (Talwar et al., 2020). Moreover, some technologies may have many constraints that negatively impact business performance and customer satisfaction. Some of these critical factors that cause a technology failure are lack of efficient technical functionality, understanding the customer behaviour and the relationship between technology and the industry, attractiveness, and lastly, but not limited to customer-oriented functionality. Another critical challenge that the marketing field has faced over the past years is the bad reputation that marketers attained over the decades (Shah & Murthi, 2021).

Nonetheless, the VR-driven marketing approach has helped establish credibility between consumers and marketing since their reputation was melted due to only profitability with fake or deceitful marketing strategies. Unlike traditional marketing approaches, VR technology presents more attractive, credible, and engaging content with real places and objects instead of bogus products. Therefore, using reliable VR technology play an essential role in changing the perceived impaired integrity that consumers hold for the marketing field. This improved positive image with a good reputation is closely related to creating a sustainable future for long-run businesses (Shah & Murthi, 2021).

Digitalization is not free and easy to adapt, deploy and maintain the entire digital platform for all shareholders. First of all, the lifecycle of digital also requires a considerable amount of budget to replace the out fashioned ones with the current technologies. The business owners' perspectives demand business owners alter their vision, mindsets, and approaches to transform their marketing strategy from a classical system to a digital platform to obtain competitive advantages among numerous rivals (Ringberg et al., 2019). They also need to have a remarkable budget to invest in the latest technologies for a more professional workplace and network with their clients and customers. Nevertheless, implementing effective digitalization is cost-effective and contributes profoundly to the business growth with more engaged loyal customers and motivated employees when the long term is projected (Taiminen & Karjaluoto, 2015). Digital marketing also offers businesses to promote their products directly without hiring costly marketing experts and distributing their digitalized tourism products or services without the middlemen's need. In other words, investment in technology, including training and adaptation, will let companies save more on the costs than the traditional methods. At the same time, they promote their products and services globally. Digital transformation also allows organizations to collaborate with their customers and clients instantly and directly to provide practical solutions that will respond to the customers' or clients' demands, needs, or expectations related to the tourism products and services. Collaboration of supply and demand sides through digital channels will enhance the business efficiency and productivity and improve consumers' satisfaction and motivations.

From the consumers' perspective, the rapid transformation of innovative technologies has also reshaped the way consumers select, order, and pay for the products. With advanced technology opportunities, consumers can reach the products and services throughout the local and the international marketplace via digital or e-commerce throughout various digital channels and platforms all year round. Digital commerce platforms and channels also benefit consumers in making a more reasonable and affordable decision before purchasing the products or services.

From the marketing point of view, technological transformation and data abundance and the numerous and diversified digitalized tools help the industries, including marketers, develop consumer-centric rather than product-centric strategies to enhance the selling opportunities for the companies, destinations, and sites (Schweer & Sahl, 2017; Shah & Murthi, 2021). Marketers can develop potentially effective marketing strategies for a suitable market selection process and developing business strategies for the companies at local and international levels (Katsikeas et al., 2019).

In this context, the digital revolution also creates significant advantages for the companies by analyzing the consumers' behaviour, needs, and expectations that will allow them to present the right product and service. Deploying and developing such sophisticated technologies enable companies as sustainable and profitable business models to have competitive advantages to outpace their rivals and improve their performance in the marketplace (Katsikeas et al., 2019). Again, companies and marketing firms need to have the applicable, suitable, and effective technologies that will enable them to conduct the deep analysis to evaluate the product's value, consumers' decision-making process, and the organization's operational power.

Virtual Reality and Tourism Marketing

The proliferation of immersive technologies has been placed VR technology on the spot of emerging technologies as a substitute marketing device. But, first of all, what is VR? Although VR technology is acknowledged as an emerging technology in many studies, the history of VR dates back as far as the 1960s. Virtual reality is composed of both software with 3D videos and hardware with a smartphone or computer and a VR headset. VR is usually defined as a computer-generated engaging simulation that creates a sense of presence on the individuals of the depicted location or environment (Li & Chen, 2019). According to the studies, VR creates effective engagement with its some critical features: first, immersion which allows the deportation from the real world to the virtual environment without the rejection of our senses; second, interactivity that allows the users can participate and control the as if they are in the depicted content, finally, a presence that breaks the location, time, and content barriers in the minds of the people and enables them to travel multiple locations around the globe, such as in the case of Matrix.

VR technology brought newer aspects to the tourism industry by expanding the opportunities to meet business owners and consumers (Guttentag, 2010; Pestek & Sarvan, 2020). Unlike the other digital technologies-driven marketing strategies, the primary functionality of VR is attracting more people and improving business growth by providing more enjoyable and satisfactory moments using VR technology. Hence, in addition to the significant characteristics, VR technology influences the travelers' perceptions, attitudes, and purchase intentions due to improved motivation and increased satisfaction, and the enhanced enjoyment they obtain with the VR environment. (Li & Chen, 2019; Yuce et al., 2020). Many studies focus on how VR physical dimensions ensure user-friendliness and easy-to-use functionality in terms of implementing it for business purposes. However, some other features such as information quality, service quality, and system quality are also decisive factors that influence the consumers' motivation and intention to visit to positively impact business growth and customer satisfaction (Yuce et al., 2020).

Furthermore, real-time interaction is also a crucial factor influencing the users' perception of a displayed content via VR environment (Lee & Chung, 2008; Steuer, 1992). VR allows users to have a real-time experience, whereas they are actively engaged with the presented contents. As Buhalis and Sinarta (2019) argued, "real-time offers dynamic engagement with connected people." VR also provides real-time content, for instance, related to a touristic site, that simulates the users' attitude and influences their decision-making process, and ultimately affects their intention to visit (Marasco et al., 2018; Yuce et al., 2020). Virtual reality carries out this achievement with its unique features, such as presenting more reliable information, authentic images, hands-on virtual experience of the destinations before purchasing. Most importantly, VR technology contains a data source that conveys the information through an immersive VR experience to the consumers (Li & Chen, 2019). Studies indicate that potential consumers are likely to book their destinations or plan to purchase them as a result of perception they received during virtual visitation (Choi, Hickerson, & Lee, 2018; Israel, Zerres, & Tscheulin, 2019; Li & Chen, 2019; Yuce et al., 2020). In particular, Although the Internet keeps connecting each business with their clients and can promote their products and services without time or place boundaries, nonetheless, immersive technologies began boosting the advances in the marketing and tourism field gradually (Buhalis & Law, 2008; Buhalis & Sinarta, 2019; Guttentag, 2010; Sharma et al., 2020; Standing et al., 2014).

Immersive technologies gained significant momentum even more with the invention of the affordable VR head-mounted glasses. VR Samsung Galaxy Head-Mounted device, invented in 2015, is integrated with a smartphone and provides an efficient, flexible, comfortable, and more enjoyable mobilized environment (Israel et al., 2019). Consumers engaged and experienced the VR contents. One of the essential characteristics that advanced VR achieved is, bringing the tourism products to the consumers' setting without time, place, and distance constraints (Israel et al., 2019; Yuce et al., 2020). One may claim that other technologies also do the same thing. However, no other technology has similar functionality, feature, or ability to create the extensive immersive and engagement on people like VR performs (Israel et al., 2019). Despite people interact with most technologies as a passive audience; however, a mobilized VR environment allows them to participate interactively in real-time as if they are part of the content. This stimulating active participation is achieved because of the unique feature of VR technology called the sense of presence.

VR has an exceptionally versatile and flexible environment to ensure that consumers are engaged with the natural objects in a virtual environment. With the advent of mobilized VR headsets and computer-generated images that provide user-friendly and easy-to-use functionalities, VR technology captured more attention for marketing purposes. Integration of smartphones with companies' and organizations' goals reshaped how tourism-related products and services are promoted. These innovative characteristics of VR technology allowed consumers to access the VR contents, which attracts people with immerse and engaging 360-degree images or videos and using a simplified cutting-edge VR headset during their stay at home.

One of the primary goals to design, develop, and adopt a VR technology in the tourism business is to improve the business potential, acquire new customers, and influence the consumers' attitude by generating more reliable, solid, and accurate contents containing 360-degree images and videos in a VR environment. It generates an immersive environment in which users are deported from the real world during a short period (Yuce et al., 2020).

VR technology also plays a critical role in acquiring and retaining customers whose attitudes, behaviour, and purchase intention change towards a tourism product. Nevertheless, some may argue that integrating an innovative immersive technology such as virtual reality for business operations as an unrealistic approach to investing for marketing purposes can be seen by some entrepreneurs. However, the implementation of VR technology in the travel and marketing field offers several alternative options, different approaches, and creative solutions based on the businesses' emerging needs (Pestek & Sarvan, 2020). Lastly, as one of the latest information and communication technologies, VR technology promises more successful marketing mediums in the landscape of the tourism industry than traditional print marketing objects such as flyers, brochures, and magazines.

As mentioned above, presence is one of the essential characteristics of VR technology. The higher VR sense of presence maximizes VR technology to its fullest potential, creates a more significant consumer experience that improves profitability, provides competitive advantages, and allows the consumers to make more informed decisions about the products and services. VR reality technology's most significant impact on consumers' decision-making process can be measured with how a quality sense of presence is produced as users experience VR content. A more sense of presence means the users achieve more profound engagement during the virtual deportation. Sense of presence, therefore, has a significant impact on customers' attitude and behavioral change, which ultimately leads to improving motivation and purchasing intention of a product.

CONCLUSION

We live in a digitalization era that has taken control of every aspect of our lives, from a drone to driverless autonomous cars. Digitalization is a process in which constant and dynamic changes occur fundamentally at an incredibly high speed, whether we realize it or not. Therefore, it demands careful consideration and planning to discover what factors influence people's desire to purchase tourism products. Moreover, technologies that create immersive experiences have become fundamentally critical emerging innovative marketing tools for businesses. VR as an immersive technology offers fundamentally new business opportunities to achieve companies, organizations', and sites' overall objectives in the tourism industry worldwide.

The ongoing development, deployment, and adaptation of digital transformation have transformed every part of our individual, society, and professional life from communication to commerce and how we learn, in particular, after Covid-19. As mentioned above, the coronavirus epidemic has harmed most businesses worldwide and resulted in a chaotic and unprecedented future. The fear of the virus spread tremendously among people, and governments applied strict lockdowns to control the outbreak. This fear triggered the cancellation of visitation activities and events all over the world. As with all chaotic situations, the global pandemic Covid-19 also presented new opportunities for the companies and businesses by leveraging their product sales or promotion using virtual events. Although Covid-19 created numerous barriers to acquiring new customers, deploying and developing customer-oriented technology allowed the marketers to overcome these challenges

Digital transformation is a savior influence on our lives profoundly during hard times. Innovative technologies can help achieve organizations' overall objectives when suitable, affordable, and consumer-centric innovative technologies are deployed, developed, and implemented quickly and effectively. Digital technologies changed how our businesses are done and performed during pandemic caused the global lockdowns. Hence, adapting and forming the most appropriate technology speedily and effectively can help the business operate efficiently, enhance its profits, and reduce its operational costs while the long-term goals are planned. There is also a significant correlation between digital transformation and customer acquisition and retention in the realm of tourism. As most studies point out, VR technology profoundly and efficiently influences customers' purchasing intention towards a tourism product or service. Lastly, adopting suitable and powerful innovative technologies also allows organizations to have competitive advantages because they develop consumer-centric business growth strategies.

With advances in innovative technologies, marketing strategies have also been evolved from traditional to modern approaches that opened up endless opportunities and benefits for the tourism industry. Integrating digital technology with the marketing sector also allowed companies to connect with the world and promote their products and services without any boundaries. Moreover, the tourism industry has experienced solid and extensive economic growth by integrating more advanced digitalization with every aspect of the business operations over the past three decades.

As a result, despite many advantages of the traditional marketing approach for businesses, with the advent of digitalization, the marketing field's role has been changed dramatically. Digital current marketing approaches allowed organizations to instantly promote and deliver their products and services without location and time barriers. Immersive technologies, however, made a fundamental shift in the marketing field to promote tourism products with more influential digital mediums. The implementation of VR has opened fascinating opportunities for all the tourism industry and its stakeholders. VR helps sustainable growth and enhances the travel industry across the globe. However, designing and implementing VR in the tourism context requires several factors, such as quality of information, user-friendly hardware, and efficient software. Next, discovering the sector's needs and demands is crucial to maximizing sectoral growth while minimizing business's adverse effects. Finally, tourism and technology are interwoven elements for the countries' wealth and welfare regardless of their economic power.

RECOMMENDATIONS

It has been a vital topic to understand the significant elements of innovative technologies that can contribute to the market field and ultimately to the tourism industry to boost the global economies and minimize the specific costs, such as marketing and maintenance. Organizations, companies, and destinations need to focus on several factors to deploy and adapt the VR technologies to get the most optimal results due to investing a significant portion of the budget on technologies. Some of these factors can be mentioned as user-friendliness, applicability, efficiency, compatibility, and suitability. Hence, it is recommended to conduct the necessary analysis of the relationship between proposed technology and marketplace by focusing on the market trend, emerging customers' needs, wants, and expectations.

LIMITATIONS

This paper reflects the conceptual representation of digitalization, digitalization-driven technologies, and marketing regarding their impact on the tourism industry. However, more empirical studies are needed to extend the solid implication areas of technologies in the tourism field.

ACKNOWLEDGMENT

I would like to express my special thanks of gratitude to my dear professors who shared their extensive knowledge, expertize and guidance in finalizing this chapter. I would also like to thank my dear wife and family who have been a great help, motivation and inspiration not only for this project but every aspect of my life.

This research received no specific grant from any funding agency in the public, commercial, or not-for-profit sectors.

REFERENCES

Abubakar, A. M., Ilkan, M., & Sahin, P. (2016). eWOM, eReferral and gender in the virtual community. *Marketing Intelligence & Planning*, *34*(5), 692–710. doi:10.1108/MIP-05-2015-0090

Agag, G. M., & El-Masry, A. A. (2017). Why do consumers trust online travel websites? Drivers and outcomes of consumer trust toward online travel websites. *Journal of Travel Research*, *56*(3), 347–369. doi:10.1177/0047287516643185

Buhalis, D. (2003). eTourism: Information technology for strategic tourism management. Pearson Education.

Buhalis, D., & Law, R. (2008). Progress in information technology and tourism management: 20 years on and 10 years after the Internet—The state of eTourism research. *Tourism Management*, *29*(4), 609–623. doi:10.1016/j.tourman.2008.01.005

Buhalis, D., & Sinarta, Y. (2019). Real-time co-creation and nowness service: Lessons from tourism and hospitality. *Journal of Travel & Tourism Marketing*, *36*(5), 563–582. doi:10.1080/10548408.2019.1592059

Choi, Y., Hickerson, B., & Lee, J. (2018). Investigation of the technology effects of online travel media on virtual travel experience and behavioral intention. *Journal of Travel & Tourism Marketing*, *35*(3), 320–335. doi:10.1080/10548408.2017.1340224

Crouch, G. I. (2011). Destination competitiveness: An analysis of determinant attributes. *Journal of Travel Research*, *50*(1), 27–45. doi:10.1177/0047287510362776

Eid, R., & El-Gohary, H. (2013). The impact of E-marketing use on small business enterprises' marketing success. *Service Industries Journal*, *33*(1), 31–50. doi:10.1080/02642069.2011.594878

El-Gohary, H. O. (2010). *The impact of E-marketing practices on market performance of small business enterprises. An empirical investigation*. University of Bradford.

Ghobakhloo, M. (2020). Industry 4.0, digitization, and opportunities for sustainability. *Journal of Cleaner Production*, *252*, 119869. doi:10.1016/j.jclepro.2019.119869

González-Rodríguez, M. R., Martínez-Torres, R., & Toral, S. (2016). Post-visit and pre-visit tourist destination image through eWOM sentiment analysis and perceived helpfulness. *International Journal of Contemporary Hospitality Management*, *28*(11), 2609–2627. doi:10.1108/IJCHM-02-2015-0057

Guttentag, D. A. (2010). Virtual reality: Applications and implications for tourism. *Tourism Management*, *31*(5), 637–651. doi:10.1016/j.tourman.2009.07.003

Israel, K., Zerres, C., & Tscheulin, D. K. (2019). Presenting hotels in virtual reality: Does it influence the booking intention? *Journal of Hospitality and Tourism Technology*, *10*(3), 443–463. doi:10.1108/JHTT-03-2018-0020

Katsikeas, C., Leonidou, L., & Zeriti, A. (2019). Revisiting international marketing strategy in a digital era: Opportunities, challenges, and research directions. *International Marketing Review*, *37*(3), 405–424. doi:10.1108/IMR-02-2019-0080

Lahiri, R., Ding, J., & Chinzara, Z. (2018). Technology adoption, adaptation and growth. *Economic Modelling, 70*, 469–483. doi:10.1016/j.econmod.2017.08.026

Law, R., Buhalis, D., & Cobanoglu, C. (2014). Progress on information and communication technologies in hospitality and tourism. *International Journal of Contemporary Hospitality Management, 26*(5), 727–750. doi:10.1108/IJCHM-08-2013-0367

Lee, K. C., & Chung, N. (2008). Empirical analysis of consumer reaction to the virtual reality shopping mall. *Computers in Human Behavior, 24*(1), 88–104. doi:10.1016/j.chb.2007.01.018

Li, T., & Chen, Y. (2019). Will virtual reality be a double-edged sword? Exploring the moderation effects of the expected enjoyment of a destination on travel intention. *Journal of Destination Marketing & Management, 12*, 15–26. doi:10.1016/j.jdmm.2019.02.003

Marasco, A., Buonincontri, P., van Niekerk, M., Orlowski, M., & Okumus, F. (2018). Exploring the role of next-generation virtual technologies in destination marketing. *Journal of Destination Marketing & Management, 9*, 138–148. doi:10.1016/j.jdmm.2017.12.002

Pestek, A., & Sarvan, M. (2020). Virtual reality and modern tourism. *Journal of Tourism Futures.*

Ringberg, T., Reihlen, M., & Rydén, P. (2019). The technology-mindset interactions: Leading to incremental, radical or revolutionary innovations. *Industrial Marketing Management, 79*, 102–113. doi:10.1016/j.indmarman.2018.06.009

Schweer, D., & Sahl, J. C. (2017). *The digital transformation of industry–the benefit for Germany. In The drivers of digital transformation.* Springer.

Seyyedamiri, N., & Tajrobehkar, L. (2019). Social content marketing, social media and product development process effectiveness in high-tech companies. *International Journal of Emerging Markets.*

Shah, D., & Murthi, B. (2021). Marketing in a data-driven digital world: Implications for the role and scope of marketing. *Journal of Business Research, 125*, 772–779. doi:10.1016/j.jbusres.2020.06.062

Sharma, A., Sharma, S., & Chaudhary, M. (2020). Are small travel agencies ready for digital marketing? Views of travel agency managers. *Tourism Management, 79*, 104078. doi:10.1016/j.tourman.2020.104078

Silvestri, L., Forcina, A., Introna, V., Santolamazza, A., & Cesarotti, V. (2020). Maintenance transformation through Industry 4.0 technologies: A systematic literature review. *Computers in Industry, 123*, 103335. doi:10.1016/j.compind.2020.103335

Standing, C., Tang-Taye, J.-P., & Boyer, M. (2014). The impact of the Internet in travel and tourism: A research review 2001–2010. *Journal of Travel & Tourism Marketing, 31*(1), 82–113. doi:10.1080/10548408.2014.861724

Stentoft, J., Adsbøll Wickstrøm, K., Philipsen, K., & Haug, A. (2020). Drivers and barriers for Industry 4.0 readiness and practice: Empirical evidence from small and medium-sized manufacturers. *Production Planning and Control*, 1–18. doi:10.1080/09537287.2020.1768318

Steuer, J. (1992). Defining virtual reality: Dimensions determining telepresence. *Journal of Communication, 42*(4), 73–93. doi:10.1111/j.1460-2466.1992.tb00812.x

Taiminen, H. M., & Karjaluoto, H. (2015). The usage of digital marketing channels in SMEs. *Journal of Small Business and Enterprise Development*, *22*(4), 633–651. doi:10.1108/JSBED-05-2013-0073

Talwar, S., Talwar, M., Kaur, P., & Dhir, A. (2020). Consumers' resistance to digital innovations: A systematic review and framework development. *Australasian Marketing Journal*, *28*(4), 286–299. doi:10.1016/j.ausmj.2020.06.014

Theodoridis, P. K., & Gkikas, D. C. (2019). *How artificial intelligence affects digital marketing. In Strategic Innovative Marketing and Tourism*. Springer.

WTTC. (2020). *Economic Impact Reports*. https://wttc.org/Research/Economic-Impact

Yuce, A., Arasli, H., Ozturen, A., & Daskin, M. (2020). Feeling the Service Product Closer: Triggering Visit Intention via Virtual Reality. *Sustainability*, *12*(16), 6632. doi:10.3390u12166632

Chapter 2
The Future Through QR Code: A Case of Its Potential on a Digital Service

Roberson Lopes Bolzan
FE, University of Algarve, Portugal

Paula Ventura
https://orcid.org/0000-0002-3199-4517
FCT, Cinturs, University of Algarve, Portugal

Silvia Fernandes
https://orcid.org/0000-0002-1699-5415
FE, Cinturs, University of Algarve, Portugal

ABSTRACT

The choice of this work arises from the interest in the topics of innovation and technology transfer in the context of launching new services to target people. The authors sought to integrate a technology that could bring more interest to a product/service, namely with the modern growth of mobile activities and apps. Among some options considered, they chose the QR code technology. With the help of a strategic plan, they evaluate whether there is a market and propensity for its widespread use in Portugal. Then, an interactive prototype of the supporting platform is presented for its validation with users. Most participants know the QR code and consider the idea interesting and promising. They even suggested add-ons such as more video functions and a greater variety of events and resources for combining. Given the challenges of modern society, the authors recognize its eventual application to real-time requests for sharing specialized information or resources in critical activities of areas such as health and tourism. Features such as augmented reality, security, and privacy are future issues to address.

INTRODUCTION

The widespread use of mobile devices and apps is boosting the market take-up of barcode scanning applications. The motivation behind this work is the interest in areas such as mobile computing, entrepre-

DOI: 10.4018/978-1-7998-7192-7.ch002

neurship, and innovation. After selecting the theme, as well as the technology to support the underlying service, we chose to apply QR code. QR means quick response, which is represented by a bar code. This designation stems from the ability of quick interpretation by mobile devices. Given the related potential and creativity, we decided to go ahead with a business idea. However, the focus of this work is on the presentation and validation of its prototype.

QR codes can have a great impact on customer satisfaction. Sharing information via QR influence people to engage in online exchanges and communities (Hossain, Zhou & Rahman, 2018). Their potential is driving organizations to implement technical approaches to business services. They have revolutionized online activities because of their usefulness and feasibility. QRs are considered as tools of communication that can be executed by customers to obtain information and/or benefit from real-time transactions. This is a strong medium to manage and innovate customer relationships.

Objectives

This work aims to approach a stage of development of a business idea underlying the future launch of a start-up company. This is a project related to the innovative offer of a product/ service, which culminates with the presentation of a prototype of a platform for sending messages in videos through QR code, called *Send & Surprise*.

In order to achieve this goal, we will analyze some of the topics that should guide prototyping according to the market, and that form the strategic plan of the project. This will give us the understanding and motivation to know if there are conditions for its adoption and use. Thus, this project culminates in the validation of the product/service through an interactive prototype.

ENTREPRENEURSHIP OF OPPORTUNITY

This idea has to do with the creation of opportunities, given the increasing use of wireless devices connected to the internet and the variety of associated applications. In opportunity entrepreneurship (discovery of a business opportunity), the entrepreneur is, above all, an expert observer. Always attentive to the needs and desires of the contemporary consumer, which include more intangible aspects (sensory, interactive, dynamic, informal).

Upon realizing the lack of a certain product, he decides to conceive and implement it. Identifying good opportunities is not a simple task and, therefore, it is noted that this profile has prior knowledge, even if not in-depth, about the market (Leite and Oliveira, 2007). On the other hand, Pessoa (2005) defines three types of entrepreneurs: corporate entrepreneur (intra-entrepreneur); start-up entrepreneur (creates new businesses/companies); and social entrepreneur (creates enterprises with a social mission).

Corporate entrepreneurship involves a process of identifying, developing and implementing new opportunities within the existing company. The start-up entrepreneur aims to give rise to a new business. He analyzes the scenario and, when faced with an opportunity, presents a new enterprise. His challenges are clear: supplying an existing demand, to which has not been given attention; seeking competitive differentials in an existing market; beating the competition; wining customers; and achieving the profitability and productivity necessary to maintain the enterprise.

Finally, another type of entrepreneur is the technological one. His profile is normally characterized by familiarity with the academic world, by a search for business opportunities in the digital and knowledge economy, by a technical culture that leads him to riskily invest in niche markets with a low survival rate (Lodi, 2000).

The QR Code is the main technology to be applied in the prototype defined in this work. Therefore, it is necessary to deepen this theme and its variants.

EXPLORING QR CODE TECHNOLOGY

The adoption of technology implies many advantages for companies and people, such as: cost reduction, availability, timeliness, usefulness and ease of use. At the end of each decade, a new technology propels us into the next era. The quick response code (QR) has revolutionized the code barrier. It is an interesting technological breakthrough, which has transformed the way consumers interact with sellers, service providers and other consumers. Even for recruitment, contact information and details (about research, projects, LinkedIn profile, etc.) of candidates can be easily accessed through a QR code reading app (Pal & Jha, 2017).

The QR code activates tags and directs them to links that can open web pages, videos, text messages, among other resources. This technology was invented by the Japanese company Denso-Wave, a Toyota subsidiary, in 1994. The main goal was to facilitate the process of cataloging automobile components. It consists of high-density bidimensional graphical images, like barcodes composed of digital squares instead of bars. The compounds of those squares come together to create codes that, in turn, host the data that will be verified by mobile devices (Bashir et al., 2013).

QR code reader applications (apps), downloadable on mobile communication devices (mobile phones, tablets, etc.) require the action of a built-in camera to decode the data. This technology allows integrate such apps with other systems or objects. QR codes are barcodes that connect us quickly from physical objects to the digital world (Bashir et al., 2013). The use of QR code is free of any license as it is an open source, defined and published as an ISO standard in 2010. Then, in 2011, the QR code became commercial for the first time in the telecommunications' sector. Today, it has gained great popularity due to mobile technology, a decisive support for its proliferation. With this technology and its mobile use, the opportunities for technology transfer are also enormous.

In the beginning, the main objective was a code to be quickly interpreted by reading equipment. But after some time, other companies began to explore different ways of using QRs so that their commercial use became widespread all over the world. These codes are changing the way we interact with people and products (magazines, books, ads, events). QR codes have also changed the way content is created and delivered (Jharotia, 2018). They provide a new channel for direct sales rewarding the advertising investments.

QR Code and its Applications

The use of QR code is increasing globally, due to its greater popularity around the world, particularly in China, Korea, Japan and the USA (Shin et al., 2012; Tarjan et al., 2011). In 2019 about 2.7 billion people used smartphones and an estimated 90% of the population will access high-speed internet in 2020. Smartphone updates have also added QR code scanning capabilities to the camera app, so these codes become an integral part of daily life. Even the latest android smartphones have made QR code scanning a native feature. Inspired by China, South Korea has also witnessed an impressive growth in the number of QR scans. India and US markets have also adopted QR to make payments and turn shopping into a unique experience (Beaconstac, 2019).

In Portugal Alipay, a leader in online and mobile payments, whose digital 'wallet' is used by millions of people, has partnered with 6 European operators to promote the interoperability of digital payments based on QR codes. Pagaqui has the exclusive use of the system in Portugal, whose project also involves the Spanish service Momopocket, the Austrian Bluecode, the Norwegian Vipps and the Finnish ePassi and Pivo that will adopt a QR code format compatible with Alipay.

The possible uses of QRs are almost infinite, as this technology is present in our daily lives in the most diverse services/products (Shin et al., 2012). Due to its versatility, it is used in several fields such as: online banking, customer service management, medical assistance, assistance for the disabled, security applications (with different types of encryption) and integrated in print ads, products, smooth surfaces, etc. Another form of QR widely used is in invoices and other documents for paying products/services, in which the user is directed to his digital invoice for its immediate payment (figure 1).

Figure 1. QR-based invoice

Futuristic stores and supermarkets that operate without staff and queues, as Amazon Go and Apple Store, also use QR codes. Before entering the store, the buyer needs to create an account and then download the app, creating a personal QR (like a digital signature). Thus, when entering the store an electronic check-in is performed that identifies the personal QR and then automatically pays the products purchased.

QR as a Tool of Digital Marketing

With QR codes, marketers can better understand which campaigns are performing well based on the number of checks (Beaconstac, 2019). URLs (website addresses) are often long, obscure and difficult to remember. That is why more companies are adopting this technology of quick recognition, due to its easiness in how people interact with digital content (Marketing charts, 2012). Whether QRs will be here in the long run is unknown, but for now it is a highly effective and valuable interactive tool.

Tracking analyses, monitoring campaigns, analyzing scans based on date, time, location and device used helps to adjust the codes of various campaigns. Exporting and integrating those analyses within Google Analytics also allows create other useful measures and innovate the campaigns/projects (figure 2).

Figure 2. QR measures

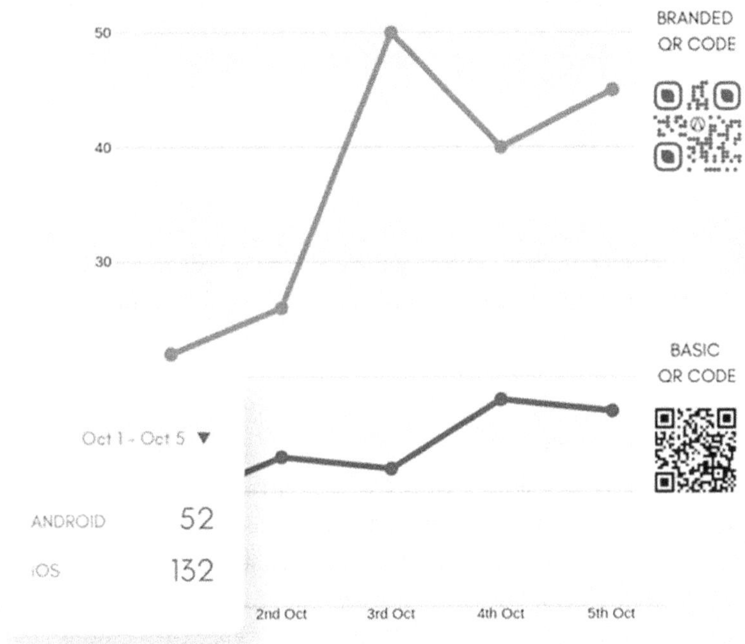

Dynamic QRs are another great advantage of this technology, as they offer versatility to edit the linked URLs according to business requirements, even after printing and distributing them. Dynamic (or smart) QRs codes allow managers to vary campaigns at different times of the day and different days. This helps campaigns to adapt to seasonal launching, special campaigns, festive offers and seasonal products, without changing the QR code in the printed material.

Based on these aspects, next section deals with the transition of the proposed idea to become a real enterprise. In this transition, the role of a strategic plan focusing on the prototype of an interactive platform based on QR code is highlighted.

STRATEGIC PLAN AND ITS RESULTS

After the theoretical bases described in the previous section, regarding several aspects that serve as basis for the idealization of this project, it is essential to consider the main steps to verify the associated business idea. With the ultimate goal of creating an innovative service underlying the launch of a start-up company.

The phase that must precede the launch of a product/service is the strategic plan, which due to its importance is required by any interested mentor or investor. Its main stages of development, within the scope of this idea, are:

1. Market analysis and characterization
2. Proposed product/service
3. Target audience
4. Competition analysis and future trends
5. Idea presentation questionnaire
6. Prototype of the idea/project
7. Prototype validation interview
8. Product implementation
9. Promotion and publicity

The following sections focus on the description of the proposed product/service, the idea presentation survey to evaluate familiarity with QR codes, prototype (model) of the proposed product and a validation interview of the prototype.

The Proposed Service

This project, *Send & Surprise*, intends to be a start-up in the area of new technologies, with a differentiating purpose in the interaction with customers through message sending (in video) among other possibilities. It allows an interaction between the offline/traditional (invitations, cards, gifts, etc.) and the online/contemporary (videos, digital platform, QR code, smartphone) on an individual and personalized way.

Emotional and affective issues are aggregated factors as another differential side of this idea. A simple message sent, either digitally (through a chat app) or by letter/printed card, is forgotten in time. But through the suggested platform, the message is delivered in the form of a video, using a QR-code tag embedded in a chosen card or gift. This has a printed QR, which can be visualized anywhere at any time, through the camera of a mobile device with web access. In addition to the object received, a carrier of a special message from a special person, it will provide a feeling of affection and closeness to who receive it even if distant.

To do it, you must access the *Send & Surprise* website and view (or download) the prepared video, where a QR-code is generated which can be printed on an object (or other items) of choice, available on the same website. The following image illustrates the steps and processes involved.

The goal of *Send & Surprise* is not send ordinary messages/videos, as most of those we often send and receive through Youtube. These are special messages regarding events, special occasions with a high degree of personalization or creativity.

It is expected that the videos sent will be made from the sender's own mobile phone, in an informal and simple way. However, in other cases the video must be professionally produced if the event requires it.

Figure 3. Sequence of the proposed app and service

Idea Presentation Questionnaire

To test the feasibility and acceptance of the idea, an online survey was applied using Google forms with multiple choice questions. These are related to familiarity and adoption degree of QR code and the proposed service. Having been available for 15 days (because of a deadline for this idea's presentation at University of Algarve), we obtained 56 responses whose data are further discussed. This is a convenience sample not representative of the population. Thus, 55 respondents recognize the use of QRs on different surfaces in their daily lives (only 1 person gave a negative answer).

Asking whether the respondents know well this type of code, 54 respondents said yes. However, knowing it does not necessarily mean that they dominate its functioning. Thus, 49 participants answered they know how a QR code works and 7 gave a negative answer. Regarding its effective use, 50 respondents answered positively, while 6 have not used it yet. In these 50 participants, who have already used a QR code, 25 did it 1 to 5 times; 16 did it 5 to 10 times, and 9 did it 10 to 15 times. The number of respondents who considered this technology easy to use was 49, while 7 considered the opposite.

About 34 respondents consider interesting to send an object with a message, using a QR code, while 19 said perhaps, and 3 do not find it interesting yet. In the question about receiving this kind of object, 37 participants find it interesting, 15 answered perhaps, and 4 gave a negative response. Half of the sample used (28) would recommend this app to friends, 24 may recommend it, and only 4 would not recommend it.

In this survey, an open non-mandatory question was added: "Regarding this idea, which other resource(s), in addition to objects or messages, would you consider relevant to include in this app?". Among the answers obtained, some more pertinent are: sending an invitation that integrates Google maps to add geo-location; advertising links associated to the object sent; photos inclusion; gift cards; codified documents such as invoices to pay; and collective messages.

It should be noted that the data collected result from a convenience sample, and therefore non-probabilistic and occasional. So, the data obtained apply only to it and are useful to generate a knowledge-base for the development of the app as it helps to define its scope and requirements.

Figure 4. Augmented reality in QR code

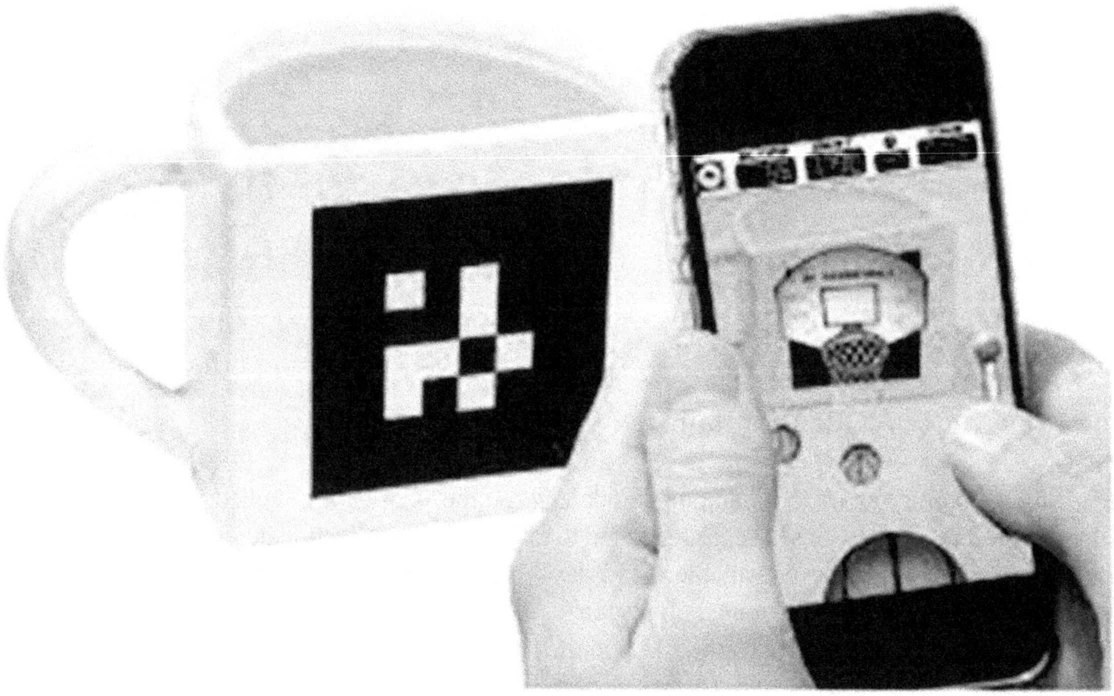

Idea Prototyping

In computing, a prototype is a software model or pattern. In this first prototype of the proposed idea, an architecture based on screens (or 'scenes') could be defined: an initial scene; intermediate scene(s), and final scene. For each of these scenes, specific routines are defined. We emphasize that the display of each scene is generic. Briefly, the application is organized as follows:

Initial interface: this is the first scene to be displayed when starting the application. There we can view the options available. Among the options, we can select the one we want and start it. When finished, it returns to the initial interface. In this step, there is an explanatory video about the platform's operation, an icon for login and another for registration.

Intermediate interface1: in this scene, the user can upload his video to the platform;

Intermediate interface2: in this step, after the video has been sent, the user can watch it on the platform. If there are no errors, it proceeds to the next scene - 'generate QR code'.

Intermediate interface3: in this phase, after the QR is generated, it is up to the user choose from among the objects available on the platform, so that his choice is sent to the recipient.

Intermediate interface4: in this scene, the user will have a first image (preview) of how the chosen object will look with the printed QR. Then, it is necessary to fill in the surprise shipping address. It should be noted that more items can be chosen (in the interface3), to avoid repeating the process for sending each item.

In the short term, the intention is to implement the *Send & Surprise* platform with augmented reality (AR) and virtual reality (VR) technologies, also known as immersive technologies (see figure 4). These have a multisensory capacity, exploring more aspects such as vision and hearing, so that the individual can feel that he is in another place. In other words, the ability to merge the real with the virtual in variable proportions for each of the new technologies, being the partial or virtual interaction, producing a 3D and dynamic scenario.

AR technology provides the user with an experience where he is aware of his location and where digital 'realities' are added to the environment. Usually these interactions are carried out in applications via smartphone which offer filters, masks, glasses, and virtual characterizations for photos and videos. VR technology, on the other hand, provides a new universe to the user, immersed and without any interaction with the real world; user experience will be unique and exclusively in a virtual world. However, to perform this experiment, a device is needed, in this case, specific glasses to create virtual immersion.

These are some of the technologies that are intended to be implemented on the proposed platform. Many other ideas can still emerge, not only around the functionality of this tool, but also turning it an indispensable tool in the user daily life.

Prototype Validation Interview

The interview had the main objective of knowing the opinion related with *Send & Surprise* application, especially to evaluate its prototype. It was an individualized interview, to 5 users from the sample, in order to validate the functionality and clarity of the prototype.

The tests were carried out informally and in parallel with the development. Such tests focused basically on the interactivity of the application, verifying if the functionalities defined were executing as planned. To obtain this feedback, six open questions were applied whose results are summarized below (we highlight here the general responses):

1. Are the layout and user interface of *Send & Surprise* friendly?

The respondents answered yes, but they suggested other color combination. They also proposed to change the font used.

2. Is it easy to navigate/interact with *Send & Surprise*?

All answered yes, as they did not find difficulties in this interaction.

3. Does *Send & Surprise* offer the products/services you need?

Although they do not perceive the proposed service as essential, most of them answered yes. However, some respondents have suggested include other options as items, such as: chocolates, t-shirts, etc.

4. Would you like to create the video directly in the platform?

They generally answered yes, if there is the function of video edition.

5. Would you like to associate photos (besides videos)?

The participants of this sub-sample answered yes, but some mentioned the inclusion of videos assembled in powerpoint style.

6. Are you comfortable with the service supported by this platform?

Although these participants had not used something similar before, they said they feel comfortable using the proposed platform and imagine its use in several events.

DISCUSSION

With new technologies, people have built a dependency of the mobile internet and its apps in daily life (Dennison et al., 2013; Hui et al., 2013). Therefore, the main objective of this work is to present an idea of a platform for sending video messages, through a QR-code tag. Before presenting it, it was necessary to review some theoretical concepts related to the creation and development of a platform for a business (start-up). These concepts include entrepreneurship, innovation, technology transfer, marketing and QR technology, being discussed in order to sustain the empirical part of this project.

Data on the use of smartphones/e-commerce in Portugal justify market demand for this type of product/service proposed. To guide its implementation into the first prototype, some steps of the strategic plan were considered. Namely within the scope of QR-code technology, a survey was applied in order to capture the familiarity with it and the acceptance/ adoption of the idea. Then, an interactive prototype of the proposed service was presented and an interview to some survey participants could give insight about it. The resulting answers help to outline further changes or innovations.

Regarding the survey, there is familiarity about QR codes having been used by most respondents, at least 1 to 5 times in the last year. It is considered an easy-to-use technology by the majority of them. However, this interaction still occurs through conventional means such as product package, concert invitation and invoice payment. Regarding the service offered, it is considered interesting to send or receive messages by QR-code. However, only 6 respondents are willing to pay for the application. Finally, regarding the interview for prototype validation, the participants find it easy to understand and interact. However, in the layout, they propose a change in color patterns and fonts for a more friendly navigation.

QR code usage not always have a significant relationship with either up-to-date electronic device knowledge or perceived usefulness (Ozkaya et al., 2015). This attribute can be taken for granted after adoption and users require more different features to increase their usage of QR. Electronic ownership (a dimension of consumer innovativeness) is one of the strongest indicators of curiosity and experience with new technologies. People who have experience with technology are more likely to have stronger self-efficacy to try out new applications.

There is a promising scenario for the implementation of an e-service like *Send & Surprise* in the Portuguese market. Nevertheless, training aimed at promoting the effective use of QR technology must evolve. Also, security and privacy of QR code applications must be taken care of on the proposed platform/service. Secure and privacy-friendly applications are today more and more important features (Wahsheh & Luccio, 2020).

IMPLICATIONS AND FUTURE WORK

Several goals underlying the development of *Send & Surprise* platform-prototype were achieved. However, there are still issues that can be tested and developed to enrich it. In the future, we intend to extend the horizon of the proposed platform as a mobile app namely on Android, iOS and Windows Phone.

Currently the main function of the platform is to send video messages by QR code activation, but we intend that it also allows sending, along with video, sponsored links creating other return sources for the business. Also, its interaction with geo-location resources can complement messages for many events. Additionally, we intend to add more languages to the platform's interface in order to broaden its geographical scope.

Over time, adding the users' database to the experience acquired with the platform, other products/services may be implemented such as: documents to pay by generated QR-code, invitations to social networks through a QR-code, etc. Given the challenges of modern society, other possibilities to consider relate to its application to quick requests for information or resources by critical activities such as in health, tourism, engineering, etc.

These are improvements we intend to implement in the *Send & Surprise* platform and resulting start-up, to be submitted to an 'innovation acceleration' program where managers, IT specialists and investors will be present.

This paper is financed by National Funds provided by FCT- Foundation for Science and Technology through project UIDB/04020/2020.

REFERENCES

Bashir, I., Naik, K., & Madhavaiah, C. (2013). Potential business applications of Quick Response (QR) codes. *Prajnan (Pune)*, *41*(4), 353–366.

Beaconstac. (2019). *The Future of QR Codes: 2019 and Beyond*. https://blog.beaconstac.com/2019/07/what-they-think-of-qr-codes-in-2019/#The-Future-of-QR-Codes:-2019-and-beyond

Dennison, L., Morrison, L., Conway, G., & Yardley, L. (2013). Opportunities and challenges for smartphone applications in supporting health behavior change: Qualitative study. *Journal of Medical Internet Research*, *15*(4), e86. Advance online publication. doi:10.2196/jmir.2583 PMID:23598614

Hossain, S., Zhou, X., & Rahman, F. (2018). Examining the impact of QR codes on purchase intention and customer satisfaction on the basis of perceived flow. *International Journal of Engineering Business Management*, *10*, 1–11. doi:10.1177/1847979018812323

Hui, S., Inman, J., Huang, Y., & Suher, J. (2013). The effect of in-store travel distance on unplanned spending: Applications to mobile promotion strategies. *Journal of Marketing*, *77*(2), 1–16. doi:10.1509/jm.11.0436

Jharotia, A. (2018). QR codes: Innovative technology for libraries in electronic environment. In Essential Technologies for Libraries in Digital Era. Lambert Academic Publishing.

Leite, A., & Oliveira, F. (2007). Empreendedorismo e novas tendências. *Estudo Edit Value Empresa Junior*, *5*, 1–35.

Lodi, E. (2000). *Empreendedorismo – Ciência, Técnica e Arte*. Instituto Euvaldo Lodi.

Marketing Charts. (2012). *QR Codes most-used Mobile Channel for Engaging Customers*. https://www.marketingcharts.com/industries/retail-and-e-commerce-22519

Ozkaya, E., Ozkaya, H. E., Roxas, J., Bryant, F., & Whitson, D. (2015). Factors affecting consumer usage of QR codes. *Journal of Direct, Data and Digital Marketing Practice*, *16*(3), 209–224. doi:10.1057/dddmp.2015.18

Pal, S. K., & Jha, K. K. (2017). Personal marketing framework based on QR code. *Scholedge International Journal of Multidisciplinary & Allied Studies*, *4*(8), 65–87. doi:10.19085/journal.sijmas040801

Pessoa, E. (2005). *Tipos de Empreendedorismo: Semelhanças e Diferenças*. https://www.administradores.com.br/infor-me-se/artigos/tipos-de-empreendedorismo-semelhancas-e-diferencas/10993

Shin, D., Jung, J., & Chang, B. (2012). The psychology behind QR codes: User experience perspective. *Computers in Human Behavior*, *28*(4), 1417–1426. doi:10.1016/j.chb.2012.03.004

Tarjan, L., Senk, I., Kovac, R., & Horvat, S. (2011). Automatic identification based on 2D barcodes. *Journal of Industrial Engineering and Management*, *2*, 151–157.

Wahsheh, H., & Luccio, F. (2020). Security and privacy of QR code applications: A comprehensive study, general guidelines and solutions. *Information (Basel)*, *11*(4), 1–23. doi:10.3390/info11040217

Chapter 3
The Digital Transformation of Companies:
An Opportunity to Co-Create Value With the Consumer

Miryam Ben Ali
University of Tunis, Tunisia

Chokri El Fidha
University of Tunis, Tunisia

ABSTRACT

The emergence of social media has given birth to a new culture in the digital era of Web 2.0 and has new forms of communication through social interactions between actors in the economic scene. In this era of digitalization, great attention is paid to the online reputation of companies. Now, company success is often measured by their ability to use social media and their level of social interaction with customers. Thanks to the development of online collaborative platforms, the world of business has seen new forms of online consumer engagement with companies and active participation in their value chains. This dynamic framework demonstrates the importance of understanding relationship that are forged online between consumer and organization. The authors try to explain the opportunity to co-create value by focusing on the relationship that may exist between the online reputation of companies and the co-creation of value with the consumer.

INTRODUCTION

The business world has undergone a real change with the birth of a new online meeting space for supply and demand. Indeed, the web has become a space of virtual socialization, based on the proximity grouping between all the actors of the economic scene. This transition to the digital world has changed the form of commercial exchanges between companies and consumers. The constant connectivity of society has fostered the emergence of a new marketing approach that is both collaborative and interactive.

DOI: 10.4018/978-1-7998-7192-7.ch003

The latest statistics, relating to trends in the use of social media around the world, testify to their dominance and underline the strategic challenge they represent for companies. Therefore, companies have accepted the digital transformation to optimize their responses to consumers (Boughzela et al, 2020). This digital revolution represents an opportunity for companies, to strengthen their social presence and get closer to the customer. At the same time, it presents a threat to their online reputation, given the huge number of Internet users connected to the giants of the Web, which are: Google, Amazon, Facebook, Apple, and Microsoft, referred to by the acronym (GAFAM).

With this digitalization of the organizational environment, the power of the consumer has continued to grow, consolidated by the abundance of information circulating on the web. The increased use of social media, and the extent to which digital technology has become a part of people's lives, has stimulated the consumer's desire to socialize by making relationships online. A rapid shift from marketing to digital marketing 2.0, focused on the savvy customer, to marketing 3.0 focused on humanism, with an awareness of social and environmental values and more recently to marketing 4.0 focused on connectivity and real-time data exchange, with the presence of a cooperative consumer (Kotler, 2016). The landscape of commerce has been disturbed by the advent of virtual communities. This intensification of social media use by firms plays an important role in the development of their online reputation (Castellano and Dutot, 2013). From now on, companies are practicing a customer-centric approach with a collaborative marketing approach that relies on the customer's involvement in the development and implementation of their communication strategies as well as in their brand building processes (Pollak et al, 2021).

The researchers' greatest attention was given to the behaviors adopted by consumers and companies on the web. This new form of sociability, marked by interactive exchanges between the actors of the economic scene, has occupied a large place in the studies of researchers in marketing and management of organizations. The major interest is about this new identity projection space and the image communicated online. Some Internet users are seduced by the proximity and co-presence online with companies which allow them to live unique social experiences (Labrecque, 2013). Since then, companies care about their online reputations, and "internet" users care about their digital identities.

Indeed, connecting Internet users and their interconnections ad armed with their knowledge and skills, has made them an information relays that both create and destroy value. Since then, all attention has been focused on the online reputation of companies and the new power of the consumer, who has become more and more autonomous. Called nowadays "consumer'actor", its autonomy and speed of action has pushed companies to integrate him in their marketing strategy as a creator of value. The world is witnessing a new economy of sharing with this new form of socialization encouraging open collaboration through value co-creation and crowdsourcing between companies and their stakeholders by bringing value mutually (Zhang et al, 2015); Palacios-Marqués, 2021). Now company and consumer together mobilize their resources, knowledge and skills for mutual gain generating collective intelligence.

Aware of this empowerment, some companies found themselves forced to switch to digital transformation to get closer to this "empowred" consumer. Since her empowerment, their worry was essentially about their online reputation and the issue of consumer power in influencing the online reputation of companies. Moreover, this dependence of companies' reputation on their use of social media forces them to develop an online presence strategy looking for notoriety through their connectivity and presence on the web (Alloing, 2013); Cadel, 2010); Sriram and Kathiravan, 2014).

Companies have been asking questions to this day, anxious about this danger to their corporate reputation. Do we really have to involve the customer to create value? Collaborate with the client? Yes, but which one? How far is social media (and corporate social media) able to engage consumers in this kind of action? Can they consider their online reputation as a lever for the value co-creation or a danger facing an empowred consumer?

This dynamic context, where companies' digital identities and their stakeholders interact, demonstrates the importance of understanding consumer behavior. The relationships that are forged online, as well as the importance of having a better prediction of consumer behavior, through their social interactions with companies, would allow for better monitoring and more proactive strategic marketing planning.

Therefore, the authors question the probable relationship that could exist between the online reputation of companies and the co-creation of value with the consumer. They want to understand the role of the company's online reputation on the behavioral intentions of the Internet user in a context of collaboration (creation of joint values) between companies and consumers.

THE ROLE OF SOCIAL MEDIA IN THE DEVELOPMENT OF EMPOWRED CONSUMER BEHAVIOR AND THE DEVELOPMENT OF THE ONLINE REPUTATION OF COMPANIES

The Empowered Consumer and Social Media

The modernity of social media has replaced the traditional needs of consumers with new needs of connectivity and interactivity, thanks to social media the world has witnessed a new category of citizens. An evolution of the generation of Internet users who search for collaboration and innovation with companies through their consumption.

Looking at Generation Y, which are the children of baby boomers and Generation X, they seem to be the most concerned with the use of social media as well as the youngest Generation Z (Mahmoud et al, 2020). Innovative, savvy, and well-informed, their passion for innovative technologies and more specifically social networks is explained by their birth in the digital world, hence their name of "Digital native". This generation uses social media with great ease, in addition to their constant connection and their incessant need to discuss with their peers, they tend to express themselves and share their lives easily on the web thus considering the web technologies as a means of acquiring and sharing knowledge (Priporas, 2020). This consumer-Internet user leads a specific lifestyle with an active cognitive process of information to cope with the stimuli he faces online. It is a mixture of an unconscious emotional and psychological mental state specific to the digital context, which allows him to develop an affective attachment through his online interactions (Mandagi and Aseng, 2021). The intention of this generation's use of social media is to be able to enhance their presence through sharing and contribute within the organizational environment through online content generation (Boughzela, 2016). These corporate networks have conveyed new forms of value exchanged between the actors of the new economic scene 2.0; that is the economy in the era of web 2.0 that use digital technologies taking advantage of online social interactions and are based on peer-to-peer exchanges in a framework that is more friendly than formal. Well-defined as a collaborative workspace of production and exchange of content, it allows interaction between the company and consumers (Mejri and Gharbi, 2016); Siano et al, 2013). The web allows to strengthen these relationships and leads consumers to collaborate by developing his own online influence group.

It is quite clear that the world has witnessed a transition to a new era of communication, marked by the ability of companies to adopt technological developments. Nowadays being on the web is no longer a choice for companies but rather a strategic way to get closer to Internet users by having more visibility on the web. The Internet user thus presents an authority through the power he possesses he has within social networks (Alloing, 2013). Therefore, the company ensures to be online and to have a good structure of its information environment. Optimizing documentary mediation on social networks has become a priority in addition to sharing and disseminating information that includes signs conforms to the values of the company, to promote a favorable opinion of Internet users. (Eouzan et al, 2017).

Some companies have opted for conveying strategies with new practices by encouraging open collaboration through crowdsourcing and co-creation (Zhang et al, 2015). The digital makes it possible to create value to those who know how to take advantage of its opportunities. They have therefore understood the new perspectives that this mobility offers in terms of social media marketing and especially the risk of not being there. This is how a large majority have aligned themselves with this new behavior of mobile users by developing their own mobile applications to get even closer to their customers, making them easier to use by enjoying an active and permanent presence. This co-creation context allows company, to empower the consumer with it through the combination integrating him in its value chain, (Vianna et al, 2020). The best examples of success that the economic scene has seen, are those of brand in the IT sector such as Dell, Apple and Microsoft who were pioneers in the application of this concept through the participation of their customers in the design and development of some products by sharing their opinions and co-designing innovative ideas, just like the Lego brand with its co-created figurines, on platforms dedicated to this such as "ideastorm" and "Lego ideas", (Nambisan and Baron, 2010); Ardeley et al, 2020). Other brands have opted to involve their customers in the customization and co-design of their products to satisfy their desire for exclusivity, particularly the sports shoes brands Nike and Adidas by the implementation of interactive digital kiosks in their store and the development of mobile applications dedicated to these operations (Rialtii et al, 2018).

Some companies remain skeptical with the belief that social media is a double-edged weapon. Between being or not being there, the danger of not ensuring that social presence and intentionally missing the right level of interaction. Many companies stay absent to this day, because of the risk of conveying their credibility and transparency to their customers and partners. This is mainly the problem of the online reputation of companies which is in part out of their control. Its important for what it symbolizes as a vector of global evaluation for the company, granting it some legitimacy and credibility reflecting the collective perception of all its stakeholders (Castellano and Dutot, 2015). The authors will study more on this concept to understand its specificities and analyze the management strategies that companies are pursuing in this new era of digital transformation.

The world has seen an exceptional acceleration in the speed of innovations, which has promoted the digital transformation in the different continents. According to the World Intellectual Property Organization (WIPO)[1], the rate of evolution of patents for inventions in the information technology sector has been increasing gradually at these recent years compared to the years (2000). In addition, the time taken to disseminate innovations is constantly decreasing from one year to the next, testifying to the reality of the speed of progression and maturity of these innovative technologies as well as the high rate of adoption of these technologies by Internet users, (Gartner, 2019). If the word "digital" is the juxtaposition of two words, it is not for nothing, since it is a question of succession and combination of social revolution (of information sharing, interaction, big data, artificial intelligence, and augmented reality). To succeed in its digital transformation, the company must prove its good agility to provide customers with a successful digital transformation by adopting a digital culture with upgrading the necessary tools and resources (Le Roux, 2017 & "Gartner"[2]).

The E-Reputation of Companies in the Digital Age

By translating to the virtual world, social media have accelerated the diffusion of online content of companies giving both an opportunity for the development of their relationships and the engagement of their customers, at the same time, an issue facing the building their e-reputation. Therefore, managing a company's online reputation comes down to managing its reputation and media coverage. Consequently, the creation of innovative communication spaces in the web allows to strengthen the relationship between the company and its stakeholders also to strengthen its online reputation (Siano et al, 2011), Sriram and Kathiravan, 2014).

In the era of digitization, a company's reputation no longer depends on its accomplishments, it is rather about these abilities to reach its stakeholders through the appropriate social interactions and innovations shared online. The company, according to some researchers, must therefore develop an online presence strategy and reach notoriety through its connectivity (Sriram and Kathiravan, 2014), Cadel, 2010). Other researchers support this proposal by justifying the dependence of a company's reputation on its employment and mode of use of social media. Corporate reputation is nothing other than the result of the interaction and collaboration between the company and its different stakeholders at the social media level (Floreddu et al, 2014). Existence on the web, is now a competitive advantage in terms of corporate reputation that many researchers call to monitor to better anticipate and increase the value of the company.

Many researchers believe that corporate e-reputation is the result of a process of building social judgment around the company based on the evaluations of its stakeholders (Siano et al, 2013). These evaluations relate to any element circulating on the web and relating to the company (Paquerot et al, 2011). However, some claim that it is a meta-opinion around the way an online company is and acts (Alloing, 2013), Alloing and Pierre, 2012)). It is consequently dependent on the subjective and collective evaluations of its stakeholders. In this sense, some researchers underline the emotional nature of the e-reputation, specifying that it is relative to the subjective beliefs and opinions around its past and future actions and is based on the emotional attractiveness of the company by its stakeholders (Ponzi et al, 2011).

Based on neo-institutional theory, corporate e-reputation seems to be formed from the signals that the company itself sends out around it in addition to other sources of external social media signals. Some researchers says that online reputation of company is an automated reconstruction of shared knowledge and information produced by online interactions, whether between the company and its customers or between consumers themselves; such an image generated online based on the assessment of available information (Pierre, 2011). Corporate e-reputation is out of control given the nature of the digital environment, which is vast, and which brings different sources of signals (According to Paquerot, 2011), Alloing, 2013). In addition, it is cumulative, given the set of accumulated evaluations that define it. Other researchers report that it is comparative in so far as it allows a classification of companies based on its strength, value and intensity (Watrick, 2002), Davies et al, 2004), Deephouse, 2000). All this underlines the specificities of corporate e-reputation about its co-construction by several actors and the difficulty of its online control which escapes the company (Rindova and Martins, 2012); Castellano and Dutot, 2015).

Known for the development of interactive relationships between different actors, the potential of the web makes possible to strengthen these links and leads consumers to collaborate by creating their own online influence group. Starting from its socially constructed nature, reputation within its social media seems to follow a process of social construction based on the perceptions of its stakeholders. It is an operating resource valued by the customer who can influence their decision-making process (Martinez and Canas, 2016). According to this, the Internet user seems to be a reputational authority through the power he possesses within social networks (Alloing, 2013). This is how the company must ensure the appropriate structuring of its information environment through the optimization of documentary mediation on social networks by sharing and spreading information in accordance with the values of the company, promoting the development of favorable opinion of Internet users.

Although the web is the reference media for marketing approach in managing relationship, but influencing strategies are no longer limited to digital media. Nowadays companies are trying to combine the different ways of media communication and web tools. Consequently, in the era of digitization, companies are trying to follow an omni-channel strategy to their digital communication by promoting its existence on social networks, websites, and blogs, in addition to traditional media communication channels. In fact, corporate social media can generate both positive and negative feelings leading consumers to react and interact with it to different degrees. In addition, the power of electronic word of mouth that customers can disseminate can impact the perception and construction of companies' online reputation. Through these interactions and social exchanges, their relationship can only progress (Hudson et al, 2016).

At the end of these observations, the Internet seems to have a strong impact on the development of companies, more specifically their online reputation, as well as on the decision-making choices of consumers. Companies are aware of the importance of their online presence and co-presence with all players in the economic scene. In the digital era, e-commerce has exploded and there is a complementarity of communication channels and techniques pushing companies to adopt this digital transformation. It is about setting up an effective social influence strategy with a participatory approach based on listening and interactivity. Therefore, companies are trying to take advantage of the opportunities of social media facilitating the propagation of information by transforming risks and generating trust with its stakeholders.

THE DYNAMIC CORPORATE E-REPUTATION VS CO-CREATION OF VALUE

The Approach to Co-Creating Value Within Social Media

Through their social co-presence, companies are more human being and more sociable in a relational dynamic, by trying to make the best use of digital technologies to better maintain their relationship with the consumer through proactive strategies adopted online.

In a mixed world that brings together the real and the virtual, these technologies have fostered an innovative collaborative framework between the different players in the economic scene through their interconnection within a context of personalized exchange between the parties. It is a process of creating joint values involving hedonic, social, learning values. Together, the company and its customers cooperate in an interactive approach of innovation where the consumer is the driving force of innovation for the company (Kaplan and Haenlein, 2010). So, the consumer can participate actively by sharing creative ideas or by sharing their own experiences while creating value in an interactive way. It is like a constant cooperation that supports the development of consumer skills (Ramaswamy, 2010). It is an Internet consumer with new connectivity needs and for whom social media presents much more than a space for socialization where it exchanges and shares with different parties and peers through different forms of social interaction. This shows the capacity of social media in connection of the different parties just through social interactions. This social dynamics of online participation of the consumer with the company is the basis of the co-creation of value which underlines the specificities of the digital environment also the potential or the power of the consumer.

The form of co-creation of value has progressed from the level of personalization to reach the creation of online content by the Internet user (user generated content, UGC). Kaplan and Haenlein (2010), consider social media as a process to strengthen the co-creation of value between companies and stakeholders. According to Moretti and Tuan (2014), it is an experience that is essentially based on the exchange and voluntary sharing of knowledge to cooperate between the company and its customers leading to the creation of value. This new Marketing 3.0 paradigm has redefined relationship marketing by highlighting the potential of Internet technologies that can be harnessed. On the other hand, he specified a new profile of the engaged consumer who is seen as an interesting human resource, and which can be translated into a financial resource (Kotler, 2016). The opportunity offered by the interactivity of digital in terms of two-way exchange (man-machine, man-man), promotes the co-creation of value between the internet user and the company. Consequently, social interaction, between the company and the Internet user within social media and virtual communities, is the starting point of the creation and extraction of value (Parahald and Ramaswamy, 2004).

By putting the consumer at the center of its strategies and by adopting the digital transformation, companies have become closer than ever to their customers, ensuring an online co-presence with them and permanent connectivity. It is noted that the participation of the consumer in the process of co-creation of value with the company can be found upstream or downstream at different stages of the development process according to the strategy followed by the company but also the degree of client expertise. Overcome the technical aspects of digital interactivity (man-machine) and focus on the mediation of social interaction through social networks and online platforms, the participatory nature of digital technologies leads, thanks to interactivity digital technology, to a content generation and co-creation of value.

In the context of knowledge marketing based on the notion of "customer knowledge, customer-company competence", the consumer's participation in the co-creation of value with the company depends, in addition to the consumer's skills, on his level of competence and his involvement (Curbatov, 2001, 2003). In fact, the Internet user is now a producer of content through what he shares, in real time, be it comments or photos and videos via his computer, smartphone or tablet. Magne and Lemoine (2015) identified a large field of action for co-creation, classifying consumer participation at different levels of the company's value chain, from the conception and design stage with idea generation to the innovation stage with the improvement of the offer until the communication and distribution stage. Whether it is a personalization, a co-production, a fabrication or an invention, companies are constantly trying to share impactful and engaging content with their customers. Aware of the issue relating to consumer power, they tend to involve them in a framework of collaborative product innovation while making the best use of the Internet's capacities, to properly organize the co-creation of potential value with this new "consumer @ctor". This knowledge marketing approach therefore considers the consumer as a service co-producer who functions as an operating resource following his interaction with the company. This is how certain marketing research works support the idea that the consumer's competence is socially constructed, presenting a dependence on the experience of the "consumer@ctor" (so called for his role of co-consumer-actor). As part of a strategic orientation of co-creation, from active consumer participation to interactive participation, companies now follow a process of skills identification followed by consumer immersion in an organizational learning process through collaboration. The potential of the consumer, long ignored, is thus enchanted in the era of cooperative enterprises which choose to bring their know-how into play with the skills of the consumer to co-create value together. Following the approach of the dominant service logic, the creation of value with the consumer is nothing other than the result of the mobilization of its own resources with those of the company. According to Vargo and Lush

(2008), it is the integration of operating resources formed by the knowledge, know-how, competence, and expertise of the parties in a dynamic approach of mobilization and activation of skills.

To this end, questions raised by the work of the literature around the co-creation of value relating to the specific targets of the latter. Indeed, the interest of integrating the consumer in the development process of the company's offer is quite clear, but is it enough to simply involve the consumer or, should we first target this? Employee them for a better attractiveness of the offer? Some researchers consider that for each level or form of co-creation there is a specific profile of the consumer belonging to the target market. Thus, many companies tend to identify the targets with which they wish to collaborate. Others opt for crowdsourcing which is a strategy of outsourcing the activity of the company (or some of its functions) by counting on the goodwill of consumers and hoping to maximize the number of ideas and optimal solutions offered on collaborative platforms.

The Participation of the Consumer Co-Creator With the Organisation

Detecting the profiles of the participants in the co-creation and knowing their motivation seems to be of great importance. Moreover, this subject continues to evoke debates in the literature. In the digital age, and thanks to the interactive specificities of the web, the relationship between the consumer and the company has undergone a revolutionary transformation which has also affected the profile of the consumer himself. Faced with this role, the consumer has been given a new name that has developed from "Consumer'actor" to "Prosumer".

These names are "neologisms" that is to say new words which do not exist in the current language, but which appeared following the creation of a common word from two words or from of the meaning of words, such as a lexical borrowing from what already exists. The term "Consumer'actor" is the result of the combination of the word "actor" with the word "consumer" by referring this to the active role, that the consumer gets with the company, and his ability to act. He is characterized by the emancipation of his lifestyle and his autonomy of choice in his decision process. This actor nowadays, seeks to have interactivity with companies by actively participating in the marketing mix of the company in addition to his requirement to have a typical customization of the offer. It is the same for the word "Prosumer" which is none other than the junction of the word "Producer" with the word "consumer" whose inventor was the American sociologist Alvin Toffler in the years "80". Ili refers to the same meaning of a consumer who has transformed socially and who tends to become more professional by designing for himself the company's offer thanks to the power and knowledge acquired by the digital revolution. All these names thus refer to the same profile of an emancipated, engaged contemporary consumer, who refuses simple passive consumption by substituting it with consumption that creates value.

Some brands in the retail sector of goods such as coffee with "Starbucks" and "Nespresso" have succeeded in engaging their communities on the web via online platforms by giving the possibility to their customers to share their experiences on the web and to earn money through their participation by product ideas labeled "community idea". Likewise, the giant of the board game "Monopoly" as well as other luxury leather goods brands have in turn been able to involve their customers by offering them the possibility of creating and personalizing their products by launching participatory contests and leaving free rein to their imaginations (Magne and Lemoine, 2015). A conscientious analysis of the profile of this "Consumer@ctor" or "Prosumer" in marketing research has made it possible to identify three types of skills (Magne and Lemoine, 2015). Based on the work of certain researchers, in this case Vargo and Lush (2004, 2008), this consumer has an instrumental competence relating to prior technical knowledge, a cognitive competence linked to the capacity to mobilize knowledge and a competence of use relating to lived experience (Curbatov and Louyot-Gallicher, 2011). As the knowledge and activities of consumers are interdependent, the skills of the consumer depend on their degree of creativity (Cova, 2008). In this sense, four customer profiles have been identified, according to their competence in the co-creation of value, namely, the short-sighted, ignorant, non-creative and organizational of corporate resources (Bonnemaizon and Batat, 2011).

Understanding what drives consumers to interact and react with businesses online comes down to understanding these motivations for social interaction with the company. Taking advantage of the great potential for viral spread that social media offers, companies are increasingly embracing relationship marketing and content marketing to further engage their customers. However, many firms find it difficult to identify and understand the motivations of their customers, ignoring that an unmotivated consumer is a consumer who is unlikely to be engaged with them. Engaging customers, whether online or offline, and ensuring interactive and collaborative exchanges are becoming vital for companies these days. But despite the efforts made by the latter, this remains a delicate or even difficult thing to achieve.

This proactive interaction of the company with consumers reflects the level of cognitive, emotional, and behavioral investment of these actors, Hollebeek (2011). Thus, companies create through this interactive communicational exchange a feeling of connection. As a result of the interpersonal dynamic that takes place online, more intimate relationships develop with the brand and the consumer develops a para-social relationship with the company. This para-social relationship is defined by the feeling developed through social interactions between the consumer and the company, which strengthens the links between them (Labrecque, 2014). This sentiment through the para-social interaction goes beyond the interaction itself and leads to consumer engagement, reflecting their strong feelings of loyalty and their willingness to generate content for the company. Consumers are seduced by the experience with the company at the level of social networks and thus develop an intimate para-social relationship enjoying closer proximity to it. Moreover, by focusing on what stimulates this behavior of co-creation of value in the consumer, the gratification theory represents a good explanatory framework insofar as it is interested in the motivations that lead the consumer to co-create. This theory states that the interactions that occur online represent a rewarding framework for the consumer in terms of the benefits that he can derive from this activity.

Sources of Consumer Motivation to Co-Create Value With the Company

The theory of uses and rewards (U&G) initiated by Blumler and Katz (1974), attests that the consumer uses social media according to his needs and his objectives based on the benefits derived in terms of information and pleasure. This theory is concerned with consumer participation in terms of sharing and delivering content. Appreciated more as an approach, this theory thus admits the existence of five categories of motivations: - the acquisition of knowledge and information - escape - entertainment - social interactions - self-improvement. The development of the intention to participate is often the translation of the consumer's motivations following their engagement with the company.

I n fact, the consumer may be motivated to participate in the co-creation of value to satisfy a need of the first or second order. In other words, he expects either a value from the activity of co-creation itself, or a value beyond the activity of co-creation. These authors consider that hedonic, financial, and learning motivations correspond to lower order needs while the motivations linked to identity building through relationships, social capital, esteem, and self-expression are relative to higher order needs (be it personal hedonism, social status acquisition or simple self-expression). Nambisan and Baron (2007,

2009), were the first to adopt in their work, the theory of gratuities to explain the reasons for the voluntary participation of consumers in the co-creation of value with the companies with which they interact in line. This theory places the consumer at the center of the experience and supports the role of interpersonal relationships in which participants demonstrate their commitment to the company. The foundations of this theory are based on needs motivation in explaining consumer behavior. Thus, in the context of co-creation, there are mainly four types of rewarding values behind consumers' co-creative behavior and their engagement in co-creation within online communities (Nambisan and Baron, (2009). According to the researchers, these motivations relate to the value of learning, the value of social integration, the value of personal development and the hedonic value. By participating an online co-creation activity, consumers tend to rate their participations based on bonuses. They will perceive the cognitive and affective advantages that may affect their participation (Lorenzo et al, 2014). These benefits derived from the value co-creation activity, revolve around economic benefits relating to cost reduction, and social and psychological benefits relating to fun and self-expression (Nambisan and Baron, 2009; Hoyer et al, 2010; Verleye, 2015). Moreover, the meeting with others and the interaction within these groups at these sharing spaces present a social motivation for participation in the co-creation of value (Füller, 2010).

Considering this classification, the author notes that the motivations for the co-creation of value form a mix of intrinsic and extrinsic motivations. The literature relating to the general framework of motivation, many researchers agree on its presentation as an energizing force which determines the form, direction, intensity, and duration of the task to be performed (Boughzela, 2016). Thus, different typologies of motivation for co-creation appear in the works of the literature. To understand the type of motivations specific to the co-creation of value, different theoretical frameworks can be mobilized.

THE COMPANY BETWEEN ITS CORPORATE E-REPUTATION AND THE CO-CREATION OF VALUE WITH THE CONSUMER

An Engaging Co-Creation of Value

Companies try to find, through these new forms of online sociability, to develop and maintain a well-set social relationship by appealing to the consumer's motivations relating to this social framework while stimulating their belonging (Moretti and Tuan, 2014); O ' Brien, 2010). In addition, the online reputation of companies has thus become an indicator of customer engagement. Managing your reputation online means managing your virtual identity, the reliability of your sharing, your online presence, and the transparency of your relationship. This whole e-reputation management and monitoring strategy relies on the customer and providing him with a favorable framework. This exchange of knowledge and skills is fostered by online stakeholder engagement, which in turn fosters collaboration, trust and the perception and sharing of value for the different stakeholders. Engaged customers are a lever for the company and a source of competitive advantage (Van Doorn, 2010). By managing customer engagement, the business can create value with these types of customers and achieve organizational goals while driving their performance.

To this end, it is necessary to manage customer engagement proactively to properly support one's power of influence around one's peers. Marketing researchers support this by arguing that the success of companies' marketing strategies comes down to their mastery and management of the customer relationship through its commitment to social media (Broodie et al, 2013). participation in the co-creation of value, within online communities, allows its participants to integrate socially by having an active role in the value chain of the company. It also allows the development of a new social identity through these interactive exchanges. In addition, this experience brings an enrichment of knowledge to its co-creators, thus representing a functional value for each of them. On the other hand, the opportunity for self-expression that this action allows only enhances their self-esteem. The development of the intention to participate is often the translation of the consumer's motivations because of his social interactive engagement with the company. Engagement begins with the connection and relational exchange between the company and the consumer which, thanks to social media technology, becomes an interactive exchange in real time. These exchanges lead to the satisfaction of the consumer who will continue to interact with the company progressing towards a state of social interactive engagement (Vivek et al, 2012); Mollen and Wilson, 2010). These Internet users are looking for pleasure through their consumption experiences and this is how their engagement is activated thanks to the benefits they perceive from the experience of co-creation. They consider their commitment to the co-creation of value to be a very enriching experience.

This interactive collaborative framework allows the creation of multiple added values for each participant, ensuring their long-term commitment. At this level, a distinction can be made between the one naturally engaged in co-creation and the one engaged through payment. The most important prerequisite for the naturally motivated person is their own interest in the task in question, which will promote the development of their natural commitment. The creativity of the person will be doubled by his intrinsic motivations (Amabile et al, 1995). Some researchers confirm this by arguing that using people who are intrinsically motivated can achieve more performance (Capelli et al, 2016). While the one who is hired for the rewards, his commitment is not going to be natural, and he will perceive this task as a job to be done and for which he will be paid (Füller, 2010). Aware of the dynamics of consumer skills and these specificities, crowdsourcing practices tend to develop mixed forms of innovation by involving both clients and non-clients of companies in the upstream or downstream innovation process to '' optimize value creation and generate innovative ideas.

From the Co-Creation of Value to the Co-Destruction of Value

These observations lead to the conclusion that value is now determined by the customer, who becomes co-creator of organizational knowledge through his consumption experience (Yi and Gong, 2013). This is a new orientation for connected companies towards the esteem needs of their customers with a satisfaction of their need, and social interactions enjoy their full attention.

However, co-creation is not always beneficial, and its process can be value-destroying rather than value-creating. Indeed, the failure of value co-creation operations can result because of several factors; mainly relating to the bad management of the actors involved (Guan et al, 2020). A healthy relationship between motivated and dynamic participants can only produce benefits for each party. The well-being of these actors, once not insured, can only lower their performance, and negatively influence the development of the process of co-creation of value between them. As a result, some companies have found themselves blocked with a disillusioned community, with a conflict of social norms, also with a dissatisfied customers who use badly the resources mobilized (Buhalis et al, 2020). These disagreements between partners and this waste of resources can lead to a process of value destruction. Harris and al (2010) have already classified in their work the co-destruction of value into a voluntary and accidental co-destruction based on the intentions of the actors involved. Consequently, an abuse of resources, whether tangible or intangible (time, physical energy, knowledge, etc.), can impact the whole context of the co-creation of value as well as the commitment and confidence of the participants (Smith, 2013).

It is an evolving process of creating value through the integration of personal resources and overcoming conflicts and technical difficulties. Moreover, the perception of the success of this collaboration still partially subjective if it depends on the expected value (Lintula et al, 2018). Some companies may witness a value contradiction with their stakeholders leading, in addition to conflicts, to the perception of insufficient value of co-creation. Faced with this, the unique involvement and engagement of customers in the development of new products and services, with a better communication strategy, makes it possible to bring more value to customers but also to gain in efficiency for companies through the outcome. Following the failure of some efforts at co-creation of value, some companies have chosen to involve their customers in a process of recovering the failed co-creation following an emotion management strategy by sending them apologies and by engaging them in a compensation system (Praveen, 2017). Other companies have opted to train customers through demonstrations, requiring little effort on their part in terms of time and innovation, for better management of the process of co-creation of value with consumers (Van den Broeke, and Paparoidamis, 2020).

CONCLUSION

With the appearance of social media, the world has seen a new form of virtual socialization that is impacting the relationship between consumers and organizations they interact with, as well as their own choice decisions. Something that has facilitated the social integration of consumers allowing them new roles on the web.

The virtual world now gives an opportunity for the company to engage its customers and jointly create value. Since value comes from online interactions and experiences, companies need to deliver satisfying virtual experiences to consumers by making the most of the potential of social media to promote their online reputation. and develop strong relationships with Internet users (Parahald and Ramaswamy, 2004); Vargo and Lusch, 2008). Some companies have adopted the digital transformation and have opted for an online presence, to face this challenge and manage their reputation well. These companies have chosen to take advantage of the interactive potential of social media, asking the collaboration of consumers for the skills they have developed online. However, others preferred not to be there, they can be found on the web through consumer shares. Between being or not being and between involving the consumer or not doing so, these are questions that managers are asking themselves these days.

Undeniably, the online presence has given companies a head start, considered a competitive advantage, allowing them to give more credibility to their online image; but this comes at a very high cost. In the era of the Internet, companies' online reputation, image and notoriety no longer depend on their marketing efforts or their accomplishments, but rather on their ability to reach the Internet user through social interactions. Hence the importance given to the management of social interactions between companies and Internet users.

This great importance given by all actors of the economic scene to online reputation underlines its weight in commercial and economic relations. Now it represents a vector of change for companies who have understood the need to adopt a digital culture by exploiting the technological tools of the Internet for a better improvement of their social image. This digitization has empowered consumers with their new ability to create content and spread information at the speed of social media. By their online coexistence, a new economic era has marked the business world based on the proactive participation of the consumer. It would be interesting to explore the identity dynamic between the online reputation of a company and the identity with the person with whom it trying to collaborate. Does promoting the online reputation of its customers allow the company to promote its own online corporate reputation?

REFERENCES

Alloing, C. (2013). La médiation documentaire sur les réseaux socio-numériques comme vecteur de l'e-réputation. La Poste, Twitter et les agents-facilitateurs. *Communication et organisation*, *43*, 73-84.

Alloing, C. (2016). *Réputation: Méditation, calcul, émotion*. CNRS Editions.

Alloing, C., & Pierre, J. (2012). *Construire un cadre d'analyse avec les SIC pour comprendre les pratiques et les enjeux de la réputation en ligne (des individus et des organisations)*. Academic Press.

Amabile, T. M., Hil, K. G., Hennessey, B. A., & Tighe, E. M. (1995). The Work Preference Inventory: Assessing intrinsic and extrinsic motivational orientations. *Journal of Personality and Social Psychology*, *66*(5), 950–967. doi:10.1037/0022-3514.66.5.950 PMID:8014837

Ardley, B., McIntosh, E., & McManus, J. (2020). From transactions to interactions: The value of co-creation processes within online brand consumer communities. *Business Process Management Journal*, *26*(4), 825–838. doi:10.1108/BPMJ-10-2019-0444

Blumer, J. G., & Katz, E. (1974). *The uses of Mass Communications Current. Perspectives on gratifications research*. Sage.

Bonnemaizon, A., & Batat, W. (2011). How competent are consumers? The case of the energy sector in France. *International Journal of Consumer Studies*, *35*(3), 348–358. doi:10.1111/j.1470-6431.2010.00937.x

Boughzala, Garmaki, & Chourabi Tantan. (2020). *Understanding how Digital Intelligence Contributes to Digital Creativity and Digital Transformation: A Systematic Literature Review*. . doi:10.24251/HICSS.2020.040

Boughzala, I. (2016). Social media and value creation: Exploring the perception of Generation Y toward corporate social networking applications use. *Journal of Organizational and End User Computing*, *28*(2), 107–123. doi:10.4018/JOEUC.2016040107

Boughzala, I., Benhayoun-Sadafiyine, L. (2020). *Étude de cas. Le DMS (Digitalization Maturity System): Instrument d'évaluation de la maturité de la transformation digitale des entreprises*. Academic Press.

Brodie, R. J., Ilic, A., Juric, B., & Hollebeek, L. (2013). Consumer engagement in a virtual brand community: An exploratory analysis. *Journal of Business Research*, *66*(1), 105–114. doi:10.1016/j.jbusres.2011.07.029

Buhalis, D., Andreu, L., & Gnoth, J. (2020). The dark side of the sharing economy: Balancing value co-creation and value co-destruction. *Psychology and Marketing*, *37*(5), 689–704. doi:10.1002/mar.21344

Cadel, P. (2010). Le marché de l'e-réputation. *Les Cahiers du numérique*, *6*(4), 111-121.

Capelli, S., Falchi, A., Hussler, C., & Sabadie, W. (2016). Co-innover avec ses consommateurs: oui, mais lesquels? De l'intérêt d'impliquer les consommateurs-membres dans le processus d'innovation des entreprises coopératives. *Gestion 2000, 33*(4), 117-141.

Castellano, S., & Dutot, V. (2013). Une analyse de l'e-réputation par analogie ou contraste avec la réputation: Une approche par les médias sociaux. *Revue française du Marketing,* (243).

Castellano, S., & Dutot, V. (2015). Designing a Measurement Scale for E-Reputation. *Corporate Reputation Review, 18*(4), 294–313. doi:10.1057/crr.2015.15

Curbatov, O. (2001). *La Construction et la Modélisation du Knowledge Marketing*. Document RODIGE.

Curbatov, O. (2003). *L'intégration du consommateur par le « Knowledge Marketing »: conception, production et consommation d'un produit personnel* (Doctoral dissertation). Université de Nice Sophia Antipolis.

Curbatov, O., & Louyot-Gallicher, M. (2011). *Le Knowledge Marketing et les compétences du consommateur au service de la co-création*. 32ème Congrès de l'Association Française de Marketing, Bruxelles, Belgique.

Davies, G., Chun, R., da Silva, R. V., & Roper, S. (2004). A corporate character scale to assess employee and customer views of organization reputation. *Corporate Reputation Review, 7*(2), 125–146. doi:10.1057/palgrave.crr.1540216

Deephouse, D. L. (2000). Media reputation as a strategic resource: An integration of mass communication and resource-based theories. *Journal of Management, 26*(6), 1091–1112. doi:10.1177/014920630002600602

Eouzan, G., Michalon, C., Guissani, A., Bridier, K., & Dupuis, J. (2017). *Webmarketing: Définir, mettre en pratique et optimiser sa stratégie digitale*. Éditions Paris ENI.

Floreddu, B. P., & Cabiddu, F. (2014). Managing online reputation: the role of social media in insurance industry. In Academy of Management Proceedings (Vol. 2014, No. 1, p. 17040). Briarcliff Manor, NY: Academy of Management. doi:10.5465/ambpp.2014.17040abstract

Füller, J. (2010). Refining virtual co-creation from a consumer perspective. *California Management Review, 52*(2), 98–122. doi:10.1525/cmr.2010.52.2.98

Füller, J., Hutter, K., & Faullant, R. (2011). Why co-creation experience matters? Creative experience and its impact on the quantity and quality of creative contributions. *R & D Management, 41*(3), 259–273. doi:10.1111/j.1467-9310.2011.00640.x

Gartner Digital Business Transformation—Gartner IT Glossary. (n.d.). Available online: https://www.gartner.com/it-glossary/digital-business-transformation

Harris, L., Russell-Bennett, R., Plé, L., & Cáceres, R. C. (2010). Not always co-creation: Introducing interactional co-destruction of value in service-dominant logic. *Journal of Services Marketing.*

Hollebeek, L. (2011). Exploring customer brand engagement: Definition and themes. *Journal of Strategic Marketing, 19*(7), 555–573. doi:10.1080/0965254X.2011.599493

Hudson, S., Huang, L., Roth, M. S., & Madden, T. J. (2016). The influence of social media interactions on consumer–brand relationships: A three-country study of brand perceptions and marketing behaviors. *International Journal of Research in Marketing, 33*(1), 27–41. doi:10.1016/j.ijresmar.2015.06.004

Kaplan, A. M., & Haenlein, M. (2010). Users of the world, unite! The challenges and opportunities of Social Media. *Business Horizons, 53*(1), 59–68. doi:10.1016/j.bushor.2009.09.003

Kotler, P., Kartajaya, H., & Setiawan, I. (2016). *Marketing 4.0: Moving from traditional to digital.* John Wiley & Sons.

Labrecque, L. I., vor dem Esche, J., Mathwick, C., Novak, T. P., & Hofacker, C. F. (2013). Consumer power: Evolution in the digital age. *Journal of Interactive Marketing, 27*(4), 257–269. doi:10.1016/j.intmar.2013.09.002

Leroux, E. (2017). Cahier: Management du tourisme durable: conciliation, commercialisation et durabilité. *Revue Management & Avenir*, (96), 117–122.

Lintula, J., Tuunanen, T., Salo, M., & Myers, M. D. (2018). When Value Co-Creation Turns to Co-Destruction: Users' Experiences of Augmented Reality Mobile Games. *International Conference on Information Systems. Association for Information Systems (AIS).*

Lorenzo-Romero, C., Constantinides, E., & Brünink, L. A. (2014). Co-creation: Customer integration in social media based product and service development. *Procedia: Social and Behavioral Sciences, 148*, 383–396. doi:10.1016/j.sbspro.2014.07.057

Magne, S., & Lemoine, F. (2015). Essai de classification des pratiques de cocréation de produits et services. *6th Meeting of the AIMS Thematic Research Group on Innovation.*

Mahmoud, A. B., Fuxman, L., Mohr, I., Reisel, W. D., & Grigoriou, N. (2020). "We aren't your reincarnation!" workplace motivation across X, Y and Z generations. *International Journal of Manpower.*

Mandagi, D. W., & Aseng, A. C. (2021). *Millennials and Gen Z's perception of social media marketing effectiveness on the festival's branding: The mediating effect of brand gestalt. Asia Pacific Social Science Review.*

Martínez-Cañas, R., Ruiz-Palomino, P., Linuesa-Langreo, J., & Blázquez-Resino, J. J. (2016). Consumer participation in co-creation: An enlightening model of causes and effects based on ethical values and transcendent motives. *Frontiers in Psychology, 7*, 793. doi:10.3389/fpsyg.2016.00793 PMID:27303349

Mejri, E., & Gharbi, J. (2016). L'impact de la valeur perçue de la Co-création sur l'engagement des consommateurs. Université Tunis El Manar. *Proceedings of the Marketing Spring Colloquy (URAM)*, 6.

Mollen, A., & Wilson, H. (2010). Engagement, telepresence, and interactivity in online consumer experience: Reconciling scholastic and managerial perspectives. *Journal of Business Research, 63*(9-10), 919–925. doi:10.1016/j.jbusres.2009.05.014

Moretti, A., & Tuan, A. (2014). *Social media marketing and relationship marketing: revolution or evolution? A first step analysis. Sinergie Italian Journal of Management, 93.*

Nambisan, S., & Baron, R. A. (2009). Virtual customer environments: Testing a model of voluntary participation in value co-creation activities. *Journal of Product Innovation Management, 26*(4), 388–406. doi:10.1111/j.1540-5885.2009.00667.x

Nambisan, S., & Baron, R. A. (2010). Different roles, different strokes: Organizing virtual customer environments to promote two types of customer contributions. *Organization Science, 21*(2), 554–572. doi:10.1287/orsc.1090.0460

O'Brien, H. L. (2010). The influence of hedonic and utilitarian motivations on user engagement: The case of online shopping experiences. *Interacting with Computers: Special Issue on User Experience, 22*(4), 344–352. doi:10.1016/j.intcom.2010.04.001

Palacios-Marqués, D., Gallego-Nicholls, J. F., & Guijarro-García, M. (2021). A recipe for success: Crowdsourcing, online social networks, and their impact on organizational performance. *Technological Forecasting and Social Change, 165*, 120566. doi:10.1016/j.techfore.2020.120566

Paquerot, M., Queffelec, A., Sueur, I., & Biot-Paquerot, G. (2011). L'e-réputation ou le renforcement de la gouvernance par le marché de l'hôtellerie. *Management Avenir*, (5), 280-296.

Pierre, J. (2011). Génétique de l'identité numérique. *Les Cahiers du numérique, 7*(1), 15-29.

Pollák, F., & Markovic, P. (2021). Economic Activity as a Determinant for Customer Adoption of Social Media Marketing. *Sustainability, 2021*(13), 3999. doi:10.3390u13073999

Ponzi, L. J., Fombrun, C. J., & Gardberg, N. A. (2011). RepTrak™ pulse: Conceptualizing and validating a short-form measure of corporate reputation. *Corporate Reputation Review, 14*(1), 15–35. doi:10.1057/crr.2011.5

Prahalad, C. K., & Ramaswamy, V. (2004). Co-creation experiences: The next practice in value creation. *Journal of Interactive Marketing, 18*(3), 5–14. doi:10.1002/dir.20015

Praveen, S. (2017). *Customer responses to failure of co-created products and services*. Academic Press.

Priporas, C. V. (2020). Smart Consumers and Decision-making Process in the Smart Retailing Context through Generation Z Eyes. In *Retail Futures*. Emerald Publishing Limited. doi:10.1108/978-1-83867-663-620201017

Ramaswamy, V. (2010). Competing through co-creation: Innovation at two companies. *Strategy and Leadership, 38*(2), 22–29. doi:10.1108/10878571011029028

Rindova, V. P., & Martins, L. L. (2012). Show me the money: A multidimensional perspective on reputation as an intangible asset. The Oxford handbook of corporate reputation, 16-33.

Siano, A., Vollero, A., Confetto, M. G., & Siglioccolo, M. (2013). Corporate communication management: A framework based on decision-making with reference to communication resources. *Journal of Marketing Communications, 19*(3), 151–167. doi:10.1080/13527266.2011.581301

Siano, A., Vollero, A., & Palazzo, M. (2011). Exploring the role of online consumer empowerment in reputation building: Research questions and hypotheses. *Journal of Brand Management, 19*(1), 57–71. doi:10.1057/bm.2011.23

Smith, A. (2013). *Smartphone ownership-2013 update* (Vol. 12). Pew Research Center.

Sriram, G., & Kathiravan, C. (2014). Effect Of Social Media And Factors Influencing A Brand's Reputation. *International Journal of Innovative Research and Studies*, *3*(8), 366–378.

Van den Broeke, M., & Paparoidamis, N. (2021). Engaging in or escaping co-creation? An analytical model. *International Journal of Production Economics*, *231*, 107917. doi:10.1016/j.ijpe.2020.107917

Van Doorn, J., Lemon, K. N., Mittal, V., Nass, S., Pick, D., Pirner, P., & Verhoef, P. C. (2010). Customer engagement behavior: Theoretical foundations and research directions. *Journal of Service Research*, *13*(3), 253–266. doi:10.1177/1094670510375599

Vargo, S. L., & Lusch, R. F. (2008). Service-dominant logic: Continuing the evolution. *Journal of the Academy of Marketing Science*, *36*(1), 1–10. doi:10.100711747-007-0069-6

Viana, M. L. D., & dos Santos, M. C. L. (2020). Design Perspectives From Co-Creation Experiences in Brazilian Complex Social Contexts. In *3rd International Conference on Dwelling Form (IDWELL 2020)* (pp. 170-179). Atlantis Press. 10.2991/assehr.k.201009.018

Vivek, S. D., Beatty, S. E., & Morgan, R. M. (2012). Customer engagement: Exploring customer relationships beyond purchase. *Journal of Marketing Theory and Practice*, *20*(2), 122–146. doi:10.2753/MTP1069-6679200201

Watrick, S. (2002). Measuring Corporate Reputation: Defining and Data. Business and Society. *Journal of Marketing*, *41*(4), 371–392.

Yi, Y., & Gong, T. (2013). Customer value co-creation behavior: Scale development and validation. *Journal of Business Research*, *66*(9), 1279–1284. doi:10.1016/j.jbusres.2012.02.026

Zhang, H., Lu, Y., Wang, B., & Wu, S. (2015). The impacts of technological environments and co-creation experiences on customer participation. *Information & Management*, *52*(4), 468–482. doi:10.1016/j.im.2015.01.008

Zollo, L., Rialti, R., Ciappei, C., & Boccardi, A. (2018). *Bricolage and Social Entrepreneurship to Address Emergent Social Needs: A 'Deconstructionist' Perspective*. Academic Press.

ENDNOTES

1 WIPO: World Intellectual Property Organization Https://www.wipo.int/portal/en/index.html

2 «Gartner»: Entreprise Américaine de référence spécialisée dans le conseil et la recherche en technologies avancées https://www.gartner.com/en

Chapter 4
The Degree of SMEs Digitalization in the Context of the European Digital United Market

Iulia Cristina Iuga
https://orcid.org/0000-0002-2831-3055
1 Decembrie 1918 University from Alba Iulia, Romania

ABSTRACT

The purpose of this study is to evaluate, based on official statistical data, Romania's situation on SME marketing adaptation to the digital economy compared to 25 other European countries. The chapter will consist of three parts: Part 1, "Digital Economy"; Part 2, "Marketing of SMEs in the Context of the Digital Age"; Part 3, "The Analysis of the Degree of Digitisation of SMEs and the Creation of Favourable Conditions for this Process in the EU: Application - Hellwig's Classic Taxonomic Method." The situation created by the COVID-19 pandemic will also be included. The author presents the main aspects of SME marketing and the new characteristics and trends of their marketing in the 'digital age'. This paper aims at the following objectives: 1) to show how the economy is influenced by new technologies and 2) to highlight Romania's position among other European countries in the application of electronic marketing techniques among SMEs.

INTRODUCTION

Humanity never met before such an increased rate of changes and a strong connection between the existent phenomena. The globalisation and continuous evolution of technology become the development real "engines", but only if they are understood and used in the right moment, in the right area, and in the measure in which they harmonise with circumstances.

The economy strongly connects to daily life, and the new technologies cannot isolate it, nor can avoid their influences. Moreover, the economy may benefit from many opportunities, by gradually adapting

DOI: 10.4018/978-1-7998-7192-7.ch004

to significant changes from performant technologies increasing usage. Nowadays, economic agents can streamline their activity more than ever and access detailed information quickly. Furthermore, consumers too become more informed and independent in making decisions and choices. This aspect imposes the granting of significant importance to marketing activities, and at the same time, their adaptation to the evolution direction of the economy.

Digitalisation is: "…the sociotechnical process of applying digitising techniques to broader social and institutional contexts that render digital technologies infrastructural" (Tilson et al., 2010). Concretely, digitalisation is the application of digital technologies and infrastructures in business, economy, and society.

The ability to internationalize has become a competitive necessity for many firms and represents an important way to survive and grow in the age of globalization (Joensuu-Salo et al., 2018). The process of SMEs internationalisation is a learning process (Schweizer 2012). Autio (2017) argues that the effect of digitalisation creates opportunities for existing SMEs to proactively rethink their internal and external interactions. Digital transformation changing the way of small and medium-sized enterprises (SMEs) create and gain value (Bharadwaj et al., 2013; Lucas et al., 2013). But, in many cases, SMEs are not fully aware of the digitalisation effects. This leads to a misconception in terms of the complexity and expenditure of digitisation solutions so that their potential economic benefits cannot be adequately estimated (Sommer 2015). On the other hand, an incorrect estimate of the adoption of digitisation could put in danger the SMEs value chain, as they are much more cost-sensitive compared to large enterprises. Therefore, an appropriate approach is needed for SMEs to estimate the potential for implementation and prioritise digital technologies (Kilimis et al.,2019).

Digitalisation encompasses a critical component: electronic commerce, which is, in essence, a selling channel (supplementary), whose essential characteristics are speed, flexibility, and transparency. Digitalisation opportunities are multiple: more extensive visibility, a broader coverage on the market, storage reduced costs, shorter delivery terms, more efficient acquisition processes, and higher customer satisfaction. E-commerce activities may generate turnovers, impossible to obtain through conventional means (such as selling at a fixed point, sales forces, fairs, and catalogues, mail-order); it may allow SMEs to access groups of new clients, digitally oriented, or extend their sales area in other regions, even beyond country borders.

Technology is continually transforming the world. Even though this offers many opportunities for those who have access to it, some barriers still exist in the online environment, which prevents users from enjoying all the desired goods and services, the online companies, and start-ups to have unlimited horizons. The governments and businesses to fully benefit of online environment's instruments.

This case study will follow Romanian SMEs' actual situation analysis on the Digital Single Market by comparing it with other 25 European states in the 2013-2019 period. The purpose of this study is to evaluate, based on official statistical data, Romania's situation on the SMEs' marketing adaptation to the digital economy.

The chapter will consist of 3 parts: Part 1. Digital Economy; Part 2. Marketing of SMEs in the context of the Digital Age; Part 3. The analysis of the degree of digitisation of SMEs and the creation of favourable conditions for this process in the EU: application - Hellwig's classic taxonomic method.

Part 1 introduces the concept of a digital economy and gives a presentation of its characteristics, concepts closely related to it, and current trends. The situation created by the Covid-19 pandemic will also be included.

Part 2 argues the importance of SMEs in the European economy and generally presents the main aspects of the marketing of small and medium-sized enterprises, as well as the new characteristics and trends of their marketing in the 'digital age', as SMEs are the most sensitive to change and adapt most easily, so they are the ones that first and foremost can and should keep up with what is happening in the economy and society.

Part 3 is a case study on the degree to which SMEs in some countries use the electronic environment to conduct marketing activities. The study is based on the application of a method that transforms statistical data, i.e., the values of certain distinct variables describing an enterprise's ability to use technologies for marketing. By processing this data, a unique ranking of states is achieved by the degree to which small and medium-sized enterprises include new technologies in the conduct of marketing activities. Based on this ranking, Romania's situation is specifically analysed and an attempt is made to explain its position in the ranking. The analysis of the current situation of Romanian SMEs in the Digital Single Market will be followed, compared to 25 other European countries. The study aims to assess, based on official statistical data, Romania's situation regarding the adaptation of SME marketing to the digital economy.

This paper aims at the following objectives:

1. To show how the economy is influenced by new technologies;
2. To highlight Romania's position among other European countries in the application of electronic marketing techniques among SMEs and the development of the conditions that favour it.

BACKGROUND

"Digitalisation" means digital technologies usage, for the change the business model of a company in a way that offers new options of income and value creation, while digital business models allow fast transboundary enlargement (Zhang et al., 2015; Holand et al., 2019). Digital transformation imposes on companies to reconsider and innovate their business models. However, small and medium-sized enterprises (SMEs) have no time or resources to experiment with new models in their businesses or apply new strategies. At the same time, the global economy increasing digitalisation offer SMEs internationalisation and scaling opportunities (Stallkamp & Schotter, 2019; Nord et al., 2020).

Parida et al. (2019) ascertain that the literature on digitalisation and connection with businesses is relatively recent. The first paper dates to 2012, and until September 2018, 106 studies appeared in 73 international journals. Bowman et al. (2019) did an empirical study on 321 European SMEs that use active social networks, big data, and information technology to innovate their business models and concluded that SMEs might take different routes to improve their performance when digital transformation changes the business model.

Zhu et al. (2003) developed a conceptual model to study electronic business adoption (e-business) at the company level, incorporating six adoption facilitators and inhibitors, based on the theoretical framework technology-organisation-environment. Investigation data from 3100 enterprises and 7500 consumers from eight European countries tested the proposed adoption model. They concluded that as the electronic businesses' intensity grows, two environmental factors – consumers' availability and the lack of commercial partners' training – become less critical while competitive pressure remains significant.

The article of Vahlne & Bhatti (2019) explores the empiric role of digital technologies of electronic businesses in the export predilection explanation of Italian SMEs and focuses on electronic business technologies' adoption and implementation, which allow enterprises to exchange information along the supply chain in order to consider the potential heterogeneities in the digitalisation path. The study results confirm the positive impact of Internet-based technologies and show that e-business technologies positively impact internationalisation only when integrated into the processes framework and conditions of organisational innovations and digital competencies investments.

Mário Franco et al. (2016) did a study in the European Union, aiming to demonstrate social networks' role in SMEs' performance in Portugal's interior region. The emerged results that studied SMEs re to social networks, especially Facebook, and the reasons associated with costs reduction influence financial indicators (increase profit) and non-financial indicators (human resources results). In another study, Montecchi & Nobbs (2017) shows, through a semi-structured series of interviews, the connection between social media and content generated by users, as well as the connection between social media and co-innovation in enterprises success. The research of Marchand et al. (2018) concludes that the proposed social media strategies are more appropriate for small enterprises. Kannan & Alice (2017) develops a framework for the key elements of the marketing strategy process, where digital technologies have a decisive impact, and Carvalhosa et al. (2017) study the proximity of an organisation with its clients if the organisation uses digital marketing techniques. Similarly, in their research, Joensuu-Salo et al. (2018) show that for Finland internationalised SMEs, the usage of marketing capacity and digitalisation is essential for their success. The internet utilisation rate has had an unprecedented dynamic during the last years. The opportunities offered by internet use are promising, especially for optimising managerial decisions, the adoption of efficient risk management and operational efficacy, innovation capacity increase, and improved client management (Benvenuto *et al.*, 2020).

COVID-19 Pandemic is a global crisis that puts small and medium-sized enterprises (SMEs) under colossal pressure to survive by requesting them to manage the crisis efficiently. SMEs adopted different digital technologies in order to face this crisis. The study of Guo et al. (2020) analyses the relation between SMEs' digitalisation and their public responses in crises using a data set from 518 Chinese SMEs' survey. The results of the study show that digitalisation may contribute to SMEs' performance improvement.

Digital Economy

The 2019-2020 pandemic has led to countries engaging in a war on three key fronts: firstly, in the health system, which has been allocated massive funds to halt the spread of the virus and to treat the sick. Secondly, economically, all countries face critical issues with great social impact. In most Western countries the economy relies primarily on domestic consumption. Isolation of people in March, April, and May and through „social distancing" had an adverse impact on the economies of those countries. In the first half of 2020, the economy contracted due to the Covid-19 pandemic. Businesses have closed and consumers have isolated, slowing down the consumption. The negative economic impact generated by the Covid-19 pandemic, already existing, is impressive. The tourism industry and transport sector make a significant contribution to GDP (in some countries) have been heavily affected. Companies were temporarily closed, employees were introduced to the "technical unemployment" system and the production was zero in some sectors. Export volumes have fallen as export markets have collapsed, with countries setting other priorities during this period. Thirdly, in terms of how to work in the future ("telework" or work from home). Some companies (banks, insurance companies) were forced by circumstances to leave their employees to work remotely from home, where business profile allowed it (Hada et al., 2020).

The economy is being increasingly influenced by globalization, the restrictive conditions enforced by the states of the world (to halt the spread of the COVID-19 virus), by recent information and communications technology, which allows to increase the efficiency of economic agents, surpass the economic disturbances and better flexibility to the changes of consumer behavior. A new form of the economy is accurately looming nowadays, also referred to as the new economy or digital economy, the network economy, the Internet-based economy, the electronic economy. A short definition is given by Mircea (2004) „ digital economy can be described as the economy relied upon knowledge, information and on Information and Communication Technology (ICT). Therefore, the new economy is the result of human interference and interaction with the personal computer, telecommunications, Internet, and Electronics, practically the economy and the technology are inseparable, given the multitude of benefits that would be brought about by the modernization of the economy.

New indicators for measuring the economy are emerging. Below is an example of classification of the indicators for gauging the digital economy by Robert D. Atkinson. Further is presented Robert D. Atkinson's classification of digital economy indicators concerning (Mircea, 2004):

- Knowledge-based jobs (number of employees in the ICT sector, educational level, etc.)
- Globalization (foreign investments, orientation towards foreign trade);
- Competition and economic dynamism (number of industry-leading companies with dramatic growth, number of newly established companies and companies that have gone bankrupt);
- Digital Economy (t percentage of adult population online, number of internet commercial domains, usage of computers and technologies in various fields, number of internet providers);
- Technological Innovation Capacity (number of jobs in technological manufacturing industries, number of engineers and scientists, number of patents, investments in research and development (% of GDP), venture capital funds (% of GDP)

A key feature of the digital economy organization is the replacement of pyramidal traditional hierarchy with the horizontal one (Ghilic-Micu B., 2004), which enhances collaboration and open communication. This propensity to remove the intermediate channels and internal communication rigors stems from the need to increase the efficiency and speed of this process, to keep up with the increasing flow of information.

Various authors have researched the constituents of digitalization in the scientific literature. For instance, Bouwman (1999) provided three types of indicators for measuring e-commerce: 1. Indicators that are related to how e-commerce is used (ease of access, computer availability, modems and, home internet availability); 2. Indicators related to the degree to which e-commerce is used (data used, types of use, products) 3. Indicators that measure the effects and implications of using e-commerce at the business level and on the entire economy. Elmer (1999) draws attention to the need for the following indicators: demand, supply, the technology used, and macroeconomic variables. Figuera (1999) develops a series of relative indicators, exclusively for e-commerce: the number of hosts on the Internet, the number of computers, modems, and mobile phones.

The use of the Internet results in a reduction in the cost of transactions, an increase in the business performance (fewer resources are employed and the costs are considerably reduced, routine tasks are handled by the service provider), and the creation of markets based on current technologies (in the present circumstances, the market not only went global but also emerges in the form of new models, of societies based on the electronic network, whose activity occurs mainly in the digital environment).

Influences on Business: Opportunities and Challenges

The progressive transition to the information society will divide enterprises into traditional and modern organizations, that use information and communication technology (ICT). First, a modern enterprise puts the customer at the center and continuously enhances its customer loyalty capacity. The rigorous pyramidal hierarchy would gradually be disabled in support of an organization based on equality and effective communication. In that manner, not only is creativity and innovation capacity-optimized but teamwork and collaboration between employees are also encouraged, hence deepening mutual reliance at work. At the same time, both how good and serviced are produced and how the value is generated and monetized are subject to innovation.

The ongoing evolution of the economy consequently imposes businesses to adjust, moreover, to find a new approach to modeling the economic activity of the organization.

Given the development of the digital means, a new term has emerged: e-business. It comprises two other new terms: e-commerce and e-payment and assumes that all three phases of a business (negotiation, payment, and delivery of the good/service) are exclusively carried out through an electronic system based on numerous technologies, techniques, services, and concepts (Leţia, 2014).

Figure 1 shows a business model that would increase the efficiency of entrepreneurs on the Internet.

Web Portals (websites) (Figure 1) are designated to attract more customers, to increase both customer loyalty and turnover, their content being structured into catalogs to be accessed as easily and usefully as possible. *Business Transactions Engines* represents the key element of a web strategy, given idea materialization (search, trade, entertainment) that aims to reach the target audience. *Virtual communities* are based on an uncomplicated psychological concept, namely, to generate to a group the power to stay united (Ghilic-Micu, 2002).

Figure 1. Key elements of an e-business (Ghilic-Micu, 2002)

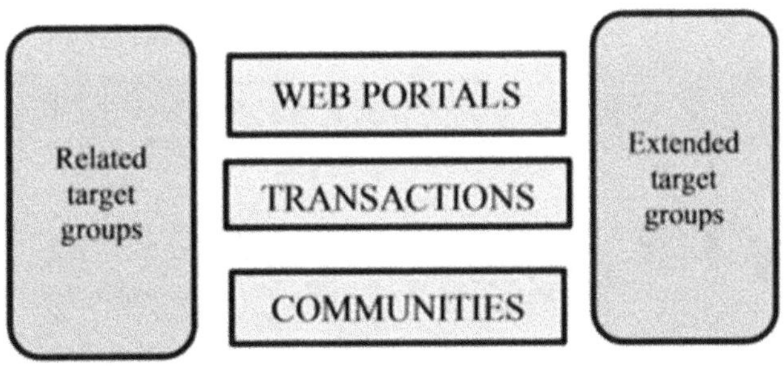

The most notable effects of the digitalization of economy on business can be listed as follows:

- a tendency for intensive innovation;
- an inclination for greater use of new sources of financing (venture capital, crowdfunding, etc.);
- recognition of the importance of intangible assets (patents, trademarks, copyrights, franchises, licenses) at the expense of tangible assets;
- the business model seeks to enhance the value of the network effects, user-generated content, and of the collection and exploitation of personal information;

- removal of border barriers in terms of trade and diversification of traditional trade forms through new channels.

The opportunities of the digital economy for business are synthetically displayed in Figure 2.

Figure 2. The facilities offered to businesses by the digital economy (Ghilic-Micu, 2002)

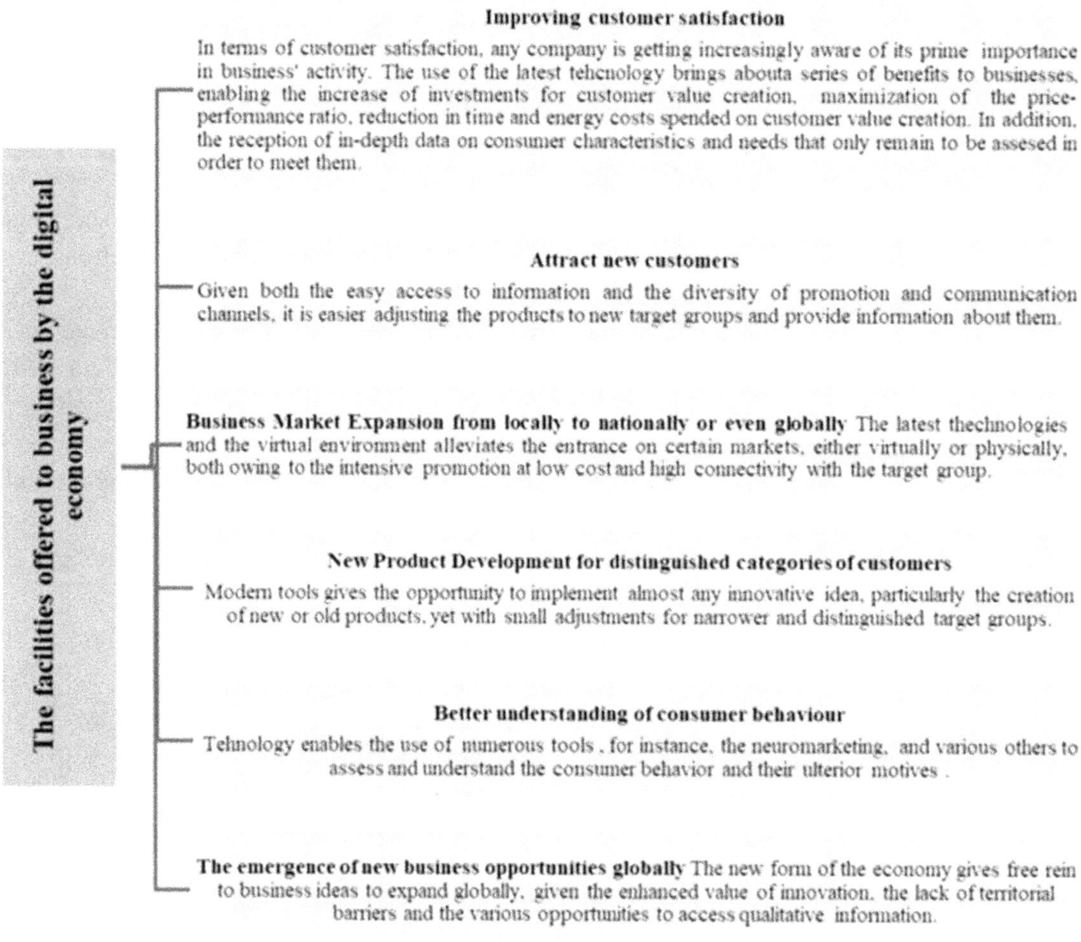

As stated above, the Internet may render numerous opportunities for organizations, if those grasp how it works and eagerly engage in taking advantage of them. However, with all opportunities, spawns a series of challenges, even threats from the online environment (Leţia, 2014).

§ The most important negative aspect of technological globalization is the intensification of economic crime.

§ States have different levels of technological development; hence certain international commercial transactions cannot be carried out under the same requirements of security and transparency.

§ Individuals in positions of authority gain even more decision-making power and influence so that the risk of committing both nondeliberate faults and internal offenses increases.
§ Gradually, the relationship between the company and the employee privacy changes.
§ The digital economy makes increasingly demanding to measure productivity as well as other traditional economic indicators, besides, an increasing number of calculations and estimations are more and more difficult to be carried out.
§ Although the ICT sector leads to the necessity of numerous workplaces, alongside the automation of many processes, the usefulness of many professions is lost, as a result, many workers are forced to change their career path and adapt to the new requirements.
§ To a certain extent, the proliferation of communication between companies and their stakeholders via digital means may lead to the capping of interpersonal communication skills and of the stability of relations between them.

The Current Situation: Data and Tendencies

All aspects of the economy are greatly impacted by digital technologies, since today they achieved the power to create and share their ideas, to generate new content and new types of entrepreneurs and markets.

Today, the number of internet users around the world is steadily increasing. The Internet traffic is doubling every 2-3 years and the mobile traffic – every year. It emerged that more than half of the existing adult population in a country are Internet users. Few countries make an exception, but also in their case, the percentage of Internet users is steadily rising. It depends on the standard of living and the stage of economic development in those countries. At the EU level, there is a rising trend in both the number of regular Internet users and the number of people who use it to search for information on certain goods and services.

Below is graphically represented (see Figure 3) the share of the Internet users (on average) in the EU and of the individuals who search online for information about the products they intend to buy online.

One can notice that yet from the past decade has existed a significant percentage of individuals who, even if they were using frequently the Internet, have taken advantage of the opportunity of finding data about the needed products. Today, the proportion does not comply with, since are way more users and increases the variety of Internet usage purposes. As a result, enterprises must adapt to the requirements and must be "present" as well in the online environment. Thus, enterprises' net turnover percentage on e-commerce is constantly increasing, as one can notice on the below graphical representation (Figure 4).

In recent years, the increase of enterprises that use the Internet proves the need and the various advantages they may take through the adjustment to the new digital economy, starting with the creation of a website which can be considered as its "virtual headquarter" until the tax payment via online services, which are used as well by governments.

The 2020 Pandemic Crisis and Digitalization

A contraction in international trade has been recorded between March and May 2020. The synchronization pattern of the recession has heightened the internal disruptions around the world. In the first semester of 2020 has been recorded a 3.2 percent contraction in trade induced by the weak demand, cross-border tourism's collapse, and the disruption generated by the closure of economic activities (in some cases, exacerbated by commercial restrictions). The retail sales index is accounted for as an aggregated measure

Figure 3. Individuals using the internet for finding information about goods and services (% of individuals aged 16 to 74)
Source: Eurostat

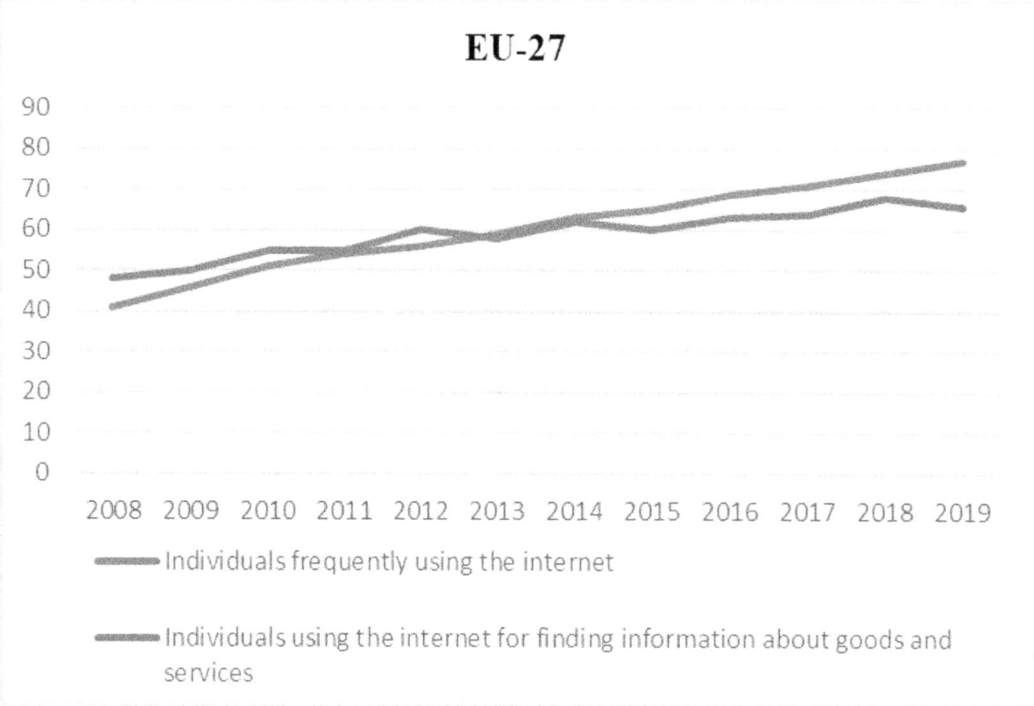

Figure 4. Share of enterprises' turnover on e-commerce - %
Source: Eurostat

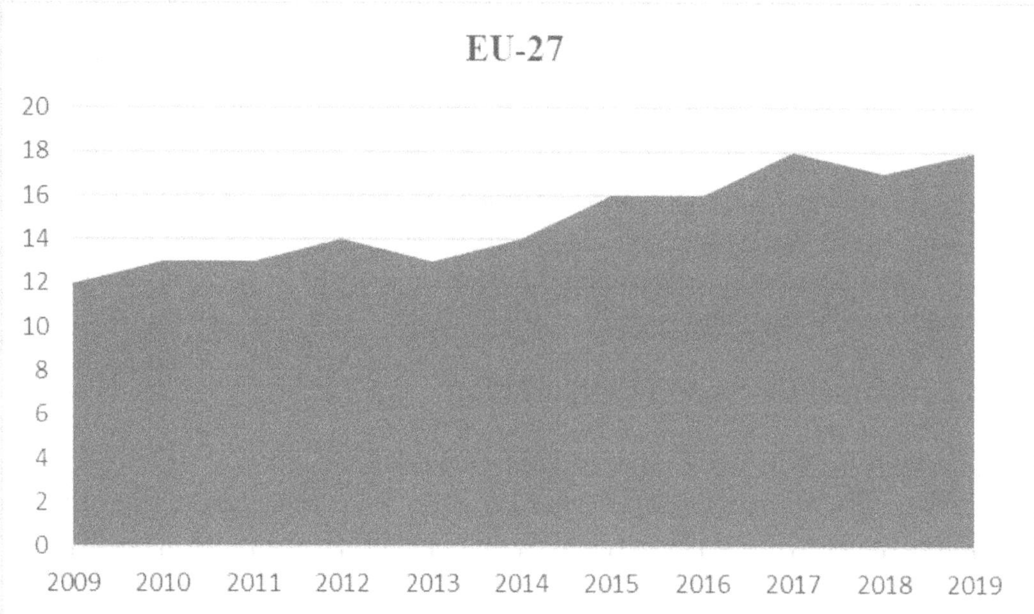

of sales of retail goods over a stated period. As retail sales are a measure of consumer demand for final goods, they are macroeconomic indicators that take the pulse of the economy and sets the tone whether for expansion or contraction. The retail sales index gauges only the changes in volume, meanwhile the corrections in price levels are excluded. One can notice in Figure 5 a decline in the Euro area's volume of retail sales, since the beginning of March 2020.

Figure 5. Retail sales Y-on-Y
Source: author's processing based on www.theglobaleconomy.com database

Policies that have been adopted by the world states since March 2020, were crucial to ensure that the partial closure of the manufacturing process (during the state of emergency) would not lead to permanent disruption of the productive capacity of the economy, damage to the financial system, and the structure of society. Therefore, national authorities assist individuals and enterprises through appropriate, specific, and short-run fiscal policy measures. Many countries have extended the loan programs for financing small and medium-sized enterprises.

As Covid-19 has caused a significant increase in depression, international transfers are projected to decrease sharply by about 20 percent in 2020. The expected decline would be the sharpest fall in recent history, largely due to a decrease in the wages and employment of migrant workers, who are likely to be more vulnerable to unemployment and the economic situation. Remittances to poor and middle-income countries are expected to fall, representing the loss of a crucial financing lifeline for many vulnerable households.

When do Crises Have Positive Sides?

Times of crisis and emergencies call forth an accelerated pace of innovation, given that the authorities are way more responsive than in normal periods to solutions that would benefit them. It was a principle valid in wars and of great chance to be for the crisis triggered by Covid-19 but would manifest differently itself (Iuga& Mihalciuc, 2020).

In terms of technological solutions primed for meeting similar needs, an analysis conducted and published in April 2020 by the European Parliamentary Research Service, established ten technologies that would be employed in the fight against the Covid-19 and have the potential to be developed at an accelerated pace. These findings are related exclusively to the medical needs of the crisis.

The importance of digitalization for companies, state institutions, and the population has increased. The demand for a vital type of service to the new working conditions, namely, of – online conference / on-line work – boomed overnight. Physically, deliveries employing autonomous robots would be a safer option for potential future isolation periods.

We can not know whether one of the aforementioned technologies would reach the impact of innovations that changed the post-war face of the world. What we are sure of, are the following: World War II lasted about six years and most innovations were ready at the end of the war. The Covid-19 crisis began to develop globally only a few months ago and likely to be the last lasting.

Today (the year 2020) we work from home. Many individuals continue working (even after the isolation period) in the work-from-home system. The main effects occur in the shift of work patterns in the industrial field, changes in the consumption structure, sales, and others.

The internet may have a tremendous economic impact until 2021. Below is displayed the statistics for 2019 (see Figure 6).

MARKETING OF SMES IN THE "DIGITAL AGE"

The Definition of SMEs and Their Role in the European Economy

Small and medium-sized enterprises have always played an important role in the economy and social life of all countries largely due to their dynamic, flexibility, adaptability, mobility, and innovative potential, and other features that lead to the development of the economy. The definition of SMEs at the European level is congruous with similar legislation. The development of small and medium-sized enterprises is one of the fundamental requirements for the healthy economic development of a country. SMEs play a crucial role in any market economy, given the fact they can promptly meet the latest trend of demand and the needs and expectations of demanding customers given the greater adaptability and creativity of small businesses. These represent a constituent of social and economic stability.

SMEs play an extremely important role in economic growth, there are three different types of enterprises, namely micro-enterprises, small enterprises, and medium-sized enterprises (see Table 1). The official definition of SMEs by the European Commission considers the following factors: staff headcount, annual turnover, and the annual balance sheet total.

It is of utmost importance to devote greater attention to SMEs, since they account for most of the existing enterprises, as the official statistics show (Table 2):

Figure 6. Enterprises selling over 50% via a website or apps (2019) and enterprises having a web site or homepage (2019)
Source: European Commission, Digital Scoreboard

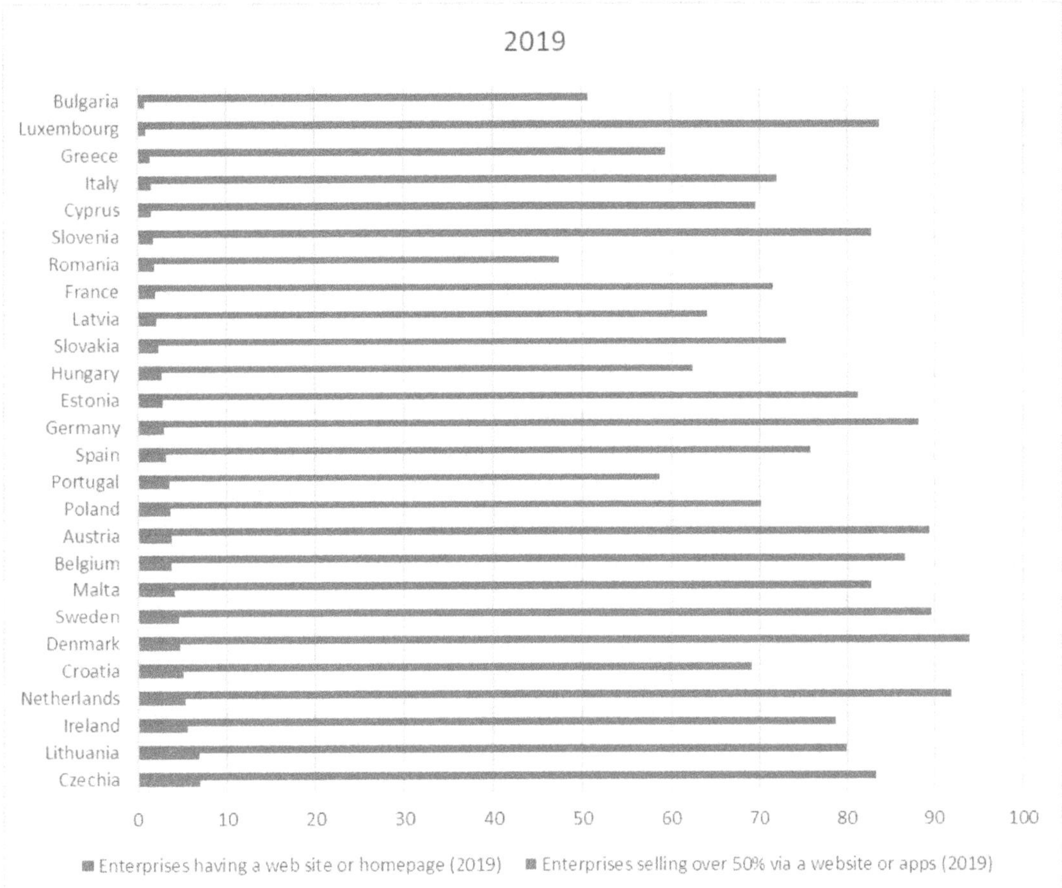

SMEs are extremely important for the proper functioning of an economy and extremely vulnerable to legislation, taxes, competition, and social policies, the European Union assists through certain measures their easy access onto the market and their barrier-free activity. A key role of SMEs lies in their numerical ability to counterbalance monopolies and oligopolies, reducing the market dominance of the large companies.

Table 1. The EC's official definition of SMEs

Types of SMEs	Headcount	Annual turnover	or	Balance sheet total
Micro-enterprises	<10	< EUR 2 million	or	< EUR 2 million
Small enterprises	<50	< EUR 10 million	or	< EUR 10 million
Medium-sized enterprises	<250	< EUR 50 million	or	< EUR 43 million

Source: Commission Recommendation of 6 May 2003 concerning the definition of micro, small and medium-sized enterprises (2003/361/CE)

Table 2. Number of micro-enterprises in the EU 28 non-financial business sector in 2019

	Micro-enterprises	**Small enterprises**	**Medium-sized enterprises**	**Large enterprises**	**Total enterprises**
Number of enterprises	22,830,944	1,420,693	231,857	46,547	24,530,050
Percentage of enterprises	93.1%	5.8%	0.9%	0.2%	100%
	Total SMEs: 24,483,496 (99.8%)				
Staff headcount	41,980,528,	28,582,254	24,201,840	47,933,208	142,697,824
Percentage of staff headcount	29.4%	20.0%	17.0%	33.6%	100%

Source: Eurostat

The share of small and medium-sized enterprises varies from country to country (see Figure 7). Concerning the number of SMEs per 1000 inhabitants (population ages 15 or above) only ten countries are below the EU average in 2017, including Romania (which ranks last on this indicator) meanwhile 18 countries exceed the European average. The large fluctuation in the number of micro-SMEs per 1000 inhabitants (ages 15 or above) is on account of various factors, such as the industrial economic structure, the adoption, and promotion of public policies which favor both self-employment and creation of enterprises, particularly micro-enterprises, the level of entrepreneurship, the general economic conditions, the fiscal policies, and the political stability.

The most beneficial effects brought about by SMEs to the economy are the following: jobs creation; formation of the middle class; increase the competitive state of markets; contribute to the GDPs; combine various factors of production; show higher adaptability and flexibility in periods of secession; have the potential of future big companies; focus on innovation; facilitate the integration of economical networks and the reduction of unemployment; ensure a superior quality of performance and satisfaction owing to the low degree of bureaucracy.

Furthermore, for building a stronger economy, the European Union aims to strengthen the entrepreneurial spirit in Europe and to create the needed requirements for the development of innovative practices that lead to the set-up and expansion of enterprises. Achieving these goals is of crucial importance in ensuring economic sustainability for social progress and environmental protection (Anghel, 2005). The European Action Plan on enterprises includes three areas of immediate intervention: encouragement of enterprises, promotion of innovative processes and change, assessment of the competitiveness of the European economy, and the inter-linkages with further policies of the European Union.

Marketing Strategies of SMEs

In order to take advantage of market opportunities and to achieve its projected objectives, an enterprise has to adopt a certain marketing strategy. Marketing strategy covers the specific guidance of an enterprise's attitude and ethics for the achievement of its objectives. The method applied for the implementation of the strategy belongs to Field Marketing. However, the marketing strategy is of paramount importance, as it connects all functions of marketing, researching market requirements, adjusting economic activity to these requirements, and meet these requirements to achieve increased efficiency for the company. As small and medium-sized enterprises are decidedly flexible and highly dependent on the management

Figure 7. Number of small and medium-sized enterprises per 1000 inhabitants (inhabitants ages 15 or above) in 2019
Source: Eurostat

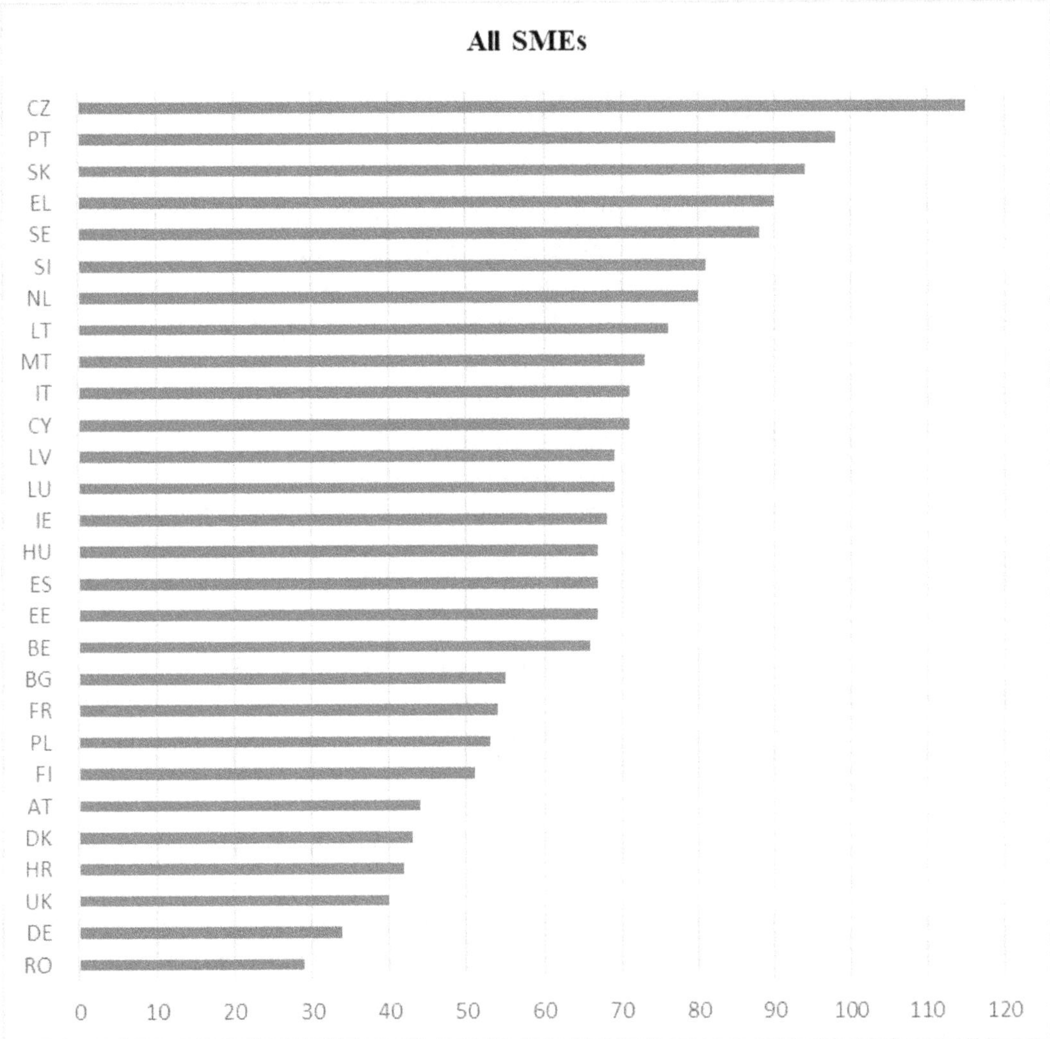

activity, they often lack strategic orientation yet show greater intuitive power. As far as the SMEs concerning emerges certain definite characteristics (Anghel, 2005) related to the marketing strategy, namely:

- The behavior and decisions of the trustee have a direct impact on the overall activity of the company.
- Management skills are at the core of the enterprise for a better entering on the market.
- The adopted strategy by the enterprise does not have a significant impact on organizational structure.
- The strategic horizon is curbed by high uncertainties.

Table 3 displays several types of marketing strategies that can be implemented by SMEs.

Table 3. Types of marketing strategies for SMEs (Anghel, 2005)

In terms of the pursued competitive advantage:	In terms of product-market criteria:	Diversification strategies:
Low pricing strategy Focus strategy Differentiation Strategy	Market Penetration Strategy Product development strategy Market Expansion Strategy	Vertical integration Horizontal Diversification Concentric Diversification Conglomerate diversification

Small and medium-sized enterprises can opt as well for strategic alliances or partnerships or for strategic withdrawal or to change their business activity, or for innovation strategy.

Key elements of the development of market strategy are the marketing plan, the business plan, the analysis of the enterprise's business portfolio (Boston Consulting Group Model and General Electric Model), SWOT analysis, and Arthur D. Little's model, etc.

SMEs's Marketing in the Context of the "Digital Age"

The digitalization of the economy offers various facilities both to consumers and manufacturers. Nowadays, with the ever-changing conditions at breakneck speed is increasingly difficult for a business to coordinate their marketing activities to the market changes. As Philip Kotler argues in his book "*Marketing Moves. A new approach to profit, growth, and renewal*" that "today's businesses must strive to meet customers' need in the most convenient possible way, through the reduction to a minimum of time and effort needed for the searching, booking, and reception of goods and services", since today the activity of any business is affected by the generalization of supply and customization of demand.

Thus, customers have an increasingly decisive role in the success of a business, and the marketing growingly depends on keeping the relationship with them.

Gradually, a new marketing paradigm is emerging bringing the holistic marketing model up to date.

The stages of paradigms evolution are represented in Figure 8.

A unique feature of holistic marketing is that it engages all stakeholders to take part in the value creation process. The ideas collected from the company, consumer, collaborators, and communities represent the end of the customer cognition, of the business' capacity, and stakeholders' resources (Figure 9).

The participants to the value creation in the digital economy are depicting a new strategic marketing mindset, which leads to the following paradigm shifts that lie at the basis of strategic marketing thinking.

Another key change called forth by the digital economy to marketing is the phenomenon of "reverse marketing" that involves "reversing" the elements of the marketing mix and not only (Figure 10).

Reverse product design: an increasing number of companies enable their customers to design virtually products, for instance, computers, jeans, and makeup products. *Reverse pricing:* customers can shift from price takers to price-setters. An example would be priceline.com, where users offer a price for certain products, services and after the information is received by traders, they will decide whether accept or not to carry out a transaction under these conditions. *Reverse advertising:* the old approach of distributing advertisements to a large-scale (broadcasting) is replaced by the dispersion of advertisements on a small-scale (narrowcasting). It means that companies started sending their advertisements and offers to individuals who show real interest and might become clients. This group would be identified with ease as individuals can choose whether to receive or not the advertisements, particularly sent by

Figure 8. Evolution of marketing paradigms (Kotler, 2009)

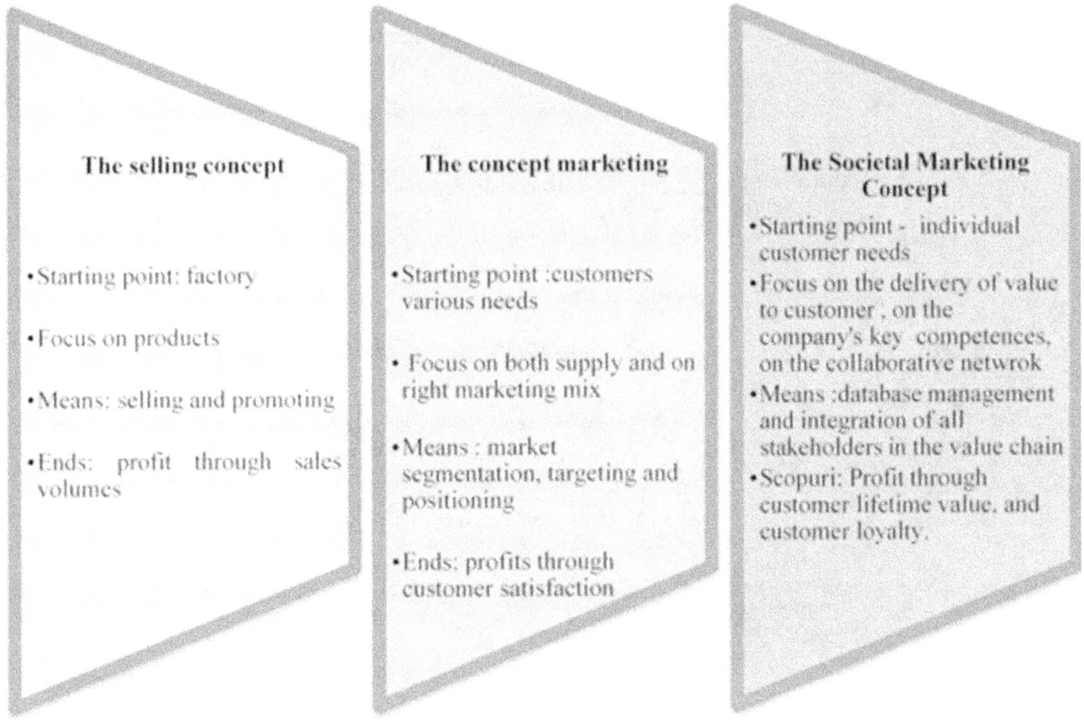

email. Moreover, users can themselves ask for informative materials concerning specific products, and services ("pointcasting"). *Reverse promotional campaigns:* customers get the chance to request offers, discount coupons, and free samples given the online marketing intermediaries. *Reverse distribution channels:* businesses have to devote increasing attention to the channels of distribution, since a growing number of daily use products and services are rendered to customers through online orders, eliminating the need of moving. *Reverse segmentation:* virtual environment enables a consumer to communicate its preferences and characteristics to campaign makers, giving the chance to use this information for an adequate segmentation. Marketing specialists must pay considerable attention to the four C's of customer: increased value for the customer, lower prices, convenience, and better communication (Kotler, 2009).

The increasingly active participation of the customer in the value creation process and the growth of its significance in this process has given rise to a new term – "Prosumer", that designates the "professional consumer", who is actively engaged in improving business' activities and decides himself what he want to purchase and how that product/service should look like.

European Countries – Brief Statistical Presentation

Hereunder the states' position is presented according to some of the digitalization indicators: concerning the coverage area of fixed internet connection, Norway and United Kingdom of Great Britain are on the best position, while Romania, Italy, and Bulgaria are at the bottom of the rankings (see Figure 11).

Figure 9. Paradigm shifts in strategic marketing (Kotler, 2009)

Iceland has the highest rate of Internet users – 99% of the population, and Romania – one of the smallest – 89%. The explanation resides in the influence of certain factors, such as living standards or coverage areas (Figure 12).

Figure 13 data show that in the United Kingdom of Great Britain, the highest percentage of Internet users, also use the Internet for online purchases. At the opposite end of the rankings is Romania, where only 21% of Internet users make online purchases, which outlines a lack of information and trust from the buyers for online transactions and contracts. Romania's average is one of the smallest in the EU, possibly due to the small number of economic agents who sell online and the SMEs' predomination in Romania's activity domains.

SMEs LEVEL OF DIGITALIZATION ANALYSIS AND THE CREATION OF FAVOURABLE CONDITIONS FOR THIS PROCESS IN UE – HELLWIG CLASSICAL TAXONOMIC METHOD

Methodology and Results

Technology is constantly transforming the world. Even though this offers many opportunities for those who have access to it, there still exists some barriers in the online environment, which prevent users

Figure 10. Reverse marketing (Kotler, 2009)

from enjoying all the desired goods and services, the online companies and start-ups to have unlimited horizons, and the governments and businesses to fully benefit of online environment's instruments.

This case study will follow the actual situation analysis of Romanian SMEs on the Digital Single Market, by comparing it with other 25 European states in the 2013-2019 period.

The purpose of this study is to evaluate, based on official statistical data, Romania's situation on the SMEs' marketing adaptation to the digital economy.

The proposed objectives are:

Figure 11. Fixed Internet connection coverage area (% households) in Europe's countries
Source: personal processing of statistic data from Eurostat

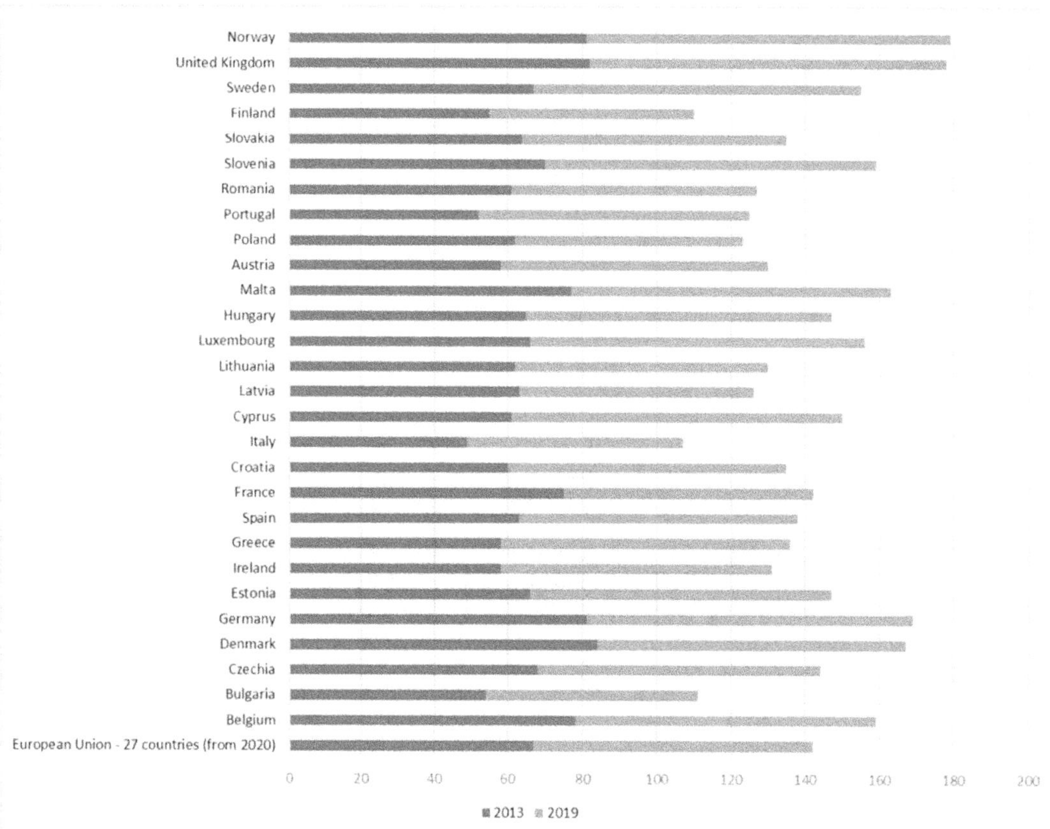

- Selecting relevant indicators to outline SMEs situation on the digital market;
- Identifying Romania's position in the obtained states' hierarchy;
- Offering explanations about Romania's position in the hierarchy;
- Finding some necessary measures and policies applicable to Romania, according to its situation in the current moment.

Hypothesis:

H_0: Romania is not in a favourable position, compared to the other states from this study since there is a need for intense development of SMEs' access to the new technologies.
H_1: Romania's situation is very good when speaking of SMEs' marketing integration in the digital economy, aiming further for stability and continuous adaptation to trends.

Further, we shall use the statistical method of the Polish statistician, Zdzislav Henry Hellwig, in order to make a hierarchy of the UE member states, depending on how much they use SMEs digital environment in marketing and how favourable are the conditions in these countries to allow such thing.

Figure 12. Internet usage of individuals (% of individuals) in European countries, 2019
Source: personal processing of statistic data from Eurostat

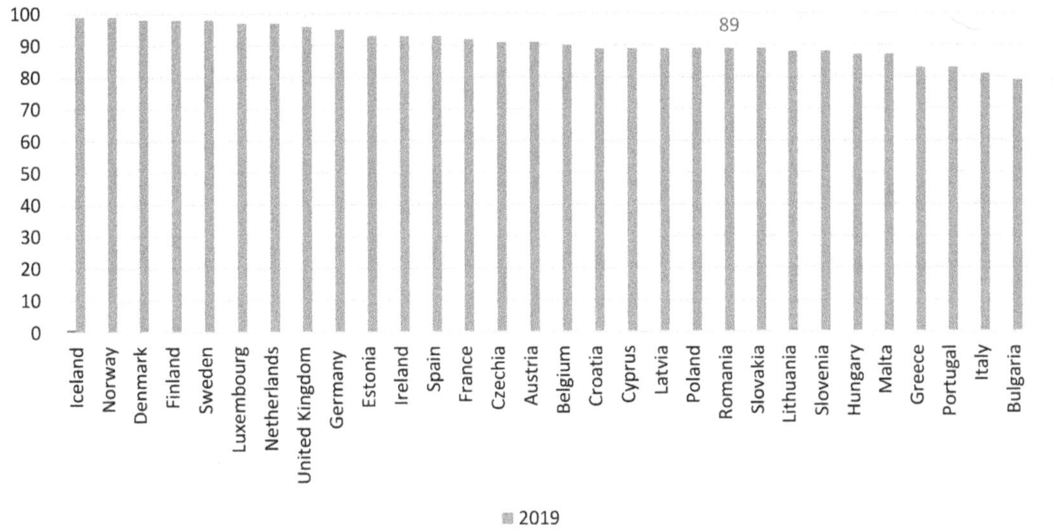

This method, named the Hellwig Classical Taxonomic Method (Hellwig, 1968) allows the hierarchy of the units (states), by processing the values of certain variables (indicators), in the case of each unit (state) included in the study. The countries selected for tooling are from continental Europe: Austria, Bulgaria, Croatia, Cyprus, Czech Republic, Denmark, Estonia, Finland, France, Germany, Greece, Hungary, Ireland, Italy, Latvia, Lithuania, Netherlands, Norway, Poland, Portugal, Romania, Slovakia, Slovenia, Spain, Sweden and United Kingdom of Great Britain.

The variables, or indicators used, are selected in such a way as to explain the SMEs marketing integration in the digital economy and the conditions in which it takes place:

1. Fixed internet connection coverage area (% households);
2. Fixed Internet expenses pegged to individual income (%);
3. Internet users (% of persons aged 16-74);
4. It Specialists (% of employed persons);
5. Using Internet for purchases (% of Internet users);
6. Offering information electronically (% of total companies);
7. Companies using social platforms (% of the total number);
8. SMEs that sell online (% of total SMEs in the country);
9. SMEs that sell online abroad (% of total SME in the country);
10. Medium income of SMEs from electronic trade (% of total income).

All data were taken from Eurostat database.

The parameters used in this method are:

m- number of diagnostic variables ($j = 1, 2, \ldots, m$),

n – number of spatial units ($i = 1, 2, \ldots, n$),

xij – diagnostic variable value with serial number j in the spatial unit with serial number i. The matrix formed of statistical observations will the following:

Figure 13. Internet purchases by individuals
Source: personal processing of statistic data from Eurostat

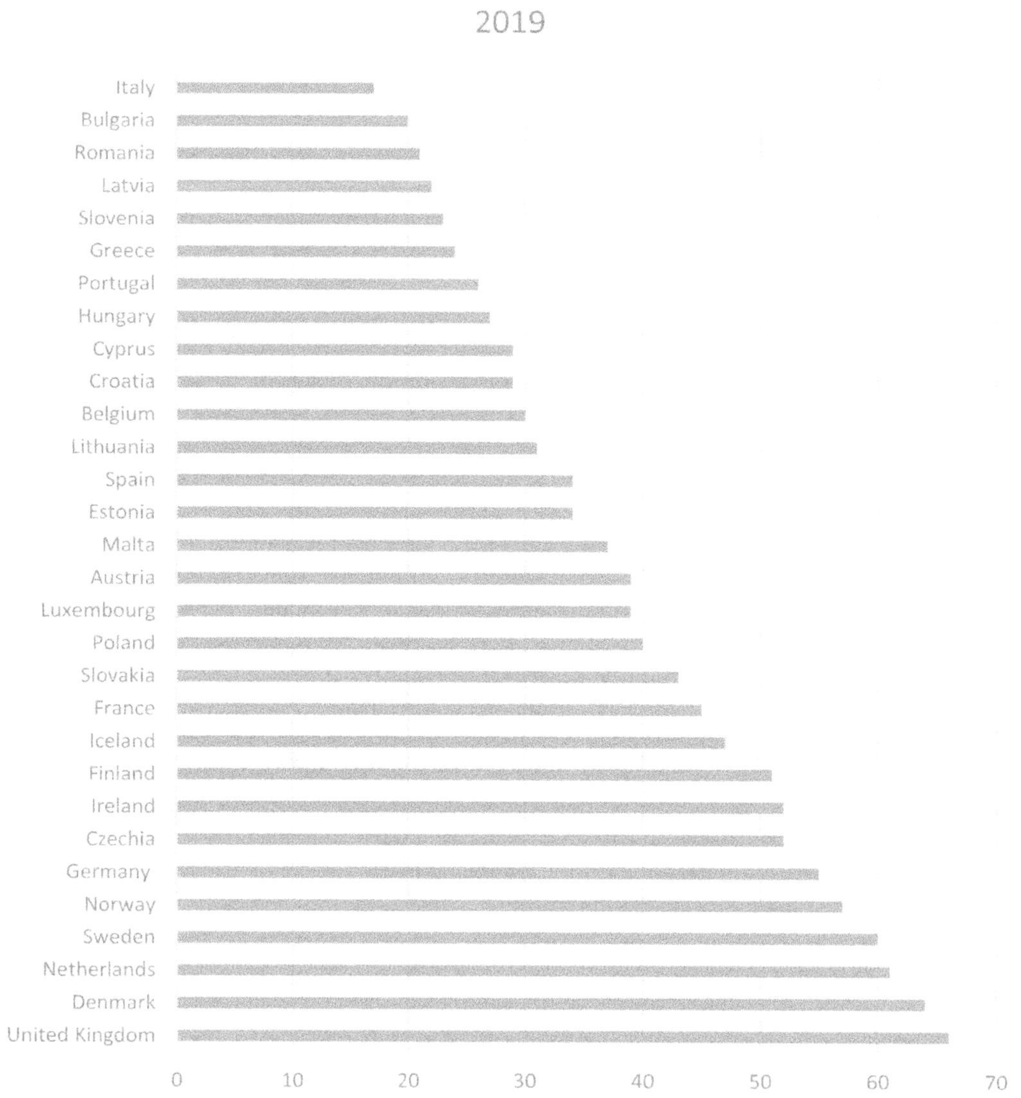

$$X = \begin{bmatrix} x_{21}x_{22}\ldots x_{2m} \\ \ldots\ldots\ldots\ldots \\ x_{n1}x_{n2}\ldots x_{nm} \end{bmatrix}$$

After collecting and organizing the statistical data, the following values will be calculated:

Table 4. Normalized values of variables

	Fixed Internet area	Internet users	IT Specialists	Using Internet for shopping	Offering electronical information	Social Platforms	SMEs that sell online	SMEs that sell online abroad	Online selling income	Internet expenses
Arithmetic average of the variable	96,04	75,85	3,68	57,62	33,12	17,26	15,91	7,43	10,34	1,53
Standard Deviation of the variable	4,25	11,92	1,36	18,20	10,52	8,45	7,12	3,22	4,83	0,66
Sum	2497,00	1972,00	95,80	1498,00	861,00	448,70	413,60	193,30	268,80	39,81
Optimal value of the variable	100,00	96,00	6,70	87,00	56,00	37,00	32,00	16,00	21,00	0,71
Normalized value of the variable j	0,93	1,69	2,21	1,61	2,18	2,34	2,26	2,66	2,21	-1,25

Source: Personal processing from Eurostat

The arithmetic average of each variable Xj:

$$\overline{x_j} = \frac{1}{n}\sum_{i=1}^{n} x_{ij}$$

Standard deviation of property Xj:

$$S_j = \left[\frac{1}{n}\sum_{i=1}^{n}\left(x_{ij} - \overline{x_j}\right)^2\right]^{1/2}$$

Furthermore, an abstract unit is created, which is characterized by the best values of each variable:

$z_{01}, z_{02}, \ldots, z_{0m}$, unde:

z_{0j}= maximum $\{z_{ij}\}$, if variable X_j is a stimulant, example in the case percentage of SMEs that sell online;
z_{0i}= minimum $\{z_{ij}\}$, if variable X_j is a destimulant, as in the case of fixed internet expenses as percentage of individual incomes:

By using these, the normalized values (Table 4) zj for each variable X_j are calculated:

$$z_j = \frac{z_{0j} - \overline{x_j}}{s_j}$$

Whereas the values from the observation matrix are also not homogeneous, they are subject of normalization, by using the following formula:

$$z_{ij} = \frac{x_{ij} - \overline{x_j}}{s_j}$$

where:

z_{ij} – normalized value of variable j for unit i;
x_{ij} – variable j value for unit i.

See the normalized values of the variables in Table 5.

Further on, the distance (difference) between each unit (country) and the abstract object with optimal values is determined. The following formula is used:

$$c_{io} = \left[\sum_{j=1}^{m} v_j \left(z_{ij} - z_{0j} \right)^2 \right]^{1/2},$$

where:

c_{i0}– generalized Euclidean distance of the object (unit) i;
v_j– variable j influence on final index – SMEs' Marketing Integration in Digital Economy

(whereas the efficacy of digital environment usage by SMEs in marketing is best expressed through online selling/total selling report, we considered as variables numbers' coefficients, directly proportional numbers (as their sum is 1) with the Pearson coefficient's values of each one of them, and the medium income of SMEs from electronical trade (% of total income).

Firstly, the squared differences $z_{ij} - z_{0j}$ were calculated, then with their help and by using the calculation formula, all generalized Euclidean distances of the objects were discovered (see Table 5).

The following step is to calculate the taxonomic indicator followed (SMEs' Level of Digitalization and the Creation of Favourable Conditions) for every state.

The calculation formula is the following:

$$d_i = 1 - \frac{c_{i0}}{c_0}$$

where:

$c_0 = \overline{c_0} + 2S_0$, named normalization factor,

$\overline{c_0} = \frac{1}{n} \sum_{i=1}^{n} c_{i0}$, named the arithmetic average of generalized Euclidean distances of the units,

Table 5. Euclidean distances calculation for countries

	Fixed Internet area	Internet users	It Specialists	Using Internet for shopping	Offering electronical information	Social Platforms	SMEs that sell online	SMEs that sell online abroad	Online selling income	Internal expenses	Generalized Euclidean distance of unit i
Austria	0,055	1,584	4,538	1,090	2,033	6,172	6,396	3,474	7,259	0,045	2,032
Bulgaria	1,386	11,833	12,432	9,466	8,684	11,448	13,655	16,815	13,762	1,445	3,440
Croatia	0,499	6,336	7,791	5,581	6,587	6,774	3,336	4,865	8,299	7,418	2,491
Cyprus	0,000	4,759	9,977	9,131	1,527	0,686	9,555	5,722	8,061	10,113	2,705
Czech Republic	0,222	2,541	3,647	3,091	6,108	10,203	1,599	1,544	0,687	0,352	1,553
Denmark	0,055	0,063	4,230	0,075	0,732	4,045	0,967	3,710	1,546	0,102	1,305
Estonia	6,708	0,704	1,748	1,331	10,446	10,662	7,897	9,458	7,147	2,751	2,342
Finland	0,499	0,176	0,000	0,365	3,262	3,583	5,705	10,040	0,000	0,033	1,548
France	0,000	1,584	5,525	0,510	2,611	8,748	5,054	6,332	4,295	0,093	1,968
Germany	0,222	1,014	4,856	0,075	0,000	6,774	1,263	4,462	5,582	0,059	1,721
Greece	0,055	7,666	15,734	4,830	3,262	5,053	13,243	15,321	16,838	3,279	3,360
Hungary	1,386	4,055	1,748	4,830	14,458	9,461	9,555	12,763	8,180	1,834	2,644
Ireland	0,887	2,281	2,379	1,739	8,684	0,056	0,000	0,000	0,172	5,140	1,232
Italy	0,055	7,666	9,518	6,955	3,614	7,404	12,837	11,256	7,037	2,751	2,864
Latvia	2,716	3,104	11,919	4,591	14,458	10,203	11,089	14,129	7,828	0,806	2,919
Lithuania	0,222	5,132	12,432	5,581	2,313	5,598	3,869	3,830	4,295	0,000	2,254
Netherlands	0,000	0,176	1,559	0,365	1,093	0,000	4,442	3,474	6,928	0,195	1,680
Norway	1,386	0,000	1,948	0,245	5,205	4,535	0,711	11,049	0,687	1,102	1,537
Poland	10,866	6,765	7,387	3,489	11,069	11,448	9,906	14,364	6,185	0,352	2,797
Portugal	0,000	6,765	9,518	5,581	1,301	8,748	3,336	6,332	2,749	5,853	2,295
Romania	6,708	13,628	9,070	14,371	10,446	13,020	11,947	19,186	11,133	9,169	3,516
Slovakia	10,866	3,407	3,647	2,041	6,108	8,748	7,897	9,080	4,295	0,352	2,270
Slovenia	1,386	4,400	1,948	3,698	4,780	6,172	5,054	3,474	1,546	2,269	1,813
Spain	1,386	3,104	6,993	3,489	3,985	3,583	5,054	9,844	8,061	9,169	2,487
Sweden	0,055	0,345	0,264	0,245	1,527	3,583	0,711	3,830	2,105	0,102	1,153
United Kingdom of Great Britain	0,000	0,253	1,748	0,000	13,744	0,126	2,843	4,729	7,259	0,806	1,836

Source: Personal processing

$S_0 = \left[\frac{1}{n} \sum_{i=1}^{n} \left(c_{i0} - \overline{c_0} \right)^2 \right]^{1/2}$, named standard deviation of generalized Euclidean distances of the units.

These values are presented in Table 6.

The values of SMEs' level of digitalization indicator and the creation of favourable conditions for this process for the countries from this study are presented in Table 7 and Chart 9.

As we can notice, the first three positions are occupied by Sweden, Ireland and Denmark, and the last positions: by Greece, Bulgaria, and the last position is occupied by Romania.

Table 6. Normalization factor

the arithmetic average of generalized Euclidean distances of the units	2,222
the standard deviation of generalized Euclidean distances of the units	0,680
normalization factor	3,581

Source: Personal processing

Table 7. Taxonomic indicator

Country	Taxonomic Indicator	Country	Taxonomic Indicator	Country	Taxonomic Indicator
Sweden	0,6781	United Kingdom of Great Britain	0,4874	Hungary	0,2618
Ireland	0,6561	France	0,4506	Cyprus	0,2448
Denmark	0,6355	Austria	0,4326	Poland	0,2190
Norway	0,5708	Lithuania	0,3706	Italy	0,2002
Finland	0,5678	Slovakia	0,3662	Latvia	0,1849
Czech Republic	0,5664	Portugal	0,3593	Grecia	0,0617
Netherlands	0,5311	Estonia	0,3462	Bulgaria	0,0394
Germany	0,5194	Spain	0,3056	Romania	0,0183
Slovenia	0,4939	Croatia	0,3044		

Source: Personal processing

Figure 14. Taxonomic indicator – comparison of Romania and 25 European states
Source: Personal processing

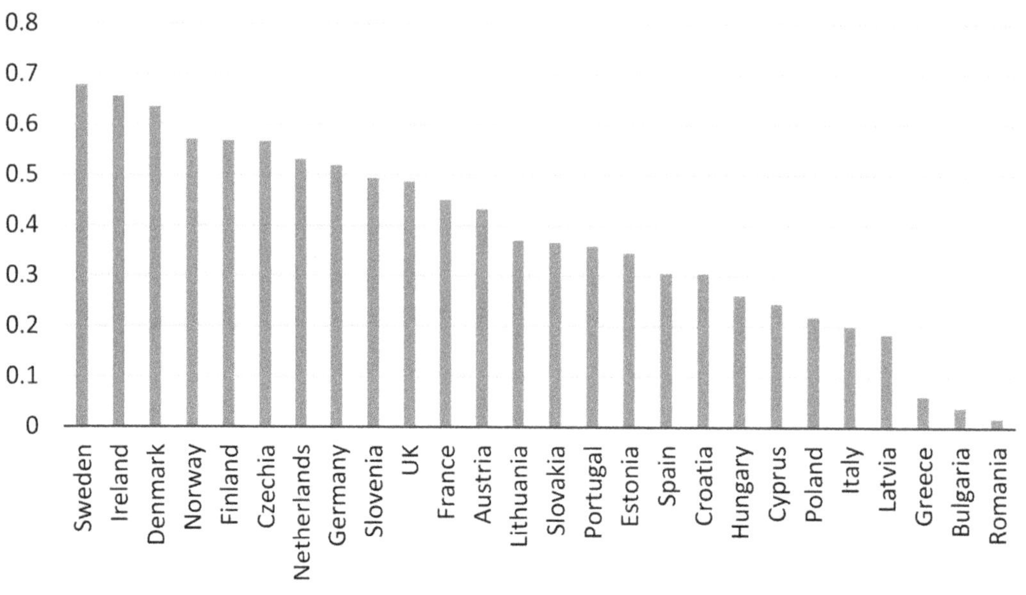

SOLUTIONS AND RECOMMENDATIONS

According to the results from the previous method application, we conclude that Romania is in a bad situation regarding the SMEs' integration in the digital economy and the creation of favourable conditions for it, by accepting the null hypothesis H_0 formulated at the beginning of this study.

Further, the situation of Romania will be analysed in detail, through concrete data and by trying to define the main causes that have led to it.

Firstly, Romania is facing a low connectivity, and the necessity of expanding the fixed networks coverage area, which is only 90% of the territory, compared to EU average of 97% (Eurostat, 2020). Therefore, we should adopt measures, which would lead to decreasing connection costs, which generally obstructs networks and infrastructure development. Anyhow, a positive aspect regarding the connectivity, is that in Romania, it has one of the best Internet access speed, exceeding the European average: the capable networks to develop a minimum of 30 Mbps are available in more than two-thirds of the Romanian households, even more than the UE average records.

Romanians are still incredulous when comes to online shopping, being in the last position at the European level (only 29% of the population is online shopping). This is a key challenge for the country since the users' trust in online shopping influences the digital economy's development rhythm. An important factor that generates this situation is the mentality of buyers and economical agents, who do not focus the attention yet on mutual trust in sale-purchase relation.

A truly digitalized economy implies businesses enjoying the opportunities and advantages offered by technologies, for both improving productivity and communicating easier with clients in order to sell products. Romania is far behind in this chapter too, since only 7,4% of SMEs sell online, and their online selling incomes are only 4,9% of total income, only 22% from the companies offer electronic information, 6,5% use social networks, and only 5,7% use Cloud services.

Such a thing may be caused either by circumstances, the general development level of Romania, by the awareness level of the innovation necessity among economy participants.

Strategies and Objectives for Digitalizing Romania

With our awareness of the necessity of implementing some reforms on digitalization, Romania had adopted in September 2014 the "National Strategy on Digital Agenda for Romania 2020", which included a set of objectives to be fulfilled until 2020. This includes a part of the objectives of the European Digital Agenda, relevant and adapted to the current situation. This strategy brought to the forefront the IT sector development, namely the implementation of some direct and indirect actions. Through this, there were also aimed the economic development, the increase of Romania's competitivity and workforce, and productivity improvements, in order to reach the region countries' level.

According to the National Strategy on Digital Agenda for Romania (Informational Society Ministry, 2020), four major domains of action were outlined:

1. Increasing efficacy and reducing costs in the public sector by ensuring a modern administration (E-Government, Cybernetic Security, Interoperability, Cloud Computing, Big Data, Open Data, and Social Media)
2. Ensuring a positive aspect of IT investments at the social level (IT in Education, Healthcare, Culture, and E-Inclusion)

3. Supporting economic growth in the private sector (ECommerce, IT Research, Development, and Innovation)
4. Ensuring social inclusion (Broadband and Digital Infrastructure Services)

This is a part of the objectives, expressed in numbers:

Table 8. Targets on digitalization

Indicators	Target UE (2020)	Target RO (2020)
Broadband coverage	100%	100%
Population that buys online	50%	30%
Population that buys online from abroad	20%	5%
SMEs that sell online	33%	20%

Source: https://www.comunicatii.gov.ro/ *(retrieved on January 21, 2021)*

As we may notice in Table 8, the targets settled for Romania are lower than those for UE, being adapted to the real possibilities of fulfilling them, and the current situation is under the levels that are necessary to reach.

According to the results of this study, Romania needs high IT development and in need of a better interfering of this domain with others, especially with the economy, namely SMEs activities, whereas they are an important employment source and contribute directly to GDB formation, and economic growth and development, even of the society.

Moreover, the activities oriented to value delivery for the buyer must be adapted to the actual trends and target group's lifestyle, which is more and more connected to the new technologies, in a time when marketing information continuously grows, because of the informed and rational decisions of buyers, and the high attention they pay to details and the way products/services are offered. Therefore, SMEs' whole activity must be well thought, actualized, and open to new opportunities, especially in marketing, which makes the company visible. Although, generally, Romania's situation is surpassed compared to the rest of European states, yet it has the potential, resources, and necessary conditions (fast network, IT specialists) to develop in this regard. An important step is the agreement on the Strategy for Digitalization, which will ensure the country a safe and gradual progression, closer to the rest of the European Union level. However, for this, is firstly necessary the awareness of change importance and new trends adaptation in a globalization era. Besides these, Romania needs to encourage more innovation and implementation of reformatory ideas, which can increase the efficacy of some processes and the productivity in any domain of activity, and lastly, the digital economy regarded as a safe source of advantages and opportunities, which could only lead to economic development and prosperity, even of the whole society, if used efficiently.

Finally, the year 2020 is over and for now, Romania does not have a strategy for the following years.

FUTURE RESEARCH DIRECTIONS

Aiming to perform a relevant study with realist and objective results, we primarily applied the quantitative research method using secondary data, i.e., official statistics annually published, processed by the author, to obtain a statistic units hierarchy. A research limit is that we did not analyse all European Member States; we included some Member States of the European Economic Area and Schengen Area in exchange. Future research directions will be in SMEs m-marketing.

CONCLUSION

This research has highlighted some ideas regarding marketing and economy actual trends, conditioned by technology development and the importance of capitalizing them among SMEs.

We may conclude that, due to the progress of information technology, the economic agents must be always prepared to adapt and must be open to innovation and change. Even though it requires a certain understanding level, the virtual environment brings many advantages to all its economic activities' participants. When speaking of marketing, not only buyers are very informed nowadays, but also the enterprises may gather fairly accurate data on buyers' preferences and necessities, to approach them easier and personalized, and to create long-term relations with them.

Nowadays, the digitalization of economic agents and society gets great attention at the European level, especially small and medium-sized enterprises, since the creation of the European Digital Single Market is initiated, together with diverse policies for encouragement and support for SMEs, which are the main economic growth force and development. Romania's situation at SMEs' integration in the digital economic evolution is relatively unfavourable, having the worst situation compared to other European states.

Digitalisation is characterized as the most important feature of the Fourth Industrial Revolution (Schwab K., 2017; Rachinger M. et al., 2018).

Scientists also focus on the spatial distribution of the digitised economy in the European Union, examining the performance of the EU as a whole and of individual Member States (Rivza et al., 2019). In this respect, one example is research regarding digital economy that has compared Poland with the other EU Member States (Moroz, 2017). A similar analysis was carried out by (Mahring et al., 2018) regarding business digitisation in Sweden. Another example, the digitisation of micro-enterprises research, compared Eastern European countries and Western Europe (Pytkovska & Korynski, 2017).

Another idea we came up with is that the "revolution" brought by the new technologies may have major effects on the economy in the future, perhaps more intense than now. It is important that people are aware of this fact and tries to control and lead this phenomenon to a more favourable path by analysing and understanding it and trying to apply it in productive ways.

The ability to implement marketing along with market orientation affects the performance of SMEs (Thi Song et al. 2017). At the same time, digitalisation is transforming the place of entrepreneurial opportunities and entrepreneurial practices (Autio 2017), thus providing new perspectives for the development of ESMS.

Lack of digital competence has been a general concern among SMEs, including a lack of knowledge and skills to apply new technologies to the work of SMEs (Marques et al. 2017). Consequently, this leads to a lack of positive attitudes, including motivation and adequate prioritisation by management for the implementation of digital technologies (Vieru et al. 2015).

The impacts of digitization on business models have been described in case studies (Neubert, 2018).

Previous research suggests that the market orientation effect on business performance is positive in contexts characterised by different levels of external turbulence of small and medium-sized enterprises, and competitive intensity (Kohli 2017).

Digital transformation means not only optimizing internal processes or incorporating new technologies, but also fundamentally changing SME business models (Loebbecke & Picot, 2015).

However, more research is needed to understand the interaction between digitalisation and the marketing capacity of small businesses in the context of globalisation.

The marketing domain is no longer “optional” for an enterprise, but it becomes vital and must dictate the starting point and the movement direction during the entire enterprise activity. Whereas it has major importance as the “bridging” between an enterprise and the market, and a general orientation, which ensures long term success, marketing needs to be adapted continuously and to be strongly connected with all other company’s activities. Moreover, each enterprise must assimilate and apply the holistic marketing idea and be able to value the opportunities through well-thought investments.

SMEs are, indeed, the economic essence by favouring a profitable and healthy environment’s development for all its participants. They easily adapt and they are very sensitive to any change or phenomenon. For this reason, I consider it essential for them to be able to access new marketing methods and techniques, based on information technology, in order to survive and ensure innovation continuity. I have proved in the official database that such a thing is understood and SMEs and their access to the new technologies are encouraged at the European level.

Anyhow, the data shows that Romania needs to work on this chapter – here the entrepreneurs are not aware of this importance, and probably they do not have favourable conditions to adapt to the so-called “new digital economy”, since there is not good coverage, nor frequent Internet users, and the ones who use it, do not use it for online shopping, at least not as other European states citizens.

In order to solve this unfavourable situation in Romania, I consider better informing necessary for both economic agents and all the persons, regarding the online environment utilization modalities in different purposes, the promotion of marketing digital techniques usage, the development of efficient laws for customer protection in online commerce, and the encouragement of this new type of commerce by implementing favourable policies.

Small and medium-sized enterprises are a key element to invest in, which require encouragement and help in order to harmoniously adapt and develop, granting the rightful attention to marketing activities, especially to opportunities and all trends generated by a potential new digital economy, in order to have a balanced economy and a flourishing society.

Changes, good or bad, must be regarded with a positive attitude, from the perspective of possible advantages brought and directed towards humanity evolution.

This research received no specific grant from any funding agency in the public, commercial, or not-for-profit sectors.

REFERENCES

Anghel, L. D. (2015). *The marketing of small and medium-sized enterprises.* Biblioteca Digitală ASE. http://www.biblioteca-digitala.ase.ro/biblioteca/

Autio, E. (2017). *Digitalisation, Ecosystems, Entrepreneurship and Policy. Perspectives into Topical Issues Is Society and Ways to Support Political Decision Making. Government's Analysis. Research and Assessment Activities Policy Brief 20/2017.* Prime Minister's Office.

Benvenuto, M., Avram, A., Sambati, F. V., Avram, M., & Viola, C. (2020). The Impact of Internet Usage and Knowledge-Intensive Activities on Households' Healthcare Expenditures. *International Journal of Environmental Research and Public Health, 17*(12), 4470. doi:10.3390/ijerph17124470 PMID:32580302

Bharadwaj, A., El Sawy, O., Pavlou, P., & Venkatraman, N. (2013). Digital business strategy: Toward a next generation of insights. *Management Information Systems Quarterly, 37*(2), 471–482. doi:10.25300/MISQ/2013/37:2.3

Bouwman, H. (1999). E-commerce: Cyber and physical environments. *Electronic Markets, 9*(1–2), 58–64. doi:10.1080/101967899359256

Bouwman, H., Nikou, S., & Reuver, M. (2019). Digitalization, business models, and SMEs: How do business model innovation practices improve performance of digitalising SMEs? *Telecommunications Policy, 43*(9), 101828. doi:10.1016/j.telpol.2019.101828

Carvalhosa, P., Portela, F., Santos, M. F., Abelha, A., & Machado, J. (2017). Pervasiveness in Digital Marketing—A Global Overview. In *Recent Advances in Information Systems and Technologies*. Springer International Publishing. doi:10.1007/978-3-319-56541-5_40

Elmer, S. (1999). Electronic Commerce - IDC. Definitions and Methodologies. In *OCDE Workshop "Defining and Measuring E-commerce"*. OECD.

Eurostat, Digital Economy, and Society Index. (2020). *Country Profile, Romania.* https://ec.europa.eu/digital-single-market/en/digital-economy-and-society-index-desi

Figuera, G. (1999). *An analysis of international Internet diffusion* (PhD Thesis). Massachusetts Institute of Technology.

Franco, M., Haase, H., & Pereira, A. (2016). Empirical study about the role of social networks in SME performance. *Journal of Systems and Information Technology, 18*(4), 383–403. doi:10.1108/JSIT-06-2016-0036

Ghilic-Micu B. (2002). Business in the Digital Economy. *Informatica Economica, 3*(23).

Guo, H., Yang, Z., Huang, R., & Guo, A. (2020). The digitalisation and public crisis responses of small and medium enterprises: Implications from a COVID-19 survey. *Front. Bus. Res. China, 14*(1), 19. doi:10.118611782-020-00087-1

Hada, T., Iuga, I., Deaconu, L., Vicol, D., & Căruţ, M. (2020). *Investment. Investment assessment. Theory. Case studies. Accounting monograph.* Pro Universitaria Publishing House.

Hellwig, Z. (1968). Application of the taxonomic method to the typological division of countries due to the level of their development and the structure of qualified personnel. *Statistical Review, 4*, 307–327.

Holand, A., Svadberg, S., & Breunig, K. J. (2019). Beyond the Hype: A Bibliometric Analysis Deconstructing Research on Digitalization. *Technology Innovation Management Review*, *9*(10), 38–50. doi:10.22215/timreview/1274

Informational Society Ministry. (n.d.). *National Strategy on Digital Agenda for Romania 2020*. https://ec.europa.eu/epale/sites/epale/files/strategia-nationala-agenda-digitala-pentru-romania-20202c-20-feb.2015.pdf

Iuga, I., & Mihalciuc, A. (2020). *Economic crises. Effects on banking systems and investment decision*. LAP Lambert Academic Publishing.

Joensuu-Salo, S., Sorama, K., Viljamaa, A., & Varamäki, E. (2018). Firm Performance among Internationalized SMEs: The Interplay of Market Orientation, Marketing Capability and Digitalization. *Administrative Sciences*, *8*(3), 31. doi:10.3390/admsci8030031

Jurkowska, B. (2014). The Federal States of Germany – Analysis and Measurement of Development Using Taxonomic Methods. *Oeconomia Copernicana*, *5*(3), 52. http://apcz.pl/czasopisma/index.php/OeC/article/view/OeC.2014.019/4316

Kannan, P. K., & Alice, L. (2017). Digital marketing: A framework, review and research agenda. *International Journal of Research in Marketing*, *34*(1), 22–45. doi:10.1016/j.ijresmar.2016.11.006

Kilimis, P., Zou, W., Lehmann, M., & Berger, U. (2019). A Survey on Digitalization for SMEs in Brandenburg, Germany. *IFAC-PapersOnLine*, *52*(13), 2140–2145. doi:10.1016/j.ifacol.2019.11.522

Kohli, A. (2017). Market orientation in a Digital World. *Global Business Review*, *18*(3_suppl), 203S–205S. doi:10.1177/0972150917700769

Kotler, P. (2009). Marketing Moves. A new approach to profit, growth, and renewal. Meteor Press Publishing House.

Leția, A. (2014). Challenges of Business Digital Environment. *Calitatea – acces la success*, *15*(S4), 111. https://www.srac.ro/calitatea/en/arhiva/supliment/2014/Q-as_Vol.15_S4_Sept-2014.pdf

Loebbecke, C., & Picot, A. (2015). Reflections on societal and business model transformation arising from digitization and big data analytics: A research agenda. *The Journal of Strategic Information Systems*, *24*(3), 149–157. doi:10.1016/j.jsis.2015.08.002

Lucas, H. C. Jr, Agarwal, R., Clemons, E. K., El Sawy, O. A., & Weber, B. (2013). Impactful research on transformational information technology: An opportunity to inform new audiences. *Management Information Systems Quarterly*, *37*(2), 371–382. doi:10.25300/MISQ/2013/37.2.03

Mahring, M., Wennberg, K., & Demir, R. (2018). Reaping Value From Digitalization in Swedish Manufactoring Firms: Untapped Opportunities? Managing Digital Transformation, 41–63.

MarchandA.Hennig-ThurauT.FlemmingJ. (2018). Social Media Resources as Strategic Determinants of Social Media Marketing Efectiveness. doi:10.2139srn.3112613

Marques, M., Agostinho, C., & Zacharewicz, G. (2017). Decentralized decision support for intelligent manufacturing in Industry 4.0. Journal of Ambient Intelligence and Smart Environments, 9(3), 299–313.

Mircea M. (2004). Dimensions and Characteristics of the Digital Economy. *Informatica Economică*, *4*(32).

Montecchi, M., & Nobbs, K. (2017). Let It Go: Consumer Empowerment and User-Generated Content—An Exploratory Study of Contemporary Fashion Marketing Practices in the Digital Age. In A. Vecchi (Ed.), *Advanced Fashion Technology and Operations Management* (pp. 294–317). IGI Global. doi:10.4018/978-1-5225-1865-5.ch013

Moroz, M. (2017). The level of development of the digital economy in Poland and selected European countries: a comparative analysis. *Foundations of Management, 9*(1), 175–190.

NeubertM. (2018). The Impact of Digitalization on the Speed of Internationalization of Lean Global. *Technology Innovation Management Review*, 8(5). Available at https://ssrn.com/abstract=3394507

North, K., Aramburu, N., & Lorenzo, O. J. (2020). Promoting digitally enabled growth in SMEs: A framework proposal. *Journal of Enterprise Information Management*, *33*(1), 238–262. doi:10.1108/JEIM-04-2019-0103

Parida, V., Sjödin, D., & Reim, W. (2019). Reviewing Literature on Digitalization, Business Model Innovation, and Sustainable Industry: Past Achievements and Future Promises. *Sustainability*, *11*(2), 391. doi:10.3390u11020391

Pytkovska, J., & Korynski, P. (2017). *Digitalizing Microfinance in Europe*. Microfinance Centre. https://www.europeanmicrofinance.org/sites/default/files/document/file/Digitalization-research-paper.pdf

Rachinger, M., Rauter, R., Müller, C., Vorraber, W., & Schirgi, E. (2018). Digitalization and its influence on business model innovation. *Journal of Manufacturing Technology Management*, *30*(8), 1143–1160. doi:10.1108/JMTM-01-2018-0020

Rivza, B., Kruzmetra, M., Gudele, I., & Foris, D. (2019). Digitalization as an essential growth factor contributing in SME development (experience of Latvia and Romania). *Agronomy Research (Tartu)*, *17*(1), 261–270. doi:10.15159/AR.19.030

Schwab, K. (2017). *The Fourth Industrial revolution*. Penguin Random House.

Schweizer, R. (2012). The internationalization process of SMEs: A muddling-through process. *Journal of Business Research*, *65*(6), 745–751. doi:10.1016/j.jbusres.2010.12.011

Sommer, L. (2015). Industrial revolution - industry 4.0. Are German manufacturing SMEs the first victims of this revolution? Journal of Industrial Engineering and Management, 8(5).

Stallkamp, M., & Schotter, A. P. J. (2019). Platforms without borders? The international strategies of digital platform firms. *Global Strategy Journal*, 1–23. doi:10.1002/gsj.1336

Thi Song, P., Le Monkhouse, L., & Barnes, B. R. (2017). The influence of relational capability and marketing capabilities on the export performance of emerging market firms. *International Marketing Review*, *34*(5), 606–628. doi:10.1108/IMR-07-2014-0235

Tilson, D., Lyytinen, K., & Sørensen, C. (2010). Research commentary-digital infrastructures: The missing IS research agenda. *Information Systems Research*, *21*(4), 748–759. doi:10.1287/isre.1100.0318

Vahlne, J. E., & Bhatti, W. A. (2019). Relationship Development: A Micro-Foundation for the Internationalization Process of the Multinational Business Enterprise. *Management International Review*, *59*(2), 203–228. doi:10.100711575-018-0373-z

Vieru, D., Bourdeau, S., & Bernier, A. (2015). Digital Competence. A Multi-dimensional Conceptualization and a Typology in an SME Context. In: *48th Hawaii International Conference on System Sciences (HICSS)* (pp. 4681–4690). IEEE. 10.1109/HICSS.2015.557

Zhang, J. J., Lichtenstein, Y., & Gander, J. (2015). Designing Scalable Business Models. Advances in Strategic Management. In *Business Models and Modelling*. Emerald Press.

Zhu, K., Kraemer, K., & Xu, S. (2003). Electronic business adoption by European firms: A cross-country assessment of the facilitators and inhibitors. *European Journal of Information Systems*, *12*(4), 251–268. doi:10.1057/palgrave.ejis.3000475

KEY TERMS AND DEFINITIONS

Digital Age: Is the time we live, characterised by people's ability to transmit information without restriction and to have access to information in a way that was impossible in the past. It is also called the "informational era."

Digital Economy: Refers to the current transformations of economic activities because of the use of digital technologies. It is also called the "new economy."

Digital Single Market: Designates the European Commission's strategy for the best possible access to the online world for individuals and businesses.

Digitalisation: Means transforming business models into numerous digital processes, which are often reduced to a combination of digital and physical.

Reverse Marketing: Is the concept of marketing where the customer searches the company and not the company searches the customer. Reverse marketing focuses on the customer approaching the sellers.

Chapter 5
Digital Transformation of Luxury Brands: Omnichannel Strategies and Implementations

Volkan Polat
Yalova University, Turkey

ABSTRACT

Competition among brands has become quite severe due to recent technological developments. These developments can bring some companies to an end, while for some companies they can turn into an opportunity, or the innovations brought by technology can open new ways for companies to work. While capturing these technological developments, companies have begun to transform these innovations into strategies. In addition to the classical marketing strategies and implementations, there are now also companies that use digital transformation in their marketing plans and actions, and they try to integrate the customer with these new types of marketing. Luxury brands have a lot of distinction from other categories with their marketing approaches and tools. Therefore, it is obvious that luxury brands must adapt to this digital transformation. This study aimed to draw a framework for their omnichannel strategies and implementations considering the characteristics of luxury brands and customers.

INTRODUCTION

Technological developments in recent years have not only improved communication channels, but also introduced new, integrated or not, marketing channels (Pauwels & Neslin, 2015). Companies have also attempted to shape these channels to provide competitive advantage for both existing and potential customers and to use them in their daily operations. Each new channel also means a new way to reach consumers. It has also enabled consumers to access alternative products and services faster, easier and at affordable prices (Melero et al., 2016).

DOI: 10.4018/978-1-7998-7192-7.ch005

It is obvious that luxury products and brands have different strategies and practices in terms of marketing compared to other product categories. The products launched by luxury brands may not always follow the classical product development steps. Neither the launch of the product on the market nor the reasons for its preference by consumers cannot be evaluated always within the framework of rational criteria (Penz & Stöttinger, 2012). Luxury brands have a lot of distinction from other categories with their marketing approaches and tools. At this point, the new strategies and implementations present the tools offered by technological transformation will undoubtedly bring different strategies and implementations for luxury brands.

However, one of the issues that needs to be discussed before all this is whether this technological transformation is right for luxury brand customers who are more classical and used to face-to-face communication. There are new discussions in the literature on this subject (Okonkwo, 2009). Although middle-aged and older people come to mind when luxury product customers are mentioned, today the millennium generation, which is experiencing rapid career and income growth, is also among the luxury product consumers. The number of customers in the young profile continues to increase day by day. Considering the prevalence and intensity of young people's access to and use of technological tools, it does not seem possible to say that the marketing strategies of luxury brands will continue with classical approaches (Giovannini et al., 2015; Han & Kim, 2020; Timperio et al., 2016). In addition, although the use of technological facilities is quite common among people above middle age, it is also increasing for older age categories. It is possible to say that digital transformation is now a part of the daily routine for all age groups, with technological products and services reflected in daily life and with easier user interfaces.

Omnichannel examines the consumer in all digital and physical channels (Bell et al., 2014). Data from all channels is collected in a pool. These data are merged, and all channels are optimized for personal communication as a result of processing information. It is a system that allows users to analyze physical stores and e-commerce stores in an integrated way to provide a single experience on all platforms. Specially, in today's world of marketing, where the use of social media and e-commerce is increasing, omnichannel aims to interact with consumers in each channel and in the most effective way. With the strategy that makes the physical store a whole with mobile applications, social media accounts, e-commerce site etc, companies can reach superior market performance by interacting with a larger audience (Gao & Su, 2018). Thus, the awareness and loyalty of the customers on the brand is increasing. For omnichannel marketing, besides recognizing the customer in digital environment, it is also very important that the customer can reach the luxury brands in the desired platform.

Therefore, it is obvious that luxury brands must adapt to this digital transformation. Omnichannel marketing is one of the most up-to-date issues of the reflection of this digital transformation on marketing strategies. Although omnichannel marketing has gained increased attention in recent years, it has not yet matured enough in its scope and applications. Especially when considered in terms of consumer behavior and business practices, the above issues are more critical for luxury brands. At this point, handling omnichannel strategies in terms of luxury brands is expected to be a guide for both researchers and practitioners. In this study, it is aimed to draw a framework for their omnichannel strategies and implementations, considering the characteristics of luxury brands and customers.

BACKGROUND

Multichannel Marketing

It is noteworthy that the number of digital channels that businesses should take part and follow for competitive advantage is increasing. Although being able to reach consumers through multiple channels is an advantage of technology, it also involves its own risks. In principle, businesses tried to adapt to this multi-channel structure with multichannel marketing strategies. Strategies that need to be implemented considering online and offline channels are gathered under multichannel strategies (Floreddu & Cabiddu, 2013). The aim here has been to reach and attract consumers through all available and usable channels as much as possible. These channels include online or offline channels such as television, radio, search engines, social networks, etc., and the number of these channels is increasing day by day. Another purpose here is to reach the location of the customer and to offer the experience desired by the consumer.

Although there are debates in the literature about whether multichannel and omnichannel marketing are different concepts or whether they are within the scope of the other, it is possible to say that there are serious differences between the two, on practice and theory (Hajdas et al., 2020; Silva et al., 2020). In the multichannel applications, some problems have emerged that need to be solved over time (Piotrowicz & Cuthbertson, 2014). The development of technology and digital channels has increased the number of channels. However, while all these channels are used in multi-channel marketing, each one is used separately and independently. For example, channels such as physical location, TV, social media are directed by separate applications and strategies. In this case, it creates confusion for consumers and difficulties in delivering desired messages by businesses.

Another issue may be that a consumer using one or more of these channels is disconnected or directed to another competitor before reaching the purchasing stage. Consumers can easily and quickly switch to another channel or switch to an alternative. Businesses cannot pressure consumers, and consumers are now much more comfortable turning to alternatives.

A misunderstood issue in the management of digital channels is physical stores. There is a false but common belief that physical stores are no longer used or that digital channels are only related to e-commerce sites. However, physical store sales still have a high share among all sales, and it is quite unreasonable to ignore it. In addition, the management of digital channels is not only aimed at increasing traffic and sales for e-trade sites. Digital channels also have a serious impact on physical store sales.

Another important issue is that consumers want to experience shopping as an experience. It can now be said that being only sales-oriented through digital channels is consumer myopia for businesses. With omnichannel strategies, strategies that create value for consumers and businesses with a more holistic perspective can be used in digital channels (Piotrowicz & Cuthbertson, 2014; Silva et al., 2020).

Omnichannel Marketing

Omnichannel marketing can be defined as the integration of all marketing channels used for a seamless experience (Bell et al., 2014; Brynjolfsson et al., 2013; Gao & Su, 2018; Verhoef et al., 2015). Customers can easily move and navigate through all channels without disconnections. Thus, it offers a holistic customer experience in line with its strategies. This experience includes not only digital channels but also face-to-face or physical store interaction. The basic understanding can be defined as perceiving and managing all channels in an integrated manner and providing an uninterrupted experience throughout the purchasing process of the consumer (Beck & Rygl, 2015; Gao & Su, 2018).

In its current meaning, omnichannel marketing first came to the agenda in 2010 and was defined as a shopping experience for consumers beyond the current approaches. The success of businesses that implemented the omnichannel strategy in the following years increased their popularity. It has gained more and more attention for both scholars and practitioners. In this direction, discussions increasingly continue in terms of its scope and conceptual framework.

Undoubtedly, the most important factor in the widespread use of omnichannel strategies is the increase in the capabilities and use of digital tools, especially mobile phones (Lawry & Choi, 2013). Mobility allows consumers to search and compare the same product or equivalent through their mobile phones, even if they enter a physical store. All these developments have led to omnichannel strategies, which were seen as an extra tool for businesses, as an inevitable reality. Because especially after 2010, serious sales declines occurred, especially in retailers who carry out physical store and online activities separately. One of the most important reasons for this was the lack of integrated systems with an integrated perspective on the management of all channels.

Thinking that omnichannel is only for big businesses at the current point is an indication that the concept is misunderstood. Today, in small or medium-sized businesses, it is undoubtedly directly or indirectly related to online channels (Brynjolfsson et al., 2013). Therefore, given their industry and capacities in omnichannel strategies, they also offer great opportunities for them. These enterprises, which frequently encounter market threats of large companies, should turn to new strategies in order to survive and gain competitive advantage.

Omnichannel Benefits and Tools - Framework

Brand consistency: Today, consumers use many different channels in coordination. Consumers demand consistent communication from the brand while browsing through physical stores, online-offline channels, and mobile devices (Bell et al., 2018). Omnichannel allows all channels to be managed with the same consistency. This will enable the brand image to be established in the minds of the consumers in the healthiest way possible.

Customer loyalty: Due to the increasing competition and ease of access to alternative products and services, consumers can easily switch with a rival brand. Many different marketing strategies are applied to create brand loyalty. Maintaining these strategies through omnichannel is very important for more effective and efficient marketing actions (Brynjolfsson et al., 2013).

Customer tracking: In the marketing context, mass tracking was quite expensive and laborious through conventional tools. On the other hand, the accuracy and diversity of the data obtained by these tools raised questions. It is possible to follow the direct or indirect connections of the target audience with the brand with omnichannel implementations. One of the most important points here is that this follow-up is carried out with personalized tools, the right customer is closely recognized with the right follow-up and the correct messages are transmitted .

Being where the customers are: Customer-centered perspective requires presence wherever the customer is. To be able to do this, it is necessary to stand by the customer through all possible channels managed from a single point. Omnichannel gives companies the opportunity to manage customer relationships in all channels with a customer-centric perspective. By monitoring the customer in all channels, it enables to follow the interactions with the customer on a single platform. It prevents the loss of information about the customer and increases the quality of customer service.

Customization of content: Traditional public and mass advertising would result in the delivery of limited message to very large audiences without the possibility of personalization. Marketing applications made by personalizing the data collected from consumers allow reaching the right consumer with the right message. Since omnichannel offers the opportunity to follow the consumers through many different channels, it enables the production of very successful and effective contents with more detailed and accurate data and the delivery of these contents to consumers through various and correct channels (Bell et al., 2014; Gao & Su, 2018).

Collecting data from every transaction: One of the most important advantages of omnichannel is that each channel used is managed individually. For this reason, the problem that the collected data is limited and transferred to a general database is eliminated. In addition, each channel used through omnichannel is used to reach consumers as well as provides the opportunity to obtain new data from consumers through the same channels. The behavior of consumers in all channels offers great potential for correct and effective marketing strategies. It provides the opportunity to collect data to give much more detailed and accurate answers about the behavior, needs and expectations of consumers, as well as general demographic data.

Customer experience: It is quite common for consumers to go to competitors when switching or using channels. Omnichannel customers can interact in a complementary way without disconnection between channels. It minimizes the disconnection between omnichannel channels and prevents customer loss.

Luxury Brands

Although there is no consensus on what exactly the concept of luxury covers, luxury brands are expressed as brands that carry one or more of the elements of prestige, status, quality and high price (Kim, 2019). Luxury brands are brands with well-known brand identity, although some of them are not very common. Brand awareness, perceived quality is high. Although it depends on the industry and customer base, it has certain sales levels and consumer loyalties. Luxury brands are brands that are above prestigious brands that contain not only physical values, but also psychological values (Kim, 2019). They can take place in many different product groups. There are luxury brands belonging to many products such as automobiles, yachts, clothing, perfume, consumer electronics, beverages, cosmetic products, etc.

The luxury products market reached a market of approximately 303 billion dollars in 2017 (statista.com, 2019). With about $ 100 billion, the US is the largest luxury product market (statista.com, 2020a). The most valuable 10 luxury brands in the world in 2020 are listed in the Table 1. below.

Luxury brands are now in demand not only in Europe and the US, but also in developing countries with the increase in national welfare levels. Especially China, gulf countries such as Dubai, Qatar and UAE are the markets where luxury brand consumption is at the forefront. Another issue is that luxury brands are not easily affected by economic crises. It was not even affected by the 2008 global economic recession. The demand for luxury brands continues to increase with an increasing momentum almost every year.

Table 1. Luxury brand values

Luxury Brand	Brand Value (in million U.S. dollars)
Louis Vuitton	51.777
Chanel	36.120
Hermès	33.008
Gucci	27.238
Rolex	7.433
Cartier	5.214
Christian Dior	5.117
Saint-Laurent/Yves Saint Laurent	3.972
Burberry	3.847
Prada	3.059

Source: (statista.com, 2020b)

TRANSFORMATION OF LUXURY BRANDS

Change in Consumer Behavior

Consumers' behavior is changing, and this causes changes in marketing approaches and strategies (Gupta, 2011). Understanding the direction and causes of change in consumer behavior is critical for companies and brands. Although the increase in Internet use and mobility is the most discussed and debated reason, there are also different reasons behind this change. Among these reasons, consumers' willingness to save more, convenience, environmental and health issues stand out (Jones Christensen et al., 2015). However, the relationship of all these reasons with the internet has become an undeniable fact.

Addressing the widespread use of the Internet solely in terms of electronic commerce also creates some obstacles to seeing the big picture. The internet and especially mobile devices have become a part of daily life. People use many tools, software and hardware that are directly or indirectly connected with the internet in many areas such as entertainment, hobby, intellectual development, health, education, etc. Therefore, the fact that companies see online channels as a medium for e-commerce and advertising reduces the opportunities brought by the internet. It is also vital for their survival, adapting to the present and the future.

In the digital world, classical approaches and practices are no longer sufficient to catch consumers. Consumers are busier and more impatient, they want their requests to come true faster. On the other hand, shopping, even on online channels, is not only seen as a product or service but also an experience. Generating loyal consumers is now more difficult than before and consumers are able to switch to competitors more quickly. As stated above, consumers' health and environmental concerns should also be considered. In addition, trying to reach consumers through a single channel can be very difficult and inefficient (Piotrowicz & Cuthbertson, 2014). Considering all these, businesses need to make more effort to understand consumer behavior. In addition to the use of technological tools, it is important not to overlook the human factor and physical facilities in terms of the balanced and successful execution of the process (Simmons, 2008).

When these requirements are examined in terms of businesses, different requirements appear. Increasing competition has revealed that businesses are more sensitive and careful about costs. Poorly managed costs make it difficult for firms to catch competitive prices. These costs may be fixed and variable costs, as well as requiring the control of inefficient expenses that do not bring income to the company. In addition, developments in supply chains and distribution channels are important in terms of making the necessary effort for the correct management of these areas. To ensure customer satisfaction, especially in the sales process and after sales, purchasing a product or service is not enough for consumers anymore.

Considering all these, it is obvious that businesses need more comprehensive and long-term strategies than existing traditional approaches and practices for their long-term success. Businesses now only build their strategies on online channels or physical stores, putting them in a risky circle. Not only for today, but also ready and well-designed approaches for potential opportunities and threats in the future will lead proactive and adaptive businesses to success. Adaptive strategies are based on response to product-market opportunities, marketing activities for responding to these opportunities, and speed of response (Oktemgil & Greenley, 1997).

Luxury Brand Challenges

Luxury brands are not just about meeting their needs for their consumers. Luxury brands can be an indicator of prestige for their consumers, an element that makes them feel privileged, and an indicator of belonging to a community (Bai et al., 2017). Luxury brands focus on identity and are defined by consumers with features such as high price and quality, aesthetic appearance and uniqueness.

A very confused issue here is that when it comes to luxury brands and products, fashion products come to mind (Kim, 2019). Luxury brands do not always consist of fashionable products. Luxury brands can be far outside of fashion and designs. Some luxury products and brands may not be well-known products or brands by the general public. Some of them may even be very different from common or fashionable products in terms of their features, contents or designs, and may be regarded as weird by people. Because some products and brands may have unusual designs and contents due to the symbolic meanings they have. This content and design also have a reflection on the relationship between brand and consumer. Therefore, designs can be maintained in the same or very similar way for many years. Therefore, they may not be affected by fashion trends and changes. Even more, they can direct and shape fashion trends.

One of the first concepts that come to mind when it comes to luxury brand is of course high price (Ko et al., 2019). Discounts and promotions on luxury brands are extremely rare. One of the prominent reasons of preference for the consumer is that the luxury product is not common, and its price is high. Even the sales prices of some products and brands can be remarkable and may be newsworthy in the mass media. Therefore, the interest attracted by the high price can also become a promotion activity for the brand. On the contrary, low prices and promotions can affect the luxury perception of brands. This may lead to both the spread of the product and a decrease in the interest of luxury brand consumers. Therefore, pricing strategies for luxury brands are very important.

When the subject is evaluated geographically, most of the luxury brands still belong to western countries such as Europe and USA. Although production has generally shifted to Asia, production for luxury brands is also made in developed countries. This situation puts into consideration that the main centers of luxury brands are located in western countries such as Europe and the US, both in terms of production and consumption. One of the reasons for this situation can be said to be the country of origin. Although the countries to which the brands belong are more prominent for consumers, this situation is slightly different for luxury brands. Luxury brand consumers pay more attention to where the brands they want to buy produce their products (Ko et al., 2019). Another reason for the geographical distribution of the production of luxury brands may be that the product ranges of luxury brands are much narrower and less variety than other brand groups. Fewer product types and the fact that these products are produced in much less number may cause issues such as production costs to be ignored. Especially, it may not be possible to change the production places of some luxury products that include handmade or hand labor.

Another issue, especially in products that require hand production or fine workmanship, is that it can take long periods of production and delivery of products to the consumer. This may affect the availability and rarity of products. However, this uniqueness also differentiates the sales process of the brands. The purchase of products can be done through private organizations or events. Therefore, the purchasing and delivery process of the product may include a separate experience for consumers.

Luxury brands can be seen as an investment tool by their consumers (Kim, 2016). Especially in some product groups, many brands can gain value over time as opposed to losing material value. This has revealed the fact that luxury brands are also used as an investment tool for investors and collectors. Therefore, while customers are competing in some cases for some products, it may not be sufficient for some brands to have only financial power. Only certain customer groups or individuals can access and buy these brands. Some brands can only be located in locations that their potential or current customers can reach. This not only facilitates the transportation of its own customers, but also leads to the segregation of consumers who are not in the potential customer category. Of course, it should be taken into consideration that the sales of some luxury brands are not made in stores or fixed locations, but in organizations such as auctions, special meetings, and invitations.

These special processes cause luxury brands to come to the fore as a lifestyle (Han & Kim, 2020). Luxury brands try to continue this in many ways. For example, if the luxury brand has products for the general consumer other than luxury products, they are careful not to associate this with the main luxury brand. Otherwise, it may have negative repercussions for the luxury brand and affect the brand value. Another point is that when it comes to luxury brands, only luxury products should not come to mind. Luxury brands that offer luxury services also apply luxury brand strategies and follow similar paths in many issues. Therefore, luxury brand management is a whole. It requires a very precise management strategy.

Although luxury brands are very strong brands, a minor negativity can cause irreparable or costly damage to the image of the brand. Therefore, with the omnichannel strategies of luxury brands, it can be both a great advantage and a serious risk for the consumer to have a seamless brand experience. For this, the omnichannel strategies of luxury brands should be handled very well and the right actions should be determined and implemented.

SOLUTIONS AND RECOMMENDATIONS

Omnichannel and Luxury Brands

Omnichannel marketing is currently one of the important developments in the marketing world. Customers can easily move between online, mobile, and in-store experiences without breaking away from brand. With omnichannel marketing, companies can deliver personalized marketing offers to their (Gao & Su, 2018; Silva et al., 2020). Customers can interact with brands on different channels, instantly switch between channels smoothly. In this way, success becomes much easier to achieve. More and more businesses offer their product or services via integrated multiple channels, including online, on-site, and mobile technologies and apps. This is the difference between multichannel marketing and omnichannel marketing (Lazaris & Vrechopoulos, 2014; Verhoef et al., 2015).

Luxury brands have different strategies and practices to follow than traditional brand strategies due to their nature (Holmqvist et al., 2020). These factors mainly stem from a lifestyle, style, thought and sense of belonging for the consumers of luxury brands, beyond just meeting their needs. Luxury brands are a sign of social identity and difference reflecting the lifestyle for consumers (Kim, 2019). Consequently, consumers may see these brands indispensable for them and therefore their sensitivity to price will be very low. And this situation causes the demand of luxury brands to not decrease even during the economic recession. But today, especially technological developments, technological transformation of companies, changes in consumer behavior, macroeconomic changes and events that affect the whole world such as Covid-19 affect luxury brands. In this transformation, luxury brands should be evaluated from different angles in order to overcome these challenges with omnichannel strategies.

Unique Sales Experience - Personalization

A very small proportion of the world's population or country's people can buy luxury brands. So, the target audience of luxury brands represents a very small proportion of the general population. Therefore, communication to be established with this small audience is quite different from mass production brands. Even if it uses the same channels as other industries, it requires much different implementations in terms of method or detail. The expectations of luxury brand consumers before, during and after sales are higher and different. Just as the products offered by luxury brands are rare and unique, so should their customer service and support be unmatched.

Here, luxury brands can collect data via omnichannel, and this data can be used to provide personalized experience for all their customers (Jocevski et al., 2019). Luxury brands can provide each consumer with a unique experience with personalized tools such as special invitations, offers, and special days. In this regard, tools called recommendation engines, especially in online channels, can be used to recommend similar products from the previous shopping history of consumers. Recommendation engines try to learn the buying habits of consumers from the products they have already purchased. In this direction, they can recommend new products suitable for their tastes, interests, or styles. In addition, with real-time analysis, consumers can recommend other products as an alternative product or as an additional product, even if they are interested in another product.

These tools can similarly be used for offline channels (Bell et al., 2018; Gao & Su, 2017). Data collected through online and offline channels can be processed and used in the provision of personalized products or services even if consumers go to physical stores. Here, the integration of different channel structures offered by omnichannel implementations will provide an important function. For example, even if the consumer has used an online channel before, it will enable the use of this information in physical store visits by the help of databases and analyzes integrated with the CRM system. This can be effective both in the provision of alternative products and services and in the sale of additional products. On the other hand, it makes it possible for the consumer to experience a completely unique and personalized shopping experience in both online and offline channels.

Another important issue here is after-sales services (Brynjolfsson et al., 2013). The personalized service concept for both online and offline channels may also apply to after-sales services. In the after-sales services, product replacement, return, malfunction, etc. may occur, as well as monitoring the satisfaction of consumers after sales is possible with omnichannel implementations. In addition, this issue is very important in terms of increasing and following the brand loyalty of consumers. Because luxury brand consumers want to feel that they are special customers not only before and during sales, but also after sales. This may include recall of special days, after-sales satisfaction surveys, as well as new product offers for certain time-based consumer products in case of expiration of the products.

It is possible to use existing consumers to reach new consumers with omnichannel tools. Because, especially the luxury brand consumers' sense of belonging to a certain group and social community can be used to reach new potential consumers. Here, it can be considered to create online or offline communities that are completely specific to current or potential consumers, perhaps with an invitation or reference. These communities are controlled or supported by omnichannel tools, providing an opportunity for both the flow of data from these communities and reaching private individuals within this community.

Internationalization – Glocalization

Another characteristic of luxury brands is that they have an international position (Fernie et al., 1997; Mir-Bernal et al., 2018). Although the general density is in developed countries, luxury brands are not limited to a specific region or country. Even If this situation is geographically concentrated in developed countries, it requires the satisfaction of a special customer group scattered around the world. The increasing demand for luxury brands, especially with the development of Asian markets, has revealed the need for luxury brands to focus not only on Europe and the USA, but also on other markets. In addition, another important point here should be considered as the emergence of not only new consumers, but also the emergence of new luxury brands, except for western countries. This situation makes the competition more difficult with the entry of new players into the market. In addition, while luxury brands need to produce a balanced and consistent brand internationally, they should also seek ways to retain their local customers. In order to appeal to online consumers with different characteristics such as different age groups, culture and language, a delicate balance must be observed.

Luxury brands need to protect the attributes and values of their identities and provide localization that will appeal to local customers in international markets and meet their expectations. In this respect, appropriate, fast and accurate solutions can be offered by combining the omnichannel approach with technological tools. Luxury brands will take the lead in localizing the contents of the tools they offer, especially through digital channels, increasing the awareness of brands and sales (Guercini & Runfola, 2015; Mir-Bernal et al., 2018). At this point, only websites should not be understood from digital tools. Social media tools, mobile applications, e-mails, search tools, electronic brochures, online real-time or artificial intelligence chat tools and robots should also be understood. Considering the widespread use of social media, it is important to create local or regional accounts as well as the global social media accounts of luxury brands. These accounts must make localized shares. At the same time, it will be beneficial to present social media or other digital ads to the right target audience, localized. For this, localized SEO content and adjustments are important. Thus, by localizing not only physical stores but also digital tools, omnichannel integrity can be achieved in a healthier way.

New Sales and Communication Channels

Online channels continue to develop and spread all over the world. The number of consumers who prefer luxury brands through online channels is increasing accordingly. Although luxury brands have very different sales channels and expectations of consumers compared to traditional products and services, online channels are a matter that should focus on luxury brands. As is known, especially old luxury brands have serious experience in physical stores and sales environments, and skills in consumer experience. They should focus on providing services to luxury brand consumers with the same quality, uniqueness and experience in online channels (Mir-Bernal et al., 2018).

The vital point in terms of omnichannel implementations is, of course, the integration of these increased channels and providing a seamless experience (Bell et al., 2014). Including only product prices and information does not provide correct integration. In particular, the details such as physical store information, stock status, communication tools of the products offered on digital channels must also be accurate and up to date. In addition, it should be ensured that consumers have an uninterrupted and successful communication process with the brand not only before and during sales, but also after sales. Because, as mentioned above, luxury brands have serious and successful experiences in physical stores, events and face-to-face communication points (Bell et al., 2018). The expectation of consumers is that this experience will continue in the increasing number of digital channels. Especially with the increase in mobility, middle-aged and older consumers also use these channels actively. Therefore, channel diversification for luxury brands should not be seen only for a certain consumer group, but omnichannel strategies should be developed with an approach that includes all existing and potential customers.

While applying omnichannel strategies, the fact that there are too many online and offline channels may cause brands to focus only on certain channels. Some may see online channels as an alternative to offline channels. The point that should not be forgotten here is that channels are not alternative to each other. The main point in omnichannel implementations is to offer a seamless and non-contradictory experience between them, no matter how many and varied the number of channels. This point is also important in order to prevent communication problems and difficulties that may arise due to the widespread use of online channels.

New Consumer Generations

Another issue is that especially new generations emerge as luxury brand consumers. Generation Y and Z (Gen Y, or Millennials, those born between 1984 and 1996; and Gen Z, those born after 1997) are increasingly present in the luxury brand market, and this rate is increasing (Timperio et al., 2016). These generations behave differently from previous generations and consumer habits are different (Han & Kim, 2020). They are more technology oriented and more creatively demanding. There are many different communication channels and communication styles. Luxury brands need to develop a communication style and language suitable for these new generations. In addition, it should not be overlooked that luxury brand consumers have higher expectations of being in touch with the brands themselves. This requires proper and relevant communication not only with new generations but also with the entire consumer community.

In the coming years, the Y and Z generations will continue to constitute a significant portion of the total consumers, with a significant purchasing power. These generations, with more entrepreneurial, liberal characteristics, are more likely to go beyond the traditional. They can be defined as early adopters as consumption habits. They have quality and value expectations in the products and services offered, and they expect the brands they use to adapt to their unique identities. The fact that products and services are easily accessible and ready for immediate consumption affects purchasing decisions. Consequently, these generations, which have many unique features of luxury brands, seem to be the most appropriate tools for luxury brands to reach them, considering their potential in the market.

Luxury Brands as Investment Tool and Secondhand Markets

Due to the uniqueness and rarity of luxury brands, some luxury brands can even be seen by consumers as an investment tool (Kim, 2016). This situation leads to the creation of a serious second-hand market for luxury brands. Luxury brands can manage the secondhand market to reach new consumers and attract more consumers in the long run. However, this situation also requires taking some precautions for luxury brands to protect their brand image and values. Because, considering the issues such as pricing of luxury brands and seeing themselves as unique by their consumers, second-hand markets should be managed and controlled properly in terms of brand image.

Secondhand markets for luxury goods are interestingly growing faster than the luxury industry (bcg.com, 2020). The widespread use of electronic commerce and social media can be shown among the reasons for the growth of these markets. Although most of luxury brands did not give importance to second-hand markets in the past, the increasing interest through these channels pushes them to focus on these markets. By narrating brands and sharing them on social media as personal identities, more consumers show interest in these markets and can be seen as an investment tool by their owners.

Studies show that consumers who want to buy second-hand luxury products want to buy these products directly from certified and luxury brands (bcg.com, 2020). This situation raises the need for luxury brands to create their own platforms for second-hand products or to integrate their existing second-hand activities with omnichannel implementations. This is important not only to meet the current demand, but also to control the second-hand market of luxury brands and eliminate a potential threat to brand images. In addition, even if it is an used product, luxury brand consumers will want to experience the identity and purchasing experience expressed by that brand. With an omnichannel infrastructure that can present the brand experience of the luxury brand in the same way, consumers will be able to access used luxury brands easily and with the same experience.

Social Awareness and Sustainability

With the change in consumer behavior, social awareness and sustainability have become an important issue for luxury brands (Jones Christensen et al., 2015; Timperio et al., 2016). Consumers can now turn to more environmentally friendly and socially aware brands. Although there may be different understandings in different product categories, socially sensitive luxury brands stand out with this image against their competitors.

Omnichannel implementations offer different alternatives not only at the point of purchasing the product but also at the point of delivering the product to the consumer. Although speed and interruption experience are prominent factors here, choosing the fastest and most suitable alternative channel can also contribute to reducing costs and leaving less carbon footprint. These advantages can be shared with consumers as part of a more sustainable environmental policy and contribute to the brand's image.

At the same time, with the purpose of social awareness and solidarity, with the campaigns to be made during or outside of the purchasing process, consumers can be offered the opportunity to be a part of this process. As it is known, luxury brands participate in many philanthropic activities and consumers want to identify these values both with the brand they prefer and with themselves. With omnichannel tools, consumers can participate in charity activities directly or indirectly, as well as follow and share their brands that engage in these activities.

Security and Privacy

A similar issue for luxury brands is that "privacy" can be very important for luxury brand consumers (Ko et al., 2016). For some luxury categories, consumers want the products and brands they buy to be known, while in others they are required to keep them confidential. In general, everyone can have privacy concerns about online channels. However, this situation becomes a more sensitive issue considering both the concern of luxury brand customers and the integration of many online and offline channels in omnichannel applications (Park et al., 2011).

Necessary technological measures should be taken to protect the privacy of consumers and consumers should be informed about this. In addition, both legal regulations and companies' own policies on privacy should be implemented for the protection of consumers. In addition, at the point of security, it is not only necessary to protect the personal information of consumers, but also to keep consumers away from problems such as fraud, counterfeiting, and fake products. Luxury brands should be able to correctly manage both the advantages and disadvantages of technological developments in this regard.

Economic Trends

As in all markets, it is necessary to consider the general economic and sociological developments in the world for luxury brands (Nunes et al., 2011). Looking at the general economic course, the slowdown in the growth rates of the countries and the decrease to single digits is an important factor for luxury brands. However, despite this trend, the luxury brands market is growing every year. The increase in the demand for luxury brands and the number of consumers is related to the increase in the welfare and economic development of the countries.

The slowdown of the economic growth, which has been discussed in the last decade, on the basis of countries, has been a driving factor for luxury brands to develop strategies for the coming years and to overcome this situation. The prominent point here is that with the technological developments and the widespread use of technology, many new potential consumers have become accessible for luxury brands as in every industry. Although countries such as the USA, European countries and Japan constitute the largest markets, especially China, South Korea and the gulf countries have also become emerging markets for luxury brands as a result of the rising economic prosperity. On the other hand, in times of economic recession, with the increasing pressure of competition, new ways of reaching and retaining consumers are sought (Bradshaw et al., 2020; Soon-hwa, 2009). Omnichannel strategies are useful tools to get ahead of competitors and gain competitive advantage at such times. Just as brands that developed innovative ways and strategies during the 2008 global recession survived and even turned this period into an advantage (Nunes et al., 2011). Likewise, in this period of economic fluctuations, brands that apply innovative and creative developments such as omnichannel can get out of this period even more profitably and growing.

Macro Developments and Covid-19

The Covid-19 pandemic has affected all countries and people of the world in every aspect of their lives and lifestyles. The world is facing such a widespread and long-lasting pandemic for the first time. It directly affected all areas of life such as education, health, trade and arts. Although studies reveal that some luxury brands and retailers are relatively less negatively affected, the category that the Covid-19 pandemic does not adversely affect is almost non-existent (Euromonitor, 2020). Because people did not reduce or delay their luxury brand purchases just for economic reasons and concerns. Especially luxury brands, which can include more authentic rituals and reach their consumers through different organizations/events, could not reach their consumers due to the risk of infection or restrictions. This situation poses a separate risk especially for the luxury wearable product categories that people directly try or use. Also, there are demand decreases due to the risk of contamination for luxury brands that offer luxury accommodation and restaurant services. In addition, although varying by country, mandatory lock-downs also directly affected many luxury brands, albeit from different categories. Another point to consider is that the pandemic does not only affect luxury brands at the point of sale. As in all industries, the pandemic has affected luxury brands in terms of production, supply and logistics. Therefore, all these effects have revealed the most difficult situation for luxury brands in recent years (D'Arpizio et al., 2020; Roggeveen & Sethuraman, 2020).

It was mentioned that luxury brands have different styles with their traditions and experiences. However, with the Covid-19 pandemic, the transition to electronic channels has ceased to be a choice for many industries and has become a necessity (Roggeveen & Sethuraman, 2020). One of the most important strategies for luxury brands to turn to electronic channels while preserving their core brand values will be omnichannel strategies. It can enable consumers who cannot go to physical stores with Omnichannel tools to reach luxury brands with the most valuable and quality experience (D'Arpizio et al., 2020). Virtual fairs and events can be organized for luxury products. Delivery of purchased products through different delivery channels, follow-up of after-sales services and customer relations can be possible with Omnichannel implementations that are integrated with each other in the most consistent and accurate way. Especially the seamless experience offered by omnichannel implementations is ideal for consumers who still want to visit physical stores, as well as for providing excellent customer service that suits the luxury brand identity.

In addition, omnichannel implementations will contribute to providing the healthiest working conditions not only for consumers but also for employees during the pandemic period. This is of vital importance both for the happiness of the employees and for the business activities not to be interrupted in this difficult period.

FUTURE RESEARCH DIRECTIONS

In this study, omnichannel strategies and implementations for luxury brands are presented in a general framework. It is obvious that this transformation will have different implementations and strategies for different types of brands (e.g. generic, global, service, public etc.). However, these are not included in the scope of this study. How this transformation will be differentiated for different type of brands may be the subject of future studies. On the other hand, since the subject of omnichannel marketing is a very new field, both theoretical and empirical research are needed in this regard. We believe that this kind of research will shed light on academics and practitioners and fill the gaps in the literature.

CONCLUSION

Luxury brands, due to their nature, can stay cautious compared to other product groups in adapting to innovations. Their traditions and expectations are among the factors that keep them in this approach. But developing technology and lifestyles push them to new implementations and tools for competition (Holmqvist et al., 2020). They adapt to new technological developments to continue to attract customers, increase their loyalty and offer them a unique experience. We see these practices and strategies under different titles in terms of omnichannel.

In their omnichannel strategies for luxury brands, brands must follow a delicate balance in order to both preserve their traditions and provide new experiences. Luxury brands, which previously stood out with their physical store experiences, now need to find the right adaptations of their omnichannel strategies to offer the same quality experience on online channels. In these adaptations, personalization is one of the most important tools and should be considered in the development of omnichannel strategies.

As brief omnichannel strategies in order to be a general approach for luxury brands;

- Consumer profiles should be determined in the most appropriate and accurate manner, and it should be taken into account that the same customer may belong to different profiles. Although there are many online and offline channels on omnichannel, not every channel is suitable for every consumer. With these profiling studies, the most appropriate combination should be used for each consumer profile.
- Communication activities through Omnichannel should not be done just for formality. Communication should provide a useful content and message to the consumer. A common and understandable language should be used to maintain integrity in all channels. In particular, the tools to be used in digital channels should be accessible from different devices and platforms as technical infrastructure. In addition, the information presented on these platforms should be consistent, accurate and up-to-date. For example, if there is different information between the website and the mobile application, if the information is not up to date, a seamless experience cannot be mentioned. All channels should be integrated with each other and working smoothly.
- When using omnichannel channels, the system should be checked and audited continuously. The efficiency and productivity of the channels should be followed. Tools/channels that do not achieve the expected goals should be determined. KPI and goals should be measured. Channels and tools that show poor or unexpected performance should be optimized with appropriate investment and regulation.

Interest to omnichannel marketing is increasing by day by. The main reason for this is to keep the customer at the maximum level by creating customer loyalty. According to a study published by the Aspect Software (2014), companies that offer a well-defined omnichannel marketing customer experience can hold more than 91% of their customers each year, compared to companies that fail to do.

The face of marketing is changing very fast with technology. These changes create new strategies, because each major company is in search of keeping more customers and gaining more new customers.

In recent years, this quest has developed much more customer-oriented approaches. Companies have begun to develop new strategies to offer their customers more personalized options. In addition, companies want to maintain their contacts with their customers whenever and wherever they want. One of the most powerful strategy for this is omnichannel marketing.

Omnichannel marketing gives the customer a chance to use all new and old technological tools and does not pass over the physical store concept. Moreover, one of the main objectives of this strategy is the uninterrupted interaction and it creates customer loyalty. Basically, this marketing type, which is one of the most popular subjects of marketing in recent years, offers a relationship model that does not detach from the customer, and strengthens it. There are many investments made by many companies to consolidate this relationship. Companies are making these investments in order to get ahead in the marketing race. The omnichannel marketing strategy has served this purpose entirely. Instead of using technology to automate processes, these companies, which are considering using technology to improve human interaction, are closer to taking a step forward with omnichannel approaches.

As a result, omnichannel marketing is an area that is currently being discussed and developing in the literature. Considering the different marketing strategies and practices of luxury brands, it is obvious that omnichannel marketing will contribute to these. Although this study is analyzed through luxury brands, it is expected that it will fill an important gap in the literature in terms of digital transformation in marketing by drawing a framework for omnichannel strategies and implementations.

REFERENCES

Bai, H., McColl, J., & Moore, C. (2017). Luxury retailers' entry and expansion strategies in China. *International Journal of Retail & Distribution Management*, *45*(11), 1181–1199. doi:10.1108/IJRDM-11-2016-0232

Beck, N., & Rygl, D. (2015). Categorization of multiple channel retailing in Multi-, Cross-, and Omni-Channel Retailing for retailers and retailing. *Journal of Retailing and Consumer Services*, *27*, 170–178. doi:10.1016/j.jretconser.2015.08.001

Bell, D. R., Gallino, S., & Moreno, A. (2014). How to win in an omnichannel world. *MIT Sloan Management Review*, *56*(1), 45–53.

Bell, D. R., Gallino, S., & Moreno, A. (2018). Offline showrooms in omnichannel retail: Demand and operational benefits. *Management Science*, *64*(4), 1629–1651. doi:10.1287/mnsc.2016.2684

Bradshaw, H. K., Rodeheffer, C. D., & Hill, S. E. (2020). Scarcity, sex, and spending: Recession cues increase women's desire for men owning luxury products and men's desire to buy them. *Journal of Business Research*, *120*, 561–568. doi:10.1016/j.jbusres.2019.07.021

Brynjolfsson, E., Hu, Y. J., & Rahman, M. S. (2013). Competing in the age of omnichannel retailing. *MIT Sloan Management Review*, *54*(4), 1–7.

D'Arpizio, C., Levato, F., Fenili, S., Colacchio, F., & Prete, F. (2020). *Luxury after Covid-19: Changed for (the) Good?* https://www.bain.com/insights/luxury-after-coronavirus/

Fernie, J., Moore, C., Lawrie, A., & Hallsworth, A. (1997). The internationalization of the high fashion brand: The case of central London. *Journal of Product and Brand Management, 6*(3), 151–162. doi:10.1108/10610429710175673

Floreddu, P. B., & Cabiddu, F. (2013). Innovating distribution channels for competitive advantage. *XXV Convegno Annuale Di Sinergie, L'innovazione per La Competitività Delle Imprese*, 265–274. doi:10.7433/SRECP.2013.17

Gao, F., & Su, X. (2017). Online and offline information for omnichannel retailing. *Manufacturing & Service Operations Management, 19*(1), 84–98. doi:10.1287/msom.2016.0593

Gao, F., & Su, X. (2018). Omnichannel service operations with online and offine self-order technologies. *Management Science, 64*(8), 3595–3608. doi:10.1287/mnsc.2017.2787

Giovannini, S., Xu, Y., & Thomas, J. (2015). Luxury fashion consumption and Generation Y consumers: Self, brand consciousness, and consumption motivations. *Journal of Fashion Marketing and Management, 19*(1), 22–40. doi:10.1108/JFMM-08-2013-0096

Guercini, S., & Runfola, A. (2015). Internationalization through e-commerce. the case of multibrand luxury retailers in the fashion industry. *Advances in International Marketing, 26*, 15–31. doi:10.1108/S1474-797920150000026002

Gupta, N. (2011). Globalization does lead to change in consumer behavior: An empirical evidence of impact of globalization on changing materialistic values in Indian consumers and its aftereffects. *Asia Pacific Journal of Marketing and Logistics, 23*(3), 251–269. doi:10.1108/13555851111143204

Hajdas, M., Radomska, J., & Silva, S. C. (2020). The omni-channel approach: A utopia for companies? *Journal of Retailing and Consumer Services*. doi:10.1016/j.jretconser.2020.102131

Han, S. L., & Kim, K. (2020). Role of consumption values in the luxury brand experience: Moderating effects of category and the generation gap. *Journal of Retailing and Consumer Services, 57*, 102249. Advance online publication. doi:10.1016/j.jretconser.2020.102249

Holmqvist, J., Wirtz, J., & Fritze, M. P. (2020). Luxury in the digital age: A multi-actor service encounter perspective. *Journal of Business Research, 121*, 747–756. doi:10.1016/j.jbusres.2020.05.038

Jocevski, M., Arvidsson, N., Miragliotta, G., Ghezzi, A., & Mangiaracina, R. (2019). Transitions towards omni-channel retailing strategies: A business model perspective. *International Journal of Retail & Distribution Management, 47*(2), 78–93. doi:10.1108/IJRDM-08-2018-0176

Jones Christensen, L., Siemsen, E., & Balasubramanian, S. (2015). Consumer behavior change at the base of the pyramid: Bridging the gap between for-profit and social responsibility strategies. *Strategic Management Journal, 36*(2), 307–317. doi:10.1002mj.2249

Kim, J. (2019). Luxury fashion goods ownership and collecting behavior in an omni-channel retail environment: Empirical findings from affluent consumers in the US. *Research Journal of Textile and Apparel, 23*(3), 212–231. doi:10.1108/RJTA-01-2019-0001

Kim, J., & Joung, H.-M. (2016). Psychological underpinnings of luxury brand goods repurchase intentions: Brand-self congruity, emotional attachment, and perceived level of investment made. *Article in Journal of Global Scholars of Marketing Science*, *26*(3), 284–299. doi:10.1080/21639159.2016.1174542

Ko, E., Costello, J. P., & Taylor, C. R. (2019). What is a luxury brand? A new definition and review of the literature. *Journal of Business Research*, *99*, 405–413. doi:10.1016/j.jbusres.2017.08.023

Ko, E., Phau, I., & Aiello, G. (2016). Luxury brand strategies and customer experiences: Contributions to theory and practice. *Journal of Business Research*, *69*(12), 5749–5752. doi:10.1016/j.jbusres.2016.04.170

Lawry, C. A., & Choi, L. (2013). The Omnichannel Luxury Retail Experience: Building Mobile Trust and Technology Acceptance of Quick Response (QR) Codes. *Marketing ZFP*, *35*(2), 144–154. doi:10.15358/0344-1369_2013_2_144

Lazaris, C., & Vrechopoulos, A. (2014). From Multichannel to "Omnichannel" Retailing: Review of the Literature and Calls for Research. *2nd International Conference on Contemporary Marketing Issues, (ICCMI)*. 10.13140/2.1.1802.4967

Melero, I., Javier Sese, F., & Verhoef, P. C. (2016). Recasting the Customer Experience in Today's Omnichannel Environment. *Universia Business Review*, *2016*(50), 18–37. doi:10.3232/UBR.2016.V13.N2.01

Mir-Bernal, P., Guercini, S., & Sádaba, T. (2018). The role of e-commerce in the internationalization of Spanish luxury fashion multi-brand retailers. *Journal of Global Fashion Marketing*, *9*(1), 59–72. doi:10.1080/20932685.2017.1399080

Nunes, J. C., Drèze, X., & Han, Y. J. (2011). Conspicuous consumption in a recession: Toning it down or turning it up? *Journal of Consumer Psychology*, *21*(2), 199–205. doi:10.1016/j.jcps.2010.11.002

Okonkwo, U. (2009). Sustaining the luxury brand on the Internet. *Journal of Brand Management*, *16*(5–6), 302–310. doi:10.1057/bm.2009.2

Oktemgil, M., & Greenley, G. (1997). Consequences of high and low adaptive capability in UK companies. *European Journal of Marketing*, *31*(7), 445–466. doi:10.1108/03090569710176619

Park, J., Song, H., & Ko, E. (2011). The Effect of the Lifestyles of Social Networking Service Users on Luxury Brand Loyalty. *Journal of Global Scholars of Marketing Science*, *21*(4), 182–192. doi:10.1080/21639159.2011.9726521

Pauwels, K., & Neslin, S. A. (2015). Building With Bricks and Mortar: The Revenue Impact of Opening Physical Stores in a Multichannel Environment. *Journal of Retailing*, *91*(2), 182–197. doi:10.1016/j.jretai.2015.02.001

Penz, E., & Stöttinger, B. (2012). A comparison of the emotional and motivational aspects in the purchase of luxury products versus counterfeits. *Journal of Brand Management*, *19*(7), 581–594. doi:10.1057/bm.2012.7

Piotrowicz, W., & Cuthbertson, R. (2014). Retail: Toward Omnichannel Retailing. *International Journal of Electronic Commerce*, *18*(4), 5–15. doi:10.2753/JEC1086-4415180400

Roggeveen, A. L., & Sethuraman, R. (2020). How the COVID-19 Pandemic May Change the World of Retailing. In Journal of Retailing (Vol. 96, Issue 2, pp. 169–171). Elsevier Ltd. doi:10.1016/j.jretai.2020.04.002

Silva, S. C., Duarte, P., & Sundetova, A. (2020). Multichannel versus omnichannel: A price-segmented comparison from the fashion industry. *International Journal of Retail & Distribution Management*, *48*(4), 417–430. doi:10.1108/IJRDM-07-2019-0232

Simmons, G. (2008). Marketing to postmodern consumers: Introducing the internet chameleon. *European Journal of Marketing*, *42*(3/4), 299–310. doi:10.1108/03090560810852940

Soon-hwa, C. (2009). Global Luxury Brands' Strategies to Fight Recession. *SERI Quarterly*, *2*(4), 108–111.

Timperio, G., Tan, K. C., Fratocchi, L., & Pace, S. (2016). The impact of ethnicity on luxury perception: The case of Singapore's Generation Y. *Asia Pacific Journal of Marketing and Logistics*, *28*(2), 217–233. doi:10.1108/APJML-04-2015-0060

Verhoef, P. C., Kannan, P. K., & Inman, J. J. (2015). From Multi-Channel Retailing to Omni-Channel Retailing. Introduction to the Special Issue on Multi-Channel Retailing. *Journal of Retailing*, *91*(2), 174–181. doi:10.1016/j.jretai.2015.02.005

ADDITIONAL READING

Bcg.com. (2020). The Secondhand Opportunity in Hard Luxury. https://www.bcg.com/publications/2020/secondhand-opportunity-hard-luxury

Euromonitor.com. (2020). The Impact of Coronavirus on Luxury Goods. https://www.euromonitor.com/the-impact-of-coronavirus-on-luxury-goods/report

Loyalty360.org. (2014). Survey: Businesses that Use Omni-channel Strategies Have Far Better Customer Retention Rates. https://loyalty360.org/content-gallery/daily-news/survey-businesses-that-use-omni-channel-strategies-have-far-better-customer

Statista.com. (2019). Most valuable luxury brands worldwide 2019, by brand value. https://www.statista.com/statistics/273135/most-valuable-luxury-brands-worldwide-by-brand-value/

Statista.com. (2020a). Value of the personal luxury goods market worldwide from 1996 to 2020. https://www.statista.com/statistics/266503/value-of-the-personal-luxury-goods-market-worldwide/

Statista.com. (2020b). Brand value of the leading 10 most valuable luxury brands worldwide in 2020. https://www.statista.com/statistics/267948/brand-value-of-the-leading-10-most-valuable-luxury-brands-worldwide/

KEY TERMS AND DEFINITIONS

Channel Management: Management of marketing channels according to firms' marketing strategies.

Consumer Generation: People born at the same time and raised with similar consumer behavior.

Digital Transformation: The process of finding solutions to social and business needs with the integration of digital technologies and the development of business processes and culture.

Luxury Brand: Brands that carry one or more of the elements of prestige, status, quality, and high price.

Multichannel: Channels include online and offline channels such as television, radio, search engines, social networks, etc.

Omnichannel: The integration of all marketing channels used for a seamless experience.

Personalization: Providing personalized products, services, or communications by collecting and analyzing data through technological tools.

Chapter 6
Digital Transformation in the Energy Industry: Strategies for Fuel Retail Companies

Emiliano Sola
Luiss University, Italy

Viviana D'Angelo
Luiss University, Italy

Francesca Capo
University of Milano Bicocca, Italy

ABSTRACT

In recent years, digital transformation has begun to significantly affect the business landscape, disrupting existing business models. In the midst of this revolution, oil and gas retail companies are experiencing a strong transformation of the whole industry, which is also driving the transformation of their processes, assets, and people. In this chapter, the authors explore how oil and gas retail companies are trying to redefine their business models by providing end-users with a wide range of smart and connected solutions. The main purpose of this work is to analyse, in the face of the digital transformation era, the potential that new technologies can unleash in mature and commoditized industries such as the one of oil and gas retail. In particular, the present work focuses on the digital transformation strategy of fuel retail companies based on the improvement of customer experience.

INTRODUCTION

Most of the companies are nowadays engaging in digital transformation, challenged by the revolution occurring in the competitive landscape and, consequently in their business models and in customer and societal needs. In the light of the new digital era, companies do need to appropriately strategize around data collection, analysis and their translation into unique customer experiences. This means that the

DOI: 10.4018/978-1-7998-7192-7.ch006

ability to handle and use data to create value for customers and for the society plays a crucial role for companies, which need to accordingly reconfigure their business processes. We define digital transformation as "the changes associated with the application of digital technology in all aspects of human society" (Stolterman & Fors, 2004: 689).

This is especially relevant in the Oil & Gas industry, whose products are represented by commodities (Sen, 1999), which is a highly dynamic sector characterized by high market volatility and fluctuating prices, affected by geopolitical events and dependent from the global value chains. In this scenario, fuel retail companies deserve attention, since the most optimistic forecasts expect that 30% of service stations could be in severe distress if their business models will not evolve (Boston Consulting Group, 2019). Indeed, they need to follow the current trend which sees the whole business environment being transformed by digital technologies (Helfat & Raubitschek, 2018).

Previous studies (Westerman, Bonnet & McAfee, 2018) found that while some industries have already embraced digital transformation in most of their activities, other industries are lagging behind. Specifically, among the industries that can be considered latecomer in engaging in digital transformation, we find the oil and natural gas industry (Kohli & Shawn, 2011), one characterized by large capital investments and thus in constant need to recover from such investments by cutting costs and, at the same time, be responsive to the changing market demands. Executives in oil and natural gas companies are facing unprecedented pressure to cut costs due to market turbulence and need advice on how to undertake digitization and execute a digital strategy.

Notwithstanding the quest for cost saving that companies in the oil and gas industry are pursuing, digitalization still constitutes a successful strategic turn for them to be undertaken, and the reason is twofold. First, digitization can be used more in general in the oil and gas industry to implement systems of predictive maintenance to monitor production assets and predict or prevent device failures, e.g. software and hardware for checking oil tanks (Nielsen *et al.,* 2017). Second, digitization can be leveraged for marketing purposes, in particular to support companies in the oil and gas industry operating in the retail business, helping them reshaping their business models, in the medium and long term, to face the rise of new non-traditional competitors (e.g. vehicle electrification companies) (Šafranić, Petljak, & Naletina, 2017) and to account for the shift in customer needs (Coelho *et al.,* 2017). Digital technologies can be effective to provide customers with innovative options like omnichannel experience and personalized offerings in order to differentiate a product that is per definition a commodity and to overcome the barriers of commodities to obtain consumers' loyalty, as they are by nature undifferentiated. The use of digital tools, apps, social media, advanced data instruments to analyse consumers' habits for fuel purchases, as well the use of these tools to develop and improve marketing communication and promotion, enables to align with other industries and to collect data on consumer behaviour, which allows to define a more effective offer and in turn benefit the sales and the economic performance. Therefore, the digital transformation, i.e. implementation of Cloud solutions, Big Data, Internet of Things, Robotic Process Automation, Artificial intelligence and Blockchain technologies, triggers the need for companies to develop new, distinctive capabilities and market solutions.

In the remainder of the chapter, we will attempt to answer the following research question: *how does digital transformation can be leveraged to improve the value proposition of fuel retailers?* In doing so, first, we will review the current state of the oil and gas industry and the current digital technologies; next, we will analyse how digital technologies can affect the oil and gas sector, in particular the fuel retail, and how such technologies can be leveraged to improve the four phases of the customer journey.

Last, final considerations and recommendations will be provided in order to address further challenges within the future generation of digital technologies.

THE OIL AND GAS INDUSTRY: AN OVERVIEW

As a mature, commoditized industry, the adoption of digital technologies in fuel retail companies is still at its very beginning. While the digitization of the infrastructures (e.g. plants and gas stations) is spreading among few pioneers (Taylor, 2020), the use of digital technologies for marketing purpose is still in the earliest days, lagging behind other industries which have been more proactive in leveraging the value of digital technologies in their marketing strategies (Willems *et al.,* 2017), such as the food and beverage industry, the fitness and nutrition industry, the movie and entertainment industry. For example, the movie and entertainment industry rely considerably on digital tools and devices to sponsor new productions, videogames, interactive experiences for consumers who, through virtual platforms, can engage with other consumers and with companies themselves (Deloitte, 2020).

In addition, it has to be noted that fuel retailers are capital intensive businesses, therefore high entry barriers hinder online retailers from entering in the market without strong investments in physical assets. In fact, competition from online retailers does not threaten the physical retailers (Lafontaine & Sivadasan, 2020). This means that physical retailers are an essential element of the industry and that digital disruption cannot revolutionize and displace the existing actors and assets by establishing data and information-based assets as a novel core resource. However, the 21st century is calling for another potential big change, led by the breakthrough industrial paradigm based on electric mobility (Deloitte, 2009), which can significantly impact the oil and gas retail business.

Companies in the oil and gas retail industry slowly proceed towards digitalization although research has pointed that digital technologies in marketing would mitigate the weakness of the commoditized industries and leverage customer satisfaction (Pasternack, 2008).

In general, the fuel retail sector shows a limited use of marketing strategies, and if any, they are limited to few rudimental marketing levers, such as pricing strategies (Rossi & Chintagunta, 2016), or customer segmentation to identify the best offer (Jung, Kwon & Yu, 2019). Their approach to customers is in line with other commodity sellers (e.g. coal, corn, potatoes) which struggle to differentiate their products in the eyes of their customers, and where a proper marketing strategy could play a crucial role in developing a unique, distinct offer, thus creating value for customers and allowing companies to gain competitive advantage. In fact, customers might be willing to pay a premium price if they perceive a differentiated, unique offer (Sharp & Dawes, 2001), with fuel retail companies reaping the benefits of such differentiated strategy (i.e. with positive results in terms of financial performance).

Extant literature has explored the use of marketing levers in the fuel retail sector. Findings reveal that the association of petrol stations with grocery stores and assistance and maintenance services improves the customer experience and generates additional revenues for the stations (Safranic, Petljak & Anletina, 2017). Notwithstanding the existing contributions on the topic, these studies have mostly overlooked the effect of digital transformation on the development of marketing strategies in the retail business of commodities. We believe that, for companies in this business, accounting for the potential of digital technologies to foster new, differentiated marketing strategies and offerings may represent a significant source of competitive advantage. On the other hand, failing to do so could stuck companies belonging to the oil and gas retail industry in a no-win costs war, eventually also threatening their long-term survival.

Where failing to embrace digitalization in marketing strategies could lead companies in the oil and gas retail industry to engage in fierce costs competition between each other, potentially with negative spillovers on the quality of services and products provided, for actors populating this industry there is more to consider than competitors. Companies must acknowledge the entire business ecosystem is shifting from a product perspective to a service perspective, as we are witnessing the phenomenon of servitization (Huikkola & Kohtamäki, 2018; Kohtamäki *et al.*, 2020). To stay in line with the shifts emerging in the business landscape, it is key also for companies in more traditional industries to provide consumers, alongside products, with engaging experiences and services. In order to do so, and transform sales centers into more experience centers, companies in the oil and gas retail industry can leverage the tools provided by the digital transformation (Kohtamäki et *al.,* 2020): for example an improved management of data about consumers' preferences can help companies create in their sales point an highly enjoyable experience for clients, who will positively remember the engagement they felt at the fuel station while fulfilling their need.

THE DIGITAL TECHNOLOGIES IN OIL AND GAS RETAIL

The technologies starring in the digital revolution can be collected into four main groups (Zaki, 2019): social media technologies, Internet of Things (IoT), human imitating technologies (AI, AR, VR), and Data Technologies. All of these technologies share the common feature of being based on mobility and ubiquitous connectivity features, which provide immediate interaction and access to a wide range of data and computing power (Lanzolla & Giudici, 2017). Below, we will provide a more detailed explanations of the different digital technologies highlighting also how they apply to the oil and gas industry and in particular how they can be leveraged to improve the customer proposition.

Social Media

The first application of digital technologies for marketing purposes is the use of social media as a mean to get in contact with consumers, in line with the past trend which consider social media as becoming part of people lives (Bronner & de Hoog, 2014). The digital experience involves both the use of digital devices such as smartphones or tablets (Solima, Della Peruta & Maggioni, 2016) in association with mobile applications developed ad hoc for oil & gas consumption (i.e. within the industry the first mobile app was developed for fuel delivery).

The wave of digitization of the industry has proceeded with the application of mobile devices for payments, which has constituted a significant change in the customer journey, involving physical and digital interactions and the use of mobile apps with personalized offerings and innovative mobile payment services.

Internet of Things

The Internet of Things (IoT) can be defined as a network of physical objects – devices, vehicles, buildings and other items embedded with electronics, software, sensors and network connectivity – that enables these objects to collect and exchange data (Atzori, Iera & Morabito, 2010). This paradigm can be framed within the so-called fourth revolution and Industry 4.0 era, which represents the second wave of digital revolution and has spurred a breakthrough transformation in the society (Teece, 2018; Helfat & Raubitschek, 2018). The IoT paradigm has brought about a significant transformation of business practices and economy and is urging companies worldwide to adapt their traditional business models to the newest technological developments.

In particular, the digital technologies for Oil & Gas companies are mainly oriented towards the development of hardware and software tools that measure, analyze and optimize process systems (Ershaghi & Omoregie, 2005). Machine Learning solutions are in general analytical systems for managing the Internet of Things (IoT) in upstream and midstream oil and gas operations (Anderson, 2017). While all of the aforementioned technologies can be used to better manage the asset lifecycle (operations optimization and predictive maintenance), it is also true that, by embracing digital transformation holistically, companies could unlock a huge value not only in terms of operations and oil explorations, but also in terms of new ways to deliver value to customers and new engagement models that provide for these customers personalized experiences and flexibility.

Another important emerging digital technology is the blockchain, best known in the cryptocurrency domain, which enables to record a list of operations, called *blocks*, that are linked using cryptography. Each block contains a cryptographic hash of the previous block, a timestamp, and transaction data (Li et *al*., 2020). This technology supports the transactions based on cryptocurrencies and can be used for a variety of purposes, payments among the others. In this respect, we could imagine the use of blockchain technologies for digital payment systems, replacing the use of the physical credit card, thus reducing the risk of card cloning (Efanov & Roschin, 2018). In fact, blockchain-based transactions are acknowledged to be extremely safe as every transaction must be validated by a network of peer users and the technology is designed as it keeps track of every transaction occurring within the network of users. According to the fuel retailer business, the Blockchain solution should have the Top-Authority role and be able to guarantee the highest transaction security, fraud protection, customer privacy management and avoidance duplication of information. In this way, from a single app, which interacts with the blockchain, it would be possible to manage payments quickly and safely.

All the solutions described so far are made possible by the implementation of an IoT technology at the point-of-sale that, with the support of machine learning and deep learning algorithms (which monitor and control the smooth running of the operations), ensures efficiency and business continuity. One example could be the creation of a dashboard that, through the correlation of data from sensors, devices, touch points and status of processing systems, outlines a representation of the quality of the customer experience offered to the user in the store.

Human Imitating Technologies

Human imitating technologies comprise all the emerging technologies based on artificial intelligence (AI), augmented reality (AR) and virtual reality (VR). The idea behind those technologies is to give to a computer or computer-controlled device the so-called cognitive computing ability, which is the capability to perform intelligent tasks such as learning or taking decisions after evaluating a situation (Gupta, Kar, Baabdullah & Al-Khowaiter, 2018), or simply giving cognitive computing.

Data Technologies

With the advent of the Internet of Things and the beginning of the Industry 4.0 revolution, a large amount of data is available real time (Ardito *et al.*, 2019). The term big data has been coined to identify such pieces of data which, because they are collected instant by instant, they are available by nature in a very large number. The main characteristics of the big data are synthetized with the 3Vs of big data, which are volume, variety and velocity (McAfee & Brynjolfsson, 2012). From one side, these characteristics enable to steadily acquire, structure and assess a great amount of data in terms of knowledge generation, decision making and forecasting (Cappa *et al.*, 2020). On the other hand, these characteristics make the process of turning data into knowledge as a very complex task due to storage, standardization, security and data quality issues.

Big data can be leveraged for marketing purposes, as collecting data about consumers' habits and behaviours enable to design personalized offers and to maximize the consumers' benefit (Carvajal *et al.*, 2017). In the oil and gas industry, big data could become more than the other technologies a valuable mean to increase the value perceived by a consumer, especially in such an industry characterized by an undifferentiated, commoditized offer. In terms of big data, the entire industry is overall pushing to develop a framework for the Digital Oil Field of the future in order to optimize the cost-effective development of oil and gas resources (Unneland & Hauser, 2005). The Digital Oil Field refers to the acquisition of high frequency data and its use to increase production efficiency, in terms of down-time, filed-wide efficiency and optimization of reservoir recovery and management.

NEW "DIGITAL - ORIENTED" BUSINESS MODELS

The Omnichannel Customer Strategy

The adoption of digital technologies could help fuel retails to adopt a more systematic approach to improve the customer experience not only by increasing the number of touchpoints, but through a holistic and strategic use of multiple channels to provide an integrated customer experience. This means that fuel retail companies could improve their omnichannel customer strategy, one able to grant a constant interaction with customers, that promptly respond to their needs and accommodate their requests. According to the World Economic Forum, an omnichannel retail strategy, in the decade 2016-2025, has the potential to create benefits worth about $20 billion for the entire economy and to unlock a value of $100 billion for the entire industry (World Economic Forum, 2017).

As mentioned, an online retail for fuel distribution is unlikely, and this is confirmed by the absence of input competition related to a possible e-commerce sale for gasoline stations (Lafontaine & Sivadasan, 2020). Furthermore, in the case of fuel retail, the physical stations are essential and represent the core of the business itself, as they offer unique advantages, i.e. the "touch and feel" experience. In fact, in the Oil & Gas industry, the threat of e-commerce is very low, as also a potential online retail would require the physical station (although we could not exclude a possible future change in the fuel supplying system). For fuel retailers, digital transformation is an opportunity to provide a more consistent and complementary "shopping" experience (e.g. cross-selling), implementing an omnichannel retail strategy through the possibility to switch between channels.

In this framework, the omnichannel strategy of a fuel retail should be designed to merge the independent in-station and digital operations, offering also exclusive advantages to improve customer satisfaction and loyalty. Digital technologies could be leveraged for example to improve the self-service refuelling, simplifying the purchasing process and reducing the risk of potential "out-of-order" of the vendor machines or "card is not readable". Also, the development of an integrated platform would enable to provide several value-added services beside the traditional purchase and fidelity program, such as tracking the fuel price and suggesting the best moment to refuelling. All in all, the improvement of the in-station experience represents a significant initiative to improve the customer experience and leverage on the privileged assets of a fuel retail.

The Importance of Digital Technologies to Customize the Offer

In order to benefit from the digital technologies, fuel retailers need to develop new skills and competencies (Van Laar *et al.,* 2019). For instance, they need to develop deep data analytic capabilities to collect and assess customer shopping habits and anticipate their preferences. In this framework, fuel retailers will also have to expand their functional expertise in such areas as digital product development, AI, blockchain, IoT and in new customer personalization platforms. To achieve a proper upskilling of the personnel in the stations, companies will need to develop ad hoc upgrading programs (Van Laar *et al.,* 2017), and to design strategies that focus on attracting and retaining new talents, including data scientists, user experience designers and software developers. In fact, being able to build a personalized offer requires new capabilities and expertise and urges companies to articulate business models that are radically different from the traditional ones. Indeed, fuel retailers may need to significantly revise the key resources and activities around which they build their value creation strategies, also forging new partnerships and establishing interactive relationships with their customers' segments.

A personalized offering system can be considered a platform to leverage advanced analytics and client data, which can be used to design and industrialize a system that offers customer incentives based on historical data. Furthermore, the Oil and Gas industry can learn from other industries and implement digital technologies to gain a better understanding of customers' preferences and buying patterns. Likewise, it could optimize pricing structures, and manage logistics and procurement accordingly. Such capabilities are expected to acquire importance in the future, enabling companies to boost their share of customer spending. According to the World Economic Forum, personalized offers, based on customers purchase history, are expected to generate $95 billion of value to migrate to omnichannel fuel retailers from other stores. Moreover, it is estimated that these specialized offers will increase same-station sales by 5% and generate an additional $6 billion for fuel retailers (World Economic Forum, 2017).

In this direction, a significant role is played by mobile apps. The development of mobile apps could allow the retailer to gain better insights into customers habits and desires, resulting in improved sales and more loyal customers. Users could choose to receive discount offers based on their mobile purchase history, which could be available on their phones while they are still on-site. Also, leveraging mobile apps may increase in-station sales to formerly fuel-only customers, who can save money on things they are likely to buy anyway.

SOLUTIONS AND RECCOMENDATIONS TO IMPROVE THE CUSTOMER EXPERIENCE IN THE FORUR PHASE OF COSTUMERS' JOURNEY

The fuel station represents the first and the only direct contact between fuel retailers and their customer base (Robinson, 2014). This means that the fuel station plays a pivotal role in the interactions between the company and its customers and in the following steps of value creation, i.e. delivery and capture. In his work, Robinson makes a comparison between the Starbucks model and the retail fuel stations. On one side, Starbuck encourages customers to stay and enjoy its products on site, thus attaching value to the experience in its entirety, rather than merely on the products sold. On the other side, gasoline stations do not usually create the conditions for customers to stay longer and enjoy the location and the experience attached to it. This means that gasoline stations do no provide customers any incentive to lengthen their stay, reducing the possibility that customers increase their spending (i.e. the longer customers stay on site, and enjoy their experience, the higher the probability they will engage into additional purchases). The Starbucks example should be a source of inspiration to transform the refuelling operation into an experience-based service. For this reason, the digital transformation and the related tools could dramatically increase the engagement of the customers, the time spent in the stations and even beyond the stations. This aspect represents one of the focal point of the customer journey based on different stages.

Todays' companies are confronted with accelerating media and channel fragmentation and omnichannel management has become the new norm. Marketing has grown more complicated over the past decade, the number of available media has grown, and customers are increasingly becoming more aware of their role (Noble, 2010). In this new era, the decision-making process is a circular journey with four phases: initial consideration; active evaluation or researching potential purchases; completing the purchase, when consumers buy products and services; post-purchase, when consumers experience the purchased items (Court *et al.,* 2009).

The First Phase: Initial Consideration

Applying the above-mentioned decision-making process to the fuel retail industry, for the first phase of the customer journey companies need to work on is improving products and services awareness, engaging customers and persuading them to consider the fuel retail brand (Lemon & Verhoef, 2016). At this level, the development of an omnichannel strategy would help to increase the number of touchpoints, trying to engage customers in the stations and eventually also in the post-purchase, once they leave the station. In this initial phase, partnerships with external actors to discover real-time geolocation of customers through wireless and interactive technologies, known as proximity marketing (Bilolo *et al.*, 2015), can strongly enhance customer engagement. New interactive forms of digital advertising together with the more traditional media such as television, radio and print media, would significantly help companies to engage customers, who are called upon to actively interact with the proposed messages.

The Second Phase: Active Evaluation

In the second phase, during which customer "actively evaluate" the alternatives proposed by the company and starts adding or removing from the basket of his/her mind the products and services which at best satisfy their needs, companies can leverage on digital platforms and mobile apps. At this stage, the company needs to foster its customers to download the mobile app, borrowing the established practices from more digitally-mature service industries, such as the airline industry and the e-commerce retails. In this way, fuel retailers can collect data about their consumers' habits and can leverage the app to stimulate additional purchases in the station or offering discounts to encourage customers to choose that gas station over a plethora of options. In this way companies can differentiate the offer of a traditionally commoditized products.

The Third Phase: Complete the Purchase

The third phase represents the moment of the purchase, during which customers refuel and shop. The traditional five minutes stop at the station is the moment when ultimately customers select the brand. This represents a crucial time interval during which the company needs to leverage the digital solutions and exploit both the physical and digital tools to increase the time spent at the station and introduce cross-selling options. In fact, by means of the data platform and mobile app, it would be possible to bundle food & beverage in the station or leveraging partnerships with other companies to sell, for example, advertising spaces. Also, an augmented reality app could send discount codes to customers in order to stimulate further purchases in the station, to extend the time spent there.

Digital tools, in this phase, could also introduce new innovative mobile payment features, limiting the use of credit cards. Such enhancement would simplify the payments by using a digital wallet, improving customer experience as the user can fuel without even leaving the car. In this framework, partnerships with fintech companies are key to accompany fuel retailers in the transition to become cashless, smoothing for customers the purchase of products and services and ultimately enhancing customers experience. Digital payments will also bring in more operational efficiency thereby reducing queues at the pumps. This may result in significant positive effects on customer retention, which constitutes a major issue for fuel retailers (indeed many customers would avoid coming to fuel stations with long queues). Also, a cashless business model would help fuel stations to ensure a smooth and fast service particularly during rush hours, when the service staff comes to be strongly under pressure, as it needs to serve as many customers as possible and make sure that no customer leaves the station before refuelling. Finally, the digital solution could also provide digital tools for companies which manage a fleet of vehicles. Those tools, for example mobile apps or platforms, could provide integrated solutions to monitor and track the fuel expenses, the kilometres and the need of car maintenance.

The Fourth Phase: Post-Purchase

The fourth phase is represented by the loyalty programs. Loyalty programs have always been a key tool for fuel retail companies to efficiently manage enlarged customer demand as well as maintaining customer retention whenever there is a tough competition among different companies (Mascarenhas, Kesavan & Bernacchi, 2006). Many fuel retailers have implemented strong loyalty and rewards program and have been able to leverage their benefits. In this context, digital tools could improve the variety of loyalty benefits by targeting the specific needs and desires of customers, along with added benefits of rewarding mechanisms (e.g. cashbacks for purchasing tickets, gifts). Rewards could be offered to customers as per their transactions over the mobile app or providing multiple amenities for customer convenience. In this respect, big data could play a pivotal role. Big data can be translated into important potential assets to provide the best experience for customers and enable companies to leverage on the increased customer loyalty, in turn triggering positive effects on their performance. The heterogeneous data collected in a single environment and in real time (personal data, images, and texts) point to the concept of data lake: a wide pool of filed data that may be used by companies to develop articulated analysis of customers' preferences and purchase habits, and may help them to design different customers' experience, (i.e. augmented reality experiences, based on the idea of gamification, such in Miloslavskaya and Tolstoy, 2016). This means that fuel retailers could exploit all the potential of data lakes to identify user preferences and purchase habits and provide them with personalized experiences. An interesting application could be for example the use of real time data to get information about the user route habits, notifying and reporting the nearest fuel station, inviting the customer to stop and engaging it by offering loyalty points, prizes and offers by playing through the app.

The circular experience does not stop at the loyalty program, as could be imagined for a customer journey shaped as a funnel. Indeed, the experience provided to customers can be conceived as cyclical. For example, with the mobile app, customers can be geo-localized to discover, or directly search, the nearest fuel station by booking a pump. In order to confirm the use of the pump the customer could scan a QR-code or entry an alphanumeric code and refuel. The experience could be fully automated partnering with mobility solution providers and leading technology companies in order to offer a connected experience.

At this point, the customer journey restarts from the beginning. It is important to highlight the circularity of such journey together with its strong customer focus. At the centre of the described circle is placed the customer, whose perspective, thanks to the digital solutions and a constantly updated data management, can become unique and personalized.

THE IMPORTANCE OF DIGITAL TECHNOLOGIES IN RESPONSE THE ELECTRIFICATION TREND

The rise of the digital era and the emerging of new technologies is simplifying this process, enabling a cost-effective information gathering customers activities, which allow companies to transform their business models targeting a personalized offer for each single customer. This transformation plays a very important role in the sector of energy commodities, with particular focus on fuel retailer, whose market is progressively shrinking and can trigger significant negative effects for those companies that will fail to make significant changes to their business models. In markets where the changes are most dramatic, such as the fuel retail industry, to stay competitive and successful in the long-term, companies need to embrace a transformation in their ways of doing business, exploiting the leverage provided by the digital transformation and adopting a complete digitization of the service station. This is particularly true in the face of the rise of electric vehicles, which will increasingly populate the future landscape of the energy industry. Indeed, while the sustainability imperative calls for the adoption of cleaner, less pollutant alternatives to traditional energy commodities, companies operating in the oil and gas industry will keep play an important role in the future of the global energy mix (Forbes, 2020). To be able to embrace this role and being competitive vis à vis other players while responding to the sustainability needs, oil and gas retailers may surely exploit digital technologies (Forbes, 2020). For example, by implementing systems of data collection and analysis, these companies may streamline their operations while considerably reducing waste and cutting their carbon footprint; also, digital innovative technologies such as big data and cloud computing can help oil and gas retailers to participate in smooth and efficient recycling processes, again lowering their ecological impact.

In this light, embracing digitalization is yet a pivot for oil and gas retailers to offer more customized, engaging experiences for their clients and it is thus a key element to develop successful marketing strategies. However, digitalization can also be a tool for these companies to become active players in the needed transition towards sustainability.

CONCLUSION AND RECOMMENDATIONS

Digital technologies have already changed the traditional relationship between channel members and customers also in the oil and gas retail industry. However, the oil and gas retail companies are still striving to develop a proper digital transformation strategy, which can help the understanding of customer engagement at every point as well as to define a customer-centred business.

In order to embrace digital transformation, is it key to disrupt the energy value chain not only at the upstream, midstream and downstream points but also at the retail level. According to the World Economic Forum (2017), there is a shift in the global demand patterns that can be translated in terms of fall of oil demand in the OECD countries, rise of electric vehicles and increase in adoption of renewables due to the development of storage capabilities. Therefore, it is extremely important for the fuel retail companies to develop and improve a digital strategy able to face the emerging environmental challenges and develop an ad hoc digital and customer-centred approach. Customers are considered the actors able to sense external changes and opportunities and to act as filters in matching the external offer with the internal technological needs. They represent the "antenna" (Caluri *et al.*, 2019) for several companies called to address the current digital transformation. For those reasons, companies seeking opportunities in an era of constant customer connectivity need to focus on two complementary activities: reshaping customer value propositions and transforming their operations using digital technologies for greater customer interaction and collaboration (Berman, 2012).

Digital transformation brings business and technology together to deliver a connected commerce experience that provides a smooth and personalized customer offering. By enabling connections and partnerships, companies are called upon to effectively bridge the digital technologies and the brick-and-mortar commerce, powering a seamless consumer experience while allowing businesses to maximize their footprint in the digital world. This is particularly relevant in the energy industry, in which products are mostly represented by commodities, whose related markets are rapidly changing. Very tough scenarios are foreseen in the future of the fuel retail market. These scenarios range from internal combustion engine vehicles remaining dominant to a landscape where electric vehicles lead the market. In the worst-case scenario, up to 80% of the fuel retailers, in certain countries, could be unprofitable in about 15 years. And even in the most positive forecasts, around 30% of service stations could be in severe distress if fuel retailers do not engage in substantial modifications of their business (Boston Consulting Group, 2020).

Therefore, it is extremely important for the Oil and Gas retail companies to develop and leverage a digital strategy based on customer proposition with particular emphasis on omnichannel customer strategy, personalized offerings and entrance in a new digital business area. The main enablers of this process, such as social media technologies, Internet of Things, human imitating technologies (AI, AR, VR), and Data Technologies, can be used to pursue different strategies and achieve specific results and have to be focused on customer centricity.

It can be concluded that the digital transformation for mature and commoditized industries, such as Oil & Gas companies, is not an option anymore, and this is particularly true in the light of the urge for actors within this industry to develop more sustainable strategies. Also, digital transformation can be a tool to leverage onto to respond to the increasingly sophisticated customer demands and competitive pressures. We have shown that the disruption of the energy value chain has to be managed not only at the upstream, midstream and downstream levels but also at the retail level, giving greater importance to customer experience and customers preferences, especially in countries where fuel retail can face a strong shrinkage of the market.

REFERENCES

Anderson, R. N. (2017). Petroleum Analytics Learning Machine for optimizing the Internet of Things of today's digital oil field-to-refinery petroleum system. In *2017 IEEE International Conference on Big Data (Big Data)* (pp. 4542-4545). IEEE. 10.1109/BigData.2017.8258496

Ardito, L., Scuotto, V., Del Giudice, M., & Petruzzelli, A. M. (2019). A bibliometric analysis of research on Big Data analytics for business and management. *Management Decision*, *57*(8), 1993–2009. doi:10.1108/MD-07-2018-0754

Atzori, L., Iera, A., & Morabito, G. (2010). The internet of things: A survey. *Computer Networks*, *54*(15), 2787–2805. doi:10.1016/j.comnet.2010.05.010

Berman, S. J. (2012). Digital transformation: Opportunities to create new business models. *Strategy and Leadership*, *40*(2), 16–24. doi:10.1108/10878571211209314

Bilolo, A., Boeck, H., Durif, F., & Levesque, N. (2015). *The impact of proximity marketing on consumer reactions and firm performance: A conceptual and integrative model*. Academic Press.

Boston Consulting Group. (2019). *Is there a future for fuel stations? Boston Consulting Group*.

Boston Consulting Group (2020). *Challenging future for fuel retailers*. Academic Press.

Bronner, F., & de Hoog, R. (2014). Social media and consumer choice. *International Journal of Market Research*, *56*(1), 51–71. doi:10.2501/IJMR-2013-053

Caluri, L., Jianu, M., Cerioli, P., & Silvestri, G. B. (2019, November). Open Innovation as Enabling Paradigm to Empower Digital Transformation in Oil & Gas Organizations. In *Abu Dhabi International Petroleum Exhibition & Conference*. Society of Petroleum Engineers.

Cappa, F., Oriani, R., Peruffo, E., & McCarthy, I. (2021). Big Data for Creating and Capturing Value in the Digitalized Environment: Unpacking the Effects of Volume, Variety, and Veracity on Firm Performance. *Journal of Product Innovation Management*, *38*(1), 49–67. doi:10.1111/jpim.12545

Carvajal, G., Maucec, M., & Cullick, S. (2017). *Intelligent digital oil and gas fields: concepts, collaboration, and right-time decisions*. Gulf Professional Publishing.

Coelho, F., Pereira, M. C., Cruz, L., Simões, P., & Barata, E. (2017). Affect and the adoption of pro-environmental behaviour: A structural model. *Journal of Environmental Psychology*, *54*, 127–138. doi:10.1016/j.jenvp.2017.10.008

Court, D., Elzinga, D., Mulder, S., & Vetvik, O. J. (2009). The consumer decision journey. *The McKinsey Quarterly*, *3*(3), 96–107.

Deloitte. (2009). *A New Era Accelerating Toward 2020 – An Automotive Industry Transformed*. Deloitte.

Efanov, D., & Roschin, P. (2018). The all-pervasiveness of the blockchain technology. *Procedia Computer Science*, *123*, 116–121. doi:10.1016/j.procs.2018.01.019

Ershaghi, I., & Omoregie, Z. S. (2005, January). Continuing-education needs for the digital oil fields of the future. In *SPE Annual Technical Conference and Exhibition*. Society of Petroleum Engineers. 10.2118/97288-MS

Gupta, S., Kar, A. K., Baabdullah, A., & Al-Khowaiter, W. A. (2018). Big data with cognitive computing: A review for the future. *International Journal of Information Management*, *42*, 78–89. doi:10.1016/j.ijinfomgt.2018.06.005

Helfat, C. E., & Raubitschek, R. S. (2018). Dynamic and integrative capabilities for profiting from innovation in digital platform-based ecosystems. *Research Policy*, *47*(8), 1391–1399. doi:10.1016/j.respol.2018.01.019

Huikkola, T., & Kohtamäki, M. (2018). Business models in servitization. In *Practices and Tools for Servitization* (pp. 61–81). Palgrave Macmillan. doi:10.1007/978-3-319-76517-4_4

Jung, H., Kwon, K. M., & Yu, G. J. (2019). Fuels sales through retail chains and their store traffics and revenue. *Asia Pacific Journal of Marketing and Logistics*, *31*(1), 2–13. doi:10.1108/APJML-04-2017-0058

Kohli, R., & Johnson, S. (2011). Digital Transformation in Latecomer Industries: CIO and CEO Leadership Lessons from Encana Oil & Gas (USA) Inc. *MIS Quarterly Executive*, *10*(4).

Kohtamäki, M., Parida, V., Patel, P. C., & Gebauer, H. (2020). The relationship between digitalization and servitization: The role of servitization in capturing the financial potential of digitalization. *Technological Forecasting and Social Change*, *151*, 119804. doi:10.1016/j.techfore.2019.119804

Lafontaine, F., & Sivadasan, J. (2020). The Recent Evolution of Physical Retail Markets: Online Retailing, Big Box Stores, and the Rise of Restaurants. In *The Role of Innovation and Entrepreneurship in Economic Growth*. University of Chicago Press.

Lanzolla, G., & Giudici, A. (2017). Pioneering strategies in the digital world. Insights from the Axel Springer case. *Business History*, *59*(5), 744–777. doi:10.1080/00076791.2016.1269752

Lemon, K. N., & Verhoef, P. C. (2016). Understanding customer experience throughout the customer journey. *Journal of Marketing*, *80*(6), 69–96. doi:10.1509/jm.15.0420

Li, X., Jiang, P., Chen, T., Luo, X., & Wen, Q. (2020). A survey on the security of blockchain systems. *Future Generation Computer Systems*, *107*, 841–853. doi:10.1016/j.future.2017.08.020

Mascarenhas, O. A., Kesavan, R., & Bernacchi, M. (2006). Lasting customer loyalty: A total customer experience approach. *Journal of Consumer Marketing*, *23*(7), 397–405. doi:10.1108/07363760610712939

McAfee, A., & Brynjolfsson, E. (2012). Big Data: The management revolution. *Harvard Business Review*, *90*(10), 60–68. PMID:23074865

Miloslavskaya, N., & Tolstoy, A. (2016). Big data, fast data and data lake concepts. *Procedia Computer Science*, *88*(300-305), 63. doi:10.1016/j.procs.2016.07.439

Nielsen, C., Lund, M., & Thomsen, P. (2017). From digital disruption to business model scalability. *ISPIM Innovations Conferencen i Wien 2017. ISPIM Conference.*

Noble, S. (2010). *It's time to bury the marketing funnel.* Steven Noble's Blog.

Pasternack, B. A. (2008). Optimal pricing and return policies for perishable commodities. *Marketing Science*, *27*(1), 133–140. doi:10.1287/mksc.1070.0336

Robinson, M. L. (2014). Building Brand Loyalty: Improving the Retail Fueling Experience. In Marketing Big Oil: Brand Lessons from the World's Largest Companies (pp. 130-135). Palgrave Macmillan.

Rossi, F., & Chintagunta, P. K. (2016). Price transparency and retail prices: Evidence from fuel price signs in the Italian highway system. *JMR, Journal of Marketing Research*, *53*(3), 407–423. doi:10.1509/jmr.14.0411

Šafranić, P., Petljak, K., & Naletina, D. (2017, January). The growing importance of petrol stations as channels for expanding the retail services. Trade Perspectives 2017 Specialization and Customer Centered Retailing.

Sen, A. (1999). *Commodities and capabilities.* Oxford University Press.

Sharp, B., & Dawes, J. (2001). What is differentiation and how does it work? *Journal of Marketing Management*, *17*(7-8), 739–759. doi:10.1362/026725701323366809

Solima, L., Della Peruta, M. R., Maggioni, V., Al-Mashari, M., & Del Giudice, M. (2016). Managing adaptive orientation systems for museum visitors from an IoT perspective. *Business Process Management Journal*, *22*(2), 10. doi:10.1108/BPMJ-08-2015-0115

Stolterman, E., & Fors, A. C. (2004). Information Technology and the Good Life BT Information Systems Research: Relevant Theory and Informed Practice. Springer US.

Taylor, M. (2020). *Energy subsidies: Evolution in the global energy transformation to 2050.* International Renewable Energy Agency.

Teece, D. (2018). Profiting from innovation in the digital economy: Enabling technologies, standards, and licensing models in the wireless world. *Research Policy*, *47*(8), 10. doi:10.1016/j.respol.2017.01.015

Unneland, T., & Hauser, M. K. (2005). Real-time asset management: from vision to engagement-an operator's experience. In *SPE Annual Technical Conference and Exhibition*. Society of Petroleum Engineers. 10.2118/96390-MS

Van Laar, E., Van Deursen, A. J., Van Dijk, J. A., & De Haan, J. (2017). The relation between 21st-century skills and digital skills: A systematic literature review. *Computers in Human Behavior*, *72*, 577–588. doi:10.1016/j.chb.2017.03.010

Westerman, G., Bonnet, D., & McAfee, A. (2018). *The Nine Elements of Digital Transformation/MIT-Sloan Management Review*. Massachusetts Institute of Technology.

Willems, K., Smolders, A., Brengman, M., Luyten, K., & Schöning, J. (2017). The path-to-purchase is paved with digital opportunities: An inventory of shopper-oriented retail technologies. *Technological Forecasting and Social Change*, *124*, 228–242. doi:10.1016/j.techfore.2016.10.066

World Economic Forum. (2017). Digital Transformation Initiative Oil and Gas Industry. Author.

Zaki, M. (2019). Digital transformation: Harnessing digital technologies for the next generation of services. *Journal of Services Marketing*, *33*(4), 429–435. Advance online publication. doi:10.1108/JSM-01-2019-0034

Chapter 7
Digital Marketing and Digital Retail Strategies in the Luxury Sector:
Critical Factors and Opportunities

Giuseppe Colella
University of Bari, Italy

Cesare Amatulli
University of Bari, Italy

ABSTRACT

Contemporary marketing strategies have shifted from unidirectional to bidirectional logic, according to which the rise of digitization and of social networks are changing the concept of marketing itself. The most impactful digital technologies have been digital platforms and brand communities, which have exposed companies and consumers alike to new challenges, such as online purchasing experiences. As a result, luxury retailers, who have traditionally resisted rapid adoption of market trends, have begun embracing digitization as part of their marketing strategies. This chapter highlights how understanding this topic is crucial amid changing global economics that are reshaping how luxury consumers interact with retailers. Through a qualitative approach based on semi-structured one-to-one interviews with experts from a leading digital marketing company, this chapter intends to illustrate the critical factors (and related opportunities) that luxury brands will look to exploit in the near future. The results highlight the pervading separation between digital technology and luxury brands.

INTRODUCTION AND RESEARCH CONTEXT

Internet expansion, digitization, and the development of social networks have disrupted the modern economy, prompting new digital business models focused on meeting the constantly evolving needs and expectations of new consumers (Teece, 2010; Wirtz, 2019). The number of people using the Internet

DOI: 10.4018/978-1-7998-7192-7.ch007

increased by 7% between 2019 and 2020, with 5.19 billion unique mobile users and 3.80 billion people using social media on mobile devices (We Are Social, 2020). Readily available access to the web of tablets and smartphones (Bruggeman et al., 2019) has brought people into greater contact with digital media (Rathnayaka, 2018). Crucially, these changes are altering the very concept of marketing itself: marketing paradigms have shifted from Marketing 2.0, oriented exclusively to consumers and based on unidirectional logic, to Marketing 4.0, of which the development of digital technologies is the key driver (Kotler et al., 2010, 2017), to the extent that a re-conception of the figure of the consumer is required. Moreover, these technologies have exposed all companies to new challenges, such as how to adopt technological innovations to better understand and address consumers' needs with respect to brand involvement, interactivity (Yu et al., 2017), and purchasing experiences in a digital context (Mosca & Chiaudano, 2020).

Digital technologies, innovations, and social media marketing activities have proliferated across the full spectrum of retail sectors (Alalwan et al., 2017; Jacobson et al., 2020)—even within the luxury sector, which has traditionally eschewed such advances (Godey et al., 2016; Kim & Ko, 2012). Such shifts have transformed the means of communicating and selling luxury brands, often transposing these activities into completely virtual contexts. This rapid growth has broad implications for companies, especially those in the luxury sector that have begun embracing digitization further redefined by technological advances in communications (Kapferer, 2015; Kim & Ko, 2012; Liu et al., 2019). However, according to Liu et al. (2019), from the perspective of accessibility and democratization, the use of digital technologies for retailing and marketing activities could conflict with the air of exclusivity that luxury brands work so hard to cultivate. In particular, luxury companies are concerned that they will be unable to guarantee key brand attributes such as quality, exclusivity, and tradition, which are considered crucial to their retail and digital marketing mix (Mosca & Giacosa, 2016; Mosca & Chiaudano, 2020). Moreover, luxury marketers have long been committed to designing a coherent luxury retail strategy that is capable of conferring uniqueness, a reputable image, and the perception of quality (Desmichel & Kocher, 2020; Kapferer & Bastien, 2012). Luxury brands must therefore strengthen their relationships with digital retail channels to offer new shopping experiences and secure their market-dominant positioning (Desmichel & Kocher, 2020; Tarnaud, 2019).

Several studies have addressed the challenges of digital transformation in the luxury sector, mainly with regard to communications (Arrigo, 2018; Colella et al., 2019; Godey et al., 2016; Kim & Ko, 2012; Kapferer & Bastien, 2012; Okonkwo, 2009). However, few studies have investigated the role of digital technologies in the luxury sector's retail strategies (Jain, 2016; Mosca & Chiaudano, 2020; Passavanti et al., 2020). Given the relative scarcity of insight, this chapter will focus on further characterizing digital transformation in the luxury retail sector. To this end, the authors develop a theoretical framework that captures the reasons behind luxury companies' decisions to delay implementing digital retail strategies. In turn, this study addresses a gap in the existing literature around the critical factors and opportunities that luxury companies must grasp when translating their retail strategies into a digital context Therefore, it aim to explain how the digital marketing mix of luxury brands can work to encourage more luxury companies to adopt digital technologies. The research in this chapter uses a qualitative-exploratory approach, based on semi-structured one-to-one interviews with experts from a leading digital marketing company. It focuses on three contributions. First, it aims to synthesize the existing literature on digital marketing in retail, particularly for luxury brands. In this way, it delineates the existing progress and gaps in the literature regarding luxury brands' implementation of digital retailing strategies, while highlighting the importance of adopting digital technologies in the luxury context. Second, it provides a comprehensive theoretical framework to help both managers and researchers understand the actions and limitations of developing digital luxury retail strategies. Finally, the authors also consider the managerial implications of such strategies and offer suggestions for future research.

BACKGROUND

Digital Marketing

In the last 20 years, the expansion of the Internet and the rapid growth of online platforms have disrupted modern retail economies, as well as the normality of human interactions (Tiago & Veríssimo, 2014). More specifically, the 'Platform Economy' has emerged as an organizational model in which several activities (social, political, and economic) become intertwined through a connection-based relationship between the market and the individual (Kenney & Zysman, 2015). New giants of the digital market have risen to the fore in the form of companies like Google, Facebook, and Amazon (Kannan & Li, 2017; Vimali & Khan, 2018), whose digital proliferation has broken down entry barriers to international markets (Javalgi et al., 2012; Katsikeas et al., 2019). Driven by digitization, these extraordinary systemic and communicative changes have given birth to new business models as brands seek to more effectively engage with consumers. Adapting to this reality is an epoch-making challenge for companies in all sectors (Hänninen et al., 2018; Ritz et al., 2019).

The significant growth of digital technologies has increased consumers' use of digital media (Smith, 2011). Companies looking to remain competitive are compelled to leverage digital marketing strategies to reach new target markets (Hänninen et al., 2018; Katsikeas et al., 2019; Smith, 2011). In this context, digital marketing can be defined as "the practice of promoting products and services using digital distribution channels via computers, cell phones, smartphones or other digital devices" (Smith, 2012, p. 86), i.e., devices that directly connect online consumers with companies through interaction processes (Kotler et al., 2009; Rathnayaka, 2018). Tools such as E-Commerce, Artificial Intelligence and the Internet of Things (IoT) thus all belong to the broader concept of digital marketing (Herhausen et al., 2020). Likewise, according to Kamal et al. (2013), social media platforms like Instagram, Facebook, and Twitter—whose activities and processes are driven by digital technology (Herhausen et al., 2020)—offer consumers the opportunity to search, create, and disseminate information and perceptions about brands.

The expansion of digital platforms has changed traditional communication models, giving companies greater opportunities to directly 'listen' to consumers (Gurău, 2008; Key & Czaplewski, 2017). According to Alalwan et al. (2017), the development of social media platforms has led to multi-dimensional communication, which allows multiple consumers to interact with and co-create brand-centered content. Consumers' all-pervasive approach to sampling new technologies (i.e., across multiple communication channels and social media applications) has introduced new levels of interactivity in the relationship between brands and consumers (Royle & Laing, 2014; Vernuccio & Ceccotti, 2015). With profound socio-economic consequences, digital platforms have surpassed the utopian predictions of the first Internet era (Haberly et al., 2019), modifying the way in which users socialize (Kenney & Zysman, 2016) and generating a strong pull away from traditional business models (Cramer & Krueger, 2016). In a modern business environment characterized by fierce competition and highly sensitive customers, digital marketing has become business-critical to brand survival and success (Melović et al., 2020).

Digital Retailing

The emergence of the Internet, digitalization and, digital technologies have changed society dramatically. The digital revolution has had significant impacts on the retail sector (Hagberg et al., 2017). Digital disruptors like the Alibaba and Amazon retail platforms are now able to reach and leverage a large number of buyers and retailers, while still extracting profit from every transaction (Reinartz et al., 2019). In response, the wider retail sector has endeavored in recent years to adapt its distribution logic. Indeed, the emphasis on physical stores has given way to multi-channel sales (physical and online) (Neslin et al., 2006) and an omnichannel logic (Rigby, 2011; Verhoef et al., 2015) that encourages overlap between online and offline retail models. Importantly, in digital retail, the emergence of new network technologies makes it necessary to periodically review the entire shopping process. In this context, the retailer's and the consumer's relationship with the purchase-decision -making process and digital technologies are changing. In this perspective, Pantano and Timmermans (2014), identified six main elements that define smart retailing:

- Ability to react quickly on the organizational side;
- Changes in Knowledge Management;
- Contact with the smart partners;
- Changes in the work of the seller on the sales side of the company;
- Access to services;
- Changes in consumption.

Recent research has looked at the use of digital marketing techniques and tools in the distribution of products and retail services (Huuhka et al., 2014; Jain, 2016; Mosca & Chiaudano, 2020; Verhoef et al., 2015; Zhu, 2019). Hagberg et al. (2016) have noted that this research has primarily focused on e-commerce. According to Verhoef et al. (2015), the evolution of digital channels has been developed separately and limited integration within companies. More broadly, the purchasing of products and services is now characterized by a high level of brand-consumer interconnectivity and interaction (Rohm et al., 2013). However, while such interactions can facilitate consumer decision-making and boost sales, the digital environment also makes it easier for consumers to transition between retailers. For instance, chatbots in retail sector "allow to pose shopping-related questions and receive answers in natural language without waiting for a salesperson or using other automated communication forms" (Rese et al., 2020, p.1), Consequently, companies must strategically strive to improve customer engagement if they are to avoid losing key prospects (Rathnayaka, 2018).

In this way, digital marketing activities are transcending brand communication and actively expanding the retail sector itself. Significantly, the digital retail market maintains an annual growth rate of 8.11%, with a forecasted turnover of $4.99 billion for 2024 (Absolute Reports, 2020). Clearly, then, there is great value for companies in translating marketing techniques into the digital language of socio-commercial activity (Hughes et al., 2016). Moreover, the digital revolution effectively requires companies to integrate Industry 4.0 technologies (e.g., Big Data analysis and IoT devices) as a means of improving consumers' online purchasing experiences and of serving as the customer's primary information and transaction points (Reinartz et al., 2019).

Digital Marketing and Digital Retail Strategies in the Luxury Sector

The modern-day luxury sector has been redefined by technological advances in communications, the shift to digitalization (Kapferer, 2015), and the development of online retailing and social media marketing (Liu et al., 2019). According to Kim and Ko (2012), luxury brands can attract friendly attention by interacting with consumers through digital platforms. In this context, marketing research has emphasized the relationship between consumers and brands (Hudson et al., 2016), and specifically their interactions and involvement in a digital context (Rohm et al., 2013). Through this digital interaction, brands aim to establish and maintain a positive consumer-brand relationship (Hudson et al., 2016).

The digitization of marketing activities is widely recognized as key to developing more efficient business models in the face of wider societal change (Cramer & Krueger, 2016). However, whereas digitization, social networking, and the Internet of Things constitute the pillars of digital marketing activities across many retail sectors, in the luxury sector, academics and marketing managers alike have not yet landed on a clear understanding of how digital communication affects consumer perceptions of luxury brands (Schivinski & Dabrowski, 2016). Heine and Berghaus (2014) have proposed an overview of possible objectives—economic, strategic, and psychological—of digital luxury marketing. In turn, psychological objectives have to consider cognitive, affective, and conative aspects (Figure 1). Finally, according to Kim and Ko (2010), digital marketing campaign objectives may include encouraging content sharing. For instance, according to Colella et al. (2019) social media offers to consumers the possibility of co-creating content with companies and sharing content by both parties. In short, digital technologies have transformed the means of communicating and selling luxury brands, often transposing these activities into completely virtual contexts.

Several studies have addressed the challenges of digital marketing for luxury brands, in particular with regard to communication activities (Arrigo, 2018; Colella et al., 2019; Godey et al., 2016; Kim & Ko, 2012; Kapferer & Bastien, 2012; Okonkwo, 2009). However, only a limited number of studies have investigated the role of digital technologies in luxury brands' retailing activities (Jain, 2016; Mosca & Chiaudano, 2020; Passavanti et al., 2020). In sum, it would appear that luxury retailers are now considering digitization an unstoppable force and are feeling increasingly compelled to adapt to the various innovative systems on offer (Passavanti et al., 2020), and in particular to integrating different digital channels into the distribution and sale of their products (Mosca & Chiaudano, 2020). Luxury brands have typically been slow to implement these technologies due to skepticism about executing retail activities in a digital context and the potential for perceived loss of quality, exclusivity, and tradition (Mosca & Giacosa 2016; Mosca & Chiaudano, 2020). Despite these initial concerns, according to Okonkwo (2010), luxury brands must exploit digital technologies and channels to preserve retail sales and market share.

According to Kepferer (2000), digital technologies can represent both an opportunity (e.g., reaching consumers in different geographical locations) and a critical factor (e.g., guaranteeing the exclusivity that is closely tied to the luxury sector). As an open-access source, the Internet presents a conflict to luxury brands: if luxury is accessible to all, some fear that it would no longer serve an exclusive niche (Liu et al., 2013) and would thus lose their dominant traits of uniqueness and quality (Desmichel & Kocher, 2020; Kapferer & Bastien, 2012). In this vein, luxury marketers have the aim of designing a coherent digital retail strategy that is capable of conferring uniqueness, a good image, and the perception of quality (Kapferer & Bastien, 2012). Therefore, luxury brands need to strengthen their relationships with digital retail channels to offer new shopping experiences and maintain a dominant position in the market (Desmichel & Kocher, 2020; Tarnaud, 2019).

Figure 1. Overview objectives of digital luxury marketing
Source: Heine & Berghaus (2014)

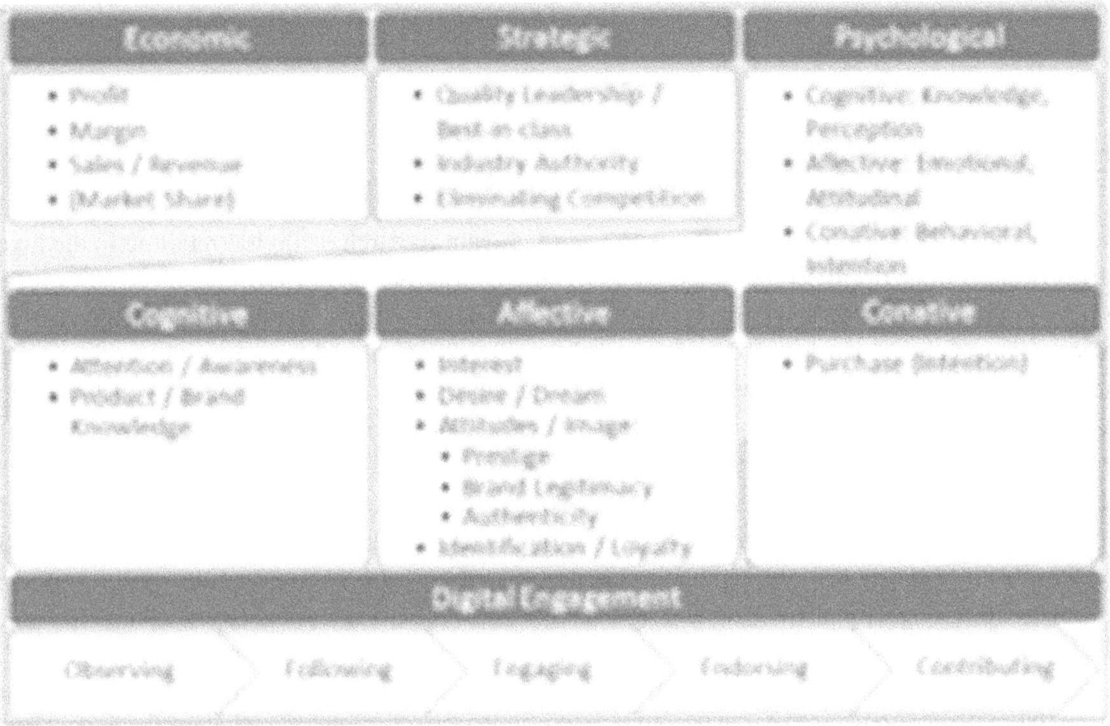

Mosca and Chiaudano (2020) have identified a sequence of four main phases that define the development of a digital luxury retailing market:

- Skepticism—the company's main activities revolve around communication (Kim & Ko, 2012; Okonkwo, 2010);
- Awareness—the company becomes more aware of the need for a complete digital strategy;
- Implementation—the company begins to integrate the first online distribution activities (Kim et al., 2015);
- Total exploitation—the company exploits the full potential of the digital channel.

Luxury companies are increasingly investing in their own e-commerce systems, which are directly connected to their websites (Kim, 2019, 2020). Interestingly, this trend coincides with the rapid growth of the online luxury retail channel, which saw a 75% increase in online luxury transactions in 2019 (Bain & Company, 2020). However, despite rising sales, many luxury companies still exhibit uncertainty about whether the online channel can offer luxury consumers the same enchanting shopping experience as their physical stores. In response, according to Kim (2019), luxury companies are becoming increasingly attentive to modern consumers' changing online habits and are looking to adopt online retail strategies. For instance, several studies have focused on the application of digital technologies (e.g., virtual shop windows, interactive environments) within physical stores (Dacko, 2017; Demirkan & Spohrer, 2014; Pantano, 2016). In this context, For example, the brand Piquadro, TheBridge, and Lancel reimagined its business model by allowing customers to make a video chat appointment with a retail associate who would shop with them in real-time. In short, there are innovative ways for luxury companies to bolster online sales while simultaneously preserving their highly valued prestige (Beuckels & Hudders, 2016) and the perception of quality.

RESEARCH METHODOLOGY

The main objective of this chapter is to supplement the scant research on digital retailing in the luxury market by examining the different critical factors and opportunities linked to digitization. Several studies have underlined how most luxury retailers focus their sales strategies primarily on a single brand or property (Desmichel & Kocher, 2020; Hagtvedt & Patrick, 2016), thereby securing the optimal brand/quality perception (Kapferer & Bastien, 2012). On the contrary, this dynamic tends to exclude the integration between retail systems and digital technologies, the resistance of which has several important limitations (e.g., luxury brands depend on exclusivity, quality and uniqueness - see Kepferer (2000); modern luxury consumer expert in digital technologies - see Kim (2019)). Against this backdrop and considering the lack of research on luxury brands' online retail strategies (Passavanti et al., 2020), this chapter intends to clarify the logic behind luxury brands' transition to a highly digitized context (Corbin & Strauss, 2015). Specifically, the authors adopt a qualitative approach to better understand the digital strategic levers that luxury retailers will have to implement within their global marketing mix.

As this chapter seeks to understand luxury brands' online retailing from a corporate perspective, emphasizing the opinions of those responsible for strategic decision-making (Wright & Crimp, 2000), the authors have gathered opinions, meanings, and key terms from relevant participants (Daymon & Holloway, 2011). The research design was based on semi-structured one-to-one interviews. This method strives to identify issues, themes, and lines of investigation. By presenting questions in a random order that follows on from participants' responses, this method also offers the flexibility needed to generate intuitions that had not been previously considered (Daymon & Holloway, 2011; Holtzhausen & Voto, 2002; Wright, 2000).

At the beginning of this study, an exhaustive literature review was conducted to better understand all the associated concepts. Once **the authors** had defined the data collection method, they were able to select the research sample. **Specifically, the sample of interviewees included four** managers **(M_{age} = 40)** employed at a leading digital marketing company specialized in online advertising and with several clients from the luxury sector. **The interviewees included the Managing Director and the Account Strategists; the average experience in the digital sector was about 14 years. Each interview lasted on average 45 minutes.** The authors created the semi-structured interview questions based on the preliminary literature review, which proved useful in conceptualizing the phenomenon of digital marketing in the luxury retail context. **The questions included theoretical and managerial aspects of the relationship between digital technology and luxury and on the next challenges for luxury brands in the digital retail sector**.

Overall, two research questions guided the analysis:

Research Question One: What is the relationship between digital technology and luxury retail?

Research Question Two: What are the critical factors and opportunities for luxury companies in their adoption of digital technologies?

SOLUTIONS AND RECOMMENDATIONS

Despite their increasing awareness of the importance of digitization to the retail sector, the relationship between luxury brands and digital technologies is not always straightforward and is often characterized by a clash between tradition and innovation. Online retail poses an immediate dilemma in terms of whether luxury brands can maintain their "dream value" in a virtual context (Chandon et al., 2016; p. 301). Based on analyses, and in line with research questions, different insights linked to criticalities and opportunities emerged to adopting digital technologies in the luxury sector. In terms of critical factors, findings point to a controversial relationship between digitization and luxury brands and an organizational gap within luxury companies in terms of digital technologies. In terms of opportunities, they equally highlight the need for adaptation to digital technologies and the support of digital communication technologies. **Table 1 provides a preliminary insight into how the interviewees at research questions answer.**

Critical Factors

The controversial relationship between digital technologies and luxury brands arises from two issues. The first is the diversity of the luxury market, which implies substantial differences in technological orientation (Ko et al., 2019). The second is luxury marketers' fear that they will be unable to guarantee an adequate level of uniqueness, image, and brand quality through technology (Desmichel & Kocher, 2020; Kapferer & Bastien, 2012). On the one hand, previous research has shown that luxury companies have now gained considerable awareness of the need to adopt new strategies related to online retail channels (Kim et al., 2015; Mosca & Chiaudano, 2020). On the other hand, the construct of awareness (of a clearly positive meaning) tends to clash with those that inhibit the process of digitizing retail, namely, the logic related to brand image and brand identity (Desmichel & Kocher, 2020; Kapferer & Bastien, 2012). Moreover, the desire to preserve the main characteristics of luxury brands—such as uniqueness, luxuriousness, or quality—often impedes the implementation of digital technologies, which threaten to diminish these deeply enshrined values and constructs.

Our analysis also highlighted the organizational gap within luxury companies in terms of implementing digital technologies. While penalizing causes and the consequent business improvements are relevant to this critical factor, the determining role is played by marketplaces. Indeed, the analysis showed that the marketplace assumes an autonomous role. Therefore, for luxury companies, having an organizational gap in terms of online retail activities represents a significant barrier in the global market. It is important to note how the problem can be found upstream of the whole system: luxury companies may have a sparse logistics system for supporting online retail, as well as an almost total absence of an e-commerce system that can handle all aspects of an online purchase (i.e., packaging, shipping, accessory services). Consequently, companies may need to consider several business-level improvements to the entire online retail system, both to deal with events like the pandemic and to satisfy consumers who are now accustomed to certain online shopping standards (Mosca & Chiaudano, 2020). Finally, another important critical factor is represented by multi-brand marketplaces (e.g., YOOX NET-A-PORTER) that exist for the purpose of selling luxury products online. These platforms often act with aggressive sales policies that divert consumers to their own sites, thereby revealing themselves as real competitors intent on increasing their own sales volumes (Ramadan, 2019).

Table 1. Excerpts interviews related at research questions

RQ. 1 Relationship between digital technology and luxury retail **RQ. 2 Critical factors and opportunities for luxury companies in digital technologies adoption**	
Critical Factors	**Opportunities**
Controversial relationship between digitization and luxury brands	**Need for adaptation to digital technologies**
"*...for luxury companies, there are constraints related to the brand image that makes the use of digital technologies and the online retail through e-commerce critical ... many online retailers, in particular on fast-fashion industry, are in full growth phases ... but for luxury brands we notice a slowness, the more prestigious they are, the less exploit to the maximum of digital technologies potential, setting different constraints that limit their application ...* " (Interviewed 1) " "*...among major luxury companies, the digital technologies implementation keep always seen as a rather weak tool, therefore at the risk of undermining the luxuriousness, its main characteristic...*" (Interviewed 2) "*...in luxury fashion industry new technologies, that is digital marketing, are still little used compared to other sectors, that is fast fast-fashion; in particular, I refer to the whole part of e-commerce where there is also a form of snobbery, considering technology as a threat...*" (Interviewed 4)	"*...in recent months there has been a strong wave of digitization; many consumers who had never made online purchases, if before they used the internet only as an information and research source for the luxury product, today they use it to complete the purchasing decision-making process...*" (Interviewed 2) "*...the consumers are increasingly connected and exigent; being luxury products, require more services than he can find on a marketplace which can be, that is Zalando, wants to have more information as possible on the brand he is interested, on all devices and on all the digital platforms uses, in order to increase the propensity to buy online and the loyalty towards the brand...*" (Interviewed 4) "*...for luxury companies, the problem is upstream, that is, logistics, distribution but above all production need an incisive strengthening... it is important, for luxury companies to fully embrace digital retail strategies, therefore mono-brand e-commerce...*" (Interviewed 4) "*...from digital marketing point of view of, luxury companies are getting closer and are exploiting what are all digital channels such as social media, digital advertising players and influencers in order to increase the online retailing activities...*" (Interviewed 1)
Organizational gap within luxury companies in terms of digital technologies.	**Support of digital communication technologies.**
"*...there are many online outlets that have made the purchase of certain luxury brands easier and more accessible, for example, the multi-brand e-commerce platforms...*" (Interviewed 4) "*...the challenges to be addressed in a digital context will mainly be linked to logistics, implementing complete e-commerce system that can handle all aspects of an online purchase, that is when I have to send you the package at home, luxury companies must manage the warehouse and must do so in order to offer the best experience on the possible market, contrasting the competition from other marketplaces platforms...*" (Interviewed 3) "*...on the theme of logistics and distribution the luxury companies, to be on a par with other consumer experiences through e-commerce activities (e.g., Amazon, Zalando), they should implement services such as free return and other similar services which must be part of an e-commerce experience, especially in these times when the consumer is now accustomed to certain standards...*" (Interviewed 2)	"*...luxury companies tend to communicate with end consumers through digital in the same logic as offline, not fully understanding the fact that the interlocutors are absolutely different ...*" (Interviewed 3) "*...the major luxury companies have reinvented themselves, modifying their productions to help people, countries in difficulty, so in this case, they have slightly abandoned the sphere of luxury based on these actions immediate, communicating through digital platforms an image of presence, social attention, and sustainability ...*" (Interviewed 4) "*...through these actions and to digital communication technologies, luxury brands got closer to a wider audience, so they no longer only had a communication with a certain high-end group of people, but they made it clear that their brand can be 'for everyone', communicating an image of simplicity that previously they failed not to communicate...*" (Interviewed 2) "*...the influencers have had a huge impact from the point of view of luxury communication and, in particular, on the retail of luxury products...*" (Interviewed 4) "*...the luxury fashion industry, through digital technology is trying to transform offline events into something more pervasive, digital and inclusive, both from the point of view of all the interlocutors of the luxury sector fashion sector that also to the final consumer; if you think the fashion shows are live on Instagram...*" (Interviewed 3)

Opportunities

Adaptation to technology represents an important theoretical construct. Several scholars have argued that the construct of technology still lacks a truly comprehensive literature due to differing levels of analysis, dimensions, and complexity (Haggerty & Golden, 2002; Orlikowski, 2000; Sproull & Goodman, 1990). Furthermore, emerging technologies are developing so rapidly that they are constantly shifting the gap between past, present, and future (Utesheva et al., 2016). The results of this study show that adopting the available digital technologies is fundamentally important to luxury companies. Indeed, adaptation to technology represents an essential lever, especially from the perspective of realizing offline shopping experiences in an online context and of the satisfaction of new digital luxury consumers (Kim, 2019). Ultimately, this means that luxury companies must seize these opportunities to close their organizational gaps around digital luxury retail, including directing serious investment to improve their digital resources.

The analysis also pointed to the opportunity to harness digital media as a means of essential support for online retailing activities. The communicative potential of digital technologies has led luxury companies and luxury marketers to rethink their business strategies to adapt to these new forms of consumer interaction and personalization (Hearn et al., 2009; Leeflang et al., 2014; Passavanti et al., 2020). Likewise, the literature has widely opined on the consolidated relationship between digital communication and luxury brands (Colella et al., 2019; Godey et al., 2016; Kim & Ko, 2012; Kapferer & Bastien, 2012; Okonkwo, 2009). Our results show that this opportunity features three important constructs: (a) image, (b) commitment, and (c) democratization. The democratization of luxury has already been the subject of several studies (Nueno & Quelch, 1998; Kapferer, 2012; Plażyk, 2015; Silverstein et al., 2003; 2008; Radón, 2012; Ramadan, 2019). According to Radón (2012), making a democratic luxury product means selling as much of it as possible, which necessarily negates the meaning of exclusivity that is so closely tied to luxury. For example, fashion influencers have used their digital communication channels to propagate a view of democratization in the luxury fashion sector. Therefore, the use of digital media and support by influencers could represent key drivers for online retailing activities. **Table 2, through the SWOT analysis tool, summarizes the different relevant factors related to digital retail strategies in the luxury sector**.

FUTURE RESEARCH DIRECTIONS

The aim of this chapter was to identify and analyze the critical factors and the opportunities afforded by digital marketing in the luxury retail sector. While several studies have shown that the paradigm is changing rapidly (Okazaki et al., 2007; Smith, 2011), especially in the fields of communication (Alalwan et al., 2017; Felix et al., 2017) and segmentation (Rutz et al., 2012; Stark, 2020), the changes wrought on online luxury retail remain less clear, and in particular the relationship between digital retail technologies and the luxury sector.

Given that technology and digitization are themes perpetually in flux, scholars need the support of fluid and dynamic research approaches. As a result, the authors found the methodological approach of qualitative research to be the most suitable for exploring the phenomenon (Cassell and Symon, 2012). By synthesizing the opinions, meanings, and key terms of the interviewees, this chapter contributes a better understanding of the criticalities and opportunities associated with digitization in the luxury retail market. Clearly, given the rapid change of digital technologies, this chapter has its limits in terms of generalizability. Specifically, the interviewees were all digital marketing experts in the luxury sector, operating an external company specializing in the open Internet. Therefore, future research might investigate digital

Table 2. SWOT analysis of the relevant factors related to digital luxury retail strategies

	Strengths	Weaknesses
Internal factors	▪ Greater attention to luxury consumers by interacting with them through digital platforms. ▪ Support of digital communication technologies. ▪ International markets coverage.	▪ The luxury market complexity. ▪ Substantial differences in technological orientation in the luxury industry. ▪ An organizational gap within luxury companies, in terms of digital technologies implementation. ▪ Complexity for luxury brands of guaranteeing an adequate level of uniqueness, image, and brand quality through technology.
	Opportunities	**Critical Factors (Threats)**
External factors	▪ Digital media as a means of essential support for online retailing activities. ▪ Strong image and social commitment. ▪ New forms of consumer interaction and personalization. ▪ Influencers as key drivers of online retailing activities. ▪ Greater relationships with digital retail channels. ▪ New shopping experiences and market-dominant positioning.	▪ Absence of a complete e-commerce system that can handle all aspects of an online purchase (i.e., packaging, shipping, accessory services). ▪ Luxury multi-brand online marketplaces ▪ The controversial relationship between digitization and luxury brands. ▪ Lower adaptation to digital technologies respect other sectors.

Source: Elaboration of the authors.

luxury retail strategies by sampling executives directly from the luxury retailers themselves. Moreover, the authors did not consider the consumer point of view in this study; future studies could adopt this perspective (qualitatively or quantitatively) to evaluate online luxury brand purchases. Finally, it would be interesting to apply the different identified constructs in a more holistic manner which would support the different theoretical frameworks developed in the current research.

CONCLUSION

This chapter explores a current problem facing marketers in the context of luxury companies. Digital platforms and digital media are already entrenched in the everyday fabric of life, and it is there that the future of the luxury retail sector will be played out. Given the current global economic scenario, luxury industry leaders must remain committed to longer-term strategic planning, including considerations of e-commerce as a business-critical channel for maintaining sales, communicating with customers, and driving new consumer activation.

ACKNOWLEDGMENT

The present research was funded by the Ministry of University and Research (MIUR) within the National Operational Programme "Research and Innovation" 2014-2020 [PON-RI 14/20] – [CCI 2014IT-16M2OP005], European Social Fund (ESF), Action I. Investments in human capital – 1. Investing in education, training and vocational training for skills and lifelong learning – 1.1 "innovative PhDs with industrial characterization".

REFERENCES

Absolute Reports. (2020). *Global Digital Retail Marketing Market Report 2020*. https://www.absolutereports.com/global-digital-retail-market-15595402

Alalwan, A. A., Rana, N. P., Dwivedi, Y. K., & Algharabat, R. (2017). Social Media In Marketing: A Review And Analysis Of The Existing Literature. *Telematics and Informatics*, *34*(7), 1177–1190. doi:10.1016/j.tele.2017.05.008

Arrigo, E. (2018). Social Media Marketing In Luxury Brands. *Management Research Review*, *41*(6), 657–679. doi:10.1108/MRR-04-2017-0134

Bain & Company. (2020). *Eight Themes That Are Rewriting the Future of Luxury Goods*. https://www.bain.com/insights/eight-themes-that-are-rewriting-the-future-of-luxury-goods/

Beuckels, E., & Hudders, L. (2016). An Experimental Study To Investigate The Impact Of Image Interactivity On The Perception Of Luxury In An Online Shopping Context. *Journal of Retailing and Consumer Services*, *33*, 135–142. doi:10.1016/j.jretconser.2016.08.014

Bruggeman, H., Van Hiel, A., Van Hal, G., & Van Dongen, S. (2019). Does The Use Of Digital Media Affect Psychological Well-Being? An Empirical Test Among Children Aged 9 To 12. *Computers in Human Behavior*, *101*, 104–113. doi:10.1016/j.chb.2019.07.015

Cassell, C., & Symon, G. (2012). Essential Guide To Qualitative Methods. In *Organizational Research*. SAGE Publications Ltd.

Chandon, J. L., Laurent, G., & Valette-Florence, P. (2016). Pursuing The Concept Of Luxury: Introduction To The JBR Special Issue On Luxury Marketing From Tradition To Innovation. *Journal of Business Research*, *69*(1), 299–303. doi:10.1016/j.jbusres.2015.08.001

Colella, G., Amatulli, C., & Martinez-Ruiz, M. P. (2019). Social Media Marketing and Luxury Consumption: A Literature Review. *International Journal of Marketing Studies*, *11*(4), 30–52. doi:10.5539/ijms.v11n4p30

Corbin, J., & Strauss, A. (2015). *Basics of qualitative research: Techniques and procedures for developing grounded theory*. Sage publications.

Cramer, J., & Krueger, A. B. (2016). Disruptive change in the taxi business: The case of Uber. *The American Economic Review*, *106*(5), 177–182. doi:10.1257/aer.p20161002

Dacko, S. G. (2017). Enabling Smart Retail Settings via Mobile Augmented Reality Shopping Apps. *Technological Forecasting and Social Change*, *124*, 243–256. doi:10.1016/j.techfore.2016.09.032

Daymon, C., & Holloway, I. (2011). *Qualitative Research Methods in Public Relations and Marketing Communications* (2nd ed.). Routledge.

Demirkan, H., & Spohrer, J. (2014). Developing a Framework to Improve Virtual Shopping in Digital Malls with Intelligent Self-Service Systems. *Journal of Retailing and Consumer Services*, *21*(5), 860–868. doi:10.1016/j.jretconser.2014.02.012

Desmichel, P., & Kocher, B. (2020). Luxury Single- versus Multi-Brand Stores: The Effect of Consumers' Hedonic Goals on Brand Comparisons. *Journal of Retailing*, *96*(2), 203–219. doi:10.1016/j.jretai.2019.09.002

Felix, R., Rauschnabel, P. A., & Hinsch, C. (2017). Elements of Strategic Social Media Marketing: A Holistic Framework. *Journal of Business Research*, *70*, 118–126. doi:10.1016/j.jbusres.2016.05.001

Godey, B., Manthiou, A., Pederzoli, D., Rokka, J., Aiello, G., Donvito, R., & Singh, R. (2016). Social Media Marketing Efforts of Luxury Brands: Influence on Brand Equity and Consumer Behavior. *Journal of Business Research*, *69*(12), 5833–5841. doi:10.1016/j.jbusres.2016.04.181

Gurău, C. (2008). Integrated online marketing communication: Implementation and management. *Journal of Communication Management (London)*, *12*(2), 169–184. doi:10.1108/13632540810881974

Haberly, D., MacDonald-Korth, D., Urban, M., & Wójcik, D. (2019). Asset Management as a Digital Platform Industry: A Global Financial Network Perspective. *Geoforum*, *106*, 167–181. doi:10.1016/j.geoforum.2019.08.009

Hagberg, J., Jonsson, A., & Egels-Zandén, N. (2017). Retail digitalization: Implications for physical stores. *Journal of Retailing and Consumer Services*, *39*, 264–269. doi:10.1016/j.jretconser.2017.08.005

Haggerty, N., & Golden, B. (2002). Theorizing technological adaptation as a trigger for institutional change. In *ICIS 2002 Proceedings of the International Conference on Information System* (pp. 247–255). Academic Press.

Hagtvedt, H., & Patrick, V. M. (2016). Gilt and Guilt: Should Luxury and Charity Partner at the Point of Sale? *Journal of Retailing*, *92*(1), 56–64. doi:10.1016/j.jretai.2015.07.004

Hänninen, M., Smedlund, A., & Mitronen, L. (2018). Digitalization in Retailing: Multi-Sided Platforms as Drivers of Industry Transformation. *Baltic Journal of Management*, *13*(2), 152–168. doi:10.1108/BJM-04-2017-0109

Hearn, G., Foth, M., & Gray, H. (2009). Applications and Implementations of New Media in Corporate Communications. *Corporate Communications*, *14*(1), 49–61. doi:10.1108/13563280910931072

Heine, K., & Berghaus, B. (2014). Luxury goes digital: How to tackle the digital luxury brand–consumer touchpoints. *Journal of Global Fashion Marketing*, *5*(3), 223–234. doi:10.1080/20932685.2014.907606

Herhausen, D., Miočević, D., Morgan, R. E., & Kleijnen, M. H. (2020). The digital marketing capabilities gap. *Industrial Marketing Management*, *90*, 276–290. doi:10.1016/j.indmarman.2020.07.022

Holtzhausen, D. R., & Voto, R. (2002). Resistance From the Margins: The Postmodern Public Relations Practitioner as Organizational Activist. *Journal of Public Relations Research*, *14*(1), 57–84. doi:10.1207/S1532754XJPRR1401_3

Hudson, S., Huang, L., Roth, M. S., & Madden, T. J. (2016). The influence of social media interactions on consumer–brand relationships: A three-country study of brand perceptions and marketing behaviors. *International Journal of Research in Marketing*, *33*(1), 27–41. doi:10.1016/j.ijresmar.2015.06.004

Hughes, M. Ü., Bendoni, W. K., & Pehlivan, E. (2016). Storygiving as a co-creation tool for luxury brands in the age of the internet: A love story by Tiffany and thousands of lovers. *Journal of Product and Brand Management*, *25*(4), 357–364. doi:10.1108/JPBM-09-2015-0970

Huuhka, A., Laaksonen, M., & Laaksonen, P. (2014). The Evolution Of New Systemic Forms In Retailing And Digital Business. *Contributions to International Business*, 239–249.

Jacobson, J., Gruzd, A., & Hernández-García, Á. (2020). Social media marketing: Who is watching the watchers? *Journal of Retailing and Consumer Services*, *53*, 53. doi:10.1016/j.jretconser.2019.03.001

Jain, S. (2016). Impact of Digitalization on Indian Luxury Market. *AIMA Journal of Management & Research*, *10*(2/4), 1–10.

Javalgi, R. G., Todd, P. R., Johnston, W. J., & Granot, E. (2012). Entrepreneurship, muddling through, and Indian internet-enabled SMEs. *Journal of Business Research*, *65*(6), 740–744. doi:10.1016/j.jbusres.2010.12.010

Kamal, S., Chu, S. C., & Pedram, M. (2013). Materialism, attitudes, and social media usage and their impact on purchase intention of luxury fashion goods among American and Arab young generations. *Journal of Interactive Advertising*, *13*(1), 27–40. doi:10.1080/15252019.2013.768052

Kannan, P. K., & Li, H. A. (2017). Digital marketing: A framework, review and research agenda. *International Journal of Research in Marketing*, *34*(1), 22–45. doi:10.1016/j.ijresmar.2016.11.006

Kapferer, J. N. (2000). How the Internet impacts on brand management. *Journal of Brand Management*, *7*(6), 389–391. doi:10.1057/bm.2000.30

Kapferer, J. N. (2015). The future of luxury: Challenges and opportunities. *Journal of Brand Management*, *21*(9), 716–726. doi:10.1057/bm.2014.32

Kapferer, J. N., & Bastien, V. (2012). *The Luxury Strategy: Break The Rules of Marketing to Build Luxury Brands* (2nd ed.). Kogan Page Ltd.

Katsikeas, C., Leonidou, L., & Zeriti, A. (2019). Revisiting international marketing strategy in a digital era: Opportunities, challenges, and research directions. *International Marketing Review*, *37*(3), 405–424. doi:10.1108/IMR-02-2019-0080

Kenney, M., & Zysman, J. (2015). Choosing a future in the platform economy: the implications and consequences of digital platforms. In *Proceedings Kauffman Foundation New Entrepreneurial Growth Conference* (*Vol. 156160*). Academic Press.

Key, T. M., & Czaplewski, A. J. (2017). Upstream social marketing strategy: An integrated marketing communications approach. *Business Horizons*, *60*(3), 325–333. doi:10.1016/j.bushor.2017.01.006

Kim, A. J. Y., & Ko, E. J. (2010). The impact of design characteristics on brand attitude and purchase intention-focus on luxury fashion brands. *Journal of the Korean Society of Clothing and Textiles*, *34*(2), 252–265. doi:10.5850/JKSCT.2010.34.2.252

Kim, A. J. Y., & Ko, E. J. (2012). Do social media marketing activities enhance customer equity? An empirical study of luxury fashion brand. *Journal of Business Research, 65*(10), 1480–1486. doi:10.1016/j.jbusres.2011.10.014

Kim, H., Choi, Y. J., & Lee, Y. (2015). Web atmospheric qualities in luxury fashion brand web sites. *Journal of Fashion Marketing and Management, 19*(4), 384–401. doi:10.1108/JFMM-09-2013-0103

Kim, J. H. (2019). Imperative challenge for luxury brands: Generation Y consumers' perceptions of luxury e-commerce sites. *International Journal of Retail & Distribution Management, 47*(2), 220–244. doi:10.1108/IJRDM-06-2017-0128

Kim, J. H. (2020). Luxury brands in the digital age: Perceived quality and gender difference. *International Review of Retail, Distribution and Consumer Research, 30*(1), 68–85. doi:10.1080/09593969.2019.1651379

Ko, E., Costello, J. P., & Taylor, C. R. (2019). What is a luxury brand? A new definition and review of the literature. *Journal of Business Research, 99*, 405–413. doi:10.1016/j.jbusres.2017.08.023

Kotler, P., Kartajaya, H., & Setawan, I. (2010). *Marketing 4.0: From Products to Customers to the Human Spirit.* John Wiley & Sons, Inc. doi:10.1002/9781118257883

Kotler, P., Kartajaya, H., & Setawan, I. (2017). *Marketing 4.0: Moving from Traditional to Digital.* John Wiley & Sons, Inc.

Kotler, P., Wong, V., Saunders, J., & Armstrong, G. (2009). *Principles of Marketing* (6th ed.). Pearson.

Leeflang, P. S., Verhoef, P. C., Dahlström, P., & Freundt, T. (2014). Challenges and solutions for marketing in a digital era. *European Management Journal, 32*(1), 1–12. doi:10.1016/j.emj.2013.12.001

Liu, S., Perry, P., & Gadzinski, G. (2019). The implications of digital marketing on WeChat for luxury fashion brands in China. *Journal of Brand Management, 26*(4), 395–409. doi:10.105741262-018-0140-2

Liu, X., Burns, A. C., & Hou, Y. (2013). Comparing Online And In-Store Shopping Behavior Towards Luxury Goods'. *International Journal of Retail & Distribution Management, 41*(11/12), 885–900. doi:10.1108/IJRDM-01-2013-0018

Melović, B., Jocović, M., Dabić, M., Vulić, T. B., & Dudic, B. (2020). The impact of digital transformation and digital marketing on the brand promotion, positioning and electronic business in Montenegro. *Technology in Society, 63*, 63. doi:10.1016/j.techsoc.2020.101425

Mosca, F., & Chiaudano, V. (2020). Digital channels and distribution in luxury market. *Marche et Organisations, 37*(1), 147–163.

Mosca, F., & Giacosa, E. (2016). Old and new distribution channels in the luxury sector. IGI Global Publisher. doi:10.4018/978-1-4666-9958-8.ch010

Neslin, S. A., Grewal, D., Leghorn, R., Shankar, V., Teerling, M. L., Thomas, J. S., & Verhoef, P. C. (2006). Challenges and opportunities in multichannel customer management. *Journal of Service Research, 9*(2), 95–112. doi:10.1177/1094670506293559

Nueno, J. L., & Quelch, J. A. (1998). The mass marketing of luxury. *Business Horizons*, *41*(6), 61–68. doi:10.1016/S0007-6813(98)90023-4

Okazaki, S., Katsukura, A., & Nishiyama, M. (2007). How mobile advertising works: The role of trust in improving attitudes and recall. *Journal of Advertising Research*, *47*(2), 165–178. doi:10.2501/S0021849907070195

Okonkwo, U. (2009). Sustaining the luxury brand on the Internet. *Journal of Brand Management*, *16*(5–6), 302–310. doi:10.1057/bm.2009.2

Okonkwo, U. (2010). Luxury online: Styles, systems, strategies. Palgrave Macmillan UK. doi:10.1057/9780230248335

Orlikowski, W. J. (2000). Using Technology and Constituting Structures: A Practice Lens for Studying Technology in Organizations. *Organization Science*, *11*(4), 404–428. doi:10.1287/orsc.11.4.404.14600

Pantano, E. (2016). Engaging consumer through storefront: Evidences from integrating interactive technologies. *Journal of Retailing and Consumer Services*, *28*, 149–154. doi:10.1016/j.jretconser.2015.09.007

Pantano, E., & Timmermans, H. (2014). What is smart for retailing? *Procedia Environmental Sciences*, *22*, 101–107. doi:10.1016/j.proenv.2014.11.010

Passavanti, R., Pantano, E., Priporas, C. V., & Verteramo, S. (2020). The use of new technologies for corporate marketing communication in luxury retailing: Preliminary findings. *Qualitative Market Research*, *23*(3), 503–521. doi:10.1108/QMR-11-2017-0144

Plażyk, K. (2015). The democratization of luxury–a new form of luxury. Studia University of Economics in Katowice, 158–165.

Radón, A. (2012). Luxury brand exclusivity strategies-An illustration of a cultural collaboration. *Journal of Business Administration Research*, *1*(1), 106. doi:10.5430/jbar.v1n1p106

Ramadan, Z. (2019). The Democratization Of Intangible Luxury. *Marketing Intelligence & Planning*, *37*(6), 660–673. doi:10.1108/MIP-11-2018-0490

Rathnayaka, U. (2018). Role of Digital Marketing in Retail Fashion Industry: A Synthesis of the Theory and the Practice. *Journal of Accounting & Marketing*, *7*(2), 1–7. doi:10.4172/2168-9601.1000279

Reinartz, W., Wiegand, N., & Imschloss, M. (2019). The impact of digital transformation on the retailing value chain. *International Journal of Research in Marketing*, *36*(3), 350–366. doi:10.1016/j.ijresmar.2018.12.002

Rese, A., Ganster, L., & Baier, D. (2020). Chatbots in retailers' customer communication: How to measure their acceptance? *Journal of Retailing and Consumer Services*, *56*, 102176. doi:10.1016/j.jretconser.2020.102176

Rigby, D. (2011). The future of shopping. *Harvard Business Review*, *89*(12), 65–76.

Ritz, W., Wolf, M., & Mcquitty, S. (2019). Digital marketing adoption and success for small businesses: The application of the do-it-yourself and technology acceptance models. *Journal of Research in Interactive Marketing*, *13*(2), 179–203. doi:10.1108/JRIM-04-2018-0062

Rohm, A., Kaltcheva, V. D., & Milne, G. R. (2013). A mixed-method approach to examining brand-consumer interactions driven by social media. *Journal of Research in Interactive Marketing*, *7*(4), 295–311. doi:10.1108/JRIM-01-2013-0009

Royle, J., & Laing, A. (2014). The digital marketing skills gap: Developing a Digital Marketer Model for the communication industries. *International Journal of Information Management*, *34*(2), 65–73. doi:10.1016/j.ijinfomgt.2013.11.008

Rutz, O. J., Bucklin, R. E., & Sonnier, G. P. (2012). A latent instrumental variables approach to modeling keyword conversion in paid search advertising. *JMR, Journal of Marketing Research*, *49*(3), 306–319. doi:10.1509/jmr.10.0354

Schivinski, B., & Dabrowski, D. (2016). The effect of social media communication on consumer perceptions of brands. *Journal of Marketing Communications*, *22*(2), 189–214. doi:10.1080/13527266.2013.871323

Silverstein, M.J., Fiske, N., & Butman, J. (2003). *Trading up: The new American luxury*. Academic Press.

Silverstein, M. J., Fiske, N., & Butman, J. (2008). *Trading Up: why consumers want new luxury goods and how companies create them*. Portfolio.

Smith, K. T. (2011). Digital marketing strategies that Millennials find appealing, motivating, or just annoying. *Journal of Strategic Marketing*, *19*(6), 489–499. doi:10.1080/0965254X.2011.581383

Smith, K. T. (2012). Longitudinal study of digital marketing strategies targeting millennials. *Journal of Consumer Marketing*, *29*(2), 86–92. doi:10.1108/07363761211206339

Sproull, L. S., & Goodman, P. S. (1990). Technology and Organizations: Integration and Opportunities. In P. Goodman & L. Sproull (Eds.), *Technology and Organizations* (pp. 254–265). Jossey-Bass Inc.

Stark, J. (2020). Digital Transformation of a Retail Store. *Digital Transformation of Industry Decision Engineering*, 73–77.

Tarnaud, N. (2019). Le Luxe Dans Le Monde d'Aujourd'hui. *Les Echos*. https://www.lesechos.fr/idees-debats/cercle/le-luxe-dans-le-monde-daujourdhui-130583

Teece, D. J. (2010). Business models, business strategy and innovation. *Long Range Planning*, *43*(2–3), 172–194. doi:10.1016/j.lrp.2009.07.003

Tiago, M. T. P. M. B., & Veríssimo, J. M. C. (2014). Digital marketing and social media: Why bother? *Business Horizons*, *57*(6), 703–708. doi:10.1016/j.bushor.2014.07.002

Utesheva, A., Simpson, J. R., & Cecez-Kecmanovic, D. (2016). Identity metamorphoses in digital disruption: A relational theory of identity. *European Journal of Information Systems*, *25*(4), 344–363. doi:10.1057/ejis.2015.19

Verhoef, P. C., Kannan, P. K., & Inman, J. J. (2015). From multi-channel retailing to omni-channel retailing: Introduction to the special issue on multi-channel retailing. *Journal of Retailing*, *91*(2), 174–181. doi:10.1016/j.jretai.2015.02.005

Vernuccio, M., & Ceccotti, F. (2015). Strategic and organisational challenges in the integrated marketing communication paradigm shift: A holistic vision. *European Management Journal, 33*(6), 438–449. doi:10.1016/j.emj.2015.09.001

Vimali, S., & Khan, K. A. (2018). Impact of Digital Marketing on Consumers Purchase. *Journal of Management, 6*(1), 51–55.

We Are Social. (2020). *Digital 2020*. https://wearesocial.com/digital-2020

Wirtz, B. W. (2019). *Digital Business Models*. Springer International Publishing. doi:10.1007/978-3-030-13005-3

Wright, L. T., & Crimp, M. (2000). *The Marketing Research process* (5th ed.). Pearson.

Yu, S., Hudders, L., & Cauberghe, V. (2017). Targeting the luxury consumer: A vice or virtue? A cross-cultural comparison of the effectiveness of behaviorally targeted ads. *Journal of Fashion Marketing and Management, 21*(2), 187–205. doi:10.1108/JFMM-07-2016-0058

Zhu, G. (2019). Precision retail marketing strategy based on digital marketing model. *Science Journal of Business and Management, 7*(1), 33–37. doi:10.11648/j.sjbm.20190701.15

KEY TERMS AND DEFINITIONS

Digital Communication: The set of marketing activities related to the promotion of a content (texts, images, videos, etc.) through the use of digital technologies such as PCs, tablets, satellites, smartphones.

Digital Marketing: Refers to all those brand promoting activities and feature a powerful tool for building, consolidating, and maintaining brand awareness through one or more digital channels.

Digital Transformation: The capability of adopting new, fast, and frequently changing digital technology to solve problems, improve experiences of customers, employees, and companies.

Luxury: It is a large and lucrative sector serving as one of the most relevant engines of growth in many countries.

Luxury Brand: It is a brand characterized by a mix of specific features such as exclusivity, uniqueness, scarcity, premium price, excellent quality, and aesthetics.

Smart Retail: New business models that allow retailers may achieve competitive advantages over their technologically lesser-integrated competitors, by enhance the customer shopping experience through the smart use of technologies for retailing purposes.

Social Media: Are interactive platforms where companies and customers can share information and contents about a brand or a product within the network.

Section 2
IoT

Chapter 8
IOTs:
An Enabler for Human and Business Activities

N. Raghavendra Rao
FINAIT Consultancy Services, India

ABSTRACT

Information technology has advanced by delivering an exponential increase in computing power. Telecommunication technology has likewise advanced communicating capabilities. Convergence of these two technologies has become possible due to the rapid advancements made in the respective technology. This convergence is termed as information and communication technology as a discipline. Many concepts are emerging in this discipline. These concepts enable business, government, and human beings to reach new realities in their required activities. Some of these concepts have created various opportunities for designing and manufacturing electronic devices. When these devices are connected to other devices and systems over the internet, this is now known as internet of things (IoT). This chapter gives a brief overview of the concepts such as cloud computing and ubiquitous and pervasive computing in the context of internet of things. Further, this chapter discusses five case illustrations with the relevance of internet of things.

INTRODUCTION

In the early years, the internet was mainly used by military and research institutions in the United States of America. Now it is being used across the globe in every activity under the sun. People prefer to be on the internet. One of the main reasons, it is simple to use. The internet is a good example of functional freedom. In principle any node can speak as a peer to any other node as long it obeys the rules of the TCP/IP protocols, which are strictly technical, not social or political. The Internet can be compared to a human language. Nether none hires a language nor no one owns a language. It is up to an individual to learn and to speak a language. People consider the internet as similar to a language. It belongs to everyone.

DOI: 10.4018/978-1-7998-7192-7.ch008

Ubiquitous and pervasive computing concepts have facilitated many manufacturers to design and develop electronic devices. Consequent to the advancements in the "Internet" many electronic devices are embedded with a feature of the "Internet". When these devices are connected to other devices and systems over the internet, are referred to as the "Internet of Things" (Daniel Kellmerit, & Daniel Obodovski, 2013)

The importance of the "Internet of Things" is that data collected and analyzed to provide insights or actions. Integration of that data depends upon the management and security of the whole system related to that data. The choice of connectivity protocol plays an important role in the "Internet of Things" (Frank Dushlmann, Jim Moorish, & Rishi M Bhatnagar, 2016).

The important requirements such as sustainability and reliability in transmitting data over distances to heterogeneous devices need the attention of the developers of the system. The efficiency of the above requirements is important because of battery-operated sensors or electrically operated sensors embedded in stationary and moving objects.

Application updates, security patches, remotely managing the operations, and maintain ace of various devices require massive scalability and flexibility. The concept of cloud computing facilitates handling the above requirements. Robust and scalable architecture is available in private and public cloud environments.

BACKGROUND

It is a general practice business model developed under information systems that follow two methods. They are "push" and "pull" methods. When information is thrust on end-users, it is considered as a "push method". The classic examples for this method are advertisements (print and electronic media), telemarketing, and information through email and snail-mail. End users when they browse websites and go through hard copies for specific information can be termed as "pull method". It has been the practice among end-users to understand the information provided under the above methods and relate to a particular context. This means end-users are proactive in the context of computing. Now attempts are being made to make the information systems proactive to the context. Now the trend is developing context-aware applications. The word "context" has its origin in the Latin verb "contexture". It means to weave together. This meaning has more relevance in context computing. The main feature in context computing is the ability to sense and process information as per the requirements of end-users. It relates to a particular context relevant to end-users. There are many definitions in respect of "context computing". They fall under two categories as "Enumeration Based" and "Role-Based". The former category talks about context in terms of its various categorization. The second category is very specific in terms of its role in context-aware computing. The essence of all the various definitions can be classified under five categories. They are (1) computing context consists of network, connectivity, communication bandwidth, and local resources. (2) User context considers profile, location, and people in the vicinity of the user. (3) Physical context includes lighting and noise levels, traffic conditions, and temperature (4) temporal context talks about the time of day, week, month, and season of the year. (5) Context history is the recording of computing, user, and physical context across the period. Further, they define context under "role-based" as the set of environmental status and settings. This either determines and application behavior or in which an application event occurs. It is interesting to the user. It can be inferred from the essence of the definitions that context-aware computing applications are developed to respond to changes in the environment in an intelligent way for the benefit of end-users. Ubiquitous and pervasive computing concepts support developing context-aware computing applications. Context-aware is also referred to as local awareness by some authors. Local aware technologies such as sensor networks enable everyday devices to become increasingly often visibly interconnected with one another and with the internet.

It is interesting to note that in the early 1990s the vision of the ubiquitous world was first introduced by Mark Weiser. In his article "The Computer of the 21st century", he described how computing technology would eventually disappear from our everyday day life and become invisible to its user. In the year 2002 Fano and Gershman have indicated that ubiquitous computing would change the way people live with technology. Further, they have observed the concept of ubiquitous computing in the information technology scenario would progressively change using everyday objects such as pencils or hinges than using a personal computer. They have also expressed that to realize these visions there would be several factors needed to be considered. The factors were such as understanding the everyday practices of people and augmenting the world through heterogeneous devices. Finally, it was required to integrate the devices through networking. This would provide a holistic user experience.

RESOURCES NEEDED FOR IOT APPLICATIONS

Coordination of various resources such as computer power, data, hardware, software, applications, devices, and internet services are required for designing the internet of things application models. The following paragraphs provide brief information related to ubiquitous, pervasive, and cloud computing. Overview of some selected devices used for IoT applications in the case illustrations discussed in this chapter is explained.

UBIQUITOUS AND PERVASIVE COMPUTING

It is interesting to note the research work related to context-aware computing started in the 1990s. The credit goes to Xerox pare laboratory and Olivetti research for initiating the research on context-aware computing.

In the mid-1990s Ubiquitous computing has also been known as pervasive computing. Ubiquitous computing refers to the blending of computing devices with environmental objects. It is a term that describes the integration of computers into practically all objects in an everyday environment endowing them with computing abilities. Ubiquitous computing is based on pervasive computing. Pervasive computing is a trend towards increasingly ubiquitous computing. It entails computing by devices connected to the environment. This enables the convergence of advanced electronic and wireless technologies, and the internet. Pervasive computing devices are handheld, very tiny, or even invisible devices which are either mobile or embedded in almost any type of object.

The environment in ubiquitous computing is a reference to location, surrounding devices, computing systems, and networks. The role of pervasive computing is to make devices adaptable to the environment. It would be apt to recall the observation of Marckweiser in the year 1991 who stated that following Moore's law, future computing environment would consist of very cheap (disposable) interacted specialized computers all around us, some embedded in our surroundings and others worn by them. Moore's law has given the name "Future Computing" for ubiquitous and pervasive computing. It can be inferred that ubiquitous computing and pervasive computing are interdependent.

Ubiquitous computing aims to design computing infrastructure to integrate them seamlessly with the environment. It can sense and process context for making a system proactive and self-tunable. Further, it supports the mobility of computing devices. Pervasive computing expects information and communication technology to be an integral part of the environment in ubiquitous computing. The demand for ubiquitous personal communication is making new networking techniques to support end-users who move in multi-complex buildings, cities, and countries.

Ubiquitous Computing and Cloud Computing

There is a common feature in ubiquitous and cloud computing. The function of both computing is to provide information services regardless of place.

The other important characteristic is to support computing capabilities and databases wherever situated globally. The resources are connected. It is complementary to each other.

CLOUD COMPUTING ENVIRONMENT

There are two types' players in the cloud computing environment. One is a service provider. Another one is making use of the services provided by a service provider. A service provider owns the various types of hardware and software. Here the software is related to system and business application software. The amount spent by a service provider for acquiring hardware and software is considered a capital expenditure or investment. A service provider applies the capital budgeting methods for evaluating the investment on the assets before deciding on the investment. There are different methods of costing for arriving at the cost service provided to the end-users. They are actual costing, cost-benefit analysis, activity costing, and opportunity costing. Profit is added to the cost of service arrived by one of the above methods. One of the methods will be applied based on the requirements of a particular user of the service (Golden B, June 2012).

DEVICES

Information and communication technology is the driving force for the production of new generation devices working on wireless technology. These devices have been providing workable solutions in virtual environment scenarios. Currently, mobile devices range in sensors, embedded controllers, pocket computers, notebooks, personal digital assistants, and mobile phones. All these devices become more useful when they support personal and business applications (Jatin Desai, 2013).

These devices can be classified under four categories. They are (1) dedicated devices – designed for a particular functionality; (2) integrated devices integration of functions in different devices, (3) modular devices- bringing devices into one shell, and (4) federated devices – connecting different parts of devices.

There are segments such as embedded systems, consumer electronics, and handheld devices that are expected to grow and support pervasive computing devices. Embedded systems are not visible to end-users. They are embedded in products and appliances. Consumer electronics have pervasive computing elements in digital cameras, video recorders, electronic books, and mp3 players/recorders with wireless modems access directly to the internet. Hand-held devices are mobile phones, pagers, PDA's, and mobile personal computers. These systems are enablers in ubiquitous computing.

PRESENT SCENARIO

In recent times handset makers have been queuing up to launch devices that have unique features. The most valued current paradigm however is the ability of business applications system developers to make use of these devices in a ubiquitous computing environment (Nabyla Daidj, 2015). Some of these devices with their unique features are developed for particular applications (Scott Shane, 2008). It may be noted that the potential for possible applications is limited by the imagination. Some of the devices available in the market are described with their special features.

BRIEF FEATURES OF ELECTRONIC DEVICES

Brief features of some of the selected electronic devices available in the electronic market are given below. They are not exhaustive.

Electronic Bracelets

This is an electronic ankle tracker bracelet system. It has a global positioning system embedded in the device. It will be helpful for people who go trekking.

Voice-enabled Mobile Phones:

This device has a feature to announce the caller's identity and also reads out Small messages (SMS). This is designed for the visually impaired, senior citizens, illiterate, and people who are not comfortable using a cellphone. It supports many different languages at the global level.

E-Book Reader

An E-Book reader is a portable reader system. It is expected to supplement conventional books. Users can carry a collection of books. Users can carry a collection of books around. It has a high-resolution electronic paper display which provides a comfortable reading experience. Users can connect to an e-book store for downloading the required material for reading.

Camera Sunglasses

This is a digital camera embedded in the frame. It can snap pictures.

Electronic Shelf Labeling

This system transmits from a retailer's product price file to wireless electronic shelf labels that are located at the product's shelf. Retailers can select among different display sizes as well as choose labels that can be mounted on peg hooks, existing fixtures, refrigerator units, and freezers.

Home Theatre Watch

Home theatre watch is designed to provide the experience of watching a film sitting in a chair at home, waiting at a doctor's clinic, or traveling on a train. It has the functionality of a watch also.

Mobile Multimedia

The mobile multimedia device provides access to a rich world of entertainment and information. It also facilitates the creation and sharing of content through this device. It has the feature of video recording.

Personal Digital Assistant (PDA)

This device is also known as a palmtop computer. This is a mobile device that functions as a personal information manager and can connect to the internet. PDA has an electronic visual display enabling it to include a web browser. Many PDAs can have access to the internet, intranets, or extranets via Wi-Fi or wireless wide area networks. Many PDAs employ touch screen technology. PDAs are used to store information that can be accessed at any time and anywhere. PDA's can be used for automobile navigation, medical and scientific purposes, educational and sporting purposes also.

Drone

A drone in a technological context is an unmanned aircraft. Drones are more formally known as unmanned aerial vehicles (UAVs) or unmanned aircraft systems (UAS). Essentially, a drone is a flying robot. The aircraft may be remotely controlled or can fly autonomously through software-controlled flight plans in their embedded systems working in conjunction with onboard sensors or GPS.

Smartphone

The main feature of a smartphone is a mobile communications device. This device optimizes in its specification and features to support one or more primary functions like music, video, gaming, pictures, browsing, mobile TV, navigation, and messaging. These devices have larger displays more powerful. It can also be mentioned that smartphones combine cell phones and PDA's into a single device that offers much of the same functionality as a basic computer.

I Phone

The iPhone offers many of the advanced features found on computer devices, but it also differs from other smartphones on the market.

Tablet

Tablets do not use a traditional keyboard and mouse as their primary forms of input. The user interface of a tablet is different than a typical laptop. For example instead of double-clicking to open a program, most applications open with a single tap.

Rental Car Recording Device

The starting mileage and ending mileage of the car used by a customer can be obtained by a person standing near the car. The customer need not spend more time at the rental car office. The rental car office will transfer the data to their database.

Graphic Information System (GIS)

There seems to be an impression among many people that computer-aided design, computer-aided cartography (CAC), and geographic information systems (GIS) are all the same because the graphic display from each of these systems is almost the same. CAC system is used to create maps from geographical objects and their descriptive attributes. It does not have analytical features. CAD system helps to generate graphic images. Remotely sensed satellite data are the source for GIS.

Compatibility Between Remote Sensing and GIS

Remote sensing systems have a very important feature for the collection and classification of spatial data. GIS is used for managing and analyzing spatial data. Thus both systems are complementary to each other. Many advancements are taking place in satellite sensors of very high resolution.

Satellite Sensors of Very High-Resolution Sensor

A sensor device that detects and responds to some type of input from the physical environment. The specific input could be light, heat, motion, moisture, pressure, or any one of a grant number of other environmental phenomena. The output is generally a signal that is converted to a human-readable display at the sensor location or transmitted electronically over a network for reading or further processing.

CASE ILLUSTRATIONS

There are many electronic devices available in the market. Many of these devices are already made use of in different contexts. The following illustrations explain making use of these devices in an innovative way for developing business models. These business models will be useful for business purposes as well as making the life of people enjoy.

Case Illustration-1

A voluntary organization in India wants to make the life of senior citizens enjoyable who live alone in their houses. They need various types of information for their day-to-day activities. They need to necessarily know about the climate conditions. Their decision to go out of their houses depends on the information about climate conditions. Senior citizens may not have the patience to browse the various websites to get the required information. A group of people at the voluntary organization have decided to identify the devices that would be more useful for senior citizens in their daily activities.

The voluntary organization has installed the devices at convenient places in their residence that will draw their attention to plan their activities. This will make the senior citizen's life easy. Climate digital display device is installed in a living room to display that day's likely temperature. A link is established to climate digital display device to a web site providing the information relating to the place where the senior citizens are living. Another digital display system has been mounted on the wardrobe. This device would suggest the types of clothes to be worn for the type of climate on that day. One more digital device has been installed at the umbrella and coat stand. The display on the system draws the senior citizen's attention whether it is required to carry an umbrella or raincoat or both (Mahamed Hisham Moubarak, 2016). The above types of information have been provided through the climate digital system by using web semantic concepts.

Discussion Related to Case Illustration-1

It is interesting to note a voluntary organization has taken the initiative to help senior citizens who live alone in their homes, make their lives enjoyable. Most of the senior citizens prefer to lead their lives independently. A group of volunteers who are associated with a voluntary organization has identified the electronic devices that would be more useful for senior citizens. This is an open innovation approach for making use of electronic devices that would facilitate the senior citizens to take care of themselves in their daily routine needs.

Case Illustration-2

Travel world services (TWS) has been in the travel agency business for over two decades in India. TWS has been providing the usual services such as holiday packages and organizing for booking air/train tickets, and transport services. Most of their clients are senior citizens. They are young in mind and they have also an adventurous spirit. In recent times many travel agencies have entered the field. Competition is becoming very tough. The management of TWS has felt the need for an innovative way to provide their services. The task of designing an innovative business model is given to a group of executives in their organization. The task group has taken up as a challenge in creating a new business model in the tourism sector. The task group had interaction with their regular clients and their younger members of their families. They inferred from their interactions with them their clients are interested in trekking and drive the cars by themselves (Bardhan I, Krishan V, Lin S, 2013). Some of them want to learn to cook Indian dishes. They have understood some of the senior citizens are interested in trekking.

New Approach Suggested by the Task Group

They have identified two types of customers among the senior age group: (1) some would like to do trekking during their vacation, and (2) another group would like to hire cars driving by themselves going around the places in India. Three types of devices have been identified for the above type of customers. Bracelet is embedded with a global positioning system. Sunglass is embedded with a digital camera. A handheld set is to be used for the process of returning rental cars.

Bracelet with GPS

This device will help them to guide the route for their trekking. In case any guidance is needed, the office in TWS can be contacted. This type of device will be useful for people even if they are not familiar with the area of places being visited by them.

Rental Car Recording Device

The starting mileage and ending mileage of the car used by the client can be obtained by a person standing near the car. The client need not spend more time at the rental car office. The rental car office will transfer the data to the database at the TWS office.

Camera in Sunglasses

A digital camera embedded in the frame facilitates a client to snap pictures while trekking.

Other Devices

Other devices such as a home theatre watch an e-book reader are provided on request from the clients.

Ubiquitous Computing at TWS

The computing infrastructure at the TWS office and the devices used by the car rental office are integrated by TWS under a ubiquitous computing environment.

Discussion Related to Case Lustration-2:

The travel service organization has taken interest in providing services to senior citizens who are interested to travel either in groups or alone. The travel services organization has identified the electronic devices used by senior citizens while trekking and driving cars without the drivers (Maish Wadhwa & Alan Harper, 2015). Especially a bracelet with GPS fitted will guide senior citizens in their trekking expedition. Books that will be of their interest are loaded into an electronic reader and provided to them. Further, they need not carry a camera for taking photos. Sunglasses fitted with digital cameras are provided to them. Travel world services have set an example for creating an open innovation travel business model (Christensen, Clayton M, Bower, Joseph L, 1995).

Case Illustration – 3

ROA mart is the largest marketer and distributor of consumer durables, consumer goods, and spare parts for tractors, medicines, and electronic devices. They have a head office in Chennai and 20 outlets across the rural places in South India. They have been in business for over three decades. Their relationship with the vendors and customers has been excellent. They have been procuring the products for their mart direct from the source of supply. The sources of procurement are from farmers, pharmaceutical companies, manufacturers of consumer durables, electronic devices, and tractor spare parts. The outlets for the sale of the procured products are retail outlets. They have also authorized distributors for some of the products procured by them. They have a tie-up with selected transporters for transporting their products to their retail outlets. They have integrated information systems for their business activities in the cloud computing environment (Claire Rowland, Martin Charier, Alfred Lui, Elizabeth Goodman, and Ann light, 2015).

Business Issue

It has been to the notice of the management that the products are not supplied to various retail outlets as per the orders placed by their customers. There is also delay in transporting the products to the customers. The management was concerned about these issues. The management was under the impression that everything was under control with the integrated information system in their company. The management has raised these issues at their weekly meetings with their executives. At the meeting, it has been decided that the junior executives who are familiar with the latest concepts in information technology should be assigned the task of finding a solution to their business issue (Humphry Hung, Y.H.Wong, & Vincent Cho, 2009)

A Solution to the Business Issue

The task force studied the exiting business process of the distribution of the products to the various outlets. After analyzing the issue from the different perspectives, the task force felt that the electronic devices are required to facilitate in getting information for the smooth flow of distribution of products to their retail outlets. The task force has identified the following electronic devices useful for their business. Open innovation initiatives among them made them think differently. Their initiative has facilitated the creation of a trading activity information system separately. The information in the new system is transferred to their existing integrated information system. This will help to have better control over the movement of their products.

Ware House

The warehouse consists of packages that are ready for dispatch, pasted with a slip containing certain characters. It is not easily decoded by human beings. A device that can read these characters is known as MICR (magnetic ink character recognition). OCR (Optical Character Recognition) is another device that is also used for this purpose. This device helps to transmit the data to a ubiquitous trading model. This facilitates the process of documentation for the packages to be dispatched (Smith, A.D, 2008).

Retail Outlet

An electronic shelf labeling system transmits information from a retailer's product size to wireless electronic shelf labels that are located on the product's shelf. Retailers can select among different display sizes as well as choose among labels that can be mounted on peg hooks and store fixtures (In Lee, 2015).

Whole Sale Group

At the time of placing orders with the formers for their products, the actual product can be viewed on a hand device with multimedia features.

Pharmaceutical Manufacturers

They can be provided with access to the database at ROA mart for the movement of their products and can know the stock position. Accordingly, dispatches can be organized by pharmaceutical manufacturers to ROA mart.

Consumer Durables

The packages of consumer durables occupy more space. The exact availability of space can be seen through a device with a multimedia feature. Executives at the head office can view the space available at the warehouse and place orders accordingly with the manufacturers of consumer durables (Smith A D, 2010).

Transporters

The movement of trucks carrying their products from Roa Mart to their outlets and their customers can be monitored through the GPRS system installed in the trucks.

Air Freight Transport

The movement of packages booked through aircraft can be traced in the websites provided by the respective air freight carriers.

Discussion Related to Case Illustration-3

ROA mart has been in the business of distributing products such as consumer and consumer durable products to retail outlets. These outlets are located at different locations in South India. Their business has been increasing year after year. ROA mart has felt that there is a need for control overstocking the products and movement of their products. RAO mart has identified the various electronic devices that will facilitate them to manage the movement of their products in their distribution business. It is also interesting to note the expiry dates of medicines are made known to pharmaceutical companies well in advance for replacement. Similarly identifying the place for storing consumer durable products can be organized after knowing the exact space available for storage. The electronic devices identified by they are useful in the logistics in managing their business. Necessity has made ROA Martin making use of the devices for developing open innovation models useful to their business (Althonayan A., & Sharif, A.M, 2010).

Case Illustration -4

Students of high schools in the rural areas in South India pursue their academic courses in Indian languages. English is also part of their courses. Many of the students are not comfortable in the English language. English is being an international language many of the students want to be more familiar with the English language. They have the ambition to study abroad for post-graduation programs. There is no proper guidance for learning the English language as per international standards. A group of educated youngsters who studied in English medium with city background wanted to help them in achieving their ambition (Aye Kok, 2016). They thought that they could go to the rural areas by rotation to teach them the English language. After visiting the rural areas, they realized it would not be possible to assemble the students in one place. It is because the villages are scattered in a district. These are not high schools in all the villages. Only some villages have high schools.

The approach followed by the group of Educated Youngsters:

The group of educated youngsters felt that they would need to find an innovative way to help them. They have discussed among themselves various options. They have given smartphones to the selected students who will be given the task of monitoring the other students. They have agreed that it would be better to provide PDA (personal digital assistants) devices to make them learn the English language. They have developed a learning tool and loaded it in the PDAS (3-Aziz S, Shamin M, Aziz M F& Avais P, 2013). They have planned to provide the students with this device. They have designed the teaching tool keeping the background of the students in their minds. At their request, a few senior citizens have taken the responsibility of contacting the students at the various villages. They have organized to assemble them at a continent place in their district. The youngsters visited the village where the students are assembled and addressed the students. They have explained and demonstrated in using the PDAs with the teaching tool developed by them

The Essence of the Teaching Tool

Most of the students have basic knowledge of the English language. They start reading an English text and click on an unknown word to see its meaning. They need to have deep knowledge of every word and framing sentences with every word. They can read a few examples and other cases of usage of the same word. They can also go through the list of words that are derived from the chosen one and later continue reading the text. At the same time, they can take notes on the words they are learning. So that they can re-read them again later. The teaching tool has the goal to give a concrete example in learning content to the user in a ubiquitous way. This is a tailor-made tool to suit a specific type of student (Lam L, 2012).

Discussion Related to Case Illustration-4

PDAs (Personal Digital Assistant) are made use in the place where internet facility is not available. A group of educated youth who had their education in the English medium has designed and developed a teaching tool as per the requirements and background of the students. Their teaching tool is more useful to the students who do not have the required guidance in learning the English language as per the international standard. The teaching tool has helped the students to pursue higher studies in well-known universities abroad. The group of educated youth has thought differently and created an open innovative teaching model with PDA.

Case Illustration – 5

Farmers in the rural part of South India mainly concentrate on growing a particular type of crop. Most of them are not familiar with the new techniques of agricultural production. They are eager to learn and make use of the new techniques in agricultural crop production.

Unfortunately, they do not know when they are expected to contact for guidance. The locations of cultivable land are scattered in the different parts of the rural area of South India. The output of the agricultural products varies based on various reasons. Some of the reasons are improper irrigation facilities, not familiar with the use of pesticides and fertilizers.

A team of agricultural scientists with doctorate degrees in agricultural science has decided to render their services to the formers who would need guidance in cultivation and marketing. This team has rich experience and knowledge in the various aspects of agricultural production and marketing. The team has planned to visit the farmlands for assessing the actual requirements for guidance. Most of the agricultural land is located at various locations. They felt it is a time-consuming process to visit the various locations of the agricultural land. They would want to discuss with the farmers, after getting an idea of the physical location of various agricultural land (Tiwari A K, 2010).

The Approach Followed by the Agricultural Scientists

The agricultural scientists have decided to use a device to know the physical appearance and location of the agricultural land. They felt drones could be used for scanning the area of cultivable land. They have hired a drone. Four cameras are filled in the drone (Hameed M A, Counsell S & Swift S, (2012). The images of the various areas have been captured. They have made use of drone in different locations for capturing the images of cultivable land

(Quazi S A, 2009).

Action Plan

The agricultural scientists have studied the images captured by them in the cameras fitted in the drone. They have stored the images and data about these images are stored in the data warehouse in the cloud computing environment. The agricultural scientists who live in a different part of the country can have access to the data for analysis and professional work. They have made use of tablets and iPhones for professional interactions among themselves. Based on their study, they have preferred a tentative plan. They sought the help of village heads for convening a meeting with the farmers. The meeting took place at a convent place agreed by all of them.

The agricultural scientists talked with the farmers. During their interaction, images of their land are shown to them. The agricultural scientists understood their problems and their requirements. They have explained many aspects of new techniques in agricultural production.

A few farmers who can grasp many aspects related to agriculture are provided with smartphones. These farmers will be in contact with the agricultural scientists. They will be given the responsibility of monitoring other farmers. The agricultural scientists felt that it would be better to provide PDAs (Personal Digital Assistants) with the information for their use. The farmers may not remember all the aspects related to the new techniques discussed at the meeting. PDAs have been provided with information to the farmers. They have also organized farmers tractors for cultivation. They are made available on the payment of nominal hire charges (Vikas Mehra, Chawla CP, Sarmistha Sharma & Sundeep Roy Dey (2011).

A farmer's tractor is fitted with GPS units inside the cabin of a farmer's tractor. GPS unit will help them for spraying less fertilizer and fewer pesticides. This will benefit the farmers in these times of rising costs of fuel, seed, and fertilizers (Hameed M A, Counsell S & Swift S, 2012).

The following information useful to farmers has been loaded in the PDAs.

1. Good Agricultural Practices:

Dissemination of knowledge about low-cost technologies is provided.

2. Deteriorating Soil Health:

Appropriate measures such as diversification, balanced fertilizers, and use of B.T.O. fertilization are explained.

3. Supplemental Life-Saving Irrigation:

Lifesaving irrigation facilities are explained to harvest and manage rainwater through BIO industrial watersheds as against exploitation of groundwater.

4. Critical Inputs:

The importance of inputs such as BIO fertilizers, Sulfur, Zinc, and Biopesticides is explained. The need for starting co-operative societies for getting the above inputs at economical prices is suggested.

5. Village Level Seed Distribution System:

Low-cost innovative seed systems will be encouraged through public and private participation models.

6. Minimize post-Harvest Losses:

Scientific storage practices are explained.

7. Storage Policy Point:

Innovative value chains for the agriculture products and strategies for improving marketing and best practices are explained.

8. Marketing:

Investment in market infrastructure and information systems is explained.

Discussion Related to Case Illustration-5

Farmers who live in the rural parts of South India do not have the required support and guidance in acquiring the latest technology in agricultural production and marketing. Qualified and experienced agricultural

Scientists have identified the devices such as PDAs, drones, and farmer's tractors with GPS fitted for the benefit of farmers. The group has created an open innovation agricultural model in updating the knowledge required for the formers in their agricultural activities year after year (Henry William Chesbrough, 2013).

CONCLUSION

Many technologies tend to be applicable only in specific industries and defined areas of operations in manufacturing or business. In the case of Information and communication technology is different. The potential of information and communication technology in business, government, and human activities are more useful. Information and communication technology provides several concepts that enable business, government, and human activities are more universal. Some of the concepts have created opportunities for designing and manufacturing electronic devices. The connectivity of these devices to other systems through the internet has created a new concept known as the internet of things, Open innovative thinking needs to be applied in identifying the electronic devices for designing and developing business models (Sanjiva Shankar Dubey, 2009). The macro-level design of business models in the IoT environment is discussed in this chapter. The usefulness of every electron device depends on the particular situation in an activity. Business models discussed in this chapter give an idea in identifying the context related to the user's benefit. The critical part of the IoT environment is establishing the link between the environment and pervasive devices (Lawrence C Miller, 2018).

REFERENCES

Althonayan, A., & Sharif, A. M. (2010). Aligning business and technology strategy within the airline industry. *International Journal of Business Information Systems*, *6*(1), 79–94. doi:10.1504/IJBIS.2010.034006

Aziz, S., Shamin, M., Aziz, M. F., & Avais, P. (2013). *The Impact of Texting/ SMS Language on Academic Writing of Students-What do we need to panic about*. Elixir Languages and Translations.

Bardhan, I., Krishnan, V., & Lin, S. (2013). Business Value of Information Technology: Testing the Interaction Effect of IT and R&D on Tobin's Q. *Information Systems Research*.

Chesbrough. (2003). *Open Innovation: The New Imperative for Creating and Profiting from Technology*. HBS Press.

Christensen, C. M., & Bower, J. L. (1995). Disruptive Technologies: Catching the wave. *Harvard Business Review*.

David, N. (2015). *Developing Strategic Business Models and Competitive Advantage in the Digital Sector*. IGI Global.

Desai. (2013). *Innovation Engine Driving Execution for Breakthrough Result*. New Delhi: Wiley India Private Limited.

Dubey. (2009). Innovation with IT. Tata McGraw Hill Publishing Company Limited.

Dushlmann, Moorish, & Bhatnagar. (2016). Enterprise IoT Strategies and Best Practices Connected to Products and Services. O'Reilly.

Golden, B. (2012, June). How Cloud Computing can Transform Business Boston. *Harvard Business Review*.

Hameed, M. A., Counsell, S., & Swift, S. (2012). A Conceptual Model for the Process of IT Innovation Adoption in Organizations. *Journal of Engineering and Technology Management*, *29*(3), 358–390. doi:10.1016/j.jengtecman.2012.03.007

Hameed, M. A., Counsell, S., & Swift, S. (2012). A Conceptual Model for the Process of IT Innovation Adoption in Organizations. *Journal of Engineering and Technology Management*.

Hung, Wong, & Cho. (2009). Ubiquitous Commerce for Creating the Personalized Market Place. IGI Global.

Kellmereit, D. (2013). *Daniel Obodovski (2013) the Silent Intelligence: Internet of Things*. DND Ventures.

Kok, A. (2016). *Cultural, Behavioral and Social Considerations in Electronic Collaboration*. IGI Global. doi:10.4018/978-1-4666-9556-6

Lam, L. (2012). An Innovative Research on the Usage of FaceBook in the Higher Education Context of Hong Kong. *The Electronic Journal of e-Learning*.

Lee, I. (2015). *RFID Technology Integration for Business Performance Improvement*. IGI Global. doi:10.4018/978-1-4666-6308-4

Mehra, Chawla, Sharma, & Dey. (2011). *New Paradigms in Business Management and Information Technology*. Kunal Books.

Miller. (2018). IOT Solutions Dummies. John Wiley & Sons Inc.

Moubarak. (2016). Internet of Things for Home Automation. Media Engineering and Technology Faculty, German University in Cairo.

Qazi, S. A. (2009). *Principles of Physical Geography*. APH Publishing Corporation.

Rowland, Charier, Lui, Goodman, & Light. (2015). *Designing Connected Products: UX for the consumer Internet of Things*. O'Reilly.

Shane. (2008). Hand Book of Technology and Innovation Management England. John Wiley & Sons Limited.

Smith, A. D. (2008). Modernizing retail grocery business via knowledge management-based systems. *Journal of Knowledge Management*, *12*(3), 114–126. doi:10.1108/13673270810875903

Smith, A. D. (2010). Retail-based loyalty card programs & CRM concepts: An empirical study. *International Journal of Innovation and Learning*, *7*(3), 303–330. doi:10.1504/IJIL.2010.031949

Tiwari, A. K. (2010). *Infrastructure for Sustainable Rural Development*. Regal Publications.

Wadhwa & Harper. (2015). *Technology, Innovation and Enterprise Transformation*. IGI Global.

ADDITIONAL READING

Attaran, M. (2020, July). Digital technology enablers and their implications for the supply chain management. In Supply Chain Forum. *International Journal (Toronto, Ont.)*, *21*(3), 158–172.

Luthra, S., Kumar, A., Zavadskas, E. K., Mangla, S. K., & Garza-Reyes, J. A. (2020). Industry 4.0 as an enabler of sustainability diffusion in the supply chain: An analysis of influential strength of drivers in an emerging economy. *International Journal of Production Research*, *58*(5), 1505–1521. doi:10.1080/00207543.2019.1660828

Nasiri, M., Tura, N., & Ojanen, V. (2017, July). Developing disruptive innovations for sustainability: a review on Impact of Internet of Things (IoT). In *2017 Portland International Conference on Management of Engineering and Technology (PICMET)* (pp. 1-10). IEEE. 10.23919/PICMET.2017.8125369

Section 3
E-Commerce

Chapter 9
Impact of Consumer Internet Self-Efficacy and User Friendliness of Websites on E-Commerce Adoption

Shirin Alavi
https://orcid.org/0000-0001-8743-6701
Jaypee Institute of Information Technology, India

Vandana Ahuja
https://orcid.org/0000-0002-4512-7203
Amity Business School, Amity University, Noida, India

ABSTRACT

The e-commerce market has grown tremendously in India over the last few years across all product categories and industry verticals. In this chapter, an attempt has been made to identify and explore the two factors that influence the success of adoption of e-commerce by apparel selling firms in India. The explored factors are the consumer internet self-efficacy (derived from compatibility) and user friendliness of websites (derived from trialability). Further, relationship between the factors and their influence on the successful adoption of e-commerce has been analysed through structured equation modelling (SEM) technique. Thus, this research study adds on to earlier research studies pertaining to innovation and diffusion theory. The findings will be helpful for the decision makers and managers in recognizing the most important circumstances under which the apparel selling firms will go for e-commerce adoption.

INTRODUCTION

In past the Indian consumers have disapproved purchasing apparels online as there is always a tendency to touch, feel and take trial of the garments prior to purchasing them. Due to this the e-commerce experts always believed that though apparel is one of the most prominent segments in retail, the consumers may

DOI: 10.4018/978-1-7998-7192-7.ch009

hold back buying them online. The huge plethora of e-commerce websites has proved this wrong. The various e-commerce companies like "Jabong", "Zovi", "Voonik", "India Rush" and "Lime road" have been able to generate a sufficient customer share. The rapid evolutions in technology and marketing have helped these companies to acquire and retain customers. These companies impose the right mix of switching barriers so that they are able to generate repeat business from their customers. The Indian market is in growth stage for products like apparel, footwear, baby care and skincare products. The present studies indicate that urban Indian consumers have become quite cognizant of fashion and the searches done on Google also confirm the same. The entire fashion market is growing at an alarming rate. In the near future the online population in India would grow stupendously further adding to the increase in sale of apparels through online medium.

In order to fascinate customers these online e-commerce companies have spent considerably on technology, automated warehouses and digital marketing. Thus we can say that future is dazzling for online clothing in India. Several factors have contributed towards this. Some of them are superior brands, special deals and discounts for various customer categories, special price categories (due to various price effects that exist in the online domain) and fabulous return policy. Further a rise in women shoppers along with growing demand for fashionable clothes will add to the revenues for these companies.

BACKGROUND

Internet

The technology and communication have been transformed by internet in a stupendous manner. It is one of the significant inventions of the present era that has completely transformed the processes and mechanisms within and outside the organizations. "The internet is world-wide mechanism for interaction between people and their computers without the regard of geographic location" (Melgarejo-Heredia, R., Carr, L., & Halford, S. 2016). Hoffman and Novak (1996) called the internet as a "huge marketing opportunity". The evolution of internet has given rise to various internet marketing techniques. These techniques enable the organizations to generate, transform, promote and trade their products in a novel manner. The usage of internet has increased considerably in the present era. The e-commerce organizations have also witnessed a phenomenal growth because of the advent of internet. The urban Indian consumers accept that internet plays a vital role in their lives (Hofacker C. F., Murphy J., 2009). These consumers use internet for conducting sale and purchase transactions but also to perform a relative examination of product features, product price and after sale service facilities.

Online Customer Experience

The familiarity with the internet is one of the most important factor which affects the online shopping and customer experience across different cultures and countries (Constantinides, E., Lorenzo-Romero, C., & Gomez, M. A. 2010). Lemke, F., Clark, M., & Wilson, H. (2011) have suggested a value- in- use approach emphasizing the importance of customer experience management in order to create a balance between the organizations offering and customers requirement. Rose, S., Clark, M., Samouel, P., & Hair, N. (2012) propose that in online environments the consumer and the firm nurture the experiences together. Further online customer satisfaction is directly reflected in repurchases made by the consumers. This repurchase intention is also a measure of online trust. Trevinal, A. M., & Stenger, T. (2014) have proposed in their research that online shopping experiences are a function of "physical, ideological, pragmatic and social dimensions". The online consumers look for more product variety and better distribution networks. The present day consumers purchase those products from internet that are quite frequently purchased, are liked by their peer group, are quite different from the products offered by competitors in that category.

E-Commerce

The E-commerce sector has grown at a very rapid pace in India. India has even left behind China in terms of number of online shoppers (Vaithianathan, S. 2010). The significant categories of electronic shopping in India include apparel, electronics, books, home appliances and shoes. E-commerce has emerged as a significant medium which helps the organizations to handle technological and organizational insufficiency (Al-Qirim, N. 2007).The technological developments help the organizations for customer engagement, better brand proliferation, improve customer care and communication. The e-commerce companies have to be quite visible, easily accessible and navigable. The organizations need to conduct constant monitoring for measuring the success of their e-commerce applications. Some of the significant parameters which need a constant check include number of visitors, product affinity, size of social media followers etc.Sharma, S., & Gutierrez, J. A. (2010) have found that e-commerce provides various benefits for organizations such as greater customer base, tapping new markets, increased communication with customers, better brand proliferation and enhanced sales. Though the number of internet users have grown in India but still it is far behind the developed nations.

Consumers Internet Self- Efficacy and E-Commerce Adoption

The Internet self-efficacy of consumers can be described as the level of confidence that an individual possesses in using the Internet.(Joyce M., Kirakowski J. 2014).The study conducted by Y.J. Joo, M. Bong, H.J. Choi (2000) depicts the importance of internet self-efficacy on the performance of students in web based instruction. The various research studies have proved that Internet self efficacy has a positive influence on the internet usage. Internet self-efficacy is a very important consumer trait which facilitates online shopping and e-commerce adoption. It also has a remarkable effect on online search performance (Hill, W. W., & Beatty, S. E., 2011).

User Friendliness of Websites and E-Commerce Adoption

Most of the researchers have concluded that user friendliness of websites has a significant impact on online shopping and e-commerce adoption. Some of the website characteristics which are important for e-commerce adoption by consumers are high level of interactivity of website domain, ease of navigation, readability of website, website reputation and reach, diversity of content, clarity of information, and degree of traffic on website(Ganguly, B., Dash, S. B., & Cyr, D. 2009, Mahadin, B., Akroush, M. N., & Bata, H. 2020).Further research studies have proved that a greater level of customer loyalty is generated if the website is updated regularly and required content diversity is maintained (Mithas et. al 2007).In a nutshell it can be summed that interactivity, feasibility, convenience and user requirements are the important attributes that organizations should keep in mind while designing websites. If the website is not up to the expectation of the consumers they are likely to switch to another website(Dadzie, K. Q., Johnston, W. J., & Pels, J. 2008).The perceived quality of website is an important determinant which can be used as a switching barrier and even gain visitor loyalty(Cristobal, E., Flavian, C., &Guinaliu, M. 2007).

Proposed Research Model and Hypotheses

The available literature on e-commerce offers several theories to investigate the determinant factors of e-commerce adoption by apparel selling firms. The four most commonly used are the "Theory of Reasoned Action (TRA); the Theory of Planned Behavior (TPB); the Technology Acceptance Model (TAM); The Diffusion of Innovation Theory (IDT)".The "Theory of Reasoned Action" developed by Fishbein and Ajzen (1975) supported that the behavior of individuals is an outcome of the intention to do so. This intention further depends on "attitude and subjective norm" (Davis, Bagozzi, &Warshaw, 1989).This model was highly criticized by researchers as it was not able to explain a situation where actual behavior and intention are extremely interrelated (Yousafzai, Foxall, & Pallister, 2010). In order to improve upon this limitation the "Theory of Planned Behaviour" was introduced by Ajzen (1991). In this theory a new construct called "Perceived Behavioral Control" was introduced. This was further criticized by various researchers as being not able to give the desired results in a situation where actual behavior and intention are extremely interrelated.

The "Technology Acceptance Model" developed by Davis in 1989 was able to improve the shortcomings of the previous models. This model also used the basic framework of "Theory of Reasoned Action". This model concluded that behavioral intention is determined by both "attitude toward" and "perceived usefulness". Further a strong criticism also came out for this model that it ignored various extrinsic and intrinsic factors of the organization.

Further "Innovation diffusion model" came up with a very new perspective i.e. a "process-oriented" perspective. This model explained in detail the process of receiving and dispersing the innovation among people (Tao, Y. H., Cheng, C. J., & Sun, S. Y, 2009).The main factors that described the pace of adoption of innovation according to "Innovation diffusion model" are "compatibility, complexity, trialability and observability".

From the above discussion the "Innovation diffusion model" is chosen as the theoretical basis for the development of our research because of the factors that explain the pace of adoption of innovation.

For the purpose of current study an **Evaluation Grid 1** (Appendix) was formulatedand circulated to a focus group of 20 participants, who were asked to rate the five determinants of the "Innovation Diffusion Model" on a scale of 1-5 (5-Excellent, 1–Poor).These respondents were practitioners from the industry who were well versed with different concepts of e-commerce and the theories behind its evolution.A free-flowing group discussion was held, and the participants were asked to actively participate in the discussion. On the basis of the rating of the experts the two most important determinants for online apparel selling e-commerce firms came out to be "*compatibility*" and "*trialability*". These two determinants were further explored by literature review in order to draw the constructs explored in this research paper.

Thus the present research paper strives to determine how the consumer internet self efficacy (derived from compatibility) and userfriendliness ofwebsites (derivedfrom trialability)impact e-commerce adoption for online apparel sellingfirms. In doing so, this research paper extends earlier research on innovation and diffusion studies by offering a new perspective. The findings will also aid the decision makers to be aware of the most important circumstances under which e-commerce adoption *for online apparel selling firms is* feasible, thus preparing management for such circumstances and future adoption decision.

Based on the literature review and the conceptual model hypothesis are formulated for the exogenous variables and the endogenous variables to explain the interrelationship between the affecting factor and their impact on the successful adoption of e-commerce for online apparel selling firms. The research model used in this study consists of two exogenous latent constructs, namely, "*Consumer Internet Self Efficacy*" and "*User Friendliness of Websites*" and an endogenous latent construct namely "*Success of e-commerce adoption*". On the basis of conceptual model the following hypotheses were formulated and investigated in the empirical analysis:

H1: Consumer Internet Self Efficacy positively affects the success of e-commerce adoption for online shopping of apparels.

H2: User Friendliness of Website positively affects the success of e-commerce adoption for online shopping of apparels.

RESEARCH METHODOLOGY

Research Instrument

The next step is to test the proposed hypothesis, for this purpose a questionnaire (Research Instrument 1) was prepared, on the basis of thorough literature review. The questionnaire was further divided into three parts. The questions related to demographic details of the respondents were mentioned in the first part of the questionnaire. The second part of questionnaire consisted of 11items on "Consumer Internet Self Efficacy" measured using a 5-point Likert scale, with choices ranging from 1 (*strongly disagree*) to 5 (*strongly agree*).The third part of the questionnaire consisted of 6 items on "User Friendliness of Websites" measured using a 5-point Likert scale, with choices ranging from 1 (*Not at all important*) to 5 (*Very Important*).

In order to gauge coherent consistencies, understanding level of questions and correct order of items, pretesting of the items was conducted. For this purpose 10 experts in e-commerce research area were contacted. All the experts had similar opinion that the questionnaire was quiet clear and easy to complete. Some of the suggestions made by experts regarding the language of the items and the overall structure of the questionnaire were included in the revised instrument. When the first draft of questionnaire was prepared there were 15 items in second part of questionnaire and 8 items in third part, but after pretesting the questionnaire, four items were dropped in second part and two in third part as they were found to be non-discriminating.

Sampling Technique and Sample Size

The study was conducted in Delhi and NCR and amongst adult Indian shoppers. The study followed a non-probability, convenience sampling design. The respondent selection was done on the basis of: a. the person resided in Delhi and NCR. b. the person is an adult c . the person is an internet user d. the person had purchased apparels online at least five times in the last one year.

The questionnaire was administered both offline and online. For online collection of data the questionnaire was drafted using Google Docs and appropriate link was mailed to respondents who fulfilled the above criteria. The respondents who fulfilled the above criteria were further selected on the basis of simple random sampling technique. It improved representativeness and discouraged multiple responses. In order to increase the number of respondents in the survey and to improve the overall response rates, up to two additional reminder invitations were typically mailed at two- to four-day intervals to those respondents who fulfilled the defined criteria but had not yet participated in the survey. A total of 600 questionnaires were distributed, of which 475 people responded, thus making the response rate to be 79%. Twenty-five questionnaires were discarded due to incomplete information, so 450 fully completed questionnaires were considered for the study. When the collection of data is done through questionnaire it is very important for researcher to see that the response rate should be more than 10 percent of the distributed questionnaires. This is important to steer clear of sample bias (Roscoe, J. T. 1975).

Sample Characteristics

Table 1 summarizes the demographic profile of the respondents. Out of 450 respondents, approximately 314 (69.7%) respondents were female and 136 (30.22%) were male. 276 respondents (61.4 percent) were in the age group of 18-25 followed by 128 respondents (28.6 percent) who were in the age group of 26-35, 45 (10%) were 36–45 years old.

Table 1. Demographic profile of the respondents

Sample Size (N)	450
Male	136
Female	314
Years of Internet Experience	9.5 years
Average number of transactions with the shopping portals in the last year	14

Source: (IGI, 2021)

MAIN FOCUS OF THE CHAPTER

Analysis of Proposed Theoretical Model

The proposed model was analyzed by two step SEM.SEM can be defined as "a second-generation multivariate technique that combines multiple regressions with confirmatory factor analysis to estimate simultaneously a series of interrelationship between the constructs of the hypothesized model".

First Step: Assessment of Reliability and Validity of Constructs

The data was analyzed using Confirmatory Factor Analysis (CFA) using AMOS that uses a co-variance based structural equation modeling (CB-SEM) for structural validation.

Composite reliability (CR) is used to measure the reliability of a construct in the measurement model. It is used to measure the overall reliability and estimates consistency of the construct itself including the stability and equivalence of construct (Hair *et al.*, 2010). A value of 0.70 or greater is deemed to be indicative of good scale reliability (Fornell and Larcker, 1981).The composite reliability of "Consumer Internet Self Efficacy" was calculated as 0.816 and "User Friendliness of Websites" as 0.874 which is above the desired criteria of 0.70 (Table 2).This depicts that both the constructs in the measurement model have good reliability.

Convergent validity shows the extent to which indicators of a specific construct converge or have a high proportion of variance in common (Hair *et al.*, 2010). It is demonstrated when factor loadings of latent to observed variables is greater than 0.50 (Hair *et al.*, 2010).The factor loading (standardized regression weights) of all observed variables are ranging from 0.60 to 0.83. This clearly indicates that observed variables or items are adequate and corresponded to their constructs. Thus construct convergent validity is confirmed.

Discriminant validity shows the extent to which a construct is truly distinct from other constructs (Hair *et al.*, 2010). The AVE extracted for the 'Consumer Internet Self Efficacy' is 0.67 and for the 'User Friendliness of Websites' is 0.71.This is above the desired levels of 0.5.Also the average variance extracted of the individual constructs are higher than the shared variances between the constructs (Table 2).Thus discriminant validity appears satisfactory at the construct level in case of both the constructs.

Second Step: Structural Assessment of Proposed Theoretical Model

The proposed structural model was evaluated with the help of various model fit indices which are depicted in Table 3. The fit indices indicate the validity of the proposed structure. For structural model analysis a wide range of fit indices are available and use of several fit indices is generally suggested. Absolute and incremental indices are the two categories of fit indices (Joreskog, K. & Sorbom, D. 1993).The absolute fit indices does not use a base line model for ascertaining the model fit and include, RMSEA, GFI, AGFI, RMR & SRMR. The incremental indices, on the other hand, uses a baseline model for ascertaining the model fit and include NFI, NNFI, CFI, PNFI.

The various fit indices indicated a good empirical validity for the proposed research model (Figure 1).The model fit indices like the comparative Fit Index (CFI), the goodness of fit index (GFI), Normed fit index (NFI), Tucker Lewis Index (TLI/NNFI) and root mean square of error approximation (RMSEA) were selected to judge the model fit (Hair *et al.*, 2010). In order to obtain an acceptable fit with data, the acceptable respective values of CMIN/df, should be less than 3, CFI,GFI, NFI and TLI should be more then 0.9 and the RMSEA value must be lower than 0.08 (Gefen, D. and Straub, D.W.2000). The CMIN/df (normed chi square) was 2.863 for the proposed model and well below 3.0 as recommended by (Wheaton et al 1997). RMSEA of less than .08 is recommended by (Mac Callum, R.C., Browne, M.W. & Sugawara, H.M. 1996), and the current model returned a RMSEA of 0.075 indicating good model fit. Hu, L.T. & Bentler, P.M., (1999) recommends CFI, GFI, NFI & NNFI should be more than 0.9 to indicate model validity. The proposed model returned 0.952, 0.890, 0.912& 0.971 for the four measures respectively indicating good fit of the proposed research model. Although the GFI value of 0.890 did not meet the verge of 0.90, its value was very close to the threshold, thus representing an acceptable model fit. A summation, of the various indices, is given in Table 3.

Table 2. Reliability and standardized regression weights

Construct	Items Description	Regression weight	Composite Reliability	Average Variance Extracted	Maximum Shared Variance
Consumer Internet Self Efficacy	Internet through a modem	0.62***	0.816	0.67	0.044
	Convenience offered	0.72***			
	Visual experience	0.81***			
	Finding information	0.68***			
	Exchange messages	0.64***			
	Like apparel selling websites	0.71***			
	Emotional satisfaction through online shopping of apparels	0.78***			
	Comfortable in navigating an e-commerce website	0.66***			
	Like e-commerce apparel selling websites offering better schemes and discounts	0.82***			
	Like e-commerce apparel selling websites which provide up-to-date information	0.79***			
	I can comfortably install an application or software	0.77***			
User Friendliness of Websites	Customer service	0.72***	0.874	0.71	0.036
	Personalized offers	0.77***			
	Large category of product comparisons	0.60***			
	Detailed product information and photo galleries of products	0.67***			
	Security and Privacy information	0.65***			
	Consumer reviews and suggestions	0.83***			

***p<0.01
Source: (IGI, 2021)

Hypothesis Testing

From Table 4 it is evident that both the proposed paths are positive and significant i.e. both consumer internet self-efficacy and user friendliness of websites affect the success of e-commerce adoption for Indian consumers in apparel segment.

Table 3. Model fit indices

	CMIN/df	RMSEA	GFI	NFI	CFI	TLI (NNFI)	P value	PCLOSE
Model	2.863	0.075	0.890	0.912	0.952	0.971	0.00	0.00

Source: (IGI, 2021)

Figure 1. Structural model (IGI, 2021)
**** p<0.01*

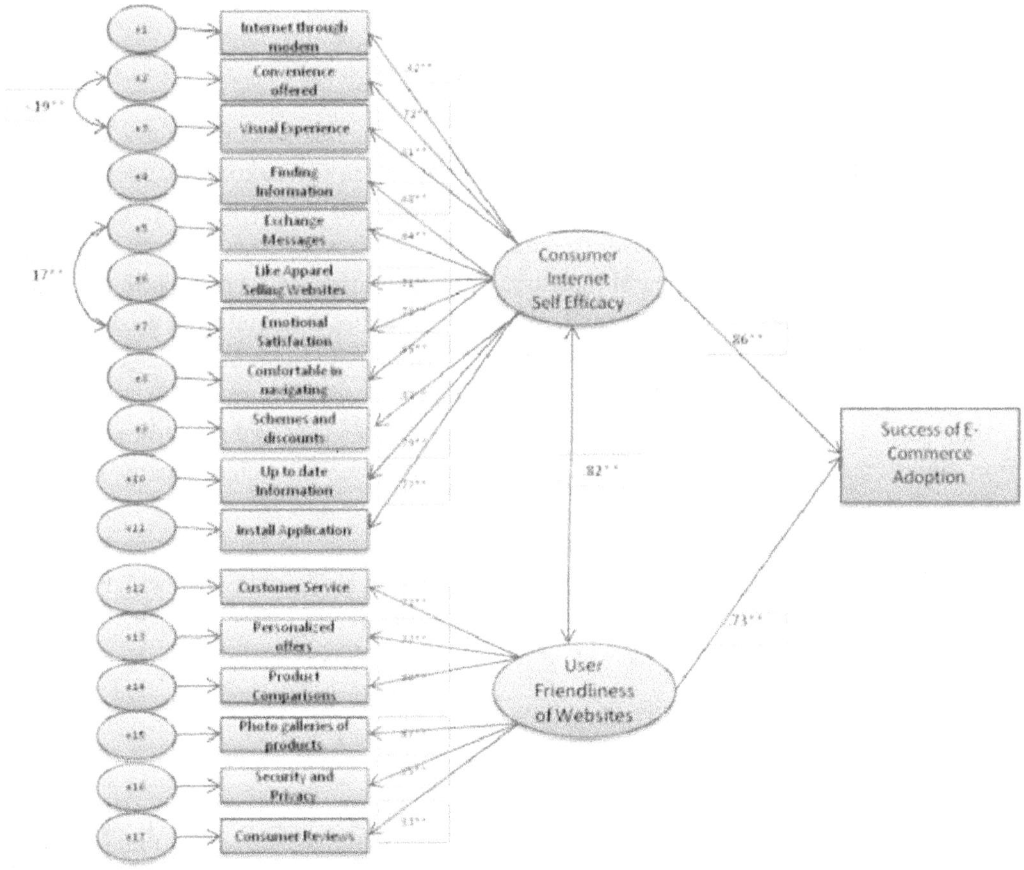

**** p< 0.01*

Table 4. Summary of results of hypothesis

Exogenous Variable	Endogenous Variable	Path Coefficient	P value	Result
Consumer Internet Self Efficacy	Success of e-commerce adoption for online shopping of apparels.	0.86	***	H1 not Rejected
User Friendliness of Websites	Success of e-commerce adoption for online shopping of apparels	0.73	***	H2 not Rejected

***p<0.01
Source: (IGI, 2021)

RESULTS

The proposed research model is corroborated through statistical findings as depicted in Figure 1. The findings support our research hypothesis 1 and 2. The construct of consumer internet self-efficacy explains 74% variance in the outcome variable and the construct user friendliness of websites accounts for 53% variance in the success of e-commerce adoption. Thus, both the proposed constructs play an important role ine-commerce adoption in Indian retail apparel sector. Also it is observed that both the factors are highly correlated (Beta Value=0.82).

CONCLUSION

This study has succeeded to appraise the factors that affect the success of e-commerce adoption in Indian retail apparel sector.It also analyses the interrelationship between the factors and their impact on the successful adoption of e-commerce using the SEMtechnique. This research paper empiricallyverifies that consumer internet self efficacy and user friendliness of websites are positively affecting the success of e-commerce adoption in Indian apparel industry. But a very important contribution is made by the study i.e. the consumers internet self-efficacy has a greater role in the adoption of e-commerce. This is the primary reason that online shopping is done by the consumers in the urban area. The organizations in Indian online apparel industry should not only focus on the user friendliness of websites but should also see whether the users are well versed in using the internet. Thus, it is the internet savvy consumer population which mostly appreciates the adoption of e-commerce in Indian apparel sector and they should be targeted accordingly.

The results are mostly unswerving with prior studies conducted in other developed countries. The study is not only useful to the apparel industry but also to other service based industries which aim to venture into e-commerce initiatives. The same research study across different industry verticals or in different countries may yield fascinating insights as well as lead to greater generalizability of the results obtained.

MANAGERIAL IMPLICATIONS

Contemporary times are witnessing the evolution of a highly computer literate and internet savvy consumer population, which spends significant volumes of time online. This generation is highly confident about traversing the internet for satisfying its hedonic agendas, for completing tasks or for merely deriving pleasure from the experience of surfing the internet. Smart managers and organisations from the e-commerce world can successfully leverage these dimensions of individual behaviour, for their benefit.

As more and more consumers get enticed by the vividness and picturesque nature of the internet, e-commerce platforms can not only induce trialability but also stimulate consumer repurchase intent. By offering convenience to the consumer, e-commerce companies can make them habitual users of the internet, and specific platforms. This prevents them from going anywhere else. Ease of accessing information and ease of navigation in the virtual spaces makes individuals regularly engage with the online media-a trait that will work out for the benefit of e-commerce organisations which want more and more consumers to buy from them.

REFERENCES

Ajzen, I. (1991). The theory of planned behavior. *Organizational Behavior and Human Decision Processes*, *50*(2), 179–211. doi:10.1016/0749-5978(91)90020-T

Al-Qirim, N. (2007). A research trilogy into e-commerce adoption in small businesses in New Zealand. *Electronic Markets*, *17*(4), 263–285. doi:10.1080/10196780701635872

Constantinides, E., Lorenzo-Romero, C., & Gómez, M. A. (2010). Effects of web experience onconsumer choice: A multicultural approach. *Internet Research*, *20*(2), 188–209. doi:10.1108/10662241011032245

Cristobal, E., Flavian, C., & Guinaliu, M. (2007). Perceived e-service quality (PeSQ) Measurement validation and effects on consumer satisfaction and web site loyalty. *Managing Service Quality*, *17*(3), 317–340. doi:10.1108/09604520710744326

Dadzie, K. Q., Johnston, W. J., & Pels, J. (2008). Business-to-business marketing practices in West Africa, Argentina and the United States. *Journal of Business and Industrial Marketing*, *23*(2), 115–123. doi:10.1108/08858620810850236

Davis, F. D., Bagozzi, R. P., & Warshaw, P. R. (1989). User acceptance of computer technology: A comparison of two theoretical models. *Management Science*, *35*(8), 982–1003. doi:10.1287/mnsc.35.8.982

Fishbein, M., & Ajzen, I. (1975). *Belief. Attitude, Intention and Behavior: An Introduction to Theory and Research Reading*. Addison-Wesley.

Fornell, C., & Larcker, D. F. (1981). Evaluating structural equation models with unobservable variables and measurement error. *JMR, Journal of Marketing Research*, *18*(1), 39–50. doi:10.1177/002224378101800104

Ganguly, B., Dash, S. B., & Cyr, D. (2009). Website characteristics, trust and purchase intention in online stores: An empirical study in the Indian context. *Journal of Information Science and Technology*, *6*(2), 22–44.

Gefen, D., & Straub, D. W. (2000). The relative importance of perceived ease-of-use in IS adoption: A study of e-commerce adoption. *Journal of the Association for Information Systems*, *1*(8), 1–31. doi:10.17705/1jais.00008

Hair, J. F., Black, B., Babin, B., Anderson, R. E., & Tatham, R. L. (2010). *Multivariate Data Analysis: A Global Perspective*. Pearson Education Inc.

Hill, W. W., & Beatty, S. E. (2011). A model of adolescents' online consumer self-efficacy (OCSE). *Journal of Business Research*, *64*(10), 1025–1033. doi:10.1016/j.jbusres.2010.11.008

Hofacker, C. F., & Murphy, J. (2009). Consumer web page search, clicking behavior and reaction time. *International Journal of Direct Marketing*, *3*(2), 88–96. doi:10.1108/17505930910964759

Hoftman, D. L., & Novak, T. P. (1996). Marketing in Hypermedia Computer Mediated Environments: Conceptual Foundations. *Journal of Marketing*, *60*(3), 50–68. doi:10.1177/002224299606000304

Hu, L. T., & Bentler, P. M. (1999). Cutoff Criteria for Fit Indexes in Covariance Structure Analysis: Conventional Criteria versus New Alternatives. *Structural Equation Modeling*, *6*(1), 1–55. doi:10.1080/10705519909540118

Joo, Bong, & Choi. (2000). Self-efficacy for self-regulated learning, academic self-efficacy, and Internet self-efficacy in Web-based instruction. *Educational Technology Research and Development, 48*(2), 5 – 17.

Joreskog, K., & Sorbom, D. (1993). *LISREL 8: Structural Equation Modeling with the SIMPLIS Command Language*. Scientific Software International Inc.

Joyce, M., & Kirakowski, J. (2014). Measuring Confidence in Internet Use: The Development of an Internet Self-efficacy Scale. In A. Marcus (Ed.), Lecture Notes in Computer Science: Vol. 8517. *Design, User Experience, and Usability. Theories, Methods, and Tools for Designing the User Experience. DUXU 2014*. Springer. doi:10.1007/978-3-319-07668-3_25

Lemke, F., Clark, M., & Wilson, H. (2011). Customer experience quality: An exploration in business and consumer contexts using repertory grid technique. *Journal of the Academy of Marketing Science*, *39*(6), 846–869. doi:10.100711747-010-0219-0

MacCallum, R. C., Browne, M. W., & Sugawara, H. M. (1996). Power Analysis and Determination of Sample Size for Covariance Structure Modeling. *Psychological Methods*, *1*(2), 130–149. doi:10.1037/1082-989X.1.2.130

Mahadin, B., Akroush, M. N., & Bata, H. (2020). The effects of tourism websites' attributes on e-satisfaction and e-loyalty: A case of American travellers' to Jordan. *International Journal of Web Based Communities*, *16*(1), 4–33. doi:10.1504/IJWBC.2020.105124

Melgarejo-Heredia, R., Carr, L., & Halford, S. (2016). The public web and the public good. In *Proceedings of the 8th ACM Conference on Web Science* (pp. 330-332). ACM. 10.1145/2908131.2908181

Mithas, S., Ramasubbu, N., Krishnan, M. S., & Fornell, C. (2007). Designing websites for customer loyalty across business domains: A multilevel analysis. *Journal of Management Information Systems*, *23*(3), 97–127. doi:10.2753/MIS0742-1222230305

Roscoe, J. T. (1975). *Fundamental research statistics for the behavioral sciences*. Academic Press.

Rose, S., Clark, M., Samouel, P., & Hair, N. (2012). Online customer experience in e-retailing: An empirical model of antecedents and outcomes. *Journal of Retailing*, *88*(2), 308–322. doi:10.1016/j.jretai.2012.03.001

Sharma, S., & Gutierrez, J. A. (2010). An evaluation framework for viable business models for m-commerce in the information technology sector. *Electronic Markets*, *20*(1), 33–52. doi:10.100712525-010-0028-9

Tao, Y. H., Cheng, C. J., & Sun, S. Y. (2009). What influences college students to continue using business simulation games? The Taiwan experience. *Computers & Education*, *53*(3), 929–939. doi:10.1016/j.compedu.2009.05.009

Trevinal, A. M., & Stenger, T. (2014). Toward a conceptualization of the online shopping experience. *Journal of Retailing and Consumer Services*, *21*(3), 314–326. doi:10.1016/j.jretconser.2014.02.009

Vaithianathan, S. (2010). A review of e-commerce literature on India and research agenda for the future. *Electronic Commerce Research*, *10*(1), 83–97. doi:10.100710660-010-9046-0

Yousafzai, S. Y., Foxall, G. R., & Pallister, J. G. (2010). Explaining internet banking behavior: Theory of reasoned action, theory of planned behavior, or technology acceptance model? *Journal of Applied Social Psychology*, *40*(5), 1172–1202. doi:10.1111/j.1559-1816.2010.00615.x

APPENDIX

Table 5. Evaluation Grid 1.Rate the following five parameters of Innovation Diffusion Model on a scale of1-5 (5-Excellent, 1–Poor).

S.No.	Parameter	Rating
1	Relative Advantages	
2	Compatibility	
3	Complexity	
4	Trialability	
5	Observability	

Research Instrument 1

Dear Respondent,

This questionnaire has been prepared as part of research in the domain of "*Impact of Consumers Internet Self Efficacy and User Friendliness of Websites on E-Commerce Adoption*". You are requested to spare some of your valuable time and fill up the questionnaire. The information provided by you will be used for research purpose only.

SECTION A: Demographics		
Q 1.	Name:	Q 2. Age:
Q 3.	Gender: (a) Male (b) Female	
Q 4.	Please indicate the duration of the usage of e-commerce for shopping apparels a. Never b. 1 year c. 2year d. 3 years e. 4 years	

Section B: Consumer Internet Self Efficacy

Q.1.Please indicate the extent to which you agree or disagree with each of the following statements by encircling one option out of 1, 2, 3, 4 and 5.

(5 -Strongly Agree; 1-Strongly Disagree)

Section C: User Friendliness of Websites

Q.1.Rate the following Website Characteristics with respect to their ability to ease the online purchase decision of apparels by encircling one option out of 1, 2, 3, 4 and 5.

(5 –Extremely Important; 1-Not at all important)

S.No	Statements	Strongly Disagree 1	Disagree 2	Neither agree nor disagree 3	Agree 4	Strongly Agree 5
1	I can easily connect Internet through a modem, ADSL, etc	1	2	3	4	5
2	I like the convenience offered by the internet	1	2	3	4	5
3	I enjoy the visual experience that the internet offers	1	2	3	4	5
4	I am comfortable in finding information by using a search engine.	1	2	3	4	5
5	The internet allows me to exchange messages with other users in discussion forums.	1	2	3	4	5
6	I like e-commerce apparel selling websites which make my information search easy	1	2	3	4	5
7	The online shopping of apparels offers me an emotionally satisfying experience	1	2	3	4	5
8	I am comfortable in navigating an e-commerce website by entering its address (URL) in the browser	1	2	3	4	5
9	I like e-commerce apparel selling websites which offer me better schemes and discounts	1	2	3	4	5
10	I like e-commerce apparel selling websites which provide me up-to-date information	1	2	3	4	5
11	I can comfortably install an application or software	1	2	3	4	5

S.No	Statements	Not at all Important 1	Low Important 2	Neutral 3	Moderately Important 4	Very Important 5
1	Customer service	1	2	3	4	5
2	Personalized offers	1	2	3	4	5
3	Large category of product comparisons	1	2	3	4	5
4	Detailed product information and photo galleries of products	1	2	3	4	5
5	Security and Privacy information	1	2	3	4	5
6	Consumer reviews and suggestions	1	2	3	4	5

Chapter 10
E-Commerce and Its Role in the Development of India's Indigenous Product Base

Javaid Ahmad Bhat
https://orcid.org/0000-0001-5703-0954
Centre of Central Asian Studies, University of Kashmir, India

Sushmita Dhar
University of Kashmir, India

ABSTRACT

This work aims to fathom how the traditional and the indigenous product base of India will change if it rides the supersonic flight of the booming e-commerce sector. E-commerce has registered unprecedented growth in the developed world, and in the developing world, the transition is more visible and is garnering a foothold in a multitude of ways. Propelled by rising smartphone penetration, 4G networks, and increasing consumer wealth, the Indian e-commerce market is expected to grow significantly. Addendum to this will be the initiatives taken to indicate the transition. One such prospective sector that will ensure this is India's traditionally produced/manufactured or exclusive homegrown products. Linking these locally vibrant products or goods in states per se with e-commerce will ensure the growth and development of the said products and will stretch their outreach both in the country and worldwide. This in turn will ensure the development of the particular regions and the country as a whole apart from carving an undaunted place in the export portfolio of the country.

INTRODUCTION

Electronic commerce or E-commerce has spread its wings across the length and breadth of developed economies, has started penetrating or assimilating in more potent and profitable sectors in developing economies, and at the same time is making its way into the other sectors of the economies and also in less developed countries. The past decade has seen the global economy's transit from the Industrial

DOI: 10.4018/978-1-7998-7192-7.ch010

Revolution 3.0 to 4.0. It will not exaggerate the actual status if we say that much of this transition is a by-product of enhanced penetration of high-end technological innovations and high-speed internet. Many people do not realize that E-commerce has been there for almost 40 years and has just become widely known in the last decade or two. By now, many of us have come to accept the notion that E-commerce is a vital piece of modern-day business. Despite being only a convenient vehicle to riches in the past, E-commerce has genuinely altered the way businesses are done (Tain and Stewart, 2007).

The work program on Electronic Commerce of the World Trade Organization (2019) defines E-commerce as the production, distribution, marketing, sale, or delivery of goods and services by electronic means. According to the Ministry of Statistics and Programme Implementation, Government of India (2019), E-commerce refers to the facilitation of trade and related practices through electronic means like via commercial internet portals and other means. Furthermore, EC encompasses several operations spread throughout the firm's value chain, including product/service marketing on the web, payment integration with consumers, secure transactions, and customer inquiries. EC is an umbrella idea to combine various applications, both present and those yet to be created (Vaithianathan, 2010).

Broadly, EC transactions can be categorized in terms of target user groups such as business-to-business (e.g., procurement over computer networks), business-to-consumer (e.g., online retailing), business-to-administration (e.g., Government and business transactions), and consumer-to-administration (e.g., filing of tax returns). However, the share of the business-to-business transactions exceeds that of business-to-consumer transactions though later being in the limelight over the recent years.

A Discussion Paper on E-Commerce in India (2014) states that E-commerce has been increasing across the world. Industry sources indicate that this growth can be sustained over a more extended period as E-commerce will continue to reach new geographies and encompass new markets. Though E-commerce has limitless opportunities to offer for many sectors, it will need a prerequisite digital revolution and a certain degree of preparedness from the economies. On the domestic front, E-commerce has witnessed exemplary growth. It will be in the fitness of things if the coverage of electronic transactions is beamed towards the traditional product base of our country. The move will not only benefit the products manufactured or grown locally which have lost their sheen amid the influx of innovative machine-made goods but will also ensure other multiple benefits for the economy as a whole. This whole process will be multi-phased and will need sound investment impetus along with infra to build up sound infrastructure for skilling of the people involved in the production/manufacturing of such products. But once accomplished, the move can revive the traditional sustainable practices and offer numerous distinctive products of high prestige value to the global and local consumer base.

LITERATURE REVIEW

Companies throughout the globe have embraced EC and have seen its benefits, including an increase in business performance. Integrating e-commerce into their value chain operations provides many benefits, including operational efficiency and income generation (Brynjolfsson and Kahin, 2000). With the advent of online retail, the quantity of scholarly articles in this field has increased proportionately. In this context, it would be highly imperative to discuss some of the studies in detail to get an insight into the growth and importance of E-commerce.

According to Damanpour and Damanpour (2001), internet communication has completely revolutionized the way firms share information with their business partners and how they do commerce. The study attempts to evaluate the main elements about the implementation of internet and E-business strategy. E-business is now an absolute necessity for any organization's long-term success. The most significant benefit of using an E-business system is to obtain an edge in a competitive market and enhance the efficiency of several company functions such as information management, integration of suppliers and vendors, better distribution, and lower transaction costs. E-business remains an advanced nations phenomenon. Currently, developing nations do not have the funds or know-how to be a part of this global phenomenon. Adjustments in present domestic rules may help resolve managerial finance.

In the words of Kalia et al. (2017), electronic commerce is gaining popularity since it provides consumers with distinct and diversified benefits. The internet has gone from being a sole communication medium to a consumer-centric e-marketplace. E-commerce prospects arise with India's tremendous development in the information and communication technology sector. By appreciating the value of E-commerce technology, being aware of one's absolved present status, and understanding how evolution works will help retailers grasp golden possibilities in the near future.

According to Bhattacharya & Mishra (2015), customers appreciate the advances brought about by e-commerce. The economy has thrived as a result of more excellent connectivity. Travel, finance, media, and various other businesses have benefited from the growth of e-commerce. Social media is used to keep clients informed about e-commerce. E-commerce businesses strive to provide their clients with an emotional and pleasurable experience. The adoption of 3G and 4G telecommunications technology will result in a rise in internet use. With several multinational corporations investing in India, India's future potential is obvious. The growing number of Facebook users in India contributes to the company's growth in digital advertising. India is heading towards the development of an internet economy with the advancement of information and communication technology.

Ravi et al. conducted a comparative study on the adoption of e-business in India and China. According to the report, the rise of e-businesses in the two nations is influenced by a variety of variables. The elements analyzed include federal legislation and policies, existing technological infrastructure, a regulatory framework that accommodates new business practices, and familiarity with a company's overall operations and climate, to name a few. After a comprehensive analysis, the study concluded that China is ahead in the infrastructure, while India is currently more prepared for e-commerce. To finish, the article says that both countries are set for fast-growing e-business, but that one obstacle to economic prosperity in both countries is poverty and disparity in connectivity between urban and rural locations.

A study conducted by (Kumar et al., 2018) investigates the problems and opportunities connected with e-commerce in India in light of the global economy. According to this study, India's pace of e-commerce growth is manageable, although slower than China and the US. The article explains how India uses ICTs, 4G technology, and many local e-commerce companies. Nevertheless, it has all of the same problems, such as poor communication infrastructure, harsh regulatory limitations, and a constructive attitude towards technology. The authors suggested that the government and business sector should implement relevant academic curriculum, update legislation, and improve ICT infrastructure to boost e-commerce development for long-term economic growth.

EVOLUTION OF E-COMMERCE IN INDIA

E-commerce analytics can provide details on how information and communication technologies have been applied in the business world. An in-depth look at how e-commerce has evolved in the past and what it looks like today can help us forecast future developments in E-commerce.

The introduction of electronic data interchange (EDI) has made it possible for businesses to conduct e-commerce transactions. EDI originated in the mid-1960s when firms in the transportation and retail industries attempted to create "paperless" workspaces (Tain and Stewart, 2007). The formation of e-commerce that serves as a business instrument for exchanging items and services on the internet initially began as a research tool. In the 1960s, the ARPANET, a precursor of the internet, was constructed for research and development purposes. When the number of hosts on the ARPANET reached 213, the term "Internet" was first used (Tain and Stewart, 2007). Throughout the 1980s, the internet retained its non-profit status. Most of the principal users were Government and university scientists and engineers (Eccleson, 1999). A significant milestone occurred in 1991 when NSFNET lifted the commercial prohibitions on network usage and opened up e-commerce opportunities.

India's E-Commerce journey started in 1999 with the advent of India's first E-commerce company Fabmart.com. The company was founded by K Vaitheeswaran, who is also known as the father of Indian E-commerce. With time, online shopping growth has flourished in India, the third-largest market for internet users. India had a significant transition in this business, starting with the print-literate workforce and concluding with telephones, radios, TVs, and computers for Internet communication and mobile phone apps. More enterprises in India are jumping on the digital bandwagon as the industry continues to develop. E-commerce is emerging as a result of the rising literacy levels in India. Today, many individuals in India buy smartphones, apparel, and books on the internet. However, e-commerce development is fueled by corporate transaction online ticket booking (Smith, 2020). The evolution of E-commerce in India took place in the following phased manner:

1st Phase of Evolution

Employment Websites: The initial phase saw the introduction of employment websites. This has a significant impact on the human resource management landscape of corporations. Before 1991, the majority of government-related firms recruited people through newspapers and publications. This was the first time that Indians encountered a novel method of job searching (Bhattacharya & Mishra, 2015).

Online Matrimony: The first online matrimonial service in India was launched in 1996. The internet matchmaking sector significantly altered Indian perceptions about arranged weddings (Bhattacharya & Mishra, 2015).

Institutional Directory: In 1996, India launched the world's first online institutional directory. The rise of these internet directories was fuelled by Liberalization, Privatization, and Globalization (LPG). These directories make it simple for buyers and sellers to connect and do business (Bhattacharya & Mishra, 2015).

2nd Phase of Evolution

Internet-Based travel: Internet-based travel flourished during this time. Numerous low-cost airlines such as Air Deccan, Spice Jet, and Jet Lite were found. The establishment of these airlines paved the way for virtual booking options. Additionally, Indian Railways has planned to launch an online reservation system. This also resulted in a significant increase in online ticket booking. Additionally, the virtualization of hotel bookings and the launch of bus booking websites attracted many clients interested in booking online (Bhattacharya & Mishra, 2015).

Social Networking: During this era, social networking sites were intertwined with the Ecommerce business. The industry's players have embraced various social networking platforms to build buzz and community involvement within their target consumer base (Bhattacharya & Mishra, 2015).

Electronic Retail: The electronic retail business has experienced tremendous growth. Electronic retail firms have added significant value to their service portfolios to please customers. Companies experiment with various permutations and combinations of business models to increase profitability, productivity, and efficiency. Flipkart, Jabong, and Yepme are all well-known names in this market (Bhattacharya & Mishra, 2015).

Figure 1. Waves of e-commerce
Source: Ernst & Young, 2013

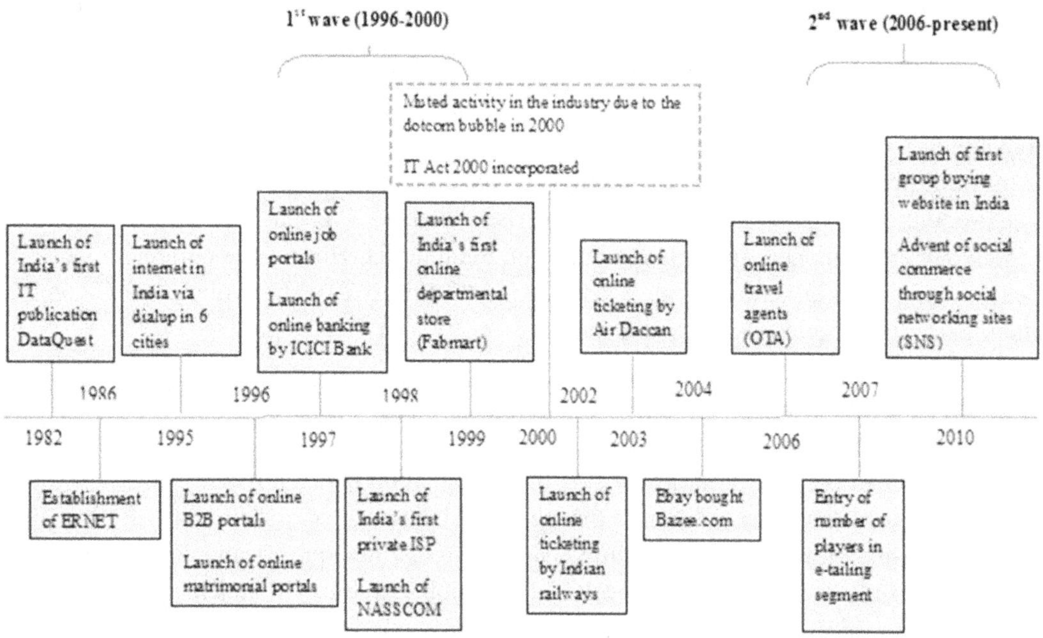

CURRENT STATUS OF E-COMMERCE IN INDIA AND WORLDWIDE

Global E-commerce is witnessing a steady upward trend. The current status of the E-commerce transactions worldwide can be figured by looking into the following pertinent figures from Statista (2019):

- The E-Commerce market encompasses the sale of physical goods via a digital channel to a private end-user (B2C).
- Revenue in the E-commerce market will amount to US$2,012,096m in 2019.

Figure 2. Models of e-commerce

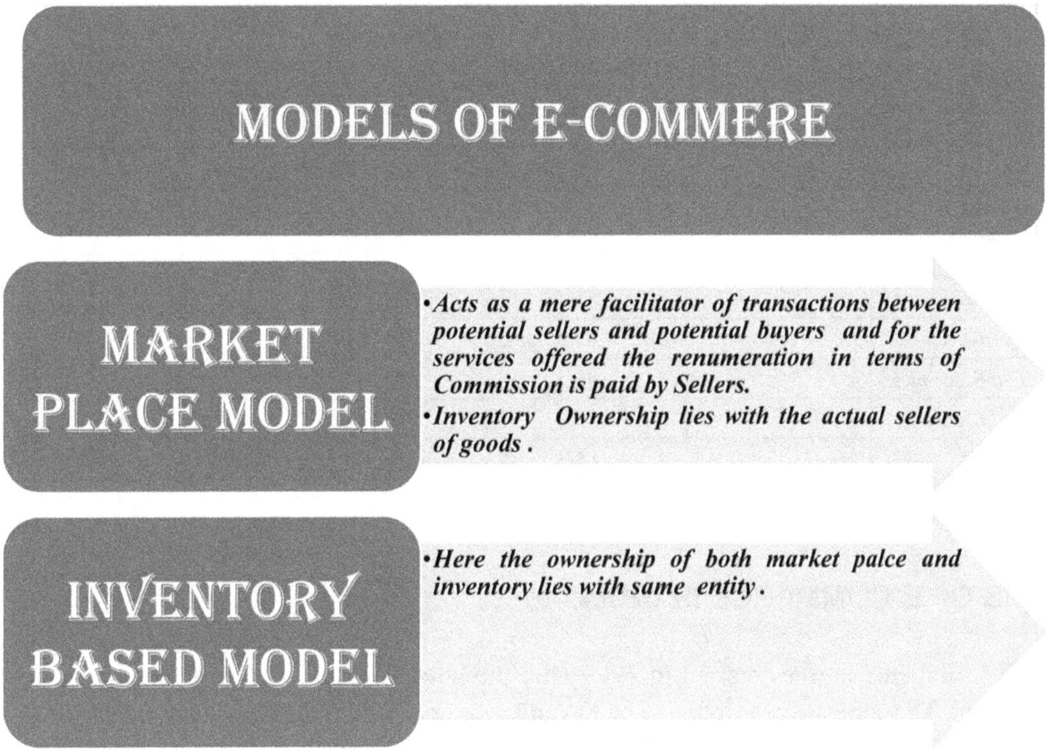

- Revenue is expected to show an annual growth rate (CAGR 2019-2023) of 8.0%, resulting in a market volume of US$2,734,414m by 2023.
- User penetration will hit the 61.8% mark by 2023 as compared to 56.2% in 2019.

Global E-Commerce Statistics of 2017 Reveals That-

- Digital buyer's penetration worldwide states 46.4% and will increase to 47.3% in 2018.
- Globally, E-commerce is a strongly growing domain with no signs of decline for 2018 and even in the following years. It remains a popular choice for investments and new businesses.
- Mobile phones will be reaching 70% of E-commerce traffic by the end of 2018.
- By the end of 2017, over two billion mobile phone or tablet users made some form of mobile commerce transactions.
- Mobile commerce was hitting US$700 billion in revenue in 2017, which is more than 300% growth over the past four years. Mobile E-commerce is growing faster than e-commerce in general.
- B2B E-commerce global sales reached $7.7 trillion in 2017. Thus, the B2B E-commerce market is twice as big as the B2C one, continuously growing.

These figures undoubtedly reveal E-commerce as an upheaval in the world economic scenario. The UNCTAD B2C E-commerce index (2019) demonstrated the following statistics: The index measures the economy's preparedness to support online shopping.

Table 1. Regional values for UNCTAD B2C e-commerce index 2018

Region	Share of Individuals Using the Internet (2018 or Latest)	Share of Individuals with an Account (15+, 2018 or Latest)	Secure Internet Servers (Normalized) (2018)	UPU Postal Reliability Score (2018 or Latest)	2018 Index Value
Africa	25	40	29	22	30
East, South, and Southeast Asia	53	59	57	59	57
Latin America and The Caribbean	59	53	53	28	46
Western Asian	75	58	49	52	57
Transition Economies	67	58	62	65	65
Developed Economies	86	93	87	82	86
World	57	60	55	49	55

Source: United Nations Conference on Trade and Development, 2019.

STATUS OF E-COMMERCE IN INDIA

India's E-Commerce journey started in 1999 with the advent of India's first E-commerce company Fabmart.com. The company was founded by K Vaitheeswaran, who is also known as the father of Indian E-commerce. E-Commerce in India is exhibiting phenomenal growth. However, growth can be attributed to multi-pronged factors, i.e., infrastructure, internet connectivity, internet penetration.

E-Commerce has transformed the way business is done in India. The Indian E-commerce market is expected to grow to US$ 200 billion by 2026 from US$ 38.5 billion as of 2017. Much growth in the industry has been triggered by increasing internet and smartphone penetration. The ongoing digital transformation in the country is expected to boost India's total internet user base to 829 million by 2021 from 560.01 million as of September 2018. India's internet economy is expected to double from US$125 billion as of April 2017 to US$ 250 billion by 2020, majorly backed by E-commerce. India's E-commerce revenue is expected to jump from US$ 39 billion in 2017 to US$ 120 billion in 2020, growing at an annual rate of 51 percent, the highest in the world (India Brand Equity Foundation, 2018). The 'Market Place Model characterizes the Indian E-commerce industry. It allows many manufacturers/traders, especially MSMEs, to advertise their products on a marketplace and benefit from increased turnover (Discussion Paper on E-commerce in India, 2014). Venture Capitalists and Private Equity firms mostly pocket the funding in the E-commerce sector and India until now, most of the budget is sourced on consolidation.

HOW E-COMMERCE WILL IMPACT DEVELOPING ECONOMIES LIKE INDIA

The UNCTAD's E-commerce and Development Report (2001), while covering the quantitative analysis of the impact of E-commerce on the Global Economy based on the assumption that E-commerce can reduce the costs of services (as services are essential inputs to other sectors of production). The partial equilibrium analysis undertaken revealed that cost reduction would push the supply curve out to the right, thereby achieving a new equilibrium where the output will increase, and prices will decline. However,

Figure 3. Advantage India

the report also revealed that when developing regions fall behind technologically, the gap between the developed and developing regions will show an upward trend. So, the information placed impetus on convergence in productivity in services, raising the competitiveness of developing countries' exports and maximizing welfare.

The impact of the E-commerce industry on developing economies like India can be traced from the fact that the "Bandwagon Effect influences customers in developing countries" and "fast adopting behaviors similar to their counterparts in more developed countries" (Discussion Paper on E-commerce in India, 2014). Besides, the growing E-commerce industry has positive spillover effects associated with it. Added to this are the increase in disposable income, income per se, mobile penetration, and internet connectivity. However, how E-commerce will prove beneficial for developing countries and to what extent it is yet to be seen is worth debatable. Developing countries like India feature traditional marketing and export channels that tend to be inefficient, dominated by multiple intermediaries. The situation can be turned around by E-commerce. The other benefits that accompany the B2B model of E-commerce, which is more in vogue, are the fall in transaction costs as the E-commerce platforms ensure the creation of consortiums of buyers and sellers and create demand-side economies of scale or network effects. Benefits like eliminating intermediaries and creating new ones in terms of independent 3rd party follow immediately (UNCTAD's E-commerce and development Report, 2001). Low barriers to entry also create profitable and lucrative prospects for new entrants accompanied by differentiated and specialized products.

The WTO report on E-commerce in developing countries, "Opportunities and Challenges for Small and Medium-sized Enterprises," stated that developing countries, particularly emerging economies, will continue to drive the growth of the global mobile phone market mainly because of the large population, low penetration rates, and rising disposable income. This implies that the E-commerce sector exhibits strong forward and backward linkages.

Advantages Garnered due to Augment of E-Commerce in India

Though E-commerce has set its footprint in India, the extent to which it excels in our country depends on our preparedness in terms of provision of better internet connectivity, infrastructure, skilling, and expansion to new and varied sectors, which are distinctive or feature traits that are unique in the setup like the traditional products of local origin–created, manufacture or grown with local, sustainable know-how.

Advantages that can be accumulated due to the augment of E-commerce in India include better resource allocation, economies of scale, improved competitiveness in sectors, better knowledge of market and product know-how, growth in employment avenues, increase in wages, and overall welfare. Though the benefits accruing due to coming up of E-commerce platforms on various fora are not visible to a bare eye, the prospects are brought enough to be deciphered.

Diverse Nature of India and E-Commerce

India is a diverse country on varied fronts, be it linguistically, geographically, or culturally. This variedness on several shows gave birth to the economically diverse India. The production activities carried out in India range from manufacturing and growth of sustainable indigenous products or products of local origin which exhibit unique and distinctive traits and possess prestige value to the High end Innovative and tech-savvy products. Since E-commerce has flourished in the field of new and innovative products and commodities, the commodities of innate nature manufactured in India are yet to board the flight of E-commerce. The study focuses on the linkage of such a traditional product base of our country with E-commerce. "It is stated that E-commerce can be aligned to the objectives of national development by providing impetus to the manufacturing sector, order consolidation and distribution, facilitating and supporting SMEs, improving outreach and access to buyers /sellers, bringing traceability and transparency in transactions, empowering consumers with information and data and finally creating job opportunities" (Discussion paper on E-Commerce in India, 2014). Besides the E-commerce sector, if de-regulated will create immense opportunities for small businesses /entrepreneurs and help them scale at almost no cost and generate employment through investment/innovation in supply chain management, warehousing, logistic services, and another ancillary sector" and inclusion of remotest customer base.

Traditional Product Base of India

By traditional product base, we mean all those commodities and goods manufactured, created, or grown in India; what makes these goods differ from the rest is the cultural and rich heritage values and domestic or local know-how attached to them. These can also be termed "Bicultural Products," i.e., the products derived from Bio-cultural heritage." India being a diverse country with diverse landscapes and cultures, is home to various outcomes associated with local knowledge accumulated by communities over the years. These products generate income for the communities and provide incentives for sustaining genetic resources and traditional knowledge. These products exhibit social responsibility and harmonious relationships through cooperation. These products generate revenue for the communities and provide incentives for supporting genetic resources and traditional knowledge in the face of external pressures and consumerism. These products being unique with high prestige value, cater to the changing demands of consumers like health, food markets, organic markets, handloom, art products, etc.

The Impetus to Indigenous Product Base Will Ensure Marching Ahead While Remaining Committed to our Roots

In 2001 Social scientist John Altman stated that to understand and address the economic development problem faced by indigenous people living on Aboriginal land in remote and regional Australia, a hybrid analytical framework that combined science, social sciences, and indigenous knowledge system was required. In tandem with this because it is the right time to undertake all possible measures to link the indigenous product base of our country with E-commerce which has already taken rapid strides. In the present context, the earlier entrants in the field of E-commerce have made substantial efforts in educating consumers, and enterprises about E-commerce besides the needed infrastructure, logistics, internet connectivity, and broadband facilities have already attained momentum and impetus with Government's policies about Digital India, E-logistics, pan India GST, E-transactions, and E-finance.

Internalizing the Indignity of our Wide Traditional and Local Goods

Though India is the fastest growing economy due to its diversity and wide geographical extend, several traditional products of one state are not known or available in another state. This situation hinders the pan India Concept and also the concept of Pan India Consumer. What will work wonders in this direction is the arrival of E-commerce via which products grown or manufactured in India can be made available to customers online. This will not only provide more choice to our consumer base but will also benefit the traditional host sector by way of increase in demand for such products and as such increase in output which in turn increase per capita income of people involved in the production process and will enhance the profitability and thereby create more avenues for expansion in production capacity and undoubtedly the increase in employment opportunities, reduction in underemployment and unemployment and welfare for all. At the same time, the linkages can create a spillover effect and provide a kick to the Tourism Industry and the state economies. Both E-commerce B2B and B2C models adjusted to the respective needs will boost equitable partnerships between local community ad E-commerce stakeholders and benefit from each other. "E-Commerce has been hailed as an opportunity for developing countries to gain a stronger foothold in the multilateral trading system (WTO Report on E-Commerce in Developing Countries, 2013).

Internationalizing our Indigenous Products

E-Commerce will provide our indigenous and local producers a platform to build Brand names and images in markets to which they have little access in the past (UNCTAD's E-commerce and development Report, 2001). Adopting E-commerce in the indigenous products arena may substantially reduce costs and inefficient trade procedures that inhibit their growth. The initiative will also expand the Export portfolio of our country. It will garner the export items whose sales will be undaunting and will get the least affected by changing world trade dynamics because of the Prestige and exotic value attached to these commodities and being price inelastic. Both internalizing and internationalizing or, in other words commercializing of these products through E-commerce portals will ensure broader markets to be catered and will have a positive impact on the economy in general and profoundly on the rural economy, employment, the standard of living, poverty elimination, and the economy as a whole.

Stretching Traditional Product Base of Country in Tandem With Minimal Carbon Footprint

The traditional methods of production and cultivation are known to be sustainable and environmentally friendly. Promoting such products through the E-commerce medium will work synchronously with the minimal carbon footprint and reduce wastes that are less hazardous than the chemical wastes generated from the production and cultivation of goods and commodities manufactured through modern scientific procedures.

The Environment and social costs associated with Bio-cultural products are also minimal, which justifies their ECO-friendly and sustainable nature.

Steps to Ensure the Benefits Arising out of Linking of Traditional Product Base of the Country to the Lucrative E-Commerce Sector

Investment Impetus

The need for capital in this industry can be met both by government funding and private investment, which in the E-commerce sector has been met by Venture capitalists and private entities willing to invest (Discussion Paper on E-Commerce in India, 2014). Venture capital will ensure easy access to finance by entrepreneurs. Since mainstream investors become nervous about the lack of profitability in the internet sector, VCs operate on the assumption that although many or most of the companies they nurture with funds will fail, some will be highly successful. Losses can be offset by profits generated through IPOs.

The Rollout of Optic Fiber across Length and Breadth of the Country alongside Assuring the Internet Connectivity and Mobile Phone Penetration and E-Means for Settling Transactions

E-Commerce is flourishing in countries that provide a suitable environment for a better regulatory framework, high-class infrastructure, and internet density. However, lower internet density remains a challenge for E-commerce (Discussion Paper on E-Commerce in India, 2014).

Linking of Both GI Tagged and non-GI Tagged Traditional Products to E-Commerce Portals

Requires prior consideration in matters like whether the product range is in tandem with consumer demand [domestic and foreign] and sticking to set domestic and international yardsticks to gain a unique position and competitive edge. On the Geographical indications, tagged products front, GOI has undertaken extraordinary measures by launching exclusive E-commerce portals like GI TAGGED "from the very land to your Hand" and mulling over collaborations with top-notch E-commerce portals to provide impetus to such products. A similar set of initiatives also need to be undertaken for non-GI tagged products and Expanding the ambit of GI tagged products. For successful marketing of these products –Branding and justified legal protection, and standardized framework can prove helpful. Creating Brands will ensure that products are differentiated and unique and enhance market share and demand and more significant market coverage. However, before looking into a worthy marketing strategy, we need to address challenges and gaps producers/farmers/artisans, and traders of these goods face.

Start-Ups as via Media to Kick Start Sought Changes

Providing enough support to emerging or budding start-ups can work wonders in the direction. A majority of E-commerce ventures are a by-product of "the first-time Entrepreneur."

Alignment of Traditional Product Base of our Country With UNCTAD's "E-Trade for All"

E-Trade for all-initiative was launched in July 2016 to make E-commerce work for development, requiring a holistic approach. It is a multi-stakeholder partnership that connects dots between beneficiary countries, partners, and donors so that everyone can maximize returns from E-commerce (UNCTAD's E-commerce and development Report, 2001). The core principles of E-trade for all envisage:

- "Demand-Driven and Bottom-Up"-Actions will be guided by the needs and interests of developing countries.
- E-Trade will facilitate interactions among all stakeholders to identify needs, gaps, and constraints to e-commerce development.
- Focused on building local knowledge and capacity.
- Emphasis on Synergies
- From collaboration to enhance efficiency and avoid duplication of work.
- Data and Facts are driven.
- Performance should be accessed through result-based management and should encompass rigorous, joint monitoring and evaluation metrics and learning from failures and good practices.
- The viable long-term impact is the goal, linking E-trade with Sustainable Development goals.

Probable Issues and Challenges that May Arise During the Process

The E-commerce industry is facing the following hurdles and challenges:

Poor last mile connectivity due to missing links in supply chain infrastructure limits access to far-flung areas (Discussion Paper on E-Commerce in India, 2014). High dropout rates on payment gateways, trust deficit in consumers, and slow adoption of online payments are compelling companies to rely on costlier payment methods. "While it is true that in theory, the internet gives SMEs new opportunities to compete because it reduces transaction costs and barriers of entry, their E-commerce business models must be adapted to their competitive strengths" (UNCTAD's E-commerce and development Report, 2001). For the pricing of these products, E-commerce companies need to remain observant of changing market situations.

Ways to do Away With Challenges

- E-commerce success depends mainly on logistics; therefore, various methods need to be adopted to meet the increased consumer demand. These include handling order fulfilment by companies themselves using in-house logistics services, outsourcing fulfilment to 3rd party logistics service providers, drop shipping, and various combinations of these methods.

- E-Finance can serve the need of new clients switching to E-commerce for catering to more customers and markets. To obtain E-trade finance and equity, investment companies from developing countries need to be registered in local, regional, and global internet-based commercial risk databases (UNCTAD'S E-commerce and development Report, 2001).
- E-Commerce can only be effective if the people managing and engaging with it have the right skills. Training can be offered to relevant entities to help them capitalize on E-commerce opportunities.
- Traditional products are also to be sourced from geographically volatile terrains, so the use of drones or miniature helicopter services can cater to transportation needs.

CONCLUSION

- Conclusively we can say that the study related to "E-Commerce and its role in the development of India's Indigenous Product base" has a sound basis to approve the linkage between the two sectors in a phased manner like:
- Phase1 – in which identification of these products alongside their delineation and standardization will be undertaken.
- Phase2 – in which sound policy initiatives are undertaken to secure the inputs and outputs of the products identified. Alongside creating a sound base for producing these items and providing incentives, suitable E-commerce models need to be chosen.
- To gauge customer demand, pilot-based surveys need to be undertaken.
- A sound insurance framework and incentivization are also needed.
- The standardized practices of production need to be adhered to prevent dilution of their uniqueness strictly.
- The flexible regulatory framework in combination with strict monitoring can help India produce several brands of its own that will be sustainable, environmentally friendly, and unique to our country.

REFERENCES

Bhattacharya, S., & Mishra, B. B. (2015). Evolution, growth and challenges in e-commerce industry: A case of india. *Sumedha Journal of Management*, *4*(1), 45–58.

Brynjolfsson, E., & Kahin, B. (Eds.). (2000). *Understanding the digital economy*. MIT Press. doi:10.7551/mitpress/6986.001.0001

Chu, S. C., Leung, L. C., Hui, Y. V., & Cheung, W. (2007). Evolution of e-commerce web sites: A conceptual framework and a longitudinal study. *Information & Management*, *44*(2), 154–164. doi:10.1016/j.im.2006.11.003

Damanpour, F., & Damanpour, J. A. (2001). E-business e-commerce evolution: Perspective and strategy. *Managerial Finance*, *27*(7), 16–33. doi:10.1108/03074350110767268

DIPP–Discussion Paper on E-commerce In India 2013-14. (n.d.). Retrieved from https://indiafdiwatch.org/wp-content/uploads/2014/01/discussionpaper.pdf

E-Commerce. (2019). *Statista.* Retrieved from https://www.statista.com/outlook/243/100/ecommerce/worldwide#market-revenue

E-commerce and Development Report. (2001). *UNCTAD Secretariat, United Nations*. Retrieved from https://unctad.org/en/docs/ecdr2001_en.pdf

E-Commerce, Government of India, Ministry of Statistics and Programme Implementation. (n.d.). Accessed January 2019, https://www.mospi.gov.in/1012-e-commerce

E-Commerce in developing countries: Opportunities and Challenges for small and medium-sized enterprises. (2013). *World Trade Organization*. Retrieved from https://www.wto.org/english/r es_e/ books _e/eco m_brochure _e.pdf

E-commerce Industry in India. (2018). *India Brand Equity Foundation.* Retrieved from https://www.ibef.org/industry/ecommerce.aspx

Global E-Commerce Trends and Statistics. (2017-2018). *Amasty Blog.* Retrieved from https://amasty.com/blog/global-e-commerce-trends-and-statistics-2017-2018/

India's first e-commerce company Fabmart.com's founder k vaitheeswaran today said. (2017, July 11). *Business Standard.* https://www.business-standard.com/article/pti-stories/india-s-first-e-commerce-company-fabmart-com-s-founder-k-vaitheeswaran-today-said-117071100874_1.html

Kalia, P., Kaur, N., & Singh, T. (2017). E-Commerce in India: Evolution and Revolution of Online Retail. In M. Khosrow-Pour (Ed.), *Mobile Commerce: Concepts, Methodologies, Tools, and Applications* (pp. 736–758). IGI Global.

Kumar, N., Anusara, J., Sarkar, M. K., Chanthamith, B., Hossin, M. A., Shah, S., & Russel, M. I. H. (2018). Challenges and opportunities of E-Commerce in india: Pathway for sustainable E-Commerce. *International Journal of Engineering Business Management*, *2*(2). Advance online publication. doi:10.22161/ijebm.2.2.1

Raven, V. P., Huang, X., & Kim, B. B. (2007). E-business in developing countries: A comparison of China and India. *International Journal of E-Business Research*, *3*(1), 91–108. doi:10.4018/jebr.2007010106

Smith, A. (2020, April 10). *Evolution and growth of eCommerce in india.* Official Blog of Hidden Brains Infotech PVT LTD. https://www.hiddenbrains.com/blog/evolution-and-growth-of-ecommerce-in-india.html#:%7E:text=India%2C%20emerging%20economic%20superpower%20and,for%20the%20growth%20of%20eCommerce.&text=The%20rising%20literacy%20rate%20and,the%20growth%20of%20e%2DCommerce

Tain, Y., & Stewart, C. (2007). History of e commerce. In A. Becker (Ed.), Electronic Commerce: Concepts, Methodologies, Tools and Applications (pp. 1–8). IGI Global. doi:10.4018/978-1-59904-943-4.ch001

Vaithianathan, S. (2010). A review of e-commerce literature on india and research agenda for the future. *Electronic Commerce Research, 10*(1), 83–97. doi:10.100710660-010-9046-0

Work Programme on Electronic Commerce, World Trade Organization. (n.d.). Retrieved from https://www.wto.org/english/tratop_e/ecom_e/ecom_e.htm

Section 4
Social Media

Chapter 11
The Impact of Social Capital and Time Spent on Facebook on Social Recognition and Attachment

Richard Ladwein
IAE, University of Lille, France

Mohamed Slim Ben Mimoun
College of Business and Economics, Qatar University, Qatar

ABSTRACT

Prior research deals rather extensively with psychological aspects related to social network sites usage. In contrast, the present study focuses on "psychosociological aspects" related to social network site usage, such as attachment to the sites. The present research seeks to determine the impact of the "need for social belonging" on the extent of a user social network and time spent on Facebook, as well as the resultant effects on social recognition and brand attachment. The research model was tested with data from 315 Facebook users using a web survey. The structural equation model in AMOS was used to test the proposed hypotheses. The results highlight the central role of social recognition in explaining attachment to Facebook. They show that the need for social belonging affects the number of friends but not time spent on Facebook. Results indicate that it is the quality of the social ties and activity on Facebook together with a feeling of social recognition that explain attachment to Facebook.

INTRODUCTION

The Internet and social networks are integral to the everyday lives of hundreds of millions of consumers (Wilcox & Stephen, 2013; Casale and Fioravanti, 2018; Bailey et al. 2021), offering to their users a massive networking opportunities and an online marketplace (Sharma and Baoku, 2013). For many people, visiting social networks sites represents their primary Internet activity (Oh et al., 2014). Facebook

DOI: 10.4018/978-1-7998-7192-7.ch011

is the most used social network site worldwide (Zheng et al. 2015) with more than 1.86 billion users (Houghton et al. 2020); it is also the fourth most popular website overall, in terms of traffic with more than 467,339,001 monthly traffic (Ahrefs.com, 2021). The massive adoption of social network sites, and Facebook in particular, leads to questions about the motivations, practices, and types of relationships that users develop with the social network sites they adopt.

Prior research deals rather extensively with motivations and psychological aspects, demonstrating that users of social network sites tend to focus closely on self-presentation (Ben Mimoun & Ammar, 2013; Wilcox & Stephen, 2013). Less research addresses psychosociological aspects related to social network site usage though, such as attachment to the sites. In this context, the objective of the present paper is to uncover the impact of an expressed need to belong on the extent of the user's social network (conceptualized as social capital) and time spent on Facebook, as well as the influences of these elements on social recognition and brand attachment.

THEORETICAL BACKGROUND

Attachment to Facebook

Consumers' relationships with brands take very different forms. Attitude toward the brand often serves to express consumers' brand relationships, but other concepts are available as well. For example, Batra, Ahuvia, and Bagozzi (2012) propose "brand love," which consumers live in an intense, deep way. Extending experiential marketing to the brand level produces the brand experience concept (Brakus, Schmitt, & Zarantonello, 2009). Other brand-related concepts seek to specify the nature of the relationship between the individual and the brand. For example, a brand commitment approach mobilizes different (emotional, cognitive, behavioral) aspects of the brand relationship (Shuv-Ami, 2012) such as brand loyalty. Escalas and Bettman (2005), study self–brand connections to characterize the way individuals appropriate the brand, in the sense that they recognize themselves in the brand. Self-image congruence (Sirgy et al., 1997) is similar to self–brand connections, in that the brands contribute to help create and socially express their users' self-concept.

Finally, the concept of brand attachment also can characterize the relationship with the brand, from an emotional perspective. Studies adopting this concept (e.g., Park, MacInnis, Eisinggerich, & Iacobucci, 2010) show that the brand attachment creates a strong emotional link between the self and the brand that is rich in meaning for the consumer. These authors also show that attachment to the brand differs from the attitude toward the brand, with greater predictive power. In particular, brand attachment can minimize the risk of disloyalty in competitive situations.

For Facebook, attachment might refer to an attachment to the brand or to the social network itself and its services. These two sides cannot be dissociated, because of the uniqueness of its offer and brand. Therefore, several distinct and specific potential determinants of attachment to Facebook, are consider. The primary focus is psychosocial determinants, including the extent of the user's network, time spent on Facebook, and feelings of social recognition. Noting the central importance of social interactions in digital networks, their direct effects on attachment to Facebook are investigated, as well as their indirect effects on brand loyalty.

Psychosocial Determinants of Attachment to Facebook

Contemporary society appears increasingly fragmented, and social networks offer a solution, in terms of providing a sense of membership (Whillans & Chen, 2018; Houghton et al. 2020). Online social networks represent a means to deal with social fragmentation. In practice, they help reconfigure modern social links (Casilli, 2010), in that social networks enable users to create new social links that complement their real-life relationships. Yang and Lin (2014) indicate that maintaining interpersonal relationships is the main purpose for most Facebook users.

Kujath (2011) highlights that young Internet users use social networks to widen their circle of acquaintances but also, and perhaps especially, to communicate in a different way with people they already know, such that they can diversify their relationships, both quantitatively and qualitatively, with their circle of acquaintances. In addition, Nadkarni and Hofmann (2012) present two main motivations for the use of Facebook, which might coexist or be expressed separately: the need to belong and the need for self-presentation. Hollenbaugh and Ferris (2014) rely on an extensive literature review to identify other motivations, such as preservation of existing social relationships, a desire to pass time, the development of new relationships, entertainment, and self-presentation. Chang and Heo (2014) specify four categories of motivations for its use: social, hedonic, utilitarian, and social intelligence. Therefore, even if not explicitly, many authors acknowledge the important influence of a need to belong on both Facebook adoption and the interpersonal relationships maintained within the social network.

Special and Li-Barber (2012) detail a need to belong as one of the main reasons to justify a presence on Facebook, and according to Baumeister and Leary (1995), the need for social belonging (need to belong) usually is expressed by a desire for frequent, sustainable interactions. In investigating this need, social ties must be considered within a digital network and the way they are implemented. Accordingly, the notion of social capital is deployed (Bourdieu, 1980). According to Bourdieu`s, (1980) definition, social capital comprises all resources connected to a sustainable network of social relationships that interact. This definition suggests a quantitative dimension of social capital, related to the size of the social network. On Facebook, the extent of a social network depends on the number of friends. One of the most recognizable characteristics of Facebook is its capacity, through its "Facebook friends" feature, to help users create and maintain networks of relationships, with moderate time and effort costs (Steinfield, Ellison, & Lampe, 2008).

Social capital also reflects the interactions among members of a social network; the more they interact socially, the more they become involved in the network and the more important the expected benefits of this interaction grow.

HYPOTHESES DEVELOPMENT

According to Yang and Lin (2014) Facebook provides a wealth of social values that meet the need for interpersonal interaction and help friends establish long-term relationships on the web site. They highlighted a positive relation between social value of Facebook and the willingness to return to and prolong the duration of stay on the social network site.

Oh et al. (2014) show empirically that people with more social interactions offer better evaluations of the use of Facebook.

Therefore, social capital is assessed according to the extent of the user's social network, whereas time spent on Facebook constitutes a means to cultivate social capital. These two elements (extent of social network and time), according to Wilcox and Stephen (2013), represent the main success factors for social networks in general. Overall, because a higher need to belong leads people to engage in more social cooperation (De Cremer & Leonardelli, 2003), the need to belong is predicted to have a positive impact on the number of Facebook friends, as well as on the time spent browsing the social network. Formally,

H1: The need to belong positively influences (a) the number of Facebook friends and (b) the time spent on Facebook.

Moreover, the number of Facebook friends likely determines the number of social interactions, and it also should increase the amount of time spent on Facebook (Orr, Sisic, Ross, Simmering, Arseneault, & Orr, 2009). Therefore,

H2: The number of Facebook friends positively influences (daily) time spent on Facebook.

Social capital also suggests that members gain certain benefits from joining a social network. Kim and Lee (2011) highlight that the more friends on Facebook people have, the more they consider themselves happy. Oh et al. (2014) indicate a positive relation between the number of friends on digital social networks and the number of positive interactions within these networks, which in turn implies an impact of social recognition (Honneth, 2013). According to Bourdieu (1980), when social capital is more important (vast and rich social interactions), it is also more effective. Thus, when a user has many friends, he or she enjoys a stronger feeling of being socially recognized and spends more time on Facebook, which further increases social recognition.

H3a: The number of Facebook friends positively influences the feeling of being socially recognized.

H3b: Time spent on Facebook positively influences social recognition.

Having numerous friends on Facebook implies, a priori, a certain level of activism (e.g., proactive searches for new friends) or popularity (Kim & Lee, 2011). Because the extent of the social network thus may confer status, it also might increase a popular user's attachment to Facebook. Furthermore, time spent on Facebook indicates involvement in the usage situation (Ellison, Steinfield, & Lampe, 2007). Therefore, impact of time spent on the social network on attachment to Facebook is expected.

H4a: The number of Facebook friends positively influences attachment to Facebook.

H4b: The time spent on Facebook positively influences attachment to Facebook.

Finally, social recognition is a source of potentially sustainable benefits, which may connect the user to Facebook. Consequently, when a feeling of social recognition is more important, people express greater attachment to Facebook.

H5: Social recognition positively influences attachment to Facebook.

To test these hypotheses, an online survey among Facebook users was administered, then the data was analyzed according to a structural equation model in AMOS. The used method is detailed in the next section.

RESEARCH METHODOLOGY

Data Collection

To test the hypotheses, a survey by questionnaire was conducted. Exclusively Facebook networks is considered, bearing in mind the popularity and market share of this site among users. Thus, the questionnaire was administered directly on Facebook, over a period of one and a half months, such that a useable sample of 315 individuals was gathered.

For the measures, first a direct count of the number of Facebook friends and daily time spent on Facebook was taken. An ad hoc two items' scale was also built to assess the feeling of social gratitude (see Table 1). Then two items from Leary Kelly, Cottrell, and Schreindorfer's (2005) scale were adopted, to measure the need for social belonging. Finally, we adapted Lacoeuilhe's (2000) scale, with four items, to measure Facebook attachment (Table 1).

To analyze the data, a structural equation model in AMOS was used. Initial results indicated that the model did not satisfy multi-normality conditions; in the initial sample, the Mardia statistics reached 17.9 (t = 9.1). Using a Mahalanobis distance, 20 extreme values were eliminated, which produced Mardia statistics of 2.9 (t = 1.6). With the elimination of the 20 outliers, the final sample consisted of 295 respondents, 67% women and 33% men. Their average age is 23 years, with a median age of 21 years and a range between 11 and 56 years.

Measurement Model

To test the quality of the measurement model, the Fornell and Larcker's (1981) approach was followed. For the multi-item measures, it is checked that their items loaded on the respective, a priori constructs at least at a 5% significance level. It is also ensured that for every construct, the Rho was greater than .50, as a check for convergent validity. Because the Cronbach's alphas varied from .77 to .88 and Jöreskog's Rho ranged from .78 to .88, evidence of good reliability is found (see Table 1).

In the check for discriminant validity, it is verified that the variance shared by different constructs was less than the average variance extracted (AVE) for each construct. The AVEs varied from .64 to .67, whereas the shared variances ranged from .266 to .445, so the constructs were sufficiently discriminated across themselves (Fornell & Larcker, 1981, pp. 45-46).

The quality of the structural equations model was satisfactory, according to well-established fit indicators, as follows: $\chi^2 = 65.498$, $p < .001$, $\chi^2/d.f. = 2.259$; goodness-of-fit index = .958, adjusted goodness-of-fit index = .920, confirmatory fit index = .964, root mean square error of approximation = .065, and standardized root mean residual = .079. That is, all the fit indicators achieve the thresholds recommended in prior literature (Hair, Black, Babin, & Anderson, 2010).

RESULTS

Need to Belong, Social Capital, and Time Spent on Facebook

As detailed in Figure 1, the results indicate that the need to belong has a positive influence on social capital, measured by the number of friends on Facebook ($\gamma = .17$; $p = .009$), in support of H1a. Yet it had no effect on time spent on Facebook ($\gamma = -.05$; $p = .395$), so H1b cannot be confirmed. Whereas, De Cremer and Leonardelli (2003) argue that a high need to belong leads people to cooperate socially, the results indicate that this cooperation is not reflected in the amount of time spent on Facebook. The absence of this predicted relationship between need to belong and time spent on Facebook led us to question the manner in which people use their time on Facebook. Some users interact more with others, but it is not because they have a high need to belong. It was posited that an increased number of friends

Table 1. Items and scales

Facebook attachment (adapted from Lacoeuilhe, 2000)	Loadings
I have a lot of affection for Facebook.	0.84
I find a certain comfort when I use Facebook.	0.76
I am very close to Facebook.	0.83
I am very attracted by Facebook.	0.78
Cronbach's Alpha:	**0.88**
Jöreskog's Rho:	**0.88**
Rho vc:	**0.64**

Social recognition	Loadings
Facebook allows me not to go unnoticed.	0.66
Facebook allows me to be more esteemed.	0.95
Cronbach's Alpha:	**0.77**
Jöreskog's Rho:	**0.80**
Rho vc:	**0.67**

indicated by people with a higher need to belong might not be associated with intense activity on the network. Whereas the number of friends on Facebook can reflect a user's popularity, which provides social capital benefits, this type of social capital is not necessarily active or activated by interactions.

In support of H2, a positive impact of the number of Facebook friends on the time spent on the social network is observed (ß = .23; $p < .001$), in line with findings by Orr et al. (2009). An increase of the number of friends led to more time spent on Facebook, and part of this time likely is dedicated to the interpersonal exchanges. At the very least, having a larger social network may oblige a person to become more knowledgeable about information posted by other members of the network, which requires spending more time on Facebook to the extent the network expands to include very active members. A particular user also might be proactive and devote more time to sharing information. As Chang and Heo (2014) show, there is a positive link between the number of Facebook friends and the disclosure of personal information on the network. Patterson (2012) also suggests that the very essence of a Facebook network is designed to enable people to disclose and exchange information with other members. If, independent of the need to belong, time spent on Facebook can be explained by the extent of social capital, it also

Need for social belonging (adapted from Leary et al., 2005)	Loadings
It bothers me a lot when other people do not include me in their projects.	0.67
I am easily affected when I feel that the others do not accept me.	0.92
Cronbach's Alpha:	**0.77**
Jöreskog's Rho:	**0.78**
Rho vc:	**0.65**

seemingly might be determined by other factors, such as social intelligence or entertainment (Chang & Heo, 2014; Hollenbaugh & Ferris, 2014).

Social Capital, Time Spent on Facebook, Social Recognition, and Attachment to Facebook

Both social capital and time spent on Facebook exerted positive impacts on social recognition. In support of H3a, more friends on Facebook causes a person to feel more socially recognized (ß = .17; $p = .009$). With the same logic, and in support of H3b, more time spent on Facebook leads to a stronger feeling of social recognition (ß = .16; $p = .017$). This notion of social recognition constitutes an emotional and esteem dimension. According to Honneth (2013), recognition is an important ontological stake that can be acquired individually or socially. In the model, it offers a strong predictor of Facebook attachment. Therefore, obtaining affection and social esteem is a means for people to strengthen their unique social identity, with influences on attachment to Facebook, such that the network could be considered as a device for managing emotional streams.

In addition to social recognition, time spent on Facebook is a good predictor of attachment to the site (ß = .26; $p < .001$), in support of H4a. This result suggests that time spent on Facebook could be considered useful, dedicated to interpersonal exchanges or self-presentation (Gonzales & Hancock, 2011). The concept of interpersonal exchanges for this study reflects a broad view, because most Facebook exchanges are time asynchronous. A user can broadcast information about him- or herself or that might be interesting to other members of the network. He or she also can gain information broadcast by others, comment on this information, and express opinions. Similarly, Orr et al. (2009) highlight the strong link between the time spent on Facebook and attitudes toward Facebook. Yet they also do not find a direct, significant relation between the number of friends and attitude toward Facebook. The results are similar (ß = .07; $p = .228$), except that attachment to is considered, rather than attitude toward, Facebook. Although, H4b must be rejected, the convergence of the results with those of Orr et al. (2009) advocate for the robustness of this part of the model.

Finally, a positive, strong impact of a feeling of social recognition on Facebook attachment is observed (ß = .35; $p < .001$), in accordance with H5.

DISCUSSION

Along with its interesting new perspectives, the present study presents certain limitations. Thus, are discussed successively, a new view on social capital, the measure of time spent on Facebook, and the determinants of a feeling of social recognition, before presenting some limitations and implications of the findings.

In this study, we adapted the Bourdieu`s (1980) definition of social capital. This definition suggests a quantitative dimension of social capital, related to the size of the social network (the number of Facebook friends). This approach could be considered as restrictive, it will be interesting to consider friendship on Facebook not only in term of quantity and but also in term of quality (Gentina et al. 2021). Time spent on Facebook appeared as a way to structure and feed this social capital, through interpersonal interactions. It would be interesting to mobilize the strength of ties in further research (Granovetter, 2000),

Figure 1.

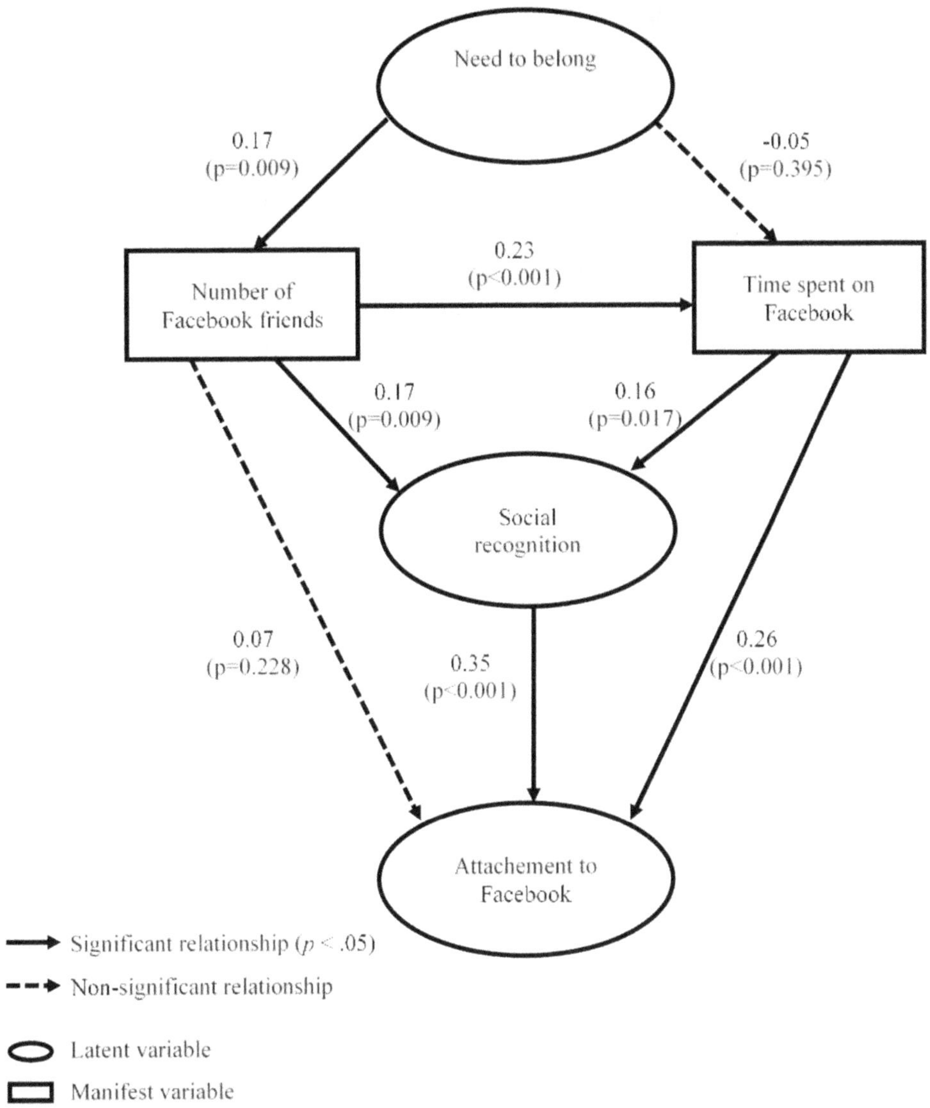

because among Facebook friends, some likely are connected with far stronger ties, while others link on the basis of very weak ties.

Ellison et al. (2007) operationalize social capital more functionally, by distinguishing among social integration in the community, a feeling of being able to count on members of the community, and the capacity to keep in touch with the community. This operationalization on Facebook would characterize the consequences of social capital in a community frame, which from one perspective is a particular case of a closed social network, consisting of redundant contacts or mutually interconnected people (Mercklé, 2011). It is not considered as particularly informative; in that it represents an exception. However, it would be interesting to take a more technical approach to personal networks that reflects not only the size of the network and the strength of the ties but also some of their structural characteristics, such as tie redundancy or the degree of centrality within a personal network.

Time spent on Facebook explained both a feeling of social recognition and attachment to Facebook, which suggests the need to investigate just how users spend their time. In addition, researchers should consider determinants of the feeling of social recognition. Users appear to consider time spent on Facebook useful, with a positive influence on feelings of social recognition and attachment to Facebook. Thus, the activities to which people dedicate their time produce positive effects for them.

However, the nature of the activities could not be specified. Further research must inventory and measure the precise activities Facebook users undertake, to discover those with the strongest impacts on feelings of social recognition or attachment to Facebook. According to some prior literature (e.g., Tosun, 2012), most social network activities involve interpersonal interactions, such as gaining information about friends' profiles and messages, reacting to these messages with likes or comments, tagging people in photos, and publishing photos or messages. These activities contribute to maintaining sociability or social ties with people the user might meet in everyday life, as well as with geographically distant connections. This source of social recognition thus depends on social esteem, which leads to self-esteem. To be socially esteemed, a person must be recognized for her or his capacities and qualities, which make her or him a unique being within the framework of a community of values (Honneth, 2013). From this perspective, activities on social networks become practices that are likely to generate gratification, in accordance with the principle of reciprocity.

MANAGERIAL IMPLICATIONS

Attachment to the brand is essential to understanding consumer behaviors. Park et al. (2010) identify attachment as a determinant of brand equity. In addition, attachment to the brand is critical, considering its predictive strength in relation to purchasing behaviors. In the present case, attachment to Facebook may be a good indicator of loyalty toward Facebook. However, even as Facebook maintains its dominant industry position, some audience erosion has begun, and some users spend less time on Facebook than they did previously. The key for the brand in coming years thus will be to encourage older users of Facebook to remain on the site, without alienating new, young adopters.

To increase attachment to its brand, Facebook also needs to enhance feelings of social belonging and perhaps differentiate communities or develop new devices to encourage users to spent more time on Facebook, to generate more interactions and stronger feelings of social recognition. Generally, the results indicate that social recognition is the main factor contributing to explain attachment to Facebook. However, the time spent on Facebook also seems to play an important role. Although the number of Facebook friends has no direct effect on attachment, it contributes to social recognition. Therefore, the extent of the social capital might not be a direct determinant of attachment, nor is it necessary to have too many "friends" on Facebook. Pushing users to accumulate friends does not necessarily lead to greater attachment to Facebook.

Rather, Facebook friends are required to create a sense of ties and develop a feeling of social recognition (Honneth, 2013). So what can managers do to encourage the creation of ties and social interactions, both with people the users already know and those separated by geography or life circumstances? Although social networks can serve to help create new relationships, most interactions are between people already in some type of relationships (Kujath, 2011). According to Patterson (2012), Facebook may appear to be a window onto others, but in truth, it is a mirror of the user. In this sense, Facebook friends represent a kind of pretext to gain a reflective view of a self-image. Through their Facebook friends, users are seeking an interaction that they can post on their wall. These interactions might be simple "likes" or comments, or they could encourage Facebook friends to share the posts, which then likely generates a stronger feeling of social recognition (Wang et al. 2021).

To encourage interactions, there must be an object of interaction; from this perspective, brand pages offer real opportunities, because Facebook and the brands present on it share the same stakes. Powers, Advincula, Austin, Graiko, and Snyder (2012) suggest facilitating conversations among Facebook users around brands, as well as between Facebook users and brands (Lin & Lu, 2011). In addition, it is not enough to prompt users to increase their number of friends; it is also necessary that these friends develop a feeling of social recognition due to high quality, interpersonal interactions. This result requires the production of valued experiences (Brakus et al., 2009), which brands might achieve by creating high quality pages that optimize possibilities for interactions among and with members.

In line with this recommendation, the role of brand community managers is essential. They should supply appealing contents. Brands should feature, on their Facebook pages, first-hand information, videos, and pictures to tell the story of the brand. They need to make the brand seem alive, such that visitors to these pages appropriate the brand and interact with and about it. They are not limited to liking the brand's page or messages formulated by the brand; they also need to interact about the related contents. A community manager thus is not a simple supplier of information; he or she also designs social interactions. If a manager cannot produce a feeling of social recognition, she or he needs to try another tactic.

CONCLUSION

This study shows that the need for social belonging affects the number of friends but not time spent on Facebook. A positive relation between the number of friends and the time spent on Facebook is noted. Thus, social capital is not inevitable, yet a large number of Facebook friends might favor more activity on Facebook, in terms of social interactions, as well as potentially social intelligence and other recreational activities (Chang & Heo, 2014; Hollenbaugh & Ferris, 2014).

Social capital and time spent on Facebook explain social recognition, which in turn explains attachment to Facebook. However, the number of friends does not explain attachment to Facebook directly, so the social network appears instrumental. Rather than the number of friends, it is the quality of the social ties and activity on Facebook, together with a feeling of social recognition, that explain attachment to Facebook. This attachment in turn may be an important source of loyalty.

To extend the study, it is recommend that further research specify the determinants of a feeling of social recognition more clearly, considering their strong explanatory power in relation to Facebook attachment. It also would be interesting to test various measures of social capital, to investigate the nature and frequency of social interactions, differentiate them using qualitative means, and identify which interactions contribute more to social recognition or favor brand attachment. Research that probes users' activities in the social network more deeply are needed, to better understand the elaboration of social recognition. In particular, it might be interesting to study the activities and roles of community managers, in their capacity to design interactions and social recognition. Finally, the stakes of these findings, related to customer loyalty and brand attachment, are crucial for ensuring the sustainability of Facebook.

REFERENCES

Ahrefs.com. (2021). https://ahrefs.com/blog/most-visited-websites/

Bailey, A. A., Bonifield, C. M., & Elhai, J. D. (2021). Modeling consumer engagement on social networking sites: Roles of attitudinal and motivational factors. *Journal of Retailing and Consumer Services*, *59*, 102348. doi:10.1016/j.jretconser.2020.102348

Batra, R., Ahuvia, A., & Bagozzi, R. P. (2012). Brand love. *Journal of Marketing*, *76*(March), 1–16. doi:10.1509/jm.09.0339

Baumeister, R. F., & Leary, M. R. (1995). The need to belong: Desire for interpersonal attachments as a fundamental human motivation. *Psychological Bulletin*, *117*(3), 497–529. doi:10.1037/0033-2909.117.3.497 PMID:7777651

Ben Mimoun, M. S., & Ammar, O. (2013). Interactions between brands and strategies of self-presentation on Facebook. *Advances in Consumer Research. Association for Consumer Research (U. S.)*, *10*, 95–97.

Bourdieu, P. (1980). Le capital social. *Actes de la Recherche en Sciences Sociales*, *31*(January), 2–3.

Brakus, J. J., Schmitt, B. H., & Zarantonello, L. (2009). Brand experience: What is it? How is it measured? Does it affect loyalty? *Journal of Marketing*, *73*(May), 52–68. doi:10.1509/jmkg.73.3.052

Casale, S., & Fioravanti, G. (2018). Why narcissists are at risk for developing Facebook addiction: The need to be admired and the need to belong. *Addictive Behaviors*, *76*, 312–318. doi:10.1016/j.addbeh.2017.08.038 PMID:28889060

Casilli, A. A. (2010). *Les liaisons numériques, vers une nouvelle sociabilité?* Editions du Seuil.

Chang, C.-W., & Heo, J. (2014). Visiting theories that predict college students' self-disclosure on Facebook. *Computers in Human Behavior*, *30*, 79–86. doi:10.1016/j.chb.2013.07.059

De Cremer, D., & Leonardelli, G. J. (2003). Cooperation in social dilemmas and the need to belong: The moderating effect of group size. *Group Dynamics*, *7*(2), 168–174. doi:10.1037/1089-2699.7.2.168

Ellison, N., Steinfield, C., & Lampe, C. (2007). The benefits of Facebook "friends:" Social capital and college students' use of online social network sites. *Journal of Computer-Mediated Communication*, *12*(4), 1143–1168. doi:10.1111/j.1083-6101.2007.00367.x

Escalas, J. E., & Bettman, J. R. (2005). Self-construal, reference groups, and brand meaning. *The Journal of Consumer Research*, *32*(December), 378–389. doi:10.1086/497549

Fornell, C., & Larcker, D. F. (1981). Evaluating structural equations models with unobservable variables and measurement error. *JMR, Journal of Marketing Research*, *18*(February), 39–50. doi:10.1177/002224378101800104

Gentina, E., Chen, R., & Yang, Z. (2021). Development of theory of mind on online social networks: Evidence from Facebook, Twitter, Instagram, and Snapchat. *Journal of Business Research*, *124*(C), 652–666. doi:10.1016/j.jbusres.2020.03.001

Gonzales, A. L., & Hancock, J. T. (2011). Mirror, mirror on my Facebook wall: Effects of exposure to Facebook on self-esteem. *Cyberpsychology, Behavior, and Social Networking, 14*(1-2), 79–83. doi:10.1089/cyber.2009.0411 PMID:21329447

Granovetter, M. S. (2000). *Le marché autrement*. Desclée de Brouver.

Hair, J. F., Black, W. C., Babin, B. J., & Anderson, R. E. (2010). *Multivariate data analysis: A global perspective* (7th ed.). Pearson.

Hollenbaugh, E. E., & Ferris, A. L. (2014). Facebook self-disclosure: Examining the role of traits, social cohesion, and motives. *Computers in Human Behavior, 30*, 50–58. doi:10.1016/j.chb.2013.07.055

Honneth, A. (2013). La lutte pour la reconnaissance. Gallimard.

Houghton, Pressey, & Istanbulluoglu. (2021). Who needs social networking? An empirical enquiry into the capability of Facebook to meet human needs and satisfaction with life. *Computers in Human Behavior, 104*.

Kim, J., & Lee, J.-E. R. (2011). The Facebook paths to happiness: Effects of the number of Facebook friends and self-presentation on subjective well-being. *Cyberpsychology, Behavior, and Social Networking, 14*(6), 359–364. doi:10.1089/cyber.2010.0374 PMID:21117983

Kujath, C. L. (2011). Facebook and MySpace: Complement or substitute for face-to-face interaction? *Cyberpsychology, Behavior, and Social Networking, 14*(1-2), 75–78. doi:10.1089/cyber.2009.0311 PMID:21329446

Lacoeuilhe, J. (2000). L'attachement à la marque: Proposition d'une échelle de mesure. *Recherche et Applications en Marketing, 15*(4), 61–77. doi:10.1177/076737010001500404

Leary, M. R., Kelly, K. M., Cottrell, C. A., & Schreindorfer, L. S. (2005). *Individual differences in the need to belong: Mapping the nomological network*. Working paper, Duke University.

Lin, K.-Y., & Lu, H.-P. (2011). Intention to continue using Facebook fan pages from the perspective of social capital. *Cyberpsychology, Behavior, and Social Networking, 14*(10), 565–570. doi:10.1089/cyber.2010.0472 PMID:21381968

Mercklé, P. (2011). *Sociologie des réseaux sociaux*. La Découverte. doi:10.3917/dec.merck.2011.01

Nadkarni, A., & Hofmann, S. G. (2012). Why do people use Facebook? *Personality and Individual Differences, 52*(3), 243–249. doi:10.1016/j.paid.2011.11.007 PMID:22544987

Oh, H. J., Ozkaya, E., & LaRose, R. (2014). How does online social networking enhance life satisfaction? The relationships among online supportive interaction, affect, perceived social support, sense of community, and life satisfaction. *Computers in Human Behavior, 30*, 69–78. doi:10.1016/j.chb.2013.07.053

Orr, E. S., Sisic, M., Ross, C., Simmering, M. G., Arseneault, J. M., & Orr, R. R. (2009). The influence of shyness on the use of Facebook in an undergraduate sample. *Cyberpsychology & Behavior, 12*(3), 337–340. doi:10.1089/cpb.2008.0214 PMID:19250019

Park, C. W., MacInnis, D. J., Eisinggerich, A. B., & Iacobucci, D. (2010). Brand attachment and brand attitude strength: Conceptual and empirical differentiation of two critical brand equity drivers. *Journal of Marketing*, *74*(November), 1–17. doi:10.1509/jmkg.74.6.1

Patterson, A. (2012). Social-networkers of the world, unite and take over: A meta-introspective perspective on the Facebook brand. *Journal of Business Research*, *65*(4), 527–534. doi:10.1016/j.jbusres.2011.02.032

Powers, T., Advincula, D., Austin, M. S., Graiko, S., & Snyder, J. (2012). Digital and social media in the purchase decision process: A special report from the Advertising Research Foundation. *Journal of Advertising Research*, *52*(4), 479–489. doi:10.2501/JAR-52-4-479-489

Sharma, G., & Baoku, L. (2013). Customer satisfaction in Web 2.0 and information technology development. *Information Technology & People*, *26*(4), 347–367. doi:10.1108/ITP-12-2012-0157

Shuv-Ami, A. (2012). Brand commitment: A new four-dimensional (4 Es) conceptualization and scale. *Journal of Customer Behaviour*, *11*(3), 281–305. doi:10.1362/147539212X13469450373155

Sirgy, M. J., Grewal, D., Mangleburg, T. F., Park, J.-O., Chon, K.-S., Clairborne, C. B., Johar, J. S., & Berkman, H. (1997). Assessing the predictive validity of two methods of measuring self-image congruence. *Journal of the Academy of Marketing Science*, *25*(3), 229–241. doi:10.1177/0092070397253004

Special, W. P., & Li-Barber, K. T. (2012). Self-disclosure and student satisfaction with Facebook. *Computers in Human Behavior*, *28*(2), 624–630. doi:10.1016/j.chb.2011.11.008

Steinfield, C., Ellison, N. B., & Lampe, C. (2008). Social capital, self-esteem, and use of online social network sites: A longitudinal analysis. *Journal of Applied Developmental Psychology*, *29*(6), 434–445. doi:10.1016/j.appdev.2008.07.002

Tosun, L. P. (2012). Motives for Facebook use and expressing "true self" on the Internet. *Computers in Human Behavior*, *28*(4), 1510–1517. doi:10.1016/j.chb.2012.03.018

Wang, T., Thai, T. D., Ly, P. T. M., & Chi, T. P. (2021). Turning social endorsement into brand passion. *Journal of Business Research*, *126*, 429–439. doi:10.1016/j.jbusres.2021.01.011

Whillans, A. V., & Chen, F. (2018). Facebook Undermines the Social Belonging of First Year Students. *Personality and Individual Differences, Vol.*, *133*(October), 13–16. doi:10.1016/j.paid.2017.03.043

Wilcox, K., & Stephen, A. T. (2013). Are close friends the enemy? Online social networks, self-esteem, and self-control. *The Journal of Consumer Research*, *40*(1), 90–103. doi:10.1086/668794

Yang, H., & Lin, C. (2014). Why do people stick to Facebook web site? A value theory-based view. *Information Technology & People*, *27*(1), 21–37. doi:10.1108/ITP-11-2012-0130

Zheng, X., Cheung, C. M. K., Lee, M. K. O., & Liang, L. (2015). Building brand loyalty through user engagement in online brand communities in social networking sites. *Information Technology & People*, *28*(1), 90–106. doi:10.1108/ITP-08-2013-0144

Chapter 12
Development of Business Through the Internet and Social Media:
The Professional Use of Audiovisual Media Technologies Through Strategic Tactics and Practices

Constantinos Nicolaou
https://orcid.org/0000-0002-6737-1653
Aristotle University of Thessaloniki, Greece

ABSTRACT

This chapter will cover development of business from and through the internet and social media. The aim of the chapter, which was set from the beginning, was twofold. The primary aim was (1) to explain the role of the effective usage of social media in the business environment and (2) to prove effective professional use-based communication process from and through audiovisual media technologies and, secondly, to become an important guide, but also a list of (new) strategic tactics and practices from and through the internet and social media, while providing a rich bibliography through literature (from theory to practice) and historical elements as a source of further study. The modern age is constantly changing, and there will always be room for improvement.

INTRODUCTION

The advancement of new communication technologies and modern phenomena in recent years has influenced the businesses worlds which are still constantly in a new and fast changing area. The international literature and empirical evidence of recent decades suggest the need for prevention (proaction) in recession as a key term, which was developed to describe either the need for business to adapt the enterprise according to developments in the external environment affecting the economic performance

DOI: 10.4018/978-1-7998-7192-7.ch012

operation (see Weick, 1979; Miller, 1987; Miller & Friesen, 1983) or/and at the level of manipulation of these developments in order to achieve the corporate and sustainability goals (see Bourgeois, 1984; Child, 1972). One such goal is considered, for example, to maintain the brand image of a business, which is not an easy task (see Nicolaou, 2011a, 2011b).

Nowadays, this specific suggestion for prevention, still remain valid in any business (including large firms as well as small and medium-sized enterprises [SMEs]). Basically, the only thing that changes is the medium and the way which now comes mainly from and through the Internet. Businesses in order to further maintain their brand image; they must expand and explore new online services. A decade ago, there were no specific check lists and templates for official, acceptable and cross-cutting (digital or e-) strategic tactics and practices from and through the Internet (and Social Media) as a guide, however, many and several professionals and practitioners in the field of business (e.g., marketing, public relations, advertising, etc.) informally used various of them for customer personas and journeys (see Sarridis & Nicolaou, 2015; Nicolaou, 2011b).

Internet is the main factor of these changes due to the new communication tools, applications and services that characterize dynamic web platform Web 2.0 (and now semantic-oriented or Web 3.0) and which are the basis for the audiovisual media technologies as new technologies (or/and Internet-based tools or Web 2.0 or Web 3.0 tools / semantic web technologies) (see O'Reilly, 2005; Heravi et al., 2012; Sarridis & Nicolaou, 2015; Nicolaou et al., 2019; Saridou et al., 2019; Prandini &Ramilli 2012; Dimoulas et al., 2019), which allow people and users to develop relationships, collaborate and interact (Hopkins & Rees, 2007; Molnár et al., 2008) with each other and eventually become active members of the (virtual) community. New technologies from and through the Internet, which are today the backbone of information and online marketplace (see Nicolaou et al., 2021b; Novgorodtseva et al. 2020; Nicolaou et al. 2019; Sarridis & Nicolaou, 2015), resulting in the main way of absolute distance communication with sound/audio media, image/picture/photograph, video and data (e.g., big data, metadata, etc.) which were enriched, merged, morphologically modified or shrunk easily without altered or/and time lacking (Sarridis & Nicolaou, 2015; Nicolaou et al., 2019; Nicolaou, 2021).

In summary, nowadays, businesses are developing based on various reported changes. Marketing scholars, practitioners, communicators, business owners, marketing managers, brand/product managers, account executives/managers/directors, marketing and business associations worldwide mostly accept these changes as well as the new conditions of our days, since they are an opportunity to review the development actions of the business (e.g., through action plan/marketing calendar actions, brief with extra smart content, etc.) (see Kwabena et al., 2020; Quinn-Allan, 2010; Sarridis & Nicolaou, 2015; Sriramesh & Hornaman, 2006; Tajvidi & Karami, 2017; Ur Rahman et al., 2020; Yannopoylos, 2011), in order to become competitive and recognizable from and through the Social Media (see Ahmad et al., 2019; Sarridis & Nicolaou, 2015; He et al., 2014; Nicolaou, 2011b; Yannopoylos, 2011). In the last few years there has been major activity through these Social Media, where people and users from all over the globe can share news, images/pictures/photographs, information about their personal life, and talk to each other, thus, began to replace traditional sources of information (Jepsen, 2006) and are becoming important networks of consumer knowledge that influence consumer behavior (de Valck et al., 2009).

This chapter will cover development of business from and through the Internet and Social Media as cutting-edge technologies. The current society in which we live is highly technologically visualized and requires, in addition to the continued use of visual media and new communication technology, to be receptive and maintain a positive outlook to every emerging innovation. Social Media have been in the spotlight for almost four (4) decades, and from now on businesses should, in addition to having to use them, be able to use them properly. In our current era, the large firms usually use Social Media by paying a large sum or/and hefty fee to specialized companies or so-called *social media gurus* to mainly improve their performance and financial sustainability of their practices (see Nicolaou & Karypidou, 2021; Kwabena et al., 2020; Ur Rahman et al., 2020; Zu et al., 2019; Barnes & Jacobsen, 2013; Rozzani et al., 2013), while the SMEs with limited resources and technical knowledge are reluctant to use them (see Ahmad et al., 2018; Ur Rahman et al. 2020; Zaki et al., 2021) or/and to use them unfortunately through amateurs, non-experts and non-specialists users of Social Media (see also Nicolaou, 2021). In this specific instant, SMEs tent to approach non-academic Social Media experts in order to offer them various paid services from and the through Social Media (e.g., creating profiles, uploading or sharing posts or/and image/picture/photograph in their own accounts/profiles, also tags, likes, followers, etc.), convincing them that Social Media are fashionable or forced due to the fact that they are used by large firms, to help them pursue their sustainability goals (see also Ye & Kulathunga, 2019; Ur Rahman et al. 2020). The well-known and famous Social Media (i.e., Facebook, Twitter, YouTube, Instagram, LinkedIn, etc.) have been and will always be free (Nicolaou & Karypidou, 2021; Sarridis & Nicolaou, 2015), and are probably the most powerful tool that a business could have without cost (Nicolaou, 2011b, p. 51) to create positive behavioral and relational outcomes among consumers through the use of them in the context of corporate social responsibility (CSR) communication (see also Cheng et al., 2021). For this reason, this chapter also refers to historical information, so that prospective readers can have a wider prospective on the whole subject; and fill this gap in the literature.

In conclusion, the aim of the chapter, which was set from the beginning, was twofold. The primary aim was (a) to explain the role of the effective usage of Social Media in the business environment; and (b) to prove that the effective professional use-based communication process from and through audiovisual media technologies, requires additional new skills and abilities as well as education/training. On the other hand, the secondly aim is to become an important guide, but also a list of (new) strategic tactics and practices to effective execution from and through the Internet and Social Media, while providing a rich bibliography through literature (from theory to practice) and historical elements as a source of further study. The modern age is constantly changing and there will always be room for improvement, not only the information that is presented but also the information that is not presented, otherwise the need for a prosperous business development strategy is still a concern.

BACKGROUND: FROM THE INTERNET TO THE SOCIAL MEDIA

The Internet first appeared in the United States of America (USA) in the decade of 1950 (Hauben & Hauben, 1997; Leiner et al., 2009). The development of computers in different computer labs around the world through a common communication code (Transmission Control Protocol / Internet Protocol - TCP/IP), created a huge network of computer systems consisting of computers and information stored on their hard drives (Kehoe, 2013; Kim, 2005; Veglis et al., 2004; Nicolaou, 2021). The continuous growth, development and evolution has created a global and international (super-)wide area network with computer interface (White, 2015; Newby et al., 2019) for connecting traffic network and data and information exchange (Koumartzis &Veglis, 2014); as computer networks and a network of people (Sarridis & Nicolaou, 2015; Chesher, 2020). Furthermore, users now use it through computers or/and other various electronic devices (e.g., see Matsiola et al., 2019; Nicolaou et al., 2021; Podara et al., 2020,

2019) as an ever-evolving culture of people, machines and everyday stories (Gauntlett, 2004) based on archetypal norms (see Booker, 2004; Lule, 2001; Parker, 2006; Phillips, 2007).

Nowadays, when people and users talk about Internet through "word of mouth" (WOM) or/and electronic word of mouth (eWOM), they refer mostly to the visible and not to the invisible part of the Internet, and especially to the World Wide Web (official name WorldWideWeb, commonly referred WWW or called just web) (Kaye & Medoff, 1999; Cohen, 2007), which was developed by Tim Berners-Lee (father of the WWW) and a group of mouthpieces in 1990; creating this technology (Berners-Lee 1999). The World, Wide and Web officially appeared in 1991, with the development of the first web browsers on it (i.e., WorldWideWeb in 1990, Line Mode Browser in 1991, etc.) (the first widely used web browser was NCSA Mosaic in 1993, while the first commercial web browser was Netscape in the same year) (see also Sarridis & Nicolaou, 2015; Giomelakis et al. 2019; Nicolaou & Karypidou, 2021), and was named Web 1.0, when DiNucci in 1999 mentioned in an article about its second version (DiNucci, 1999); as Web 2.0. The impetus for this new term by the author, was mainly the visual evolution of simple web pages, with the addition of attractive graphics and highlighted hyperlinks, as an innovation. The appearance of this innovation on the World Wide Web changed the 3W (i.e., world, wide and web) to 3C (collaboration, contribution and community) (Davies et al., 1998), and led to the creation of Generation C (GenC) (see also Nicolaou & Karypidou, 2021). This generation is not included in the genealogical generations, but it is a term used in the literature to describe our movement to 3C (see Hardey, 2011; Gazi et al., 2014). People and users who (hypothetically) belong to this generation are the *active online users*, who now produce and distribute information and are not just readers and consumers of content (e.g., branded content) and digital copy, thus facilitating collaboration and exchange (information and knowledge) between them (see Baron, 2008; Blank & Reisdorf, 2012; Bruns, 2007; Kennedy et al, 2007; Slot & Frissen, 2007). The term Web 2.0 was enacted from 2007 onwards, with the formal conceptual definition of the definition by the Organization for Economic Cooperation and Development (OECD), which focused on the model of content production and contribution from simple users (OECD, 2007). Also, since 2001 there has been talk of the semantic web as the evolution of the original world wide web (as the second version of the web), with conceptual roots from 1960, where it is now widely known as Web 3.0 (see Crosslin, 2011).

Moreover, on the other hand, Internet is a global communication system which changes the way we live our everyday lives, in the way we work, communicate and entertain our-selves, with a series of technological innovations and new services ranging from electronic mail (or e-mailing or e-mail or email or mail) (email from here on) (see Veglis, 2018) that was first sent in the late 1970s (online service) to web browsers (e.g., Google Chrome, Firefox, Microsoft Edge, etc.) (software application) and search engines (e.g., Google, Yahoo!, etc.) (software system) that are designed to carry out web searches (Internet searches) (see Pintér, 2008; Kincsei, 2008; Nicolaou, 2021, 2011b; Sarridis & Nicolaou, 2015), while at the same time it is a global network which is independent from where you live, and a place where one can have access to multiple things, disregarding nationality, social orientation and national language (Nicolaou, 2011a, 2011b). Due to the above, through the Internet it is now possible to express opinions in combination with other sources or/and forms of communication, resulting in the formation of new forms of communication and new cultures, creating a new society (see Molnár et al., 2008; Nicolaou, 2021, 2011b). This new society varies in different ways from the ending way of life due the audiovisual media technologies, such as for example the functioning and evolution of the Internet which occurs through (a) websites; (b) interactive websites or/and weblogs/blogs (e.g., interactive documentary, etc.); (c) online social networks (OSNs), social media and platforms (e.g., LinkedIn, Facebook, Twitter, etc.); (d) audiovisual platforms with interactivity (e.g., YouTube, Vimeo, Netflix, etc.) as content-hosting or/and video-sharing websites which can be moved into the software as a service (SaaS) model (e.g., a video posted on YouTube to transport you to the Netflix); (e) sound platforms (e.g., Mixcloud, SoundCloud, etc.); (f) image/picture/photograph or/and video sharing social networking service (e.g., Pinterest, Instragram, TikTok, etc.); and (g) Internet applications and services (e.g., Internet relay chat or/and multimedia messaging apps/social messaging/social chat, such as Skype, Viber, Facebook Messenger, WhatsApp, Snapchat etc.); so-called as 'Social Media' by the general public (see Nicolaou & Karypidou, 2021; Nicolaou et al. 2021a, 2021b, 2019; Podara et al., 2021; Nicolaou & Kalliris, 2020; Matsiola et al., 2018, 2015; Zachos et al., 2018; Sarridis & Nicolaou, 2015; Nicolaou, 2021, 2011a, 2011b; Dimoulas et al., 2019), as virtual communities. The virtual communities are the epitome of an ongoing trial of changing the social solidarity (see Pintér, 2008; Kincsei, 2008; Nicolaou, 2011a, 2011b; Sarridis & Nicolaou, 2015; Gajjala, 2008; Oldenburg, 1991; Habermas,1971; Gouldner, 1976) where people and users can create free mainly their own virtual profile through email and develop a (social) network of communication so they can communicate, interact and discuss from and through the Social Media (see also Sarridis & Nicolaou, 2015; Nicolaou, 2011b; Campos-Freire, 2008). At this point, we should mention that GeoCities was the first (unofficial) social network in 1994 and SixDegrees in 1997 as the first Social Media - before the term "social" was even discovered; while followed by the first wiki in 1995 as the first web application as well as emerged the weblogs/blogs in 1998 as the first full-format multimedia websites (see Nicolaou & Karypidou, 2021).

Social Media as audiovisual media technologies are governed by various demands and requirements, such as functional, data and non-functional requirements (Avouris, 2000, pp.133-168), which focus on communication, community-based input, interactive computer-mediated technologies that facilitate the creation or/and sharing of information, ideas, career interests and other forms of expression through virtual communities and networks (see Nicolaou & Karypidou, 2021; Matsiola et al., 2018, 2015; Sarridis & Nicolaou, 2015; Nicolaou, 2011b). Furthermore, they are based on the dynamic web platform Web 2.0 (see O'Reilly, 2009, 2007, 2005), where content is mostly the product of the non-corporate users themselves; as user-generated content (UGC) (Haenlein & Kaplan, 2009; Molnár et al., 2008; Bruns, 2006). Also, the people as social media users can (a) interact through them without specialized knowledge on computers and networks (Pisani & Piotet, 2009; Sarridis & Nicolaou, 2015) for a greater two-way interaction, discussion and conversation (Hopkins & Rees, 2007, pp.13-14); and (b) easily produce and contribute their own audiovisual content that make it available for thousands of other social media users and get feedback in just a few minutes, by using open or/and free software and application (such as e.g., social software) (see Owen et al. 2006; Dabbagh & Reo, 2011) as potential producers (Matsiola et al., 2018, 2015; Sarridis & Nicolaou 2015; Hopkins & Rees, 2007); due Social Media have user-friendly interfaces through usability heuristics (e.g., user control, consistency, error prevention, etc.) and interaction design (e.g., visibility, constraints, mapping, etc.). Finally, it should be mentioned that they are mainly divided into the following categories as terms (some of them have already been mentioned above): (a) Blogging; (b) Social Networking; (c) Microblogging; (d) Media Sharing; (e) Social News & Social Bookmarking; (f) Ratings & Reviews; (g) Forums; and (h) Virtual Worlds (see Zarrella, 2009).

THE NEED FOR THE USE OF SOCIAL MEDIA: FROM THEORY TO PRACTICE

The continuous technological developments in our everyday lives combined with personal involvement of the same people and users as active online users, have highlighted the need of Social Media which established their presence from 2006 onwards (Ajjan & Hartshorne, 2008; Sarridou & Nicolaou, 2015; Nicolaou et al., 2021b, 2019; Nicolaou & Karypidou, 2021). More specifically, it started mainly in 2003 with the appearance of MySpace, while it becomes more intense from 2005 onwards, when Hi5 and Facebook appeared in 2004, YouTube in 2005 and Twitter in 2006 (see Kwak et al., 2010; Nicolaou, 2011a, 2011b; Sarridis & Nicolaou, 2015; Boyd & Ellison, 2007). Based on the international literature and empirical evidence and data of recent decades (Bourgeois, 1984; Lane & Lubatkin, 1998; Miller, 1988; Teece et al., 1997; Weick, 1979), it is a justified move in the context of the adoption of prevention in the field of business, which is summarized in the need to investigate new trends and approaches that influence choice of communication tactics and practices to formulate ideal strategic tactics and practices to effective execution (see Nicolaou, 2011b; Sarridis & Nicolaou, 2015).

Nowadays, we live in a world where new communication technology and society evolve over time (Kincsei, 2008), resulting in evolution of new technologies and modern phenomena (i.e., Social Media), while, on the other hand, numerous scientific fields, such as the Marketing, the Public Relations as well as the Advertising, to swing and risk losing their reputation, value and role (see Nicolaou, 2011b; Sarridis & Nicolaou, 2015). However, this does not seem to be the case, because these new technologies, and in particular Social Media as audiovisual media technologies, are the ideal communication tool for transmission of messages, for realizing the ideal strategic tactics and practices of these sciences (Sarridis & Nicolaou, 2015; Nicolaou 2011a, 2011b). The only crucial change is the fact that instead of referring to the authentic and classic form of these scientific fields, we now refer to the field of e-Business, e-Marketing, e-Public Relations, and so on (see Sarridis & Nicolaou, 2015; Nicoli & Komodromos, 2013; Nicolaou, 2011a; 2011b), which arose from the demand for better use of triptych Information Communication Technologies (ICTs). In summary, we can say with absolute certainty that Social Media are a modern revolution with multiple-multimodal functions of symmetrical communication and dialogue with two-way concessions (see also Roper, 2005), who create new trends, attitudes and stereotypes as well as new multiple forms with access to *comprehensive multimedia communication* (Nicolaou, 2011b, p. 43) with people and users as active online users from and through the Internet with multimodal content and digital copy (i.e., online and offline texts, images/pictures/photographs, sounds/audio medias - audio in the form of sound, or audio recordings, certain sounds, music's/songs, sound effects [sfx] etc. - as well as in the combined format of the mentioned in the form of animations, or videos into a single presentation) (see Nicolaou et al., 2021b), such as the media websites which add a cumulative value through the contribution of users (Antonopoulos et al., 2015, p. 48) that may even influence public opinion (Antonopoulos & Veglis 2013; Spyridou et al., 2013).

In order to be able to use the Social Media; and especially marketing scholars, practitioners, communicators, business owners, marketing managers, brand/product managers, account executives/managers/directors, marketing and business associations worldwide, they must keep in mind some of the rules, which are governed and reflected (a) on the relevant literature review and corresponding findings of previous studies and researches (see Quinn-Allan, 2010; Haenlein & Kaplan, 2009; Melcrum, 2007; Safko & Brake, 2009; Nicolaou & Karypidou, 2021; Sarridis & Nicolaou, 2015); as well as (b) by the users/members themselves - mainly by the users/members of the (modern) Internet forums (e.g., torrent community portals/forums) from the middle of the 1990's and the beginning of the 2000's (millennium)

- as informal norms in them (see Nicolaou & Karypidou, 2021). At this point, we should mention that most of the potential users of the torrent community portals/forums, where most of them were banned or/ and closed due to universal legislative reforms and copyright laws mainly in the mid-2000s worldwide, moved to YouTube and mainly to Twitter, due to the fact that they were allowed to keep their anonymity behind a digital avatar, or a persona (something that is still valid until today in several Social Media at the time of writing this chapter) (Nicolaou & Karypidou, 2021) as were the specific culture in these Internet forums (see also Sarridis& Nicolaou, 2015; Nicolaou, 2011a, 2011b; Gajjala, 2008). Additionally, many potential users who had no issue sharing their true identity (whether they hid it or not initially, e.g., on Twitter) moved notably to Snapchat mainly from 2014 onwards, then to Instagram which allowed users since mid-2016 to create live stories and live streaming, and then to TikTok mainly from 2018 onwards, which became widely known worldwide during the first period of global quarantine in March 2020 of the COVID-19 pandemic (see Nicolaou & Karypidou, 2021). In summary, due to the constant changes and upgrades that took place over the last decade on Social Media, a vast number of users has become non-academic Social Media experts, leading to what we nowadays refer to bloggers, vloggers, instagrammers, youtuberers, tiktokers and so on, with large audiences, who are now considered the modern key figures; so-called influencer or *social media influencer* (SMI) (see also Cheng et al. 2021; Coates et al., 2020; Kádeková & Holienčinová, 2018; Konstantopoulou et al., 2019; Nicolaou & Karypidou, 2021).

The most fundamental rules as organizational factors influencing the strategic tactics and practices of business, as they are highlighted out, are: (a) the communication should take the form of conversation and not monologue or/and narration from and through audiovisual media technologies; (b) the participants in them (i.e., the person/s or group/team of people behind them as community managers, social media managers or/and administrators, copywriter, etc.) should behave as people with emotions, feelings, empathy and critical thinking, and not as inanimate machines (i.e., robots) with automated written or/ and verbal responses due to well-behaved scenarios that are usually applied recklessly in business call centers, believing that they offer "better" customer service and experience as customer personas and journeys - do not forget that you are addressing humans; (c) the honesty, transparency and trust are the most essential, fundamental and important triptych values; and finally (d) the issue and subject to be raised should always be about attraction and interaction, and not promotion, which will arise if done correctly (see also Sarridis & Nicolaou, 2015; Nicolaou, 2011a, 2011b). Furthermore, they should be aware of the use of Social Media Optimization (SMO), which partially function as Search Engine Optimization (SEO) (Nicolaou & Karypidou, 2021; Sarridis & Nicolaou, 2015).

Before referring to SEO and SMO, we should refer to the search engines that can be used in two (2) equally important ways in the business environment (Ištvanić et al., 2017). Search engines are programs that allow keyword searches in databases (with millions of web pages, websites, etc.) and (see Veglis et al., 2004, pp. 115-137). This search sometimes fails, and the solution comes from and through SEO (see also Giomelakis &Veglis, 2021), which is one of the two-ways that helps businesses show search results (see also Bhandari & Bansal, 2018; Berman & Katona, 2013; Burghardt et al., 2012). In the meantime, the solution is realized through minor changes at specific points (in the encryption) of the code or/and during the development or/and design of the website, it can help significantly (Sarridis & Nicolaou, 2015), e.g., increase the performance of an official website (or a web page) of a business in the search results, without having to make a generously payment to the respective companies that manage or/and own search engines (see Trengove et al., 2011, pp. 120-121) through a pay-per-click campaign (PPC) (see also Giomelakis &Veglis, 2021). An illustrative example is having a business (other than its official website) e.g., a solid and serious weblog/blog (see Du & Wagner, 2006), which should be frequently updated with information relevant to its subject matter (and with the corresponding keywords that are relevant to our topic - something that search engines take very seriously), resulting in a simple and easy solution in terms of SEO of its website (Sarridis & Nicolaou, 2015), without much to no cost. In addition, if the business wants to pay, the solution is the search engine marketing (SEM), which is the second way that helps businesses show search results. SEM allows e.g., marketers to buy inventory in search results, usually in the form of advertising in multiple forms, such as online and offline text, image/picture/photograph, or video ads) (see Terrance et al., 2017; Ištvanić et al., 2017); and is called display advertising (see Ištvanić et al., 2017). On the other hand, SMO is a way of attracting new visitors/ audiences to the business's official website, and can be done for example through adding social links or/ and buttons, such as RSS feeds or/and share buttons in the branded content or/and the promotion of the activity of the business from and through all the Social Media of the business (e.g., through status update, posts, tweets, blog posts, memes, quote, etc.) (see Sarridis & Nicolaou, 2015; Nicolaou, 2011a, 2011b).

Social Media also provides excellent opportunities for the development of "*synchronous and asynchronous two-way communication fostering high levels of audience engagement and privileging users with more control over communication and ultimately the relationships they choose to pursue*" (Quinn-Allan, 2010, pp. 52-53) with multiple uses, depending on the message they convey to the target audience as well as the possibility of better prevention and timely adaptation to social demands and trends (Nicolaou 2011b, Sarridis & Nicolaou 2015). Furthermore, they enable the creation of a 24-hour presentation with interactive multimedia display (combination of online and offline text, image/picture/photograph, sound/audio media, and video) to build a good brand image, in order (a) to interact with people and users (audience/s from here on) in the world from and through the Internet; (b) to eliminate geographical restrictions and easy monitoring of the environment; (c) to collect different kind of information to identify the real needs and problems faced by the various categories of the public and audiences, resulting in the promotion of appropriate suggestions and solutions (Nicolaou, 2011b, pp. 43-44); as well as (d) to create, build and maintain symmetrical communication and dialogue with two-way concessions (see also Roper, 2005) - business must more care about feedback and comments from audiences that emerge from and through them, because Social Media is a powerful communication tool for dialogue (see also Sancar, 2013).

STRATEGIC TACTICS AND PRACTICES FROM AND THROUGH THE SOCIAL MEDIA

The use of Social Media can develop new innovative business actions, business initiatives, implement business pilot programs or/and create partnerships (see Piñeiro-Otero & Martínez-Rolán, 2016; Sarridis & Nicolaou, 2015; Weber, 2009), of course it is enough to use the right strategies tactics and practices. A typical example of such a business innovation, is the start of an e-action or/and e-business. The golden section of this venture is the creation of close and long-term relationships as well as the creation and building of prestige and brand image through formal and healthy communication from and through audiovisual media technologies (Sarridis & Nicolaou, 2015; Nicolaou, 2011a, 2011b). The key word of success is interactivity with the audience with whom we should personally communicate with them constantly (Nicolaou, 2011b; Culbertson, 1991; Haley, 1985). If we achieve this, the doors open automatically to success in the business environment. In summary, using four (4) simple small on the job steps, such as (a) describing the audience and (b) justifying the needs and interests to interact with them; (c) determining first how to approach them; and finally (d) choosing the right and most appropriate Social Media (Thackeray et al., 2012); success is widespread.

The most popular practice on Social Media for business activity is native advertising through specialized multimodal content (i.e., through quote, memes, etc.) as function, which the number one factor for a successful commercial policy or/and ad campaign (Sarridis & Nicolaou, 2015; Nicolaou, 2011a, 2011b), while directly or/and indirectly affects people's thoughts, emotions and feelings from and through audiovisual media technologies and audiovisual content (audiovisual media communications) (see Nicolaou, 2020; Nicolaou & Kalliris, 2020; Nicolaou et al., 2021b). The types of advertisements from and through the Internet using Social Media as communication tool in the business environment are sufficient (Sarridis & Nicolaou, 2015), while the selection of a particular advertisement form is always based on the target audience, to which they are addressed (Arens et al., 2011).

In summary, whichever Social Media are being used, businesses should always keep in mind some important steps and tips as check list(s) and template(s) for their correct management and successful use to effective execution, which should apply to all Social Media, without exception:

1. people must have a profile account, while businesses and companies page account;
2. if we are referring to businesses, the profile picture should represent them;
3. either you have a profile account or/and a page account (depending, of course, on which Social Media we refer), it should be continuously updated and structured with a systematic flow of information in time and quantity, but always sparingly;
4. the information should be original and with interesting branded content that deserves to be reproduced, notified and shared;
5. create different content and digital copy with customizations for each Social Media respectively, and avoid transferring simple and unedited information (e.g., from the official website of your business as an announcement or a post on Facebook or/and Twitter, or from Facebook to Twitter or/and vice versa, etc.); also the content should be targeted to your respective audience, - do not forget that content and targeting are the two (2) main pillars of success in the business environment from marketing strategy to effective execution;
6. make the most of the possibilities offered by the "hashtag"—written with a # symbol— from the familiar digital powerups (keywords displayed keys) that are associated and used with corresponding prompts in forums or/and online discussions; which became widespread when the first appeared and proposed on Twitter in a 2007 tweet by Christopher Reaves Messina (https://twitter.com/chrismessina/status/223115412), and then on almost all Social Media respectively (e.g., Instagram, Facebook, LinkedIn, etc.); to presented your content both your audience and beyond your audience (e.g., to friends / acquaintances of your audience, etc.);
7. create official and exclusive hashtags for your business (which would be good to be legally secured their protection);
8. in the description point (bio) that exists on all Social Media, there should be a relevant link that leads to the official website or there should be ways of contacting the business (e.g., email, contact phone, etc.) or/and including the official hashatgs (because they help in SEO and SMO);
9. it is very important for business
    a. to monitor the progress of their social media posts, in order to understand what their audience likes and dislikes, but and what days and hours their posts are most popular; as well as the business keywords (e.g., the official hashtags) both competition and sector, through useful

analytics tools (some useful tools are Mention, Google Alerts and Hootsuite) (some Social Media offers this service or/and through other providers);
   b. to know web position assessment of the their official website and Social Media (e.g., through Google search or Alexa ranking); and
   c. to make Social Media evaluation for presence, activity, influence, etc. (here tools, such as Klout, PeerIndex and Kreed, become relevant);
10. do not send recklessly messages to your audience from and through the Social Media;
11. motivate and give incentive to your audience to create content and participate in your Social Media;
12. respond immediately to comments or/and messages from your audience, and of course, not standardized / automated;
13. ask the opinion of your audience (e.g., through a question, quiz or/and gallop/poll), and listen to them, because they share their perspectives, insights and knowledge, or/and generate value from and through audiovisual content development;
14. reward your loyal audience with offers, discounts or/and vouchers and gifts, in the context of customer relationship management (CRM);
15. in the same context (i.e., through CRM), create at regular intervals events or/and contests with gifts;
16. promote services and fewer products through ad campaigns, native advertisements or/and updates to your audience or/and to a targeted audience depending on the demographics you choose, through the corresponding service which is now offered on almost all Social Media; and final
17. it would be good not to sell (e.g., products) and of course, not to expose your business. (see Podara et al., 2021; Dimoulas et al., 2019; Piñeiro-Otero & Martínez-Rolán, 2016; Sarridis & Nicolaou, 2015; Nicolaou, 2011a, 2011b; Scott & Jacka, 2011; Weber, 2009)

In conclusion, the Social Media (as audiovisual media technologies) forma way of formal and healthy communication and enhance a strong relationship between a business and its audience (see also Nicolaou, 2020; Nicolaou & Kalliris, 2020). Furthermore, the field of Social Media is an interdisciplinary subject and refers finally to a few, to the right and competent professionals and practitioners mainly in the field of business (e.g., marketing, public relations, advertising, etc.) (see Quinn-Allan, 2010; Yannopoylos, 2011; Sarridis & Nicolaou, 2015; Sriramesh & Hornaman, 2006; Nicolaou, 2011b). Finally, it can be said with fair certainty that one of the purposes of Social Media through strategic tactic and practices in a business is to gain and maintain the organizational legitimacy and this perhaps is achieved only with the moral capacity, knowledge and technical skills and abilities of that person who really deals with them (e.g., as community managers, social media managers or/and administrators, copywriter, etc.) (see also Nicolaou et al., 2021a, 2021b, 2019; Nicolaou & Kalliris, 2020; Sarridis & Nicolaou, 2015, Quinn-Allan, 2010; Yannopoylos, 2011).These of kind knowledge, abilities and skills should be continuous, up-to-date and lifelong, through the appropriate education and training (see also Nicolaou et al. 2021b, 2019; Nicolaou & Kalliris, 2020; Nicolaou, 2020).

CONCLUSION

The continuous and rapid development of new communication technology has adjusted our everyday lives. Social Media, as digital intermediaries, are a great tool as well as a great opportunity for development for modern business. It is a field that raises the interest of most businesses for a long time, due to the advantages they offer, while avoiding to spend large sums of money - creating a Social Media account is mainly free (see also Campos-Freire, 2008; Nicolaou, 2011b; Sarridis & Nicolaou, 2015).

Technology in general, will always continue to influence businesses and therefore Social Media should be used open-mindedly in order to be able to establish a formal and healthy communication worldwide network (see Nicolaou, 2020; Nicolaou & Kalliris, 2020). It is theoretically possible through their use, to urge and help businesses to develop a healthy relationship with their audience (see Sarridis & Nicolaou, 2015; Nicolaou, 2011a, 2011b). Furthermore, businesses should from now on, in addition to having to use them, will have to use them properly; otherwise, the need for a prosperous business development strategy will continue to be a concern (see also González-Tosat & Sádaba-Chalezquer, 2021).

The purpose of this chapter was to capture the development of business, and provide a synopsis of (new) strategic tactics and practices to effective execution from and through the Internet and Social Media, through a rich bibliography. Also, become an important guide, as in on-the-job training. Hence, the steps and tips as check list(s) and template(s) for their correct management and successful use of cutting-edge technologies are straightforward.

In summary, Social Media aims are humans (see also Sarridis & Nicolaou, 2015; Nicolaou, 2011a, 2011b). Thus, businesses must first understand and therefore interact with them without any exploitation. Humans, as mentioned above, (a) exchange information in their social environment from and through the Internet and Social Media; and (b) create, build and maintain (i) symmetrical communication and dialogue; as well as (ii) relationships (see Sarridis & Nicolaou, 2015; Nicolaou, 2020).

In conclusion, what should be noted is that there will always be room for further improvement of strategic tactics and practices for the development of a business through business actions, using the theoretical approaches correctly as key basic business principles from and through audiovisual media technologies. Finally, the modern and visual-centric era we live in requires us to be always receptive to any innovation that arises, and as we live in a changing world.

REFERENCES

Ahmad, S. Z., Ahmad, N., & Bakar, A. R. A. (2018). Reflections of entrepreneurs of small and medium-sized enterprises concerning the adoption of social media and its impact on performance outcomes: Evidence from the UAE. *Telematics and Informatics*, *35*(1), 6–17. doi:10.1016/j.tele.2017.09.006

Ahmad, S. Z., Bakar, A. R. A., & Ahmad, N. (2019). Social media adoption and its impact on firm performance: The case of the UAE. *International Journal of Entrepreneurial Behaviour & Research*, *25*(1), 84–111. doi:10.1108/IJEBR-08-2017-0299

Ajjan, H., & Hartshorne, R. (2008). Investigating faculty decisions to adopt Web 2.0 technologies: Theory and empirical tests. *The Internet and Higher Education*, *11*(2), 71–80. doi:10.1016/j.iheduc.2008.05.002

Antonopoulos, N., & Veglis, A. (2013). The evolution of the technological characteristics of media websites. *Proceedings of the 4th Annual Asian Conference on Media and Mass Communication (MediAsia 2013)*, 130-146.

Antonopoulos, N., Veglis, A., Gardikiotis, A., Kotsakis, R., & Kalliris, G. (2015). Web Third-person effect in structural aspects of the information on media websites. *Computers in Human Behavior, 44*, 45–58. doi:10.1016/j.chb.2014.11.022

Arens, W., Arens, C., Weigold, M., & Schaefer, D. (2011). *Advertising (M)*. McGraw-Hill/Irwin.

Avouris, N. (2000). *Introduction to Communication Human – Computer* [Εισαγωγή στην Επικοινωνία Ανθρώπου – Υπολογιστή]. Diavlos.

Barnes, N. G., & Jacobsen, S. (2013). Adoption of social media by fast-growing companies: Innovation among the Inc. 500. *Journal of Marketing Development and Competitiveness*, *7*(1), 11–17.

Baron, N. (2008). *Always On*. Oxford University Press. doi:10.1093/acprof:oso/9780195313055.001.0001

Berman, R., & Katona, Z. (2013). The role of search engine optimization in search marketing. *Marketing Science*, *32*(4), 644–651. doi:10.1287/mksc.2013.0783

Berners-Lee, T. (1999). *Weaving the Web: The Past, Present and Future of the World. Wide Web by Its Inventor*. Orion Business Publishing.

Bhandari, R. S., & Bansal, A. (2018). Impact of Search Engine Optimization as a Marketing Tool. *Journal of Business Research*, *7*(1), 24–36. doi:10.1177/2278682117754016

Blank, G., & Reisdorf, B. C. (2012). The Participatory Web: A user perspective on Web 2.0. *Information Communication and Society*, *15*(4), 537–554. doi:10.1080/1369118X.2012.665935

Booker, C. (2004). The Seven Basic Plots: Why We Tell Stories. *Continuum*.

Bourgeois, L. III. (1984). Strategic Management and Determinism. *Academy of Management Review*, *9*(4), 586–596. doi:10.5465/amr.1984.4277347

Boyd, M. D., & Ellison, B. N. (2007). *Social Network Sites: Definition, history and scholarship*. Michigan State University.

Bruns, A. (2006). Towards Produsage: Futures for User-Led Content Production. In F. Sudweeks, H. Hrachovec, & C. Ess (Eds.), Proceedings Cultural Attitudes towards Communication and Technology (pp. 275–284). Academic Press.

Bruns, A. (2007). The Future is User-Led: The Path Towards Widespread Produsage. In A. Hutchinson (Ed.), *Proceedings of perthDAC 2007: The 7th International Digital Arts and Culture Conference* (pp. 68–77). Curtin University of Technology. https://eprints.qut.edu.au/12902/

Burghardt, M., Heckner, M., & Wolff, C. (2012). The many ways of searching the web together: A comparison of social search engines. In D. Lewandowski (Ed.), *Social information research* (Vol. 4). Emerald Group Publishing Limited.

Campos-Freire, F. (2008). Las redes sociales trastocan los modelos de los medios de comunicacióntradicionales. *Revista Latina de Comunicación Social*, *63*, 287–293.

Cheng, Y., Chen, Y.-R. R., & Hung-Baesecke, C.-J. F. (2021). Social Media Influencers in CSR Endorsement: The Effect of Consumer Mimicry on CSR Behaviors and Consumer Relationships. *Social Science Computer Review, 39*(4), 744–761. Advance online publication. doi:10.1177/0894439320987184

Chesher, C. (2020). How Computer Networks Became Social. In Second International Handbook of Internet Research (pp. 105-126). Springer. doi:10.1007/978-94-024-1555-1_4

Child, J. (1972). Organization Structure, Environment and Performance: The Role of Strategic Choice. *Sociology, 6*(1), 1–22. doi:10.1177/003803857200600101

Coates, A. E., Hardman, C. A., Halldord, J. C. G., Christiansen, P., & Boyland, E. J. (2020). "It's Just Addictive People That Make Addictive Videos": Children's Understanding of and Attitudes towards Influencer Marketing of Food and Beverages by YouTube Video Bloggers. *International Journal of Environmental Research and Public Health, 17*(2), 449. doi:10.3390/ijerph17020449 PMID:31936672

Cohen, J. E. (2007). Cyberspace as/and space. *Columbia Law Review, 107*, 210–256.

Crosslin, M. (2011). When the Future Finally Arrives: Web 2.0 Becomes Web 3.0. In M. J. W. Lee & C. McLoughlin (Eds.), *Web 2.0-based e-learning: Applying social informatics for tertiary teaching* (pp. 380–393). IGI Global. doi:10.4018/978-1-60566-294-7.ch020

Culbertson, H. M. (1991). Role Taking and Sensitivity: Keys to Playing and Making Public Relations Roles. *Journal of Public Relations Research, 3*(1-4), 37–65. doi:10.12071532754xjprr0301-4_2

Dabbagh, N., & Reo, R. (2011). Back to the future: Tracing the roots and learning affordances of social software. In M. J. W. Lee & C. McLoughlin (Eds.), *Web 2.0-based e-learning: Applying social informatics for tertiary teaching* (pp. 1–20). IGI Global. doi:10.4018/978-1-60566-294-7.ch001

Davies, L. B., Shield, L., & Weininger, M. J. (1998). Godzilla can MOO, can you? MOOs for construction, collaboration & community and research. *Language Teaching, 22*(2), 16–21.

de Valck, K., van Briggen, G., & Wierengan, B. (2009). Virtual communities: A marketing perspective. *Decision Support Systems, 47*(3), 185–203. doi:10.1016/j.dss.2009.02.008

Dimoulas, C. A., Veglis, A. A., & Kalliris, G. (2019). Semantically Enhanced Authoring of Shared Media. In Advanced Methodologies and Technologies in Media and Communications (pp. 277-289). IGI Global. DOI: doi:10.4018/978-1-5225-7601-3.ch022

DiNucci, D. (1999). Fragmented future. *Print, 53*(4), 32–33.

Du, H. S., & Wagner, C. (2006). Weblog success: Exploring the role of technology. *International Journal of Human-Computer Studies, 64*(9), 789–798. doi:10.1016/j.ijhcs.2006.04.002

Gajjala, R. (2008). *Avatar research ethics*. Air-L Archive. http://listserv.aoir.org/pipermail/air-l-aoir.org/2008-March/016057.html

Gauntlett, D. (2004). Web Studies: What's New. In D. Gauntlett & R. Horsley (Eds.), *Web.Studies* (2nd ed., pp. 3–23). Bloomsbury Academic.

Gazi, A., Cordeiro, P., Starkey, G., & Dimitrakopoulou, D. (2014). 'Generation C' and audio media: A cross-cultural analysis of differences in media consumption in four European countries. *Participations, 11*(2), 239–257.

Giomelakis, D., Karypidou, C., & Veglis, A. (2019). SEO inside Newsrooms: Reports from the Field. *Future Internet, 11*(12), 261. doi:10.3390/fi11120261

Giomelakis, D., & Veglis, A. (2021). Theory and Practice of Search Engine Optimization. In Encyclopedia of Organizational Knowledge, Administration, and Technology (pp. 1354-1367). IGI Global. doi:10.4018/978-1-7998-3473-1.ch093

González-Tosat, C., & Sádaba-Chalezquer, C. (2021). Digital Intermediaries: More than New Actors on a Crowded Media Stage. *Journalism and Media, 2*(1), 77–99. doi:10.3390/journalmedia2010006

Gouldner, A. (1976). *The Dialectic of Ideology and Technology*. Seabury Press. doi:10.1007/978-1-349-15663-4

Habermas, J. (1971). *Knowledge and Human Interests*. Beacon Press.

Haenlein, M., & Kaplan, A. M. (2009). Users of the world, unite! The challenges and opportunities of Social Media. *Business Horizons, 53*, 59–68.

Haley, R. I. (1985). *Developing effective communication strategy: A benefit segmentation approach*. Wiley.

Hardey, M. (2011). Generation C: Content, Creation, Connections and Choice. *International Journal of Market Research, 53*(6), 749–770. doi:10.2501/IJMR-53-6-749-770

Hauben, R., & Hauben, M. (1997). *Netizens: On the History and Impact of Usenet and the Internet*. IEEE Computer Society Press.

He, W., Wang, F. K., & Zha, S. (2014). Enhancing social media competitiveness of small businesses: Insights from small pizzerias. *New Review of Hypermedia and Multimedia, 20*(3), 225–250. doi:10.1080/13614568.2014.889225

Heravi, B. R., Boran, M., & Breslin, J. (2012). Towards social semantic journalism. In *Sixth International AAAI Conference on Weblogs and Social Media*. Dublin: AAAI Press.

Hopkins, P. J., & Rees, M. J. (2007). Creating a Branded Information Environment with Social Media: positioning Bond University within Web 2.0. In *Library Services and IT Services papers*. Paper 16. http://epublications.bond.edu.au/library_pubs/16

Ištvanić, M., Milić, D. C., & Krpić, Z. (2017). Digital Marketing in the Business Environment. *International Journal of Electrical and Computer Engineering Systems, 8*(2), 67–75. doi:10.32985/ijeces.8.2.4

Jepsen, A. (2006). Information Search in Virtual Communities: Is it Replacing Use of Off-Line Communication? *Journal of Marketing Communications, 12*(4), 247–261. doi:10.1080/13527260600694308

Kádeková, Z., & Holienčinová, M. (2018). Influencer Marketing as a modern phenomenon creating a new frontier of virtual opportunities. *Communication Today, 9*(2), 90–106.

Kaye, B. K., & Medoff, N. J. (1999). *The World Wide Web: A Mass Communication Perspective*. Mayfield Publishing Company.

Kehoe, B. P. (2013). *Zen and the Art of the Internet*. Tredition Classics.

Kennedy, G., Dlagarno, B., Gray, K., Judd, T., Waycott, J., Bennett, S., Maton, K., Kerri-Lee, K., Bishop, A., Rosemary, C., & Churchward, A. (2007). The net generation are not big users of Web 2.0 technologies: Preliminary findings. ASCILITE, 517-525.

Kim, B.-K. (2005). *Internationalising the Internet: The Co-evolution of Influence and Technology (New Horizons in the Economics of Innovation)*. Edward Elgar Publishing Ltd. doi:10.4337/9781845426750

Kincsei, A. (2008). Technology and society in the information age. In R. Pintér (Ed.), *Information Society: From Theory to Political Practice*. Gondolat - ÚjMandátum.

Konstantopoulou, A., Rizomyliotis, I., Konstantoulaki, K., & Badahdah, R. (2019). Improving SMEs' competitiveness with the use of Instagram influencer advertising and eWOM. *The International Journal of Organizational Analysis*, *27*(2), 308–321. doi:10.1108/IJOA-04-2018-1406

Koumartzis, N., & Veglis, A. (2014). Internet Regulation and Online Censorship. *International Journal of E-Politics*, *5*(4), 66–81. doi:10.4018/ijep.2014100104

Kwabena, A. E., Li, K., Bonsu, O. A. M., Faamaa, O. B., & Alexander, B. (2020). Effects of Social Media on Firm Performance and Customer Relations-Evidence from Ghana. *Business and Economic Review*, *10*(1), 101–111.

Kwak, H., Lee, C., Park, H., & Moon, S. (2010), What is Twitter, a social network or a news media? *WWW '10: Proceedings of the 19th international conference on World wide web*, 591–600. 10.1145/1772690.1772751

Lane, P., & Lubatkin, M. (1998). Relative Absorptive Capacity and Inter-Organizational Learning. *Strategic Management Journal*, *19*(5), 461–477. doi:10.1002/(SICI)1097-0266(199805)19:5<461::AID-SMJ953>3.0.CO;2-L

Leiner, B., Cerf, V., Clark, D., Kahn, R., Kleinrock, L., Lynch, D., Postel, J., Roberts, L., & Wolff, S. (2009). A brief history of the internet. *Computer Communication Review*, *39*(5), 22–31. doi:10.1145/1629607.1629613

Lule, J. (2001). *Daily News Eternal Stories: The Mythological Role of Journalism*. Guilford Press.

Matsiola, M., Dimoulas, C., Kalliris, G., & Veglis, A. A. (2015). Augmenting User Interaction Experience through Embedded Multimodal Media Agents in Social Networks. In Social Media and the Transformation of Interaction in Society (pp. 188-209). IGI Global. doi:10.4018/978-1-4666-8556-7.ch010

Matsiola, M., Dimoulas, C., Kalliris, G., & Veglis, A. A. (2018). Augmenting User Interaction Experience Through Embedded Multimodal Media Agents in Social Networks. In Information Retrieval and Management: Concepts, Methodologies, Tools, and Applications (pp. 1972-1993). IGI Global. doi:10.4018/978-1-5225-5191-1.ch088

Matsiola, M., Spiliopoulos, P., Kotsakis, R., Nicolaou, C., & Podara, A. (2019). Technology-Enhanced Learning in Audiovisual Education: The Case of Radio Journalism Course Design. *Education Sciences*, *9*(1), 62. doi:10.3390/educsci9010062

Melcrum. (2007). *How to use social media to engage employees*. Melcrum Publishing.

Miller, D. (1987). The Structural and Environmental Correlates of Business Strategy. *Strategic Management Journal*, *8*(1), 55–76. doi:10.1002mj.4250080106

Miller, D. (1988). Relating Porter's Business Strategies to Environment and Structure: Analysis and Performance Implications. *Academy of Management Journal*, *31*(2), 280–308.

Miller, D., & Friesen, P. (1983). Strategy-Making and Environment: The Third Link. *Strategic Management Journal*, *4*(3), 221–235. doi:10.1002mj.4250040304

Molnár, S., Kollányi, B., & Székely, L. (2008). Social networks and the network society. In R. Pintér (Ed.), *Information Society: From Theory to Political Practice*. Gondolat - ÚjMandátum.

Newby, T. J., Stepich, D. A., Lehman, J. D., Russell, J. D., & Leftwich, A. T. (2019). *Educational Technology for Teaching and Learning* (4th ed.). Pearson Education.

Nicolaou, C. (2011a). *Public Relations and New Technologies* [Unpublished CIPR Professional PR Diploma Thesis]. Chartered Institute of Public Relations, London, UK.

Nicolaou, C. (2020). Communication Skills through Audiovisual Media and Audiovisual Content. *ΣΚΕΨΥ, 7*(1), 166-174.

Nicolaou, C. (2021). Qualitative methods research through the Internet Applications and Services: The contribution of audiovisuals media technology as technology-enhanced research. *International Research in Higher Education, 6*(1). doi:10.5430/irhe.v6n1p1

Nicolaou, C., & Kalliris, G. (2020). Audiovisual Media Communications in Adult Education: The case of Cyprus and Greece of Adults as Adult Learners. *European Journal of Investigation in Health, Psychology and Education*, *10*(4), 967–994. doi:10.3390/ejihpe10040069

Nicolaou, C., & Karypidou, C. (2021). Generations and Social Media: The case of Cyprus and Greece. In *Proceedings of the 7th International Scientific Conference.*

Nicolaou, C., Matsiola, M., & Kalliris, G. (2019). Technology-Enhanced Learning and Teaching Methodologies through Audiovisual Media. *Education Sciences*, *9*(3), 196. doi:10.3390/educsci9030196

Nicolaou, C., Matsiola, M., Karypidou, C., Podara, A., Kotsakis, R., & Kalliris, G. (2021b). Medias Studies, Audiovisual Media Communications, and Generations: The case of budding journalists in radio courses in Greece. *Journalism and Media*, *2*(2), 155–192. doi:10.3390/journalmedia2020010

Nicolaou, C., Podara, A., & Karypidou, C. (2021a). Audiovisual media in education and Generation Z: Application of audiovisual media theory in education with an emphasis on radio. In *Proceedings of the 6th International Scientific Conference on Communication, Information, Awareness and Education in Late Modernity* (pp. 294-302). Institute of Humanities and Social Sciences.

Nicolaou, C. A. (2011b). *Public Relations: Future and New Technologies* [Δημόσιες Σχέσεις: Μέλλον και Νέες Τεχνολογίες of Greek language] [Unpublished Bachelor's Thesis]. University of Nicosia, Nicosia, Cyprus.

Nicoli, N., & Komodromos, M. (2013). *Principles of Public Relations*. University of Nicosia Press.

Novgorodtseva, A. N., Tomyuk, O. N., Dyachkova, M. A., & Piankova, M. P. (2020). Online marketplace: Student consumer strategies. *Economic Consultant*, *32*(4), 41–53. doi:10.46224/ecoc.2020.4.5

O'Reilly, T. (2005). *What is Web 2.0?* https://www.oreilly.com/pub/a/web2/archive/what-is-web-20.html

O'Reilly T. (2007). What Is Web 2.0: Design Patterns and Business Models for the Next Generation of Software. *Communications & Strategies*, 17-37.

O'Reilly, T. (2009). Battelle John, Web Squared: Web 2.0 Five Years On. *Web 2.0 Summit*, 1-15.

OECD. (2007). *Participative Web and User-Created Content: Web 2.0, Wikis, and Social Networking*. OECD.

Oldenburg, R. (1991). *The Great Good Place*. Paragon House.

Owen, M., Grant, L., Sayers, S., & Facer, K. (2006). *Social Software and Learning*. Futurelab. https://www.nfer.ac.uk/media/1820/futl57.pdf

Parker, P. (2006). *The Art and Science of Screenwriting* (2nd ed.). Intellect.

Phillips, A. (2007). *Good writing for Journalists*. SAGE Publications, Inc.

Piñeiro-Otero, T., & Martínez-Rolán, X. (2016). Understading Digital Merketing – Basics and Actions. In MBA: Theory and Application of Business and Management Principles. Springer.

Pintér, R. (2008). *Information Society: From Theory to Political Practice*. Gondolat- ÚjMandátum.

Pisani, F., & Piotet, D. (2009). La alquimia de las multitudes: cómo la web estácambiando el mundo (No. Sirsi). Barcelona: Paidós.

Podara, A., Giomelakis, D., Nicolaou, C., Matsiola, M., & Kotsakis, R. (2021). Digital Storytelling in Cultural Heritage: Audience Engagement in the Interactive Documentary New Life. *Sustainability*, *13*(3), 1193. doi:10.3390u13031193

Podara, A., Matsiola, M., Nicolaou, C., Maniou, T. A., & Kalliris, G. (2019). Audiovisual consumption practices in post-crisis Greece: An empirical research approach to Generation Z. *Proceedings of the International Conference on Filmic and Media Narratives of the Crisis: Contemporary Representations*.

Podara, A., Matsiola, M., Nicolaou, C., Maniou, T. A., & Kalliris, G. (2020). Transformation of television viewing practices in Greece: Generation Z and audio-visual content. *Journal of Digital Media & Policy*. doi:10.1386/jdmp_00034_1

Prandini, M., & Ramilli, M. (2012). Raising Risk Awareness on the Adoption of Web 2.0 Technologies in Decision Making Processes. *Future Internet*, *4*(3), 700–718. doi:10.3390/fi4030700

Quinn-Allan, D. (2010). Public relations, education, and social media: Issues for professionalism in the digital age. *Asia Pacific Public Relations Journal, 11*(1), 41–55.

Roper, J. (2005). Symmetrical Communication: Excellent Public Relations or a Strategy for Hegemony? *Journal of Public Relations Research, 17*(1), 69–86. doi:10.12071532754xjprr1701_6

Rozzani, N., Rahman, R. A., Mohamed, S. I., & Yusuf, S. N. S. (2013). Applying technology: Issues in microfinance operations. *Middle East Journal of Scientific Research, 17*(3), 374–381.

Safko, L., & Brake, D. K. (2009). *The social media bible: tactics, tools and strategies for business success*. John Wiley & Sons.

Sancar, G. A. (2013). Political Public Relations 2.0 and the Use of Twitter of Political Leaders in Turkey. *Online Journal of Communication and Media Technologies, 3*(1), 181–194. doi:10.29333/ojcmt/2417

Saridou, T., Panagiotidis, K., Tsipas, N., & Veglis, A. (2019). Towards a semantic-oriented model of participatory journalism management: Perceptions of user-generated content. *Journal of Education, Innovation, and Communication, 1*(1).

Sarridis, I., & Nicolaou, C. (2015, December). *Social Media: (Correct) Professional Use* [Μέσα Κοινωνικής Δικτύωσης: Η (σωστή) Επαγγελματική Χρήση τους of Greek language] [Paper presentation]. The 2nd Student Conference of the Department of Applied Informatics—University of Macedonia on Modern Entrepreneurship & Informatics Technologies, Thessaloniki, Greece.

Scott, P. R., & Jacka, J. M. (2011). *Auditing Social Media: A Govermance and Risk Guide.* IIARF.

Slot, M., & Frissen, V. (2007). Users in the 'Golden' age of the information society. *Observatório Journal, 1*(3), 201–224. doi:10.15847/obsOBS132007153

Spyridou, L.-P., Matsiola, M., Veglis, A., Kalliris, G., & Dimoulas, C. (2013). Journalism in a state of flux: Journalists as agents of technology innovation and emerging news practices. *The International Communication Gazette, 75*(1), 76–98. doi:10.1177/1748048512461763

Sriramesh, K., & Hornaman, L. B. (2006). Public Relations as a Profession: An Analysis of Curricular Content in the United States. *Journal of Creative Communications, 1*(2), 155–172. doi:10.1177/097325860600100202

Tajvidi, R., & Karami, A. (2017). The effect of social media on firm performance. *Computers in Human Behavior, 115*, 105174. doi:10.1016/j.chb.2017.09.026

Teece, D., Pisano, G., & Shuen, A. (1997). Dynamic Capabilities and Strategic Management. *Strategic Management Journal, 18*(7), 509–533. doi:10.1002/(SICI)1097-0266(199708)18:7<509::AID-SMJ882>3.0.CO;2-Z

Terrance, A. R., Shrivastava, S., & Kumari, A. (2017). Importance of Search Engine Marketing is the Digital World. *ICITKM, 14*, 155–158. doi:10.15439/2018KM24

Thackeray, R., Brad, L., Neiger, B. L., & Keller, H. (2012). Integrating Social Media and Social Marketing: A Four-Step Process. *Health Promotion Practice, 13*(2), 165–168. doi:10.1177/1524839911432009 PMID:22382492

Trengove, A., Malczyk, A., & Beneke, J. (2011). *Internet Marketing*. GetSmarter.

Ur Rahman, R., Ali Shah, S. M., El-Gohary, H., Abbas, M., Haider Khalil, S., Al Altheeb, S., & Sultan, F. (2020). Social Media Adoption and Financial Sustainability: Learned Lessons from Developing Countries. *Sustainability, 12*(24), 10616. doi:10.3390u122410616

Veglis, A. (2018). *Email. In The SAGE Encyclopedia of Surveillance, Security, and Privacy*. SAGE Publication, Inc.

Veglis, A., Abraham, E., & Pomportsis, A. (2004). *Research and Information Collection on the Internet* [Έρευνα και Συλλογή Πληροφοριών στο Διαδίκτυο of Greek language]. Tziolas Publications.

Weber, L. (2009). *Marketing To The Social Web: How Digital Customer Communities Build Your Business*. John Wiley & Sons. doi:10.1002/9781118258125

Weick, K. (1979). *The Social Psychology of Organizing* (2nd ed.). Addison-Wesley.

White, R. (2015). *How Computers Work: The Evolution of Technology* (10th ed.). Que Publishing.

Yannopoylos, P. (2011). Impact of the Internet on Marketing Strategy Formulation. *International Journal of Business and Social Science*, *2*(18).

Ye, J., & Kulathunga, K. M. M. C. B. (2019). How does financial literacy promote sustainability in SMEs? A developing country perspective. *Sustainability, 11*(10), 2990. doi:10.3390u11102990

Zachos, G., Paraskevopoulou-Kollia, E.-A., & Anagnostopoulos, I. (2018). Social Media Use in Higher Education: A Review. *Education Sciences*, *8*(4), 194. doi:10.3390/educsci8040194

Zaki, A. M., El-Gohary, H., & Edwards, D. (2021). Understanding Ethical and Other SMEs Internationalisation Determinants and Its Impact on Business Performance: A Primary Attempt to Understand Malaysian SMEs Internationalisation. *International Journal of Customer Relationship Marketing and Management*, *12*(1), 1–27. doi:10.4018/IJCRMM.2021010101

Zarrella, D. (2009). *The Social Media Marketing Book*. O'Reilly Media.

Zu, X., Diao, X., & Meng, Z. (2019). The impact of social media input intensity on firm performance: Evidence from Sina Weibo. *Physica A*, *536*, 122556. doi:10.1016/j.physa.2019.122556

Chapter 13
Brand Humour Advertisements on a Social Network Platform and Their Impact on Online Consumer Engagement:
The Case of Instagram

Tooba Ali Akbar
Qatar University, Qatar

Hatem El-Gohary
https://orcid.org/0000-0001-6139-7054
Qatar University, Qatar

ABSTRACT

Past studies on humour have predicted that the right humour technique can attract attention and lead to organic engagement from the viewer. However, limited research has been conducted concerning the use of humour by brands on social media. Based on Speck's taxonomy of humour, this research aims to clarify whether online brand humour advertisements have an impact on consumer engagement on a visual social media platform like Instagram. This chapter analyses the influence of comic wit and satire on product involvement, brand familiarity and gender, and their impact on online consumer engagement on the social network platform. A survey was developed and distributed online and a total of 216 participants from Qatar voluntarily filled out the questionnaire. Data was then analysed using SPSS and structural equation modelling. Results provide evidence that both humour techniques have a significant impact on consumer engagement when product involvement is mediating their relationship. Managerial implications of the results and future research prospects are also discussed.

DOI: 10.4018/978-1-7998-7192-7.ch013

INTRODUCTION

In recent years, online marketing and advertisement research has become the centre of many empirical studies due to internet penetration and the increasing number of social network sites and users (El-Gohary and El-Gohary, 2016; Krawford, 2011; El-Gohary and Eid, 2012). Several studies on the attitude towards advertisements demonstrate that humour creates a positive effect on consumers by breaking through the advertisement clutter. Many researchers studying the effect of humour in traditional media, such as television and print media (Eisend, 2009; Gulas and Weinberger, 2006) have reached this conclusion; however, little research has been conducted regarding the use of humour in digital media.

Researchers have been intrigued by the complexity of humour; however, the effect of humour in brand communication and advertising remains an under-researched area in marketing literature. According to Eisend's meta-analysis of humour effects (2009), there are some inconsistencies in research findings of the impact of humour, such as humour leading to higher attention generation towards the advertisement and brand in question. However, because of mixed results, it remains unclear how online brand humour influences consumer motivation to engage with the brand online. Therefore, humour is perceived by most brands and researchers as a very usable but complex and unpredictable tool. As the use of humour in advertising is prevalent, it is crucial to improve our understanding of consumers' responses to brand humour on social media platforms by acknowledging that different humour types lead to different results. This study examines whether different humour types on social media networks, specifically Instagram, contribute to consumer engagement.

The research objectives of this study are to examine the role that comic wit and satire humour techniques play in a brand advertisement on a social media platform and how it can affect consumers' choice to engage with such a post on the platform. Furthermore, this research work will help in the examination of other important factors that can affect the relationship between social media brand advertisements and online consumer engagement. This study will address the gap in literature by scrutinising the role of brand familiarity, product involvement, and gender in creating online consumer engagement.

BACKGROUND

Most businesses these days are facing with an "attention-deficit" from consumers. Attention-deficit is a phenomenon that describes consumers' lack to attention to brand messages and cues. Due to an overwhelming amount of information coming from various sources, consumers end up absorbing a small percentage of that information.

Commercial brands are constantly developing different communication strategies to approach their target market electronically (El-Gohary et al., 2013). Social Network Sites have especially been a game changer in providing brands with an effective communication channel to interact with their target audience in an efficient and timely manner to increase brand awareness (Christodoulides, 2009). Social Network platforms offer consumers the tools to be expressive. Due to this reason, social media and more specifically, social network sites have become essential for brands to manage consumer experience and loyalty with their brand (Christodoulides, 2009).

Traditional media has a captivated audience that has little choice but to watch the ad being shown on their television screens. However, on social media, consumers are considered an active audience and are given the choice to skip ads that they are not interested in. Moreover, the platform providers understand the importance of curating the website according to consumer needs. For instance, Instagram videos advertisements are set to mute as a standard setting and can be unmuted by the user if required. Some consumers would continue scrolling through their newsfeed without turning the sound on if the ad did not capture their interest. Similarly, users can skip advertisements that are embedded in Instagram stories. Therefore, it is not surprising that the impact of advertisements may vary in different media platforms due to their varying features for consuming and creating content online. As the use of social network sites is on the rise among consumers, brands now consider social media as an important medium for marketing and developing strategies. Many businesses rely on humour to advertise their products due to its effectiveness, yet, the causes for a humour technique's success or failure in advertising are not fully understood. (Kellaris & Cline, 2007).

In literature, most used definitions of humour describe it as a communication tool or activity that leads to mirth (Scheel, 2017). Butterfield and Booth-Butterfield (1991) interpret humour as a "verbal or nonverbal form of communication that stimulates laughter or joy". However, humour is not always received as a positive process leading to laughter, as it has also been defined as "an incongruent communicative process that can evoke a variety of emotions in the producer, receiver or both" (Gervais and Wilson 2005). Albeit humour appears frequently in brand messaging, its usage remains debatable due to mixed findings of its effectiveness and its complex nature. As most research studies over the years that have looked at humour did not recognize humour as a multifaceted subject and categorized all humour types under one umbrella, therefore, there is not unanimously or commonly established taxonomy of humour. (Catanescu and Tom, 2001).

Apart from definitions, several theories have emerged to address how, why, or why not humour works. Some theories have been developed to understand and categorize humour, which differ among humour research groups. Berger (1976, 1993) classified humour by taking different theories into consideration. According to Berger's typology, humour can be activated by various techniques such as exaggeration, mockery, repetition, and incongruity. In order to come up with his typology of humour, Berger analysed jokes and stated that some techniques might not be funny on their own and must complement one another to create humour, yet there is always one dominant mechanism of humour in play. Berger hypothesized that humour types or techniques fall into four categories: language, action, identity, and logic. He further stated that these categories were comprehensive and had 45 mutually exclusive techniques. Since Berger's typology was based on jokes, but without specifying which kind of media the typology was for, Buijzen and Valkenburg (2004) formulated a new typology by modifying it for the analysis of audio-visual humour. Building on Berger's typology, Buijzen and Valkenburg categorized humour into eight types to make it appropriate for television commercials. These types are slapstick humour, surprise, irony, clownish behaviour, misunderstanding, parody, satire and miscellaneous. This typology was formulated not only to distinguish between television commercials, but to also show different techniques used for diverse audience groups. Another widely cited theory used to explain humour effects is the theory of incongruity. Taking the theory of incongruity into view, people tend to find humour in things that have an element of surprise. Since the time of Aristotle, theory of incongruity has been the most used and widely accepted philosophy. It is also the most extensively used mechanism in humour advertisements. Forabosco (1992) described incongruity as a deviation from a cognitive reference model, where resolution and cognition are mechanisms of the process of humour. According to this theory, comprehension of humour is necessary for it to be funny. It also requires thought to understand a situation and incongruence in order to experience humour in that situation.

A second widely cited theory approach used by researchers is grounded on the Elaboration Likelihood Model (ELM). According to ELM, receivers process information via the central or peripheral routes. The model explains how the level of involvement changes the receiver's attitude (Petty and Cacioppo, 1986). The central route of persuasion is used to process serious information. For instance, when a viewer has a high level of involvement, the central route is activated. Whereas, the peripheral route is activated in a low-involvement situation where the viewer does not process the information based on its strong argument, rather, the viewer looks for other sources. Most scholars believe that humour is comprehended through the peripheral route as viewers rely on their emotions and feeling of amusement to process the advertisement containing humorous content. On the contrary, some researchers argue that since advertisements containing humour increase viewers' level of attentions as compared to non-humorous advertisements (Eisend, 2009), therefore increased attention will lead to the activation of the central route for cognitive processing.

Researchers over the years have studied humour and classified it into categories based on theories, different humour techniques or applied humour (Catanescu and Tom, 2001). At present, the most prevalent theory used to understand humour is Speck's (1991) taxonomy of humour. This taxonomy is popular among humour researchers as it sheds light on different types of mechanisms of humour. Speck's humorous message taxonomy has recently been applied in Barry and Graca's (2018) study of humour effectives in video advertisements played on YouTube. Similarly, Leonidas et al., (2009) analysed the effects of situational factors such as culture and product type on humour in TV advertisements in Greece while applying Speck's Humorous Message Taxonomy.

Incongruity-Resolution Theory

Incongruity is defined as the lack of congruence with what is considered logical or suitable. Incongruity-resolution is to resolve something that is absurd. Although incongruity-resolution is a dominant theory used to understand different mechanisms of humour, there is no precise definition for it.

According to the Incongruity-Resolution theory, processing humour is a type of interpretation of information. Humour is experienced by the receiver when there is an incongruity between expectation of what is about to unfold and what actually happens, resulting in people laughing at unexpected things. This theory emphasizes the importance of cognition in order to find humour in the subject. The incongruity resolution path gets activated when the content of the advertisement differs from what is generally accepted. Advertisements using incongruity-resolution usually consist of problem-solving leading to a comical resolution. Most humour processes employed by advertisers rely on incongruity-resolution (Alden & Hoyer, 1993) as some scholars believe that it increases audience's attention towards the advertisement. Moreover, for an incongruity to be hilarious, the setting must not be threatening and should consist of playful and harmless peculiarities. An example of such an incongruity would be talking objects or animals. For humour to work, the incongruity must be understood and resolved. Incongruity-resolution humour is thus a process, which depends on the manipulation of knowledge or the norm.

Arousal-Safety Theory

A version of release theory, the Arousal-Safety theory suggests that viewers feel an initial tension, which is followed by relief upon realization that there is no real harm or a negative consequence.

Advertisements involving Arousal-safety humour usually create a positive emotional response amongst the viewers (Speck, 1991). Some of the humour types capitalizing on arousal-safety consist of innocence of children, fear and relief, and melodrama. Commercials containing humour built on arousal-safety theory consists of scenes where the subjects barely escape tense situations, creating suspense amongst the viewers, which quickly fades away and is replaced by relief once the stressful situation turns into something trivial. Laughter is produced due to the swing in the emotional response. The affective model is centred on the postulation that a positive state comprising of joy experienced by people will result in them ridding themselves of any exposure to negative elements.

Humorous Disparagement Theory

Disparagement humour is the oldest humour mechanism based on the theory of Superiority. Disparagement theories imply that humour is a tool used for criticism and hostility without facing serious negative consequences. Disparaging humour is laughter at somebody else's expense. When United Airlines became the target of criticism for dragging one of its passengers by dragging him out of the plane; one of the competitors tweeted "we beat competition, not you". Similarly, another competitor poked fun at United Airline's injuries by stating "drags on our flights are not allowed." (Chicago Tribune, 2017). This humour disguises criticism in a cloak of humour so it appears harmless to the audience. It challenges the bounds of what is socially acceptable by making humour out of things that might not be socially acceptable in normal circumstances. An example of disparagement humour would be that sexism is looked down upon and unacceptable but the presence of sexist jokes in commercials is prevalent. Satire and self-depreciating humour are the most used forms of disparaging humour in advertising.

The three humour mechanisms can occur alone or in combination. Based on the three theories, Speck categorized humour into 5 types: comic wit, sentimental humour, satire, sentimental comedy, and full comedy.

The present study is based on Speck's approach to humour mechanisms and borrowing from his framework called the Humorous Message Taxonomy, which categorizes humour into five types:

- Comic wit,
- Sentimental Humour,
- Satire,
- Sentimental Comedy, and
- Full comedy.

CONCEPTUAL FRAMEWORK AND HYPOTHESES DEVELOPMENT

The conceptual framework shows the hypothesized relationship between consumer engagement and brand humour. It hypothesizes if brand familiarity and product involvement can influence the relationship between humour types and online consumer engagement.

From Speck's five types of humours, comic wit and satire were chosen for analysis in this study, as they are the most commonly adopted humour types in advertisements (Beard, 2008). Comic wit is a creative yet simple style of humour that is only based on incongruity-resolution (Meyer, 2000). Whereas,

Table 1. Taxonomy of humour types

Humour Types	Arousal-safety	Incongruity-resolution	Humorous disparagement
Comic wit		X	
Sentimental humour	X		
Satire		X	X
Sentimental comedy	X	X	
Full comedy	X	X	X

Source: Speck (1991)

satire is a humour technique which combines humorous disparagement and incongruity resolution to create humour. Some studies have shown that humorous messages containing comic wit, that are obvious for consumers to comprehend, reach their communication goals faster as compared to complex humour types (Anand and Sternthal, 1990). Moreover, information that is not congruent at first is recalled more often than congruent information (Heckler and Childers,1992).

Satire on the other hand, makes playful mockery as the basis of the message for the viewer to experience humour. Humorous disparagement is activated in a way that one party in the ad feels superior to the other party at their expense. (Martin 2007). Research has also shown that while viewers try to reconcile the incongruity in a message/ad (comic wit/satire), new links are created in the brain related to that message, resulting in new paths and revising the brand schema or creating a new brand schema if the person is not acquainted with the brand. In this case, brand familiarity mediates the relationship between a viewer's reaction to a humorous ad and engagement with the brand after viewing the ad (Sjödin & Törn, 2006).

Although the impact of humorous advertisements on consumer attitudes has been a vital research subject among academics, most researchers relied on fictitious brands to test their hypotheses. However, since the probability of consumers being exposed to completely new brands is minimal, taking a fictitious brand to test reactions to humour in the ad is unrealistic. Therefore, this research will also look at brand familiarity as a mediator while testing humour effects on online consumer engagement (Chung and Zhao, 2011).

The second mediator considered for this study is product involvement. It is typically agreed upon within the marketing practitioners' community that advertisements for high-involvement products should not use humour techniques in their messages as this can lead to results contrary to what is anticipated. However, the effect of humour also depends on the humour technique in question. If humour is found to be more effective in gaining attention or leading to high recall and comprehension, marketers should then use it in their advertising message. (Chung & Zhao, 2003)

Lastly, This study will also look at the effect of gender on the relationship between humour techniques and online consumer engagement. Gender is being investigated as studies have shown that men and women react differently to humour (Schwarz, Hoffmann and Hutter, 2015).

Comic Wit

Comic wit purely relies on the incongruity-resolution method without activating any other mechanism. Previous research studies have found that comic wit is the most popular type of humour used in advertisements (Barry and Graça, 2018). Viewers, while attempting to resolve the incongruity, create new paths to process information (Heckler and Childers, 1992), increasing their involvement with the ad directly and the brand indirectly. Moreover, comic wit is a positive humour technique that usually has a simple ad message, making it easier for consumers to absorb information as compared to other humour techniques such as satire, full comedy etc. (Anand and Sternthal, 1990).

Research on humorous advertisements shows that incongruency leads to surprise, which plays an important positive impact in creating humour (Yoon, H. J. (2018). Once the humour is successfully understood and the incongruency is resolved, it leads to greater perceived humour. According to Eisend's meta-analysis (Eisend, 2011), humour that is perceived can result in the individual liking the advertisement and the brand in in question. The element of surprise or incongruity in an advertisement that leads to humour can also enhance consumer engagement (Wang, 2006).

As comic wit is expected to leave a positive impression on the viewer and due to its simplicity and straightforwardness in conveying a message, we can hypothesise that:

H1: Comic wit humour appeal applied in Instagram brand advertisements will have a positive impact on online consumer engagement.

Satire

Satire is another humour type that combines elements from incongruity resolution and disparagement humour. Satire can either lead to identification with the victim of the joke or detachment from the victim. Satire can either bring together the audience or create a division between them, depending on the opinion being communicated in the ad. If the audience does not have the view as shared in the ad, they will not identify with the ad or even the brand. (Stern, 1996) The right type of humour can encourage communication and engagement, but the wrong humour can just as easily hinder it. Past research studies have suggested that viewers can form a positive or negative attitude towards an advertisement which can also affect their attitude towards the brand and other measures of advertisement such as engagement with the brand (Eisend, 2018). We assume that this can also be applied to humour techniques used in online social media brand advertisements.

Considering all factors and the risk involved in using satire as humour technique in ads, we hypothesise that:

H2: Satire humour appeal applied in Instagram brand advertisements will have a negative impact on online consumer engagement.

Perceived Product Involvement

While the word "involvement" has many definitions in consumer behaviour psychology, researchers agree that messages of high involvement will be more relevant, thus causing greater consequences or connections as compared to low involvement messages (Petty and Cacioppo 1979). The notion of involvement has been looked at in new consumer behaviour research studies as an important moderator for information processing communication messages. (Petty and Cacioppo 1981, 1983). Moreover, cues and stimuli, such as comic wit or satire humour in this study, in a consumer's surrounding can function as situational sources of involvement. Furthermore, research has noted that attitude formed during high involvement are often extended to attitude towards the brand. Furthermore, the nature of the product has an impact of the reaction towards the humour treatment used in an ad.

Built on the Elaboration Likelihood Model, the product's perceived relevance to the consumer is one of the main variables that motivate the consumer to process the ad. Previous studies (Chung and Zhao, 2002) testing the moderating role of personal involvement in traditional media on the effect of humour found that humour has shown to create undesirable effects on memory and attitude for high-involvement products and positive effects for low-involvement products. On social media, we expect that product involvement will mediate the relationship between humour and consumer engagement.

H3: Product involvement mediates the relationship between comic wit and consumer engagement

H4: Product involvement mediates the relationship between satire and consumer engagement

Brand Familiarity

Brand familiarity reflects the level of information or knowledge a consumer might have regarding a certain brand. These knowledge structures exist in the memory of the consumer that are linked with the brand (Kent & Allen, 1994). According to the theory of Schemata, prior knowledge of a stimulus helps in easier retrieval and processing of information from their schema. A schema is a structure of links and nodes about the stimulus. (Taylor, Peplau and Sears, 2000). Familiarity towards a brand can increase due to a consumer's personal interaction with a brand or by listening to friends and family mentioning the brand. Brand familiarity has an impact on the consumer's motivation to interact with the brand (Baker et al., 1986). Moreover, the effort required to process information from a familiar brand is much less as compared to an unfamiliar one, making them more amiable. (Delgado-Ballester et al., 2012). Consequently, we can assume that when a consumer is exposed to a humorous ad, he or she will be more likely to interact with the post if the ad is about a familiar brand.

Therefore, it is postulated that:

H5: Brand Familiarity mediates the relationship between comic wit and consumer engagement.

H6: Brand Familiarity mediates the relationship between satire and consumer engagement.

Consumer Engagement

Brodie et al. (2011) have defined consumer engagement as "a psychological state that occurs through interactive and co-creative customer experience with a brand". On social media, consumer engagement is viewed as the fundamental measure of market effectiveness. Whereas humour is defined as "a means of providing pleasure, initiating social interactions with both familiar and unfamiliar audiences" (Lynch, 2002). If consumers agree with the humour, they are more likely to engage with the post containing the humour.

In the context of engagement, the use of humour in advertisements can encourage consumers to interact with the brand's advertising post. Advertisements that consist of creativity and arouse positive emotions have shown a higher chance of capturing the viewer's interest and have a higher probability of being shared online (Teixeira, 2012; Wang, 2006). This demonstrates that although sharing intent of online users depends on their personal choices, however, it is much more likely that advertisements that sustain the viewer's interest will be engaged with, and the inclusion of humour in those advertisements can thus lead to higher consumer engagement (Cox, 2015).

Humorous advertisements can invoke favourable feelings in the viewer. Literature supports the argument that brands that evoke favourable feelings through their advertisement have a higher probability of engaging consumers with the brand (Wang, 2006).

Based on the literature discussed, we postulate that:
H7: Product involvement positively influences online consumer engagement.
H8: Brand familiarity positively influences online consumer engagement.

Gender

Gender is a social construct that is interwoven with all facets of human behaviour. Across various studies, both genders have shown behavioural patterns different from each other. Men and women have also been found to have a varying sense of humour. Both genders have shown to appreciate different types of humour mechanisms. Studies focusing on humour appreciation have mainly indicated that the male gender is more likely than the female gender to enjoy humour encompassing aggressive content, whereas females are more likely to appreciate illogical or absurd humour structures. Both genders have shown to react differently in behavioural studies.

Thus, it is hypothesised that:
H9: Gender moderates the relationship between comic wit (***H9a***),
Product involvement (***H9b***),
Brand familiarity (***H9c***),
Satire (***H9d***) and
Consumer engagement.

Figure 1. Conceptual framework

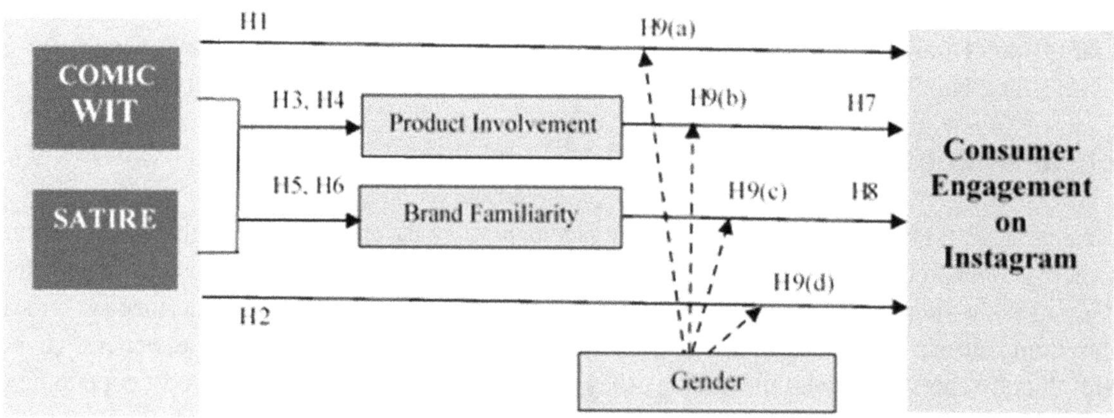

METHODOLOGY AND RESEARCH DESIGN

The data for this study was collected through a questionnaire. A survey was prepared for the measurement of the constructs proposed in the conceptual framework. The questionnaire was created using an online survey software, Google Forms. As most respondents of the study were Qatar University students belonging to the age group of 18 to 24 years, most Instagram users also belong to a similar age bracket. Therefore, using convenience sampling in this study can be justified because of the overlap of audience age group for Instagram and respondents of this study. Before the distribution of the survey, a sample was sent out to a few individuals for pre-testing of the language used and general coherence of the questionnaire. Based on their suggestions, a few changes were made to address wordings and structure of the survey. As the study focuses on Instagram, before the survey begins, respondents are asked if they use the specified social network. The survey automatically ends for those that do not have an account on the platform.

The development of the questionnaire was done by relying on well-established and validated measures. Some of the measurement items had to be adapted to the framework of the research. However, due to time constraints, the survey was only distributed in the English language.

Table 2. Measurement scales

Variable	Items	Source
Satire/Comic wit	1. I found the advertisement to be funny. 2. I understood the context of the advertisement. 3. Relying on humour to execute this advertisement made sense to me. 4. The humour applied to the advertisement made it entertaining. 5. I enjoyed the advertisement because of its humorous style. 6. The humour in the advertisement grabbed my attention.	Modified from Spielmann (2014), Speck (1991)
Product Involvement	1. Relevant. 2. Exciting. 3. Important. 4. Appealing. 5. Consumed by me regularly. 6. Preferred over other brands offering similar products.	Modified from Zaichkowsky (1994)
Brand Familiarity	1. I am familiar with the brand shown in the advertisement. 2. I have used the brand shown in the advertisement. 3. I am able to identify this brand from its logo. 4. I feel the values of this brand are close to me. 5. I like this brand. 6. After seeing the advertisement, I feel emotional closeness to the brand.	Modified from Kent & Allen (1994)
Consumer Engagement	1. Visit the brand page? 2. Click on the advertisement for more information? 3. Follow the brand's Instagram page? 4. Want to leave a comment/like under the brand's post? 5. Tag other users on the brand's post? 6. Want to create posts about the brand advertisement?	Modified from Schivinski, B., Christodoulides, G., & Dabrowski, D. (2016)

Data Collection

A total of 216 surveys responses were collected, of which 189 respondents completed the survey, whereas 27 respondents did not use Instagram and their responses were excluded. Convenience sampling method and snowballing technique were used to invite respondents to participate in the study. The link of the questionnaire was shared on social media and shared through WhatsApp service. An email was also sent out to Qatar University students to fill out the survey.

As convenience sampling method was adopted for survey distribution, consequently, most respondents were from Qatar University. As 70% of the student population at the university consists of females, it

Table 3. Demographic breakdown of respondents

Categories	*Subcategories*	*Frequency*	*Percent*
Gender	Male	60	31.7
	Female	129	68.3
Age	18-24 years	92	48.7
	25-29 years	73	38.6
	30-34 years	21	11.1
	35-40 years	3	1.6
Education	High school	23	12.2
	Bachelors	123	65.1
	Masters	42	22.2
	Doctorate	1	.5
Employment Status	Employed	109	57.7
	Student	76	40.2
	Unemployed	3	1.6
Monthly Income	Below 5000	99	52.4
	5000 – 10000	71	37.6
	10000 – 15000	12	6.3
	15000 and above	7	3.7

also reflected in the survey results. According to the demographic breakdown of Instagram users, 51% of the users are females, whereas 49% males also use the social media application. Moreover, 30% of the audience on the social media app is between the ages of 18 to 24 (Clement, 2020). As the statistics show, Instagram is typically popular among the younger generation, therefore the questionnaire being filled out mainly by university going students was suitable for the study. Since the target audience of the study were Instagram users, a screening question was added before the survey began to ensure all participants had an Instagram account. Most of the participants were females (129) whereas the biggest age group that completed the survey ranged between the age of 18 to 24 years.

DATA ANALYSIS

The demographic variables included in this study were gender, age, education, employment status and monthly income. These variables give us an impression of the average respondent for the study. The following table illustrates the frequency and percentage of the subcategories of the respective demographic variables.

Descriptive Statistics

Before analysing data, all data recorded through Google Forms was extracted and entered SPSS (Statistical Package for the Social Sciences). After data entry, the data was cleaned and coded so further statistical tests and data analysis could be conducted on it. With the help of frequency tables in SPSS, any missing values or errors present in the data were identified and removed. Descriptive statistics tests including central tendency measured by mean and the measure of dispersion (standard deviation) were carried out. Single composite scores of the constructs were calculated by averaging the associated measurement items.

Table 4 illustrates the mean and standard deviation of the constructs used in the study.

Table 4. Descriptive statistics

Humour Technique	Construct	Mean	Std. Deviation
Comic wit	Brand Humour	2.2037	.75585
	Product Involvement	2.3695	.79783
	Brand Familiarity	2.2381	.67200
	Consumer Engagement	2.4974	.89826
Satire	Brand Humour	2.2328	.74667
	Product Involvement	2.3598	.78506
	Brand Familiarity	2.2363	.68438
	Consumer Engagement	2.5035	.92156

Inferential Statistics

To test and verify the reliability of the constructs in the study, Cronbach's alpha was calculated. Cronbach's alpha measures the internal consistency in a set of items in a construct. It is used to gauge at the reliability of the scale. It is important to measure internal consistency of a scale before running further tests as internal consistency indicates whether the items of a construct are measuring the same concept. The larger Cronbach's α value ensured the internal consistency among the constructs (Nunnally, 1978). All the constructs' Cronbach's α had high values ranging between 0.926 and 0.829 which is in the acceptable range (>0.70) (Hair et al., 2019; Hamad et al., 2018; El-Gohary and Eid, 2013; El-Gohary et al., 2021, 2012, 2009, 2008a, 2008b; El-Gohary 2012, 2011, 2009a, 2009b, 2010a, 2010b; Hamad et al., 2015; El-Gohary et al., 2009a, 2009b; Eid and El-Gohary, 2013; 2014; etc.). As the results showed significant homogeneity among all constructs, it was deemed acceptable to conduct further data analysis.

Confirmatory Factor Analysis (CFA)

To test to the relationship between measurement items of a research scale and constructs in a study, a confirmatory factor analysis is conducted. As data has been collected through questionnaires, it is important to test the reliability and validity of these measurement items. The proposed conceptual model; impact of different humour techniques used by brand advertisements and its contribution to consumer

Table 5. Measure of construct reliability

Humour Technique	Construct	Cronbach's alpha	No. of items
Comic wit	Brand Humour	.898	6
	Product Involvement	.894	6
	Brand Familiarity	.822	6
	Consumer Engagement	.915	6
Satire	Brand Humour	.908	6
	Product Involvement	.901	6
	Brand Familiarity	.829	6
	Consumer Engagement	.926	6

engagement, and its hypothesized relationships are tested through structural equation modelling (PLS-SEM) using SmartPLS.

Convergent Validity and Reliability

To test the construct reliability of the model, Cronbach's alpha and composite reliability values were assessed. As the constructs had values above 0.70 for both tests, construct reliability was established. To test the convergent validity, Average variance extracted (AVE) was used as an indicator of the amount of variance identified by a construct in comparison to the amount of variance due to an error in the measurement. An AVE reading of 0.50 and above is required for the construct to have convergent validity. (Hair et al., 2019; El-Gohary 2012; and Hamad et al., 2015). Mainstream of factor loading values were higher than 0.70, which indicate that it is acceptable.

Discriminant Validity

In PLS-SEM method, Heterotrait-Monotrait Ratio (HTMT) is a measure of discriminant validity. HTMT estimate the correlations among constructs (Hair et al, 2019). Values below 0.90 indicate the presence of discriminant validity. As shown in the table below, majority of the HTMT values were below 0.90.

Table 6. Discriminant validity (HTMT)

	Brand Familiarity	Comic Wit	Consumer Engagement	Product Involvement	Satire
Brand Familiarity					
Comic wit	0.934				
Consumer Engagement	0.726	0.691			
Product Involvement	0.887	0.794	0.873		
Satire	0.924	0.895	0.768	0.856	

Structural Model Analysis and Hypothesis Testing

The structural model was examined after confirming the validity of the measurement model as suggested by Hair et al, (2019).

Figure 2.

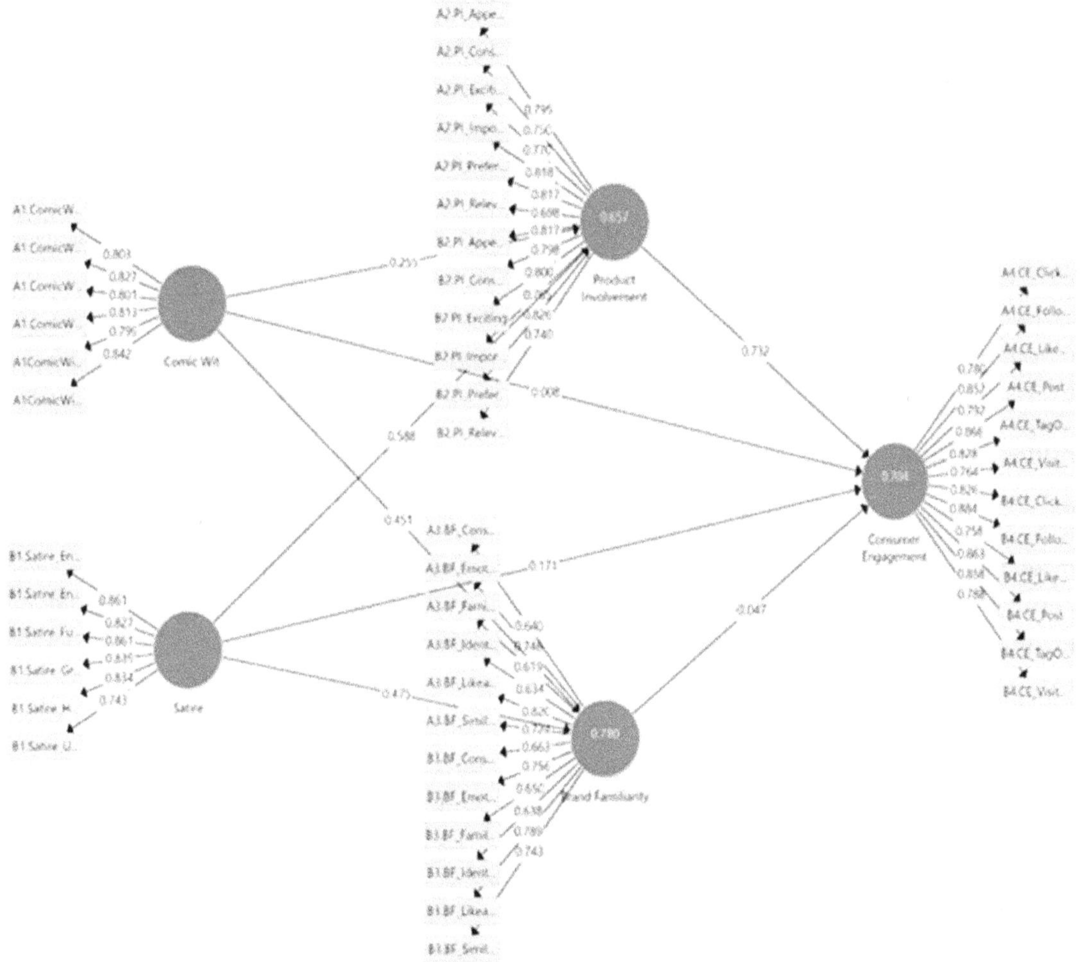

1. Direct Effect

In the two-tailed tests, the t value is considered to be statistically significant if such value ranged between -1.96 and +1.96, and in the same time, the p-value is less than 0.05 as suggested by Byrne (2013). As illustrated in Table 7, five out of eight paths were statistically significant at $p<0.01$. Comic wit and satire did not have any significant effect on consumer engagement and thus, hypotheses H1 and H2 were not supported. In addition, brand familiarity did not positively influence online consumer engagement and thus, hypothesis H8 was not supported. However, product involvement significantly and positively influences online consumer engagement and thus, hypothesis H7 was supported.

Table 7. Direct effect of the structural model

Direct Paths	*Path coefficients (β)*	*T statistics*	*P Values*	*Results*
Comic wit -> Brand Familiarity	0.451	4.279	0.000*	significant
Comic wit -> Product Involvement	0.255	2.695	0.007*	significant
Comic wit -> Consumer Engagement	0.008	0.075	0.940	insignificant
Satire -> Brand Familiarity	0.475	4.461	0.000*	significant
Satire -> Product Involvement	0.588	6.095	0.000*	significant
Satire -> Consumer Engagement	0.171	1.106	0.269	insignificant
Brand Familiarity -> Consumer Engagement	-0.047	0.296	0.767	insignificant
Product Involvement -> Consumer Engagement	0.732	6.076	0.000*	significant

Note: *p<0.01, based on two-tailed test; t=1.96

2. Indirect Effect (Mediation):

Table 8 shows that the effect of comic wit and satire on consumer engagement was significant through the mediation of product involvement and thus, hypotheses H3 and H4 were supported. However, the effect of comic wit and satire on consumer engagement was not significant through the mediation of brand familiarity and thus, hypotheses H5 and H6 were not supported.

Table 8. Structural model analysis (indirect effect)

Direct Paths	*Path coefficients (β)*	*T statistics*	*P Values*	*Results*
Comic wit -> Brand Familiarity -> Consumer Engagement	-0.021	0.287	0.774	insignificant
Satire -> Brand Familiarity -> Consumer Engagement	-0.022	0.290	0.772	insignificant
Comic Wit -> Product Involvement -> Consumer Engagement	0.187	2.266	0.024*	significant
Satire -> Product Involvement -> Consumer Engagement	0.431	4.204	0.000**	significant

Note: **p<0.01, *p<0.05, based on two-tailed test; t=1.96

3. Moderating Effect:

To analyse if gender played any role in impacting comic wit, satire, product involvement and brand familiarity and to identify if this also affects consumer engagement, another model was run which is illustrated below:

Figure 3.

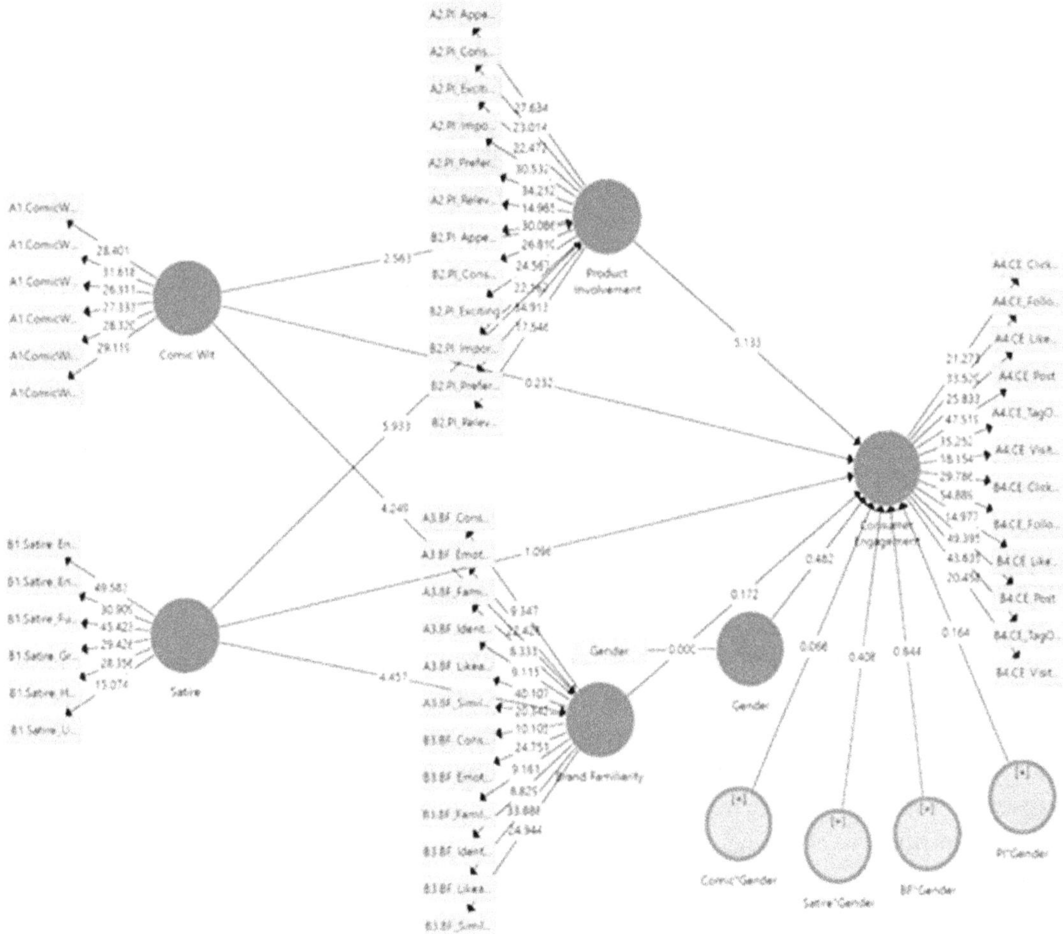

The moderating effect of gender was found to be statistically insignificant (as shown in Table 9). This means that H9a, Hb, H9c, H9d were not supported. Based on this, gender does not have any impact on the strength of the relationship between comic wit, satire, product involvement, brand familiarity to affect consumer engagement.

Table 9. Structural model analysis (moderating effect)

Direct Paths	*Path coefficients (β)*	*T statistics*	*P Values*	*Results*
Comic wit*Gender -> Consumer Engagement	-0.007	0.066	0.948	insignificant
Satire*Gender -> Consumer Engagement	0.066	0.408	0.684	insignificant
PI*Gender -> Consumer Engagement	0.025	0.164	0.870	insignificant
BF*Gender -> Consumer Engagement	-0.145	0.844	0.399	insignificant

Coefficient of Determination (R^2):

R^2 (coefficient of determination) is normally used to evaluate the descriptive power of the structural model in PLS. Coefficient of determination can range from 0 to 1 as illustrated by Hair et al. (2019). A higher R^2 value indicates a better prediction power. As shown in Table 10, the r square value of .704 indicated that around 70.4% of the variation in consumer engagement was explained by the entire predictor construct, e.g., comic wit, satire, brand familiarity and product involvement.

Table 10. R square - coefficient of determination ()

Latent Variables	*R Square*	*R Square Adjusted*	*Comment*
Brand Familiarity	0.780	0.778	High
Satire	0.704	0.698	Moderate
Product Involvement	0.657	0.654	Moderate

RESULTS AND CONCLUSION

This study makes several contributions to advertising literature in addition to the work of other scholars in the field (e.g. Raghubansie and EL-Gohary, 2021; Raghubansie et al., 2013; Ur Rahman et al., 2020; Zahiri et al., 2018; Millman and El-Gohary, 2011; Tafheem et al.,2022; El-Gohary, 2012; etc.). Firstly, it is one of the first few works to study the impact of online brand humour on a social network platform. This research study will provide researchers with a better understanding of how different humour mechanisms can contribute to consumer engagement on visual platforms like Instagram. The study analysed two types of humour mechanisms from Speck's taxonomy. Both humour mechanisms are based on incongruity-resolution theory, but satire also has an element of disparagement which can sometimes lead to negative reactions. In addition, other factors like the mediating role of product involvement, brand familiarity and the moderating role of gender were also analysed.

While satire and comic wit are most frequently portrayed in commercials, researchers have previously discussed that satirical humour mechanisms can provoke a negative reaction from the audience. However, this conclusion was not supported by Instagram's brand humour advertisements in the current study.

Findings indicate that both humour techniques have a significant effect on brand familiarity and product involvement. However, comic wit and satire do not have a direct impact on online consumer engagement. Results also show that brand familiarity did not positively affect online consumer engagement. Conversely, product involvement has a positive effect on online consumer engagement. Previous studies in marketing literature have argued that humorous advertisements work better for unfamiliar brands. Yet, most studies have not considered different humour techniques and their mechanisms like this study.

Furthermore, studies in the past have highlighted that advertisement humour received a better reception by males than females. Males have also shown to influence humour in previous research studies. The same results were not significant in this study. This could be due to two reasons; previous studies have generalised humour techniques as one construct. Second, studies have shown that the social media platform impacts its effectiveness. Finally, this research was conducted with Instagram as a medium, whereas previous studies have mainly looked at television ads and print media advertisements.

Research Contributions

Humour advertisements are evolving and gaining momentum, as most scholars have concluded that they lead to positive brand attitudes. However, no research specifically categorised humour into two types and applied them to one of the most popular social media platforms, Instagram. Moreover, the moderating role of brand familiarity and product involvement has been studied separately on traditional media advertisements, but research has shown that context-type affects the consumer's response. This research extends the literature on the implementation of humour in online advertisements. As the use of social media networks increases amongst consumers and brands alike, it has become necessary for brands to understand what can grow their brand's visibility and engagement on the platform. Advertising on social media has become a direct way to reach your target audience. Even though all social media platforms offer advertising solutions, it is not necessary for brands to use them all. When making ad placement decisions, marketers can look at the most popular platform for their target audience.

Managerial Implications

The results of this research further indicate the importance of understanding the impact of factors that lead to online consumer engagement. This study shows that brand humour employed in ads alone cannot lead to online consumer engagement. As the results show, comic wit and satire had no direct impact on consumer engagement. However, product involvement significantly influences the relationship between both humour types and consumer engagement. It is vital for marketers to realize that unaided humour is not sufficient to create engagement on an online platform. The fact that product involvement helps to influence consumer engagement suggests that humorous advertisements on Instagram are best for consumers that the products are relevant to. To implement these suggestions, Instagram gives marketers with sophisticated tools to manage their advertisements on the platform by choosing their targeting options. Moreover, since gender did not have any impact on consumer engagement, marketers can use Instagram's precise targeting options to reach audience based on their interests (product involvement), rather than other demographics like gender.

As previously discussed, interactions that take place on such platforms are usually controlled by the consumers and marketing managers have less control on the flow of the conversation unlike traditional media, therefore, brand managers should take reins of their campaigns by better understanding their audience's motivations to engage with their page or Instagram posts.

Past studies have highlighted the role humorous advertisements can play to generate attention; however, not enough research has been performed to understand the evolving world on social network sites. The outcomes of this research can be helpful to marketers who are unable to create engagement on their social network sites. Humour techniques have been popular, but not all styles of humour work. It is necessary that businesses choose the appropriate humour technique and give more attention to the consumers of their specific brand.

This study can help marketers decide if they can organically engage with their target audience through a humorous brand advertisement on Instagram. As Instagram is mostly used by millennials and Gen-Z, brands targeting this demographic can investigate the type of humour techniques that promotes organic consumer engagement.

Last, this study categorises humour into two types does not consider people's differences in their sense of humour. Humour involves a complex delivery, and a sense of humour can vary from person to person. If a certain individual finds an advertisement funny, another might view it in a negative light (Maples et al. 2001).

LIMITATIONS AND FUTURE RESEARCH

The study has filled some theoretical gaps in literature, but it also has its limitations that can be addressed in future studies. As the idea of the study was to analyse the impact of two humour techniques, each respondent was asked to answer questions using a similar brand and similar questions about two different types of humour techniques. This led to huge cross-loadings in the factor analysis. Moreover, the results cannot be generalized to the whole population as the respondents were mostly university students and young people who have recently joined the workforce. Nonetheless, the social network site in question is also most popular among young individuals. Furthermore, as noted by Goodrich (2013), older audience watches online advertisements more intently than young adults. This study did not have a lot of respondents belonging to an older age group.

Due to the limitation of time and resources, the sample size of respondents was small and not all humour techniques suggested by Speck (1991) were tested. It is an avenue that can be explored in future research studies where sentimental comedy and full comedy can also be tested. Future research can also study the impact of other important factors that might affect online consumer engagement like income, educational background, and cultural values. Other constructs of marketing can also be tested to see their effect on online consumer engagement such as brand loyalty, emotional motivation etc. Another future research suggestion would be to conduct a comparative study between two popular social network sites such as Instagram and twitter and analyse how the audience reacts to different humour techniques.

CONCLUSION

In conclusion, this research addressed the effect of online brand humour advertisements on consumer engagement. It aimed to fill a gap in literature about the role humorous advertisements can play on interactive social media platforms like Instagram. This research studied the impact of external factors like brand familiarity, product involvement and even a person's gender and how these factors affect humour comprehension and consumer interaction with Instagram brand advertisement posts. People's perceptions of humorous advertisements were studied through the distribution of an online questionnaire.

Results showed that similar to traditional advertisements, product involvement could influence the relationship between humour techniques (comic wit and satire) and consumer engagement. Other factors did not directly have an impact on consumer engagement. This research study has also contributed to better understanding of engaging organically with users through humour in advertisements.

REFERENCES

Alden, D. L., Mukherjee, A., & Hoyer, W. D. (2000). The effects of incongruity, surprise and positive moderators on perceived humour in television advertising. *Journal of Advertising*, *29*(2), 1–15. doi:10.1080/00913367.2000.10673605

Anand, P., & Sternthal, B. (1990). Ease of message processing as a moderator of repetition effects in advertising. *JMR, Journal of Marketing Research, 27*(3), 345–353. doi:10.1177/002224379002700308

Baker, W., Hutchinson, J., Moore, D., & Nedungadi, P. (1986). *Brand familiarity and advertising: effects on the evoked set and brand preference.* ACR North American Advances.

Barry, J. M., & Graça, S. S. (2018). Humour Effectiveness in Social Video Engagement. *Journal of Marketing Theory and Practice, 26*(1-2), 158–180. doi:10.1080/10696679.2017.1389247

Beard, F. K. (2008). *Humour in the advertising business: Theory, practice, and wit.* Rowman & Littlefield.

Berger, A. A. (2017). *An anatomy of humour.* Routledge. doi:10.4324/9781315082394

Bijmol, T. H., Leeflang, P. S., Block, F., Eisenbeiss, M., Hardie, B. G., Lemmens, A., & Saffert, P. (2010). Analytics for customer engagement. *Journal of Service Research, 13*(3), 341–356. doi:10.1177/1094670510375603

Booth Butterfield, S., & Booth-Butterfield, M. (1991). Individual differences in the communication of humorous messages. *Southern Journal of Communication, 56*(3), 205–218. doi:10.1080/10417949109372831

Brodie, R. J., Ilic, A., Juric, B., & Hollebeek, L. (2013). Consumer engagement in a virtual brand community: An exploratory analysis. *Journal of Business Research, 66*(1), 105–114. doi:10.1016/j.jbusres.2011.07.029

Buijzen, M., & Valkenburg, P. M. (2004). Developing a typology of humour in audio-visual media. *Media Psychology, 6*(2), 147–167. doi:10.12071532785xmep0602_2

Chattopadhyay, A., & Basu, K. (1990). Humour in advertising: The moderating role of prior brand evaluation. *JMR, Journal of Marketing Research, 27*(4), 466–476. doi:10.1177/002224379002700408

Christodoulides, G. (2009). Branding in the post-internet era. *Marketing Theory, 9*(1), 141–144. doi:10.1177/1470593108100071

Chung, H., & Zhao, X. (2003). Humour effect on memory and attitude: Moderating role of product involvement. *International Journal of Advertising, 22*(1), 117–144.

Cline, T. W., & Kellaris, J. J. (2007). The influence of humour strength and humour—message relatedness on ad memorability: A dual process model. *Journal of Advertising, 36*(1), 55–67.

Cox, K. (2015). *Hashtag or Crashtag: Should I use hashtags in my marketing campaign?* Retrieved September 28, 2019 from http://www.tmpmagnet.co.uk/blog/2015/03/hashtagor-crashtag-should-i-use-hashtags-in-my-marketingcampaign

Delgado-Ballester, E., Navarro, A., & Sicilia, M. (2012). Revitalising brands through communication messages: The role of brand familiarity. *European Journal of Marketing, 46*(1/2), 31–51. doi:10.1108/03090561211189220

Djambaska, A., Petrovska, I., & Bundaleska, E. (2015). Is Humour Advertising Always Effective? Parameters for Effective Use of Humour in Advertising. *Journal of Management Research, 8*(1), 18–36. doi:10.5296/jmr.v8i1.8419

Eid, R., & El-Gohary, H. (2013). The Impact of E-Marketing Use on Small Business Enterprises' Marketing Success: The Case of UK Companies. *Service Industries Journal, 33*(1), 31–50. doi:10.1080/02642069.2011.594878

Eid, R., & El-Gohary, H. (2014). Testing and Validating Customer Relationship Management Implementation Constructs in Egyptian Tourism Organizations. *Journal of Travel & Tourism Marketing, 31*(3), 344–365. doi:10.1080/10548408.2014.883348

Eisend, M. (2009). A meta-analysis of humour in advertising. *Journal of the Academy of Marketing Science, 37*(2), 191–203. doi:10.100711747-008-0096-y

El-Gohary, H. (2010). Expanding TAM and IDT to understand the adoption of E-Marketing by small business enterprises. *International Journal of Customer Relationship Marketing and Management, 1*(3), 56–75. doi:10.4018/jcrmm.2010070105

El-Gohary, H. (2010, October). E-Marketing-A literature Review from a Small Businesses perspective. *International Journal of Business and Social Science, 1*(1), 214–244.

El-Gohary, H. (2010a). *E-Marketing: Towards a Conceptualization of a New Marketing Philosophy - Book Chapter. In E-Business Issues, Challenges and Opportunities for SMEs: Driving Competitiveness*. IGI Global.

El-Gohary, H. (2010b). *Exploring E-Marketing as a tool for globalisation: the case of Egyptian small business enterprises. In Electronic Globalized Business and Sustainable Development through IT Management: Strategies and Perspectives*. IGI Global.

El-Gohary, H. (2011). *Electronic Marketing Practises in Developing Countries: The case of Egyptian business enterprises*. VDM Verlag Dr Müller.

El-Gohary, H. (2012). *The impact of E-Marketing Practices on Marketing Performance: A Small Business Enterprises Context*. LAP Lambert Academic Publishing.

El-Gohary, H. (2012). *Transdisciplinary Marketing Concepts and Emergent Methods for Virtual Environments*. IGI Global.

El-Gohary, H. (2012). Factors affecting E-Marketing adoption and implementation in tourism firms: An empirical investigation of Egyptian small tourism organizations. *Tourism Management, 33*(5), 1256–1269. doi:10.1016/j.tourman.2011.10.013

El-Gohary, H., Edwards, D., & Huang, J. (2013). Customer Relationship Management (CRM) Practices by Small Businesses in Developing Economies: A Case Study of Egypt. *International Journal of Customer Relationship Marketing and Management, 4*(2), 1–20. doi:10.4018/jcrmm.2013040101

El-Gohary, H., & Eid, R. (2012). DMA Model: Understanding Digital Marketing Adoption and Implementation by Islamic Tourism Organizations. *Tourism Analysis, 17*(4), 523–532. doi:10.3727/108354212X13473157390885

El-Gohary, H., & Eid, R. (2013). *E-Marketing in Developed and Developing Countries: Emerging Practices*. IGI Global. doi:10.4018/978-1-4666-3954-6

El-Gohary, H., & El-Gohary, Z. (2016). An Attempt to Explore Electronic Marketing Adoption and Implementation Aspects in Developing Countries: The Case of Egypt. *International Journal of Customer Relationship Marketing and Management*, *7*(4), 1–26. doi:10.4018/IJCRMM.2016100101

El-Gohary, H., O'Leary, S., & Radway, P. (2012). Investigating the Impact of Entrepreneurship Online Teaching on Science and Technology Degrees on Students attitudes in Developing Economies: The case of Egypt. *International Journal of Online Marketing*, *2*(1), 29–45. doi:10.4018/ijom.2012010103

El-Gohary, H., Thayaseelan, A., Babatunde, S., & El-Gohary, S. (2021). An Exploratory Study on the Effect of Artificial Intelligent Enabled Technology on Customers Experience in Banking Sector. *Journal of Technological Advancements*, *1*(1), 1–17. doi:10.4018/JTA.20210101.oa1

El-Gohary, H., Trueman, M., & Fukukawa, K. (2008). The Relationship between E-Marketing and Performance: Towards a Conceptual Framework in a Small Business Enterprises Context. *Journal of Business and Public Policy*, *2*(2), 10–28.

El-Gohary, H., Trueman, M., & Fukukawa, K. (2008). E-Marketing and Small Business Enterprises: A review of the methodologies. *Journal of Business and Public Policy*, *2*(2), 64–93.

El-Gohary, H., Trueman, M., & Fukukawa, K. (2009). E-Marketing and Small Business Enterprises: A Meta Analytic Review. *Journal of International Business and Finance, 1.*

El-Gohary, H., Trueman, M., & Fukukawa, K. (2009). E-Marketing and Small Business Enterprises: A review of the literature from 1993 to 1997. *International Business & Technology Review.*

El-Gohary, H., Trueman, M., & Fukukawa, K. (2009). Understanding the factors affecting the adoption of E-Marketing by small business enterprises - Book Chapter. In E-Commerce Adoption and Small Business in the Global Marketplace (pp. 237–258). Academic Press.

Field. (2009). *Discovering Statistics Using SPSS*. Sage Publications.

Forabosco, G. (1992). Cognitive aspects of the humour process: The concept of incongruity. *Humor: International Journal of Humor Research*, *5*(1-2), 45–68. doi:10.1515/humr.1992.5.1-2.45

Ford, T. E., Richardson, K., & Petit, W. E. (2015). Disparagement humour and prejudice: Contemporary theory and research. Humour. *International Journal of Humour Research*, *28*(2), 171–186.

Gervais, M., & Wilson, D. S. (2005). The evolution and functions of laughter and humour: A synthetic approach. *The Quarterly Review of Biology*, *80*(4), 395–430. doi:10.1086/498281 PMID:16519138

Gulas, C. S., & Weinberger, M. G. (2006). *Humour in advertising: A comprehensive analysis*. ME Sharpe.

Hair, J. F., Black, W. C., Babin, B. J., & Anderson, R. E. (2019). *Multivariate data analysis: A global perspective* (8th ed.). Cengage Learning EMEA.

Hamad, H., Elbeltagi, I., & El-Gohary, H. (2018). An Empirical Investigation of Business-to-Business E-Commerce Adoption and its Impact on SMEs Competitive Advantage: The Case of Egyptian Manufacturing SMEs. *Strategic Change: Briefings in Entrepreneurial Finance*, *27*(3), 209–229. doi:10.1002/jsc.2196

Hamad, H., Elbeltagi, I., Jones, P., & El-Gohary, H. (2015). Antecedents of B2B E-Commerce Adoption and its Effect on Competitive Advantage in Manufacturing SMEs. *Strategic Change*, *24*(5), 405–428. doi:10.1002/jsc.2019

Heckle, S. E., & Childers, T. L. (1992). The role of expectancy and relevancy in memory for verbal and visual information: What is incongruency? *The Journal of Consumer Research*, *18*(4), 475–492. doi:10.1086/209275

Hollebeek, L. D., Glynn, M. S., & Brodie, R. J. (2014). Consumer Brand Engagement in Social Media: Conceptualization, Scale Development and Validation. *Journal of Interactive Marketing*, *28*(2), 149–165. doi:10.1016/j.intmar.2013.12.002

Holme, J., & Marra, M. (2002). Having a laugh at work: How humour contributes to workplace culture. *Journal of Pragmatics*, *34*(12), 1683–1710. doi:10.1016/S0378-2166(02)00032-2

Hurley, A. E., Scandura, T. A., Schriesheim, C. A., Brannick, M. T., Seers, A., Vandenberg, R. J., & Williams, L. J. (1997). Exploratory and confirmatory factor analysis: Guidelines, issues, and alternatives. *Journal of Organizational Behavior*, *18*(6), 667–683. doi:10.1002/(SICI)1099-1379(199711)18:6<667::AID-JOB874>3.0.CO;2-T

Jiang, T., Li, H., & Hou, Y. (2019). Cultural differences in humour perception, usage, and implications. *Frontiers in Psychology*, 10.

Johnson, R. B., & Onwuegbuzie, A. J. (2004). Mixed methods research: A research paradigm whose time has come. *Educational Researcher*, *33*(7), 14–26. doi:10.3102/0013189X033007014

Juckel, J., Bellman, S., & Varan, D. (2016). A humour typology to identify humour styles used in sitcoms. *HUMOUR*, *29*(4), 583–603.

Kaplan, A. M., & Haenlein, M. (2010). Users of the world, unite! The challenges and opportunities of Social Media. *Business Horizons*, *53*(1), 59–68. doi:10.1016/j.bushor.2009.09.003

Kazecki, J. (2012). Laughter in the Trenches – Humour and the Front Experience in German First World War Narratives. Cambridge Scholar Publishing.

Kent, R. J., & Allen, C. T. (1994). Competitive interference effects in consumer memory for advertising: The role of brand familiarity. *Journal of Marketing*, *58*(3), 97–105. doi:10.1177/002224299405800307

Krawford, K. (2011). *Digital Technologies Effect on Humans and Societies*. Academic Press.

Krishnan, H. S., & Chakravarti, D. (2003). A process analysis of the effects of humorous advertising executions on brand claims memory. *Journal of Consumer Psychology*, *13*(3), 230–245. doi:10.1207/S15327663JCP1303_05

Lee, Y. H., & Lim, E. A. C. (2008). What's funny and what's not: The moderating role of cultural orientation in ad humour. *Journal of Advertising*, *37*(2), 71–84. doi:10.2753/JOA0091-3367370206

Millman, C., & El-Gohary, H. (2011). New Digital Media Marketing and Micro Business: A UK perspective. *International Journal of Online Marketing*, *1*(1), 41–62. doi:10.4018/ijom.2011010104

Nielsen, M. (2015). *The influence of product type, humour type, brand attitude, and gender on humour effectiveness in ads* (Doctoral dissertation).

Nunnally, J. C. (1978). *Psychometric Theory* (2nd ed.). McGraw-Hill.

Petty, R. E., & Cacioppo, J. T. (1986). The elaboration likelihood model of persuasion. In *Communication and persuasion* (pp. 1–24). Springer.

Petty, R. E., Cacioppo, J. T., & Schumann, D. (1983). Central and peripheral routes to advertising effectiveness: The moderating role of involvement. *The Journal of Consumer Research*, *10*(2), 135–146. doi:10.1086/208954

Raghubansie, A., & El-Gohary, H. (2021). Digital Advertising Creative Processes and Innovation in UK SME Advertising Agencies: An Empirical Investigation of Viral Advertising. *Scientific Journal for Financial and Commercial Studies and Research, Faculty of Commerce*, *2*(1), 75-116.

Raghubansie, A., El-Gohary, H., & Samaradivakara, C. (2013). An Evaluation of the Viral Marketing Research. *International Journal of Online Marketing*, *3*(4), 1–27. doi:10.4018/ijom.2013100101

Ramli, N. A., Latan, H., & Nartea, G. V. (2018). Why should PLS-SEM be used rather than regression? Evidence from the capital structure perspective. In *Partial least squares structural equation modelling* (pp. 171–209). Springer. doi:10.1007/978-3-319-71691-6_6

Romeo, E. J., & Cruthirds, K. W. (2006). The Use of Humour in the Workplace. *The Academy of Management Perspectives*, *20*(2), 58–69. doi:10.5465/amp.2006.20591005

Samels, P. (2017). *Advice on Reliability Analysis with Small Samples - Revised Version. Technical Report*. ResearchGate.

Scwarz, U., Hoffmann, S., & Hutter, K. (2015). Do men and women laugh about different types of humour? A comparison of satire, sentimental comedy, and comic wit in print ads. *Journal of Current Issues and Research in Advertising*, *36*(1), 70–87. doi:10.1080/10641734.2014.912599

Sek, Y. W. (2016). *An Empirical Study of Learners' Acceptance of Open Learner Models in Malaysian Higher Education (Doctor of Philosophy)*. RMIT University.

Sheel, T. (2017). Definitions, Theories, and Measurement of Humour. In *Humour at Work in Teams, Leadership, Negotiations, Learning and Health* (pp. 9–29). Springer. doi:10.1007/978-3-319-65691-5_2

Sjödin, H., & Törn, F. (2006). When communication challenges brand associations: A framework for understanding consumer responses to brand image incongruity. *Journal of Consumer Behaviour: An International Research Review*, *5*(1), 32–42. doi:10.1002/cb.44

Souiden, N., Chtourou, S., & Korai, B. (2017). Consumer attitudes toward online advertising: The moderating role of personality. *Journal of Promotion Management*, *23*(2), 207–227. doi:10.1080/10496491.2016.1267676

Speck, P. S. (1991). The humorous message taxonomy: A framework for the study of humorous ads. *Current Issues and Research in Advertising*, *13*(1-2), 1-44.

Spielmann, N. (2014). How funny was that? Uncovering humour mechanisms. *European Journal of Marketing, 48*(9/10), 1892–1910. doi:10.1108/EJM-07-2012-0393

Stathooulou, A., Borel, L., Christodoulides, G., & West, D. (2017). Consumer branded# hashtag engagement: Can creativity in TV advertising influence hashtag engagement? *Psychology and Marketing, 34*(4), 448–462. doi:10.1002/mar.20999

Sterntal, B., & Craig, C. S. (1973). Humour in Advertising. *Journal of Marketing, 37*(4), 12–18. doi:10.1177/002224297303700403

Tabacnick, B. G., & Fidell, L. S. (2007). *Using Multivariate Statistics*. Pearson Education.

Tafheem, N., El-Gohary, H., & Sobh, R. (2022). Social Media User-Influencer Congruity: An Analysis of Social Media Platforms Parasocial Relationships. *International Journal of Customer Relationship Marketing and Management, 13*(1), 1–29.

Ur Rahman, R., Shah, S., El-Gohary, H., Abbas, M., Khali, S., Al Altheeb, S., & Sultan, F. (2020). Social Media Adoption and Financial Sustainability: Learned Lessons from Developing Countries. *Sustainability, 12*(24), 27–52. doi:10.3390u122410616

Wang, A. (2006). Advertising engagement: A driver of message involvement on message effects. *Journal of Advertising Research, 46*(4), 355–368. doi:10.2501/S0021849906060429

Warre, C., Barsky, A., Mcgraw, A. P., & MacInnis, D. (2018). Humour, Comedy, and Consumer Behaviour. *The Journal of Consumer Research*.

Weinberger, M. G., & Gulas, C. S. (1992). The impact of humour in advertising: A review. *Journal of Advertising, 21*(4), 35–59. doi:10.1080/00913367.1992.10673384

Williams, B., Onsman, A., & Brown, T. (2010). Exploratory Factor Analysis: A Five Step Guide for Novices. *Journal of Emergency Primary Health Care, 8*(3), 1–13. doi:10.33151/ajp.8.3.93

Yoon, H. J. (2018). Creating the mood for humour: Arousal level priming in humour advertising. *Journal of Consumer Marketing, 35*(5), 491–501. doi:10.1108/JCM-01-2017-2074

Zahiri, S., El-Gohary, H., & Hussain, J. (2018). Internet Marketing Adoption by Iranian Distribution Industry: An Attempt to Understand the Reality. *International Journal of Customer Relationship Marketing and Management, 9*(2), 33–61. doi:10.4018/IJCRMM.2018040103

KEY TERMS AND DEFINITIONS

Comic Wit: A type of humour technique that includes incongruity and an element of surprise.

Instagram: An online social media network platform for users to follow other profiles and share pictures and videos with their followers.

Online Consumer Engagement: Online interaction between consumer and company that is initiated by the consumer.

Satire: A type of humour technique that includes incongruity and harmless puns.

Section 5
Specialised Research Areas

Chapter 14
Phygital Customer Experience Mixed Approach of Augmented Reality and Customer Experience (DCX) in the Context of Heritage Tourism

Nedra Bahri Ammari
IHEC of Carthage, Tunisia

Ines El Hassoumi
ENAU, Tunisia

ABSTRACT

What if customer experience was the primary driver of digital transformation? Indeed, new hybrid experiences have emerged thanks to daily-life technologies that fused both digital and physical worlds. This kind of experience uses applications and connected objects (IoT) to adapt and respond to consumer needs. Augmented reality and virtual reality are one of the most functionally and emotionally memorable phygital experiences that create value for customers. In this chapter, the authors chose heritage tourism as the study field for different reasons. While the adoption of augmented and virtual reality is gaining grownd, cultural heritage sites have started to consider the possibilities offered by these new and innovative technologies. This industry is starting to integrate AR and VR in several ways to attract more people. However, it is necessary to study how modern technology can be developed and implemented in a meaningful way to improve the tourist's experience. An AR- and VR-based mobile application has been developed and tested at Antonine's Baths in Carthage, Tunisia.

INTRODUCTION

The emergence of the internet has incited marketing researchers to study its effects on our consumer

DOI: 10.4018/978-1-7998-7192-7.ch014

society. Practitioners are increasingly interested in electronic commerce (Galan and Sabadie, 2001). Nevertheless, this type of commerce led to the emergence of a new form of hybrid experience or phygital experience that combined both the digital and the phygital to diversify tourism products. More particularly, visitors to archaeological sites are no longer passive; they have certain expectations and wish to participate actively in their cultural experience. Therefore, they require information and entertainment through innovation and creativity (Hoyer et al., 2020), in addition to multisensory stimulation (Li et al., 2019; Pine and Gilmore, 1999).

Indeed, this experience uses augmented reality software with connected objects to ensure adaptation and optimization to consumer needs. Accordingly, augmented reality came to the fore as an experience that offers memorable and satisfying phygital experiences that serve the functional and emotional needs of customers while creating value. The use of augmented reality contributes to improving the relational, hedonic and aesthetic dimensions of the digital customer experience. It has become a relevant interactive tool in marketing, increasingly used in different contexts.

The emergence of these interactive technologies has completely revolutionized the tourism industry (Buhalis and Law 2008), and converted traditional business channels (Wang & Liao, 2007). The competitive and financial viability of tourism organizations depends now on the innovation of the service provided, in this case: benefit to visitors (Neuhofer et al, 2014; Tussyadiah, 2014). AR has transformed guided tours by incorporating a new form of apps that deliver a unique immersive experience (Qin et al, 2021). The latter will allow the visitor to get involved in its unfolding, and, *in fine*, to live an experience enriched in emotions (Bruner and Kumar, 2005).

The use of augmented reality offered solutions in ifferent fields like: medicine, commerce, education, and architecture (Datcu et al., 2015). However, the development of AR applications to market cultural heritage is scarce despite the potential of this sector and its importance in attracting more visitors. Then, the aim of this chapter is to present the different facets of AR and the components of digital experience (the tourist experience) and to develop an application dedicated to market the archaeological sites of Antonine's Baths of Carthage in Tunisia. The innovation of this work consists in offering a new user experience inside archaeological sites in order to create a new link between the visitor and the heritage.

AUGMENTED REALITY

Faust et al., (2012) define AR as "the superposition of virtual objects (computer-generated images, texts, sounds, etc.) on the user's real environment" (p 1164). For a long time, heavy and bulky devices (Rese et al., 2017) have hampered AR. However, with the widespread of smartphones, the interest of developers, retailers and consumers in augmented reality has increased dramatically. AR is brought to consumers in different ways such as mobile navigation applications (Qin et al, 2021; Javornik et al., 2016) as well as innovative learning tools in cultural heritage tourism (Moorhouse et al., 2017). Azuma (1997) identifies three attributes of an augmented reality tool; association of virtual and real objects, fostering interaction between users in real time and saving information in three dimensions (3D).

In addition, AR is an interactive technology that combines the physical and the digital by overlaying virtual annotations such as information, images and sound in real time (Javornik 2016). Theoretically speaking, AR is an interactive technology that modifies the physical environment with the help of superimposed virtual elements. This virtual layer, placed between the physical environments and the user, can add textual information, images, videos or other virtual elements. The devices that allow this superposition are smartphones or tablets, portable objects (screens on the head), fixed interactive screens or projectors (Carmigniani et al., 2011). Azuma et al's. (2001) definition of AR by, recognized as the most accepted definition, emphasizes not only coexistence between the virtual and the real in the same space, but also interactive alignment and mutual superposition of computer generated sources with physical reality. It emphasizes anchoring AR as a real time and an interactive solution. Morton Heilig, who named the feature films «Sensorama» (Carmigniani et al., 2011), developed the first AR attempts in the 1950s in cinematography. In the 1960s, Ivan Sutherland developed the first AR prototype at Harvard that allowed three-dimensional graphics to be viewed using a holographic projection. In the 1970s and 1980s, research institutes, NASA, the aviation industry, and other industrial centers continued to develop wearable devices, digital displays, and 3D graphics with AR.

The scientists Caudell and Mizell coined the term in the aviation industry in the 1990s, developing an AR support system for workers doing wiring (Azuma et al., 2001; Carmigniani et al., 2001; Carmigniani et al. al., 2011). Since the 1990s, AR has received increased attention in computing, in the aeas of virtual reality, 3D technology and mobile technology (Azuma et al., 2001; Van Krevelen and Poelman, 2010; Preece et al., 2015; Wilson et al., 2018; Chylinski et al., 2020). However, conditions have changed since the 1990s. Indeed, technological advancement, lower associated costs, increased mobility and portability of AR and its integration into the existing digital landscape, Global Positioning System (GPS) and Near Field Communications (NFC) have increased both the usefulness and the relevance of AR. Today's digital environment enables the deployment of AR technology for marketing purposes at various points of contact with consumers, particularly in retail, mobile and online (Qin et al., 2021).

Table 1. Summary of definitions of augmented reality

Authors	*Definitions*
Azuma et al., (2001)	*"The AR system complements the real world with virtual (computer generated) objects that appear to coexist in the same space as the real world, the AR system has the following properties: combines real and virtual objects in a real environment, runs interactively in real time and registers real and virtual objects with each other "*
Reitmayr et Drummond (2006)	*"Augmented reality (AR) is a promoter user interface technique for mobile, wearable computing and location-based systems".*
Zhou et al., (2008)	*"Augmented reality (AR) is a technology that enables computer-generated virtual imagery to exactly overlay physical objects in real time. Unlike virtual reality where the user is completely immersed in a virtual environment, AR allows the user to interact with visual images using real objects seamlessly. "*
Van Krevelen et Poelman (2010)	*"Augmented reality is a technology to create a next-generation reality-based interface and moves from laboratories around the world to various industries and consumer markets. AR complements the real world with virtual (computer generated) objects that appear to coexist in the same space as the real world".*
Carmigniani et al., (2011)	*"Augmented Reality (AR) is a direct or indirect real-time view of a real physical environment that has been enhanced or enhanced by adding information generated by a virtual computer. Augmented reality is both interactive and recorded in 3D and combines real and virtual objects".*

Source: *Javornik (2016)*

AUGMENTED REALITY AND ITS IMPORTANCE

In recent years, products have been used and tested by different AR applications and in different contexts. So far, augmented reality is used on smart devices and large interactive screens (Javornik, 2014). Thus, augmented reality applications allow consumers to visualize a virtual product in a physical environment.

Moreover, it allows access to additional digital content by scanning a product logo or associated image that turns into a video on the screen (Javornik, 2016). In addition, according to Javornik, (2016), large interactive screens can show a greater view of the physical environment on the screen to which virtual elements are added, for example an AR campaign in a shopping center with the aim of raising awareness about endangered species, showing these species on large screens that look to be walking around the mall.

For Carmigniani et al. (2011), AR applications are different from the concepts they portray. Under this perspective, Preece et al., (2015) claim that the ability of augmented reality to enhance physical reality is technically effective, as it encompasses virtual elements about people, products or the environment. Then, graphically enhancing a person refers to the improvement of a view of someone else or of a self. In addition, an improved sight of another person can be provided by augmented reality glasses (Google glasses ...). However, such applications are considered to be rare in the marketing arena due to limited access. On the other hand, applications for enhanced self-view or self-augmentation have been more widely disseminated in the form of virtual mirrors or virtual trials (Javornik, 2016). AR applications have appeared in marketing practice since the late 2000s (Javornik, 2016), resulting in new opportunities for consumer engagement (Scholz and Smith, 2016; Flavian et al., 2019b) as well as mobile and retail marketing (Javornik, 2016; Qin et al, 2021).

Augmented Reality (AR) has become a relevant interactive technology in marketing and often developed in the form of smart device applications. Its ability to superimpose virtual elements onto the physical environment such as: information or images which can interact with the physical environment in real time, offers new possibilities for the dessimination of content to consumers. As its use increases, there is a growing need to better understand its impact on consumer behavior and the experience it provides. AR has become a new technology available to retailers that allows them to interact with their customers in a unique and vivid way (Javornick, 2016; Yim et al., 2017). Although AR is still in its infancy in consumer markets, spending on AR is expected to reach $ 60 billion by 2020 (Porter and Heppelmann, 2017). Augmented reality aims to connect the real world to the virtual world (Rauschnabel et al., 2015). In the same line of thought, Azuma (1997) asserts that augmented reality integrates computer-generated objects into the real world and provides people with real-time interactions. The ability of AR to superimpose virtual elements onto a physical environment, which can interact with the physical environment in real time, opens up new possibilities for businesses to deliver content to consumers. In turn, the functions offered by augmented reality can change a number of consumer activities, including product testing, virtual testing, information retrieval and acquisition (Javornik, 2016).

The innovative aspect of the technology has a positive effect on an individual's intention to experience and use AR (Flavian et al., 2019). Indeed, people who demonstrate a greater capacity for innovation show a greater intention to use new technologies (Krey et al., 2019). Thus, the innovation of AR is decisive in guiding the choice of people looking for innovations and new ideas and technologies (Hong, Lin, and Hsieh, 2017). This technology helps meet the needs of visitors who crave the imagination to understand and appreciate the benefits associated with new technology.

The Dichotomy Between Augmented Reality and Virtual Reality

Although virtual reality and augmented reality are both evolving interface systems for displaying digital information, they are two distinct technologies with fundamental differences in the type of computer systems required to use them. . Indeed, virtual reality (VR) is described as an immersive human-computer interaction in which an individual can explore and interact with a three-dimensional computer-generated environment (Fan et al., 2020; Kung, 2020; Lee et al., 2020). A VR experience is typically accomplished through the use of a head mounted stereoscopic display (HMD) which completely replaces the user's real physical world view with an interactive synthetic environment (Silva et al., 2018). The term virtual reality was not popularized until the late 1980s, when Jason Lanier, founder of VPL Research, developed the first VR products available on the market, including the Dataglove and EyePhone head-mounted display (Lauria and Ford-Morie, 2015). AR is a relatively new form of person-machine interaction that superimposes computer-generated information onto a person's real-world view, creating an illusion where virtual and real objects coexist in the same space (Ong and Nee, 2004). Therefore, AR can be differentiated from VR, since the former covers digital information in a real environment, rather than replacing it completely. In addition to combining real and virtual information, a true AR system should work interactively in real time and seamlessly align the natural world and virtual objects with each other (Azuma et al., 2001; Kipper and Rampolia, 2013; Flavian et al., 2019a).

Figure 1. Milgram's continum (Milgram et Kishino, 1994)
Source: *Bastide, (2017)*

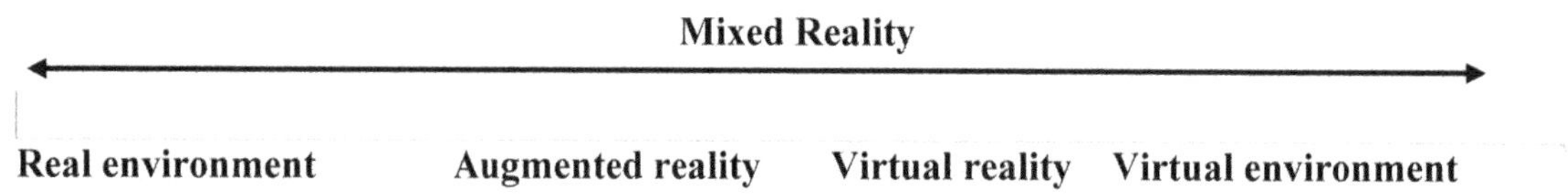

AR is a variation of virtual reality (VR), where virtual objects are superimposed onto the real environment (Azuma, 1997). It should meet three requirements: combine virtual and real objects in a real environment, perform interactively and in real time, and register real and virtual objects with each other. In other words, AR should record or correct the alignment of the virtual world with the real world (Azuma, 2001). VR technology creates a virtual environment presented to our senses in such a way that we experience it as if we really were there. Conversely, AR refers to the incorporation of virtual objects into a real three-dimensional scene. To ensure a consistent overlap of objects, AR systems must estimate, in real time, the position and orientation of the virtual object (Linowes & Babilinski, 2017). One of the most common methods of making such an estimate is to use markers in the real scene. These markers will be identified by cameras and compared to previously defined models.

Today, several experts agree that augmented reality will be more widely adopted than virtual reality (Gallagher, 2016), thanks in particular to its accessibility on portable devices (mobile phones, tablets and laptops) and its use in multiple business contexts (Research and Markets, 2016).When making decisions, consumers often rely on mental imagery to produce images that reflect products and experiences (Pearson et al., 2015). One of the main advantages of AR is its ability to generate a clear representation of a product combining the real world and the virtual world (Heller et al., 2019). Then, AR can provide consumers with a visual representation of a product or experience allowing them to unload mental imagery during the decision-making process.

THE Attributes of Augmented Reality

Azuma (1997) identifies three characteristics of augmented reality namely:

- *Interactivity*: human interactions involve an element of interactivity (Heeter, 1992). According to Yim et al., (2017), the definition of interactivity describes two complementary points of view, needed to understand interactivity in augmented reality experience, namely: the technological result and user perception. Additionally, interactivity is the ability to control what the user sees by combining the real world with the virtual world. Interactivity comes from the capacity of the technological system to allow individuals to interact much easier with content (Hoffman and Novak, 2009). Consumer perceptions can be influenced by components of the technology that drives speed, mapping, similarity of control in the virtual and real world in which content can be manipulated by the user (Steuer, 1992).
- *liveliness*: the clear and detailed representation of an image (often superimposed in 3-D) in combination with the real world and the virtual world. Steuer, (1992) defines liveliness as "the capacity of a technology to produce a sensorially rich mediated environment". It combines the sensory experience of real and imaginary objects to create a clear image in an individual's mind (Lee, 2004). From a technological point of view, liveliness can be increased by enriching the quality of the information provided while increasing the number of sensory dimensions (Li et al., 2002). In an online environment, liveliness is often associated with aesthetic appeal and the quality of product display (Flavian et al., 2017; Griffith & Gray, 2002).
- *novelty*: it denotes the unique and specific information provided to the user combining the real world and the virtual world each time an individual uses augmented reality. Massetti, (1996) defines novelty as a situation where an individual sees something new, unique and different. Berlyne et al. (1993) suggest innovation as a combination of new and unusual stimuli.

AUGMENTED REALITY IN THE HERITAGE TOURISM SECTOR

Augmented Reality's Contribution to the Heritage Tourism Sector

Historically, tourism has been viewed as a tool to stimulate a country's economic growth (Ko and Stewart, 2002). With technological developments, the implementation of ICT in the tourism industry is crucial for the survival and sustainability of heritage sites especially archaeological sites. Then, the effective use of smart technologies that add value to the tourist experience (Carlsson and Walden, 2010; Cranmer et al, 2016; Deloitte, 2013) represents a competitive advantage. Internet and communication technologies have contributed to the efficient dissemination of all content on cultural heritage creating attractiveness and social and economic value (Glaeser, Kolko, and Saiz, 2001; Del Vecchio et al., 2018). This dissemination can reach a wider audience thanks to attractive mobile applications. Indeed, AR technology is used in the tourism sector with the aim of improving the tourism experience. According to He et al. (2018), "Augmented reality has revolutionized the world of interactions between humans and technology with increasing attention in tourism and cultural heritage research".

Then, its use allows them to enhance their knowledge in a fun way on a site, a museum or other tourist attractions (Arnaboldi et al., 2021), to improve and create unique and memorable tourist experiences (Yovcheva et al, 2013; Crespo et al, 2009; Leue et al, 2015), and to create value (Cranmer et al, 2016). This is possible thanks to the availability of smart technologies such as smartphones and mobile applications (Do et al., 2020). Indeed, these latter make it possible to offer attractive and customized experiences directly to the general public, on devices that they already carry with them (Tussyadiah et al., 2018).

Applications that previously required specialized hardware at each point of use can now be delivered via a smartphone (Do et al., 2020). In order to guarantee a more attractive digital / phygital experience for visitors to archaeological sites, it is interesting to create augmented reality mobile applications with cultural heritage means / tools, in this case: historical images and information.

THE DIGITIZATION OF CUSTOMER EXPERIENCE OR DCX

Batat, (2018) draws attention to the importance of digitizing customer experience since it allows for meeting the needs of new hyper-connected consumers who want to switch from one channel to another to compare, understand and buy a product or service. The author defines the digital customer experience as "the key to a winning strategy for the digital transformation of companies". Indeed, digitization and the presence of connected technologies aim to extend the digital experience within the brand's points of sale, to renew and customize the shopping experience (Fan et al., 2020; Roy et al., 2016), and create a rewarding shopping experience (Shankar et al., 2011). This consequently improves the overall shopping experience (Fan et al., 2020; Ladhari et al., 2019; McLean and Wilson 2019; Shankar et al., 2011). According to Guépet and Salgado (2016), digital transformation represents an opportunity which contributes to the optimization of customer experience through digital tools by making it interactive and unique and this by ensuring the collection and control of data (information) on customer behavior. The digitization of customer experience (DCX) requires, first, the establishment and integration of new contact channels such as mobile and connected objects in order to ensure "limitless" customer journeys. Second, it needs a good knowledge of customers and the implementation of technologies in several forms and a multitude of interactive applications (tablets and interactive screens, control terminals, mobile applications, smart phones, etc.). These allow consumers to access knowledge provided free of charge (Bathelot, 2016). DCX encompasses all of the interactions that an individual is likely to have with a business, including a specific product, in this case: an application. The emergence of these interactive technologies has completely transformed the tourism industry (Buhalis and Law 2008).

Technologies have revolutionized travel behaviors, such as decision-making and information seeking (Wang et al, 2014), and the transformation of traditional business channels. To remain competitive and financially viable, tourism organizations have to now innovate in terms of services provided and added value to visitors (Neuhofer et al, 2014). The potential of augmented reality has manifested itself in several sectors, in this case the heritage tourism sector. AR has transformed guided tours by incorporating a new form of apps that deliver a unique immersive experience (Lee et al., 2020). The latter will allow the visitor to get involved in its unfolding, and, ultimately, to live an experience enriched with emotions (Bruner and Kumar, 2005).

APPLICATION TO VISIT ANTONINE'S BATHS IN CARTHAGE

General Presentation

Throughout the 20th century, the emergence of new adaptive and interactive technologies completely transformed the tourism industry (Buhalis & Law 2008).

To remain competitive and financially viable, tourism organizations have to find new ways to deliver improved (Neuhofer & al, 2014; Tussyadiah, 2014), enriched and unique services (Yovcheva et al, 2013). The aim is to offer value-added services (Garcia-Crespo et al, 2009). In particular, new technologies have offered new ways of delivering cultural content. These technological advances have important repercussions on the tourism sector as cultural heritage contributes to the creation of social and economic value (Glaeser, Kolko & Saiz, 2001).

Accordingly, we present an application that offers a new visit experience based on augmented and virtual reality techniques. In general, a mobile application is a computer program, "executable from the operating system of a smartphone or a touchscreen tablet" (Bathelot, 2016) intended for free or paid use. In addition, augmented reality consists of "superimposing virtual imagery on a physical environment" (Been-Lirn, 2013, p. 109). Indeed, augmented reality (AR) allows the user to see virtual objects (audios, 2D or 3D images, videos, etc.) linked with a real world. Therefore, Augmented Reality complements reality, rather than completely replaces it '(Rampolla, 2013).

Inversely, Virtual Reality (VR) is a technology that allows a total immersion in a digital and artificial world. It is a reproduction of the real world or a totally imaginary universe.

According to Jean Segura, specialist in synthetic imagery and virtual uses, virtual reality can be defined as "all the techniques and systems which give man the feeling of entering synthetic universes created on the internet".

Virtual reality allows users to perform, in real time, a certain number of actions defined by one or more computer programs and to experience visual, auditory or haptic sensations.

Application Architecture

To introduce augmented reality and virtual reality into our application, we integrate the following components into the architecture (see figure 1):

- *Smartphone*: compatible with the virtual mask of "Google Cardboard" . This phone can be inserted inside the mask to ensure VR. It also allows the user to view the catalog in AR
- *VR mask:* it is the Virtual Reality device which will allow immersion of users in the 3D environment
- *Catalog*: is the marker of Augmented Reality

Game Design Document (GDD)

As our application shares several common characteristics with video games (such as graphics, storyline and gameplay) we have developed the Game Design Document "game specifications" to present all the elements that should make up this new application. .

In this GDD, we focus on the two main scenes namely the AR scene and the VR scene.

AR Scene: this scene shows from the catalog (that contains the marker images) a 3D model or a video of the archaeological site, consists of an AR camera and three buttons:

- Information button: to display a text containing a description of the site.
- Capture button: to take a screenshot of the AR experience and share it on social networks.
- Exit button: to exit the AR experience and return to the welcome scene.

Figure 2. Physical architecture of the application

In the AR experiment Control is done with the AR camera and the target image (marker). After detection of the marker by the camera, the user observes the 3D model or a video of the archaeological site superimposed on the target image.

VR Scene: this scene presents a 3D environment and 3D objects of the archaeological site that allow the movement of the user, following an interaction by sight. In the VR experience, control is made through sight. The user has a viewfinder, a reticle in the center of the screen that allows them to interact with the interactive elements of the application. A graphical indication, in the form of a circular loading bar, specifies the progress of their interaction with the observed item to the users. After a second and a half, the bar fills up and the interaction is confirmed. Movement occurs automatically as soon as the user interacts with specific elements.

Application Interfaces

The integration of augmented reality technology into our application aims to enable archaeological sites such as Antonine's Baths of Carthage to reach a wider audience. The aim is to serve up valuable information for users that improves their historical knowledge and increases their levels of entertainment throughout the visit.

Then, in our application we used augmented reality to superimpose virtual elements, in real time, on target images from the catalog. This catalog will be made available to visitors at the entrance of the archaeological site. In other words, by scanning images on paper with a mobile phone, the visitor will be able to visualize 3D objects, videos or audios about the Antonine's Baths of Carthage such that they were in antiquity (see figure 3).

We have chosen Unity3D supported by the Vuforia kit as development tools. Unity3D is a cross-platform game engine (smartphone, Mac, PC, video and web game consoles) developed by Unity Technologies. It is one of the most common in the video game industry. It has the particularity of offering a free license called "Personal" without engine access limitation. Vuforia is a software development kit (SDK) that enables the creation of augmented reality applications in Unity. It uses Computer Vision technology to recognize and track planar images (Image Objectives) or simple 3D objects in real time.

Figure 3. AR interface of the application

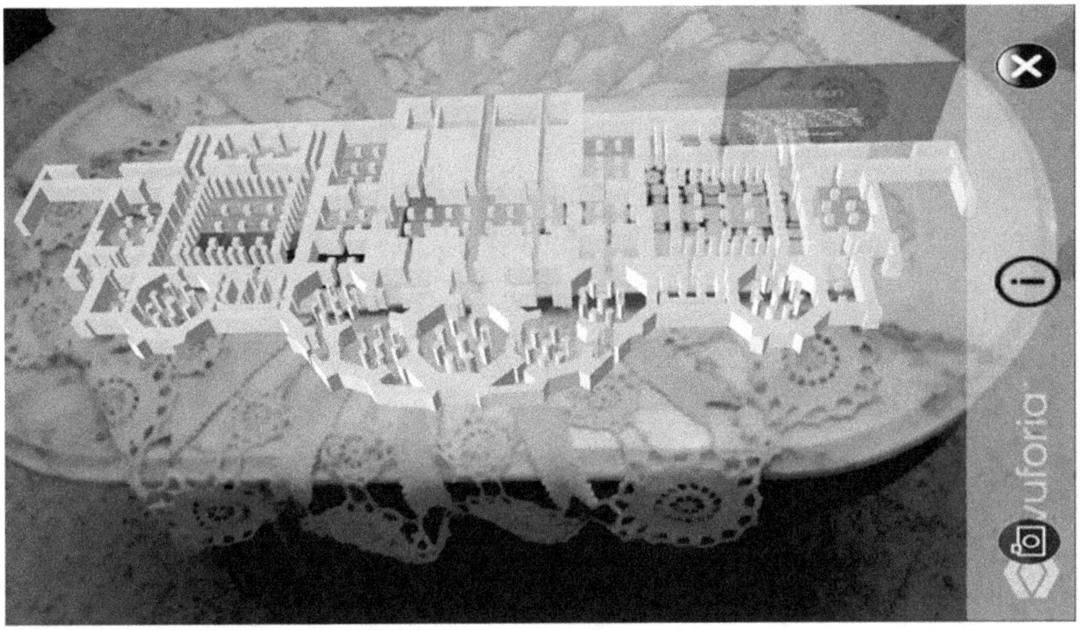

To have a good detection result and real-time monitoring, we have to choose a good target marker. Moreover, a marker can be considered practical and useful if the mediation support (mobile device with a camera) is able to easily capture and visualize it.

First, we used the prefabricated "ARCamera" which is inserted into our AR scene. This camera will be attached to the webcam of our mobile. When the AR scene loads, the camera of our mediation support will recognize the marker and display the related objects (a 3D model or a video of the archaeological site).

Then we inserted the second prefab: "ImageTarget" which will display the target image that we created and import it into Unity, from the Vuforia site.

On the other hand, the VR interface allows the user to take a virtual tour of the 3D environment of the archaeological site namely Antonine's Baths in Carthage (See figure 4). To create this interface, we imported the Google VR SDK into Unity, which creates mobile VR applications for Android. The Google VR SDK package for Unity contains several elements. In our VR scene, we used the following Google VR prefabs:

- *GvrReticlePointer*: this prefab adds a reticle based on the interactive user's gaze. It behaves like a small pointer in space that throws itself correctly into the scene where the user's focus should be. It turns into a reticle when the camera's "raycast" passes through an object or a valid element
- *GvrEditorEmulator:* This prefab contains an instance of the script
- *GvrViewer:* controls VR mode settings

The two technologies used, namely Augmented Reality (AR) and Virtual Reality (VR), are now increasingly used in several sectors and they are becoming known to the general public. Our project is part of the enhancement of Tunisian heritage via digital tools. It consists in creating an interactive and

Figure 4. VR interface of the application

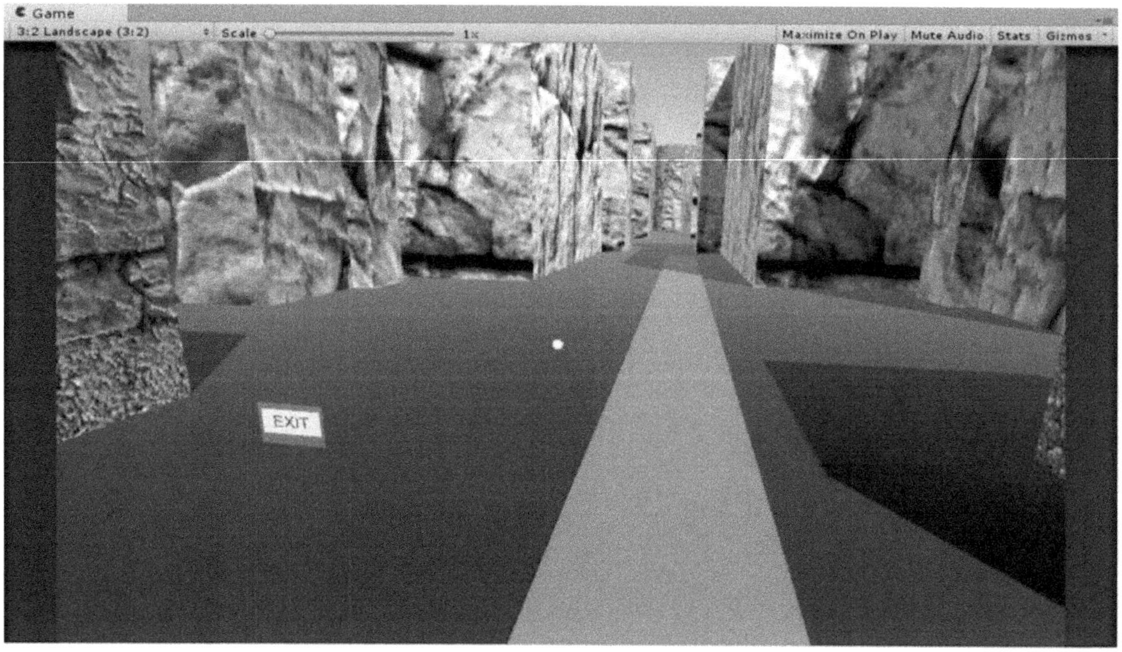

immersive mobile application to enrich the visit to an archaeological site using AR and VR technologies (Lee et al., 2020; Qin et al., 2021).

This application was developed with the aim of raising awareness of the general public and especially young people, about promoting tourism and participating in the safeguarding of the country's heritage.

CONCLUSION

Although cultural heritage sites have used traditional means such as dashboards, brochures and maps to share information, visitors find these disinteresting and not motivating enough. Alternatively, cultural sites can adopt smart technologies to bring more liveliness to their static environment and take full advantage of the benefits to highlight all the heritage sites detailed to visitors. Today's visitor is no longer a passive consumer of service, they ask for more information, entertainment, active participation and multisensory stimulation in combination with innovative design elements (Pine and Gilmore, 1999; Bruner et Kumar, 2005).

Developing and experimenting this application in the archaeological site "Antonine's Baths in Carthage", has shown that visitors really seek customized emotional experiences. They want to relive the experience and learn more about their heritage in a fun way. According to previous research, the presence in museums and archaeological sites has shown as an increased need for: learning, involvement and participation (Sheng and Chen, 2012), education (Conti, Pencarelli and Vesci, 2017), social interaction (Nowacki, 2010), customized information, emotional and relational engagement with the cultural place (Poria, Reichel and Biran, 2006). Then, this consumer and their tastes should be identified in order to continually improve their experiences. The anthropological and historical dimensions of archaeological sites are unique and complex. Therefore, technological improvement should be approached in a customized way (Pietroni and Adami, 2014). The case of the technology examined in this chapter.

As implications to organizations operating in the tourism industry, the context of heritage tourism is sensitive given that the majority of those who visit historic sites are either specialists in the field or tourists. Through an augmented reality application, companies in the tourism industry could reach a wider target and encourage more people to take an interest in sites and cultural heritage. AR applications appear to enhance the sensory richness of the experience and should therefore be viewed as a potentially valuable tool for creating effective interactions with consumers. The innovative nature of augmented reality technology helps, among other things, professionals to identify people who are likely to adopt innovations in information technology rather than others (Heller et al., 2019). These people can then serve as thought leaders to facilitate the diffusion of a new technology.

Moreover, these technologies are attracting a new audience to archaeological sites such as young people, children, etc. So this will inevitably have economic repercussions on the touristic organizations located around these sites like restaurants, hotels, guest houses, etc.

REFERENCES

Arnaboldi, M., Melisa, L. & Lema, D. (2021). The participatory turn in museums: The online facet. *Poetics*. doi:10.1016/j.poetic.2021.101536

Azuma, R., Baillot, Y., Behringer, R., Feiner, S., Julier, S., & MacIntyre, B. (2001). Recent advances in augmented reality. *IEEE Computer Graphics and Applications*, *21*(6), 34–40. doi:10.1109/38.963459

Azwna, R. (1997). A survey of augmented reality. *Presence (Cambridge, Mass.)*, *6*(4), 355–385. doi:10.1162/pres.1997.6.4.355

Bastide, E. H. (2017). *L'influence de la réalité augmentée sur l'expérience de magasinage mobile: le cas de l'application Make-up Genius de L'Oréal, Mémoire en Science de Gestion*. Université du Québec à Montréal.

Batat, W. (2011). The coming out of the «new consumer»: Towards the theorisation of the concept in consumer research. *Advances in Consumer Research. Association for Consumer Research (U. S.)*, *9*, 304–312.

Batat, W., & Frochot, I. (2014). *Le Marketing Expérientiel. Comment concevoir et stimuler l'éxpérience client*. Dunod.

Bathelot, B. (2016). *Définition: Réalité augmentée*. Récupéré sur Définitions marketing: http://www. definitions-marketing. com/definition/realite-augmentee

Berlyne, D. E., Margaret, M. A., Salapatek, P. H., & Judith, L. L. (1963). Novelty, complexity, incongruity, extrinsic motivation, and the GSR. *Journal of Experimental Psychology*, *66*(6), 550–567. doi:10.1037/h0045767 PMID:14087632

Bruner, I. C., & Anand Kumar, A. (2005). Explaining Consumer Acceptance of Handheld Internet Devices. *Journal of Business Research*, *58*(5), 553–558. doi:10.1016/j.jbusres.2003.08.002

Buhalis, D., & Law, R. (2008). Progress in information technology and tourism management: 20 years on and 10 years after the Internet—The state of eTourism research. *Tourism Management, 29*(4), 609–623. doi:10.1016/j.tourman.2008.01.005

Carlsson, C., & Walden, P. (2010). Supporting Tourists at the Bomarsund Fortress with a Mobile Value Service. *Journal of Information Technology Theory and Application, 11*(1), 43–56.

Carrnigniani, J., Furht, B., Anietti, M., Ceravolo, P., Damiani, E., & Ivkovic, M. (2011). Augmented reality technologies, systems and applications. *Multimedia Tools and Applications, 51*(1), 341–377. doi:10.100711042-010-0660-6

Chylinski, M., Heller, J., Hilken, T., Keeling, D. I., Mahr, D., & De Ruyter, K. (2020). Augmented reality marketing: A technology-enabled approach to situated customer experience. *Australasian Marketing Journal, 28*(4), 374–384. doi:10.1016/j.ausmj.2020.04.004

Datcu, D., Lukosch, S., & Brazier, F. (2015). On the Usability and Effectiveness of Different Interaction Types in Augrnented Reality. *International Journal of Human-Computer Interaction, 31*(3), 193–209. doi:10.1080/10447318.2014.994193

Dieck, T. (2017). Value of Augmented Reality at Cultural Heritage Sites: A Stakeholder Approach. *Journal of Destination Marketing & Management, 6*(2), 110–117. doi:10.1016/j.jdmm.2017.03.002

Dieck, T. M. C., & Jung, T. (2016). Value of augmented reality to enhance the visitor experience: A case study of Manchester Jewish Museum. *Review of Tourism Research, 7*, 1–5.

Do, H.-N., Shih, W., & Ha, Q.-A. (2020, August). Effects of mobile augmented reality apps on impulse buying behavior: An investigation in the tourism field. *Heliyon, 6*(8), e04667. doi:10.1016/j.heliyon.2020.e04667 PMID:32923709

Fan, X., Chai, Z., Deng, N., & Dong, X. (2020). Adoption of augmented reality in online retailing and consumers' product attitude: A cognitive perspective. *Journal of Retailing and Consumer Services, 53*(March), 101986. doi:10.1016/j.jretconser.2019.101986

Faust, F., Roepke, G., Tiago, C., Fernanda, A., Marcelo, F., Gomes, G., & Deise, A. (2012). Use of augmented reality in the usability evaluation of products. *Work (Reading, Mass.), 41*(1), 1164–1170. doi:10.3233/WOR-2012-0298-1164 PMID:22316877

Flavian, C., Ibanez-Sanchez, S., & Orus, C. (2017). The influence of online product presentation videos on persuasion and purchase channel preference: The role of imagery fluency and need fortouc. *Telematics and Informatics, 34*(8), 1544–1556. doi:10.1016/j.tele.2017.07.002

Flavian, C., Ibanez-Sanchez, S., & Orus, C. (2019a). The impact of virtual, augmented and mixed reality technologies on the customer experience. *Journal of Business Research, 100*, 547–560. doi:10.1016/j.jbusres.2018.10.050

Flavián, C., Ibáñez-Sánchez, S., & Orús, C. (2019b). Feeling Confident and Smart with Webrooming: Understanding the Consumer's Path to Satisfaction. *Journal of Business Research, 47*, 1–15.

Galan, J. P., & Sabadie, W. (2001). *Les déterminants de la satisfaction de l'internaute: une étude exploratoire*. 17ème congrès international de l'Association Française de Marketing, Deauville.

Gallagher, D. (2016). Virtual reality is cool; this may be bigger; augmented reality devices like microsoft's HoloLens are still a work in progress, but they may bear more fruit for investors. *Wall Street Journal.*

García-Crespo, A., Chamizo, J., Rivera, I., Mencke, M., Colomo-Palacios, R., & Gómez-Berbís, J. M. (2009). SPETA: Social pervasive e-Tourism advisor. *Telematics and Informatics*, *26*(3), 306–315. doi:10.1016/j.tele.2008.11.008

Glaeser, E. L., Kolko, J., & Saiz, A. (2001). Consumer city. *Journal of Economic Geography*, *1*(1), 27–50. doi:10.1093/jeg/1.1.27

Griffith, D. A., & Gray, C. C. (2002). The falacy of the level playing field. *Journal of Marketing Channels*, *9*(3-4), 87–102. doi:10.1300/J049v09n03_05

Han, D. I., Dieck, M. C., & Jung, T. (2018). User experience model for augmented reality applications in urban heritage tourism. *Journal of Heritage Tourism*, *13*(1), 46–61. doi:10.1080/1743873X.2016.1251931

Heller, J., Chylinski, M., De Ruyter, K., Mahr, D., & Keeling, D. L. (2019). Touchning the untouchable: Exploring multi sensory augmented reality in the of online retailing. *Journal of Retailing*, 1–16.

Hong, J. C., Lin, P. H., & Hsieha, P. C. (2017, February). The effect of consumer innovativeness on perceived value and continuance intention to use smartwatch. *Computers in Human Behavior*, *67*, 264–272. doi:10.1016/j.chb.2016.11.001

Javornik, A. (2014). Classifications of augmented reality uses in marketing. *Proceedings of the IEEE International Symposium on mixed and augmented realities.* 10.1109/ISMAR-AMH.2014.6935441

Javornik, A. (2016). Augmented reality: Research agenda for studying the impact of its media characteristics on consumer behavior. *Journal of Retailing and Consumer Services*, *30*, 252–261. doi:10.1016/j.jretconser.2016.02.004

Javornik, A., Rogers, Y., Moutinho, A. M., & Freeman, R. (2016). Revealing the Shopper Experience of Using a" Magic Mirror" Augmented Reality Make-Up Application. *Conference on Designing Interactive Systems*, 871-882. 10.1145/2901790.2901881

Kipper, G., & Rampolla, J. (2013). *Augmented reality: An emerging technologies guide to AR*. Elsevier.

Krey, N., Chuah, S. H.-W., Ramayah, T., & Rauschnabel, P. A. (2019). How functional and emotional ads drive smartwatch adoption: The moderating role of consumer innovativeness and extraversion. *Internet Research*, *29*(3), 578–602. doi:10.1108/IntR-12-2017-0534

Kung, W.-S. (2020). Reconceptualizing the digital humanities in Asia: New representations of art, history and culture (vol. 2). Springer. doi:10.1007/978-981-15-4642-6

Ladhari, R., Gonthier, J., & Lajante, M. (2019). Generation Y and online faschion shopping: Orientations and profiles. *Journal of Retailing and Consumer Services*, *48*, 113–121. doi:10.1016/j.jretconser.2019.02.003

Lauria, R. M., & Ford-Morie, J. (2015). *Virtuality: AR as metamedia and herald of future realities. In Communication and Technology*. CPI Books.

Lee, H., Jung, T. H., Dieck, M. C. T., & Chung, N. (2020). Experiencing immersive virtual reality in museums. *Information & Management*, *57*(July).

Lee, K. M. (2004). Presence explicated. *Communication Theory*, *14*(1), 27–50. doi:10.1111/j.1468-2885.2004.tb00302.x

Lemon, K. N., & Verhoef, P. C. (2016). Understanding Customer Experience throughout the Customer Journey. *Journal of Marketing*, *80*(6), 69–96. doi:10.1509/jm.15.0420

Li, H., Daugherty, T., & Biocca, F. (2002). Impact of 3D advertising on product knowledge, brand attitude and purchase intention: The mediating role of presence. *Journal of Advertising*, *31*(3), 43–57. doi:10.1080/00913367.2002.10673675

Linowes, J., & Babilinski, K. (2017). *Augmented reality for developers: Build practical augmented reality applications with unity*. Packt publishing.

Massetti, B. (1996). An empirical examination of the value of creativity support systems on idea generation. *Management Information Systems Quarterly*, *20*(1), 83–97. doi:10.2307/249543

McLean, G., & Wilson, A. (2019). Shopping in the digital world: Examining customer engagement through augmented reality mobile applications. *Computers in Human Behavior*, *101*, 210–224. doi:10.1016/j.chb.2019.07.002

Moorhouse, N., Tom-Dieck, C. & Jung, T. (2017). Augmented reality to enhance the learning experience in cultural heritage tourism: An experiential learning cycle perspective. *e-Review of Tourism Research*, *8*, 1–5.

Neuhofer, B., Buhalis, D., & Ladkin, A. (2014). A Typology of Technology-Enhanced Tourism Experiences. *International Journal of Tourism Research*, *16*(4), 340–350. doi:10.1002/jtr.1958

Ong, S. K., & Nee, A. Y. C. (2004). A brief introduction of VR and AR applications in manufacturing. In *Virtual and augmented reality applications in manufacturing* (pp. 1–14). Springer. doi:10.1007/978-1-4471-3873-0_1

Porter, M. E., & Heppelmann, J. E. (2017, Nov.). *Why every organisation needs an augmented reality strategy. Havard Business Review*.

Preece, J., Sharp, H., & Rogers, Y. (2015). Interaction design beyond human computer. Academic Press.

Rauschnabel, P. A., Brem, A., & Ivens, B. S. (2015). Who will buy smart glasses? Empirical results of two pre-market entry studies on the role of personality in individual awareness and intended adoption of google glass wearables. *Computers in Human Behavior*, *49*, 635–647. doi:10.1016/j.chb.2015.03.003

Rese, A., Baier, D., Geyer-Schulz, A., & Schreiber, S. (2017). How augmented reality apps are accepted by consumers: A comparative analysis using scales and opinions. *Technological Forecasting and Social Change*, *124*, 306–319. doi:10.1016/j.techfore.2016.10.010

Roy, P. A., Ponnam, A., & Mandal, S. (2017). Comprehending technology attachment in the case of smart phone-application: An empirical study. *Journal of Electronic Commerce in Organizations*, *15*(1), 23–43. doi:10.4018/JECO.2017010102

Scholz, J., & Smith, A. N. (2016). Augmented reality: Designing immersive expenences that maximize consumer engagement. *Business Horizons*, *59*(2), 149161. doi:10.1016/j.bushor.2015.10.003

Shankar, V., Smith, A. K., & Rangaswamy, A. (2003). Customer satisfaction and loyalty in online and offline environments. *International Journal of Research in Marketing*, *20*(2), 153–175. doi:10.1016/S0167-8116(03)00016-8

Silva, J. N. A., Southworth, M., Raptis, C., & Silva, J. (2018). Emerging applications of virtual reality in cardiovascular medicine, JACC. *Basic to Transitional Science*, *3*(3), 420–430. doi:10.1016/j.jacbts.2017.11.009 PMID:30062228

Steuer, J. (1992). Defining virtual reality: Dimensions determining telepresence. *Journal of Communication*, *42*(4), 73–93. doi:10.1111/j.1460-2466.1992.tb00812.x

Tscheu, F., & Buhalis, D. (2016). Augmented Reality at Cultural Heritage sites. In A. Inversini & R. Schegg (Eds.), *Information and Communication Technologies in Tourism 2016 ENTER* (pp. 607–619). Springer. doi:10.1007/978-3-319-28231-2_44

Tussyadiah, L. P. (2014). Toward a Theoretical Foundation for Experience Design in Tourism. *Journal of Travel Research*, *53*(5), 543–564. doi:10.1177/0047287513513172

Van Krevelen, D. W. F., & Poelman, R. (2010). A survey of augmented reality technologies: Applications and limitations. *The International Journal of Virtual Reality: a Multimedia Publication for Professionals*, *9*(2), 1–20. doi:10.20870/IJVR.2010.9.2.2767

Wilson, P. F., Stott, J., Warnett, J. M., Attridge, A., Smith, M. P., & Williams, M. A. (2018). Museum visitor preference for the physical properties of 3D printed replicas. *Journal of Cultural Heritage*, *32*(July–August), 176–185. doi:10.1016/j.culher.2018.02.002

Yim, M. Y., Chu, S. C., & Sauer, P. L. (2017). Is augmented reality technology an effective tool for e-commerce? An interactivity and vividness perspective. *Journal of Interactive Marketing*, *39*, 89–103. doi:10.1016/j.intmar.2017.04.001

Yovchevam Z., Buhalism D., & Gatzidis, C. (2013). Engineering Augmented Tourism Experiences. In Information and Communication Technologies in Tourism 2013. Springer.

Chapter 15
Intelligent Customer Experience in a Connected Commerce Environment

Afnen Gam
IHEC of Carthage, Tunisia

Nedra Bahri Ammari
IHEC of Carthage, Tunisia

ABSTRACT

The objective of this research is to examine the relationship between the smart customer experience and behavioral brand loyalty through relationship variables (satisfaction, trust, and brand attachment) in the retail sector. Behavioral brand loyalty was examined through positive word of mouth (proselytism), the client's intention to continue the relationship with the brand, and resistance to price increases in the context of connected commerce. A questionnaire was administered face-to-face to 302 French consumers who used smart technology during their shopping experiences. The results obtained suggest that brand attachment explains behavioral loyalty to the brand. Also, the satisfaction and trust that result from a smart customer experience have a positive effect on the customer's attachment to the brand. Finally, only the relationship that stipulates the existence of a significant link between satisfaction and proselytism has not been verified.

INTRODUCTION

Faced with an over-informed customer, with evolving behavior, and dependent on interactive technology, companies are worried about adopting new technologies to make it easier for them to buy. Moreover, retailers are trying to make their physical stores digitized in which they integrate smart technologies: interactive tablets and screens, interactive and virtual windows, order kiosks, interactive mirrors, mobile applications, interactive augmented reality technologies…(Nikhashemi et al., 2021; McLean & Wilson, 2019; Picot-Coupey, 2013). Indeed, the digitization of points of sale is dramatically changing the experi-

DOI: 10.4018/978-1-7998-7192-7.ch015

ence of customers in stores and the way they buy (Bennett et al., 2015). Nowadays, providing customers with an experience is essential for creating links with customers (Batat, 2018-2020; Berthiaume, 2015; Wei et al., 2019), and one of the central objectives of current retail environments (Huré et al., 2011; Shankar et al., 2011). However, customers are increasingly looking for a personalized relationship with their favorite brands that essentially lies in providing a seamless experience with them. One of the ultimate goals of experiential marketing is, moreover, the creation of interactivity, which is nowadays ensured by technological tools. Thus, the smart customer experience is a means of creating an interaction between the customer and the brand (Nikhashemi et al., 2021; Wei et al., 2019; Kim et al., 2017; Mosquera et al., 2018; Batat, 2018, 2020). Mosquera et al., (2018) state that the most important technological challenge for brands is to take advantage of the interaction that exists between the brand and the customer and to understand the preferences of the latter to provide a smart experience of personalized shopping. This will help to build customer loyalty (Ladhariet al., 2019; Renko et al., 2014). The existing studies dealing with smart technologies are conceptual and focus on the adoption of these tools by retailers such as the work of Pantano & Viassone (2014); Bennett et al., (2015); Voropanova et al., (2016); Willems et al., (2017); Fuentes et al., (2017). Although smart technology allows the company to gain a competitive advantage (Jain et al., 2017; Inman et al., 2017), and to offer its customers memorable and engaging experiences (Batat, 2018-2020; Kim et al., 2017; Bodhani, 2012; Gretzel et al., 2015; Pantano & Di Pietro, 2012), it remains however mixed empirically (Roy et al., 2017). Nonetheless, Roy et al., (2017) highlighted the lack of rigorous empirical studies on smart customer experience in the retail context, and its impact on customer behavior (Roy et al. 2017; Homburg et al., 2017; Keyoor & Sunil, 2019).The effects of the smart customer experience on satisfaction, trust, brand attachment and brand loyalty remain scarce. We will therefore try through our research to shed better theoretical and managerial light by answering the following problem: To what extent can the smart customer experience affect behavioral brand loyalty in the context of retail sales? Thus, to respond to this problem, a research model has been developed that interacts between the smart customer experience, satisfaction, trust, attachment to the brand and loyalty.

In the following paragraphs, we will first present a review of the literature on the acceptance of technological innovations. We will then detail our research methodology, and we will develop and discuss the results obtained.

LITTERATURE REVIEW

Smart Retailing

Smart retailing or connected commerce allows the reinvention of retail and the customer experience of the 21st century. Bèzes, (2019) and Roy et al., (2017) define smart distribution as being "An interactive and connected retail system that supports seamless management of different customer contact points to customize the customer experience at different points of contact". This system highlights a set of interactions between different parts of the retail world (customers, retailers, products, brands, smart objects "smart technologies" and retail channels…) The goal is to merge the digital and physical worlds to generate greater value for both customers and businesses, thereby improving the quality of purchasing experiences (Pantano& Timmermans, 2014). Indeed, Kim et al., (2017) argue that the explosion of smart technologies has provided retailers with innovative and beneficial ways to transform the buying experience of the new "hyper-connected and over-informed" consumer (Druguet et al., 2015). Thus, connected commerce is a technological solution that allows retailers to manage omnichannel customer experiences well and has many benefits for both customers and retailers (Priporas et al., 2017; Vrontis et al., 2017; Bèzes, 2019; Ladhari et al., 2019).With smart technologies, connected commerce allows retailers to improve consumer buying experiences and remain competitive by following new retail strategies (Priporas et al., 2017). In other words, smart commerce aims to provide transparent customer experiences using the technologies available to it (Roy et al., 2017), and to promote retailer performance and service quality (Pantano, 2014; Pantano et al., 2018; Belanche et al., 2020). As well, the retailer can benefit from smart commerce and new technologies that will enable them to acquire new capabilities in terms of "monitoring, optimization and autonomy" (Porter et al., 2014), to collect real-time information on customers (Pantano et al., 2010, 2018), to ensure good control of the omnichannel experience and avoid "free-riding" (Bèzes, 2019).

Digitization of Retail Outlets/Physical Stores (WEB in Store)

The development of technologies and the intensification of their uses, the emergence of a new consumer able to use several channels simultaneously, have led to the birth of connected commerce, and it is in this context that there has been the emergence of a new marketing discipline that is "digitalization" (Abaidi, 2010). The latter is not only the modernization of traditional trade but also a tool for increasing commercial efficiency and optimizing the customer experience (Bathelot, 2017). Indeed, digitization is defined by Guépet et al., (2016) as the "digitization of physical channels". Hence, the birth of the notion of the "WEB in-store" consists of introducing digital technologies and content within the point of sale to expand the offer and improve the customer experience. Besides, retailers are opting for digitalization and are developing their online stores, since this is a renewal of physical outlets after the threat of online channels and the emergence of the phenomenon of show rooming. (Materne et al., 2017; Guépet et al., 2016). The digitalization of retail outlets has encouraged several brands to follow this trend and to ensure a commercial ubiquity that consists of considering e-commerce channels, m-commerce, and the physical retail outlet as complementary (Picot-Coupey, 2013). Indeed, using a technological tool (smartphone, tablet, computer..), the customer becomes able to buy any type of product, anywhere and at any time (Fuentes et al ., 2017). According to Materne et al., (2017), the digitalization of retail outlets makes it possible to meet the needs of consumers in physical commerce and puts the customer at the center of interest of merchants. These same authors conclude that the goal of the implementation of smart technologies and mobile devices in stores is to ensure the continuity of an experience initiated on the internet thus a digitalization of the customer experience (McLean & Wilson, 2019).

Digitization of the Customer Experience

Batat, (2018) draws attention to the importance of digitalizing the customer experience as it helps meet the needs of new hyper-connected consumers who want to switch from one channel to another to compare, understand and buy a product or service. It defines the digital customer experience as "the key to a winning strategy for the digital transformation of companies".Indeed, digitalization and the presence of connected technologies aim to extend the digital experience at the retailer's points of sale, to renew and personalize the shopping experience (Ladhariet al., 2019; Roy et al., 2016), and creating a rewarding buying experience (Shankar et al., 2011; El Abed et al., 2017). As a result, the overall purchasing experience has improved (Shankar et al., 2011). According to Guépet & Salgado (2016), digital transformation is an opportunity that helps optimize the customer experience through digital tools by making it interactive and unique, by ensuring data collection and control (information) relating to customer behavior. The digitalization of the customer experience requires, first, the establishment and integration of new contact channels such as mobile and connected objects to ensure "limitless" customer journeys. Secondly, a good knowledge of customers and the implementation of retail technologies in several forms (interactive tablets and screens, control stations, mobile applications, etc.), and finally the development and maintenance of the brand presence on social networks to communicate a good image to consumers (Casaló et al., 2020; McLean & Wilson, 2019). Likewise, Ghali et al., (2016) have demonstrated through an exploratory study with a group of Tunisian distributors that the use of digital technologies by retailers aims to personalize consumer experiences and immerse customers in consumer experiences exceptional and memorable. According to Dacko (2017), innovative retailers use smart technologies such as augmented reality to provide consumers with immersive experiences, create interactive ads, and make the shopping experience more entertaining and attractive. Besides, a study by Poncin et al., (2017) shows that using gamification mechanics makes the customer experience more playful, interactive and compelling.

Smart Technologies

Technology has always played an important role in the reinvention of retail trade (Renko et al., 2014), so the past decade has been marked by a growing interest in the adoption of many technological innovations in retail. Following the digitalization of the commercial function, companies must make new digital tools available to their omnichannel customers (Guépet et al., 2016), to improve the atmosphere of traditional outlets and make them more attractive (Chylinski et al., 2020; Inman et al., 2017; Poncin et al., 2014; Pantano et al., 2014; Pantano &Di Pietro, 2012), to facilitate and enrich the customer experience by providing personalized sales services (Roy et al., 2017). Beck (2015) defines smart technologies as technical tools and interactive media offered by the company and useful to both the customer and the salesperson. It is a set of technologies that support a new form of collaboration and value creation that supports innovation, entrepreneurship, and competitiveness. Similarly, Roy et al., (2017) conceptualize these technologies with this definition "connected or synchronized smart objects that create value or devices that interact with each other, detect the environment, and guide and control their functions autonomously".Gretzel et al., (2015a, 2015b) define technology as an infrastructure that encompasses several intelligent computing technologies (RFID radio frequency identification tags, sensors, actuators, mobile devices) allowing consumers to make smarter purchasing decisions. In its study, Bèzes (2019) looked at the characteristics of the technologies available to the customer and emphasized that these technologies should not only be used to illuminate, facilitate and help the customer in his choice especially in the evaluation phase of the alternatives of his purchasing process but in addition to ensure the autonomy of the customer (Belanche, 2020).In addition, they must aim to stimulate, personalize and enrich the customer experience, thus increasing the level of sales. The interactivity of these technologies is also one of the most important characteristics because it allows maintaining and strengthening the relationship between the customer and the brand (Casaló et al., 2020). Nevertheless, Pantano &Di Pietro (2012) state that the main feature of smart technologies is their ability to provide up-to-date information on products and services available at the point of sale that is useful to both consumers and retailers.

HYPOTHESIS DEVELOPMENT

The Relationship Between Smart Customer Experience and Satisfaction

Customer satisfaction is positively influenced by their experiences (Meyer & Schwager, 2007; Pantano& Di Pietro, 2012; Kilani, 2016; Jain et al., 2017; Wei et al., 2019), cumulative lived with the brand (Khelil & Bouslama, 2013; Bahri-Ammari et al., 2016). Materne et al., (2017) focused their study on the digitized customer experience and declared that the latter is more interesting than a simple non-digital experience. They add that satisfaction is the variable most positively impacted by the digitization of the customer experience. Furthermore, Fuentes-Blasco et al. (2017) state that technological innovation in the retail experience has a positive impact on satisfaction. Roy et al. (2017) add that customer satisfaction is a mediator between the smart customer experience and future behaviors. They also show that the smart customer experience has a direct and positive effect on customer satisfaction.

H1: the smart customer experience has a positive effect on satisfaction

The Relationship Between Smart Customer Experience and Trust in the Brand

Morgan & Hunt (1994), and Sirieix & Dubois, (1999) state that trust results from past experiences and positive encounters with a brand. In other words, trust can evolve based on the customer's past, present and future experience with a brand. These authors suggest the existence of a link between past experience with the brand (frequency, recency and age of the experience) and trust (Wei et al., 2019). In addition, in their study, Inman & Nikolova, (2017) stress that retailers should focus on managing the customer experience using smart technologies as it can influence consumer trust in the brand. Hence the second hypothesis which states that:

H2: the smart customer experience has a positive effect on trust in the brand

The Relationship Between Satisfaction and Trust in the Brand

Sirieix &Dubois (1999) as well as Delgado-Ballester et al., (2001) consider satisfaction as a factor allowing to reinforce trust. They add that trust results from customer satisfaction through past experiences with the brand. These authors claim "satisfaction from experience with the brand influences consumer trust in the brand." As a result, studies by Sirieix &Dubois (1998), Sirieix and Dubois (1999), Delgado-Ballester et al., (2001), BellaajGargouri &Akrout (2008), and Cheikho, (2015) confirm the existence of a link between customer satisfaction and trust in the brand.

H3: consumer satisfaction has a positive effect on trust in the brand

The Relationship Between Satisfaction and Brand Attachment

Ben Khelil &Bouslama (2013) and Ben Khelil &Bahri-Ammari (2014) describe satisfaction as an antecedent of brand attachment. Indeed, Aurier et al., (2001), Smaoui (2008), and Bahri-Ammari (2012) reveal that customer satisfaction is a factor that explains attachment to the brand since a satisfied customer can be emotionally attached to the brand. Thomson et al. (2005) assert that an individual attached to a brand is "generally satisfied by it", hence, satisfaction is considered to be a determinant and a basis of brand attachment.

H4: customer satisfaction positively influences their attachment to the brand

The Relationship Between Trust in the Brand and Attachment to the Brand

Many authors consider trust as an antecedent and a determining factor in the brand attachment (Aurier et al., 2001; Smaoui, 2008). Garbarino & Johnson (1999) assert that trust allows the benevolent maintenance of good long-term relationships between stakeholders, and stimulates the development and sustainability of relational exchanges. Chaudhuri and Holbrook (2001) also testify to the existence of a link between trust and emotional attachment to it. In addition, Aurier et al., (2001), Khelil & Bouslama (2013), Ben Khelil & Bahri-Ammari (2014), and Bahri-Ammari et al., (2016) were able to establish and test the positive and significant relationship between brand trust and brand attachment. Hence the fifth hypothesis:

H5: trust in the brand has a positive effect on brand attachment

The Relationship Between Satisfaction and Proselytism

Maxham &Netemeyer (2002), and Brown et al., (2005) state that there is a relationship between consumer satisfaction and the disclosure of positive word of mouth about the brand; since a satisfied customer is more likely to positively engage with word-of-mouth. The more satisfied the customer, the more positive word-of-mouth they express about the brand. Roy et al., (2017) state that the innovative nature of retail technologies arouses consumer interest and generates more positive word of mouth and this will depend on the satisfaction of customers with their experiences with the technology smart. Besides, studies by Ben Khelil & Bouslama (2013), San-Martín (2015), Bahri-Ammari et al., (2016), Roy et al., (2017), Fuentes-Blasco et al., (2017), Wei et al., (2019) confirm the existence of a positive and significant relationship between satisfaction and proselytizing.

H6: Satisfaction positively affects Proselytism

The Relationship Between Satisfaction and the Intention to Continue the Relationship With the Brand

Anderson & Sullivan (1993) claim that satisfaction is a predictor of the customer's intention to continue the relationship with the brand. Furthermore, the likelihood of a customer's repeat purchase of the same brand and their intention to continue their relationship with them depends on their satisfaction (Bloemer & Kasper, 1995; Joachim, 2019; Keyoor & Sunil, 2019). In their study, McQuitty et al., (2000) argue that the customer continues his relationship with the same brand and develops an intention to return regularly if he has had a very satisfactory consumption experience. Several researchers have confirmed the existence of a significant and positive relationship between customer satisfaction and their intentions to continue a relationship with the brand (Zeithaml et al., 1996; Mittal et al., 1999; Joachim, 2019). Hence the seventh hypothesis:

H7: Satisfaction positively affects the customer's intention to continue the relationship with the brand

The Relationship Between Brand Attachment and the Components of Brand Loyalty

Numerous studies claim that brand attachment is a predictor of brand loyalty (Chaudhuri & Holbrook, 2001; Bahri-Ammari et al., 2016). In this sense, Bellaaj-Gargouri & Akrout (2008) confirm that attachment has a significant and direct effect on brand loyalty. Bahri-Ammari, (2012)a nd Keyoor & Sunil, (2019) mentioned that the consumer's attachment to the brand explains his intention to pursue a long-term relationship with the same brand and his willingness to make financial sacrifices to obtain it. According to some authors, brand attachment promotes consumer brand loyalty (Bellaaj-Gargouri & Akrout, 2008).

H8. Attachment to the brand has a positive impact on behavioral loyalty

The Relationship Between Brand Attachment and Proselytizing

Cristau (2001) argues that brand attachment indicates a lasting emotional and psychological relationship that affects the development of positive word-of-mouth or proselytizing. Besides, a consumer attached to a brand encourages the brand and speaks positively about it to those around him (Bahri-Ammari, 2012; Wei et al., 2019). Indeed, several authors claim proselytism is a consequence of the consumer's attachment to a brand (De Matos & Rossi, 2008; Bahri-Ammari, 2012).

H8.1: Attachment to the brand positively affects proselytism

The Relationship Between Attachment to the Brand and the Intention to Continue the Relationship with the Brand

Belaid & Temessek-Behi (2010) state that brand attachment expresses the consumer's desire to maintain a nostalgic link with the brand and this through his consumption. These authors add that a high level of brand attachment manifests itself in the customer's desire to rely on it and to maintain the relationship with it. This manifests itself in repetitive buying behavior. Also, Khelil et al., (2013) and Keyoor & Sunil, (2019) argue that brand attachment determines the willingness of consumers to continue the relationship over the long term.

H8.2: Attachment to the brand positively affects the intention to continue the relationship with the brand.

The Relationship Between Brand Attachment and Resistance to Price Increases

Marketing literature shows that customers attached to a brand pay a premium for their attachment (Bahri-Ammari et al., 2016). Indeed, a customer attached and strongly committed to a brand is one who devalues any competing brand by developing a negative attitude towards it (Raju & Unnava, 2002). Thomson et al., (2005) argue that brand attachment explains the consumer's intention to pay a premium price for the brand and his willingness to continue paying the asking price. Several authors claim that the more the customer is attached to a brand, the more he develops resistance to rising prices, the more he accepts high prices to obtain the brand and the less sensitive he is to the prices of the competition (Aaker, 1996; Raju & Unnava, 2002). In this direction, Bahri-Ammari et al., (2016) and Nikhashemi et al., (2021) state that a customer attached to a brand is a customer who is willing to pay more for it.

H8.3: Brand attachment positively affects resistance to price increases

Figure 1. Conceptual model

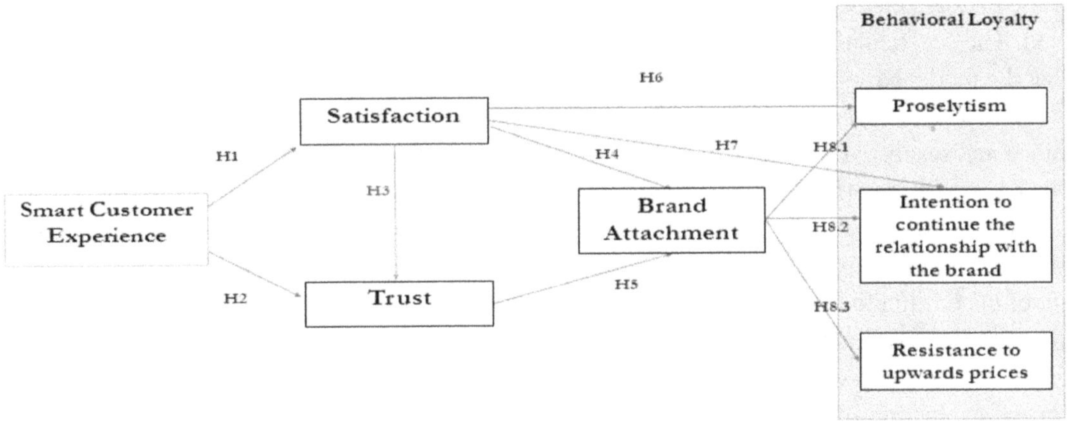

METHODOLOGY

The measurement scales were taken from the literature according to their adaptability to the retail context, their reliability, and their psychometric qualities. These are The smart customer experience (5 dimensions & 16 items; Roy et al., 2017); satisfaction (6 items; Montoya-Weiss et al., 2003; Bennett et al., 2005; Harris &Goode, 2004); trust (3 dimension & 8 items; Gurviez & Korchia, 2002); attachment to the brand (5 items; Lacoeuilhe, 2000); proselytism (3 items; Cristau, 2003); intention to continue the relationship (3 items; Maxham & Netemeyer, 2002); and resistance to price increases (3 items; Gurviez (1999). The five-point LIKERT scale was used.

The quantitative method was based on collection via a survey administered face to face with the presence of an interviewer in the field. In our study, the sampling method chosen is the judgment method or "reasoned sample". The selected population is made up of 302 French consumers who have used smart technology in their shopping experiences. This population consists mainly of young men and women customers of the ZARA, McDonald's, and SAMSUNG brands.

RESULTS

The analysis and interpretation of the results obtained were made using the software «SPSS» in its twenty-first version and SMART PLS 3.0 and this to test the hypotheses of our research.

The values of Cronbach's alpha are satisfactory (>0.7) (Nunnally, 1978; Nunnally & Bernstein 1994). The reliability indicator RHÔ takes values between 0.768 and 0.938 (>0.7) (Lacroux, 2011). So the internal consistency and reliability of all the variables that make up our model are verified. Convergent validity (Fernandes, 2012), measured by the Average Variance Extracted (AVE), shows that all the average variances extracted (AVE) have valued between 0.620 and 0.859 (> 0.5). Discriminant validity is established by checking that the shared variance between the constructs is lower than the average variances extracted (Fornell & Larcker, 1981; Gurviez & Korchia, 2002). The results present satisfactory coefficients, which respect the required standards. Two coefficients were measured to evaluate the quality of the measurement model is primarily concerned with its explanatory and predictive power. These are the coefficient of determination of the dependent variables (R^2) and the Stone-Geisser coefficient Q^2 of the endogenous variables of the model (Fernandes, 2012). The technique of "Blindfolding" was adopted. The coefficient Q^2, as well as the R^2, takes positive values other than zero, from which we can say that the model has good predictive validity. The q^2 effect makes it possible to evaluate the predictive relevance of each exogenous construct for an endogenous construct. the thresholds set to interpret the relevance are, respectively, the values of 0.02 (small), 0.15 (medium), and 0.35 (large).

The degree of the effect of smart customer experience and satisfaction on trust is small. While the size of the attachment satisfaction effect is small since q^2 is close to 0. The size of the attachment trust effect is medium because $q^2 > 0.15$. Satisfaction has no effect on proselytizing since the value of q^2 is negative; in addition to Q^2, the exclusion of satisfaction is greater than that in the case of the inclusion of this variable. Finally, the removal of satisfaction has a small effect on the customer's intention to continue a relationship with the brand since then.

For the evaluation of the quality of the structural model, goodness indices GOF and SRMR were used. The results revealed a GoF = 0.5655129> 0.36 acceptable according to Wetzels et al., (2009). The structural model is thus considered to be of good quality. The value of 0.02 of the found SRMR shows that our structural model has a good fit.

DISCUSSION, CONTRIBUTION AND IMPLICATIONS

The objective of this research is to examine the relationship between the smart customer experience and behavioral brand loyalty through relationship variables (satisfaction, trust, and brand attachment) in the retail sector. Thus, in order to respond to this objective, a conceptual model has been designed and hypotheses developed. The first hypothesis of the model confirms the work of Roy et al., (2017) which stipulates that customer satisfaction is a mediator between the smart customer experience and his future behaviors. In addition, Materne et al., (2017) find that "customer satisfaction induced by the customer experience offered through digitization is greater than customer satisfaction induced by the customer experience in physical commerce". In this direction, the results of studies by Poncin & Mimoun (2014) and Fuentes-Blasco (2017) show that the introduction of technological innovations in the retail experience increases the level of customer satisfaction. The second hypothesis assumes that there is a link between smart customer experience and trust. Sirieix & Dubois (1999) and Morgan and Hunt (1994) have also studied this relationship and claiming that past experience with the brand is significantly related to the level of trust. The third hypothesis tested raises the significant and positive relationship between satisfaction and trust. This corroborates with the results of Sirieix &Dubois (1999), Boyer & Nefzi (2008), and Cheikho (2015). However, Belaid &Temessek Behi (2010) have studied the relationship in its reverse causal direction and state that the higher the satisfaction with a brand, the more the consumer trusts that brand. The fourth hypothesis emphasizes the existence of a relationship between satisfaction and attachment to the brand in accordance with the results of Thomson etal., (2005), Smaoui (2008), Bahri-Ammari (2012), Khelil & Bouslama (2013), and Ben Khelil & Bahri-Ammari (2014). However, Belaid & Temessek-Behi (2010) have studied the relationship in its reverse causal direction and confirm that the higher the attachment to a brand, the greater the customer satisfaction for that brand. This relationship has not been shown, which shows that the causal link must be reversed.The fifth hypothesis states the existence of a significant positive relationship between trust and attachment to the brand in accordance with the results of Aurier et al., (2001) and Smaoui (2008). In addition, Ben Khelil & Bahri-Ammari (2014) tested this relationship on two product categories (a food product and a cosmetic product) and stipulate that this relationship is not confirmed in the case of a food product brand. However, the relationship between satisfaction and word of mouth (proselytism) has not been validated. This is contrary to the results of other research, which demonstrates the existence of a positive and significant link between customer satisfaction with their experiences and word of mouth in the retail context (Batat, 2018-2020; Bahri-Ammari et al., 2016; Fuentes-Blasco et al., 2017; Roy et al., 2017). The seventh hypothesis states that there is a significant positive relationship between satisfaction and the customer's intention to continue a relationship with the brand. This result confirms the literature with the exception of the study by Bahri-Ammari et al., (2016) who report that satisfaction does not imply the intention to continue the relationship. The eighth hypothesis, which studies the relationship between brand attachment and behavioral loyalty to it, is confirmed. This corroborates with the results of studies by Bellaaj-Gargouri & Akrout (2008) and Joachim, (2019) which focus on the direct, significant, and positive effect of brand attachment on the facets of long-term loyalty since a customer attached to a brand behaves in a cooperative and loyal manner with it. However, Belaid & Temessek-Behi (2010) have studied the relationship in its reverse causal direction and confirm that the higher the attachment to a brand, the greater the customer satisfaction for that brand. This relationship has not been shown, which shows that the causal link must be reversed. The fifth hypothesis states the existence of a significant positive relationship between trust and attachment to the brand in accordance with the results of Aurier et al., (2001) and Smaoui (2008). In addition, Ben Khelil & Bahri-Ammari (2014) tested this relationship on two product categories (a food product and a cosmetic product) and stipulate that this relationship is not confirmed in the case of a food product brand. . However, the relationship between satisfaction and word of mouth (proselytism) has not been validated. This is contrary to the results of other research which demonstrates the existence of a positive and significant link between customer satisfaction with their experiences and word of mouth in the retail context (Batat, 2018-2020; Bahri-Ammari et al., 2016; Fuentes-Blasco et al., 2017; Roy et al., 2017). The seventh hypothesis states that there is a significant positive relationship between satisfaction and the customer's intention to continue a relationship with the brand. This result confirms the literature with the exception of the study by Bahri-Ammari et al., (2016) and Nikhashemi et al., (2021) who report that satisfaction does not imply the intention to continue the relationship. The eighth hypothesis, which studies the relationship between brand attachment and behavioral loyalty to it, is confirmed. This corroborates with the results of studies by Bellaaj-Gargouri &Akrout (2008) which focus on the direct, significant, and positive effect of brand attachment on the facets of long-term loyalty since a customer attached to a brand behaves in a cooperative and loyal manner with it.

The Theoretical Contribution: This study is the first to develop a conceptual model examining the relationship between the smart customer experience and behavioral brand loyalty through relational variables such as satisfaction, trust, and brand attachment in the context of smart retail technologies. The first academic contribution of our research is the synthesis of previous work dealing with the same concepts that we have studied in our research. In addition, the smart customer experience is a new concept little studied in the literature and addressed by Roy et al., (2017) which is the first one to have developed a scale of measurement of this concept that we also used. This work provided an opportunity to empirically study the different smart technologies in the retail context and examine the consequences of the smart customer experience and its effect on behavioral brand loyalty. This study contributes to

Table 1. Testing hypotheses

Hypotheses	B	t	*P Values*	Hypotheses Validation
ATT -> ICR	0.448	8,794	0,000	Confirmed
ATT -> PRO	0.639	15,812	0,000	Confirmed
ATT -> RUP	0.534	12,909	0,000	Confirmed
TRST -> ATT	0.535	9,442	0,000	Confirmed
SCE -> TRST	0.253	3,862	0,000	Confirmed
SCE -> SAT	0.651	14,587	0,000	Confirmed
SAT -> ATT	0.148	2,374	0,018	Confirmed
SAT -> TRST	0.379	5,563	0,000	Confirmed
SAT -> ICR	0.335	5,945	0,000	Confirmed
SAT -> PRO	0.010	0,207	0,836	Rejected

***p ‹ 1%

the literature on the integration and use of smart technologies within the points of sale, by demonstrating the influence of the customer experience using these innovative technological on its relationship with the brand (satisfaction, trust, brand attachment, and behavioral loyalty to the brand). The empirical study showed that the smart customer experience positively affects satisfaction and trust, which in turn positively influences brand attachment. Thus, significant and positive relationships between brand attachment and proselytism, intent to pursue a relationship with the brand, and customer resistance to price increases were approved.

Managerial Contributions: The results of our research allow us to provide a series of recommendations for retailers to better manage their retail businesses. One of the major roles of this work is to emphasize the importance of the smart customer experience in developing satisfaction, trust, attachment, and behavioral loyalty to a brand. We have shown that smart customer experience affects customer satisfaction and trust, This leads retailers to offer their customers satisfying experiences given that satisfaction and trust imply consumer attachment to and loyalty to the brand through a positive word of mouth, her intention to pay more for the brand, and her intention to pursue a relationship with it. Companies must then be aware of the importance of integrating new technologies into their physical outlets. In this perspective, they have an interest in providing consumers with a satisfying and memorable smart experience that promotes customer loyalty. Retailers must also focus on improving customer satisfaction to take advantage of greater profitability resulting from re-chat behaviors, increased customer retention, and positive word-of-mouth disclosure (Rust et al., 1995; Gomez et al., 2004). In order to protect and grow their customer portfolios, retailers need to create and maintain relationships between the brand and its customers in order to promote a good brand image (Belaid &Temessek-Behi, 2010). Given that improving customer satisfaction and developing customer attachment is a way for companies to maintain lasting relationships with their customers, they must satisfy them and make them attached to the brand in order to be able subsequently to retain them (Mohsan et al., 2011). It is also recommended that managers and sellers in direct contact with customers communicate emotionally with customers in order to strengthen their attachment (Bellaaj-Gargouri, & Akrout, 2008).

REFERENCES

Aaker, D. A. (1996). Measuring Brand Equity Across Products And Markets. *California Management Review, 38*(3), 102–120. doi:10.2307/41165845

Agustin, C., & Singh, J. (2005). Curvilinear effects of consumer loyalty determinants in relational exchanges. *JMR, Journal of Marketing Research, 42*(1), 96–108. doi:10.1509/jmkr.42.1.96.56961

Anderson, E. W., Fornell, C., & Lehmann, D. R. (1994). Customer satisfaction, market share, and profitability: Findings from Sweden. *Journal of Marketing, 58*(3), 53–66. doi:10.1177/002224299405800304

Anderson, H., & Jacobsen, P. N. (2000). Creating loyalty: Its strategic importance in your customer strategy. *Customer Relationship Management, 55*, 67.

Aurier, P., Benavent, C., & N'goala, G. (2001). Validité discriminante et prédictive des composantes de la relation à la marque. *Cahiers de Recherche du CREGO*, (8), 51–70.

Bahri-Ammari, N. (2012). The effects of loyalty program quality on word-of-mouth recommendations intentions. *International Journal of Economics and Management Engineering, 6*(4), 619–628.

Bahri-Ammari, N., Van Niekerk, M., Khelil, H. B., & Chtioui, J. (2016). The effects of brand attachment on behavioral loyalty in the luxury restaurant sector. *International Journal of Contemporary Hospitality Management*.

Batat, W. (2018). *Concevoir et améliorer l'expérience client digitale: Le Triangle de l'Expérience Digitale pour réussir la transformation digitale-Le Blue Sunflower Marketing pour innover efficacement-L'approche Physical 2030 pour performer*. Editions Eyrolles.

Batat, W. (2020). How can art museums develop new business opportunities? Exploring young visitors' experience. *Young Consumers, 21*(1), 109–131. doi:10.1108/YC-09-2019-1049

Belaid, S., & Behi, A. T. (2011). The role of attachment in building consumer-brand relationships: An empirical investigation in the utilitarian consumption context. *Journal of Product and Brand Management, 20*(1), 37–47. doi:10.1108/10610421111108003

Belanche, D., Casaló, L. V., & Flavián, C. (2020). Frontline robots in tourism and hospitality: Service enhancement or cost reduction? *Electronic Markets*, 1–16.

Bellaaj-Gargouri, R., & Akrout, F. (2008). Nostalgie et fidélité du consommateur: le rôlemédiateur de l'attachement à la marque. *Proceedings of International Congress Marketing Trends*, 7.

Ben Khelil, H., & Bahri-Ammari, N. (2015). Brand Attachment and its Effects on Proselytism and the Resistance to Change: Comparative Study between Two Categories of Products. *Nedra, Brand Attachment and its Effects on Proselytism and the Resistance to Change: Comparative Study between Two Categories of Products*.

Ben Khelil, H., & Bouslama, N. (2013). *L'impact de la perception de la qualité du service sur le prosélytisme: Cas des fournisseurs de service Internet en Tunisie* [The Impact of the Perception of the Quality of the Service on Proselytism: Case of Internet Service Suppliers in Tunisia]. Academic Press.

Bennett, D. R., & El Azhari, J. (2015). *Omni-Channel Customer Experience: An Investigation Into The Use Of Digital Technology In Physical Stores And Its Impact On The Consumer's Decision-Making Process*. Academic Press.

Bennett, R., Härtel, C. E., & McColl-Kennedy, J. R. (2005). Experience as a moderator of involvement and satisfaction on brand loyalty in a business-to-business setting 02-314R. *Industrial Marketing Management*, *34*(1), 97–107. doi:10.1016/j.indmarman.2004.08.003

Bèzes, C. (2019). What kind of in-store smart retailing for an omnichannel real-life experience? [English Edition]. *Recherche et Applications en Marketing*, *34*(1), 91–112. doi:10.1177/2051570718808132

Bloemer, J. M., & Kasper, H. D. (1995). The complex relationship between consumer satisfaction and brand loyalty. *Journal of Economic Psychology*, *16*(2), 311–329. doi:10.1016/0167-4870(95)00007-B

Boyer, A., & Nefzi, A. (2008). La relation entre la perception de la qualité et la fidélité. *La Revue des Sciences de Gestion*, *234*(6), 37–48. doi:10.3917/rsg.234.0037

Brown, T. J., Barry, T. E., Dacin, P. A., & Gunst, R. F. (2005). Spreading the word: Investigating antecedents of consumers' positive word-of-mouth intentions and behaviors in a retailing context. *Journal of the Academy of Marketing Science*, *33*(2), 123–138. doi:10.1177/0092070304268417

Casaló, L. V., Flavián, C., & Ibáñez-Sánchez, S. (2020). Be creative, my friend! Engaging users on Instagram by promoting positive emotions. *Journal of Business Research*. Advance online publication. doi:10.1016/j.jbusres.2020.02.014

Chaudhuri, A., & Holbrook, M. B. (2001). The chain of effects from brand trust and brand affect to brand performance: The role of brand loyalty. *Journal of Marketing*, *65*(2), 81–93. doi:10.1509/jmkg.65.2.81.18255

Cheikho, A. (2015). *L'adoption des innovations technologiques par les clients et son impact sur la relation client-Cas de la banque mobile* (Doctoral dissertation). Université Nice Sophia Antipolis.

Cristau, C. (2001). *Définition, mesure et modélisation de l'attachement à une marque comme la conjonction de deux dimensions distinctes et concomitantes(la dépendance et l'amitié vis-à-vis de la marque)*. Academic Press.

Dacko, S. G. (2017). Enabling smart retail settings via mobile augmented reality shopping apps. *Technological Forecasting and Social Change*, *124*, 243–256. doi:10.1016/j.techfore.2016.09.032

Delgado-Ballester, E., & Munuera-Alemán, J. L. (2001). Brand trust in the context of consumer loyalty. *European Journal of Marketing*, *35*(11/12), 1238–1258. doi:10.1108/EUM0000000006475

Fernandes, V. (2012). En quoi l'approche PLS est-elle une méthode a (re)-découvrir pour les chercheurs en management?. *M@ n@ gement*, *15*(1), 102-123.

Fuentes-Blasco, M., Moliner-Velázquez, B., Servera-Francés, D., & Gil-Saura, I. (2017). Role of marketing and technological innovation on store equity, satisfaction and word-of-mouth in retailing. *Journal of Product and Brand Management*, *26*(6), 650–666. doi:10.1108/JPBM-07-2016-1279

Garbarino, E., & Johnson, M. S. (1999). The different roles of satisfaction, trust, and commitment in customer relationships. *Journal of Marketing*, *63*(2), 70–87. doi:10.1177/002224299906300205

Gretzel, U., Werthner, H., Koo, C., & Lamsfus, C. (2015). Conceptual foundations for understanding smart tourism ecosystems. *Computers in Human Behavior*, *50*, 558–563. doi:10.1016/j.chb.2015.03.043

Gurviez, P., & Korchia, M. (2002). Proposition d'une échelle de mesure multidimensionnelle de la confiance dans la marque. *Recherche et Applications en Marketing*, *17*(3), 41–61. doi:10.1177/076737010201700304

Harris, L. C., & Goode, M. M. (2004). The four levels of loyalty and the pivotal role of trust: A study of online service dynamics. *Journal of Retailing*, *80*(2), 139–158. doi:10.1016/j.jretai.2004.04.002

Heilbrunn, B. (2001). *Les facteurs d'attachement du consommateur à la marque* (Doctoral dissertation). Paris 9.

Henseler, J., Dijkstra, T. K., Sarstedt, M., Ringle, C. M., Diamantopoulos, A., Straub, D. W., & Calantone, R. J. (2014). Common beliefs and reality about PLS: Comments on Rönkkö and Evermann (2013). *Organizational Research Methods*, *17*(2), 182–209. doi:10.1177/1094428114526928

Homburg, C., Jozić, D., & Kuehnl, C. (2017). Customer experience management: Toward implementing an evolving marketing concept. *Journal of the Academy of Marketing Science*, *45*(3), 377–401. doi:10.100711747-015-0460-7

Huré, E., & Cliquet, G. (2011, September). Du multicanal au transcanal: le point de vue du consommateur. In *Actes du 14e Colloque Étienne Thil, Roubaix* (pp. 1-19). Academic Press.

Inman, J. J., & Nikolova, H. (2017). Shopper-facing retail technology: A retailer adoption decision framework incorporating shopper attitudes and privacy concerns. *Journal of Retailing*, *93*(1), 7–28. doi:10.1016/j.jretai.2016.12.006

Jain, R., Aagja, J., & Bagdare, S. (2017). Customer experience–a review and research agenda. *Journal of Service Theory and Practice*, *27*(3), 642–662. doi:10.1108/JSTP-03-2015-0064

Kilani, N. (2016). *Étude de l'expérience vécue sur trois canaux d'achat différents et son impact sur la relation marque-consommateur dans le cas des marques de luxe*. Academic Press.

Kim, H. Y., Lee, J. Y., Mun, J. M., & Johnson, K. K. (2017). Consumer adoption of smart in-store technology: Assessing the predictive value of attitude versus beliefs in the technology acceptance model. *International Journal of Fashion Design, Technology and Education*, *10*(1), 26–36.

Lacoeuilhe, J. (2000). L'attachement à la marque: proposition d'une échelle de mesure. Rechercheet Applications en Marketing, 15(4), 61-77.

Lee, J. H., Phaal, R., & Lee, S. H. (2013). An integrated service-device-technology roadmap for smart city development. *Technological Forecasting and Social Change*, *80*(2), 286–306. doi:10.1016/j.techfore.2012.09.020

Lemoine, J. F., & Onnée, S. (2001). Vers une meilleure compréhension du statut" d'actionnaire individuel-client. *Gestion*, *2000*(4), 127–138.

Mahad, M., Mohtar, S., & Othman, A. A. (2015). Disposition to trust, interpersonal trust and institutional trust of mobile banking in Malaysia. *Journal of Management Info*, *8*(1), 1–14. doi:10.31580/jmi.v8i1.45

Materne, S., & Charry, K. (2017). *Digitalisation des commerces traditionnels: une amélioration du parcours client pour les consommateurs?* Academic Press.

Maxham, J. G. III, & Netemeyer, R. G. (2002). A longitudinal study of complaining customers' evaluations of multiple service failures and recovery efforts. *Journal of Marketing*, *66*(4), 57–71. doi:10.1509/jmkg.66.4.57.18512

McQuitty, S., Finn, A., & Wiley, J. B. (2000). Systematically varying consumer satisfaction and its implications for product choice. *Academy of Marketing Science Review*, *10*(1), 231–254.

Mercier, J., & Roux, E. (2017). L'attachement à la marque: mesure unidimensionnelle ou tridimensionnelle? *Centre d'étude et de recherché en gestion d'Aix-Marseille*, 1-38.

Meyer, C., & Schwager, A. (2007). Understanding Customer Experience. *Harvard Business Review*, *85*(2), 116. PMID:17345685

Morgan, R. M., & Hunt, S. D. (1994). The commitment-trust theory of relationship marketing. *Journal of Marketing*, *58*(3), 20–38. doi:10.1177/002224299405800302

Mosquera, A., Olarte-Pascual, C., Ayensa, E. J., & Murillo, Y. S. (2018). The role of technology in an omnichannel physical store: Assessing the moderating effect of gender. *Spanish Journal of Marketing-ESIC*.

Neuhofer, B., Buhalis, D., & Ladkin, A. (2015). Smart technologies for personalized experiences: A case study in the hospitality domain. *Electronic Markets*, *25*(3), 243–254. doi:10.100712525-015-0182-1

Nikhashemi, S. R., Knight, H. H., Nusair, K., & Liat, C. B. (2021). Augmented reality in smart retailing: A (n)(A) Symmetric Approach to continuous intention to use retail brands' mobile AR apps. *Journal of Retailing and Consumer Services*, *60*, 102464. doi:10.1016/j.jretconser.2021.102464

Pantano, E., & Di Pietro, L. (2012). Understanding consumer's acceptance of technology-based innovations in retailing. *Journal of Technology Management & Innovation*, *7*(4), 1–19. doi:10.4067/S0718-27242012000400001

Pantano, E., & Timmermans, H. (2014). What is smart for retailing? *Procedia Environmental Sciences*, *22*, 101–107. doi:10.1016/j.proenv.2014.11.010

Pantano, E., & Viassone, M. (2014). Demand pull and technology push perspective in technology-based innovations for the points of sale: The retailers evaluation. *Journal of Retailing and Consumer Services*, *21*(1), 43–47. doi:10.1016/j.jretconser.2013.06.007

Picot-Coupey, K. (2013). Les voies d'avenir du magasin physique à l'heure du commerce connecté. *Gestion*, *38*(2), 51–61. doi:10.3917/riges.382.0051

Picot-Coupey, K., Ekaterina, V., & Cliquet, G. (2016, October). Coproduction de services enmagasin: impact des objets connectés sur la productivité du consommateur. *18ème colloque E. Thil.*

Pine, B. J., & Gilmore, J. H. (1998). Welcome to the experience economy. *Harvard Business Review*, *76*(4), 97–105. PMID:10181589

Poncin, I., Garnier, M., Mimoun, M. S. B., & Leclercq, T. (2017). Smart technologies and shopping experience: Are gamification interfaces effective? The case of the Smart store. *Technological Forecasting and Social Change, 124*, 320–331. doi:10.1016/j.techfore.2017.01.025

Poncin, I., & Mimoun, M. S. B. (2014). The impact of "e-atmospherics" on physical stores. *Journal of Retailing and Consumer Services, 21*(5), 851–859. doi:10.1016/j.jretconser.2014.02.013

Poujol, F., & Siadou-Martin, B. (2010, October). De l'OC des vendeurs à la fidélité à l'entreprise: Le rôle modérateur de la propension relationnelle du client. In *Colloque Etienne Thil, La Rochelle* (pp. 7-8). Academic Press.

Purani, K., Kumar, D. S., & Sahadev, S. (2019). e-Loyalty among millennials: Personal characteristics and social influences. *Journal of Retailing and Consumer Services, 48*, 215–223. doi:10.1016/j.jretconser.2019.02.006

Raju, S., & Unnava, H. R. (2002). *The effects of brand commitment on the evaluation of competitive brands*. ACR North American Advances.

Renko, S., & Druzijanic, M. (2014). Perceived usefulness of innovative technology in retailing: Consumers′ and retailers′ point of view. *Journal of Retailing and Consumer Services, 21*(5), 836–843. doi:10.1016/j.jretconser.2014.02.015

Roy, S. K., Balaji, M. S., Sadeque, S., Nguyen, B., & Melewar, T. C. (2017). Constituents and consequences of smart customer experience in retailing. *Technological Forecasting and Social Change, 124*, 257–270. doi:10.1016/j.techfore.2016.09.022

San-Martín, S., Prodanova, J., & Jiménez, N. (2015). The impact of age in the generation of satisfaction and WOM in mobile shopping. *Journal of Retailing and Consumer Services, 23*, 1–8. doi:10.1016/j.jretconser.2014.11.001

Scholz, J., & Duffy, K. (2018). We ARe at home: How augmented reality reshapes mobile marketing and consumer-brand relationships. *Journal of Retailing and Consumer Services, 44*, 11–23. doi:10.1016/j.jretconser.2018.05.004

Shankar, V., Inman, J. J., Mantrala, M., Kelley, E., & Rizley, R. (2011). Innovations in shopper marketing: Current insights and future research issues. *Journal of Retailing, 87*, S29–S42. doi:10.1016/j.jretai.2011.04.007

Sirieix, L., & Dubois, P. L. (1999). Vers un modèle qualité-satisfaction intégrant la confiance? *Recherche et Applications en Marketing, 14*(3), 1–22. doi:10.1177/076737019901400301

Smaoui, F. (2008, January). Les déterminants de l'attachement émotionnel à la marque: effet des variables relationnelles et des variables relatives au produit. In *Proceedings of the 2008 Marketing Trends Congress* (pp. 17-19). Academic Press.

Thomson, M., MacInnis, D. J., & Park, C. W. (2005). The ties that bind: Measuring the strength of consumers' emotional attachments to brands. *Journal of Consumer Psychology, 15*(1), 77–91. doi:10.120715327663jcp1501_10

Wei, W., Qi, R., & Zhang, L. (2019). Effects of virtual reality on theme park visitors' experience and behaviors: A presence perspective. *Tourism Management*, *71*, 282–293. doi:10.1016/j.tourman.2018.10.024

Willems, K., Smolders, A., Brengman, M., Luyten, K., & Schöning, J. (2017). The path-to-purchase is paved with digital opportunities: An inventory of shopper-oriented retail technologies. *Technological Forecasting and Social Change*, *124*, 228–242. doi:10.1016/j.techfore.2016.10.066

Zeithaml, V. A., Berry, L. L., & Parasuraman, A. (1996). The behavioral consequences of service quality. *Journal of Marketing*, *60*(2), 31–46. doi:10.1177/002224299606000203

APPENDIX

Figure 2.

Chapter 16
Generation Z's Media Use and Preferences as a Foundation for a Destination Media Planning Process

Andrijana Kos Kavran
https://orcid.org/0000-0002-1441-0321
Polytechnic of Medjimurje in Cakovec, Croatia

Daniel Herman
https://orcid.org/0000-0001-9399-6297
Polytechnic of Medjimurje in Cakovec, Croatia

ABSTRACT

The purpose of this chapter is to explore the media use and preferences of Generation Z as a foundation for destination media planning. This chapter used a quantitative method with a questionnaire used as primary data source with a sample of 299 respondents. Data were analysed using descriptive statistic method. The results showed that the majority of Generation Z uses and prefers online media while at the same time offline media shouldn't be ignored. This chapter provides recommendations for the destination marketing organizations (DMOs) and media planners to better understand the media habits of Generation Z to use them as a valuable input for destination media planning.

INTRODUCTION

This chapter seeks to present and explore the media use of the Generation Z, to explore the media preference of the Generation Z and to create the media planning guidelines and recommendations for destination media planners when targeting Generation Z. As technology is a vital part of Generation Z's life, it perceives and consumes the information through it, which makes its tendency more individualized (Tafonao et al., 2020). With this in mind media planners should learn the differences in media use

DOI: 10.4018/978-1-7998-7192-7.ch016

and preference of this generation in comparison with previous generations (Millenials, Generation X, Baby Boomers and Silent generation), because not every generation is alike, nor should they be treated by marketers in the same way (Williams & Page, 2011).

A new generation is becoming a very important member of the market from the consumption perspective. It is called Generation Z and follows previous very important generation Y or Millenials. This young generation members are individuals born in the 1994 and after (until 2010) and are around 26 years old in 2020. Generation Z has experienced technology development from the first day it was born. Smartphones and other smart devices made them quite different from other previous generations. Members of Generation Z represent the new tourist as they are considered to be the new actors on the demanding tourism market. They represent the most important future guests (Dimitriou & AbouElgheit, 2019) while at the same time are likely to transform tourism and destinations (Robinson & Schänzel, 2019). When it comes to planning the trip they highly use different media and channels. Tourist arrivals (the number of persons (tourists) who registered and realized nights in an accommodation establishment) to Croatia for the year 2018 show that of the 18,667,000 arrivals, 2,160,698 were aged 15-24 years or 11,57% (Croatian Bureau of Statistics, 2018).

In comparison with other generations Williams and Page (2011) revealed that for Silent Generation (aged 71-91) marketers should use formal written and face-to-face conversation and reach them through traditional media (radio, television, billboards, magazines and direct mail). However, this generation is increasingly becoming more tech savy. In terms of communication with generation of Baby Boomers (aged 55-73) direct mail, e-mail and face-to-face conversation should be used. For them, TV is still a major media route, they use Internet and mobile technology but don't have high understanding of functions beyond simple voice calls and SMS. On the Internet, social networks can be effective as well as blogs. In terms of communication, the next generation – Generation X (39-54) is not always easy to reach, especially by using TV as a media. Communication methods for this generation include the Internet, e-mail, word-of-mouth, social events and direct mail. When targeting Generation Y or Millenials (23-38) marketers should use magazines, Internet sites, TV and radio programs and video games. This generation also uses e-mail, voice mail, direct mail and newspapers. Interest in television is less for Millenials than any other generation. If they do watch, they watch on their schedule, not the networks.

Earlier research of media use and preferences of Generation Z show an increasingly interest in this topic so this chapter represents a certain extension. A continuous follow up is needed for marketers and media planners to get to know this generation and to adapt to their preferences. The research in the scope of this chapter is conducted among Croatian Generation Z as the lack of similar research is noted in this country. The objective of this chapter is to provide the basic theoretical background about the Generation Z, its media use and preferences and destination media planning as a part of a media strategy. This chapter uses descriptive explorative study and the empirical research on the media use and preferences of Generation Z using an online questionnaire among members of the Generation Z.

Croatia is an EU country which highly depends on tourism, with the highest ratio of travel receipts to GDP in 2019 – 19.4%, confirming the importance of tourism in this country (https://ec.europa.eu/eurostat/statistics-explained/pdfscache/1171.pdf). This and above mentioned data stresses the need of proper destination promotion strategy as Generation Z is becoming a very important tourist target group for Croatia. When planning a destination promotion strategy for Generation Z, destinations should apply the principles of the integrative approach. Their media strategy should contain the combination of those various media channels which collectively will create a communication channel for delivering the desired key messages targeted to the Generation Z at the lowest costs.

This paper is structured in the following way. Firstly, the main theoretical background on Generation Z and destination media planning is provided. Secondly, the methodology and research results are presented, and finally recommendations for destination media planners are provided.

THEORETICAL BACKGROUND

Generation Z's General Characteristics

Every generation is under the influence of time in which it grows and develops. The members of each generation share the same basic cultural, political and economic experiences and similar life views and values (Kotler et al., 2014). According to Dimock (2019) different generations are defined according to their year of birth (Figure 1).

Figure 1. The definitions of different age generations
Source: Dimock, M. (2019). Defining generations: Where Millennials end and Generation Z begins, Pew Research Center, Retrieved May 11, 2020, from: https://www.pewresearch.org/fact-tank/2019/01/17/where-millennials-end-and-generation-z-begins/

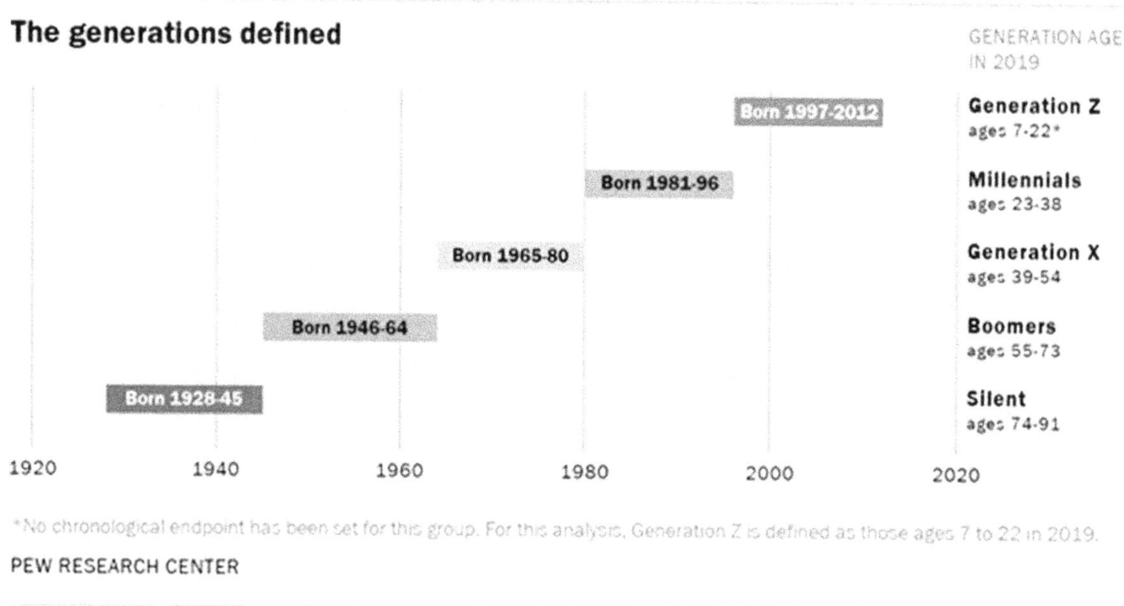

While there is no commonly accepted definition of Generation Z, most researches agree that the Generation Z, also known as Baby Bloomers, Tweens, Post Millenials and iGeneration, was born after 1994 (Williams & Page, 2011) and are around 26 years old in 2020. Generation Z is the first generation that was exposed to the Internet technology from birth (Yadav & Rai, 2017) and that was another characteristic of this generation that labeled them as a "Mobile and App Native" Generation (Persada et al., 2020). Besides the strong exposure to the technology, they also faced global terrorism, school violence, economic uncertainty, recession, mortgage crisis (Williams & Page, 2011) increased inequality, job insecurity and social media presence (Robinson & Schänzel, 2019). Mandelbaum (2016) states that Generation Z members are always connected, influential, have evolving needs and prefer to do-it-yourself ideas and in-person communication, aspire to career goals, have more entrepreneurial style, and have respect and are apparently loyal. They are also individualistic, less focused, multi-taskers, tend to have higher expectations (Beall, 2017), and are always ready to share their experiences publicly (Slivar et al., 2019).

Wood (2013) states that four trends characterize Generation Z as consumers: 1) A focus on innovation, 2) An insistence on convenience, 3) An underlying desire for security, and 4) A tendency toward escapism. Innovation refers to the fact that Generation Z has an innate comfort with the virtual world and as consumers are likely to feel that constant innovation is a given. Convenience is connected to their lack of exposure to "from scratch" consumption and the increased pressure on today's youth to achieve at young ages is likely to be reflected in an increased reliance on convenience in both product attributes, product delivery, product experience and product messaging. Economically difficult times are underlying their need for security so Generation Z may feel more careful and discriminating in where they spend their money. Their desire for an opportunity to escape is likely to be facilitated by technological advances that 1) make entertainment products like video games more real and compelling, 2) offer greater 24-7 access to social networks, and, 3) offer greater mobility in devices that offer escapism.

Born into a digital age and with increasing international travel, this young generation is likely to transform tourism and destinations, as they will soon be the adults occupying leadership positions and become the financiers of tourism and travel (Robinson & Schänzel, 2019). Generation Z represents the most important future guests and travellers in the hospitality and tourism global market and it should be noted that this new generation is significantly different in various ways compared to previous generations, especially when it comes to how they plan and organize their vacation trips and other forms of travel (Dimitriou & AbouElgheit, 2019), and the way they use different media in the information search about a certain destination.

Generation Z's Media Use and Preferences

Marketing on the right channel is no longer enough, marketers should be specific about the exact marketing platform and the exact device (Dimitriou & AbouElgheit, 2019).

Smartphones are absolutely central to lives of Generation Z. This group was spending an average of 4 hours and 15 minutes per day on their mobiles by the end of 2018. Nearly 97% of them own a smartphone.

Generation Z is constantly online, connected to the internet, social media, and all kinds of websites, reading, checking, comparing, analyzing, and evaluating options, information and ideas in order to ensure they are making the most out of the whole experience (Dimitriou & AbouElgheit, 2019). Generation Z utilizes social media and other applications to strengthen the bond between friends and family. Twitter, Instagram, and other social media applications have become rather popular in the Generation Z. As a result, the increase in technology usage, cause Generation Z to spend more time with their smartphones, and social media have made online relations developed into a new norm (Husein et al., 2017).

According to the Trifecta Research (2015) Generation Z is connected and conscientious. They are always online but are on the other hand worried that people their age spend too much time connected to the digital devices. Technology brands are important to them but that doesn't mean they want the latest gadget. They still watch TV more than two hours a day but on the other hand favor YouTube. They still love Facebook but are simultaneously cautious about what they post on social media. Generation Z is happy and comfortable shopping online but they prefer shopping offline and even 67% of them would rather shop in stores. As of media habits the rising popularity of Netflix is noticeable among Generation Z as well as YouTube as opposed to traditional TV - the amount of time they spend on Netflix and YouTube websites combined equates to 59% versus traditional TV at 29%. From a music perspective, broadcast radio continues to cede share to digital streaming and Spotify is gaining on Pandora. Tweens (8-12 years old) average 2:26 a day watching TV and videos, 1:18 a day playing games, and 51 minutes listening to music. While watching TV and videos (at 2:38 a day on average) and gaming (1:21 per day) are still popular among teens (13-19 years old), listening to music (1:54 per day) and using social media (1:11 per day) appear to gain importance once young people enter the teenage years, adding to the total amount of time teens spend with media (Figure 2).

Figure 2. Time spent in each media activity

Source: Trifecta research (2015): http://trifectaresearch.com/wp-content/uploads/2015/09/Generation-Z-Sample-Trifecta-Research-Deliverable.pdf

Among Tweens		Among Teens	
Watching TV/DVDs/videos	2:26	Watching TV/DVDs/videos	2:38
Playing video, computer, or mobile games	1:19	Listening to music	1:54
Listening to music	:51	Playing video, computer, or mobile games	1:21
Reading	:29	Using social media	1:11
Using social media	:16	Doing other activities on computer/mobile device	:32
Doing other activities on computer/mobile device	:13	Browsing websites	:36
Browsing websites	:12	Reading	:28
Video-chatting	:06	Video-chatting	:13
Going to the movies	:02	Going to the movies	:03
Total screen media	4:36	**Total screen media**	**6:40**
Total media	5:55	**Total media**	**8:56**

According to the Global Web Index research (2018) top five online activities of Generation Z are mostly related to mobile phones, and include the following: visiting/using social network (95%), using a chat or instant messaging service (92%), watching a video clip or visiting a video-sharing sites (91%), visiting or using a search engine (90%), visiting an online retail sites or stores (79%). As smartphones are very important to Generation Z, they're becoming more tech-savvy and more privacy-aware. 60% say they're concerned about how their personal data is being used by companies and 53% say they prefer to be anonymous when online. Generation Z is 12% more likely than average to be blocking ads. An overabundance of ads online is the biggest frustration (49%), with close to a majority also saying they block ads because they are annoying/irrelevant (48%). Watching TV and video content is the second most important reason for using the internet amongst Generation Z, making them 20% more likely than general internet users to hold this view. Social networking and messaging apps represent the most heavily used app categories amongst Generation Z.

According to the research by Levak and Baric Selmic (2018), members of Generation Z in Croatia use the internet on a daily basis and several times a day. Also, most of them access the internet via a smartphone, and the two most used app social networks for them are Facebook and Instagram. While evaluating the particular social networks, Instagram and Snapchat are the most popular ones. Regarding the most used communication apps according to the same research, the most used ones are Messenger and WhatsApp. Duffett (2017) stated that the teenagers who spend 2 or 3 hours daily on the social media are likely to have favorable cognitive, affective and behavioral stance regarding the marketing communications, so the conclusion can be that the social media is one of the most preferable digital communication channels for connecting with Generation Z. The Millennials, the generation before the Generation Z, regarding the Duffet (2014) finds Facebook as the main social media channel with a positive influence in the buying process so the change in the social media preferences in comparison with Generation Z is visible.

There are few things marketers have to have in mind when market to Generation Z. They want to be communicated with visually and with short, bite-sized content. This is a generation that knows how to search and find exactly what they want, so when expectations aren't met, they don't give a second chance. Their limited attention span means brands can never stop working for their business and, since they don't like being sold to, marketers need to find ways to deliver relevant, engaging and immediately beneficial experiences (Trifecta Research, 2015).

Destination Media Planning

Destination media planning is one of the most important part of a successful promotion strategy for a destination. Destinations should apply the principles of the integrative approach while planning a successful promotion strategy, which means that the media mix should include both traditional and online media channels. Destination media strategy must contain the combination of those various media channels which collectively will create a communication channel for delivering the desired key messages targeted to the specific audience and markets at the lowest costs. Using all the benefits of the available media channels will increase the percentage of meeting the media goals which are also a part of the media strategy creation. The following section will explain the definition of a tourism destination, media strategy and planning in a tourism destination, as well as the importance of choosing the right media mix channels.

2.3.1. The definition of a Tourism Destination

For a better understanding of the importance regarding the media channel planning in a destination, it is necessary to understand the definition of a destination. The term destination by UNWTO (2007, 14) is defined as following: „a local tourism destination is a physical space in which a tourist spends at least one overnight. It includes tourism products such as support services and attractions and tourist resources within one day's return travel time. It has physical and administrative boundaries defining its management, and images and perceptions defining its market competitiveness". Żemła (2016, 2) also cites the definition of the destination by the UNWTO as "the fundamental units of analysis in tourism". In general, analysis of targeted audience and markets have to be applied in the field of planning the destination media channels and have to be used as a foundation for further destination communication activities.

Buhalis (2000, 1) defines the destination as "amalgams of tourism products, offering an integrated experience to consumers'", while Goeldner (2003, 466) defines it as "a particular geographic region within which the visitor enjoys various types of travel experiences". Both authors pointed out the importance of the experience for the visitors, and the main task of the destination regarding the promotion should be combining the most suitable media channels through which can targeted visitors get its key communication messages. Those key communication messages must entice tourists to visit the destination, which confirms the definition of the Flagestad (2002, 3) who stated that "the destination is a function of tourists' choice – a place or region where tourists choose to go". Key communication messages of a destination should persuade visitors to become their first destination choice.

There are many definitions of the destination, but it is important to conclude that there is no universally accepted one. It cannot be stated with certainty that the destination does nor doesn't have a physically established border, but it is important to mention that destination is "the location where tourists choose to travel outside of their place of residence" (Mariutti, 2013, 13).

Morrison (2019) defines that the following is crucial for understanding the definition of destination: destination can be everything from a small city to the largest country in the world and its tourists must be able to find overnight accommodation. Also, the product of the destination should be available for visitors, and the destination must be organized by the coordinating organizational structure (Destination Marketing Organizations (DMO-s)). From the promotional perspective, the destination should promote itself to attract tourists, and branding of the destination must be strong enough so the tourists can have a perception about what the destination is and what it has to offer. Those definitions are a base for better understanding of the process of media channel planning in a destination.

Media Planning Process

Crucial part of every marketing plan of a destination is a media plan which consists of various media channels that destinations choose to deliver its key messages to the targeted audience. Media can offer a way of communicating information to the desired audience and it can help informing and entertaining them. Also, the destination can use media to socialize with the targeted audience which represents a way for connecting with them (Katz, 2017). According to Sissors & Barron (2010, 2) "media exist primarily to deliver message content—entertainment, information, and advertisements to a vast audience". Destinations should use all the benefits from media, but the content and the media should be chosen carefully to avoid unnecessary costs. The biggest mistake a destination can make is to choose all the media without the preliminary analysis focused on the preferences of the targeted audience.

The following part of the paper shows the steps in the destination media planning process according to Tellis & Ambler (2007). The first step for the destination is to set marketing objectives by planning sales value and market share of the destination. Second step is focused on defining who the targeted audience for the destination will be and what are their preferences and habits. Third step is focused on the decision for the media selection. This decision is the most complex one in the media planning process because the selection should be aligned with defined marketing objectives and within the budget. When the media is selected, destinations should set the media objectives which coincide with defined market objectives and then the focus should be on scheduling the media. In this step it's important to pick the right timing, placements and size or length of the promotional campaigns. The penultimate step is media buying and budgeting. Destination media buying is a process focused on making a final decision on the spreading the budget to the various media channels. When the campaigns are set up, the person in charge of the destination campaigns should focus on evaluation and effectivity through the measurement. This step should not be skipped because it can give the measurable results which are the base for the campaign optimization and improvements.

According to Sissors & Baron (2010) before the creation of a media plan for a destination promotional campaign, the media planners should know which media to choose for placing the ads for the campaign, when and how often during the month should ads be served to the targeted audience on chosen media channels, what is the budget for the each media and where the ads should be placed regarding the placements on the media channels. Also, destination media planners should know which markets and regions should be covered by the media.

Destination media planning process is often leaded by the DMO-s or the marketing agency who is in charge of process and they are called media planners, as stated in the section above. It often happens that the goals of the destination promotional campaigns are not properly defined, so the representatives of the destination should work with the marketing agency or the person who is responsible for the media planning on setting clear objectives. Objectives can be defined as desired results achievable in a short time, so in promotional sense in a destination media planning process, objectives are desired results from the destination promotional campaigns which are conducted through the media. Objectives have to be defined as SMART, which means every media objective as marketing objective has to be specific, measurable, achievable and also relevant. It's important to set up the time frame for achieving the objectives and if they are set up correctly, the success for the destination is easier to achieve (Chartered Management Institute, 2011).

Media Strategy

Media strategy is the fundamental part of the destination marketing strategy. Porter (1996, 64-68) defines strategy as a "creation of a unique and valuable position, involving in different set of activities". For Porter strategy is also focused on "combining activities and nothing more than a marketing slogan that will not withstand competition". Based on strategy definitions and according to the topic of this work, strategy has to be a foundation for a destination promotion. Destination marketing strategy involves different set of activities, so the media strategy is a part of it.

Strategy is known from the wars, and all the successful battles were successful by virtue of properly defined strategy. Many warrior leaders tested different kinds of tactics to support the implementation of the defined strategies, so that should be the right tactic for the destinations too. Those tactics are essential for the marketing strategy which is the main document for the destination promotion.

Marketing strategy must also include basic marketing elements and decisions. Those are, by Slater & Olson (2001, 1056) "decisions relating to market segmentation and targeting, and the development of a positioning strategy based on product, price, promotion and distribution decisions". On the other side, Personal et al. (2012) are describe that Kotler's marketing strategy consists of "identifying markets and customers' needs in those markets. Also, the part of the destination marketing strategy is "planning products which will satisfy the needs of these markets and organizing marketing resources, so as to match products with customers in the most efficient and effective way possible."

Destination media strategy can be explained as a scope of actions chosen from possible alternatives with one goal: obtaining the destination media objectives. The destination media strategy document includes selection of the targeted markets, media objectives and media which will be used for the destination promotional campaign with the expenses. As well, the following answer should be given in the document: "how the destination media plan will accomplish the stated objectives"? (Sissors & Baron, 2010). As it is stated, all of the basic communication documents as destination media plan and destination media strategy should contain those basic elements. If they are not defined, the media strategy will not be effective for the destination.

Media Channels

Today destinations have various types of media to choose from. They differ according to the reach and coverage, audience size, expenses of advertising, legitimacy and much more. Destination should make a connection with its targeted audience through the media channels, and the decision has to be made based on a research of the habits and preferences of the targeted audience.

Sissors and Baron (2010) mention four types of media channels which can destinations use: traditional mass media, nontraditional media, digital media, and specialized media. Traditional Mass Media according to Wimmer & Dominick (2014, 2) are „any form of communication transmitted through a medium (channel) that simultaneously reaches a large number of people". According to Blakeman (2014, 1) nontraditional media can be defined as media "used as an alternative choice to more traditional mass media vehicles directed at a mass audience. The goal of nontraditional media is to present brand promotion in ways and in places consumers least expect them". Sissors & Baron (2010, 13-14) consider online media as media that "includes any communications medium where there is a real-time interaction between the user and the content producer via the Internet." Specialized media according to the same authors are special-interest consumer media "that are often referred to as niche media because of their focus on special-interest ", targeted to specific interests of its audience.

Destination media channels are shown in the Table 1 bellow, and examples, advantages and disadvantages are refined by the authors.

As it is shown above, destinations have a large variety of available media channels. All of them have its advantages and the disadvantages, but to gain the quality results, a combination of media channels should be used. Focus just on particular media channels can assure short-time results, but destination media planners should focus on integrative approach while planning the media.

METHODOLOGY

The main objective of this chapter was to explore the media use and preference of the Generation Z in Croatia and to create the media planning guidelines and recommendations for destination media planners when targeting Generation Z. For this purpose, a qualitative descriptive study was conducted during October and November 2019 in Croatia among students who were aged 18-25 at the moment of research. The main criteria to participate in the study were the generational identities ie. the age of the respondents. The sample was intentional and chosen based on the availability of units for testing. The sample consisted of 318 subjects, but the answers of only 299 of them were used for the analysis, as they represented the Generation Z.

An online questionnaire was designed using Google forms and distributed through Loomen e-learning platform and Facebook social network. The starting point of the questionnaire design were studies mentioned in the theoretical background. The questionnaire consisted of four parts with single choice questions as most frequent questions posed. The first part of the questionnaire consisted of questions that were related to information search of Generation Z using online and offline media channels. The second part consisted of questions related to use and preference of TV and radio as a media channels, while the third part consisted of questions related to use and preference of online and print media. The last part of the questionnaire included socio-demographic data (age, gender and county of residence).

Table 1. Destination media channels

Destination media channels	Examples	Advantages	Disadvantages
Traditional Mass Media	Radio, television, newspapers, magazines and billboards, books, journals	Immediate delivery of messages Reaching mass audience Relatively low costs Ability to deliver advertisements to special kinds of audiences Integrity	Limitations in delivering key communication messages Relatively hard for destination to differentiate Fewer people prefer traditional media Sometimes political conditioned Hard to measure the audience and results
Nontraditional Media	Out of home venues such as video screens in airport waiting areas, elevators, gas pumps and any other place where the video screen can display content to the audience, any other alternative media and outdoor media that relies on innovation like package designs, in-store ads, POP displays, guerrilla marketing	Creativity in promotion Ability of personalization Effective targeting Interactive media Relatively low costs	Problems with identifying the brand or message Smaller reach compared to the mass media Hard to target segments Insufficient ad frequency Hard to measure the audience and results (ROI)
Online Media	Websites, Social Media, Search Engine Marketing, Audio and video online platforms, E-mail, PPC, podcasts, forums, smartphones, tablets, VR systems, digital TV,	Low costs Reaching large audience and easy segmented targeting Creativity, interaction and personalization Allows instant two-way communication Easy to measure results and audience	Problems with identifying the brand or message because of the competition Large period for delivering results Increasing budgets for paid advertising GDPR restrictions and security problems Dependability on technology
Specialized Media	Special-interest consumer magazines, B2B publications, films, trade shows, convention exhibits, CDs, flash drives, handbills, direct mail, catalogs, newspaper inserts, event tickets, seats, uniforms, naming rights, cinemas,	Extensive reach and frequency Selective audience because of the special-interest focus Ads can be seen in relevant areas to the products or services offered Creativity and innovation Can be saved and stored	One-way communication Lack of feedback and control Insufficient message frequency Smaller reach compared to the mass and online media Hard to measure the audience and results (ROI)

Source: authors work based on Sissors & Baron (2010); Wimmer & Dominick (2014) and Blakeman (2014).

After the collection, data were downloaded from Google forms and imported into IBM SPSS Statistics 20. Every answer was assigned with a code, so the coding process started. After the coding, all analyses were performed using SPSS.

RESULTS

Demographics

The average respondent in a sample is a female (71,91%), age 20 -25 (51,63%) from Varazdin County. The demographic profile of respondents is provided in Table 2.

Table 2. Demographic profile of respondents (n=299)

Characteristics	%
Gender	
Male	28,09
Female	71,91
Age	
18-20	48,37
20-25	51,63
County	
Bjelovar-Bilogora	1,19
Osijek-Baranja	2,38
Pozega-Slavonia	1,19
Sisak-Moslavina	2,38
Split-Dalmatia	1,19
Varazdin	34,52
Zadar	1,19
Zagreb	4,76
Brod-Posavina	1,19
The City of Zagreb	14,29
Istria	1,19
Karlovac	3,57
Koprivnica-Krizevci	8,33
Krapina-Zagorje	1,19
Medimurje	21,43

Source: authors work according to the research

From the age range of the respondents, it is evident that all of them belong to the Generation Z so the results bellow can be taken as a basis for destination media channels planning.

Figure 3. Media channel preference while searching for information
Source: authors work according to the research

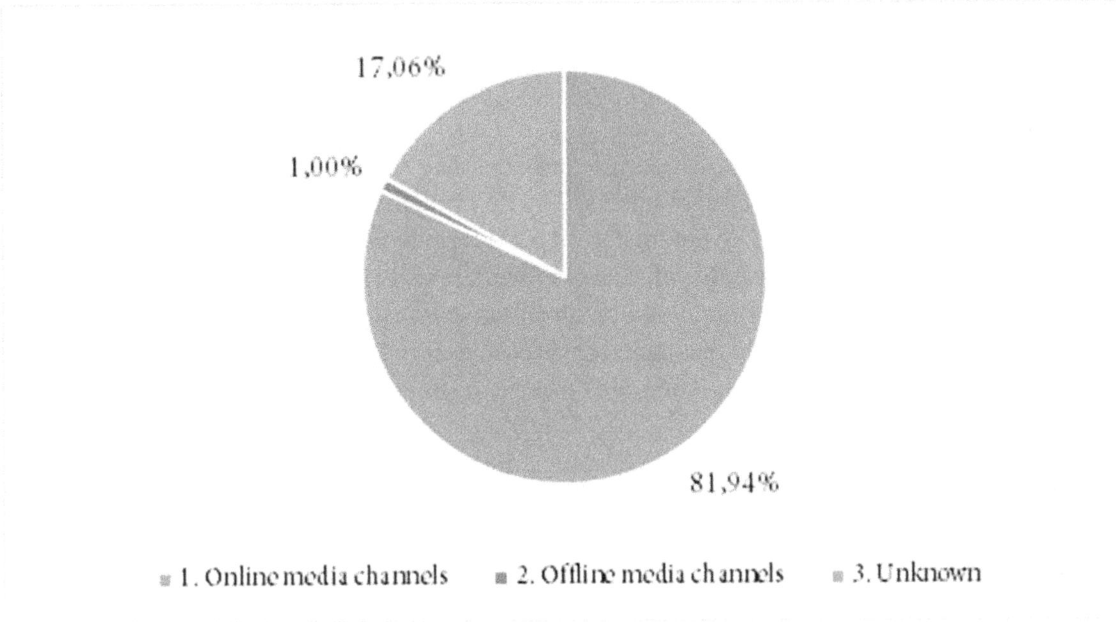

Figure 4. Trusting in the information that can be found, seen and heard on/in the media
Source: authors work according to the research

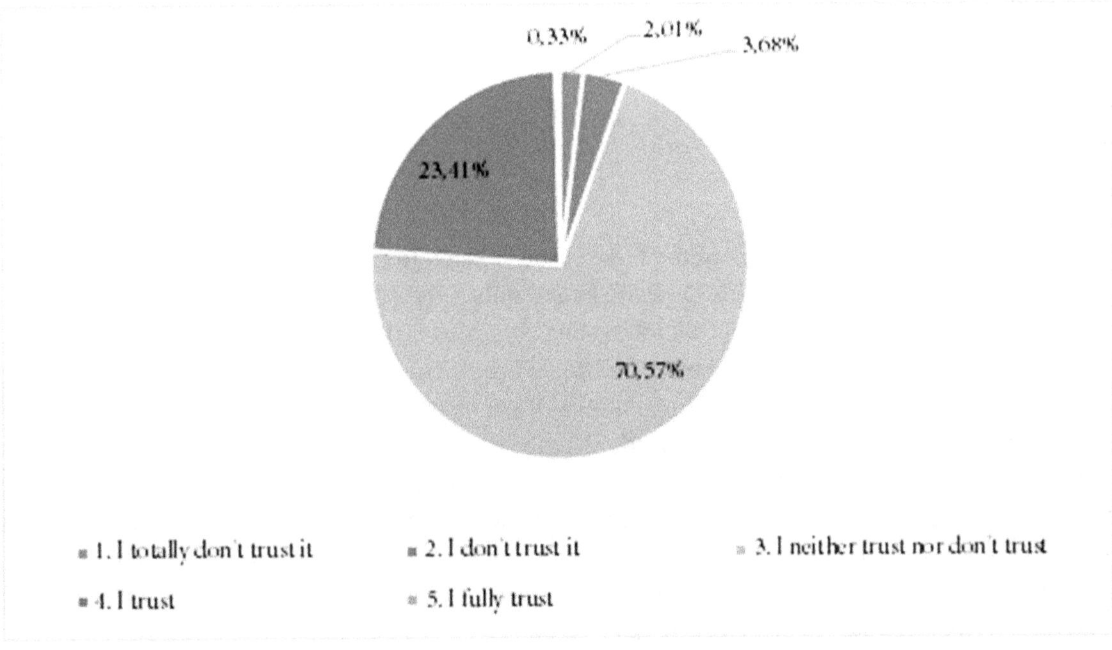

Information Searching Using Online and Offline Media Channels

Out of 299 respondents, 81,94% of them prefer online media when searching for information, 1% of them prefer offline media and 17,06% of respondents did not answer the question (Figure 3).

The Figure 3 shows that the Generation Z prefer online media channels while searching for an information.

Most of the respondents (70,57%) are indifferent regarding the information found, seen, or heard in the media. Of the total number of respondents, 23,41% of them trust the information found, seen or heard in the media, 2,01% of them do not trust at all the information found, seen or heard in the media, and only 0,33% of them totally trust the information found, seen, or heard in the media (Figure 4).

The paper provided introductory information about information searching using online and offline media channels. It can be concluded that the Generation Z uses online media channels while searching for an information but they neither trust nor don't trust in information that can be found, seen, or heard on/in the media.

The following papers will explore the results regarding the television, radio, print media (offline) and online media as media channels.

TV as a Media Channel

Regarding watching TV, 31,44% of the respondents watch TV from one to three hours daily, 12,37% of them do not watch TV and 23,75% of the respondents watch TV less than 30 minutes a day. Almost half of them (43,14%) changes the TV station if the commercial is shown, but that depends on its content. TV is mostly watched on the TV set (74,25%) and 6,69% of the respondents watch TV on the smartphone. Although the high percentage of watching the TV on the TV set, 74,27% of the respondents watches YouTube and Vimeo videos and only 25,15% of them watches TV program. Despite the great rise of IGTV service on Instagram, only 0,61% of respondents watch the content on IGTV. Also, 61,20% of them do not have paid subscriptions to the digital television platform, but of those who have, the most common ones are Netflix and HBO.

Radio as a Media Channel

According to the research, members of the Generation Z listen to the radio for less than half an hour a day (40,80%). More than 3 hours a day the radio listens only 5,69% of the respondents and 14,38% of the respondents do not listen to the radio at all. Interesting cognition is that 30,43% of the respondents change the radio station if they hear a radio ad on it, and 34,78% of them will change the radio station when the ad is released according to its content. Only 28,09% of the respondents will not change the radio station while the ad is played at all. The radio is mostly listened to in the car (68,90%), on the radio at the home (9,70%), online on the computer (6,69%), and on the online radio on the smartphones (3,68%). More than half of the respondents (51,17%) listen to the music online using YouTube, and 22,41% of them listen to the radio directly at the website of the radio application on the smartphone. Online streaming platforms like Spotify or Deezer are used by only 8.70% of respondents, and the surprising fact is that only 0,33% of the respondents listen to the radio in the car.

Print Media as a Media Channel

The respondents read printed newspapers less than half an hour a day (49,38%), only 9,36% of them read newspapers one hour daily and 37,79% of the respondents do not read the printed newspapers at all. More than half of them notice print ads (64,21%) in the newspapers but they generally do not read them (61,20%). The percentage of those who will read the print ad regarding its content is 33,78% and the percentage of those who do not buy print media is 74,58%. If the cover of the print media is fully formatted in the form of an advertisement, 20,07% of the respondents will not read the ad or buy the newspapers, 34,45% of them will read or buy and 45,48% of them will read the ad or buy the newspapers depending on its content. Those who read print media read them mostly at home (37,12%) and in a café (17,39%).

Online Media as a Media Channel

When the respondents were asked to say how much time a day they spend on the internet, the average answer was more than three hours a day (62,54%). 30,10% of the sample spends more than one hour and less than three hours a day on the internet and only 1,67% of the respondents spend less than 30 minutes on the internet daily. The concerning fact is that the 54,52% of the respondents have an ad blocker installed in their web browsers, but 88,96% of the sample notices ads on online media regardless of using the ad blocker. More than half of the respondents (78,26%) said that they were bothered by ads in online media and 17,39% of the respondents said that it depends on the content of the ad. The daily time spent on the specific online media platform is provided in Table 3.

Table 3. Time spent on each online media platform

Daily time	Facebook (%)	Instagram (%)	Twitter (%)	LinkedIn (%)	Snapchat (%)	YouTube (%)	Tinder (%)	Skype (%)
Up to 1 hour	**46,82**	24,08	7,02	6,35	23,41	32,78	2,68	12,37
Up to 2 hours	30,10	**34,11**	1,67	1,34	1,67	**33,11**	0,67	2,01
Up to 5 hours	13,38	23,08	1%	0,67	1,34	25,08	0,33	0,33
Up to 10 hours	3,34	7,02	0	0	0,67	6,02	0	0
More than 10 hours	2,34	4,01	0	0	0	1,34	0	0
I don't use the platform	4,01	7,69	**90,30**	**91,64**	**72,91**	1,67	**96,32**	**85,28**

Source: authors work according to the research

As it is provided in the Table 3., Facebook is mostly used up to 1 hour daily so as Twitter, LinkedIn, Snapchat, Tinder, and Skype. The only two online platforms used up to 2 hours a day are Instagram and YouTube.

Figure 5. Media platforms used by generation Z
Source: authors work according to the research

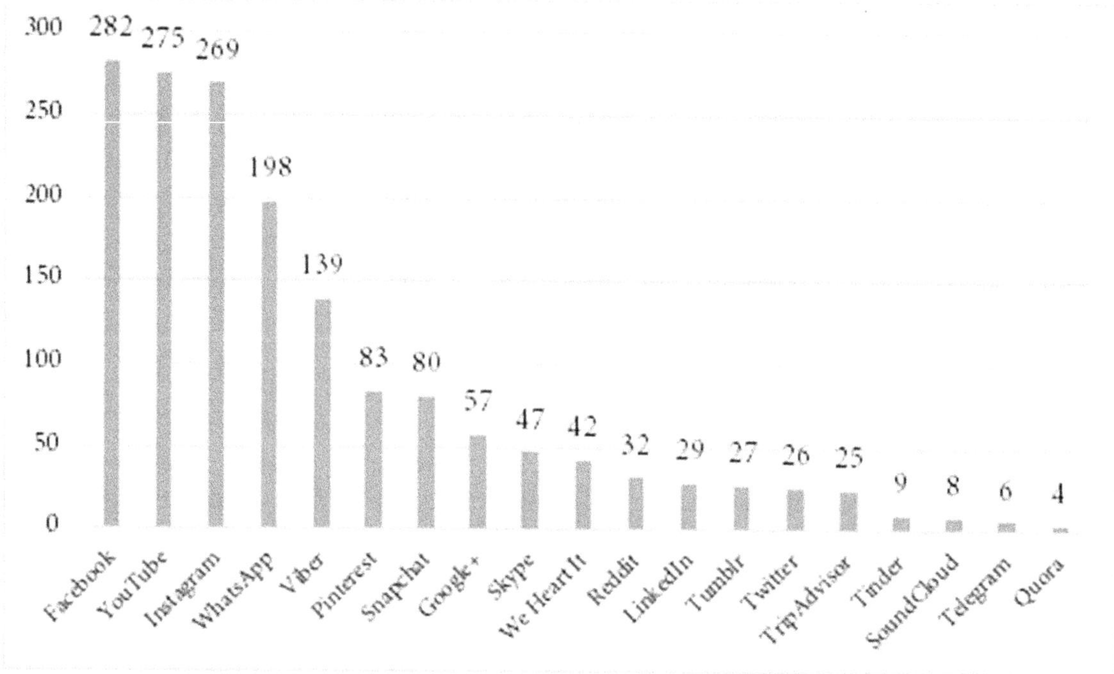

Figure 6. Online media platforms where generation Z searches for information
Source: Authors work according to the research

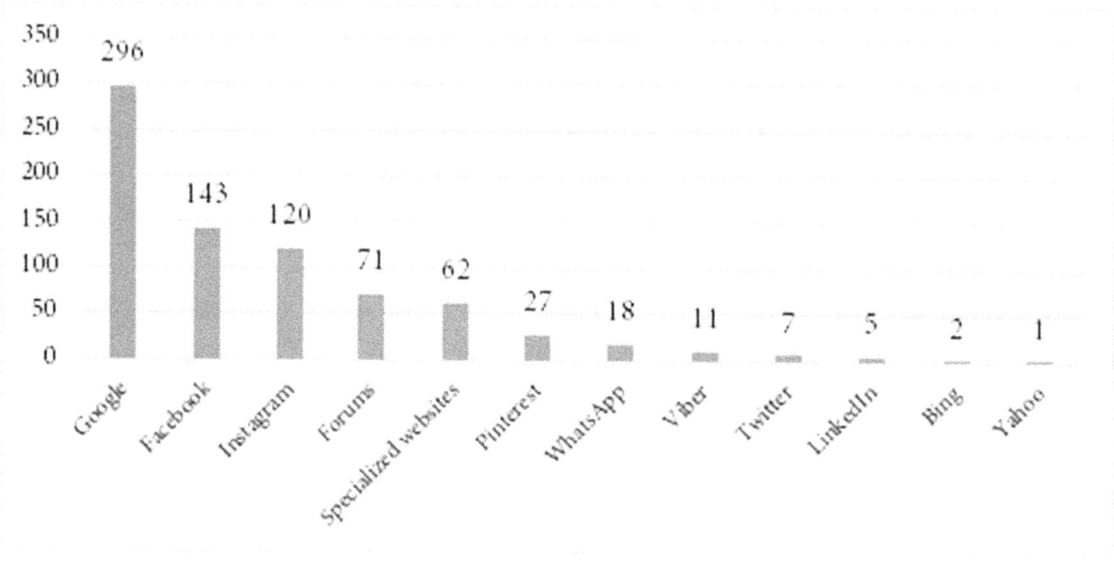

On the question "Will a digital platform full of ads distract you from reading or using it?", 67,22% of the respondents said that it will and 25,08% of the respondents said that reading or using a digital platform full of ads depends on the content of the ad. Most of the sample (88,29%) notices ads on digital platforms, but 62% of the respondents do not read ads on digital platforms.

Although, 32,78% of the sample read the ads depending on their content. Almost half of the respondents (49,50%) said that if the homepage of a digital platform is full of ad placements, it will distract them from reading or buying a subscription for the platform but 39,46% of the respondents said the decision on it depends on the content of the digital platform homepage. Regarding the device on which digital platforms are mostly used, 82,61% of the sample use them on a smartphone, 15,38% of them use them on a computer, and 0,33% of them use a tablet.

The following figure shows the usage of online media platforms by the Generation Z (Figure 5).

As can be seen, the most used media platforms by Generation Z are Facebook, YouTube, Instagram, WhatsApp and Viber. The following figure shows where does Generation Z search for information (Figure 6).

It is visible from the results that the main web browser for searching the information is Google, but the Generation Z for the information research also uses social media platforms like Facebook and Instagram. Forums and specialized websites are also used.

CONCLUSION

This paper showed the importance of bearing in mind which media Generation Z uses and prefers. The research results represent a valuable input for destination media planners. The findings indicate that the Generation Z prefers online media when searching for information while at the same time are indifferent regarding the information found, seen or heard and don't trust them. Regarding offline media, Generation Z still watches TV but almost half of them changes the TV station when the commercial is shown. On the other hand, a respectable majority likes to watch online video platforms like YouTube and Vimeo. Almost a half of Generation Z still listens to a radio in the car and the third of them will not change the radio station while the ad is playing. YouTube is also very popular platform for Generation Z to listen to the music online. Generation Z still reads the printed newspapers and more than half of them notice print ads but generally do not read them.

The findings also indicate that Generation Z spends quite a lot of daily time on internet (3 hours) which confirms the Levak and Baric Selmic (2018) research results about the daily use of the internet. The concerning fact is that the half of the respondents have an ad blocker installed in their web browsers, but in the same time, majority of them notice ads on online media regardless of using the ad blocker. This information confirms the findings of Global Web Index research (2018) that Generation Z is more privacy-aware and concerned about the use of their data from other companies. As for the offline media, Generation Z also gets bored by ads on online media. Instagram, Facebook, YouTube, WhatsApp and Viber are the most popular media platforms among Generation Z, while Twitter, LinkedIn, Snapchat, Tinder, and Skype are less significant for them. In comparison Duffett (2017) in his research also stated that the social media is one of the most preferable digital communication channels for connecting with Generation Z, especially Messenger and WhatsApp.

Research results also show that the main web browser for searching the information is Google, but the Generation Z for the information research also uses social media platforms like Facebook and Instagram.

The findings are mostly in line with Trifecta Research (2015) and the Global Web Index research (2018). Previous research results also indicated that online channels are the ones where Generation Z spends a certain amount of time during the day and prefer social media channels like Facebook, Instagram and Snapchat, which is in line with the results of this study. Generation Z prefers online channels for communication, so this can be an opportunity for advertisers to spread a message about their products or services in the destination. The Millennials, the generation before the Generation Z according to Duffet (2014) finds Facebook as the main social media channel with a positive influence in the buying process so the change in the social media preferences in comparison with Generation Z is visible also in this study.

This chapter pointed out that while Generation Z prefers and mostly uses online media, offline media shouldn't be ignored by destination media planners. Therefore, the recommendations for media planners are provided.

RECOMMENDATIONS

In the process of destination media planning, if destination media planners would like to reach and engage Generation Z, they should not focus on only one type of online or offline media channels, but on the combination of both of them. The main source for searching an information for the Generation Z are online media channels, therefore the destination media planners have a great opportunity to present the information about the destination on the right place where they search for it.

As it is shown in the research, the Generation Z neither trust or don't trust the information found, seen or heard on/in the media, so the information presented in the ads about the destination has to be honest, accurate, testable, relevant and presented in the language that Generation Z understands.

While planning a destination media channel mix, TV should be one of the destination media channels, but it is important that the ads planned for the TV promotional campaigns are focused on honesty and integrity. Also, YouTube as an online media channel has to be the most important video channel which will give the destination media planners the opportunity to show the destination and its benefits in a creative and innovative way.

As the Generation Z spends most of the day listening to the music, destination media planners should also include radio as an online media channel. They mostly listen to the radio while driving in a car, so the destination media planners have to include radio ads that also have to be interesting enough for them to not to change the radio station. YouTube is another important ad placement because members of Generation Z have a habit of listening to music using that online media channel. Generation Z does not like the interruption, so destination media planners have to focus on creating the ads that will not make negative impact which will result with changing the radio station or channel.

Print media also has to be included in the destination media plan. A key component of the successful offline media campaign like advertisements in print media is an interesting visual design of the ad regarding the fact that the Generation Z will read or buy the newspaper depending on its content. Destination media planners should be careful when placing the ad on the front cover of the magazine or newspaper because they are likely not to read or buy the newspaper if the content is tedious or if it is not different from the other advertisers. Generally, distinguishing from other destinations in terms of the promotion will gain success for the destination.

Key media channel for the destinations should be online media because of the high percentage of the daily internet access and usage by the Generation Z. The crucial part of the successful online promotional campaign will be also the design of the ads regarding the usage of ad blockers on web browsers. As the Generation Z largely notices ads on online media, but they are bothered by those ads, innovation in design and using nontraditional placements and forms of ads is desirable. Destination media planners should include Facebook, Instagram and Snapchat social media platforms in the destination media plan regarding the time that Generation Z is spends on them daily. YouTube as an online video-sharing platform is a great communications channel and gives the destination the opportunity to gain interest and desire to visit the destination to its target audience.

When planning a destination promotional campaign in the online digital media platforms, it is desirable not to place ads on the homepages that are full of ad placements. Generation Z does not like and are not likely to notice or read the ads placed on those placements. It is also important that the ad design is suitable for display on mobile devices regarding the high percent of using the digital platforms on the smartphones. Generation Z likes to communicate using WhatsApp and Viber communication platforms which also offer options for promotion, and specialized websites and forums should be represented in the destination media plan.

In the destination media planning process, destination media planners should take care of the placements, the design of ads, the language the destination is communicating with its targeted audience. It is essential to communicate with the Generation Z at the time when they want and where they want. They will notice innovation, social awareness and quality stories. The storytelling should also be used as a method to gain awareness and trust. Those recommendations are a basis for a successful destination promotional campaign to reach the Generation Z.

Further research should be focused on understanding every phase of the Generation Z's travel decision making and their media preference and profiling it as a future tourist. Another field of research should be the comparison of different generation segments and their media use. Future research could also benefit from deeper analysis of every channel Generation Z uses, that are mentioned in this chapter.

REFERENCES

Beall, G. (2017). *8 Key Differences between Gen Z and Millennials*. Retrieved May 8, 2020, from Huffington Post:https://www.huffingtonpost.com/george-beall/8-key differencesbetweenb12814200. html?guccoun ter=1

Buhalis, D. (2000). Marketing the competitive destination of the future - Growth strategies for accommodation establishments in alpine regions. *Tourism Management*, *21*(1), 91–116. doi:10.1016/S0261-5177(99)00095-3

Croatian Bureau of Statistics. (n.d.). Retrieved May 15, 2020, from: https://www.dzs.hr/Hrv_Eng/publication/2019/SI-1639.pdf

Dimitriou, C. K., & AbouElgheit, E. (2019). Understanding generation Z's social decision-making in travel. *Tourism and Hospitality Management*, *25*(2), 311–334. doi:10.20867/thm.25.2.4

Dimock, M. (2019). *Defining generations: Where Millennials end and Generation Z begins*. Pew Research Center. Retrieved May 11, 2020, from: https://www.pewresearch.org/fact-tank/2019/01/17/where-millennials-end-and-generation-z-begins/

Duffett, R. G. (2015). Facebook advertising's influence on intention-to-purchase and purchase amongst Millennials. *Internet Research*, *25*(4), 498–526. doi:10.1108/IntR-01-2014-0020

Duffett, R. G. (2017). Influence of social media marketing communications on young consumers' attitudes. *Young Consumers*, *18*(1), 19–39. doi:10.1108/YC-07-2016-00622

Eurostat. (2020). *Tourism statistics*. Retrieved April 20, 2020, from: https://ec.europa.eu/eurostat/statistics-explained/pdfscache/1171.pdf

Flagestad, A. (2002). *Strategic success and organizational structure in winter sports destinations. A multiple stakeholder approach to measuring organizational performance in Scandinavian and Swiss case studies*. ETOUR.

Global Web Index. (2019). *The youth of the nations: Global Trends Among Gen Z*. Retrieved April 28, 2020, from: https://assets.ctfassets.net/inb32lme5009/7wDIuSsLOnSxTUqPmRb081/603b8ffb77757549d39034884a23743c/The_Youth_of_the_Nations__Global_Trends_Among_Gen_Z.pdf

Goeldner, C. R., & Ritchie, J. R. B. (2003). *Tourism: principles, practices, philosophies*. Willey.

Husein, K., Wiweka, K., Kurniawati, R., & Adnyana, I. N. (2017). *The profile and behavior of "SMART TOURIST' (Generation Z) in travel decision making*. 4th World Research Summit for Tourism and Hospitality, Orlando, FL.

Kotler, P., Keller, K. L., & Martinovic, M. (2014). *Upravljanje marketingom*. Mate.

Levak, T., Baric Selmic, S. (2018). Escaping the "virtual promenade" – new trends in use of social networks by members of generation "Z". *Media, Culture and Public Relations*, *9*(1-2), 37-55.

Mandelbaum, A. (2016). *What Should Your Hotel Know About Generation Z?* Retrieved April 27, 2020, from: https://lodgingmagazine.com/what-should-your-hotel-know-about-generation-z/

Mariutti, F. G., Giraldi, J. D. M. E., & Crescitelli, E. (2013). The image of Brazil as a tourism destination: An exploratory study of the American market. *International Journal of Business Administration*, *4*(1), 13–22.

Morrison, A. M. (2019). *Marketing and Managing Tourism Destinations*. Routledge.

Persada, S. F., Ivanovski, J., Miraja, B. A., Nadlifatin, R., Mufidah, I., Chin, J., & Perwira Redi, A. A. N. (2020). Investigating Generation Z' Intention to Use Learners' Generated Content for Learning Activity: A Theory of Planned Behavior Approach. *International Journal of Emerging Technologies in Learning*, *15*(4), 179–194. doi:10.3991/ijet.v15i04.11665

Robinson, V. M., & Schänzel, H. A. (2019). A tourism inflex: Generation Z travel experiences. *Journal of Tourism Futures*, *5*(2), 127–141. doi:10.1108/JTF-01-2019-0014

Slivar, I., Aleric, D., & Dolenec, S. (2019). Leisure travel behavior of generation Y & Z at the destination and post-purchase. *E-Journal of Tourism*, *6*(2), 147–159. doi:10.24922/eot.v6i2.53470

Tafonao, T., Saputra, S., & Suryaningwidi, R. (2020). Learning Media and Technology: Generation Z and Alpha. *Indonesian Journal of Instructional Media and Model*, *2*(2), 89–100. doi:10.32585/ijimm.v2i2.954

Trifecta Research. (2015). *Generation Z Media Consumption Habit*. Retrieved May 5, 2020, from: http://trifectaresearch.com/wp-content/uploads/2015/09/Generation-Z-Sample-Trifecta-Research-Deliverable.pdf

Williams, K. C., & Page, R. A. (2011). Marketing to the Generations. *Journal of Behavioral Studies in Business*, *3*(1), 1–18.

Wood, S. (2013). *Generation Z as consumers: Trends and innovation*. Institute for Emerging Issues: NC State University. Retrieved May 5, 2020, from: https://iei.ncsu.edu/wp-content/uploads/2013/01/GenZConsumers.pdf

Yadav, G. P., & Rai, J. (2017). The Generation Z and their Social Media Usage: A Review and a Research Outline. *Global Journal of Enterprise Information System*, *9*(2), 110–116. doi:10.18311/gjeis/2017/15748

Zemla, M. (2016). Tourism destination: The networking approach. *Moravian Geographical Reports*, *24*(4), 2–14. doi:10.1515/mgr-2016-0018

ADDITIONAL READING

Duffett, R. (2020). The YouTube Marketing Communication Effect on Cognitive,Affective and Behavioural Attitudes among Generation Z Consumers. *Sustainability*, *2020*(12), 5075. doi:10.3390u12125075

Haddouche, H., & Salomone, C. (2018). Generation Z and the tourist experience: Tourist stories and use of social networks. *Journal of Tourism Futures*, *4*(1), 69–79. doi:10.1108/JTF-12-2017-0059

Robinson, V. M., & Schänzel, H. A. (2019). A tourism inflex: Generation Z travel experiences. *Journal of Tourism Futures*, *5*(2), 127–141. doi:10.1108/JTF-01-2019-0014

Tolani, K. C., & Sao, R. (2020). Influence of Micro-Celebrities on Generation Z: Perception, Customer Engagement, and Career Option. In A. Shrivastava, G. Jain, & J. Paul (Eds.), *Circular Economy and Re-Commerce in the Fashion Industry* (pp. 54–72). IGI Global. doi:10.4018/978-1-7998-2728-3.ch007

KEY TERMS AND DEFINITIONS

Destination Marketing Organizations: An organization located in the tourism destination that deals with its marketing activities.

Generation Marketing: A communication approach that considers the differences between certain group of people based on their age.

Generation Z: Generation of people born after 1994, that are around 26 years old in 2020.

Media Planning: A process of identifying and selecting different media channels for a product or a brand to use in the communication campaign.

Media Preferences: Attitudes of people towards different kind of media.

Offline Media: Communication media that use traditional technologies for information exchange.

Online Media: Communication media that use internet technologies for information exchange.

Tourism Destination: An area that is highly dependent on tourism activity.

APPENDIX

QUESTIONNAIRE

Habits of using online and offline media of generation Z

1. What type of media do you prefer when looking for information?
   a) Online Media
   b) Offline Media
   2. Do you trust the information you find / see / hear on / in the media?
   a) I don't completely believe it
   b) I don't believe it
   c) I neither believe nor believe
   d) I believe
   e) I fully believe
   3. Do you trust more information you find / see / hear on / in online or offline media?
   c) Online Media
   d) Offline Media

TV

4. How much time a day do you spend watching TV?
   a) Less than half an hour
   b) 1 hour
   c) More than 1 hour and less than 3 hours
   d) More than 3 hours
   e) I don't watch TV
   5. What national TV programs do you watch?
   a) HRT1
   b) HRT2
   c) Doma TV
   d) RTL
   e) RTL2
   f) CMC
   g) Nova TV
   h) HTV4
   i) Jabuka TV
   j) N1 TV
   k) TV channel AL Jazeera Balkans
   l) Z1 TV
   m) Kockica
   n) I don't watch TV

6. If you watch TV, what local TV shows do you watch?
7. If you watch TV, which foreign TV programs do you watch?
8. Which promotional TV ad, for which product / service / company and on which TV channel is the last one you remember?
9. Do you change the TV program when a TV ad appears on it?
a) Yes
b) No
c) Depending on the content of the ad
d) I don't watch TV
10. Do you have a subscription to any digital television platform? If so, which one? (Netflix, HBO, Pickbox ...)
a) Netflix
b) HBO
c) Pickbox
d) I don't have a subscription
11. Where do you usually watch TV programs?
a) Television
b) Mobile phone
c) Tablet
d) Desktop computer or laptop
e) I don't watch TV
12. What do you watch more? TV programs or YouTube / Vimeo ..?
a) TV programs
b) YouTube / Vimeo
c) IGTV
d) I don't watch TV / Youtube / Vimeo

RADIO

13. How much time a day do you spend listening to the radio?
f) Less than half an hour
g) 1 hour
h) More than 1 hour and less than 3 hours
i) More than 3 hours
j) I don't listen to the radio
14. Which national or regional Croatian radio stations do you listen to?
a) Narodni radio
b) Otvoreni radio
c) Antena Zagreb
d) Radio Kaj
e) Radio 101
f) Soundset Plavi
g) Hrvatski Radio

h) Radio Student
i) Laganini.fm
j) Enter
k) Extra FM
l) Yammat FM
m) I don't listen to the radio
15. If you listen to the radio, which local radio stations do you listen to?
16. If you are listening to the radio, which foreign radio stations are you listening to?
17. Which radio ad for a product / service / company do you remember? Also state the name of the radio station where you heard the ad.
18. Do you change the radio station when an ad starts playing on it?
e) Yes
f) No
g) Depending on the content of the advertisement
h) I don't listen to the radio
19. You usually listen to the radio on / in?
a) Radio in the car
b) Radio receiver at home
c) Online on your computer
d) Offline on the computer
e) Online on your smartphone
f) Offline on a smartphone
g) Online on a tablet
h) Offline on a tablet
i) On the TV
j) I don't listen to the radio
20. If you listen to the radio online, you listen to it more often?
a) Directly on the web / application radio page
b) Online streaming platform
c) I mostly listen to YouTube
d) I don't listen to the radio

PRINT MEDIA

21. How much time a day do you spend reading the print media?
a) Less than half an hour
b) 1 hour
c) More than 1 hour and less than 3 hours
d) More than 3 hours
k) I don't read the print media
22. Which Croatian print media do you read?
a) Jutarnji List
b) Večernji List

c) 24 sata
d) Gloria
e) Bug
f) Cosmopolitan
g) Playboy
h) Globus
i) Lider
j) Meridijani
k) Nacional
l) National Geographic Hrvatska
m) PCchip
n) PC Play
o) Poslovni dnevnik
p) Privredni vjesnik
q) Regionalni tjednik
r) Slobodna Dalmacija
s) Telegram
t) Sportske novosti
u) Men'sHealth
v) Elle
w) Vidi
x) I don't read the print media

23. If you are reading print media, list some of the local print media that you are reading.

24. If you are reading print media, list some of the foreign print media you are reading.

25. Do you notice ads in the print media?
a) Yes
b) No

26. Do you read ads in the print media?
a) Yes
b) No
c) Depending on the content of the ad
i) I don't read the print media

27. Which printed advertisement for a product / service / company do you remember? Also provide the name of the print media from which you remember the ad.

28. Do you buy print media?
a) Yes
b) No

29. Will a cover that is fully formatted in the form of an advertisement distract you from reading / buying print media?
a) Yes
b) No
c) Depending on the content

30. Where do you read the print media most often?

a) At home
b) In a cafe
c) At the kiosk
d) At the college
e) During the trip (car, bus, train)
f) I don't read the print media

ONLINE PLATFORMS AND MEDIA

31. How much time a day do you use the internet?
a) Less than half an hour
b) 1 hour
c) More than 1 hour and less than 3 hours
d) More than 3 hours
e) I don't use internet
32. Mark online social media networks you use in everyday life.
a) Facebook
b) Instagram
c) Twitter
d) LinkedIn
e) Flickr
f) Foursquare
g) TripAdvisor
h) Google+
i) Tinder
j) Pinterest
k) Quora
l) SoundCloud
m) Tumblr
n) We Heart It
o) Yelp
p) WhatsApp
q) Viber
r) KiK
s) WeChat
t) Skype
u) Snapchat
v) Telegram
w) Reddit
x) YouTube
y) Vine
z) Xing
aa) Meetup

bb) Vero
cc) Vimeo
dd) TikTok
ee) I don't use online social networks

33. Do you have AdBlocker installed in your web browsers? (plugin that prevents ads from appearing in a web browser)

a) Yes
b) No

34. Do you notice ads on social media platforms? (video, text, banners ...)

a) Yes
b) No

35. Do ads on social media bother you? (video, text, banners ...)

a) Yes
b) No
c) Depending on the content

36. Indicate which ad, for which product / service / company and on which social media you remember. List the one that you remember.

37. Where do you search for information online?

a) Google
b) Bing
c) Facebook
d) Instagram
e) Yahoo
f) LinkedIn
g) Forums
h) Specialized online portals
i) Twitter
j) Pinterest
k) WhatsApp
l) Viber
m) I do not search for information online

38. Indicate how much on average do you spend per day on each social media platform. (1. I do not use the platform, 2. Up to 1 hour, 3. Up to 2 hours, 4. Up to 5 hours, 5. Up to 10 p.m., 6. More than 10 hours).

a) Facebook
b) Instagram
c) Twitter
d) LinkedIn
e) Snapchat
f) YouTube
g) Tinder
h) Skype

39. Will a digital platform full of ads distract you from reading / using it?

d) Yes

e) No
f) Depending on the content
40. Which Croatian news platforms do you read/use?
a) jutarnji.hr
b) večernji.hr
c) 24sata.hr
d) telegram.hr
e) net.hr
f) miss7.24sata.hr
g) miss7zdrava.24sata.hr
h) gastro.hr
i) putoholičari.rtl.hr
j) bengeri.com
k) lider.hr
l) croatiaweek.com
m) croportal.net
n) direktno.hr
o) dnevnik.hr
p) punkufer.dnevnik.hr
q) zadovoljna.dnevnik.hr
r) dnevno.hr
s) index.hr
t) nacional.hr
u) narod.hr
v) nezavisni.hr
w) slobodnadalmacija.hr
x) tportal.hr
y) vijesti.hr
z) njuškalo.hr
aa) novac.hr
bb) hrturizam.hr
cc) poslovniturizam.com
dd) poslovni.hr
ee) bug.hr
ff) netokracija.com
gg) pcchip.hr
hh) gol.hr
ii) sportske.jutarnji.hr
jj) newsbar.tv
kk) croatia.hr
ll) croatia-times.hr
mm) putovnica.net
nn) turizaminfo.hr

oo) coolinarika.com
pp) buro247.com
qq) cafe.hr
rr) jutarnji.hr/dobrahrana
ss) journal.hr
tt) kuharica.hr
uu) mojfaks.com
vv) naturala.hr
ww) recepti.hr
xx) srednja.hr
yy) womeninadria.com
zz) jeftinije.hr
aaa) ispravi.me
bbb) cosmopolitan.hr
ccc) jutarnji.hr/globus
ddd) gloria.hr
eee) menshealth.hr
fff) playboy.hr
ggg) story.hr
hhh) I do not read Croatian news websites

41. If you are reading online media, list some of the local ones you are reading.

42. If you are reading online media, list some of the national ones you are reading.

43. Do you notice ads in online media?

44. Do you read ads in online media?
a) Yes
b) No
c) Depending on the content

45. Which online ad for a product / service / company do you remember? Also provide the name of the online media from which you remember the ad.

46. Will a cover/homepage that is fully formatted in the form of an advertisement deter you from reading / purchasing a subscription on online media?
a) Yes
b) No
c) Depending on the content

47. Which device do you use the most to read online media?
a) Computer
b) Smartphone
c) Tablet
d) I don't read online media

DAILY FREQUENCY OF ONLINE AND OFFLINE MEDIA

48. How much time a day do you spend reading / watching / listening to? (1. I don't read / watch / listen to, 2. Up to 1 hour, 3. Up to 2 hours, 4. Up to 5 hours, 5. Up to 10 p.m., 6. More than 10 hours)

a) TV
b) Radio
c) Print media
d) Online platforms
e) Online media

SOCIO-DEMOGRAPHIC DATA

49. Gender

a) Female
b) Male
50. Age
a) 18-20
b) 21-25
c) 26-30
d) 31-35
e) 36-40
f) 41-45
g) 46-50
h) 51-55
i) 56-60
j) 61+
51. What is your place of residence?
52. Employment status.
a) Elementary school student
b) University Student
c) Part-time employment
d) Full-time employment
e) Retired

Chapter 17
Critical View of Multiple Channels Retailing

Richard Ladwein
University of Lille, France

Thouraya Ben Achma
University of Lille, France

Mohamed Slim Ben Mimoun
College of Business and Economics, Qatar University, Qatar

ABSTRACT

The aim of this chapter is to better understand the gap that exists between the literature dealing with multiple channels shopping behavior and the actual shoppers' behavior. Adopting a critical analysis of a large literature of research articles dealing with consumer behavior and retailing in a multiple channel context, covering the period from 2002 to 2020, this chapter identifies an important gap in the literature: generally the authors define the different situations of multiple channels retailing (e.g., multichannel, crosschannel, and omni-channel) from the company point of view, and the main distribution channels presented in the literature review do not reproduce the richness of variety of channels available to the shoppers. Implications for future research related to multiple channel retailing and shopping behavior are discussed.

INTRODUCTION

Advanced digitalized technologies have profoundly changed the shopping behavior as well as the retail industry (Alexander et al., 2020; Blom et al., 2017; Sun et al., 2020). The shoppers are currently able to buy services and goods using more than one channel making retailing evolving from multi-channel concept toward the concepts of cross-channel and omni-channel (Balasubramanian et al., 2005 ; Ansari et al., 2008 ; Avery et al., 2012 ; Beck and Rygl, 2015; Verhoef et al., 2015).

DOI: 10.4018/978-1-7998-7192-7.ch017

Furthermore, the worldwide situation marked by the different type of crisis: economic crisis, ecological crisis, social and the COVID 19 sanitary crises; in addition to the level of unemployment due to mass lay-offs have contributed to the development of new forms of shopping behaviors and to consumer empowerment characterized by the research of the best deal throw the integration of new channels in the shopping journey. Consumers are increasingly using shopping channels non-controlled by conventional retailers. They could be new digital channels, as peer to peer online platforms (Jang et al., 2021), second-hand digital platforms (Luo et al. 2020; Zou & Jiang, 2020), or social media e-commerce (Kim & Kim, 2018); or old physical channels as flea markets (Sherry, 1990) or farmer markets (Brown, 2001).

Through a fast scrolling of the literature review related to multiple channels retailing, we can observe that generally the authors define the different situations of multiple channels retailing (e.g. multichannel, crosschannel and omni-channel) from the company point of view and the main distribution channels presented in the literature review do not reproduce the richness of channels variety available to the shoppers. Researches present mostly a model of shoppers switching amid the different channels of one retailer (Verhoef et al., 2007; Konus et al., 2008 ; Schröder and Zaharia, 2008 ; Dholakia et al., 2010 ; Cao and Li, 2015 ; Lee et al., 2019) and few researches discuss the free-riding shopper behavior who consist on a shopper using different channels from different retailers in a same shopping journey (Heitz-Spahn, 2013).

The aim of this paper is to better understand the gap that exists between the literature dealing with multiple channels shopping behavior and the actual shoppers' behavior. Adopting a critical analysis of a large literature of research articles dealing with consumer behavior and retailing in a multiple channel context, covering the period from 2002 to 2020, we identify important gap in the literature that future researches need to investigate.

LITERATURE REVIEW

How to imagine nowadays a company with only one channel? Multichannel has now established itself as a distribution model. According to Frazier (1999), "the multi-channel strategy is becoming the rule rather than the exception".

Due to technological advances, competition, and new consumer expectations, companies believe it is imperative to sell their products through a multitude of distribution channels (Bilgicer, Jedidi, Lehmann & Neslin, 2015).

Consumers multiply the channels and means of communication to make their purchases (Dholakia et al., 2010). During their shopping journey, consumers traditionally bought in the physical store, but nowadays companies have multiplied the distribution channels including physical stores, online stores, catalogs, call-centers, mobile phones, social media… (Shen et al., 2018; Neslin and Shankar, 2009). These different distribution channels are common places through which consumers can interact with companies and make their purchases (Neslin et al., 2006).

In the literature related to the multiplicity of channels, three concepts are used to describe a multiple channel distribution system and a multiple channel shopping behavior: the multichannel, the cross-channel and the omnichannel, but the boundaries between these 3 concepts are sometimes blurred.

According to Beck and Rigl (2015), multichannel distribution consists of selling products or services through more than one channel without interaction between the different channels from the consumer's point of view and/or without integration between them from the retailer's point of view.

In the logic of multichannel distribution, which was in vogue during the first decade of the present millennium, retailers multiplied their distribution channels but considered each channel independent of other channels. There was therefore no interaction between the different channels since each channel was considered to be autonomous, with specific management and serving its own customers segments (Vanheems, 2015). In this context, developing and managing separate channels has often provided consumers with fragmented and inconsistent shopping experience (Sun et al., 2020).

As a consequence to the critics addressed toward the multichannel retailing, a new concept has emerged: the cross-channel. The cross-channel could be seen as a response to the changes that appeared in consumer's behavior who began to migrate from one channel to another within the same shopping journey (Vanheems, 2015). Consumers migrate from one channel to another through the different phases of their decision-making process. They tend to go through several channels (physical store, online store, catalogs ...) to collect as much information as possible on the desired product or service, then make a decision and choose to place their order through the channel that suits them better.

The cross-channel has gradually replaced the multichannel which has become insufficient to offer a pleasant consumption experience to consumers. Indeed, consumers migrate from one channel to another in order to adapt their objectives through each step of their decision-making process and this navigation should offer them a homogeneous and pleasant consumption experience (Verhoef et al., 2015).

The increasing digitalization conducts to a continuous change in the retailing context and consumer behavior specifically with the development of new ubiquitous distribution and communication channels such as the mobile channel and social medias. A direct result of this development of new channels is the emergence of the omnichannel retailing and shopping behavior (Du et al., 2019; Pak et al., 2020).

Generally, in comparison with multichannel and cross-channel, omnichannel offers more channels to consumers. We can cite new channels as mobile, connected objects, social medias, interactive terminals ... It should be noted that omnichannel integrates both distribution channels and communication channels. Some channels are used by consumers to place their orders while other channels are mainly used by consumers to communicate with the company.

Rigby (2011, p. 67) was the first to introduce the term Omnichannel presented as "an integrated sales experience that melds the advantage of physical stores with the information richness of online shopping." According to Verhoef et al. (2015, p. 176), omnichannel management refers to "the synergetic management of the numerous available channels and customer touchpoints, in such a way that the customer experience across channels and the performance over channels is optimized."

According to Rodriguez-Torrico, et al. (2017), an omnichannel strategy allows consumers to shop across channels anytime and anywhere offering to customers a unique and comprehensive seamless shopping experience eliminating the limits between channels. Miquel-Romero, et al. (2020), added that the omnichannel retailing encompasses the abolition of borders between shopping channels to the elimination of boundaries between communication channels altering the concepts of push and pull communication channels.

According to Poirel (2008), the most difficult for a multiple channels company is not adding multiple channels but rather the creation of links between them so as to have an integrated system which provides the consumer a seamless and unified shopping experience (Verhoef and al, 2015 ; Du et al., 2020 ; Cheah et al., 2020 ; Lee et al., 2019 ; Rodriguez-Torrico et al., 2017 ; Adivar et al., 2019 ; Shen et al., 2018).

Although multiple channel distribution is gaining more and more attention from businesses as well as academia, few attempts tried to synthesize the academic research relating to this field. In the present paper, we proceed to a synthesis of the main researches related to this domain.

METHODOLOGY

A wide literature review focusing on the topic of shopping in a multiple channels' context shows that the researches are numerous but on the other hand there are very few attempts to synthesize the academic research relating to this field. We can for example cite the synthesis of academic articles proposed by Beck and Rygl (2015) that is based on articles published between 1997 and 2013, and therefore does not take into account the most recent publications. For this reason, we decided to enrich this literature review.

Indeed, we proceeded to a structured overview of the area of multiple channels shopping by using a systematic literature review in order to provide a knowledge base for future research.

We mainly used Google Scholar search engine, EBSCO, Proquest and Sciencedirect databases and opted for articles published in English and in French in scientific journals whose contributions are peer-reviewed and accepted by referees.

We have chosen the main following keywords to obtain contributions related to the subject of our research: « multichannel retailing», « multichannel shopping behavior », « omni-channel », « omnichannel shopping behavior », « cross-channel ».

Once all the contributions obtained using these keywords have been gathered and after a careful reading of these works then after eliminating those that are not relevant to our subject of analysis, we obtained mainly 43 researches published between 2002 and 2020 that we presented in the table below.

DISCUSSION

The information in the table represents a synthesis of the 43 articles published from 2002 to 2020 and dealing with multiple channel retailing and shopping. It summarizes the main concepts used by these articles (e.g. multichannel, crosschannel or omnichannel), the definitions given to these main concepts as well as the channels investigated.

First, considering the main concepts, we can observe that majority of articles are dealing with multichannel (25 articles), that twelve articles are dealing with omnichannel but only six are dealing with crosschannel and three others are using neither of this main concepts explicitly (they are talking about consumers switching between channels or use the term multiple channels). We can observe also that the concept of crosschannel is always associated and presented in opposition to multichannel. However, the concept of omnichannel is associated five times to multichannel. We can also realize that a unique article (Beck and Rygl, 2015) compares the three concepts at the same time, confirming the importance of the gap that we are covering through the present research.

In addition it is possible to observe a chorological evolution of the concepts, if the use of the multichannel concept covers all the period from 2002 to 2020, the use of crosschannel covers the period from 2007 to 2017 and the use of omnichannel start only on 2014 (but as indicated previously, the concept was first introduced by Rigby in 2011).

Considering the definitions of the main concepts and the importance given to the consumer in the approaches used by the 43 articles, it is possible to observe that only five articles are explicitly consumer centric (Gupta et al. 2004; Kumar and Venkatesan, 2005; Poncin, 2008; Blazquez, 2014; Rodriguez-Torrico et al. 2017). However, 18 articles are using the terms consumer behavior, shopping or shopper behavior without being consumer centric. In contrast, fifteen articles are explicitly business centric and the majority of them used the term customers' management. In addition, majority of articles are dealing

Table 1. Synthesis of academic articles in the multiple channel context

Authors	*Year of publication*	*Journal*	*Concepts*	*Definitions*	*Channels investigated*
Blazquez	2014	International Journal of Electronic Commerce	Multichannel retailing	**Multichannel retailing**: use of multiple distribution channels by companies.	Physical stores, online stores, mobile commerce, social networks (as communication channels),
Heitz-Spahn	2013	Journal of Retailing and Consumer Services	Multichannel retailing, Cross- channel consumer, Cross-channel free-riding behavior	**Multichannel retailing**: multiple distribution channels offered by companies to their consumers which increases channel choices in purchase situation. **Cross-channel consumer**: consumer who switch channels and retailers. **Cross-channel free-riding behavior**: consumer who switch channels and retailers during the decision making stages. This consumer use one retailer's channel to prepare a purchase and then switch to another retailer's channel to purchase.	Physical stores, online stores, mobile commerce
Hickman et al.	2020	The International Review of Retail, Distribution and Consumer Research	Omnichannel retailing	**Omnichannel retailing**: « … is an emerging approach to retailing that responds to the changing nature of how customers shop in alternation between online and offline shops, and the increasing use of digital devices (e.g. smartphones and tablets), as a consequence retailers are focusing and establishing a seamless integrated approach to their services ».	Physical stores, online stores, mobile commerce
Cao	2014	International Journal of Electronic Commerce	Multichannel retailing, Cross-channel retailing	**Multichannel retailing**: using multiple channels separated « creating the silo effect where lack of communication or coordination between operations leads to, for example, poor customer satisfaction... ». **Cross-channel retailing**: using integrated channels where « retailers had moved to align their brand, product offering and marketing message to offer a uniform customer experience across channels... ».	Physical stores, online stores, mobile commerce, kiosks
Emrich et al.	2015	Journal of retailing	Multichannel retailing, multichannel customer management, multichannel assortment integration	**Multichannel retailing**: multiple distribution channels offered to consumers. **Multichannel customer management**: multichannel retail strategies to manage multichannel customer. **Multichannel assortment integration**: the coordination of assortments between channels.	Physical stores, online stores
Konus et al.	2008	Journal of retailing	Multichannel shopper segments	**Multichannel shopper segments**: homogeneous groups of shoppers on the base of their channel orientation considering the search and purchase phases of their shopping process.	Physical stores, online stores, catalogs
Verhoef et al.	2007	International Journal of Research in Marketing	Multichannel customer, research shopper phenomenon, cross-channel synergy	**Multichannel customers**: customers using multiple shopping channels during their shopping process. **Research shopper phenomenon**: the tendency of consumers to research the product in one channel and then purchase it through another channel. **Cross-channel synergy**: synergetic effects between search and purchase in two different channels.	Physical stores, online stores, catalogs
Anderl et al.	2016	Journal of retailing	Online customer journey	**Online customer journey**: all contacts of any individual customer with a retailer over all online marketing channels prior to a potential purchase decision.	Online channels
Ansari et al.	2008	Journal of Marketing Research	Multichannel customer management, customer channel migration	**Multichannel customer management**: a pivotal component in firm's marketing strategy. **Customer channel migration**: switching between channels.	Online channels, catalogs
Schröder and Zaharia	2008	Journal of retailing and consumer services	Multichannel retailing, multichannel customer behavior, shopping motives of the customers of a multi-channel retailer	**Multichannel retailing**: retailers offering their customers the opportunity to buy their goods through different channels. **Multichannel customer behavior**: shopper behavior in different channels belonging to one retailer. **Shopping motives of the customers of a multi-channel retailer**: «… shopping motives determine whether the customer seeks information on a product in one channel and then buys the product in the same channel, or whether he/she spreads these activities over two channels ».	Physical stores, online stores, catalogs
Bilgicer et al.	2015	Journal of retailing	Multichannel retailing, multichannel customer management, social contagion	**Multichannel retailing**: retailers selling their products through multiple channels. **Multichannel customer management**: multichannel retail strategies. **Social contagion**: the impact of a customer's network of peers and influencers on a customer behavior (the impact of social contagion on the adoption of a new channel is studied in this article)	Physical stores, online stores
Verhoef et al.	2015	Journal of retailing	Multichannel retailing, omni-channel retailing, multichannel customer management, omni-channel management	**Multichannel retailing**: retailing through multiple channels. Major research on multichannel retailing consider 3 channels (stores, online websites and traditional direct marketing channels for example catalogs). In multichannel retailing, the channels are separated with no overlap. **Multichannel customer management**: managing customers in a multichannel context. **Omnichannel**: omni-channels involves more channels than multi-channel (advent of new digital like mobile channels). The borders between channels disappear in omni-channel. In omni-channel, « …the different channels and touchpoints are used constantly, interchangeably and simultaneously by both customers and firms to facilitate the customers' retail experience ».The channels are integrated and are providing « seamless retail experiences ». **Omnichannel management**: «the synergetic management of the numerous available channels and customer touchpoints in such a way that the customer experience across channels and the performance over channels is optimized ». The different channels interact with each other and are used simultaneously.	Physical stores, online stores, direct, marketing (catalogs), mobile channels (smartphones, tablets, mobile applications), social medias (as communication channels), touchpoints

continued on following page

Table 1. Continued

Authors	Year of publication	Journal	Concepts	Definitions	Channels investigated
Melis et al.	2015	Journal of retailing	Multichannel retailing, online buying experience	**Multichannel retailing:** retailing through more than one channel (offline channels and online channels). **Online buying experience:** familiarity with the online shopping environment.	Offline stores, online stores
Venkatesan et al.	2007	Journal of Marketing	Multichannel shopping	**Multichannel shopping:** shopping through multiple channels.	Physical stores, online stores
Neslin et al.	2006	Journal of Service Research	Multichannel customer management, multichannel retailing, multichannel shopping, channel data integration	**Multichannel customer management:** « the design, deployment, coordination, and evaluation of channels through which firms and customers interact, with the goal of enhancing customer value through effective customer acquisition, retention, and development ». **Multichannel retailing:** retailing through multiple channels. **Multichannel shopping:** shopping through multiple channels. **Channel data integration:** coordinating the objectives, the design and the deployment of channels to create synergies.	Physical stores, online stores, catalogs
Balasubramanian et al.	2005	Journal of Interactive Marketing	Multichannel environment, channel choice	**Multichannel environment:** using multiple channels for shopping. **Channel choice:** the choice of channels at various stages of shopping.	Physical stores, online stores
Neslin and Shankar	2009	Journal of Interactive Marketing	Multichannel customer management	**Multichannel customer management:** « the design, deployment, coordination, and evaluation of channels through which firms and customers interact, with the goal of enhancing customer value through effective customer acquisition, retention, and development ».	Physical stores, online stores, catalogs
Cao and Li	2015	Journal of retailing	Multichannel retailing, cross-channel integration	**Multichannel retailing:** retailing through multiple channels. **Cross-channel integration:** « cross-channel integration is the degree to which a firm coordinates the objectives, design, and deployment of its channels to create synergies for the firm and offer particular benefits to its consumers ».	Physical stores, online stores, catalogs, mobile commerce, call centers, social medias (as communication channels)
Piotrowicz and Cuthber	2014	International Journal of Electronic Commerce	Multichannel retailing, omnichannel retailing, channel integration, information technology	" ...**omnichannel** concept is perceived as an evolution of **the multichannel**. While the multichannel implies a division between the physical and online store, in the omnichannel customers move freely between the online (PC), mobile devices, and physical store, all within a single transaction process".	Physical stores, online stores, mobile commerce, social networks (as communication channels)
Dholakia et al.	2010	Journal of Interactive Marketing	Multichannel and multimedia consumer behavior	**Multichannel and multimedia consumer behavior:** « ... as technology advances, consumers are increasingly shopping across a variety of channels and communication media.	Physical stores, online stores, phone
Sands et al.	2016	Journal of Retailing and Consumer Services	Multichannel retailing, multichannel consumer segments	**Multichannel retailing:** « Multichannel retailing comprises the set of activities involved in selling goods or services to consumers through more than one channel ». **Multichannel consumer segments:** homogeneous groups of consumers on the base of their channel orientation considering the different stages of the shopping process.	Physical stores, online stores, mobile commerce, social medias (as communication channels)
Kumar and Venkatesan	2005	Journal of Interactive Marketing	Multichannel shoppers, multichannel shopping behavior	**Multichannel shoppers:** customers who make a purchase in more than one channel. **Multichannel shopping behavior:** purchase behavior across multiple channels.	Sales persons, direct mail, telephone sales, online sales
Poncin	2008	Reflets et Perspectives de la vie économique	Multichannel consumer behavior	**Multichannel consumer behavior:** consumer combining multiple channels during one shopping process.	Physical stores, online stores, catalogs
Vanheems	2009	Décisions Marketing	Multichannel retailing, channel integration	**Multichannel retailing:** the use of multiple channels by a company to sell its products and services. **Channel integration:** the coordination between the different channels of a company.	Physical stores, online stores, catalogs
Poirel et al.	2008	Revue Française de Gestion	Multichannel retailing, Multichannel distribution strategy, channel integration	**Multichannel retailing:** simultaneously distribute products and services through several distribution channels. **Multichannel distribution strategy:** «The multichannel distribution strategy is not about juxtaposing channels, but rather fostering links in order to achieve an integrated system ». **Channel integration:** « what counts in the multiple distribution strategy is not so much the number of channels to be set up as the coordination of the channels between them ».	Physical stores, online stores
Sullivan and Thomas	2005	Journal of Marketing	Customer channel migration	**Customer channel migration:** « A dynamic process in which a current customer repeatedly makes choices to frequent one of a retailers channel options ».	Physical stores, online stores, catalogs
Gupta et al.	2004	International Journal of Electronic Commerce	Consumer channel switching	**Consumer channel switching:** switching behavior from offline to online channels.	Physical stores, online stores
Wallace et al.	2004	Journal of Retailing	Multiple channel retailing	**Multiple channel retailing:** « Multiple channel retailers simultaneously employ an array of channels consisting of retail stores, mail order catalogs, and web sites often targeting the same customer ».	Physical stores, online stores, mail order
Schoenbachler and Gordon	2002	Journal of Consumer Marketing	Multichannel shopping behavior, multichannel strategy	**Multichannel shopping behavior:** shopping from multiple channels. **Multichannel strategy:** « ...the key to successful multi-channel marketing is to focus on managing the customer contact points rather than the channel ».	Physical stores, online stores, catalogs

continued on following page

Table 1. Continued

Authors	Year of publication	Journal	Concepts	Definitions	Channels investigated
Coelho and Easingwood	2004	The Service Industries Journal	Multiple channel strategy	**Multiple channel strategy:** « A multiple channel strategy is employed when a firm makes a product available to the market through two or more channels of distribution ».	Physical stores, online stores, catalogs, call centers, telephone, digital TV
Stone et al.	2002	Journal of Database Marketing	Multichannel customer management, multichannel strategy	**Multichannel customer management:** « The multichannel customer management is the use of more than one channel or medium to manage customers in a way that is consistent and coordinated across all the channels or media used ». **Multichannel strategy:** « The multichannel strategy is one that provides numerous customer touch-points at which products and services are purchased or serviced across several distribution channels ».	Physical stores, online stores, telephone, mobile commerce, interactive TV
Zhang et al.	2010	Journal of Interactive Marketing	Multichannel retailing	**Multichannel retailing:** « Multichannel retailing is the set of activities involved in selling merchandise or services to consumers through more than one channel ».	Physical stores, online stores, catalogs, call centers, TV home shopping, mobile commerce
Adivar et al.	2019	Journal of Retailing and Consumer Services	Omnichannel retailing	**Omnichannel retailing:** « Omni-channel retailing ensures an integrated process that provides an integrated outlook of a product or service to the consumer in terms of purchase, return, and exchange in each channel. Retailers can use a wide range of technologies to trace and track consumer behavior across physical and online channels, understanding each consumer and providing a personalized shopping experience in omni-channel retailing ».	Physical stores, online stores, catalogs, mobile commerce, social medias (as communication channels), TV
Lee et al.	2019	Industrial Marketing Management	Omnichannel retailing, customer engagement	**Omnichannel retailing:** « Omnichannel retailing refers to retailing that involves a synergetic integration of channels for the purpose of creating a unified brand experience for customers, regardless of the channel or stage they are enduring the purchasing process ». **Customer engagement:** « Customer engagement refers to the level of a customer's or prospective customer's interactions and connections with a brand's or firm's offerings and/or activities ».	Physical stores, online stores
Li et al.	2018	Decision Support System	Omnichannel retailing, multichannel retailing	**Omnichannel retailing**: full channel integration, synergetic channels. **Multichannel retailing**: the presence of retailers across diverse channels.	Physical stores, online stores, mobile commerce
Rodriguez-Torrico et al.	2017	Computers in Human Behavior	Omnichannel retailing	**Omnichannel retailing:** « …providing shoppers with a unique, complete, and seamless shopping experience that eliminates the barriers between channels. »	Physical stores, online stores, mobile commerce
Beck and Rygl	2015	Journal of Retailing and Consumer Services	Multichannel retailing, Cross-channels retailing, omni-channel retailing	**Multichannel retailing**: Selling products or services through more than one channel without interaction between the different channels from the point of view of the consumer and without integration between the latter from the point of view of the retailer **Cross-channels retailing**: a partial interaction/integration between the different channels. **Omnichannel retailing**: a full interaction/integration between the different channels.	Physical stores, catalogs, telephone, online stores, mobile commerce
Sun et al.	2020	International Journal of Information Management	Multichannel retailing, Omnichannel retailing, Digitalization	**Multichannel retailing:** the presence of retailers across diverse channels. **Omnichannel retailing:** « …which aims to integrate all the physical and digital channels tightly »	Offline channels and online channels
Li et al.	2017	International Journal of Electronic Commerce	Channel migration, cross-channel competition, multichannel environment, Online channel adoption	**Multichannel environment:** « in the multichannel environment, customers can shop from multiple channels offered by firms competing in the same industry ». **Customer channel migration**: switching between channels.	Offline channels, Catalog, online channels
Rodriguez-Torrico et al.	2017	Computers in Human Behavior	Omnichannel consumer behavior, mobile devices, online devices	**Omnichannel shopping behavior**: purchase behavior across multiple channels simultaneously.	Offline channels, online channels, mobile channels
Cheah et al.	2020	Journal of Retailing and Consumer Services	Omnichannel retailing, Consumer empowerment, channel integration	**Omnichannel retailing:** « … it allows retailers to leverage synergies and synchronize their interactions with consumers across multiple channels.	Offline channels and online channels
Yurova et al.	2016	Journal of retailing and Consumer Services	Multichannel consumer, Omnichannel consumer	**Omnichannel consumer:** « … who shops for products and services using mobile, online and traditional retail channels ».	Physical channels, catalog, online channels, mobile commerce
Du et al.	2019	International Journal of Production Economics	Omnichannel	**Omnichannel:** « … an increasing number of companies are transforming into omnichannel operations, a new retail mode that emphasizes the interplay between channels and consumers.	Offline channels, online channels, mobile commerce

with a consumer switching between the different channels of one retailer (Konus et al., 2008 ; Verhoef et al., 2007; Schröder and Zaharia, 2008 ; Dholakia et al., 2010 ; Cao and Li, 2015 ; Lee et al., 2019 etc…) and few studies present the free-riding consumer behavior who consist on a consumer using one retailer's channel to prepare a purchase and then switch to another retailer's channel to purchase (Heitz-Spahn, 2013).

Third concerning the channels investigated, thirteen opposed offline to online channels, thirteen associated catalogs to offline and online channels, and seventeen associated mobile channels to offline and online channels. It should be noted that some articles have taken social networks into account as communication channels that allow consumers to get in touch with the company or to collect opinions or to share their experiences with virtual communities. However, the table shows that although many studies contribute to the multichannel/omnichannel shopping domain, no study has yet taken into account the non-conventional channels that emerged in recent decades or that have always existed (physical vs digital). Indeed, omnichannel consumers are nowadays switching between a range of various channels available and used during their shopping experiences. These channels are the conventional ones (physical stores, online stores, mobile channels, catalogs …) which are controlled by companies but multiple other "non-conventional channels" are also available to consumers. In this multiple channel context, companies have some control over all the channels they manage, on the other hand, several other distribution channels are a little bit or not at all controlled by companies such as the peer to peer channels, the second hand channels, the flea markets, the black market channels…

CONCLUSION

Based on a systematic literature review, the present paper shows the gap existing between the channels considered in the literature and those that actually considered by shoppers in multiple channel shopping behavior. Indeed, there is a plethora of shopping solutions used by consumers during their shopping journey but rarely considered in the literature.

The challenge of engaging customers across the channels of one retailer (Lee et al., 2019) is very hard to achieve: tracking consumer behavior across both physical and virtual environments (Chen et al., 2018) and gather information about the consumers in order to deliver a seamless shopping experience (Verhoef et al., 2015) is a more realistic challenge in the context of empowered customers who have regained control of their decision-making processes from retailers (Heitz-Spahn, 2013).

Accordingly, academia should move to a more customer-centric approach and future research should focus more on the omni-channel shopping with consumer lenses to understand the different shopping motives and the different patterns of consumption of this empowered consumer.

However, future studies could make an inventory of all the distribution channels (conventional and non-conventional) available to consumers and to explore the determinants and the motivations linked to the shopping consumer behavior in a multiple channel context.

REFERENCES

Adivar, B., Hüseyinoglu, I. O. Y., & Christopher, M. (2019). A quantitative performance management framework for assessing omnichannel retail supply chains. *Journal of Retailing and Consumer Services*, *48*, 257–269. doi:10.1016/j.jretconser.2019.02.024

Alexander, B., & Cano, M. B. (2020). Store of the future: Towards a (re)invention and (re)imagination of physical store space in an omnichannel context. *Journal of Retailing and Consumer Services, 55*, 101913. doi:10.1016/j.jretconser.2019.101913

Anderl, E., Schumann, J. H., & Kunz, W. (2016). Helping firms reduce complexity in multichannel online data: A new taxonomy-based approach for customer journeys. *Journal of Retailing, 92*(2), 185–203. doi:10.1016/j.jretai.2015.10.001

Ansari, A., Mela, C. F., & Neslin, S. A. (2008). Customer channel migration. *JMR, Journal of Marketing Research, XLV*(1), 60–76. doi:10.1509/jmkr.45.1.60

Balasubramanian, S., Raghunathan, R., & Mahajan, V. (2005). Consumers in a multichannel environment:product utility, process utility, and channel choice. *Journal of Interactive Marketing, 19*(2), 12–30. doi:10.1002/dir.20032

Bilgicer, T., Jedidi, K., Lehmann, D. R., & Neslin, S. A. (2015). Social Contagion and Customer Adoption of New Sales Channels. *Journal of Retailing, 91*(2), 254–271. doi:10.1016/j.jretai.2014.12.006

Blazquez, M. (2014). Fashion Shopping in Multichannel Retail: The Role of Technology in Enhancing the Customer Experience. *International Journal of Electronic Commerce, 18*(4), 97–116. doi:10.2753/JEC1086-4415180404

Blom, A., Lange, F., & Hess, R. L. Jr. (2017). Omnichannel-based promotions' effects on purchase behavior and brand image. *Journal of Retailing and Consumer Services, 39*, 286–295. doi:10.1016/j.jretconser.2017.08.008

Brown, S. (2001). Marketing-The retro revolution. *Sage (Atlanta, Ga.).*

Cao, L. (2014). Business Model Transformation in Moving to a Cross-Channel Retail Strategy: A Case Study. *International Journal of Electronic Commerce, 18*(4), 69–96. doi:10.2753/JEC1086-4415180403

Cao, L., & Li, L. (2015). The impact of cross-channel integration on retailers' sales growth. *Journal of Retailing, 91*(2), 198–216. doi:10.1016/j.jretai.2014.12.005

Cheah, J.H., Lim, X. J., Ting, H., Liu, Y., & Quach, S. (2020). Are privacy concerns still relevant? Revisiting consumer behaviour in omnichannel retailing. *Journal of Retailing and Consumer Services.*

Chen, Y., Cheung, C., & Tan, C. (2018). Omnichannel business research: Opportunities and challenges. *Decision Support Systems, 109*, 1–4. doi:10.1016/j.dss.2018.03.007

Coelho, F. J., & Easingwoo, C. (2004). Multiple Channel Systems in Services: Pros, Cons and Issues. *Service Industries Journal, 24*(5), 1–29. doi:10.1080/0264206042000276810

Dholakia, U. M., Kahn, B. E., Reeves, R., Rindfleisch, A., Stewart, D., & Taylor, E. (2010). Consumer Behavior in a Multichannel, Multimedia Retailing Environment. *Journal of Interactive Marketing, 24*(2), 86–95. doi:10.1016/j.intmar.2010.02.005

Du, S., Wang, L., & Hu, L. (2019). Omnichannel management with consumer disappointment aversion. *International Journal of Production Economics, 215*, 84–101. doi:10.1016/j.ijpe.2018.05.002

Emrich, O., Paul, M., & Rudolph, T. (2015). Shopping benefits of multichannel assortment integration and the moderating role of retailer type. *Journal of Retailing*, *91*(2), 326–342. doi:10.1016/j.jretai.2014.12.003

Frazier Gary, L. (1999). *Organizing and managing channels of distribution. Journal of the Academy of Marketing Science* , 27.

Gupta, A., Su, B. C., & Walter, Z. (2004). An Empirical Study of Consumer Switching from Traditional to Electronic Channels: A Purchase-Decision Process Perspective. *International Journal of Electronic Commerce*, *8*(3), 131–161. doi:10.1080/10864415.2004.11044302

Heitz-Spahn, S. (2013). Cross-channel free-riding consumer behavior in a multichannel environment: An investigation of shopping motives, sociodemographics and product categories. *Journal of Retailing and Consumer Services*, *20*(6), 570–578. doi:10.1016/j.jretconser.2013.07.006

Hickman, E., Kharouf, H., & Sekhon, H. (2020). An omnichannel approach to retailing: Demystifying and identifying the factors influencing an omnichannel experience. *International Review of Retail, Distribution and Consumer Research*, *30*(3), 266–288. doi:10.1080/09593969.2019.1694562

Jang, S., Farajallah, M., & So, K. K. F. (2021). The effect of quality cues on travelers' demand for peer-to-peer ridesharing: A neglected area of the sharing economy. *Journal of Travel Research*, *60*(2), 446–461. doi:10.1177/0047287519897998

Kim, N., & Kim, W. (2018). Do your social media lead you to make social deal purchases? Consumer-generated social referrals for sales via social commerce. *International Journal of Information Management*, *39*, 38–48. doi:10.1016/j.ijinfomgt.2017.10.006

Konus, U., Verhoef, P. C., & Neslin, S. A. (2008). Multichannel shopper segments and their covariates. *Journal of Retailing*, *84*(4), 398–413. doi:10.1016/j.jretai.2008.09.002

Kumar, V., & Venkatesan, R. (2005). Who are the multichannel shoppers and how do they perform?: Correlates of multichannel shopping behavior. *Journal of Interactive Marketing*, *19*(2), 44–62. doi:10.1002/dir.20034

Lee, Z. W. Y., Chan, T. K. H., Chong, A. Y. L., & Thadani, D. R. (2019). Customer engagement through omnichannel retailing: The effects of channel integration quality. *Industrial Marketing Management*, *77*, 90–101. doi:10.1016/j.indmarman.2018.12.004

Li, J., Konus, U., Langerak, F., & Weggeman, M. C. D. P. (2017). Customer Channel Migration and Firm Choice: The Effects of Cross-Channel Competition. *International Journal of Electronic Commerce*, *21*(1), 8–42. doi:10.1080/10864415.2016.1204186

Li, Y., Liu, H., Lim, E. T. K., Goh, J. M., Yang, F., & Lee, M. K. O. (2018). Customer's reaction to cross-channel integration in omnichannel retailing: The mediating roles of retailer uncertainty, identity attractiveness, and switching costs. *Decision Support Systems*, *109*, 50–60. doi:10.1016/j.dss.2017.12.010

Luo, N., Wang, Y., Zhang, M., Tao, N., & Tu, J. (2020). Integrating community and e-commerce to build a trusted online second-hand platform: Based on the perspective of social capital. *Technological Forecasting and Social Change*, *153*, 119913. doi:10.1016/j.techfore.2020.119913

Melis, K., Campo, K., Breugelmans, E., & Lamey, L. (2015). The impact of the multichannel retail mix on online store choice: Does online experience matter? *Journal of Retailing*, *91*(2), 272–288. doi:10.1016/j.jretai.2014.12.004

Miquel-Romero, M.-J., Frasquet, M., & Molla-Descals, A. (2020). The role of the store in managing postpurchase complaints for omnichannel shoppers. *Journal of Business Research*, *109*(3), 288–296. doi:10.1016/j.jbusres.2019.09.057

Neslin, S. A., & Shankar, V. (2009). Key Issues in Multichannel Customer Management: Current Knowledge and Future Directions. *Journal of Interactive Marketing*, *23*(1), 70–81. doi:10.1016/j.intmar.2008.10.005

Neslin, S. C., Grewal, D., Leghorn, R., Shankar, V., Teerling, M. L., Thomas, J. S., & Verhoef, P. C. (2006). Challenges and opportunities in multichannel customer management. *Journal of Service Research*, *9*(2), 95–112. doi:10.1177/1094670506293559

Park, J., Dayarian, I., & Montreuil, B. (2020). Showcasing optimization in omnichannel retailing. *European Journal of Operational Research*. Advance online publication. doi:10.1016/j.ejor.2020.03.081

Piotrowicz, W., & Cuthbertson, R. (2014). Introduction to the Special Issue Information Technology in Retail: Toward Omnichannel Retailing. *International Journal of Electronic Commerce*, *18*(4), 5–15. doi:10.2753/JEC1086-4415180400

Poirel, C., & Bonet Fernandez, D. (2008). La stratégie de distribution multiple à la recherche de synergies entre canal physique et canal virtuel. *Revue Française de Gestion*, *34*(182), 155–170. doi:10.3166/rfg.182.155-170

Poncin I, (2008), Le comportement multicanal du consommateur est-il une simple évolution ou constitue-t-il une véritable révolution ? *Reflets et perspectives de la vie économique*, *47*, 43-51.

Rigby, D. (2011). The Future of Shopping. *Harvard Business Review*, *89*, 65–76.

Rodriguez-Torrico, P., Cabezudo, R. S. J., & San-Martin, S. (2017). Tell me what they are like and I will tell you where they buy. An analysis of omnichannel consumer behavior. *Computers in Human Behavior*, *68*, 465–471. doi:10.1016/j.chb.2016.11.064

Sands, S., Ferraro, C., Campbell, C., & Pallant, J. (2016). Segmenting multichannel consumers across search, purchase and after-sales. *Journal of Retailing and Consumer Services*, *33*, 62–71. doi:10.1016/j.jretconser.2016.08.001

Schoenbachler, D. D., & Gordon, G. L. (2002). Multi-channel shopping: Understanding what drives channel choice. *Journal of Consumer Marketing*, *19*(1), 42–53. doi:10.1108/07363760210414943

Schröder, H., & Zaharia, S. (2008). Linking multi-channel customer behavior with shopping motives: An empirical investigation of a German retailer. *Journal of Retailing and Consumer Services*, *15*(6), 452–478. doi:10.1016/j.jretconser.2008.01.001

Sherry, J. F. Jr. (1990). A Sociocultural Analysis of a Midwestern Flea Market. *The Journal of Consumer Research*, *17*(June), 13–30. doi:10.1086/208533

Stone, M., Hobbs, M., & Khaleeli, M. (2002). Multichannel customer management: The benefits and challenges. *Journal of Database Marketing & Customer Strategy Management*, *10*(1), 39–52. doi:10.1057/palgrave.jdm.3240093

Sun, Y., Yang, C., Shen, X. L., & Wang, N. (2020). When digitalized customers meet digitalized services: A digitalized social cognitive perspective of omnichannel service usage. *International Journal of Information Management*, *54*, 102200. doi:10.1016/j.ijinfomgt.2020.102200

Thomas, J. S., & Sullivan, U. Y. (2005). Managing Marketing Communications with Multichannel Customers. *Journal of Marketing*, *69*(4), 239–251. doi:10.1509/jmkg.2005.69.4.239

Vanheems, R. (2009). Distribution multicanal- pourquoi les clients mixtes doivent faire l'objet d'une attention particulière? *Décisions Marketing*, *55*, 41–52. doi:10.7193/DM.055.41.52

Venkatesan, R., Kumar, V., & Ravishanker, N. (2007). Multichannel shopping: Causes and consequences. *Journal of Marketing*, *71*(2), 114–132. doi:10.1509/jmkg.71.2.114

Verhoef, P. C., Kannan, P. K., & Inman, J. F. (2015). From Multi-Channel Retailing to Omni-Channel Retailing: Introduction to the special Issue on Multi-channel Retailing. Academic Press.

Verhoef, P. C., Neslin, S. A., & Vroomen, B. (2007). Multichannel customer management: Understanding the research-shopper phenomenon. *International Journal of Research in Marketing*, *24*(2), 129–148. doi:10.1016/j.ijresmar.2006.11.002

Wallace, D. W., Giese, J. L., & Johnson, J. L. (2004). Customer Retailer Loyalty in the Context of Multiple Channel Strategies. *Journal of Retailing*, *80*(4), 249–263. doi:10.1016/j.jretai.2004.10.002

Yurova, Y., Rippé, C. B., Weisfeld-Spolter, S., Sussan, F., & Arndt, A. (2016). Not all adaptive selling to omni-consumers is influential: The moderating effect of product type. *Journal of Retailing and Consumer Services*. Advance online publication. doi:10.1016/j.jretconser.2016.01.009

Zhang, J., Farris, P. W., Irvin, J. W., Kushwaha, T., Steenburgh, T. J., & Weitz, B. A. (2010). Crafting Integrated Multichannel Retailing Strategies. *Journal of Interactive Marketing*, *24*(2), 168–180. doi:10.1016/j.intmar.2010.02.002

Zou, T., & Jiang, B. (2020). Integration of primary and resale platforms. *JMR, Journal of Marketing Research*, *57*(4), 659–676. doi:10.1177/0022243720917352

Chapter 18
The Conceptualization of the E-Service Quality:
A Review of the Literature

Ramzi Ben M'rad
Higher School of Economic and Commercial Sciences of Tunis, Tunisia

ABSTRACT

Several research studies have focused on the conceptualization, measurement, and management of service quality and their effects in electronic environments. Most of them are based on a classic paradigm, which consists in relating the quality of e-service to customer satisfaction and loyalty. The prescribing intent of the e-service as a plausible consequence of the quality of the e-service has not received enough interest from the researchers. Along these lines, this chapter examined the direct effect of the quality of the e-service on the prescribing intention of the e-service by the consumer as well as the indirect effect through a mediating variable, which is the perceived online value of the consumer.

INTRODUCTION

The growth of online sales has created strong competition in the online market space, and hence the need for a change in the direction of online commerce, with a greater focus on other means of marketing. differentiation, rather than low prices (Kim and Kim 2010). Benaroch and Appari (2011) have pointed out that the emergence of the electronic service paradigm goes beyond simple service automation to include differentiation by the quality of the services offered ". Santouridis et al. (2012) argued that the major challenge that many companies face concerns the correct management of the processes associated with customer service.

The quality of service is well recognized in the literature as an important factor that allows companies to have various strategic advantages, such as the increased ability to attract and retain customers. Benaroch and Appari (2011) have pointed out that the provision of quality service creates a significant competitive advantage, which helps ensure effective differentiation and long-term profitability gains. The need for studies to better understand the quality of service in a digital context is recognized by several

DOI: 10.4018/978-1-7998-7192-7.ch018

authors (Blut et al, 2015, Chen et al. 2013; Carlson and O'Cass, 2011). To this end, researchers should pay more attention to conceptualizing the quality of e-service and analyzing its consequences.

In this chapter, we will define the concept of the quality of an electronic service, noting its specificities and its differences from the quality of a traditional service. We will endeavor to highlight the dimensions and the underlying attributes of this concept, by analyzing the theoretical basis relating to the conceptualization of the quality of e-service.

THE QUALITY OF THE E-SERVICE

With the development of the Internet and technology, the website takes the place of physical business units. The perceived usefulness of the site and of the new electronic environment constitutes an important part of the company's image. The increase in the number of electronic services can also affect the interaction and purchasing behavior of businesses and consumers (Yang, 2001; Santos, 2003). At the same time, consumers have become more sensitive to the quality of service thanks to the competitive and comparable system of electronic commerce. As a result, issues relating to e-commerce, e-service, e-service quality and measurement of that quality have started to arouse the interest of marketers.

Thus, we will propose to define the concept of electronic service or e-service, highlighting its differences from the traditional service. We will then define the quality of e-service, by noting its points of difference relative to the traditional quality of service.

From Traditional Service to Electronic Service

According to Hoffman and Bateson (1997), "the term service refers to acts, efforts, processes or performances".

Several authors have identified salient intrinsic characteristics of services, namely, intangibility, heterogeneity, and inseparability.

- Services are intangible, as they are seen as an act on the part of the provider and an experience for the recipient (Zeithaml et al, 1988).
- Services are heterogeneous since they are based on an impersonal relationship and a subjective and situational assessment (Sabadie and Vernette, 2003).
- Services are characterized by inseparability, in that their production, distribution and consumption processes are simultaneous (Eiglier and Langeard, 1987).

Zeithaml et al (2013) argue that: "although traditionally retail customer service has been associated with the direct interaction between service personnel and customers, developments in information technology have given rise to this called electronic services or e-service".

Rowley (2006) defined electronic service as "acts, efforts or performances whose delivery is mediated by information technologies, including the Web, information kiosks and mobile devices". The service and interaction that occurs online is known as e-service (Ho and Lin, 2010). Information flows and good experiences between businesses and consumers are delivered through e-commerce (Santos, 2003).

Websites are considered as service environments in which customers form perceptions of online service experiences through their cognitive and affective responses to web interface signals.

A website provides the framework or conditions under which service encounters take place between a service provider and a customer and where the service is produced and consumed simultaneously (Eroglu et al. 2003). When customers buy products online, search for information, or view video clips, they interact with service providers through websites as a technology platform for service delivery. Therefore, online service is essentially an interactive self-service process in which users rely on the online service delivery platform to meet their individual needs.

Interactions mediated by Internet technologies are more useful and enjoyable when users feel that the service process is in their control (Jiang et al., 2010). By its very nature, service involves social interactions between clients and between clients and service providers (Brady and Cronin, 2001).

The online environment lacks some characteristics of traditional physical environments but has its own advantages, such as temporal and spatial flexibility (Eroglu et al., 2003). Online merchants can also create visual appeal to attract customers by manipulating physical factors such as colors, graphics and layout (Eroglu et al., 2003), which correspond to design factors in the typology by Baker et al. (1994).

Eroglu et al. (2003) examined the atmospheric qualities of a virtual store, which they defined as the sum of all visible and audible signals. To date, few researchers have explored how website design factors affect customer experiences.

Websites can not only allow customers to establish their own service meetings through interactions on the website, but also provide social interactions on behalf of a company's service staff. Interacting with a computer during a service process implies that users have control over the process and can produce and consume the service without the direct involvement of service personnel. Thus, the sense of control of the service process and the environment is at the center of the notion of web interactivity in a service context (Chen and Yen, 2004). Leveraging interactivity on the web, service companies can design their websites in a way that allows users to personalize the e-service interface and improve the fit between their preferences and the online service experience (Kang and Lee, 2015). Therefore, a key aspect of the service interface design is to allow users to customize the website so that they feel in control of the service process.

The site as a medium of interaction plays the role of a service person helping customers if necessary. Social interaction plays an important role in the consumption process (Argo et al., 2008). Online, computer-mediated interactions replace interpersonal and human interactions common in physical service environments (Bitner et al., 2000, Dabholkar, 1996, Meuter et al., 2005). Social presence has become a central element in research on virtual environments, as well as an important design goal of online social interactions (Hassanein & Head, 2007).

As the computer as a social actor paradigm (CASA) suggests (Moon, 2000), humans tend to view computers as social actors; Therefore, human-computer interactions can take the place of human interactions during service delivery without losing much emotional value. Thus, in the design of interfaces, service providers should integrate social factors so as to elicit strong positive affective reactions from users (Cyr et al., 2009).

The study of Youn Jung Kang and Won Jun Lee (2016) considers sense of control and social presence as key web interface features that influence users' e-service experiences. With an experimental study, the authors show how the experiences of users' sense of control and social presence, affect the perceived quality of their online service experiences and their intention to revisit the service platform. They view the sense of control as a functional attribute and social presence as a social factor in an electronic service environment.

From Quality of Service to Quality of E-Service: Definition and Specifics

There has long been a strong interest among management researchers in trying to understand and assess customer perceptions of quality. This interest was primarily motivated by the need to strengthen relationships between companies and customers. This may explain the relevance of the concept of quality of service, which has been emphasized by researchers in the field of marketing.

Indeed, many definitions of traditional quality of service, or interpersonal service experience, have been proposed in the literature. The most adopted is that of Parasuraman et al. (1988) who define it as "a global judgment, or an attitude, as to the superiority of the service".

Many authors have examined the dimensionality issues of traditional perceived quality and have identified several dimensions that consumers consider when evaluating service quality.

Many authors have examined the dimensionality issues of traditional perceived quality and have identified several dimensions that consumers consider when evaluating service quality.

Eiglier and Langeard (1987) identified three dimensions, namely:

- "the quality of the output" or of the service itself, the result of servuction;
- "the process" or operating rules of servuction;
- "the quality of each element of the servuction system".
- Grônroos (1990) identified two dimensions:
- "technical quality" result of the act of service and
- "functional quality" service delivery process.
- Prasuraman et al (1988) evoked five dimensions contributing to the formation of the judgment of the quality of service, in this case:
- "tangible elements": appearance of physical elements, equipment, personal, and communication materials;
- "reliability": ability of the service provider to offer the promised service in an exact, precise and trustworthy manner, serious and fair performance.
- "responsiveness / helpfulness": willingness to help consumers and provide prompt service.
- "assurance": competence and courtesy of employees, credibility and security.
- "empathy": easy access, good communication and understanding of the customer.

The contributions of this different research were drawn from the paradigm of disconfirmation relating to tangible products which states that "quality is the result between what is perceived and the expected performance" (Bressolles, 2002).

Specifically, the SERVQUAL model of Parasuraman et al (1988) considers "the quality of service as being a gap between the level of service expected and the level of service perceived by the consumer". (Figure 3)

The transposition of the concept of quality to the field of e-service has resulted in several definitions. In this regard, Santos (2003), Ho and Lin (2010), argue that the quality of e-service, "is the way in which consumers decide on overall ratings and judgments regarding the excellence and quality of the service. provision of e-services in the virtual market. ". Zeithaml et al (2002), Parasuraman, Zeithaml * and Malhotra (2005) define e-service quality as "the extent to which a site facilitates the efficient and effective shopping, purchase and delivery of products or services. "

Figure 1. The model SERVQUAL of Parasuraman, Zeithaml et Berry
Source: Parasuraman and al (1988)

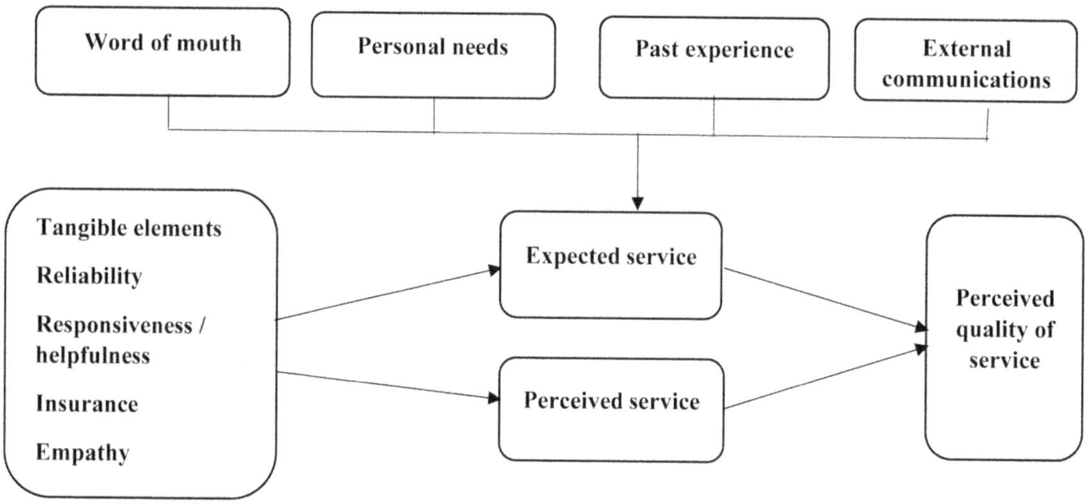

Wolfinbarger and Gilly (2003) consider the quality of e-service as "the process of the transaction including the search for information, navigation on the site, interactions with customer service, delivery and the satisfaction inherent in the product. ordered."

E-quality could be defined as "the set of main attributes in the context of e-commerce that make customers perceive quality service" (Parasuraman et al. 2005; Boshoff, 2007).

An online shopping experience therefore includes several phases: information research, valuation of the property, decision-making, completion of the transaction, delivery and possibly contact with customer service. The electronic quality of service is a rather transactional quality, it includes elements of pre- and post-service experience evaluation (Bressolles, 2006).

One of the most important differences between traditional service quality and electronic service quality is the replacement of interpersonal interaction with human-machine interaction coupled with the absence of human contact (Bressolles, 2006). The encounter between a client and a company can now be seen as a dynamic and interactive relationship at the center of which is technology (Dabholkar, 2000).

The lack of human interaction during the online experience, means that determinants such as competence, courtesy, cleanliness, comfort, flexibility, all significant in a traditional service encounter, are not really relevant. However, determinants such as accessibility, communication, credibility, comprehension, appearance and availability are equally applicable to both e-commerce and traditional commerce (Cox and Dale, 2001). Other features unique to the Internet make the application of traditional dimensions of quality of service inappropriate. These dimensions sometimes do not consider all the subtleties necessary to assess the quality of electronic services.

Sabadie and Vernette (2003) evoked the differences between the management of a traditional service and that of an electronic service, focusing on the attributes of a service, namely: intangibility, inseparability and heterogeneity.

They argue that the intangibility of services is consolidated in a virtual environment and in the case of electronic services. In addition, the heterogeneity of services is ensured by means of the Internet, which makes it possible to standardize the provision of service thanks to the automation of the transactions carried out and to personalize the offer using the interactive functions of the website and informational databases. Finally, they add that the production, distribution and consumption of a traditional or electronic service are simultaneous. This makes the quality of service highly dependent on its delivery conditions and the consumer's choice of all parameters relating to its relationship with the company and / or the brand on the website.

Although they may overlap, the quality of e-service can differ substantially from the quality of service. The e-service lacks people-to-people contact and can pose perceived high risk and privacy issues for customers (Bitner, Brown, & Meuter, 2000; Dabholkar 1996). Thus, the results of the quality of service cannot be easily transposed to the domain of the quality of e-service. The efficiency of transaction and information has been recognized as two main achievements of e-services (Parasuraman and Zinkhan, 2002).

The Dimensions of E-Service Quality

The spectrum of research relating to the quality of e-service is increasingly broad (Sweeney and Lapp, 2004). Researchers are working intensively on this and contributions have been made in this area (Francis, 2007). There is a great deal of research on the quality of e-service (Loiacono et al., 2000; Li et al., 2000; van Riel et al., 2001; Yoo and Donthu, 2001; Wolfinbarger and Gilly, 2003; Yang et al., 2003; Parasuraman et al., 2005; Cristobal et al., 2007; Hadwich et al., 2010; Akinci et al. ., 2010; Rolland and Freeman, 2010;...).

Based on the meta-study of Blut et al. (2015) on the quality of e-service, we found that there are differences in the conceptualization of the quality of an e-service.

Indeed, the perception of the quality of the e-service could differ according to the sector and the product. Nevertheless, they highlight certain salient attributes testifying to the functional quality of the e-service.

THE FUNCTIONAL DIMENSION OF THE QUALITY OF E-SERVICE

Blut et al. (2015) have synthesized the dimensions of e-service quality into four main dimensions, of a functional nature.

1. The first dimension is the design of the website, which refers to all elements of the consumer experience related to the site (except customer service), including navigation, search for information, order processing, shipment tracking, product availability, product and price offerings, system customization and availability.
2. The second dimension is fulfilment, which includes activities that ensure that customers receive what they think they ordered based on the display and description offered on the website and / or the delivery of the right product. at the right price (correctly invoiced), in good condition, on time.
3. The third dimension is customer service, which refers to a helpful and responsive service that responds to customer inquiries and returns / complaints during or after the sale.
4. The fourth dimension of security / confidentiality, which is defined as the security of credit card payments and the confidentiality of information shared during or after the sale

Table 1. Definition of the constructs used in the meta-analysis (quality of e-service)

Construct	Definition	Attributes	Source
Website design **Execution** **Consumer service** **Security**	Includes all elements of the consumer experience on the site (except for customer service), including navigation, information search, order processing, shipment tracking, product availability, product offering and pricing, customization and system availability (adapted from Holloway and Beatty, 2008). Customers receive what they thought they ordered, based on the display and description provided on the website; And delivery of the right product at the right price (correctly billed) in good condition, on time (Holloway & Beatty, 2008). Helpful and responsive service that responds to customer inquiries and feedback / complaints promptly during or after the sale (Holloway & Beatty, 2008). The security of credit card payments and the confidentiality of information shared during or after the sale (Holloway & Beatty, 2008).	• Quality of website information • Website organization / design / navigation •Purchasing process • Competence / ease of use of the website • Product selection • Availability of stocks of goods • Personalization • System availability • Delivery delay • Order precision • Delivery requirement • Billing accuracy • Quality of the goods • Level of service • security	Holloway and Beatty (2008); Parasuraman, Zeithaml, and Malhotra (2005); Wolfinbarger and Gilly (2003) Holloway and Beatty (2008); Parasuraman, Zeithaml, and Malhotra (2005); Wolfinbarger and Gilly (2003) Holloway and Beatty (2008); Parasuraman, Zeithaml, and Malhotra (2005); Wolfinbarger and Gilly (2003) Holloway and Beatty (2008); Parasuraman, Zeithaml, and Malhotra (2005); Wolfinbarger and Gilly (2003)

Source: Blut et al. (2015)

Website Design

Website design is the first dimension of e-service quality that has received the most attention in the literature. The first conceptualizations had a very narrow focus and focused mainly on attributes related to the website interface (Wolfinbarger and Gilly, 2003).

According to Bressolles (2006), "the design or the graphic style of the site refers to the richness of representation of the mediatized environment, induced by its formal characteristics, in other words, its graphics, colours, the use of images., icons, animations, videos, windows embedded in the screen, etc. ".

Wells et al (2011) noted that the website helps to report the quality of online sales. According to Zhou et al (2009), a high-quality website demonstrates not only a salesperson's ability, but also interest in customers. Chen et al (2013), Mpinganjira (2015) considered the visual appearance of the website as a sub-dimension of the quality of the platform, and one of the factors associated with the quality of the environment of the stores in line. Visual appeal is associated with such things as the use of colours, graphics, and layout (Thielsch and Hirschfeld 2012; Phillips and Chaparro 2009).

According to Mercy Mpinganjira (2015), the information quality sub-dimension, on the other hand, concerns the content of the platform. Bressolles (2006) defines the quality and quantity of information as "the perceptions of the Internet user concerning the quality and quantity of commercial or technical information on products and services, the service provider or the sales contract».

Rowley (2006) pointed out that the electronic service should be seen as an information service. When customers visit a merchant website, they are looking for information about the products on offer and the company itself. The quality of the information provided, determined by its suitability for decision-making and the speed of its circulation, influences customers' perceptions of the quality of service offered by websites (Chen et al 2013). Failure to ensure that information on sites is up to date only serves to portray a picture of neglect (Küster and Vila, 2011).

Research has indicated that many of the early measures of service quality do not take into account the entire purchasing process (Holloway and Beatty 2008). Bauer, Falk and Schmidt (2006) state that the online purchasing process includes four phases, an information phase, an agreement phase, a realization phase and an after-sales phase. They argue that the attributes used by online shoppers differ from their needs in different phases. The attributes related to the design of the website are of major importance during the early stages of the buying process. Customers at this stage have a major interest in product information. The easier the information accessed, the more positively the website will be evaluated (Holloway and Beatty 2008). Customers in this phase are interested in the quality of the information provided, the aesthetics of the site when making a purchasing decision, the fluidity of the purchasing process, and navigation on the site., product selection, merchandise availability, pricing information, information personalization and permanent site availability.

Another dimension of e-service quality, according to Mpinganjira (2015), encompasses website ease of use and personalization.

Bressolles (2006) considers interactivity as a means "allowing the customer to define and model himself the offer most suited to his needs, to have a privileged relationship with the brand, to modify the content and the shape of the mediated environment in real time. ". In addition, it defines ease of use or usability on a website as "the way the Internet user perceives and interacts with the site; is it easy to navigate the site? ".

In offline retail, when shoppers walk into a store, they can expect direct interaction with sellers. They also can touch and feel products that interest them. In electronic commerce, the interaction takes place on the site. Customers must rely on themselves to find interesting products, evaluate them and close the deal. Therefore, the ease granted by the website to customers to complete their consumption experience and the offer of services tailored to their needs, are two factors that can help to indicate the quality or lack thereof. (Zavareh et al 2012; Ladhari, 2010).

Regarding ease of use, Akrimi and Khemakhem (2014) pointed out that an easy-to-use website is one that responds quickly to orders. For example, when a customer clicks on a link, the pages should be able to load fairly quickly. Online systems that respond to orders slowly can be very frustrating for customers. Ease of use also indicates the user-friendliness of the system. Studies of human and computer interactions often recognize the need for system developers to have the mind of the user and not just be supported by technical capabilities. A user-friendly website does not require excessive mental effort on the part of the customer (Alomari et al. 2012).

The concept of personalization is about considering each customer and, in some ways, unique from others. Bressolles (2006) defines personalization as "the possibility for the seller to adapt the content and design of the site according to the expectations and profile of the customers. "

A store's ability to provide a shopping experience that considers diverse needs is indicative of its responsiveness. Pappas et al (2014) pointed out that merchant websites can enrich the online store experience for customers by having a system capable of using customer data to filter website content and deliver to customers only content that is relevant to them.

Empirical results from the study by Blut (2016) reveal that website design perceptions directly contribute to overall perceptions of the quality of electronic service and are directly influenced by the quality of a site's information. Web, website aesthetics, availability of goods, price quotations, website personalization, system availability. Contrary to the author's expectations, attributes such as: the buying process, convenience of the site, and product selection did not affect the perceptions of the site's design.

Realization (Execution)

The second dimension is order fulfilment, which refers to the ability of the merchant website to ensure that customers receive what they thought they ordered. It mainly concerns the stage of completion of the purchasing process (Bauer, Falk and Hammerschmidt 2006). In this phase, customers have already placed their orders, and want to receive what they expected. Therefore, attributes related to the accuracy of order fulfilment, order timing and condition of delivered products are of major importance.

Customers expect the online store to ensure that the display and description provided on the website is accurate and that the right products are delivered at the right prices (correctly billed), in good condition and on time. timely. Mpinganjira (2015) considers the reliability of execution as a main sub-dimension of the results of the interaction of customers with a merchant website, which in turn, constitutes a dimension of the quality of the e-service. Research by Markus Blut (2016) has shown that, perceptions of execution directly contribute to general perceptions of the quality of electronic service and are directly influenced by the speed of delivery provided by the website, the accuracy of the order, and delivery conditions.

Realizing that when shopping online, the customer is ultimately interested in getting the purchased product, Akter et al (2010) see quality issues related to order fulfilment as an important outcome of online interaction with customers. One of the main issues that worries customers when it comes to order fulfilment for products purchased online is the reliability of the store in delivering products on time and without error (Chen et al 2013).

Customer Service

The third dimension, customer service, relates to online customer service, before, during or after the online ordering (Bauer, Falk and Hammerschmidt 2006). It includes attributes related to the general service level of the online store and the management of return policies. Although online stores do not offer personal contact, they can still provide a number for customer service or the option of contacting service employees via email. Holloway and Beatty (2008) indicate that reliable service support, combined with fair and well-communicated return / exchange policies, is an important attribute for customer satisfaction. Therefore, they assume that the level of service and management of return policies contributes to the perception of a high level of customer service from the merchant website.

The study by Markus Blut (2016) found that perceptions of customer service contribute directly to general perceptions of the quality of electronic service and are directly influenced by the level of service of a merchant website and the management return policies.

Security / Privacy Protection (Confidentiality)

The fourth dimension is the security / privacy of an online store, which refers to customer concerns about possible security and privacy gaps.

According to Bressolles (2006), "security involves protecting the user from the risks of fraud and financial loss on the site. Respect for privacy involves the protection of personal data and not to share, or resell, this information collected on consumers. "

Customers frequently avoid online stores when they feel their credit card payment is insecure and their information during or after the sale is not private. Online shoppers expect online stores to protect them from fraud, theft, and spam after an online purchase. In this context, Blut (2016) has shown that, perceptions of security / privacy directly contribute to the general perception of the quality of electronic service and are directly influenced by the security and privacy of an online store. The studies by Liao et al (2011) as well as that by Featherman et al. (2010) widely recognize privacy concerns as a major factor affecting customer confidence in online shopping in general. This study therefore includes the protection of privacy as an important area that may affect the customer's assessment of the quality of the services provided by online stores.

THE HEDONIC DIMENSION OF QUALITY

Van der Heijden (2004) can be considered as the pioneer in the analysis of the importance of the hedonic role of a website. This author defines the hedonic dimension as that which emphasizes the playful aspect of the adoption of information systems, which encourages their prolonged use.

Hoffman and Novak (1996) evoke the state of flow experienced by the Internet user while browsing the Internet, which manifests itself "by a continuous sequence of responses facilitated by the interactivity of the machine, which is intrinsically pleasant, which is accompanied by a loss of self-awareness which strengthens the self "

Boulaire and Mathieu (2000), Bressolles (2002) specify that "the hedonistic state of the site is associated with the sensations, emotions and fantasies felt by an Internet user following an online experience". J, Gharbi et al. (2003) define emotional state as "an emotional response, which can be described as pleasure, stimulation or dominance, to a set of stimuli influencing an individual's perception".

A number of authors have argued that the hedonic element or enjoyment is one of the key dimensions of e-commerce. Vazquez-Casielles et al. (2009) concerning travel agencies, and Shamdasani et al. (2008), in relation to e-banking, included a hedonic element as part of the quality of service. Hausman and Siekpe (2009) also incorporated the entertainment factor into their e-quality scale. The results show that all the factors studied are important for purchase and return intentions. Lin and Hsieh (2011) introduced enjoyment as a relevant dimension of IT quality in their SSTQUAL scale. Their results show that the hedonic dimension has become a necessary part of electronic commerce.

Likewise, Ha and Stoel (2009, 2012) proposed an atmospheric or experiential dimension in their model of website quality and found that this dimension was essential to customer satisfaction and purchase intention in the retail sale of clothing.

Considering the model developed by Parasuraman et al. (2005), Bauer et al. (2006) argued that a hedonic dimension was necessary to build e-quality, proposing a five-dimensional model, called eTransQual. Using the same scale, Yang et al. (2004) proposed and tested hedonic quality as another dimension of the quality of electronic service.

As a result, Lin and Hsieh (2011) defined jouissance in their SSTQUAL scale as "perceptions of pleasure encountered during the delivery and outcomes of self-service technologies". Since self-service technologies have been accused of negatively impacting consumer habits, the hedonic dimension could reduce these negative perceptions by creating pleasurable experiences for customers and thus achieve customer satisfaction. (Shamdasani et al. 2008).

Finally, given that the functional and hedonic qualities focus on different aspects of electronic quality (Yang et al. 2004), Maria Del Mar Alonso-Almeida, Merce Bernardo, Josep Llach, Frederic Marimon (2013) have shown that the quality functional as well as hedonic quality are positively related to higher levels of e-service quality.

THE MEANS-END CHAIN THEORY APPLIED TO THE QUALITY OF E-SERVICE

The meta-analytical review by Blut et al. (2015) aimed to develop a conceptual framework linking the different components of e-service quality to its results (see Figure 5). This framework is rooted in the theory of the means-ends chain (Gardial et al., 1994).

Drawn from the literature relating to customer satisfaction (Mittal, Ross, and Baldasare, 1998) and quality of service (Parasuraman, Zeithaml and Berry 1985), the multi-attribute approach (Blut et al. al, 2015) provides the conceptual basis for understanding the quality of e-service.

Theoretically, the multi-attribute approach is rooted in the means-ends chain theory, which describes how customers rate their consumption experiences (from specific means to more abstract ends) (Gardial et al 1994; Jung and Kang 2010; Zeithaml 1988).

The theory of the means-ends chain represents the theoretical basis for the hierarchical conceptualization of the quality of electronic service (Gardial et al., 1994, Blut et al, 2015). This theory assumes that consumers retain information about the product in memory, at several levels of abstraction (Parasuraman, Zeithaml and Malhotra, 2005). She suggests that consumers can evaluate their experiences (with an online store) in terms of very specific and concrete events (at the attribute level), which can then be synthesized and linked to higher order dimensions, the latter being relatively more abstract (Johnson, 1984, Blut, 2016). For example, customers can rate their consumer experiences in terms of very specific online store attributes, such as 'online assortment width', which can then be linked to higher order performance dimensions., such as "website design".

According to this theory, each specific attribute is associated with a higher-order dimension, and each dimension is associated with an overall higher-order summary construct, such as: the overall quality of the e-service. The overall quality of e-service is then associated with key outcomes such as customer satisfaction, customer redemption intentions and word of mouth behaviour (Parasuraman, Zeithaml and Malhotra, 2005).

According to this theory, it is essential for understanding the quality of e-service to include:

1. the different attributes included in the conceptualization of the construct,
2. the number of higher order dimensions related to the attributes, and
3. the type of relationship between attributes and dimensions, which can be either Reflective (the direction of causality is from dimensions to attributes) or formative (the direction of causality is: from attributes to dimensions). Means-ends chain theory suggests a formative relationship between attributes and dimensions, as clients evaluate attributes first before forming their more abstract judgments on different dimensions. (Blut et al, 2015, Blut, 2016)

The meta-study by Blut et al. (2015) suggests that the e-service quality construct should cover sixteen attributes that can be attributed to four dimensions.

1. The first dimension is the design of the website, which refers to all elements of the consumer experience related to the site (except customer service), including navigation, search for information, order processing, shipment tracking, product availability, product and price offerings, system customization and availability.
2. The second dimension is fulfilment, which includes activities that ensure that customers receive what they think they ordered based on the display and description offered on the website and / or the delivery of the right product. at the right price (correctly invoiced), in good condition, on time.
3. The third dimension is customer service, which refers to a helpful and responsive service that responds to customer inquiries and returns / complaints during or after the sale.
4. The fourth dimension of security / confidentiality, which is defined as the security of credit card payments and the confidentiality of information shared during or after this date.

Figure 2. Conceptualizing the quality of e-service
Source: Blut et al. 2015)

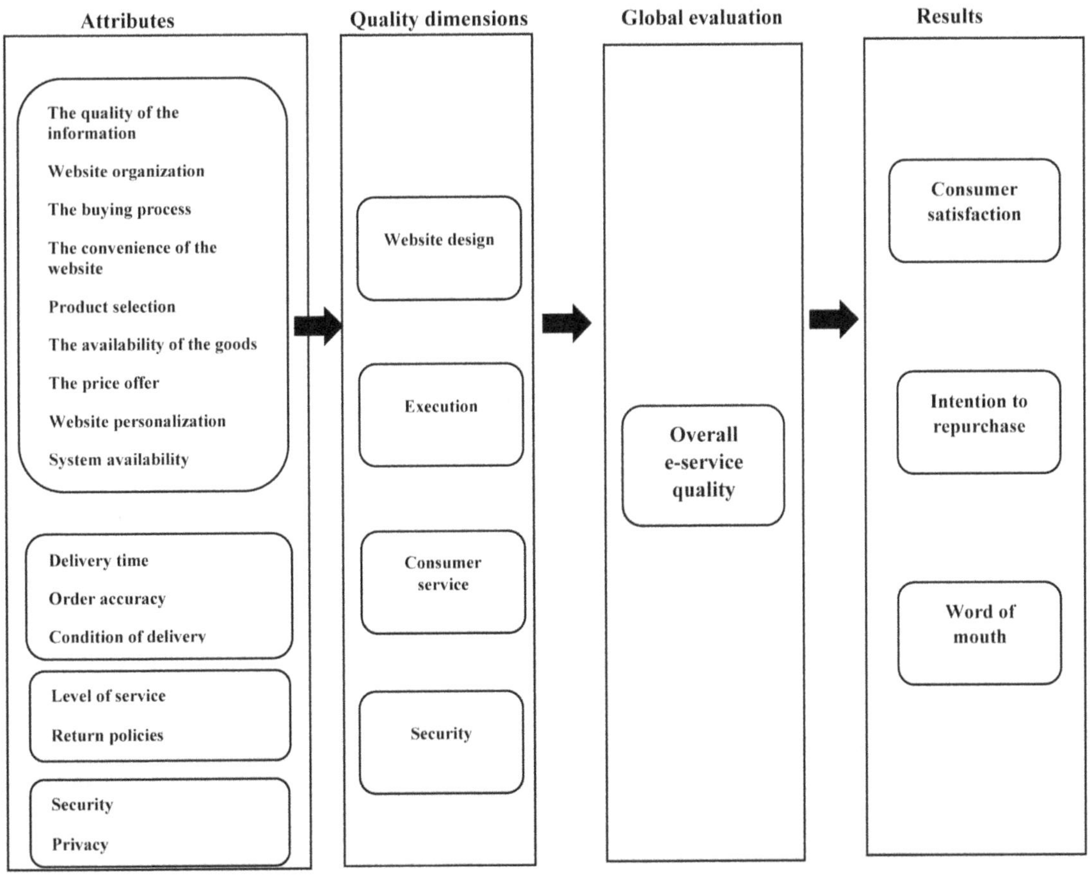

In the context of e-service, the key question is to determine the relative weight (relative importance) given to each attribute and each dimension, both conceptually and empirically. (Blut et al, 2015).

There is disagreement in the literature on the specific dimensions that make up the quality of e-service. In the basic conceptual framework, attributes are associated with dimensions. The dimensions are associated with the quality of the overall e-service, which is associated with outcomes such as customer satisfaction, redemption intentions, and word of mouth (Blut et al, 2015)

CONCLUSION

It seems essential that online merchants constantly improve the quality of their services to adequately meet the needs of their customers. To deliver superior service quality, managers need to analyse customer perceptions and their assessment of online customer service. Electronic service quality refers to "the extent to which a site facilitates the efficient and effective shopping, purchase and delivery of products or services." (Parasuraman, Zeithaml & Malhotra, 2005). The concept is defined in a way broad to encompass all phases of customer interaction with a merchant website, in this case: information research, privacy policies, website navigation, ordering process, interaction with the customer service, delivery, return policies and satisfaction with the product ordered (Wolfinbarger & Gilly, 2003).

Most researches have brought out certain predominant attributes, attesting to the functional quality of e-service, which Blut et al. Brock (2015) have synthesized into four main dimensions, namely:

1. Website design, which refers to all elements of the consumer experience related to the site (except customer service), including navigation, information search, processing orders, shipment tracking, product availability, product and price offerings, system customization and availability.
2. Fulfilment, which includes activities that ensure that customers receive what they think they ordered based on the display and description offered on the website and / or the delivery of the right product at the right price (correctly invoiced), in good condition, within the time promised.
3. Customer service, which refers to a helpful and responsive service that responds to customer inquiries and returns / complaints during or after the sale.
4. Security / confidentiality, which is defined as the security of credit card payments and the confidentiality of information shared during or after the sale.

Other authors have argued that the hedonic element or enjoyment is one of the key dimensions of e-commerce. Boulaire and Mathieu (2000), Bressolles (2002) specify that "the hedonistic state of the site is associated with the sensations, emotions and fantasies felt by an Internet user following an online experience".

The theory of the means-ends chain represents the theoretical basis for the hierarchical conceptualization of the quality of electronic service (Blut et al, 2015). This theory suggests that consumers can evaluate their experiences (on a merchant website) in terms of very specific and concrete events (at the attribute level), which can then be synthesized and linked to higher order dimensions, the latter being relatively more abstract (Blut, 2016).

REFERENCES

Adam, S., Mulye, R., & Deans, K. R. (2001). The evolution of relationships in e-marketing. In J. N. Sheth, A. Parvatiyar, & G. Shainesh (Eds.), *Customer Relationship Management: Emerging Concepts, Tools and Applications* (pp. 135–142). Tata McGraw-Hill.

Adam, S., Mulye, R., Deans, K. R., & Palihawadana, D. (2002). e-Marketing in perspective: A three country comparison of business use of the internet. *Marketing Intelligence & Planning*, *20*(4), 243–251. doi:10.1108/02634500210431649

Akıncı, S., Atılgan-Inan, E., & Aksoy, S. (2010). Re-assessment of E-S-Qual and E-RecS-Qual in a Pure Service Setting. *Journal of Business Research*, *63*(3), 232–240. doi:10.1016/j.jbusres.2009.02.018

Alonso-Almeida, Bernado, Llach, & Marimon. (2013). Building loyalty through functional and hedonic quality. *Industrial Management & Data Systems*, *114*(3), 387–404.

Bauer, H. H., Falk, T., & Hammerschmidt, M. (2006). A transaction process-based approach for capturing service quality in online shopping. *Journal of Business Research*, *59*(7), 866–875. doi:10.1016/j.jbusres.2006.01.021

Benghozi. (2003). De l'intermédiation à la prescription: le cas de la Télévision. Revue Française de Gestion, 29(402), 205-227.

Blut, M., Chowdhry, N., Mittal, V., & Brock, C. (2015). E-Service Quality: A Meta-Analytic Review. *Journal of Retailing*, *91*(4), 679–700. doi:10.1016/j.jretai.2015.05.004

Bressolles, G. (2006). La qualité de service électronique: NetQu@l Proposition d'une échelle de mesure appliquée aux sites marchands et effets modérateurs. *Recherche et Applications en Marketing*, *21*(3), 19–45. doi:10.1177/076737010602100302

Carlson, J., & O'Cass, A. (2011). Developing a framework for understanding e-service quality, its antecedents, consequences, and mediators. *Managing Service Quality*, *21*(3), 264–286. doi:10.1108/09604521111127965

Cheema, U., Rizwan, M., Jalal, R., Durrani, F., & Sohail, N. (2013). The trend of online shopping in 21st century: Impact of enjoyment in TAM model. *Asian Journal of Empirical Research*, *3*, 131–141.

Cox, J., & Dale, B. G. (2001). Service quality and e-commerce: An exploratory analysis. *Managing Service Quality*, *11*(2), 121–131. doi:10.1108/09604520110387257

Cristobal, E., Flavian, C., & Guinaliu, M. (2007). Perceived e-service quality (PeSQ) Measurement validation and effects on consumer satisfaction and web site loyalty. *Managing Service Quality*, *17*(3), 317–340. doi:10.1108/09604520710744326

Dabholkar, P. A., Shepherd, C. D., & Thorpe, D. I. (2000). AComprehensive Framework for Service Quality: An Investigation of Critical Conceptual and Measurement Issues through a Longitudinal Study. *Journal of Retailing*, *76*(2), 139–173. doi:10.1016/S0022-4359(00)00029-4

Demangeot & Broderick. (2007). Conceptualising consumer behaviour in online shopping environments. *International Journal of Retail & Distribution Management*, *35*(11), 878-894.

Eroglu, S. A., Machleit, K. A., & Davis, L. M. (2003). Empirical testing of a model of online store atmospherics and shopper responses. *Psychology and Marketing*, *20*(2), 139–150. doi:10.1002/mar.10064

Gharbi, J. (1998). *Etude des facteurs qui influencent les processus décisionnels des consommateurs lors d'un achat sur Internet* (Thèse de doctorat). Ecole des Hautes Etudes Commerciales, Université de Montréal.

Grégory, B., Francois, D., & Deans, K. R. (2015). An examination of the online service-profit chain. *International Journal of Retail & Distribution Management, 43*(5), 727–751.

Hadwich, K., Georgi, D., Tuzovic, S., Büttner, J., & Bruhn, M. (2010). Perceived quality of e-health services: A conceptual scale development of e-health service quality based on the C-OAR-SE approach. *International Journal of Pharmaceutical and Healthcare Marketing, 4*(2), 112–136. doi:10.1108/17506121011059740

Hirschman & Holbrook. (1982). Hedonic consumption: Emerging concepts, methods and propositions. *Journal of Marketing, 31*, 397-408.

Hoffman, D. L., & Novak, T. P. (1996). Marketing in hypermedia computer-mediated environments: Conceptual foundations. *Journal of Marketing, 60*(3), 50–68. doi:10.1177/002224299606000304

Holloway, B. B., & Beatty, S. E. (2008). Satisfiers and Dissatisfiers in the Online Environment: A Critical Incident Assessment. *Journal of Service Research, 10*(4), 347–364. doi:10.1177/1094670508314266

Jarvenpaa, S. L., & Todd, P. A. (1996). Consumer reactions to electronic shopping on the World Wide Web. *International Journal of Electronic Commerce, 1*(2), 59–88. doi:10.1080/10864415.1996.11518283

Khalifa, M., & Liu, V. (2007). Online consumer retention: Contingent effects of online shopping habit and online shopping experience. *European Journal of Information Systems, 16*(6), 780–792. doi:10.1057/palgrave.ejis.3000711

Ladhari, R. (2010). Developing e-service quality scales: A literature review. *Journal of Retailing and Consumer Services, 17*(6), 464–477. doi:10.1016/j.jretconser.2010.06.003

Li, Y. N., Tan, K. C., & Xie, M. (2002). Measuring web-based service quality. *Total Quality Management, 13*(5), 685–700. doi:10.1080/0954412022000002072

Lin, C.-P., & Bhattacherjee, A. (2010). Extending technology usage models to interactive hedonic technologies: A theoretical model and empirical test. *Information Systems Journal, 20*(2), 163–181. doi:10.1111/j.1365-2575.2007.00265.x

Loiacono, E. T., Watson, R. T., & Goodhue, D. L. (2000). *Webqual: a web site quality instrument*. Working paper 2000-126-0, University of Georgia.

Muller, T. E., Tse, D. K., & Venkatasubramaniam, R. (1991). Post consumption emotions: Exploring their emergence and determinants. *Journal of Consumer Satisfaction, Dissatisfaction & Complaining Behavior, 4*, 13–20.

Parasuraman, Zeithaml, & Malhotra. (2005). E-S-QUALA Multiple-Item Scale for Assessing Electronic Service Quality. *Journal of Service Research, 7*(3), 213–233. doi:10.1177/1094670504271156

Parasuraman, A., Zeithaml, V. A., & Berry, L. L. (1988). SERVQUAL: A multiple-item scale for measuring consumer perceptions of service quality. *Journal of Retailing, 64*(1), 12–40.

Rolland, S., & Freeman, I. (2010). A new measure of e-service quality in France. *International Journal of Retail & Distribution Management*, *38*(7), 497–517. doi:10.1108/09590551011052106

Rowley, J. (2006). An analysis of the service literature: Towards a research agenda. *Internet Research*, *16*(3), 339–359. doi:10.1108/10662240610673736

Shamdasani, P., Mukherjee, A., & Malhotra, N. (2008). Antecedents and consequences of service quality in consumer evaluation of self-service internet technologies. *Service Industries Journal*, *28*(1), 117–138. doi:10.1080/02642060701725669

Srinivasan, S. S., Anderson, R., & Ponnavolu, K. (2002). Customer loyalty in e-commerce: An exploration of its antecedents and consequences. *Journal of Retailing*, *78*(1), 41–50. doi:10.1016/S0022-4359(01)00065-3

Van der Heijden, H. (2004). User acceptance of hedonic information systems. *MIS Quarterly & The Society for Information Management*, *28*(4), 695–704.

Van Riel, A. C. R., Liljander, V., & Jurrie¨ns, P. (2001). Exploring consumer evaluations of e-services: A portal site. *International Journal of Service Industry Management*, *12*(4), 359–377. doi:10.1108/09564230110405280

Wolfinbarger, M., & Gilly, M. C. (2003). Etailq: Dimensionalizing, measuring and predicting etail quality. *Journal of Retailing*, *79*(3), 183–198. doi:10.1016/S0022-4359(03)00034-4

Yang, Z., Jun, M., & Peterson, R. T. (2004). Measuring customer perceived online service quality. *International Journal of Operations & Production Management*, *24*(11), 1149–1174. doi:10.1108/01443570410563278

Yang, Z., Peterson, R. T., & Cai, S. (2003). Services quality dimensions of Internet retailing: An exploratory analysis. *Journal of Services Marketing*, *17*(7), 685–701. doi:10.1108/08876040310501241

Yoo, B., & Donthu, N. (2001). Developing a scale to measure the perceived quality of an internet shopping site (SITEQUAL). *Quarterly Journal of Electronic Commerce*, *2*, 31–47.

Chapter 19
Brand Purpose and Purpose-Driven Marketing:
The New Digital

Emrah Gülmez
https://orcid.org/0000-0002-4850-9725
Anadolu University, Turkey

ABSTRACT

With the changing and transforming world, the relationship between consumers and brands began to change and transform. Nowadays, it is not enough for brands to produce quality products or provide quality service for consumers. Now, consumers expect brands to be sensitive to social, ecological, economic, or health problems. This situation has enabled the two concepts to become important and popular today: brand purpose and purpose-driven marketing. Brand purpose is the "why" the brand exists. And purpose-driven marketing is a marketing trend that aims to connect brands with their consumers through common social goals. It seems that the concepts of brand purpose and purpose-driven marketing will be more common in marketing communication. The notion of purpose will change the commercial dynamics of brands in the same way that digitalization transformed the way people buy and sell stuff. This is exactly why purpose is the new digital.

INTRODUCTION

The digitalizing world has completely changed both brands and consumers. Brands aim to attract consumers' attention and create a positive attitude towards them by using media, especially digital media. With the development of digital media, it has become easier for brands to reach and interact with consumers. On the other hand, since digital media is cheaper than conventional media and because of the advertising clutter caused by brands' infinite desire to connect with the consumers, consumers can avoid ads. Or the advertisements created by brands may disappear in the advertising crowd.

Besides all these, brands still want to create long-lasting relationships with their customers. But, consumers' expectations from brands are completely different from 10 or 20 years ago. Today, consumers

DOI: 10.4018/978-1-7998-7192-7.ch019

do not evaluate or choose a brand only with the features of its products or the prestige of using it. These factors are not enough for a brand to be preferred by consumers. In a world of nearly infinite choice, consumers increasingly base their purchasing decisions on factors beyond price and product benefit. They look to how brands articulate their ideals; not simply the corporate culture, but how they aspire to benefit customers and the world. (TED 2012 Ads Worth Spreading Report as cited in Hsu, 2017, p. 373). Especially the Millennial generation (Gen Y) and Gen Z, born into the digital world or grew up in the digital world, establish a different relationship with brands than other generations. The Millennial generation (Gen Y) and Gen Z, which are stated to be more sensitive to social events, sustainability, and the future of the world, can easily share these ideas with the whole world with the help of digital media.

Therefore, for a brand, what it produces or what service it offers to consumers is not enough in today's world. As mentioned above, consumers are different now. Nowadays, as the reflections of today's trends, they want to know everything about a corporation or a brand. The consumer's request for information can be about the contents of a product of a brand, as well as about the sustainability and environmentalism works of that brand. And especially with the help of digital media, consumers can get every information they want to know about a brand in seconds.

With the effects of all these, we are seeing a lot of prosocial consumers today. Pro-social consumers are increasingly connecting with brands that serve the purpose of making the world better. They are consuming the products of these brands and benefit from their services. Especially, through digital and social media, they are sharing and recommending these brands with other pro-social consumers with similar sensitivities.

So, the changing needs of consumers, new habits, social and environmental sensitivities, and way of perceiving the world compel brands to change, to renew their understanding of marketing, and to show more attention to consumers and the realities of the world than ever before. As Simon Sinek (2011 as cited in Hsu, 2017, p. 373) said, "People don't buy what you do; they buy why you do it. And what you do simply proves what you believe.". It seems that brands that can achieve this will continue to be in the lives of consumers in the future, too. However, it is possible to say that the future is not very bright for brands that are not concerned with the social, political, environmental, and cultural sensitivities of the consumer. Many current studies and researches confirm this situation. For example, according to global marketing, communication, and media agency Havas Media Group's Meaningful Brands 2019 Research, people wouldn't care if 77% of brands disappeared (Meaningful Brands Research Report, 2019). That means consumers say "I don't care if that brand is out of my life tomorrow". People say this for 77% of the brands they use. It's a very dramatic result for brands' future. And also considering that Havas Meaningful Brands 2019 research was conducted in 30 different countries with the participation of 350,000 consumers, including 1800 brands, it is becoming clear how serious the situation is for brands in a global sense. Besides, the Havas Media Group's Meaningful Brands research, which has been conducted since 2008, reveals that this remarkable rate of 77% has increased every year for 11 years (Akkılıç, 2020). So, many things are changing rapidly in the world of marketing globally. But before everything else, the consumers are changing, so brands have to keep up with this change.

As another result of the Meaningful Brands Research 2019, 77% of consumers prefer to buy from companies that share their values. Consumers expect brands to understand and empathize with them. They want brands to care about what they value and to protect those values (Meaningful Brands Research Report, 2019).

However, another important piece of data from Meaningful Brands Research 2019 is as follows: 55% of consumers believe companies have a more important role than governments today in creating a better future. So, while consumers are ready to give up 77% of the brands, it can be seen that their trust in brands is at least more than their trust in governments in terms of having a better future. Therefore, consumers have expectations from brands in terms of creating a better world and future. In this sense, a product or service is no longer just a product or service. It is something more than that. Consumers want more interesting, more useful, or more meaningful content/services apart from brands' usual offers. So, from Boomers to Gen Z, people expect more from brands. This situation seems to be inversely proportional to the age of the consumer. In other words, as consumers get younger, their expectations from brands increase. According to Meaningful Brands Research 2019, %63 of Boomers, %76 of Gen X, %84 of Gen Y, and %87 of Gen Z want and expect more from brands (Meaningful Brands Research Report, 2019).

One of the important areas where the footsteps of this change in consumers are heard is the Cannes Lions International Festival of Creativity, which is known as one of the world's largest creativity, advertising, and brand communication competitions and can be said to give the most prestigious award in the field of advertising. Especially, two concepts became more prominent in the festival in 2019: Brand Purpose and Creative Use of Technology. Topics such as technology, artificial intelligence, data, consumer experiences, privacy, breaking the mold, sustainability, social benefit, and diversity were on the agenda this year. But, brand purpose and creative use of technology were the star topics and headlines of the festival in 2019. In this context, it can be said that we have entered a period when the context is much more important than advertising. As mentioned above, one of the important findings of Meaningful Brands Research 2019 is that particularly the new generation consumer expects something much bigger from the product or service.

In this context, the term "Lovemark", which was created by Kevin Roberts (2005), CEO of Saatchi and Saatchi, is in a way changing shape today. Roberts' (2004) lovemark theory suggests that to create a lovemark and build customer loyalty, a company must go beyond creating a brand. According to Roberts, a lovemark is defined as a deep emotional connection that distinguishes a lovemark experience from a brand experience. Roberts asserted that lovermarks are brands, events, and experiences that people passionately love (Roberts, 2006, p. 15 as cited in Cho, 2011, p. 14). However, it can be said that the concept of lovemark has also transformed, considering that 77% of the consumers will not care if the brands disappear tomorrow, which is an important finding of the Havas Media Group Meaningful Brands 2019 research. Now, more than loving a brand, consumers want to meet with brands that have purposes similar to theirs. Consumers want brands to strive for the same or similar purposes as theirs. The task of communication and marketing professionals is to ensure that the brand is in the remaining 23%, not the 77%, which consumers would not care if the brand disappears from their life, taking into account the Havas Meaningful Brands Research.

All of these bring up the concepts of brand purpose and purpose-driven marketing. And this consumer trend has led more brands to embrace brand purpose in marketing their products to the target audience.

Within this context, in this section, the concepts of brand purpose and purpose-driven marketing, which affect all marketing/brand management and communication areas, will be discussed, and the conceptual background of these concepts will be presented with successful examples in the world.

BACKGROUND OF BRAND PURPOSE

First, let's define the concept of purpose. Spence (2009, p. 29) define purpose as a definitive statement about the difference you are trying to make in the world. In addition to this, Collins and Porras (2005 as cited in Spence, 2009, p. 28) define "core purpose" as an organization's fundamental reason for being. An effective purpose reflects the importance people attach to the company's work - it taps their idealistic motivations - and gets at the deeper reasons for an organization's existence beyond just making money.

In this context, brand purpose is brand ideal and it is an organization's inspirational and motivational reason for being, the higher-order it brings to the world (Stengel, 2011 as cited in Hsu, 2017, p. 374).

A brand's purpose explains why the brand exists and the impact it seeks to make in the world (Hsu, 2017, p. 374). It is a higher-order reason for a brand to exist than just making a profit. Besides the what, ie the company's products, and the how, ie resource planning such as defining structures, budgets, processes, etc., strategies include and usually start with the why (Kullnig, Obermüller & Aichhorn, 2020, p. 9).

As it can be seen, the "why" question is at the core of the brand's purpose. Of course, the main purpose of brands is to make a profit to survive. Because brands are not non-profit organizations. And of course, consumers are well aware of this. They don't criticize any brand with a question like "why are you making a profit?". But especially today, consumers want an answer to this question: "Why do you exist in this world and my life?".

In his book "Start With Why", Simon Sinek (2009) recommends brand and marketing professionals and also everyone to start with the question "why", as the title of the book suggests. Sinek states that people don't buy what the brands do, they buy why the brands do it and what the brands do only serves to prove that. Simon Sinek visualized this situation in a diagram called "The Golden Circle".

The concept of The Golden Circle was inspired by the golden ratio - a simple mathematical relationship that has fascinated mathematicians, biologists, architects, artists, musicians, and naturists since the beginning of history (Sinek, 2009, p. 41). Like the golden ratio, which offers evidence of order in the seeming disorder of nature, The Golden Circle finds order and predictability in human behavior. Put simply, it helps us understand why we do what we do. The Golden Circle provides compelling evidence of how much more we can achieve if we remind ourselves to start everything we do by first asking why.

You can see The Golden Circle diagram and its elements in Figure 1 (Sinek, 2009, p. 41).

As you can see above, The Golden Circle elements are listed from outside to inside as "What", "How" and "Why". Sinek has briefly defined these elements as follows (Sinek, 2009, p. 43):

- **WHAT:** Every single company and organization on the planet knows WHAT they do. This is true no matter how big or small, no matter what industry. Everyone is easily able to describe the products or services a company sells or the job function they have within that system. WHATs are easy to identify.
- **HOW:** Some companies and people know HOW they do WHAT they do. Whether we call them a "differentiating value proposition," "proprietary process" or "unique selling proposition," HOWs are often given to explain how something is different or better. Not as obvious as WHATs, many think these are the differentiating or motivating factors in a decision. It would be false to assume that's all that is required. There is one missing detail. It is exactly this:
- **WHY:** Very few people or companies can clearly articulate WHY they do WHAT they do. WHY doesn't mean to make money - that's a result. By WHY, it is meant to emphasize what is your purpose, cause, or belief? WHY does your company exist? WHY do you get out of bed every morning? And WHY should anyone care?

So, the "Why" question is important and it is the core of The Golden Circle diagram. Not only for marketing and branding but also all the phases of life, Why is a key question. So this alternative perspec-

Figure 1. The golden circle diagram

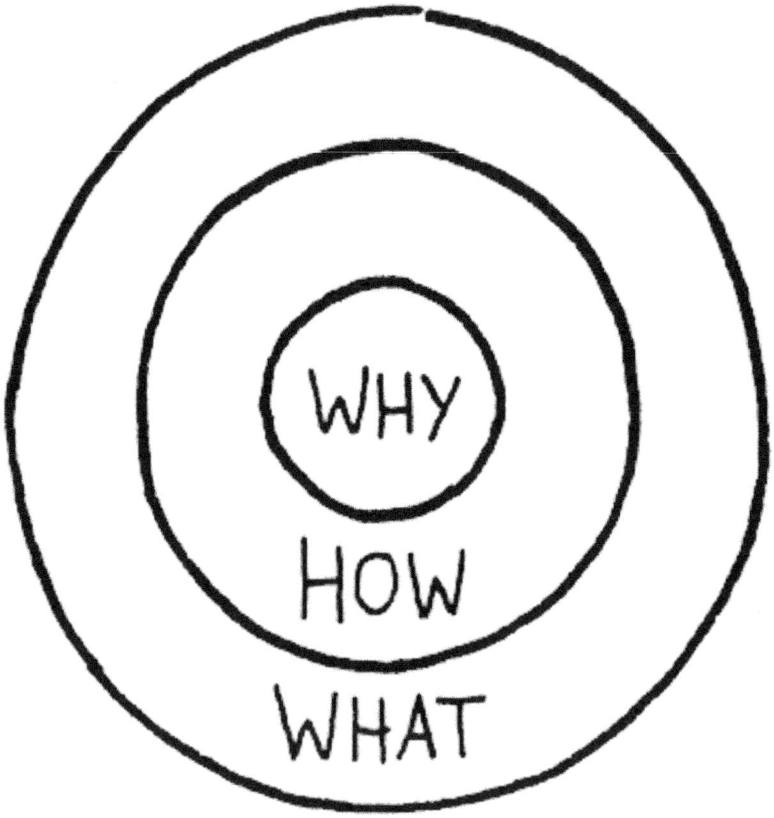

tive is not just useful for changing the world. There are practical applications for the ability to inspire, too. It can be used as a guide to vastly improving leadership, corporate culture, hiring, product development, sales, and marketing. It even explains loyalty and how to create enough momentum to turn an idea into a social movement (Sinek, 2009, p. 42).

The Golden Circle diagram is the reverse of how most brands think from a brand and marketing point of view. And, it can be said that the philosophy and approach in The Golden Circle diagram is the starting point of brand purpose. Because brands should put the Why question at their core and try to look for an answer for it.

Importance of Brand Purpose

The world of brands is getting more crowded day by day and so, competition is increasing. Nowadays, it is not easy for new brands to exist in the market as compared to 20 years ago. It can be said that this situation is valid not only for new brands but also for established brands. Competition is now much tougher for them too. For brands to differentiate themselves from their competitors and adapt to competition, they must adapt all elements of marketing management to today's conditions and consumer trends. And these upgrades, updates, and improvements need to be done in a realistic, sincere, insightful, persuasive way, not just to tick the to-do list. Because the consumer can easily understand what is sincere and what is not; who wants to draw attention to a problem to solve it or who makes it just to keep up with trends.

Today, it is not possible for brands to easily distinguish themselves from their competitors by using methods developed in the previous years. First of all, it is much more difficult for brands to find a USP (Unique Selling Proposition) for a product or service. Besides, even if a brand finds a USP (Unique Selling Proposition) for a product or service, it takes only a few months for its competitor to produce a product with similar features and almost the same quality, with the help of today's technologies. Therefore, the products have become the same. While the products are getting similar, the consumers are changing and differentiating from each other. So, positioning the brand on user personality is not effective as in the past, too. As mentioned in the introduction, it has become more important for a brand to be able to create meaning in consumers' life, especially for Gen Y and Gen Z. With identical products and poor connection with consumers, brands are having difficulty finding a place in today's world. For this reason, brands should be able to add meaning and value to the lives of consumers. This is where brand purpose comes into play.

Consumers want sincerity and integrity. Brands that determine their brand purpose appropriately and accurately can establish sincere communication with the consumers. But brands should also understand that brand purpose is not a temporary trend. Therefore, brands should not see the brand purpose as a trend but should internalize it so that they can reflect it sincerely to the consumer. Because the purpose of the brand enables brands to understand the consumer and find a place in the consumer's life. When a brand finds a place in the consumer's life, it becomes more than just a whim or a trend. It shows that as a brand, you live the same life as consumers. This means loyal customers for the brand. Because it is not possible to create customer loyalty with old methods due to changing consumer sensitivities about the world. Brand purpose also offers brands a great opportunity to achieve this.

Consumers tend to prefer brands that contribute to life, create value, in other words, have a clear brand goal. This of course also affects sales. Jim Stengel (2011, p. 15) states that the data from a ten-year-growth study of more than 50,000 brands around the world show that companies with ideals of improving people's lives at the center of all they do outperform the market by a huge margin. And also it revealed that (Aziz, 2017):

- The 50 highest-performing businesses are the ones driven by 'brand ideals' (his term for purpose).
- These 50 businesses grew three times faster than their competitors.
- An investment in them would have been 400 percent more profitable than an investment in the S&P 500.

Another example of the impact of brand purpose on sales is from Unilever. In 2015, Unilever said that "brands with purpose' are growing at twice the speed of others in their portfolio. Dove, Ben & Jerry's and Comfort were all achieving above-average growth, with high single and double-digit sales over the past three years". Paul Polman, the ex-CEO of Unilever, states that "in a volatile world of growing social inequality, rising population, development challenges and climate change, the need for businesses to adapt is clear, as are the benefits and opportunities (Spary, 2015).

Brand purpose is not only an important concept for creating customer loyalty, but also for internal communication, corporate culture, and employee management. In addition to the desire of consumers to prefer brands that add value to the world, it is seen that people also want to work for brands that add value to the world. They want to work for a company that does not only value employees' work but also has a deeper reason for being other than making a profit. And as mentioned before, it is especially true for millennials, and many research findings support this.

For example, according to one of the key findings of The Deloitte Millennial Survey (2016), millennials would prioritize the sense of purpose around people rather than growth or profit maximization. Millennials recognize that financial success is one of the elements that characterize a "leading organization," but on its own it is insufficient. Profit is combined with three others of the "Four Ps": people (employees and wider society); products; and purpose, which, in combination, provide a platform for long-term success.

And also, according to Cone Communications, 75% of millennials are willing to take a pay cut to work for a values-driven company. So when it comes to attracting and retaining purpose-driven talent, leading with "why" might be the most effective HR strategy you can deploy (Pontefract, 2017).

Another example about Millennials' work expectations in the future is Gallup's research named "How Millennials Want to Work and Live (2016). In Gallup's research, it is found that Millennials tend to particularly value certain aspects of the employee experience: Millennials don't just work for a paycheck - they want a purpose. So, for millennials, work must have meaning. Their compensation is important and must be fair, but they're motivated more by mission and purpose than a paycheck.

So, the purpose is a very effective tool for increasing employee engagement, too. As millennials now make up the largest generation in the workforce, "purpose" is becoming an important criterion for evaluating potential job choices.

As a result of all this, brand purpose is now seen as an element of the marketing mix. Not an ordinary man, Philip Kotler, a best-seller writer of marketing books, has added the Purpose as a fifth to the four Ps (product, price, place, and promotion). He explains that this is because if a company has the interest of customers, employees, and the supplier aligned to its business then it will make everyone happy thus will improve the overall profitability of the business and that is why, Purpose, should also form the core of the business (Anand, 2013). Therefore, just as brand managers strive to be holistic while shaping their brands' marketing strategies, they should also make this effort to set goals. Just as all elements of the marketing mix need to be managed in a consistent, harmonious, and supportive way, decisions about all elements should be made by considering the new element, the purpose. Therefore, the purpose must be reflected in all elements of the marketing mix.

Differences Between Purpose and Vision, Mission, Values, and Positioning

Considering that brand purpose is a relatively new concept, it can be thought that it can be confused with many concepts. In this context, it should be briefly discussed at what points it differs from the concepts of marketing and brand communication. In particular, addressing the relationship and differences between purpose and vision, mission, values, and positioning will make the concept of purpose clearer in mind.

- **Purpose:** First of all, as mentioned above, the purpose is the 'Why' the brand exists. It sits at the core of a brand's identity. It is the essence of the brand, what it stands for, the inspirational reason the brand exists beyond making a profit (Kramer, 2017 as cited in Mirzaei, Webster & Siuki, 2021, p. 2). For example, Nike's purpose is to unite the world through sport to create a healthy planet, active communities, and an equal playing field for all (Nike Official Website-Purpose, 2021).
- **Vision:** Vision is the "Where" the brand wants to get to. It's your goal, and what you expect to find when you arrive at the destination. It is your destination, at a point in the near or distant future. It is

a vivid, imaginative conception or view of the world once your purpose has been fulfilled (Spence, 2009, p. 96). For example, Ikea's vision is to create a better everyday life for many people (Ikea Official Website-Vision and Business Idea, 2021).

- **Mission:** Mission is the "What" the brand should do to get there. It addresses how to undertake a strategy to fulfill the purpose (Spence, 2009, p. 96). A mission statement tends to be internally focused on the brand, whereas a purpose statement is outwardly focused on whom the brand is trying to serve (Hsu, 2017, p. 374). For example, Nike's mission is "To bring inspiration and innovation to every athlete in the world. If you have a body you are an athlete" (Nike Official Website-About Nike, 2021).
- **Values:** Values are the "How" the brand acts to achieve its goal. Values are the 'How' the brand would like to behave to get there. What is the organizational culture of a company or an organization? And what are the qualities or behaviors it prizes (Aziz, 2017)? For example, these are Walmart's values: Service to the Customer, Respect for the Individual, Strive for Excellence, and Act with Integrity (Walmart Official Website-Values, 2021).
- **Positioning:** Positioning is "How" the brand differentiate itself from their competitors. Positioning term was firstly used by Ries and Trout in 1972. Ries and Trout wrote a three-part series of articles for Advertising Age in 1972 and the name of one of them is The Positioning Era Cometh (Ries & Trout, 1972). Then, the themes discussed in that series of articles inspired their later book, Positioning: The Battle for Your Mind published in 1981. They indicate the positioning concept of the oversimplified message is further developed into their theory of "owning a word in the mind." (Ries & Trout, 2001, p. 9).

So, as it can be seen clearly, the purpose is the core of all these marketing terms. It's the beginning of shaping your brand. So it can affect every decision about these concepts for a brand. A brand transformation firm, Brand New Purpose, has visualized all these concepts mentioned above in Figure 2 (Brand New Purpose Official Website, 2013).

Some brands express their purpose as a mission. The semantics of the label is irrelevant. What's important is that a brand's purpose shines through and elevates it into rich emotional territory. This doesn't mean that the brand doesn't have to compete on functional benefits. Of course, it does, but its purpose gives it that edge and credibility that brands without purpose lack (Madden, 2017, p. 13).

Finding the Brand Purpose

As stated in the introduction, today, it is seen that consumers expect not only quality products or services but also a purpose from brands. However, it should be noted that a brand may find its purpose not as easy as it seems. In this context, Doug Levy (2013 as cited in Wind & Hays, 2016, p. 56) suggests to the brand professionals that "to discover a brand's purpose, brand stewards must delve into what motivates them, and what role they see for the goods they put out in the world.

For the purpose to be believable, there are two fundamental checkpoints that a brand needs to deliver on: credibility and authenticity (Madden, 2017, p. 14).

Credibility is important because as said before, the purpose must be real and sincere. Consumers can easily distinguish between the real and the fake ones. For this reason, brands should not pretend to care about consumers' troubles and sensitivities; they should either really care about them or find a brand purpose that they care about.

Figure 2. Differences between purpose and vision, mission, values, and positioning

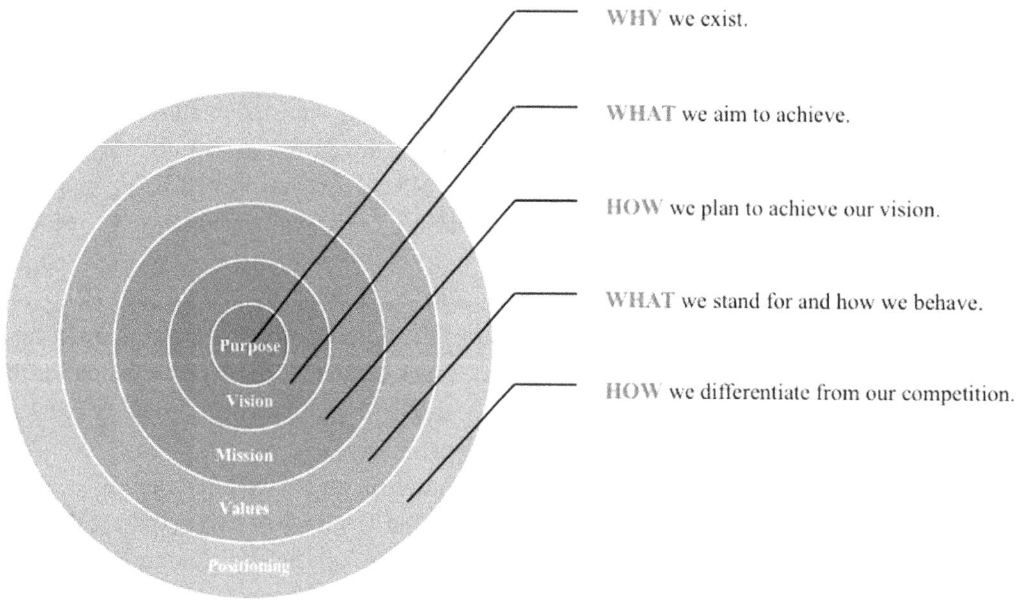

Authenticity is also an important concept in terms of brand purpose. That's why we talk about "Finding" your why rather than "Choosing" or "Strategizing" your why. Because, consumers are not excited to hear the purpose of a brand that has been voiced, owned, made by certain efforts and projects carried out by one or more brands, once again by your brand. For this reason, there is no place for the "Me, Too" strategy in the brand purpose.

Besides these, Havas Global CEO David Jones provides three simple rules for purpose-driven brands (Keohane, 2016):

- **Forget 'Image Is Everything' And Embrace 'Reality Is Everything'**

Brands need to create a reality around what they do – it does not need to be perfect, but it does need to be honest.

- **Do Good to Do Well**

Old-world Corporate Social Responsibility saw companies 'gave back' to society without a lot of concern about what they 'took out' (and how they took it out) in the first place. In the new world of Purpose-driven brands, how the business impacts its stakeholders internally and externally is baked into the operating model. Success generates profits that allow the organization to continue operating so long as its purpose remains relevant. Doing well is a by-product of doing 'good'.

- **Out Behave the Competition**

Eighty percent of brand building is through behavior, not marketing. People want to know what a company stands for, and they want to see evidence that the company is delivering on that promise.

For a new brand, establishing brand purpose can be relatively easy compared to a brand that has already been in the market for years. Afdhel Aziz (2017) describes some methodologies for a decades-old brand that has well-established attributes - but no clear brand purpose at its heart:

1. **An "Archaeological Dig":** A deep-dive into the history and heritage of the brand, the story of the founders, its reason for coming into existence in the first place.
2. **A Brand Evaluation:** Looking at a brand's strengths (what you are good at) and passions (brand passion points), and their intersection with how the brand can be of service to the world.
3. **Ask Your Employees:** Finding out the stories of why they are proud to work for your company or brand often unearths the real value that they see in the work that they do. Even if you have hundreds of thousands of employees scattered around the world, the technology exists in the form of platforms like VisionLab which allow you to collate feedback extremely quickly.
4. **Ask Your Customers:** Similarly, asking your customers (and associated stakeholders like retailers, suppliers, and other partners) can help unearth valuable insights as to the distinctive, own-able higher-order purpose for your business.

Along with the context, timing, and execution of your strategy, there needs to be a meaningful reason behind why a brand pursues a cause. This meaning is the "belief" that lies within the brand (Brand Master Academy-How to Discover Your Brand Purpose, 2019).

Michael Dale (2015) summarized the main pillars of finding brand purpose in Figure 3.

As can be seen above, the brand purpose stands at the intersection of 3 elements: What You Are Passionate About, What The World Needs, and What You Are Good At.

What you are passionate about is about finding brand passion and what you care about most. There likely are ready-made consumers that feel the same way. And it can be a good opportunity to connect to them at a deeper and emotional level.

What the world needs is about the realities of the world's today and future. It is important to truly care about the world, be able to act together, and be able to think about the future. Especially in today's world where environmental, social, political, and economic problems are seen in many parts of the world, it is necessary to seek answers to the real needs of the world.

What you are good at is about you and your brand's special talents. It is necessary to consider where else the competencies and abilities of the brand can be transferred.

By integrating these sources of research and data, a brand can uncover a compelling brand purpose that can help it future-proof itself for generations to come.

Successful Brand Purpose Examples

Many successful brands in the world define their brand purposes through the sensitivities, expectations of the consumers, the connection they have established with life, they present themselves to the consumers through these, and these presentations are appreciated by the consumers. Now let's examine a few examples of successful brands with the right brand purpose.

Figure 3. Finding brand purpose

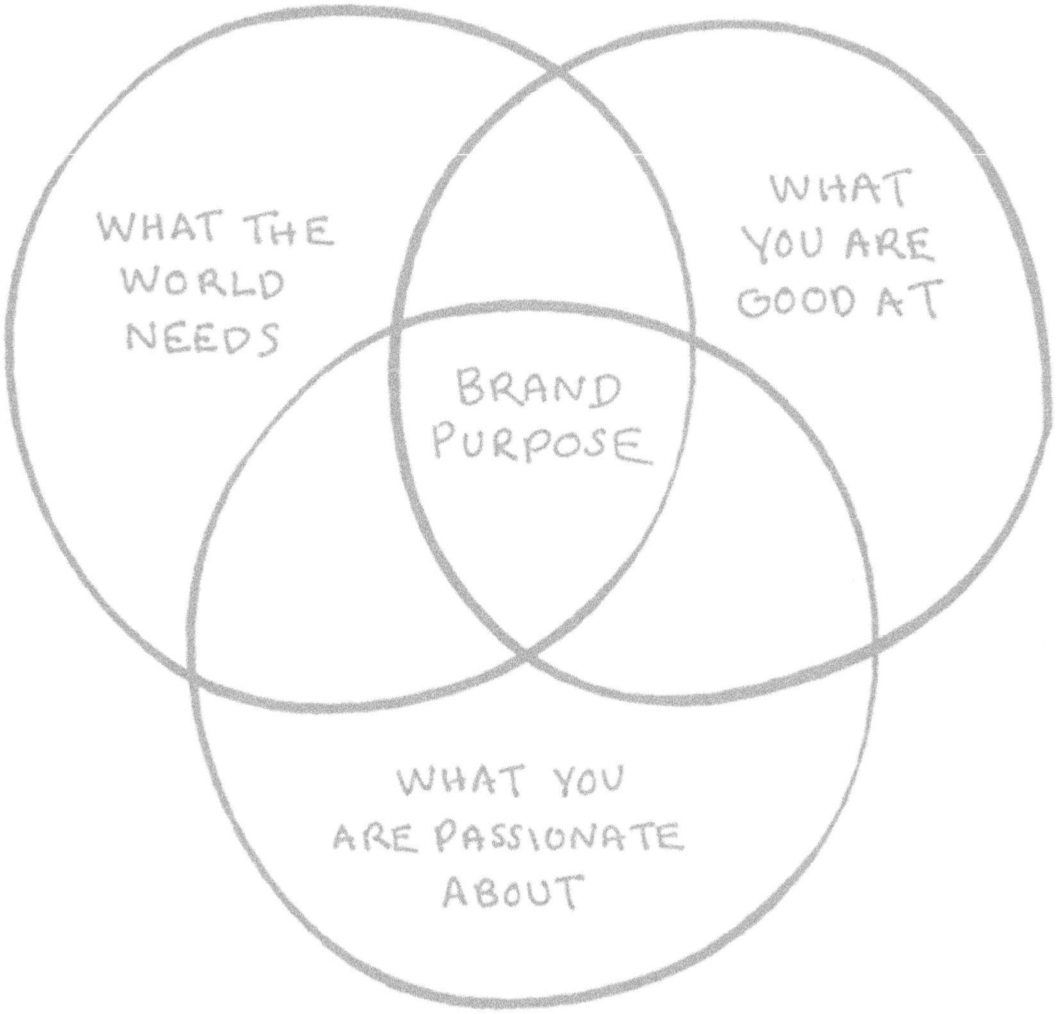

Patagonia

Patagonia is one of the best examples when it is talked about brand purpose. Patagonia, a California-based outdoor apparel and equipment company, describes itself as a designer of outdoor clothing and gear for the silent sports: climbing, surfing, skiing, and snowboarding, fly fishing, and trail running (Patagonia Official Website, 2021). It has staked its entire reputation on being a brand that lives its purpose – from its products and company culture to its support of more than 1,000 grassroots environmental organizations around the world (Rogers, 2018).

Although Patagonia's brand purpose is not clearly stated on its official website, considering all its activities, projects, and marketing practices - all of which will be mentioned in the purpose-driven marketing section - it can be said that in fact, its brand purpose is to make the world livable in the future. It is written on their official website that "At Patagonia, we appreciate that all life on earth is under threat of extinction. We're using the resources we have—our business, our investments, our voice, and our imaginations—to do something about it" (Patagonia Official Website-Business Unusual, 2021).

Figure 4. Patagonia's business unusual

So, they describe their brand as business unusual. And it can be said that it is true. Because Patagonia is in business to save our home planet (Patagonia Official Website-Business Unusual, 2021).

Nike

Nike is one of the most successful sports brands in the world. There are, of course, many reasons behind this success. However, one of the most important reasons why Nike has been able to sustain its success for many years is the importance given to the concept of brand purpose.

When entering the official website of Nike, it is seen that the "purpose" title stands alone, not under any title. When you click on the title a Purpose, it directs you to purpose.nike.com. In other words, Nike did not design a small title within its website but designed a separate micro-website to convey its brand purpose to consumers. It also has the following note at the top of the page: Purpose moves us.

Nike stated its brand purpose as follows: Our purpose is to unite the world through sport to create a healthy planet, active communities, and an equal playing field for all (Nike Official Website-Purpose, 2021).

Besides, it has stated the activities and practices it has done to achieve this goal under the titles Equality, Community, Manufacturing, Environment, Product (Nike Official Website-Purpose, 2021).

Nike is a brand that has managed to differentiate itself from rival sports brands. Nike owes this to the acceptance of the brand purpose by the consumers, that is, the brand purpose being "real" and the ability to reflect the brand purpose to the marketing communication activities.

Figure 5. Nike's brand purpose

Dove

Dove is another good example for brand purpose. Dove defines itself on its official website as "the home of real beauty". And also it is stated that "Whatever you're looking for - products to provide you with the care you need, tips and advice ranging from hair care to skincare, to underarm care – everything you see here is designed to make you feel beautiful (Dove Official Website, 2021).

It can be said that Dove's brand purpose is caring for the real beauty and life. Although not directly stated in this way, it is possible to draw this inference from what is written on the official website: "We care about all women, female-identifying and non-binary people. We want to redefine beauty standards and help everyone experience beauty and body image positively. We care about the future generation: helping girls build positive self-esteem through the Dove Self-Esteem Project, ensuring the world they enter is removed of toxic beauty standards. We care about how we make our products and what goes into them, about the impact we have on our planet and how we can strive for a better, more sustainable way of being" (Dove Official Website-About Dove, 2021).

Dove endeavors to realize its brand purpose with many projects and activities mentioned here. In particular, it continues to attract attention all over the world with its successful marketing communication works - which will be discussed in more detail in the purpose-driven marketing section - for more than 10 years.

The Body Shop

The Body Shop is a cosmetic brand, but as the Body Shop calls it "Not your average cosmetic company". It first opened its doors in 1976. Its approach to beauty was radically different from the big players in the beauty industry. It was simple – ethically sourced and naturally-based ingredients from around the

Figure 6. Dove: Care that goes further

world, in no-nonsense packaging you could easily refill. Products and beauty rituals made for every body, that made women feel good in their skin – never promising to make them look like someone else (The Body Shop Official Website-Story, 2021).

As it can be understood from above, it has a very successful brand purpose. On its official website, its brand purpose is stated as "We're a brand with a lot to say. This is what we believe". The Body Shop's brand purpose is defined as "We exist to fight for a fairer, more beautiful world. This is our purpose, and it drives everything we do. We believe in the beauty of the planet and the good in people, but our world needs work. Nature is suffering at our hands, whole species have become extinct in our lifetimes, and our society remains desperately, deeply unfair, and unequal. Today, this fight is still at the heart of everything we do" (The Body Shop Official Website-Brand Purpose, 2021).

Figure 7. Body Shop's brand purpose

The Body Shop has a nearly half a century history and is one of the rare brands that continues in the same way as it started its adventure.

Crayola

Crayola is a brand famous for its crayons and it has inspired artistic creativity in children for more than 100 years - since the first box of Crayola crayons rolled off the assembly line in 1903. Since 1903, the Crayola brand has grown into a portfolio of innovative art tools, crafting activities, and creative toys that give kids the power to express all that inspires them as they explore, discover, play, pretend, and dream (Crayola Official Website-Company, 2021).

Crayola states its brand purpose as "to help parents and educators raise creatively-alive kids". Crayola wants to help kids ask those "what if?" questions that keep them curious. So, Crayola's goal is to free the "What If?" questions in kids' minds (Crayola Official Website-Brand Essence, 2021).

Crayola explains how they do all of these (Crayola Official Website-Brand Essence, 2021):

1. First, by believing that we can help unleash the originality in every child.
2. Second, by offering tools that inspire kids to express what they're thinking.
3. Finally, to create products that will help kids free their "what if?" questions, Crayolians need to be kid-inspired.

Figure 8. Crayola's brand essence

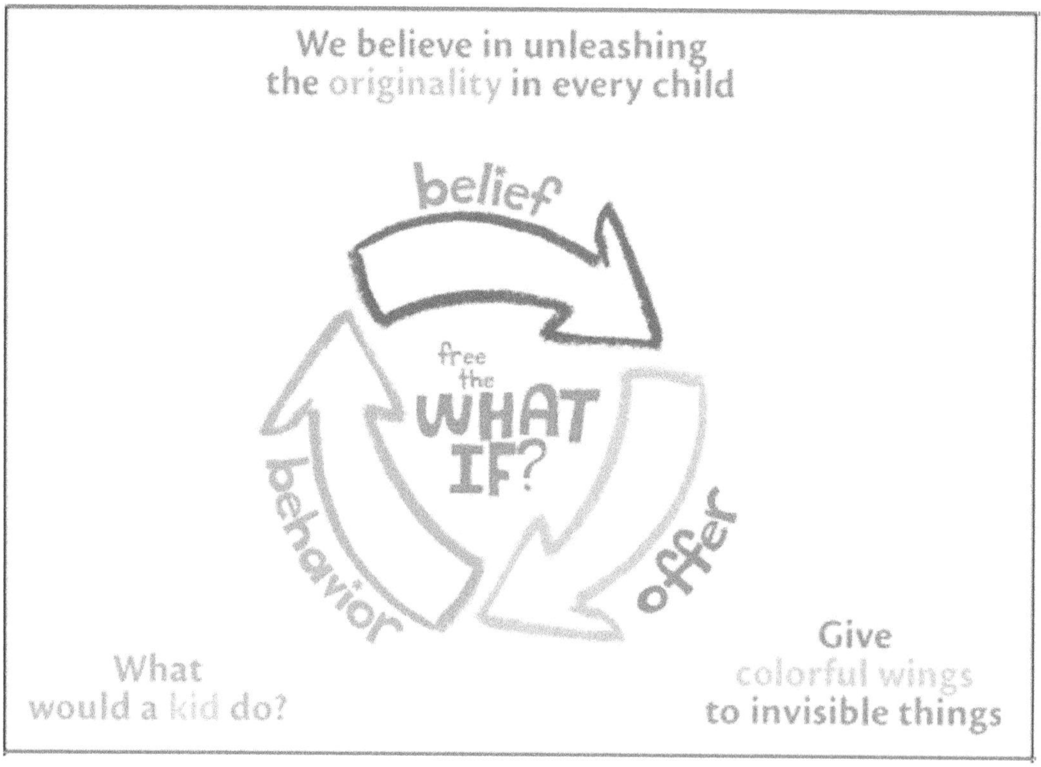

Crayola, inspires children to dream for over a century. It still invites children to step out of the ordinary and imagine the extraordinary. So Crayola believes that "What if?" is the greatest question in the world, a question that makes the impossible permissible. It's also a question that helps Crayolians think more like kids – their Nr. 1 consumer (Crayola Official Website-Brand Essence, 2021).

BACKGROUND OF PURPOSE-DRIVEN MARKETING

Philip Kotler (2011) indicates that consumers may be the major driving force that pressures companies to change their marketing practices as consumers share Word of Mouth information through blogging, tweeting, and emailing about positive and negative behaviors of companies. He states that companies move from Marketing 1.0, the period when they view consumers choosing brands based on functionality, to Marketing 2.0 where the choice is made on emotional criteria, and now, to Marketing 3.0 with the emphasis on companies' social responsibility. Because now, consumers demand that the brand they bought have a common purpose with them, and more importantly, brands take an active role in social problems. So, Kotler, Kartajaya, and Setiawan (2010) call Marketing 3.0 the value-driven era, which recognizes consumers as value-driven people with minds, hearts, and spirits and as potential collaborators. Also, the objective of Marketing 3.0 is to make the world a better place as the Millennials.

In this context, marketing efforts are also changing shape. It is not enough for a brand to adopt the concept of brand purpose, which is explained in detail in the first chapter; that brand must be able to convey the brand's purpose to consumers. This brings up the concept of purpose-driven marketing.

Purpose-driven marketing is a marketing trend that aims to connect brands with their consumers through their brand purpose. It is a type of marketing where the brand connects with its customers on causes they both believe in. The brand's messaging aligns with the customer's beliefs and, in turn, that customer believes in and supports that brand.

In purpose-driven marketing, the aim is to introduce the brand purpose to the consumers with certain marketing and marketing communication efforts. Therefore, for a brand to realize a purpose-driven marketing practice, it must establish a brand purpose by making strategic decisions in terms of brand management.

Of course, there are lots of purpose-driven marketing tools, but one of the most preferred by brands is ads. According to the ad ratings service database of advertisement effectiveness agency, System1, in November 2018, purpose-driven ads were often emotional winners, particularly in the US market (Ewing, 2018). It can be said that this is not a temporary situation according to System1 research findings. It is indicated that the last few years have seen a surge of interest in the idea of brand purpose - the belief that global brands have a wider positive role to play in society and that embracing this will be an effective form of long-term marketing (System1 Official Blog, 2018). And also another research by System1 reveals that one in five of the most powerful TV ads now focuses on "brand purpose", with 20% of the most effective and emotive ads from 100 marketing categories in the UK and US linking company brand to a wider cause (Everett, 2019).

Of course, the effectiveness of the ads will vary depending on many factors. However, it can be said that an advertisement made within the scope of purpose-driven marketing by a brand that has determined its brand purpose accurately and realistically, finds a response in the consumers.

Certainly, as mentioned earlier, advertising as a promotional tool is the most visible and most interesting, but only one of the instruments that can be used for purpose-driven marketing. A brand should be able to reflect the brand purpose to all elements of 4Ps, the marketing mix. In other words, product, price, placement, and promotion decisions should be made with the brand purpose in mind.

One of the successful examples in which the product is handled within the scope of purpose-driven marketing is The Body Shop, which is also mentioned under the title of successful brand purpose examples. The Body Shop states the features of its products on its official website as follows: "We create naturally-inspired beauty products from sustainably sourced ingredients from all around the world. We always stand up and campaign for what's right." (The Body Shop Official Website-Company (2021).

Figure 9. The Body Shop ingredients map

And also, Patagonia can be shown as a successful example where the price is handled within the scope of purpose-driven marketing. Since 1985, Patagonia has pledged 1% of sales to the preservation and restoration of the natural environment. They stated that "We give back for every sale. We've pledged 1% of sales to the preservation and restoration of the natural environment.". Also, in 2002, they created a non-profit corporation, 1% for the Planet, to encourage other businesses to do the same (Patagonia Official Website-One Percent For the Planet, 2021). So, Patagonia's customers know that 1% of the money they pay for any Patagonia product is used for a good cause.

Figure 10. Patagonia %1 for the planet program

Besides, Amazon is a good example for place and distribution. In addition to using many elements of the marketing mix correctly, Amazon is also one of the most sustainable and innovative brands in distribution. Amazon is trying to build the most sustainable transportation fleet in the world. In support of The Climate Pledge, Amazon is committed to achieving net-zero carbon across its operations by 2040, a decade ahead of the Paris Agreement. To achieve this goal, Amazon is transforming its transportation network. Along with custom electric delivery vehicles, Amazon is exploring new technologies, alternative fuels, and delivery methods that deliver packages to customers in a more sustainable way. Amazon currently operates thousands of electric vehicles worldwide and is redesigning its delivery stations to service electric vehicles—ranging from the electrical design to the physical layout. Last year, Amazon delivered more than 20 million packages to customers in electric delivery vehicles across North America and Europe and will continue building on that momentum in 2021 (Amazon Official Website-News, 2021). So 100,000 electric delivery vans which are just made for Amazon's distribution network, will save millions of metric tons of carbon per year.

Examples of purpose-driven marketing concepts in terms of promotion will be given in the following pages.

Differences Between Purpose-Driven Marketing and Cause Marketing and Corporate Social Responsibility

Purpose-driven marketing and cause marketing and corporate social responsibility may seem interchangeable, of course, they have some differences from each other.

First of all, cause marketing is, for the most part, against something. Purpose, on the other hand, tends to lean into support for something. Many brands are against environmental pollution, but Seventh Generation's purpose is to help people live a more natural and chemical-free life. A major retailer may sponsor the Sierra Club's efforts against deforestation; Patagonia makes saving the environment its corporate mission (Lenderman, 2015).

Figure 11. Amazon's custom electric delivery vehicle

Also, cause marketing is usually short-term and campaign-driven. It's like when a brand chooses a charitable cause for a period of, say, a month and promotes that cause during the campaign. The brand may partner with a charity they support and collect proceeds or donate proceeds via their business (Frieman, 2020). On the other hand, purpose is a long term strategy and it is not just campaign-driven. It is an essential principle rooted in a brand (Hsu, 2017, p. 373).

Besides, cause marketing historically relies on corporate giving, whereas for many up-and-coming companies today, purpose lies at the heart of their entire business model. Purpose-driven brands incorporate beliefs and values into the very core of their business. They are baked into the culture, business operations, and long-term initiatives. A purpose is re-interpretable in nearly countless ways. It may or may not be tied to a specific cause. Often, it is broader and more aspirational (Kopervas, 2019).

Where cause marketing is "tacked on" to a brand, purpose is part of the blueprint. It is foundational. The associated mission is not a single goal that can be achieved simply. It's something that lends itself to numerous smaller goals that contribute to a larger ongoing effort. Purpose infuses business decisions with a particular ethos that can take many forms (Kopervas, 2019). So, purpose is bigger than cause.

Besides, corporate social responsibility is defined as "context-specific organizational actions and policies that take into account stakeholders' expectations and the triple bottom line of economic, social, and environmental performance." (Aguinis, 2011, p. 855 as cited in Aguinis & Glavas, 2012, p. 933). Also, The Financial Times defines corporate social responsibility as "a business approach that contributes to sustainable development by delivering economic, social and environmental benefits for all stakeholders." The key point is "sustainable development." (Pontefract, 2017). On the other hand, of course, sustainability is important but an organization does not solely stand for improving sustainable development. In this manner, purpose is "broader" than corporate social responsibility. As already said many times, it is what a brand stands for. It ought to be thought of as how it provides its various services in totality (Pontefract, 2017).

Cause marketing or corporate social responsibility practices can be outputs of a good brand purpose. However, these are tools that will have an effect on their own for a short time or only for solving a particular problem. As mentioned before Purpose-driven marketing is a long-term strategy and it has a broader scope. As already said, a great purpose should manifest itself in everything a brand does: from product development to customer experience, to how it should conduct its marketing.

Purpose-Washing

While talking about the concept of purpose-driven marketing, we should mention another new concept related to this concept: Purpose-washing.

Purpose-washing refers to presenting your brand as if it operates according to a larger purpose when in reality it only operates to serve itself (McGilvary, 2020).

As stated earlier, purpose is about beliefs. When a purpose that has not been internalized by the whole organization is turned into marketing activity, it cannot be expected that consumers will not feel it's fake. In other words, any marketing activity that is done to show off eyes and gain sympathy will not only be ineffective but will also negatively affect the current perception and image of consumers. Because consumers expect empathy, not sympathy from brands. Consumers want a sincere approach to the joys, happiness, expectations, worries, sadness, and anger they experience in their daily lives.

So, as Carolyn Tate, writer of the Purpose Project indicates that just because a company has a purpose statement does not mean they're on purpose. Having a purpose statement is one thing. Truly believing in it and activating it is quite another. When the 'purpose promise' does not match the 'purpose experience' there's a very real risk that it will be seen as a pithy advertising line instead of the raison d'être. An investment in purpose can actually do more harm than good if it's not brought to life (Tate, 2016). And all your efforts can easily turn into a purpose-washing.

When a purpose comes from a place, a genuine place, an organization realizes the negative impact that they are having on the earth and does something about it. Unfortunately, because of the diminishing trust caused by organizations 'washing,' their audience with messages of do-goodery- genuine good is being lost in the noise (Rees-Rogers, 2019).

Examples of Successful Purpose-Driven Marketing Practices

As stated before, there are very successful brand purpose examples. But one of the most important things for a brand is meeting its purpose with consumers. To achieve this, the most important tool of brands is of course purpose-driven marketing practices. Let's briefly examine some successful purpose-driven marketing practices.

Patagonia: Worn Wear

As stated in successful brand purpose examples, Patagonia is a very good example of brand purpose. Patagonia's brand purpose is to make the world livable in the future. In their words, Patagonia is in business to save our home planet (Patagonia Official Website-Business Unusual, 2021).

Patagonia is good at purpose-driven marketing practices, also. After the legendary campaign, "Don't Buy This Jacket" as part of its "Common Threads Initiative", Patagonia announced its experiential marketing initiative, Worn Wear Program. It started in 2017 and is still going on.

Worn Wear program practices and promotes sustainability by offering free repair services, online repair tutorials, discounts for trading in used Patagonia brand apparel, and opportunities to share stories of one's adventures in repaired or long-lived garments through its micro-website, wornwear.patagonia.com. Also, they made a film about this campaign named Worn Wear – a Film About the Stories We Wear (Patagonia Official Youtube Channel- Worn Wear: a Film About the Stories We Wear, 2021).

At Worn Wear Program, Patagonia encourages consumers' emotional attachment to their products and the relationship of those products with their lives (Simpson, 2015 as cited in Michel and et al., 2019, p. 166). Through the Worn Wear Program, customers were encouraged to take pride in the signs of wear on their apparel by learning how to mend tears from sewing tutorials on its website. Free repairs were offered via a mobile pop-up to events across the United States and Europe. A truck equipped with sewing machines, supplies, and staff skilled in the refurbishing of clothing provided repairs to the apparel of any brand and stimulated interest in Patagonia and its initiatives (Michel and et al., 2019, p. 166).

Besides these, there is a shopping section named Recrafted Collection in the Worn Wear website where Patagonia puts together used clothes for sale (Patagonia Official Website-Worn Wear Recrafted, 2021). So, these are clothes made from other clothes. There is also another section for products that have some sort of flaws and defections, which is named Seconds Collection and Patagonia sells the products in this section by "Everybody Makes Mistakes" message (Patagonia Official Website-Worn Wear Seconds, 2021).

All of these are accurate and creative purpose-driven marketing practices that integrate with the brand purpose successfully.

The Body Shop: Forever Against Animal Testing

The Body Shop was already stated many times in this chapter. To recap, The Body Shop's brand purpose is defined as "We exist to fight for a fairer, more beautiful world. This is our purpose, and it drives everything we do. We believe in the beauty of the planet and the good in people, but our world needs work. Nature is suffering at our hands, whole species have become extinct in our lifetimes, and our society remains desperately, deeply unfair, and unequal. Today, this fight is still at the heart of everything we do" (The Body Shop Official Website-Brand Purpose, 2021).

So, to make all these real, The Body Shop made lots of campaigns, programs, and projects. They listed all of them under the title of Our Activism (The Body Shop Official Website-Activism, 2021). And their last campaign is Forever Against Animal Testing. They started this campaign in 2017 and the campaign is still going on.

At Forever Against Animal Testing campaign, The Body Shop and Cruelty Free International are working towards a worldwide ban on animal-tested cosmetics… forever (The Body Shop Official Website-Forever Against Animal Testing, 2021).

Figure 12. Patagonia worn wear tour poster
Source: (Patagonia Official Website-Business Unusual, 2021)

Figure 13. Forever against animal testing sign the petition poster
Source: The Body Shop, 2018

Forever Against Animal Testing campaign was met with an intense response and reached huge success. On October 4th, 2018, World Animal Day, The Body Shop and Cruelty Free International took 8.3 million signatures against cosmetic animal testing to the United Nations Headquarters in New York

City, to create a global framework to end animal testing while advancing the United Nations' sustainable development agenda (The Body Shop Official Website-Forever Against Animal Testing, 2021).

The celebration of these signatures is a culmination of more than 30 years of advocacy between The Body Shop and Cruelty Free International. The joint effort is the most ambitious campaign ever against cosmetic animal testing and serves as a model to inspire action from businesses, governments, and citizens. The petition signatures, collected from supporters around the world in just 15 months, call on the countries of the UN to formalize an international framework to end cosmetic animal testing, everywhere and forever (The Body Shop Official Website-Forever Against Animal Testing, 2021).

Also, through Forever Against Animal Testing campaign, The Body Shop wants to engage their consumers which are more connected and concerned about the campaign. It is also supported by the series make up The Body Shop which is a product that is 100% Cruelty Free Make Up. To avoid using animals, The Body Shop uses poor technology using synthetic leather in testing its products, both cosmetics, body treatments, and skincare (Manggiasih, 2019, p. 40).

Warby Parker: Buy A Pair, Give a Pair

Warby Parker is a glasses brand that can be called young. The brand goal of Warby Parker, which was founded in 2010, is very clear: To offer people glasses at affordable prices. Because everyone has the right to see. The brand explains its purpose exactly as follows: "We believe that buying glasses should be easy and fun. It should leave you happy and good-looking, with money in your pocket. We also believe that everyone has the right to see." (Warby Parker Official Website-History, 2021).

To achieve this goal, they launched a program named "Buy A Pair, Give a Pair". They explain the reason for the realization of this program as follows. "Almost one billion people worldwide lack access to glasses, which means that 15% of the world's population cannot effectively learn or work. To help address this problem, Warby Parker partners with non-profits like VisionSpring to ensure that for every pair of glasses sold, a pair is distributed to someone in need (Warby Parker Official Website-History, 2021).

To help address the problem as mentioned, they work with a handful of partners worldwide to ensure that for every pair of Warby Parker glasses purchased, a pair of glasses is distributed to someone in need. There are two models they employ (Warby Parker Official Website-Buy A Pair Give A Pair, 2021).

1. Empowering adult men and women with training opportunities to administer basic eye exams and sell glasses for ultra-affordable prices (This accounts for the majority of their distribution).
2. Directly giving vision care and glasses to school-age children in their classrooms, where teachers are often the first to spot issues.

"Buy a Pair, Give a Pair" program continues and it has been so successful that over eight million pairs of glasses have been distributed through the program (Warby Parker Official Website-Buy A Pair Give A Pair, 2021).

Effects of Digital Transformation on Purpose-Driven Marketing

In the 80s and 90s, communication between consumers and brands was one way. Brands used to present their promises to consumers through their advertisements. Consumers' attitudes towards these advertisements could only be measured by post-test research. So, brands would evaluate their advertisements with

Figure 14. Buy a pair, give a pair program by Warby Parker
Source: Warby Parker, 2013

tests made to very few people. Therefore, consumers probably had a lot to say in this communication, but there was no channel to make their voices heard. The voice of the consumer was small, whispering, and could be talked over quite easily or simply be ignored. Then, the digital revolution came along and conversations went online which started in the beloved 90s' chat rooms like mIRC, AOL, etc. Then, consumers started talking about everything including ads, too. They started to voice their opinions and they quickly realized the power in their numbers. In just a few years, with the advent of social media, especially Facebook and Twitter, consumers' voices became heard much more. And with this digital transformation, brands couldn't ignore this.

Digital transformation encompasses the profound changes taking place in society and industries through the use of digital technologies (Agarwal et al., 2010; Majchrzak et al., 2016 as cited in Vial, 2019, p. 118). It is the holistic transformation of humans, business processes, and technology that provide more effective and more efficient services in line with the opportunities provided by rapidly developing information technologies and changing social needs.

Digital transformation is a concept that completely changes business processes from marketing to sales, from production to human resources. The state, the private sector, and individuals, in short, everyone is actually a part of this change.

So, both consumers and brands have changed by digital transformation. Digital media, mobile and social media are some of the digital transformation technologies and as it is said before, consumers can communicate with each other easily by using them. They have the chance to express their opinions and share them via social media tools.

Brands, on the other hand, started to take place on social media institutionally. They started to communicate with consumers through their official Twitter, Facebook, and Instagram accounts. Thanks to social media, they had the opportunity to receive feedback from consumers on many issues from their marketing communication applications to their new products. They presented their new Ad or PR campaigns to consumers via social media as well as conventional media. In fact, after a while, they produced "works" just for social media, not for conventional media.

On the other hand, consumers' - especially the Millennials- opinions sometimes relate to the social, economic, political, etc. problems in the world, sometimes to brands, and sometimes to both. As they share their sensitivities, desires, and reactions about social and economic problems in the world, their future, and the future of the world on social media, it has been necessary for brands not to remain silent on this issue and to do something about them. The rising voice of the Millennials, who have a high interest and sensitivity towards these issues, on social media have forced the brands to take action.

And with the cumulative effect of this whole process, brands could not ignore the sensitivities of consumers. First of all, brands either determined the brand purpose according to zeitgeist or revised the brand purpose. Later, brands started to carry out communication and marketing practices to achieve this brand goal. The cultural and sociological effects of this digital transformation as well as the technological, combined with the power of social media and the sensitivities of the Millennials, and the concept of purpose-driven marketing has become one of the most important concepts of recent times.

For this reason, digital transformation, especially digital media, mobile and social media, which are digital transformation technologies, have a great impact on purpose-driven marketing. Any communication and marketing activity carried out by brands within the scope of purpose-driven marketing can be found on social media. Even brands can perform these activities using social media and digital media tools.

Finally, as Raja Rajamannar (2021), Mastercard Chief Marketing and Communications Officer said, "purpose-driven marketing is an increasingly important differentiator. With so many digital platforms for a brand to showcase its values, engaging new technologies will multiply the impact". With the emergence of new technologies and new channels, digital transformation will continue and purpose-driven marketing will take place in brand new channels.

CONCLUSION

In the new era, conscious consumers and increasing competition conditions encourage companies to pay more attention to social problems. Protecting natural resources that were unconsciously consumed in the past, preventing environmental pollution, using production techniques that respect animal rights, and supporting each individual to have equal living conditions have now become the target of not only governments or non-governmental organizations, but also brands.

So, these situations have brought out the "brand purpose" and "purpose-driven marketing" concepts. As stated before, brand purpose is the purpose of a brand to exist. It is the answer to the question of why the brand exists. Beyond the usual brand definitions, it is what contributes to society, life, and the world in terms of cultural, economic, political, and social aspects. Purpose-driven marketing, on the other hand, is the marketing practices made by the brand to realize brand purpose.

It seems that the concepts of brand purpose and purpose-driven marketing are being discussed at an increasing level by marketing and brand communication practitioners. The concept of "brand purpose", which also marked the Economist session of Cannes Lions 2019, will be the one the industry discusses the most in the coming years. Due to the sensitivities and interests of the consumer, especially Gen Y and Gen Z, which differ sharply from other generations, it seems that more attention will be drawn to issues such as finding the right purpose for a brand, being able to inject the purpose into the veins of the brand, actualizing the purpose and infusing it into the consumers. Therefore, it is obvious that in the coming years, marketing and brand practitioners will seek answers to questions to be asked on these issues.

On the other hand, this search should not make brands fall into the purpose-washing trap. Brand purpose is important not only in terms of the marketing and branding world, but also in terms of really caring about the world, acting together, and thinking about the future. Especially in today's world where environmental, social, political, and economic problems are seen in many places, brands should deal with these issues sincerely. Brands should not pretend to care about these issues. These problems should really, sincerely be cared about so that the consumer can internalize the brand and the brand does not purpose-wash with its campaign.

A purpose-led brand has to live up to its purpose. Its purpose becomes a guiding light in everything the brand does. It gives the brand immense focus and a long-term vision. It also provides a clear competitive edge against brands that focus primarily on product differentiation (Madden, 2017, p. 14). A higher purpose is like a higher power. It's both inside us and outside of us. It's both the guiding north-star, ever-present yet never reachable, and it's also the glue of the organization, the thing that drives strategy and that drives every company decision. A higher purpose is about the betterment of humankind and mother earth. It's noble, just, moral, and ethical (Tate, 2016). A great purpose should manifest itself in everything a brand does: from product development to customer experience, from placement strategy to how it should conduct its marketing.

It should also be added that brand purpose is not a law. It can change with time. Also, the purpose doesn't have to be about massive problems such as social justice, climate change, or inequality. Brands have the opportunity to solve problems from the 'every day to the epic' (Aziz & Jones, 2016).

Besides all these, so, as Max Lenderman (2015) said, "purpose is the new digital." The notion of purpose will change the commercial dynamics of brands in the same way that digital transformed (and is still transforming) the way people buy and sell stuff. In other words, just like marketers had to learn to grapple with the massive implications of digital, we need to understand the profound implications of purpose which are equally transformative.

REFERENCES

Agarwal, R., Gao, G., DesRoches, C., & Jha, A. K. (2010). Research commentary -The digital transformation of healthcare: Current status and the road ahead. *Information Systems Research*, *21*(4), 796–809. doi:10.1287/isre.1100.0327

Aguinis, H. (2011). Organizational responsibility: Doing good and doing well. In S. Zedeck (Ed.), *APA handbook of industrial and organizational psychology* (Vol. 3, pp. 855–879). American Psychological Association. doi:10.1037/12171-024

Aguinis, H., & Glavas, A. (2012). What we know and don't know about corporate social responsibility: A review and research agenda. *Journal of Management*, *38*(4), 932–968. doi:10.1177/0149206311436079

Akkılıç, S. (2020). *Anlamlı Marka Olabilmek, Kalabalıkların Kültürü ve Anti-Prensesler...* http://serhatakkilic.com/2020/01/anlamli-marka-olabilmek-kalabaliklarin-kulturu-ve-anti-prensesler/

Amazon Official Website-News. (2021). https://www.aboutamazon.com/news/transportation/amazons-custom-electric-delivery-vehicles-are-starting-to-hit-the-road

Anand, N. (2013). *Kotler adds a 5th P to his set of four – Purpose.* https://www.dnaindia.com/business/report-kotler-adds-a-5th-p-to-his-set-of-four-purpose-1812393

Aziz, A. (2017). *Brand Purpose 101: Everything you wanted to know but were afraid to ask.* https://medium.com/@afdhelaziz/brand-purpose-101-everything-you-wanted-to-know-but-were-afraid-to-ask-21593fb37d33

Aziz, A., & Jones, B. (2016). *Good Is the New Cool: Market Like You Give a Damn.* Regan Arts.

Brand Master Academy-How to Discover Your Brand Purpose. (2019) https://brandmasteracademy.com/brand-purpose/#discover

Brand New Purpose Official Website. (2013). http://brandnewpurpose.com

Cho, E. (2011). Development of a brand image scale and the impact of lovemarks on brand equity. *Graduate Theses and Dissertations.* 11962. Available at https://lib.dr.iastate.edu/etd/11962, doi:10.31274/etd-180810-4450

Collins, J. C., & Porras, J. I. (2005). *Built to last: Successful habits of visionary companies.* Random House.

Crayola Official Website-Brand Essence. (2021).https://www.crayola.com/about-us/company/brand-essence.aspx

Crayola Official Website-Company. (2021). https://www.crayola.com/about-us/company.aspx

Dale, M. (2015). *How to uncover your brand purpose.* https://medium.com/@firebrand_design/how-to-uncover-your-brand-purpose-9dc420e550f1

Dove Official Website. (2021). https://www.dove.com/us/en/home.html

Dove Official Website-About Dove. (2021). https://www.dove.com/us/en/stories/about-dove.html

Everett, C. (2019). *'Brand purpose' delivering ad impact but Nike dissent demonstrates its dangers.* https://www.mycustomer.com/marketing/strategy/brand-purpose-delivering-ad-impact-but-nike-dissent-demonstrates-its-dangers

Ewing, T. (2018). *10 Insights From Ad Ratings.* https://system1group.com/blog/ad-ratings-has-arrived-10-effectiveness-insights-from-system1s-new-service

Frieman, E. (2020). *Cause marketing vs purpose-driven marketing.* https://keymedium.com/cause-marketing-vs-purpose-driven-marketing

How Millennials Want to Work and Live. (2016). https://www.gallup.com/workplace/238073/millennials-work-live.aspx

Hsu, C. K. J. (2017). Selling products by selling brand purpose. *Journal of Brand Strategy, 5*(4), 373–394.

Ikea Official Website-Vision and Business Idea. (2021). https://www.ikea.com/gb/en/this-is-ikea/about-us/vision-and-business-idea-pub9cd02291

Keohane, K. (2016), *The Case For Purpose Driven Brands.* https://www.brandingstrategyinsider.com/the-case-for-purpose-driven-brands/#.YBl3oHczZn5

Kopervas, G. (2019). *Cause Marketing vs. Purpose-Driven Brands.* https://www.20nine.com/cause-marketing-vs-purpose-driven-brands

Kotler, P. (2011). 'Reinventing marketing to manage the environmental imperative'. *Journal of Marketing, 75*(4), 132–135. doi:10.1509/jmkg.75.4.132

Kotler, P., Kartajaya, H., & Setiawan, I. (2010). *Marketing 3.0: From Products to Customers to the Human Spirit.* John Wiley & Sons, Inc. doi:10.1002/9781118257883

Kramer, M. (2017). Brand purpose: The navigational code for growth. *Journal of Brand Strategy, 6*(1), 46–54.

Kullnig, C., Obermüller, A., & Aichhorn, K. (2020). Improving campaign performance using purpose marketing: Case study of Run For The Oceans. *Journal of Brand Strategy, 9*(1), 7–17.

Lenderman, M. (2015). *Cause vs. Purpose: What's the Difference?* https://sustainablebrands.com/read/product-service-design-innovation/cause-vs-purpose-what-s-the-difference

Levy, D. (2013). My View of the Future. *WFoA Advertising 2020 Project.* https://wfoa.wharton.upenn.edu/perspective/douglevy/

Madden, C. B. (2017). *Path to Purpose.* Sunday Lunch Pty Ltd.

Majchrzak, A., Markus, M. L., & Wareham, J. (2016). Designing for digital transformation: Lessons for information systems research from the study of ICT and societal challenges. *Management Information Systems Quarterly, 40*(2), 267–277. doi:10.25300/MISQ/2016/40:2.03

Manggiasih, S. S. D. P. (2019). Public relations campaign "Forever against animal testing" by the body shop. *International Journal of Humanities and Social Science Research., 5*(3), 39–44.

McGilvary, L. (2020). *How to avoid purpose-washing and create a more purposeful brand.* https://adage.com/article/industry-insights/how-avoid-purpose-washing-and-create-more-purposeful-brand/2270546

Meaningful Brands Research Report. (2019). https://s3.amazonaws.com/media.mediapost.com/uploads/MeaningfulBrands2019.pdf

Michel, G. M., Feori, M., Damhorst, M. L., Lee, Y. A., & Niehm, L. S. (2019). Stories we wear: Promoting sustainability practices with the case of Patagonia. *Family and Consumer Sciences Research Journal, 48*(2), 165–180. doi:10.1111/fcsr.12340

Mirzaei, A., Webster, C. M., & Siuki, H. (2021). Exploring brand purpose dimensions for non-profit organizations. *Journal of Brand Management*, 1–13.

Nike Official Website-About Nike. (2021). https://about.nike.com

Nike Official Website-Purpose. (2021). https://purpose.nike.com

Patagonia Official Website. (2021). https://www.patagonia.com/home

Patagonia Official Website-Business Unusual. (2021). https://www.patagonia.com/business-unusual

Patagonia Official Website-One Percent For the Planet. (2021). https://www.patagonia.com/one-percent-for-the-planet.html

Patagonia Official Website-Worn Wear Recrafted. (2021). https://wornwear.patagonia.com/recrafted

Patagonia Official Website-Worn Wear Seconds. (2021). https://wornwear.patagonia.com/seconds

Patagonia Official Youtube Channel-Worn Wear. A Film About the Stories We Wear. (2021). https://youtu.be/z20CjCim8DM

Pontefract, D. (2017). *Stop Confusing CSR With Purpose.* https://www.forbes.com/sites/danpontefract/2017/11/18/stop-confusing-csr-with-purpose/#377b8ed31904

Rajamannar, R. (2021). *What can marketers learn from 2020 to lead digital transformation in the new year?* https://www.mastercard.com/news/perspectives/2020/what-can-marketers-learn-from-2020-to-lead-digital-transformation-in-the-new-year

Rees-Rogers, P. (2019). *Greenwashing, purpose-washing, woke-washing and your brand.* https://www.linkedin.com/pulse/greenwashing-purpose-washing-woke-washing-your-brand-pia-rees-rogers

Ries, A., & Trout, J. (1972). The positioning era cometh. *Advertising Age, 24*, 35-38. http://www.ries.com/wp-content/uploads/2015/09/Positioning-Articles002.pdf

Ries, A., & Trout, J. (2001). *Positioning*. McGraw-Hill.

Roberts, K. (2005). *Lovemarks: The future beyond brands.* New York: Powerhouse Books.

Roberts, K. (2006). *The lovemarks effect: Winning in the consumer revolution.* Powerhouse Books.

Rogers, C. (2018). *Patagonia on why brands 'can't reverse into purpose' through marketing*. Marketing Week.

Sinek, S. (2009). *Start with why: How great leaders inspire everyone to take action* (1st ed.). Penguin Group.

Sinek, S. (2011). *Start with why: how great leaders inspire everyone to take action* (Reprinted ed.). Penguin Group.

Spary, S. (2015). *Unilever says 'brands with purpose' are growing at twice the speed of others in portfolio.* https://www.campaignlive.co.uk/article/unilever-says-brands-purpose-growing-twice-speed-others-portfolio/1345772

Spence, R. (2009). *It's Not What You Sell, It's What You Stand for: Why Every Extraordinary Business Is Driven by Purpose*. Penguin Group.

Stengel, J. (2011). *Grow: How ideals power growth and profit at the world's greatest companies*. The Crown Publishing Group.

System1 Official Blog. (2018). https://system1group.com/blog/purpose-marketing-meet-the-brand-thats-quacked-it

Tate, C. (2016). *Purpose-washing. Is it the new green-washing?* https://carolyntate.co/purpose-washing-is-it-the-new-green-washing/

TED Ads worth spreading report. (2012). https://wooshii.com/blog/author/wooshiiricardo/page/60/

The Body Shop. (2018, December 21). *The Body Shop and Cruelty Free International Campaign to end cosmetic product and ingredient animal testing globally once and for all.* Cision Canada. https://www.newswire.ca/news-releases/the-body-shop-and-cruelty-free-international-campaign-to-end-cosmetic-product-and-ingredient-animal-testing-globally-once-and-for-all-625675423.html

The Body Shop Official Website-Activism. (2021). https://www.thebodyshop.com/en-gb/about-us/activism/a/a00015

The Body Shop Official Website-Brand Purpose. (2021). https://www.thebodyshop.com/en-gb/about-us/our-story/brand-purpose/a/a00003

The Body Shop Official Website-Company. (2021). https://careers.thebodyshop.com/content/About-Us-The-Body-Shop/?locale=en_GB

The Body Shop Official Website-Forever Against Animal Testing. (2021). https://www.thebodyshop.com/en-gb/about-us/activism/faat/a/a00018

The Body Shop Official Website-Story. (2021). https://www.thebodyshop.com/en-gb/about-us/our-story/a/a00002

The Deloitte Millennial Survey. (2016). https://www2.deloitte.com/us/en/pages/about-deloitte/articles/millennials-shifting-business-purpose.html

Vial, G. (2019). Understanding digital transformation: A review and a research agenda. *The Journal of Strategic Information Systems*, *28*(2), 118–144. doi:10.1016/j.jsis.2019.01.003

Walmart Official Website-Values. (2021). https://careers.walmart.com/values

Warby Parker. (2013, February 13). *Shiagi.* http://shiagi.com/warby-parker/

Warby Parker Official Website-Buy A Pair GiveA Pair. (2021). https://www.warbyparker.com/buy-a-pair-give-a-pair

Warby Parker Official Website-History. (2021). https://www.warbyparker.com/history

Wind, Y. J., & Hays, C. F. (2016). *Beyond advertising: Creating value through all customer touchpoints.* John Wiley & Sons.

ADDITIONAL READING

Agrawal, M. (1995). Review of a 40-year debate in international advertising: Practitioner and academician perspectives to the standardization/adaptation issue. *International Marketing Review*, *12*(1), 26–48. doi:10.1108/02651339510080089

De Mooij, M. (2003). Convergence and divergence in consumer behaviour: Implications for global advertising. *International Journal of Advertising*, *22*(2), 183–202. doi:10.1080/02650487.2003.11072848

De Mooij, M., & Hofstede, G. (2010). The Hofstede model: Applications to global branding and advertising strategy and research. *International Journal of Advertising*, *29*(1), 85–110. doi:10.2501/S026504870920104X

Green, R. T., Cunningham, W. H., & Cunningham, I. C. (1975). The effectiveness of standerdized global advertising. *Journal of Advertising*, *4*(3), 25–29. doi:10.1080/00913367.1975.10672591

Hamel, G., & Prahalad, C. K. (1985). Do you really have a global strategy? *The International Executive*, *27*(3), 13–14. doi:10.1002/tie.5060270306

Pae, J. H., Samiee, S., & Tai, S. (2002). Global advertising strategy: The moderating role of brand familiarity and execution style. *International Marketing Review*, *19*(2), 176–189. doi:10.1108/02651330210425024

Robertson, R. (1992). *Globalization: Social theory and global culture* (Vol. 16). Sage.

Szymanski, D. M., Bharadwaj, S. G., & Varadarajan, P. R. (1993). Standardization versus adaptation of international marketing strategy: An empirical investigation. *Journal of Marketing*, *57*(4), 1–17. doi:10.1177/002224299305700401

Chapter 20
An Investigation of Advertising Agency Creative Managers' Perspectives on the Impact of Digital Threats and Opportunities:
The Case of UK SMEs – It Is Tricky; How Does a Brand Leopard Change Its Spots?

Antonius Raghubansie
British Council, UK

Chandrani A. Samaradivakara
Lancaster University, UK

ABSTRACT

UK advertising agency managers' perspectives on the impact of digital media (threats and opportunities) on their roles and models of managing are explored in this chapter. In the context of digital creative strategy, and the advertising industry specifically, there is far less published work, much of which has been in the context of larger, often global agencies rather than on independent SMEs. This interpretive research reviews the literature then employs semi-structured in-depth interviews with creative managers within a range of UK SME advertising agencies to analyse their views and responses to digital media. The study finds four key themes which illustrate how managers in SME advertising agencies have responded: 1) digital media as a pre-test laboratory, 2) unclear boundaries among the actors within the nodes of the agency social network, 3) fewer financial resources but more dedication to creative concepts, and 4) reduction in customer information processing costs. Relationships with larger agencies are being redeveloped as opportunity, but SMEs also represent a threat to agencies through innovation.

DOI: 10.4018/978-1-7998-7192-7.ch020

INTRODUCTION

The stereotypical views of an advertising agency made up of groups of people, involved in energetic exchange of ideas is an old one and while still partly valid, increasingly out of touch today (Cohen, 2020; Hackley and Hackley, 2019). The very core of what is classified as "advertising" itself has experienced considerable change. It can mean turning a bus station into a bedroom for a day, sharing emails of Gorillas playing drums to Phil Collins' music, posting Carlsberg's photo examples of "probably best in the world" on Facebook, Instagram and WhatsApp. Advertising tools which were perceived as emerging have quickly established themselves as part of the creative agency's arsenal (Carah and Brodmerkel, 2021; Hackley and Tiwsakul, 2011). These have had profound effects, particularly among SME agencies that make up the largest proportion of the new interactive advertising agencies.

Ad spend was reducing consistently over the decades running up to and post the millennium. However, new platforms and types of ads, especially online have had sharp growth, consistently, despite the shocks of recession, Brexit and the pandemic. Budgets spent grew from £5 billion a decade ago to more than £15 billion now (Advertising Association, 2020). At the same time advertising agencies and brand owners have much to do in truly meeting the opportunities delivered by digital. Technology leaders are delivering the platforms but the creatives are still to respond fully, or to develop management processes that give confidence to brands (Bharadwaj et al, 2013). The increase in mobile (phones, tablets, streaming etc) will drive another wave of wireless social connections, marketing opportunities and new business structures (Carah and Brodmerkel, 2021; Hackley and Tiwsakul, 2011).

In other words, the advertising industry recognises that digital is delivering a creative eruption that has and will continue to change business models (Harms, Bijmolt and Hoekstra, 2017). One such business model in advertising agencies came out of the 1960s, from Doyle Dane Bernbach (DDB) agency who had developed iconic, globally acknowledged work for brands like Volkswagen. To achieve this, they created the art director and writer combination which changed the industry, became the new paradigm (Busca and Bertrandias, 2020; Mallia and Windels, 2011). The changes which digital is heralding are on a similar scale as in the 1960s (Raghubansie and El-Gohary, 2021).

At a macro level, they represent threats particularly to the established agencies and opportunities to the new (El-Gohary, 2012; El-Gohary and El Gohary, 2016). Today, viral marketing (VM) probably best illustrates this change as it happens. Viral marketing refers to the online sharing of marketing campaigns (videos, emails, images) from consumer to consumer (Huh et al, 2020; Raghubansie, El -Gohary and Samaradivakara, 2013). It is the closest to the conventional form of TV advertising (Fard and Marvi, 2019; Southgate, Westoby and Page, 2010). Very often, there is a two-way relationship between today's viral and TV with some virals starting online and then coming to TV and vice versa (Raghubansie, El -Gohary and Lewis, 2014). VM perhaps best illustrates how the changes to the paradigm are emerging (Eckler and Bolls, 2011; Makrides, Vrontis, and Christofi, 2020). Some indicators show that interactive, or web-based, independent agencies combine the whole of their work into one brief (Carson and Springer, 2012; Raghubansie and El-Gohary, 2021). In other words, beyond the DDB model of writer/creative director, towards a cooperative model, based on teams. What other changes are taking place? How will creative roles and processes develop? Given that most of these agencies are small or medium-sized enterprises and tend to be independent, what is the nature of their operation compared to larger firms? How do they construct relationships to larger agencies?

These questions are considered in this paper and contribute to the hitherto limited literature on advertising SMEs within the UK. This study examines the phenomena of viral marketing and its impact on the developmental process of creative work. Through this exploration creative directors and heads of digital also explain their organisational responses. The question of size and competition with established advertising agencies is also investigated. The purpose is to show how creative design processes are changing and how SME agencies are developing different management systems in response. This is done from a broad perspective, focussing on macro issues of creative processes and managerial responses.

The paper starts with a clarification of the prior research and the gaps to ground the work. There is then a discussion of large and SME advertising agencies and the nature of their behaviour, ending with the research questions to be investigated. The rationale for conducting qualitative interviews with digital directors/ heads of digital is then outlined. The preliminary findings of this exploratory paper are then discussed, followed by conclusions, recommendations, limitations and suggestions for further study.

LITERATURE REVIEW

An advertising agency usually has six departments, account services, planning, media buying, finance, production and creative (Turnbull and Wheeler, 2017). Larger agencies may separate out corporate central services such as human resources, research, online and traffic. The latter would tend to appear under production in SME agencies (Grabher, 2002), moving across departments to ensure the client timeframe is met. The creative department is made up of designers (often including a web designer), production artists, art directors and copywriters, all of whom report to the creative director (de Gregorio and Windels, 2020). Within smaller agencies, departments may not exist but teams would serve those functions, outsource or draw upon an extended organisation. Some may be classed as boutique outfits which offer bespoke services that could include digital creative work such as viral marketing (Horsky, 2006; Turnbull and Wheeler, 2017).

The literature on SME advertising agencies and their creative responses to digital media is not as yet focussed into a body of work where clear theoretical and operational constructs are evident (El-Gohary, 2012; Hamad, Elbeltagi and El-Gohary, 2018). Within the broader SME literature there are many studies taking multiple theoretical positions, investigating a wide range of issues (El-Gohary and Eid, 2012; El-Gohary and El-Gohary, 2016, Hamad et al, 2015). Makrides, Vrontis and Christofi (2020) assess how brands could be built globally using digital tools. Within the UK, the advertising industry has shown a social class bias in its personnel choices (McLeod, O'Donohoe and Townley, 2009). The attitudes of people to management systems within SME organisations was the focus of Blackburn and Kovalainen (2009) who conclude that the introduction of such mechanisms, is perceived as unnecessary but also that people believe that it could inhibit the employee's own opportunities and output. There are a number of studies of advertising agencies from an economic perspective; mainly evaluating classical market structures (see Arzaghi et al, 2012). Pehlivan et al, 2013 explore outsourcing and the way technology has changed the established processes and concepts. Liu-Thompkins (2019) reviews a decade of online advertising research but still capturing these core themes.

There are many areas that one could focus on. However, this study explores the impact of digital media on the systems, structures and processes surrounding the creative function within the agency. It is usually the heart of the business generating the concepts and campaign outputs (de Gregorio and Windels, 2020; McLeod, O'Donohoe and Townley, 2009). The paper has focused on the roles played by Creative Directors and Heads of Digital. In the outward facing aspect of their roles, these creative managers pitch for new business and are the sources of creativity (Malli and Windels, 2011; Turnbull and Wheeler, 2017). They lead and supervise teams, recruit people, work cross-functionally, and negotiate and manage creative budgets (de Gregorio and Windels, 2020). Finally, they are responsible for creative and digital strategy, organising the creative processes, supporting the development of creative concepts for campaigns and for approving creative ideas and final outputs (Lee and Lau, 2020; McLeod, O'Donohoe and Townley, 2011). These are the roles that are the focus of this study.

The Social Network Perspective

This paper does not adopt a psychology or economic perspective (for example complexities such as social class, ethnic minorities, immigrants etc.). Those two streams have been dominant in the advertising literature (Busca and Bertrandias, 2020; Liu-Thompkins, 2019) but the viewpoint of SMEs remains limited (Arzaghi et al, 2012; Raghubansie and El-Gohary, 2021; Raghubansie, El-Gohary and Lewis, 2014). Social network theory has been used to understand various organisational issues within large and SMEs (See Huh et al, 2020; Perry-Smith and Shalley, 2003 for a wide-range of framework applications). These studies have developed explanations of individual and group behaviour but they are primarily a fixed perspective on the social network phenomena (Hu and Zhang, 2017; Huang et al, 2019). There are particular questions. What is the nature of this new, specialist, digital role within mainly SME advertising agencies? These relationships are embedded in a social network, a network made instant, unstable, threatening and exciting by digital technologies (Busca and Bertrandias, 2020; Zahiri, El-Gohary and Hussain, 2018).

The Large Agency and the SME Agency

The domain of control has rested with large, traditional agencies; however, that movement towards a consumer pull model (Liu-Thompkins, 2019) rather than the push of old media, is evident. Another dimension to this is the consumers, some of whom are acting as "agencies" for pay in some cases (e.g. blogging, seeding) and for free in most others (Raghubansie, El-Gohary and Lewis, 2014). In other words, the industry landscape has changed and is changing (Raghubansie and El-Gohary, 2021). The integration of digital and creative content is a two-way process. It is not only a media platform but a creative device in itself, requiring a different type of interaction between the two elements and the target audience (Huh et al, 2020; Raghubansie, El -Gohary and Samaradivakara, 2013). The loss of influence of the creative process among conventional agencies is documented but how SME advertising agencies have actually done represents a gap in the literature (Griffin, Morrison and Sheehan, 2009; Liu-Thompkins, 2019).

A global and established brand like Pepsi agreed to a US TV show making TV ads for them while its large, established agency was uninvolved. This was indicative of a trend where the big agencies are seeing work taken out of their purview (into the domain of their audiences as here) or to specialists who deliver different creative responses and strategies (Cara and Brodmerkel, 2021). Size and culture may be playing a large part of this (Cohen, 2021; Mallia and Windels, 2011).

How Do Large Agencies Become Set in a Pattern?

Reference was made above to the paradigm shift that Bernbach and his agency DDB made in the 1960s, also to the threat of digital which, in Kuhnian terms is seeking to replace the existing, accepted practices within the industry. This is a pendulum swing which will see in the future the establishment of another norm as agencies rush to adopt the new or emerging business model based on the idea that legitimacy and conformity work together (Baptista, 2009; Fard and Marvi, 2019). Much of this is related to agency size, its age and to what extent it is entrenched in institutional behaviour (Carson and Springer, 2012; Harms, Bijmolt and Hoekstra, 2017). Incumbents are less likely to immediately embrace an emerging system (Hamad, Elbeltagi and El-Gohary, 2018). In contrast, new advertising agencies are quite often digital, smaller and take as factors for start-up, disagreements with large, established agencies over creative strategy and process (Horsky, 2006; Raghubansie and El-Gohary, 2021).

Digital Media and Advertising

Truong, McColl and Kitchen (2010, p.711) conclude that "a distinction is made between digital content delivered through traditional channels – television, radio, and digital media diffused through the internet or mobile where interaction is permitted and encouraged". It is these last two verbs which make digital advertising including viral marketing (VM) a threat to brands – the loss of control of the message, the public dissemination by "unauthorised persons" of messages that could harm their reputation (Fard and Marvi, 2019; Raghubansie, El-Gohary and Samaradivakara, 2013). Digital media forms such as VM provide users the opportunity to create content, instantaneously, independent of supervision and to a large extent, in their own control (Eckler and Bolls, 2011; Raghubansie, El-Gohary and Lewis, 2014). On the other hand, there is valuable insight which is being given freely by the consumer (Huh et al, 2020); many become brand advocates and actively share positive messages about a product or service, growing brand awareness or recruiting potential members of the target audience (Griffin, Morrison and Sheehan, 2009; Carah and Brodmerkel, 2021).

The established advertising agencies such as WPP, Saatchi and Saatchi, which have dominated the global advertising industry for decades, have found themselves playing catch-up and they have had to learn fast. The advertising industry has changed much in response to digital technologies with many new entrants. Specialist agencies have emerged which offer mainly digital advertising services, competing with incumbents (Busca and Bertrandias, 2020).

Digital technologies are associated with disruption in business process and in management models (Bharadwaj et al, 2013). The implications of creative process and organisational changes in the film industry (Pardo, 2013) and tourism (El-Gohary and El-Gohary, 2016). Hackley and Tiwsakul's (2011) exploration of the changing identity of advertising professionals in the digital age (Hackley and Hackley, 2019). Conflict among individuals is examined (de Gregorio, Cheong and Kim, 2012) and conflict within the broader advertising network (Grant, McLeod and Shaw, 2012). Grabher's seminal work (2001 and 2002) proposed a set of "ecologies" of advertising agencies as villages and clusters brought together by projects. His work links to the broad social network within which advertising managers operate, the extension of which has been exponential with the growth of digital. Scholarly attention to the UK advertising sector has been far less with empirical studies addressing SMEs particularly sparse (Raghubansie, El-Gohary and Lewis, 2014).

The Standard Creative Campaign Strategy

The interruption model of traditional advertising is based on pushing a message into the space of the consumer, (Raghubansie, El-Gohary and Samaradivakara, 2013). It is about building awareness in a uni-directional manner (Liu-Thompkins, 2019). While this is the dominant approach to advertising delivery, user generated content (UGC) and digital connectedness are pointing to a shift of power from brands towards target audiences (Carah and Brodmerkel, 2021). Social media sites such as Facebook have finally developed a way to monetise its business; Twitter is facing that dilemma still, Linked-in to a lesser extent (Makrides, Vrontis and Christofi, 2020). The growth has been so fast that the business models are being developed in parallel, or hindsight (Raghubansie and El-Gohary, 2021). The platform for much of that explosive growth is the rapid diffusion of online messages, supported by offline activity (Huang et al, 2019). Viral marketing is a prime example and a central pillar of that agenda (Raghubansie, El-Gohary and Lewis, 2014). These challenges to the dominant model mean changes to the existing structure of agencies.

The established model of media buying is also under threat with competing models emerging, pointing to a more fluid future with multi-modal frameworks in place (Hackley and Hackley, 2019; Truong, McColl and Kitchen, 2010). Where people have led the purchase of advertising space in the past, those processes are being increasingly automated by computing (Huang et al, 2019; Griffin, Morrison and Sheehan, 2009). With the emergence of so called "big data", the intelligence is available and making the process very different (Boyd and Crawford, 2012; Clemons, Barnett and Appadurai, 2007; Huh et al, 2020). Bearing in mind that media buying utilises the largest share of advertising budgets, this is a major change. Younger, small and medium sized agencies with a strong digital profile are better placed to respond, though the resources required would make larger agencies better able to drive change in the longer term (Raghubansie and El-Gohary, 2021).

The New SME Advertising Agencies and a New Model

As we have seen the larger, established agencies are not organised to respond to a digital environment (Raghubansie and El-Gohary, 2021). The agency of current times has to respond to client needs which extend across traditional and new media (Carah and Brodmerkel, 2021). The growth of smaller, independent, specialist agencies, hybrids, and experiments do demonstrate this very well (Hackley and Hackley, 2019; Truong, McColl and Kitchen, 2010). Expertise in social media and cross-platform capability are two essentials for interactive agency survival in the next decade (Lee and Lau, 2018; Pardo, 2013).

The new digital agency organises itself around a principle of fluidity, using functional diversity teams with different competencies into play when required, where creative issues have to be resolved (Raghubansie and El-Gohary, 2021). Such multiplicity of capabilities can lead to a greater pool of creative ideas, enhanced solutions to creative briefs as well as innovations in process (Hackley and Hackley, 2019; Turner and Wheeler, 2017). In other words, the traditional separation between creatives and other teams in the agency is gradually being dissolved.

"Creative Content is King"

This phrase is based on the view that digital creative content should be about the creation of stories which are compelling and distinct (Raghubansie, El-Gohary and Lewis, 2014). The German car brand, BMW was ahead of its time when it started to use films on the web to develop its brand personality and positioning. The improvement of video has allowed advertisers to create more nuanced work which has not been possible before (see Golan and Zaidner, 2008 seminal work). There were creative issues compared to other medium such as glossy print which had greater richness. There was also the issue of trackability of viral advertisements across the internet, measurement of impact and control (Huang et al, 2019).

Viral marketing videos generally deliver creative content which is fun and interesting, encouraging peer-peer transmission (Raghubansie, El-Gohary and Samaradivakara, 2013). It is a mixture of commercial messages with content that will also engage the audience in an experience (Raghubansie and El-Gohary, 2021). However, it has wider applications especially in the digital sphere where brands have pursued target audiences wherever they are (Fard and Marvi, 2019). YouTube has facilitated part of this engagement with target audiences, for example Dove's ground-breaking "evolution" video being watched by over 2.5% of the world. The spread of the video was facilitated by email, which was the primary tool to initiate viral marketing distribution a decade ago (Raghubansie, El-Gohary and Lewis, 2014). Social media has since taken over much of that role also facilitated sharing and has largely replaced email in the distribution element for virals (Carah and Brodmerkel, 2021). These examples illustrate unique engagement approaches, deep understanding of customer behaviour and global appeal characteristics (see San Jose-Cabezudo and Camarero-Izquierdo, 2012; and a seminal study from Porter and Golan's, 2006). How the creative managers have created the campaign to meet the needs of great content and great storytelling is still an area that shows a paucity of research. There has been a focus on the digital platforms and the technology rather than the creative process.

The Work Culture

In an industry dominated by powerful individuals, there is a depreciation of the individualistic element characterising the processes, the structures and the management of the organisations (de Gregorio and Windels, 2020; Mallia and Windels, 2011). Reference was made to this above in the form of a different culture in SME advertising agencies – a group orientation (Chatman and Spataro, 2005). Does this change the nature of planning and design process? What are the systems emerging which address the potential conflict and disagreement that could emerge where the clear decision-maker is no longer as clear as before?

Research Questions

From the literature above, it is clear that there are substantial gaps within the body of existing work. There are questions which digital as a whole has brought to the advertising industry.

RQ1: What are the changes which digital has brought to the creative process of SME advertising agencies and the factors behind these?

RQ2: How are the agency and process management models changing as a result of this?

METHODOLOGY

Applying the social network perspective, this interpretive research uses ten semi-structured in-depth interviews with creative managers within a range of SME advertising agencies to inductively analyse the views and responses to digital media platforms. In investigating the views and human interactions within a changing environment, a qualitative approach which engages the participants is a suitable one (Bryman and Bell, 2019). The study is exploring a relatively new and undeveloped research topic among a sample population which is difficult to access (Thomas and Harden, 2008; Raghubansie, 2014). Other methods such as focus groups do result in quicker results, cheaper but one to one depth interviews have some superiority relating to the quality of the output, the richness and deep insight (Stokes and Bergin, 2006).

The social network perspective has been applied to study the interactions (called "edges") of people ("actors") in a social structure (Wellman and Berkowitz, 1988). These original ideas were supplemented by the addition of "embeddedness" within the social system (Granovetter, 1985), so this study deliberately chooses agencies within London, where more than two thirds of the advertising industry is located as well as agencies outside, including the largest digital agency outside London (Raghubansie and El-Gohary, 2021).

In this study, process changes are explored within creative teams on the one level, and within the broader sub-category of SME agencies within the advertising industry. Of particular relevance is the influence of a pattern of expectations/ behaviour on the nodes (individual creative team members), perceived belonging to groups, the idea of evolutionary change, self organising systems and a pattern of dynamics across the whole (Huh et al, 2020). There is at the heart of the social network perspective, an empirical focus on the individuals within the network and the relationships among them (Hu and Zhang, 2017). There is too a focus on places and function, as well as how groups deal with barriers between themselves (Bryman and Bell, 2019). These present opportunities and also restraints on what can be achieved by the group.

Data Analysis- Thematic Framework

Content analysis is employed to describe the impact viral marketing has had on creative development and management processes with the view of making a theoretical contribution (Elo and Kyngäs, 2008). There are three key stages – the data preparation (video recorded, transcripts), structuring (data categorisation) and then the discussion (Bryman and Bell, 2019). The data is coded firstly into related categories, then further organised into analytical themes reflecting the key issues in the research and the literature (Raghubansie, 2014). Themes are developed through the application of the constant comparison method.

Data collection and analysis were iterative (Dey, 1993). There was top down, thematic coding, with a coding system to guide the whole (Bryman and Bell, 2019). Data coding was conducted by the researcher. Discussions and feedback assisted greater reflexivity (Elo and Kyngäs, 2008). The data collection sessions took up from about 40 to 60 minutes each, generating substantial data sets, in excess of 20, 000 words. Before, during and after each interview notes were made of key points in the interview and reflections (Bryman and Bell, 2019). Participants' company profile and background were researched in the recruitment stage and then printed before the meetings to prepare. Transcripts were checked for errors and Excel was used to conduct initial coding and sub-categorization, following Elo and Kygnas (2008).

RESULTS

The study finds four key themes which illustrate how managers in SME advertising agencies have responded: 1) digital media as a pre-test laboratory, 2) unclear boundaries between corporate and advertising strategy, 3) less financial resources but more dedication to creative concepts and, 4) reduction in customer information processing costs. Relationships with larger agencies are being re-developed as opportunity (specialist support role) but they also represent a threat to less current agencies (in terms of knowledge, speed and creative partnerships). Many independent, smaller firms are expected to become acquisition targets for medium sized and larger, global agencies.

The Social Network Perspective

In contrast to prior work (Perry-Smith and Shalley, 2003), this study has found that the social network is not fixed but much more fluid and dynamic within the SME digital agencies investigated here (closer to Huh et al, 2020). The social network within which creative teams and agencies operate has been made unstable by digital technologies, consistent with Hackley and Hackley, (2019) and Raghubansie and El-Gohary (2021). The edges of creative teams and the actors within are considerably different to that seen in established agencies consistent with the study conducted by Mallia and Windels (2011) and de Gregorio, Cheong and Kim (2012).

There is evidence of self –organising (Huang et al, 2020) but also of actors de-institutionalising themselves either from having worked client side or departed from a traditional advertising agency. This latter finding is novel from the viewpoint of the social network interactions that this process must require. The nodes have been extended to a wider creative team, in some cases with heads of digital not being located in the creative team but playing cross agency roles, outside of creative processes (agreeing with Raghubansie and El-Gohary, 2021). This links well with Granovetter's (1985) idea of varying degrees of influence based on the extent of embeddedness in the network.

While that is within the social network dynamic within the agencies themselves, in terms of the industry social network, those agencies outside of London perceive this as a distinction, in social network theory the places and functions differ (Hu and Zhang, 2017) and they value the relatively low level of embeddedness within the overall structure. A complex picture emerges of the nature of relationships within the network at this level (like Zahiri et al, 2018). While it is not the domain of this study to examine market structures, there are some key issues which link to the second research question (models). One Head of Digital commented on successful campaigns,

People that are doing well, they are almost not corporate entities.

Participants felt that there is a different way of delivering creative value. At the same time, most said that they are seeing more work coming from traditional agencies. While they have continued to compete, it is a situation which is yet to resolve itself, common in social networks which are experiencing major change (Huh et al, 2020).

This study did not investigate the nature of conflict within these emerging social networks, within teams and the industry network, but it is clear that there is considerable tension between the digital lead, creative teams and other groups (Grant, McLeod and Shaw, 2012). There is a substantial education role within agencies as well as brand owners before creative concepts can be pitched consistent with both Turnbull and Wheeler (2017). In other words, the role of the digital advertising executive is as much an internal training support (agreeing with Lee and Lau, 2018) as well as the creative function, coming out much clearer than in Hackley and Tiwsakul's (2011) or Grabher's (2001 and 2002) studies.

From the social network perspective, there is a more fluid dynamic which has brought out additional links to places, barriers and other relationships, beyond the creative team agreeing with Raghubansie, El-Gohary and Lewis (2014). These do represent opportunities as well as constraints to the way the teams can operate.

Digital Media and Advertising

The viral effect that you are talking about gives you an opportunity to do six different things without paying for media. If one of them takes off, then you get the media you would have got in the first place. – Creative Director

It is not like a book. It does not end. You can always evolve; taking things to the end and see what comes out... keep running and running with it and never stopping – Head of Digital

It is about how you interact with that medium – launching apps, podcasts, and videos to back up events. I suppose it is the cherry on the cake – Head of Marketing

The comment from these participants evidence a key theme in the analysis, where digital media has become a test laboratory for creative ideas, agreeing with the work of de Gregorio, Cheong and Kim (2012). Creative managers believe that digital advertising makes creative work a series of stories which the target audience can engage with. The possibilities for further dissemination of those stories are exponential based on the technology available and the creative concept on which the campaign is based. This is equivalent to a "media imaginarium" that is accessible to both creatives and target audiences in a process of co-creation. While the new agencies see this as liberating, the traditional agencies who outsource digital work to specialist SME agencies, do not agree. However, this may be coming from the brand owners themselves. The data shows a common theme across all the interviews pointing to clients who refuse to give permission. Most brands are not prepared to give away control. This idea will be further discussed under business models.

At the same time, the most common theme in the analysis is consumer freedom. When combined with the technological platforms available to consumers to communicate with brands and among themselves, there is a disconnect (Hackley and Hackle, 2019). The choice among target audiences to engage with a brand relies with the consumer, with software providing content to the consumer when they require it, reinforcing the findings of San Jose-Cabezudo and Camarero-Izquierdo, (2012). The popularity of subscriptions, following and feeds, including viral videos to personal web pages (Facebook or Twitter) has made this an even greater challenge for brands (Huh et al, 2020 have proven this to). These technologies are effectively digital butlers delivering to the needs of individuals what they want then they do. Participants pointed to the cultural relationship of this behaviour to the consumers' consumption of media and goods and services in line with the work of Harms, Bijmolt and Hoekstra (2017).

The Standard Creative Campaign Strategy

It is evident from the interviews that specialist agencies offer mainly digital advertising services (in line with Hackley and Hackley's argument, 2019). Four of the participants have moved out of conventional agency settings into new businesses. The business models have changed considerably consistent with Bharadwaj et al, (2013). Similar findings are evident as with Clemons, Barnett, and Appadurai (2007) in terms of the failure of the interruption model to connect in a digital framework. With multi-modal frameworks in place (Makrides, Vrontis and Christofi, 2020; Truong, McColl and Kitchen, 2010) across the networks, there is opportunity to turn agencies outwards towards the audience as one participant observed, "It is about flexibility... You are never going to get to the end of it".

Planning has been very linear in campaign development but the data here shows a clear narrative of integration of creative ideas, corporate vision and management processes with very indistinct boundaries within the formal structures of the smaller independent agencies. This is more consistent with the general literature on organisation culture of SMEs (Van de Vrande et al, 2009). Much of this is also aligned with the nature of decision-making within SMEs (Van de Vrande, 2009) but not within advertising. The dominance of the writer/ creative director model set out by DDB (Mallia and Windels, 2011) has institutionalised the separation of functions within advertising agencies (Baptista, 2009). However, in responses to most questions, interviewees made reference to looser groupings of resources around client needs, compared to the difficulties of maintaining a static, hierarchical model common in bigger agencies, in the face of the need for speed (also Hackley and Hackley, 2019).

Content is King

The views of creative managers coalesce around creativity and distinction, confirming Lee and Lau (2018). They believe that this is the greatest response that they can make to the behaviour of consumers – the creative concept should be novel or the appeal unique (Raghubansie and El-Gohary, 2021). This is viewed as the essential strategy to encourage consumers to share the "story" (Golan and Zaidner, 2008).

"Marketing is word of mouth. The way you inspire people to talk of you can differ quite radically. Inspiring buzz is a delicate balance" – Head of Creative Technology

The idea of an exchange mechanism facilitating peer-peer conversation is captured in the comment from a CD whose previous role was in a large global agency, before moving to his new role in a new SME, "The viral effect is anything that has some kind of social currency". The latter point is a novel insight into how digital has affected the creative process. In other words, it is not the technological platforms but the creative idea and digital media output, agreeing with Truong, McColl and Kitchen (2010).

The Large Agency and the SME Agency

A lack of constraining institutional practices has helped the SME agency to develop multiple responses to digital media (like Turnbull and Wheeler, 2017). A theme around rewards (personal benefit as opposed to social) was common but represented in different ways. There is an advertising pay per view model already successfully running in one agency which is rolling out to two other continents at this point. The use of a monetary exchange process in online currency appears to encourage rewarded engagement – access to the buy services, information etc as credits accumulate. There is a reward system similar to the games model and even on mobile phones in the form of videos and advertising sharing for credit and free messages (similar to Harms, Bijmolft and Hoekstra, 2017).

Within the SME agencies there is a celebration of consumer responses to digital ads. They deliberately lower the processing costs (cognitive pressure, volume), the privacy costs (using public systems - YouTube), the infrastructure (broadband and wifi) and better guidance as found by Pehlivan et al (2013). Most of all, they do link with the idea of great content but also message fit to the consumer interest supporting Raghubansie, El-Gohary and Lewis, (2014). One medium sized agency has a 24-hour monitoring of the internet around the world and moves content wherever people are and based on the time they are browsing or sleeping. They perceive the Consumer as a traveller, seeing online as a country to visit, online as a short trip to get away and recharge agreeing with Carah and Brodmerkel, (2021). Consumers are also encouraged to submit themselves to soft domination to satisfy their own needs and in so doing submit to colonisation of their personal time and space, beyond the suggestions of Cohen (2020).

The New SME Advertising Agencies and a New Model

Among these new agencies, consistent with other SMEs, they do have less financial resources. However, they have been dedicating more funding to creative concepts. This is movement away from the conventional pattern, where media is the largest element of the budget (similar to Cohen, 2020).

The below points to a trend which represents a threat and opportunity for the agencies, small or large, new and old, perhaps best captured in the commentary of a CD, "In a way, they had reverse engineered. They had thought of doing the online recruitment first, then it finally led to the TV ad". A similar theme to the funding model above, has manifested in the creative process as well (building on the work of Raghubansie, El-Gohari and Lewis, 2014).

Managing Advertising Process:

- Conventional Ad Testing – Cinema, Control groups, Focus groups, Local testing
- Digital Ad Testing – Online channels with the same methods as conventional, Different platforms (social media, private groups), Global

The Culture

"It is tricky, how does a brand leopard change its spots?" observed one interviewee when asked about the responses of larger agencies and large brand owners. Most people noted that they worked in teams and supported each other as found by Chatman and Spataro (2005). The result was creative outputs that reflected the power of partnership, consistent with theories of an emergent social network, functional diversity and early institution building (also, Huang et al, 2019). However, a divergent view in the data refers to a major challenge of working alongside colleagues as well. "You always find in digital that you have to educate the market, which is also your internal audience as much as you are developing the campaign itself". This view was common in all the interviews. It is not the typical explanation of a creative idea to a client or to a colleague; it is that and technical training, as well as operating as a source of cutting edge thinking. As a different role, there is some disquiet among digital creatives on how this affects their relationships with other members of their own team. There is a higher risk with clients, who in "say we want to be like Old Spice. Then when you share some ideas; they say not quite like that. Then there is a retreat and then it is back to what is known". This strand could potentially mark a clear difference of roles within creative teams, with implications for the co-creative approach (see Lee and Lau, 2018).

Another point linked to relationships within teams has to do with connections to other teams in larger agencies which are being re-developed as opportunity (the SME as in a specialist role). At the same time, the participants recognised that they are distinctly different in operation and are aware that they represent a threat to less current agencies (in terms of knowledge, speed and creative partnerships).

CONCLUSION AND RECOMMENDATIONS

There are threats and opportunities across much of the technological, creative and management changes which have been found in this study. The data analysis revealed challenges to the traditional advertising agency, both creative and structural, viewed as opportunities by SME agencies. There are emerging visions of a future model constructed around core brand understanding, target audience engagement and a business structure that positions the agency in a network role as member of the public. There are practical aspects of these new models such as the emergence of a virtual reward system, including monetary currencies. This is closely linked to the pay per view model, except it is the reverse process where consumers are paid to view ads. Interestingly, there are also indications that the now "established" digital advertising agencies, be they larger, medium or small themselves need to reconsider their roles in relation to other nodes within the advertising industry network. There is agreement across the interviews that the consumer has a multitude of ways to interact with brands, and therefore they have little initial cost output, be that in time, tolerance or silence. Perhaps the greatest threat to SMEs and even more so to traditional agencies is the emergence of new models of operation for example, in the Mobile phone companies forming a network similar to the role of traditional advertising agencies.

- Creativity seems to be the main concern. The change of processes, of team working and of business structures is a complex network around this idea.
- The social network within teams, agencies and the industry is very fluid and shows many different edges and actors taking on different roles.
- The use of specialists and a loose network of extended resources could mean major change in the ways in which agencies are managed.
- Many independent, smaller firms are expected to become acquisition targets for medium sized and larger, global agencies. Global agencies have been developing their own competencies and in-house digital services.
- Finally, many agencies are no longer seeing digital as a separate function or role; they see it as another part of the whole offer within an agency. They also see it as mainstream rather than separate, as essential rather than optional.

Limitations, Managerial and Policy Implications and Direction for Future Research

It is a cross-sectional, exploratory, qualitative study and therefore the findings and conclusions are indicative in the context.

The sample is drawn mainly from the South of England rather than across the whole of the UK.

This paper really only looked at one function within SME advertising agencies but there are other departments that may have different views or could change the interpretation of those presented here.

Viral marketing is used as a starting point from which to explore a range of issues but it is just one phenomena within a range of others.

Managerial and Policy Implications:

This study does not only point to digital advertising's ability to allow customers to interact and increase brand awareness, but also to the need to re-examine current models on which smaller and larger agencies operate.

There are lessons for "coopetition" with SME agencies and for using them as building ground for new business models and develop an industry social network exchange process.

There are some very different issues emerging here – is it acceptable for mobile phone companies to become agencies as we have seen recently? Are they too big and hold too much data already? An issue for regulators?

Future Research Agenda

Creative responses to digital challenges require learning at a pace which is a different function in itself. This is a potentially rich vein of research opportunity.

Clearly, relationships among advertising professionals and among target audiences are much more interactive than the static model previous social network studies have shown. How is the link to the digital network important in understanding consumers? In being creative?

The advertising and media industry is an incestuous one; does this mean that the social network ties are different from what we have seen in prior work? The emergence of digital firms has been mainly among SMEs, how do they link to the broader creative networks? Was this necessary to be responsive to the threat of digital?

There are many advertising agencies which seem to operate like independent SMEs but the vast majority are owned by the top four, which operate like holding companies. How are these different from independents? What SME characteristics do they possess?

From the literature review, it is also clear that the extant work requires meta-analysis to evaluate the state of research, the various themes and conceptual contributions and gaps therein.

This paper examined the intermediaries in the creative process; there are consumer perspectives and client views that would enhance understanding.

REFERENCES

Advertising Association. (2020). *UK advertising trends, Advertising Matters.* Available from adassoc.org.uk

Arzaghi, M., Berndt, E. R., Davis, J. C., & Silk, A. J. (2012). The unbundling of advertising agency services: An economic analysis. *Review of Marketing Science.*, *10*(1), 1546–5616. doi:10.1515/1546-5616.1164

Baptista, J. (2009). Institutionalisation as a process of interplay between technology and its organisational context of use. *Journal of Information Technology*, *24*(4), 305–319. doi:10.1057/jit.2009.15

Bharadwaj, A., El Sawy, O. A., Pavlou, P. A., & Venkatraman, N. (2013). Visions and Voices on Emerging Challenges in Digital Business Strategy. *Management Information Systems Quarterly*, *37*(2), 633–661. doi:10.25300/MISQ/2013/37.2.14

Blackburn, R., & Kovalainen, A. (2009). Researching small firms and entrepreneurship: Past, present and future. *International Journal of Management Reviews*, *11*(2), 127–148. doi:10.1111/j.1468-2370.2008.00254.x

Boyd, D., & Crawford, K. (2012). Critical questions for big data: Provocations for a cultural, technological, and scholarly phenomenon. *Information Communication and Society*, *15*(5), 662–679. doi:10.1080/1369118X.2012.678878

Bryman, A., & Bell, E. (2019). Business Research Methods (5th ed.). Oxford University Press.

Busca, L., & Bertrandias, L. (2020). A Framework for Digital Marketing Research: Investigating the Four Cultural Eras of Digital Marketing. *Journal of Interactive Marketing*, *49*(1), 1–19. doi:10.1016/j.intmar.2019.08.002

Carah, N., & Brodmerkel, S. (2021). Alcohol marketing in the era of digital media platforms. *Journal of Studies on Alcohol and Drugs*, *82*(1), 18–27. doi:10.15288/jsad.2021.82.18 PMID:33573719

Carson, M., & Springer, P. (2012). *Pioneers of Digital: Success Stories from Leaders in Advertising, Marketing*. Kogan Page.

Chatman, J. A., & Spataro, S. E. (2005). Using Self-Categorization Theory to Understand Relational Demography-Based Variations in People's Responsiveness to Organizational Culture. *Academy of Management Journal*, *48*(2), 321–331. doi:10.5465/amj.2005.16928415

Clemons, E. K., Barnett, S., & Appadurai, A. (2007). The Future of Advertising and the Value of Social Network Websites: Some Preliminary Examinations. *ACM International Conference Proceeding Series, Ninth International Conference on Electronic Commerce*, 267-76. 10.1145/1282100.1282153

Cohen, A. C. (2020). Seeing the market: Performative sensemaking and the case of advertising agencies and their clients. *Consumption Markets & Culture*, *23*(5), 481–505. doi:10.1080/10253866.2019.1625775

de Gregorio, F., Cheong, Y., & Kim, K. (2012). Intraorganizational Conflict within Advertising Agencies. *Journal of Advertising*, *41*(3), 19–34.

de Gregorio, F., & Windels, K. (2020). Are Advertising Agency Creatives More Creative Than Anyone Else? An Exploratory Test of Competing Predictions. *Journal of Advertising*, *1*(1), 1–10. doi:10.1080/00913367.2020.1799268

Dey, I. (1993). *Qualitative Data Analysis: A User-Friendly Guide for Social Scientists*. Routledge.

Eckler, P., & Bolls, P. (2011). Spreading the virus: Emotional tone of viral advertising and its effect on forwarding intentions and attitudes. *Journal of Interactive Advertising*, *11*(2), 1–11. doi:10.1080/15252019.2011.10722180

El-Gohary, H. (2010). E-Marketing - A literature Review from a Small Businesses perspective. *International Journal of Business and Social Science*, *1*(1), 214–244.

El-Gohary, H. (2012). Factors affecting E-Marketing adoption and implementation in tourism firms: An empirical investigation of Egyptian small tourism organizations. *Tourism Management*, *33*(5), 1256–1269. doi:10.1016/j.tourman.2011.10.013

El-Gohary, H., & Eid, R. (2012). DMA Model: Understanding Digital Marketing Adoption and Implementation by Islamic Tourism Organizations. *Tourism Analysis*, *17*(4), 523–532. doi:10.3727/108354212X13473157390885

El-Gohary, H., & El-Gohary, Z. (2016). An Attempt to Explore Electronic Marketing Adoption and Implementation Aspects in Developing Countries: The Case of Egypt. *International Journal of Customer Relationship Marketing and Management*, *7*(4), 1–26. doi:10.4018/IJCRMM.2016100101

Elo, S., & Kyngäs, H. (2008). The qualitative content analysis process. *Journal of Advanced Nursing*, *62*(1), 107–115. doi:10.1111/j.1365-2648.2007.04569.x PMID:18352969

Fard, M. H., & Marvi, R. (2019, Aug.). Viral marketing and purchase intentions of mobile applications users. *International Journal of Emerging Markets*.

Golan, G. J., & Zaidner, L. (2008). Creative Strategies in Viral Advertising: An Application of Taylor's Six-Segment Message Strategy Wheel. *Journal of Computer-Mediated Communication*, *13*(4), 959–972. doi:10.1111/j.1083-6101.2008.00426.x

Grabher, G. (2001). Ecologies of creativity: The Village, the Group, and the heterarchic organisation of the British advertising industry. *Environment & Planning A*, *33*(2), 351–374. doi:10.1068/a3314

Grabher, G. (2002). The Project Ecology of Advertising: Tasks, Talents and Teams. *Regional Studies*, *36*(3), 245–262. doi:10.1080/00343400220122052

Granovetter, M. (1985). 'Economic Action and Social Structure: The Problem of Embeddedness'. *American Journal of Sociology*, *91*(3), 481–510. doi:10.1086/228311

Grant, I., McLeod, C., & Shaw, E. (2012). Conflict and advertising planning: Consequences of networking for advertising planning. *European Journal of Marketing*, *46*(1/2), 73–91. doi:10.1108/03090561211189248

Griffin, G., Morrison, D. K., & Sheehan, K. B. (2009). Note from Guest Editors: Perspectives from Digital Creativity. Journal of Interactive Advertising, 9(2), 1-3. doi:10.1080/15252019.2009.10722150

Hackley, C., & Hackley, A. R. (2019). Advertising at the threshold: Paratextual promotion in the era of media convergence. *Marketing Theory*, *19*(2), 195–215. doi:10.1177/1470593118787581

Hackley, C., & Tiwsakul, R. (2011). Advertising Management and Professional Identity in the Digital Age. In M. Deuze (Ed.), *Managing Media Work* (pp. 209–216). Sage.

Hamad, H., Elbeltagi, I., & El-Gohary, H. (2018). An Empirical Investigation of Business-to-Business E-Commerce Adoption and its Impact on SMEs Competitive Advantage: The Case of Egyptian Manufacturing SMEs, Strategic Change. *Briefings in Entrepreneurial Finance*, *27*(3), 209–229.

Hamad, H., Elbeltagi, I., Jones, P., & El-Gohary, H. (2015). Antecedents of B2B E-Commerce Adoption and its Effect on Competitive Advantage in Manufacturing SMEs. *Strategic Change*, *24*(5), 405–428. doi:10.1002/jsc.2019

Harms, B., Bijmolt, T. H., & Hoekstra, J. C. (2017). Digital native advertising: Practitioner perspectives and a research agenda. *Journal of Interactive Advertising*, *17*(2), 80–91. doi:10.1080/15252019.2017.1357513

Horsky, S. (2006). The changing architecture of advertising agencies. *Marketing Science*, *25*(4), 367–383. doi:10.1287/mksc.1060.0198

Hu, J., & Zhang, Y. (2017). Discovering the interdisciplinary nature of Big Data research through social network analysis and visualization. *Scientometrics*, *112*(1), 91–109. doi:10.100711192-017-2383-1

Huang, H., Shen, H., Meng, Z., Chang, H., & He, H. (2019). Community-based influence maximization for viral marketing. *Applied Intelligence*, *49*(6), 2137–2150. doi:10.100710489-018-1387-8

Huh, J., Kim, H., Rath, B., Lu, X., & Srivastava, J. (2020). You reap where you sow: A trust-based approach to initial seeding for viral advertising. *International Journal of Advertising*, *39*(7), 963–989. doi:10.1080/02650487.2020.1718823

Interactive Advertising Bureau. (2019). *2019 Full year digital ad spend results.* Author.

Lee, P. Y., & Lau, K. W. (2018). A new triadic creative role for advertising industry: A study of creatives' role identity in the rise of social media advertising. *Creative Industries Journal*, *11*(2), 137–157. doi:10.1080/17510694.2018.1434362

Liu-Thompkins, Y. (2019). A Decade of Online Advertising Research: What We Learned and What We Need to Know. *Journal of Advertising*, *48*(1), 1–13. doi:10.1080/00913367.2018.1556138

Makrides, A., Vrontis, D., & Christofi, M. (2020). The gold rush of digital marketing: Assessing prospects of building brand awareness overseas. *Business Perspectives and Research*, *8*(1), 4–20. doi:10.1177/2278533719860016

Mallia, K. L., & Windels, K. (2011). Will changing media change the world? An exploratory investigation of the impact of digital advertising on opportunities for creative women. *Journal of Interactive Advertising*, *11*(2), 30–44. doi:10.1080/15252019.2011.10722183

McLeod, C., O'Donohoe, S., & Townley, B. (2009). The elephant in the room? Class and creative careers in British advertising agencies. *Human Relations*, *62*(7), 1011–1039. doi:10.1177/0018726709335551

McLeod, C., O'Donohoe, S., & Townley, B. (2011). Pot noodles, placements and peer regard: Creative career trajectories and communities of practice in the British advertising industry. *British Journal of Management*, *22*(1), 114–131. doi:10.1111/j.1467-8551.2010.00705.x

Pardo, A. (2013). Digital Hollywood: How Internet and Social Media Are Changing the Movie Business. In *Handbook of Social Media Management* (pp. 327–347). Springer Heidelberg. doi:10.1007/978-3-642-28897-5_19

Pehlivan, E., Berthon, P. R., Pitt, L. F., & Chakrabarti, R. (2013). When outsourcing fragments: Customer creativity and technological transmutations. *Production Planning and Control*, *24*(4-5), 284–293. doi:10.1080/09537287.2011.648541

Perry-Smith, J. E., & Shalley, C. E. (2003). The Social Side of Creativity: A Static and Dynamic Social Network Perspective. *Academy of Management Review*, *28*(1), 89–106. doi:10.5465/amr.2003.8925236

Porter, L., & Golan, G. J. (2006). From subservient chickens to brawny men: A comparison of viral advertising to television advertising. *Journal of Interactive Advertising*, *69*(2), 30–38.

Raghubansie, A. D. (2014). Chasing ghosts: problems of participant recruitment from among innovators/practitioners in the UK advertising industry. *International Multidisciplinary Academic Conference.*

Raghubansie, A. D., & El-Gohary, H. O. A. S. (2021). Digital Advertising Creative Processes and Innovation in UK SME Advertising Agencies: An Empirical Investigation of Viral Advertising. *Scientific Journal for Financial and Commercial Studies and Research*, *2*(1), 75-116.

Raghubansie, A. D., El-Gohary, H., & Lewis, C. (2014). Revising Extant Frameworks of Viral Marketing: Implications from Empirical Investigations of Digital Advertising Creative Managers' Practice in the UK. *ISBE 2014 Conference, The Future of Enterprise: The Innovation Revolution*.

Raghubansie, A. D., El Gohary, H., & Samaradivakara, C. (2013). An Evaluation of the Viral Marketing Research. *International Journal of Online Marketing*, *3*(4), 1–30. doi:10.4018/ijom.2013100101

San José-Cabezudo, R., & Camarero-Izquierdo, C. (2012). Determinants of opening-forwarding email messages. *Journal of Advertising*, *41*(2), 97–112. doi:10.2753/JOA0091-3367410207

Southgate, D., Westoby, N., & Page, G. (2010). Creative determinants of viral video viewing. *International Journal of Advertising*, *29*(3), 349–368. doi:10.2501/S0265048710201221

Stokes, D., & Bergin, R. (2006). Methodology or 'methodolatry'? An evaluation of focus groups and depth interviews. *Qualitative Market Research*, *9*(2), 26–36. doi:10.1108/13522750610640530

Thomas, J., & Harden, A. (2008). Methods for the thematic synthesis of qualitative research in systematic reviews. *BMC Medical Research Methodology*, *8*(1), 45. https://www.biomedcentral.com/1471-2288/8/45/

Truong, Y., McColl, R., & Kitchen, P. (2010). Practitioners' perceptions of advertising strategies for digital media. *International Journal of Advertising*, *29*(5), 709–725. doi:10.2501/S0265048710201439

Turnbull, S., & Wheeler, C. (2017). The advertising creative process: A study of UK agencies. *Journal of Marketing Communications*, *23*(2), 176–194. doi:10.1080/13527266.2014.1000361

Van de Vrande, V., De Jong, J. P., Vanhaverbeke, W., & De Rochemont, M. (2009). Open innovation in SMEs: Trends, motives and management challenges. *Technovation*, *29*(6), 423–437. doi:10.1016/j.technovation.2008.10.001

Wellman, B., & Berkowitz, S. D. (1988). Introduction: Studying Social Structures. In B. Wellman & S. D. Berkowitz (Eds.), *Social Structures: A Network Approach* (pp. 1–14). Cambridge University Press.

Zahiri, S., El-Gohary, H., & Hussain, J. (2018). Internet Marketing Adoption by Iranian Distribution Industry: An Attempt to Understand the Reality. *International Journal of Customer Relationship Marketing and Management*, *9*(2), 33–61. doi:10.4018/IJCRMM.2018040103

Chapter 21
Transformation of WOM (Word of Mouth) From Traditional to Digital and Current Recommendations for e-WOM

Mustafa Şehirli
https://orcid.org/0000-0002-4800-0283
The University of Health Sciences, Turkey

ABSTRACT

The conceptual and technological transformation of word of mouth (WOM) is one of the most effective and old factors in customers' purchasing decisions. Although digital WOM is expressed as e-WOM, it is similar to traditional WOM, but it differs in the perception of trust, as well as in speed and scope. It affects the fate of companies both positively and negatively. For this reason, it is essential for marketers to inactively and proactively develop e-WOM strategies that are as personalized as possible to ensure that a positive mark is left on the customers. This study demonstrates the e-WOM strategies and tactics that are relevant today to provide guidance to marketers.

INTRODUCTION

In today's world, shopping has become an activity on its own, rather than just being a needed activity. People shop to meet their psychological, social, and physical needs. Socialization has become an important aspect of shopping. Studies are demonstrating that people buy more than usual when they are with their friends. For this reason, marketers are obliged to ensure that they emphasize the social aspect of shopping. Therefore, WOM has become more prevalent in marketing; WOM replaces advertising and promotions. WOM is an interpersonal transfer of information about the sale of products and services beyond the information or advertisements provided by companies that affect personal decisions (Brown et al., 2007). In this environment of intense competition, customers trust their friends or other customers rather than companies and enjoy the comfort of belonging to a community by behaving like

DOI: 10.4018/978-1-7998-7192-7.ch021

others. Moreover, consumers generally rely on informal personal communication rather than official or organizational sources in their purchasing decisions (Bansal & Voyer, 2000).

On the other hand, digitalization is progressing extremely rapidly with the stimulation brought on by the global pandemic. While concepts, applications, operations, and almost everything else is being moved to online platforms, marketing tools are also being digitalized. Of course, WOM, which requires interpersonal interaction in purchasing decisions, has also evolved as e-WOM. One of the most comprehensive definitions for e-WOM is as the following: "any positive or negative statement made by potential, actual, or former customers about a product or company, which is made available to a multitude of people and institutions via the Internet" (Hennig-Thurau et al., 2004).

Today, e-WOM is faster and more effective than traditional WOM. There are not many people left who shop before reading reviews of the product or service to be purchased. Under these circumstances, understanding and correctly managing e-WOM has become the new front for marketers to positively influence the purchasing and loyalty decisions of customers.

E-WOM is significantly different from traditional WOM, but it can be diversified as positive and negative, just like traditional WOM. These differences include advantages and disadvantages. For example, it can be both an advantage and a disadvantage that it spreads very fast, can be saved, and the low level of trust compared to traditional WOM is certainly one of the biggest handicaps. Although there are similarities between them, the reasons for its occurrence and even its effects are different. Besides these two basic types of WOM, it can also be diversified according to the way it manifests. For example, the e-WOM defined as social e-WOM is specific to social media, and there are certain differences between it and e-WOMs made on e-commerce websites or platforms.

There is a wealth of literature on the determinants involved in the emergence of e-WOM. These determinants emphasized in studies are well-known concepts such as loyalty, satisfaction, and trust. Many of these origins are similar to traditional WOM.

Extensive research has studied the outcomes of e-WOM; the most obvious is the outcome of purchasing decisions. In other words, WOM has a direct impact on sales numbers, which is the lifeblood of companies and customer loyalty in the long run.

In this chapter, the concepts mentioned above are discussed within the framework of previous studies. The main goal of this section is to provide practical and vital suggestions about e-WOM to today's managers and academics based on prior studies. Thus, a number of up-to-date and effective methods are presented that will enable marketers to obtain advantages in the intense competition to influence customers. In the following sections, the importance of traditional WOM is addressed briefly, which is then followed by a discussion regarding the transformation of WOM to e-WOM and the definition and the scope of e-WOM, including its effects and antecedents. This chapter aims to support academics and managers in digitally enabling customers to influence other customers (WOM), which is one of the most fundamental ways to gain and retain customers. The final section is devoted to providing advisory suggestions.

The Historical Transformation of Marketing and the Transformation and Reemergence of WOM

The most recent and well-known change that has emerged in marketing is humanization. Marketers attempt to treat customers as individuals and persuade them to make purchases and to stay loyal by adding value and humanity-based touches to their approaches. Traditional methods are gradually being replaced by personal and human-centric methods. This new approach, which is defined as hearts, minds, and souls by Kotler et al. (2017), came together with digitalization, which resulted in a whole new approach that is both humane and technological. The marketing mix that is evolving McCarthy's 4P to Lautherborn's 4C was redefined by Kotler et al. (2017) as co-creation, currency, communal activation, and conversation. Aydın (2019), on the other hand, defined the marketing mix with 8E: experience, entertainment, effort, exchange, emotions, expression, every time, everywhere. Many processes or tools in marketing have undergone metamorphoses or have been replaced by new ones.

For instance, the customer persuasion process has changed the most. The most important instrument of this field can be summarized as promotions in traditional marketing, which have begun to give way to WOM, which is an older, more personal, and more humane concept. The first definitions of WOM were made in the 1960s. Katz and Lazarsfeld (1966) defined WOM as the sharing of market information among customers, which has a profound impact on customers' attitudes about products and services.

In other words, communications and advertisements that target the masses were replaced by ones that target individuals' needs and desires and by presenting them as an experience that is specific to them. The rest is handled by the customers, who share the experience they've had with others. One of the greatest reasons behind the effectiveness of WOM is the fact that in the digital age, sharing information is expanding and accelerating like never before, and many products and services are becoming very alike as a result of competition. Confirming this, the source information (sender) in WOM (i.e., the person who performs the WOM) usually does not have any interest in this situation or the behavior of the person they affect with the WOM (Schiffman & Kanuk, 1997).

Any WOM performed by customers who have undergone a positive experience will have a larger effect with zero expenses than advertisements that are carried out with large budgets. In particular, the effects of e-WOM spread exponentially. However, the effects of negative WOM can be much more severe. WOM is extremely important, persuasive, and effective in business life (Bristor, 1990). According to one of the earliest sources, WOM was twice as effective as radio and four times more effective than personal selling, which was the most effective sales channel at the time (Katz & Lazarsfeld, 1955). It is obvious that this situation significantly favors WOM, and it is continuing by changing mediums and increasing. Methods that customers have on hand for communicating with each other, sharing, and collecting information regarding products and services are one of the most important factors for WOM, and these have changed significantly in the past decade (Hennig-Thurau et al., 2010). Face-to-face communication is giving way to online communication, and this is affecting the decision-making processes of companies and their sales (Barnes & Jacobsen, 2014). These changes led to the development of e-WOM. Before discussing the concept of e-WOM in detail, it is useful to discuss the origins and effects of traditional WOM.

Antecedents and Effects of Face-to-Face (Traditional) WOM

The history of WOM as a practice of commercial communication must be as old as the history of commerce. Therefore, the number of academic studies on WOM is also quite high. WOM has been defined from different perspectives, and its origins and effects were discussed comparatively.

First, in the eyes of customers, WOM is much more reliable than other traditional media channels (i.e., advertising, TV, and radio; Cheung & Thadani, 2012) because people trust each other more than companies (Nieto et al., 2014). Moreover, WOM creates higher levels of empathy and persuades customers more effectively compared to traditional advertisements (Bickart & Schindler, 2001).

Examination of the literature on traditional WOM, or WOM, reveals that its antecedents could include concepts such as trust, satisfaction (or dissatisfaction with the product/service), attitude toward the product or service, and engagement. Customers rely on WOM to reduce risk, increase trust, and spread WOM communications to prevent injustices by sharing information, to show how knowledgeable they are, or to garner financial benefits. There are two sides to WOM: a sender and a receiver. The reasons for performing WOM may differ for each of them.

If individuals engaging in WOM are people who do not personally know one other or people who are not in a direct relationship, the risks come to the forefront via the expertise of these individuals regarding the subject and their level of knowledge. In particular, there is an inverse U-shaped relationship between the knowledge level of the receiver and the behavior of seeking WOM. This means that if the receiver has high or low levels of knowledge, they will have a higher tendency to seek WOM. Additionally, the higher expertise and knowledge of the individual providing the WOM, the higher its effectiveness tends to be. On the other hand, there is an inverse relationship between the risk perceived by the receiver and the level of knowledge. The higher the perceived risk, the greater the tendency for seeking WOM (Bansal & Voyer, 2000).

However, if both parties are in a direct relationship, the strength of the intimacy between them becomes the factor of importance (Brown & Reingen, 1987). The better they know each other, the stronger the effect of WOM will be.

Of course, looking at the general effects of WOM, the greatest effect is the one it has on the customer's intentions toward making purchases. WOM plays an active role in customers' decision mechanisms and purchasing behavior (Kumar et al., 2010). This is especially true for sectors directly related to the experience, such as tourism and hospitality. WOM is one of the most important resources that reduce the perceived risk of purchasing by consumers (Murray, 1991). Moreover, it causes attitude-related changes in brand awareness and value. According to Bansal and Voyer (2000), the effect of WOM in purchasing decisions is influenced by noninterpersonal forces (i.e., receiver's expertise, receiver's perceived risk, and sender's expertise) and the effect of the interpersonal forces (i.e., ties strength and how actively WOM is sought).

After evaluating the traditional WOM in a general manner, it is necessary to discuss the concept of e-WOM, which is its digitized form, to reveal the differences between it and traditional WOM.

Differences Between E-WOM and WOM in the Digitization Process

Although it was born from traditional WOM, e-WOM is quite different. Before examining the differences, it would be beneficial to understand what e-WOM is. Other than the overarching definition above, some definitions of E WOM that address different dimensions are:

- Consumer-generated, consumption-related communication that employs digital tools and is directed primarily to other consumers" (Babić Rosario et al., 2019).
- The positive or negative information obtained from other consumers about products and services (Forman et al., 2008).
- Referrals in online message boards, blogs, and online communities (Choi et al., 2012).
- İnformation and suggestions about products and services received online from peers (Dellarocas et al., 2007).

Thus, an umbrella definition of e-WOM would include all of the content provided by online customers, although it is possible that such content does not include direct recommendations (Babić Rosario et al., 2019). However, e-WOM should not be confused with similar concepts associated with it. Some of these are (1) general information sharing, (2) WOM, (3) critics' reviews, (4) advertising, (5) user-generated content (UGC), (6) electronic recommendation systems, (7) online search rankings, and (8) observational learning (MacInnis, 2011, as cited in Babić Rosario et al., 2019). In other words, e-WOM is a concept that is intertwined with activities such as technical information sharing, advertising, and grading by companies or individuals but is a wider concept than them.

The differences between WOM and e-WOM can be summarized as prevalence (e.g., e-WOM reaches a larger audience), form (e.g., traditional is face-to-face), and source (WOM has a definite source while e-WOM is generally anonymous). Communication in e-WOM is not as reassuring as face-to-face communication. However, it allows access to many more individuals, and since it stays in circulation for a long time, it can reach many people. Therefore, negative e-WOM, in particular, can be very harmful and even destructive for companies (Ismagilova et al., 2017). The differences between traditional WOM and e-WOM are shown in Table 1.

Table 1. Differences between WOM and eWOM

	WOM	eWOM
Credibility (Trust)	The receiver of the information knows the communicator (positive influence on credibility)	Anonymity between the communicator and the receiver of the information (negative influence on credibility)
Privacy	The conversation is private, interpersonal (via dialogs), and conducted in real time	The shared information is not private and, because it is written down, can sometimes be viewed by anyone and at any time
Diffusion speed	Messages spread slowly. Users must be present when the information is being shared	Messages are conveyed more quickly between users and, via the Internet, can be conveyed at any time
Accessibility	Less accessible	Easily accessible

Source: Huete-Alcocer (2017).

In addition to the information provided in Table 1, e-WOM may be more effective in decreasing risks and increasing trust because, with WOM, opinions generally reach customers through third parties, which means that information may have changed (Huete-Alcocer, 2017). Another concept that is not included in the table is temporality. E-WOM also has no time constraints, so its effect may extend over a longer period of time (Babić Rosario et al., 2019). While WOM is only in spoken or written format, e-WOM is spread over many more formats (e.g., written, audio, and visual). Therefore, many definitions and statements made for e-WOM are currently out of date. For example, the word "statement," which has been used frequently before, is more of a literary expression.

Of course, the results of e-WOM have greater effects on business life compared to its origins. These effects will be discussed in the following section.

Factors Determining the Effects and Degree of e-WOM

Apart from the determinants of WOM, the content of the e-WOM message, the characteristics of the sending source, and the recipient also influence the effects of e-WOM. However, customers are expected to be satisfied or dissatisfied with the product or service they have received to engage with e-WOM. In this context, engaging in e-WOM is correlated with satisfaction, which in turn is correlated with online convenience. The three primary factors that affect online convenience are possession, transaction, and evaluation (Duarte et al., 2018). In other words, factors such as proper stock management, shipping conditions, packaging, subscription, return, and warranty conditions are the most important reasons for convenience, and in turn, for e-WOM.

This section includes information directly related to WOM as opposed to providing convenient services and quality. In one of the many studies on WOM or e-WOM, Sundaram, Mitra, and Webster (1998) listed the reasons that cause people to engage in WOM:

- Altruism (positive WOM): The drive to help others without the need for personal gain
- Product involvement: A genuine commitment to a product
- Self-enhancement: The desire to make oneself appear good in the eyes of other individuals
- Helping the company: The motivation to help a company
- Altruism (negative WOM): The motivation to protect others
- Anxiety reduction: The desire to alleviate anger, anxiety, and frustration
- Vengeance: The willingness to take revenge on the company for a bad experience
- Advice seeking: The need to seek advice to solve problems

In another study, the motivations behind making and receiving e-WOM were listed under two similar yet separate categories. While the motivations for making e-WOM include altruism, self-enhancement, venting feelings, social benefits, and economic incentives (e.g., receiving discounts), people are motivated to seek e-WOM due to risk reduction, social approval, reduction of search time and effort, getting product (usage) information, and social interaction benefits (Ismagilova et al., 2017).

While demonstrating the relationship between e-WOM and brand value, Sijoria, Mukherjee, and Datta (2018) referred to previous studies and listed the following antecedents of e-WOM:

- Argument quality: The nature of the information in the shared message
- Trust: Confidence, reliability, credibility towards the message
- Loyalty: The loyalty of customers to the brand in question
- Satisfaction: Positive impressions and experiences
- Social relationship: The association among the people
- Tie-strength: The level of intensity of the social relationship between consumers or the degree of overlap of two individuals' friendship that varies greatly across a consumer's social network
- Interpersonal influence: The degree of influence of peers, society, and others on an individual

Next, these items are discussed under the significant categories.

Characteristics of People in E-WOM

The personality or attitudinal characteristics of the people who make or make use of e-WOM determine its effects. The main characteristics are people's desire for social interaction, desire to benefit from economic incentives, interest in other consumers, and their potential to improve their self-worth (Choi et al., 2012; Hennig-Thurau et al., 2004). Following a large-scale literature review, Babić Rosario et al. (2019) performed a comprehensive study on e-WOM within the framework of MOA (motivation, opportunities, and ability) and in three stages (creation, exposure, and evaluation) from the perspective of both the customers (senders and receivers) and marketers. In the first stage, creation, the primary motivations of customers to make e-WOM's include altruism, the desire to help others and the social value of interaction with the community, fun and pleasure, expressing one's identity, balance restoration, venting, retribution (e.g., seeking revenge if one believes they were treated unjustly), incentives, and rewards. Opportunities define the circumstances and opportunities for e-WOM; they include access to devices, the internet, and e-WOM platforms. Its formats are texts, ratings, images, ratings, scales, and likes. Ability defines the possibilities and assets available at its disposal, which includes knowledge and expertise, product familiarity, and skills. The primary motivation in the stage of exposure to or use of e-WOM includes receiving personal services, achieving high levels of knowledge, eliminating uncertainties and risks, preventing possible problems, making use of free time, and being exposed to e-WOM unintentionally. The factors that affect the motivations of individuals while evaluating e-WOM include personal factors (high cognition or the need to be unique) and cultural characteristics, trust in the source, and the qualities of the message (e.g., simplicity, clarity). The opportunities and ability used in evaluating are similar to the factors in other stages.

People with a high social media presence are less likely to provide negative e-WOM, while people with a higher tendency to show their knowledge provide negative e-WOM more often. Additionally, individuals who tend to expect a response from the brand (i.e., deal proneness) after their negative experience are more likely to make negative e-WOM (Dutta et al., 2019).

Further, people are more engaged and motivated when they retain control in digital advertisements. A person's intention to provide e-WOM increases as the viewing time of an advertisement increases. On the other hand, viewers get more positive impressions from advertisements where they are given the opportunity to end the advertisement, which has positive effects on e-WOM (Belanche et al., 2019).

Finally, the customers doing e-WOM can be put into five categories: effective, meticulous, quality evaluators, prudent critics, and quick pessimists (Gottschalk & Mafael, 2017).

The Nature of the e-WOM Message

The content of the message and the way it is delivered also determines the effect of e-WOM. For example, the effect will be greater if the message directly contains the information needed. Contrary to what was expected, a study revealed that e-WOM information on shopping websites affects online consumers' purchase intentions more than the recommendations by their friends. This information is helpful in terms of information reliability, information usefulness, and information adoption. The reason for this is the high amount of information and readiness of the information, as well as such information being detailed and specific (Erkan & Evans, 2018).

Furthermore, the higher the frequency (i.e., how often) and timing (i.e., the closer to the measurement of satisfaction) of when the message was posted online increases the effect it will have (Raassens &

Haans, 2017). To attract consumers, digital content must be concise, vibrant, and interesting. Moreover, such content must be created using big data analysis to ensure that it is based on the true interests of users (Bu et al., 2020).

For the receiver's part of e-WOM, the quality (its clarity, comprehensibility, and objectivity) and frequency of e-WOM have a positive effect on online buyers' trust in the electronic environment (e-trust), while for the sender's part, the content and intensity of e-WOM positively affects the loyalty felt toward the brand in the electronic environment (e-loyalty). Thus, these four variables affect purchasing decisions through the concepts of e-trust and e-loyalty (Bulut & Karabulut, 2018).

Prior studies indicate that the usefulness of the information in question (and its reliability) is one of the most important moderator effects in the acceptance of e-WOM (Liu & Zhang, 2010). Besides the usefulness of information for individuals, certain other factors also come into play in this context. For instance, Brackett and Carr (2001) introduced a new model by adding a new variable (credibility) to the model previously developed by Ducoffe (1996) to determine the value of advertisements in digital media. The variables in this model are entertainment, informativeness, irritation, and credibility. Based on the effects it creates, e-WOM could also be considered a type of advertisement. Therefore, the factors that determine the impact of digital advertisements are also valid for e-WOM.

Entertainment expresses the escapism, diversion, aesthetical pleasure, and emotional relief contained in a WOM message (Ducoffe, 1996). The more entertaining the message, the better it will attract people's attention and influence them. Informativeness is how informative an advertisement is, and this information enables customers to find the best option among the alternatives (Ducoffe, 1996). Therefore, information about the product and service in an e-WOM positively influences its effect. Irritation is the displeasure caused by the WOM message on the recipients. This is related to whether it contains any crimes, insults, or excessive manipulation (Ducoffe, 1996). Irritation can vary based on many factors, such as product category and channel. Considering that authoring an e-WOM is hardly difficult, it is very likely for such messages to be irritating. Credibility was added to the model post facto, and it is believed to have a direct effect on the value of the advertisement (Brackett & Carr, 2001). In other words, the WOM expresses the extent to which someone perceives the opinions of others as convincing, correct, and realistic (Nabi & Hendriks, 2003).

After evaluating the most often used models to understand the effects of e-WOM, Cheung and Thadani (2012) proposed a more comprehensive model. This model, shown in Figure 1, has five essential components: communicators (sender), stimuli (message), receivers (receiver), responses (receiver response), and contextual factors (platform).

The message sent from the communicator (sender) over the platform creates a reaction in the receiver. This reaction takes the form of responses, such as purchase intentions or behaviors. In this model, the variable that needs to be explained separately from other models, especially the WOM model, is the contextual factor variable, which is the platform on which the e-WOM takes place. The quality and credibility of the platform have a great influence on the impact of e-WOM. The effect of this trust on the platform is even more profound than the trust that companies create on their web pages (Bickart & Schindler, 2001). This is not limited just to the platform, as there is a general relationship between e-WOM and the channel it was made on. While blogs and social networks are effective in improving perceptions and general attitudes towards the brand, SMS are particularly effective for personal information, and forums are much more effective channels to increase credibility (Gvili & Levy, 2016). Since they contain only concise information, the information levels of online comment boards are low. However, their irritation is also quite low (Gvili & Levy, 2016).

Figure 1. An integrative framework of the impact of eWOM communication
Source: Cheung, & Thadani, (2012.

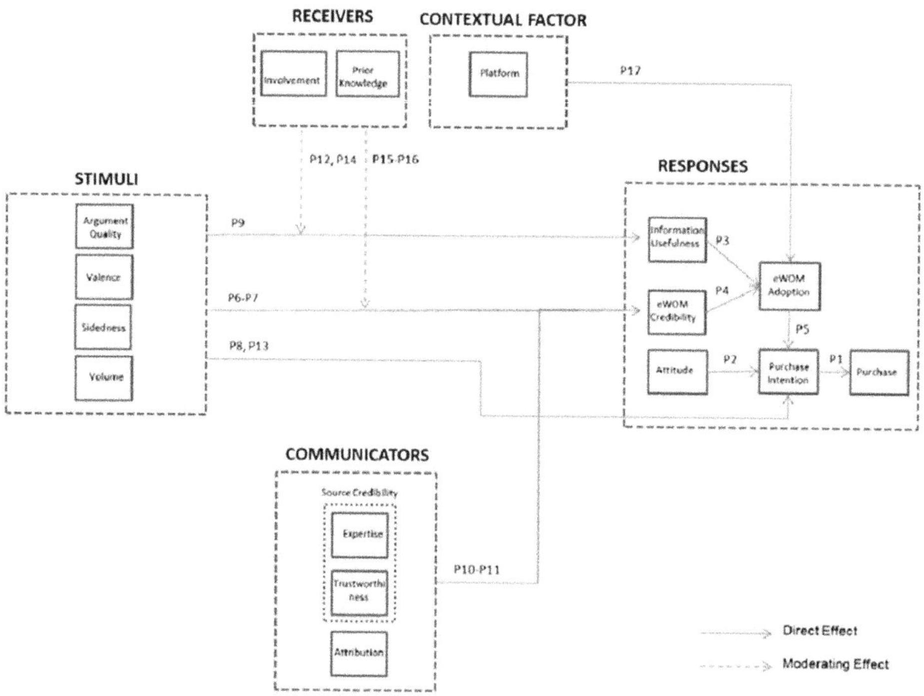

Online communities that come together based on a certain product (i.e., fan communities) are generally interested in sharing lively and entertaining information, while communities that gather based on services generally aim to produce and develop knowledge (Choi et al., 2019).

TRUST AND E-WOM

For e-WOM to be effective, users must first trust the commenting sender. The biggest handicap of e-WOM is the low level of trust inherent in it. For example, authors could write positive reviews of their books on Amazon, and the fake accounts found on TripAdvisor have shaken the trust of the customers (Pihlaja et al., 2017). After examining a large number of hotel reviews, Belarmino and Koh (2018) identified differences regarding valuations. For the same hotel, the number of star ratings was very high on the hotel's, but was lower on the travel agency's page, and was the lowest on third party websites. All of this information negatively affects people's sense of trust when it comes to e-WOM.

Two of the most studied concepts in understanding the effects of e-WOM are the credibility of sources and interpersonal interaction (Cheung & Thadani, 2012). In a customer-based study carried out over TripAdvisor, four factors significantly impacted the credibility and effect of e-WOM. These factors are the number and quantity of e-WOM, the credibility of the source, consumer engagement, and the perceived credibility of e-WOM (Reyes-Menendez et al., 2019).

Trust is divided into cognitive and affective trust, and both of these aspects influence one another. Cognitive trust originates from the authority and responsibility of the information provider, while emotional trust originates from the warmth, openness, and sincerity of the information provider (Johnson & Grayson, 2005). Unlike in WOM, the sender is not an intimate individual who is known for a long time; certain visible information is used to establish trust, such as the information provided under their profile (Xu, 2014). For example, information or opinions approved by many people affect consumers' decisions much more than detailed information (Cantallops & Salvi, 2014). This bandwagon effect is one of the most important factors in play in the digital realm. If someone's opinion is approved by a large group, users will become more likely to believe that the opinion in question is true and the product is good (Xu, 2014). To meet the need for credibility, senders create profiles on many sites. According to Van Der Heide (2008), there are two profile features that affect the formation of a sense of trust about that person the most. These features are the sender's reputation and profile picture. Reputation is determined by how many other users find the sender credible and how many of them find their opinions beneficial. This information and the person's appearance intuitively affect the users' sense of trust in the sender (Xu, 2014). Thus, both cognitive and affective trust are directly affected. Moreover, affective trust can develop independently of cognitive trust. In other words, users can develop trust in the commenter based on the profile picture, and this can even occur before the formation of cognitive trust (Steinbrück et al., 2002). As an additional detail, when the comments are negative, users tend to pay more attention to the commenter's profile (Xu, 2014).

SOCIAL E-WOM

There are two primary types of social e-WOM. The first is made by unfamiliar people on websites, and the other is made through social media with familiar individuals (Yan et al., 2018). Social e-WOM can be defined as the type of e-WOM made with familiar people or people who are recognizable from their profile on social media. Social e-WOM has more credibility. Or, as is the case on TripAdvisor, commenters frequently contact one another, which provides them some level of familiarity and increases trust (Hennig-Thurau et al., 2013). Although there are studies showing opposite results, it is generally accepted that trust increases in direct proportion to familiarity (McKnight et al., 2004). In other words, the stronger the bond (i.e., connection, acquaintance) between people in the e-WOM environment, the higher the credibility of e-WOM. However, women prefer more open and available social cues in the environment, which is the source of information (e.g., the profile of the commentator) compared to men. Moreover, the effects of intimacy and social proof are higher on social media than on websites (Yan et al., 2018). For this reason, many companies implement appropriate marketing practices. For example, Amazon allows users to log into the book reviews page along with their social media pages. This allows the readers to share content with each other (C2C). Likewise, Spotify and Airbnb have allowed comments that are linked to Facebook profiles (Pihlaja et al., 2017).

According to Park, Shin, and Ju (2019), the two sides in attachment theory (avoidance of attachment and anxiety about not attachment) directly affect e-WOM, while self-surveillance and social supervision are only effective indirectly. In other words, people who do not want to be attached to others adopt e-WOM to a lesser extent, while those who do not want to lose their attachments adapt it to a greater extent. Additionally, both self-surveillance and social surveillance show their effects on e-WOM through attachment styles. Therefore, whether a user seeks to control others due to their motive of independence or seeks to observe them and fit in, their involvement in e-WOM increases.

Social e-WOM is slightly different from e-WOM. Social e-WOM applies to social media platforms where membership is restricted, and content providers are known to purchasers. In relation to traditional e-WOM platforms that allow the publishing of anonymous reviews, social e-WOM has several unique features, including the target audience, information credibility, source assessment, and interpersonal relationships (Pihlaja et al., 2017).

EFFECTS AND RESULTS OF E-WOM

E-WOM is extremely influential on many customers' decisions to purchase a product or service, and it alters companies' financial, institutional, or operational results. The Dave Carrol incident in 2008 shows how effective e-WOM is. After his song that humorously complained about how United Airlines damaged his guitar and were completely indifferent to the issue was watched by 150,000 people on the first day, the company lost 180 million USD in three weeks. Another example from GAP relates to managerial decisions. After changing their blue background logo in 2010, the brand GAP received more than 2000 comments on Facebook criticizing the well-known logo, and a Twitter account formed to protest the new logo reached 5000 followers. The company then had to give up on changing its logo (Ismagilova et al., 2017).

Thus, e-WOM can go viral and turn into mass movements. These viral marketing effects can also be used by companies to achieve positive effects. However, such movements tend to be more effective if they are created as a result of a natural trend among the customers (and such effects tend to be generally grave). However, the resulting statistics for e-WOM are very striking, regardless of whether it creates a massive effect. This is because consumer reviews are trusted 12 times more than the descriptions provided by manufacturers (Ismagilova et al., 2017). For this reason, 91% of those between 18 and 34 place as much stock in online reviews as personal recommendations, and 93% of consumers indicate that online reviews influence their purchasing decisions (Kaemingk, 2020). Fifty or more reviews per product can lead to a 4.6% increase in conversion rates. E-WOM communications lead to an average of 18% uplift in sales (Ismagilova et al., 2017). Of course, when there are negative e-WOMs, the sales will decrease accordingly. However, e-WOM extends beyond purchasing decisions and changes the customers' attitudes. There are well-known and significant results among these attitudes, such as the purchasing intention, trust, dedication, intention to recommend, product/service, or brand knowledge level. These are all powerful variables that determine the destiny of a brand. In addition to these, there is a direct and linear relationship between e-WOM and brand value (Sijoria et al., 2018), using opportunities presented (Bai et al., 2017), ethnocentrism (Sun et al., 2020), and willingness to pay and price perceptions (Nieto-García et al., 2017).

In summary, customers leave comments about products and services for other customers to obtain and use to make purchasing decisions, also known as e-WOM. Companies also use this structure to listen to customers and understand their needs, to improve their products and services, and to provide feedback to their customers (Huete-Alcocer, 2017). However, extensive networks store information and user behaviors in an extremely large database, which further increases the visibility, accessibility, and readability of e-WOM data. Thus, in the future, e-WOM communication will become easier and play a more important role in influencing consumer purchasing decisions (Cheung & Thadani, 2012).

SOLUTIONS AND RECOMMENDATIONS

This section provides some practical suggestions for managers to increase the effect of positive e-WOM and prevent negative e-WOM.

Managers must be open to e-WOM and expand their channels to receive all messages, including negative e-WOMs. In particular, using written, visual, and aural formats can provide effective participation for e-WOM, so investments should be made in technologies that have these features.

There are thousands of reviews on the internet, even for ordinary products. Moreover, additional information, such as other relevant statistics or author reviews, is included on websites such as Amazon or TripAdvisor in addition to regular comments (Gottschalk & Mafael, 2017). It is easy to lose one's footing in this depth of information. Therefore, e-WOMs must be classified, and separate strategies must be developed for each category (Zhao et al., 2019). Hennig-Thurau et al. (2004) developed a segmentation model for their e-WOM customers and demonstrated that the customers who have made e-WOM decisions accordingly achieved a higher number of sales. For companies, using a single template while managing the e-WOM structure might result in many missed opportunities. For this reason, marketing managers must act according to the e-WOM structures of their customers and, if possible, influence them with personalized web pages. To this end, they must determine the e-WOM types that their customers prefer through surveys and online reviews. In this context, Gottschalk and Mafael (2017) stated the precautions and suggestions that should be taken according to e-WOM types (see Table 2).

Furthermore, the number of friends, the characteristics of friends, and the posts that are made can also provide information about a person's character traits. This means that digital media can provide social and interpersonal evidence to evaluate others (Utz, 2010).

A company culture that responds quickly and accurately to e-WOM should be established. This culture must be people-oriented and personalized. Even if artificial intelligence technologies are being employed, customers should be contacted using humane language. Different channels should be used for different messages and effects. While e-WOMs that contain a lot of information can leave positive effects on the general attitudes of people, they can also facilitate work that is carried out by users, especially in practical applications. For example, while closer relationships are used for products that contain higher emotional content, using social media over wider audiences for more functional products may enhance e-WOM (Gvili & Levy, 2018). In addition, it is especially important to use entertaining messages to increase persuasiveness and credibility. Marketers need to set up control systems to ensure that information delivered to customers is always correct. Thus, the credibility and entertainment of e-WOM will also increase (Gvili & Levy, 2016).

User-friendly online advertisements that allow users to participate should be designed. Moreover, correct advertisements should be targeted to correct individuals by making proper use of segmentation (Belanche et al., 2019).

Applications that promote customers to perform positive e-WOMs (e.g., promotions, discounts, providing information about altruism, sharing entertaining posts, competitions with awards, practical information) should be implemented (Babić Rosario et al., 2019). For example, 85% of the first commenters on Amazon are those who have received free books or other similar promotions (Pinch & Kesler, 2011). Honesty and candor should be taken as the basis while undertaking such efforts. Loyal customers should be identified, contacted, and thanked, and they should be encouraged to perform e-WOM communications (Sijoria et al., 2018).

Table 2. Cluster summary and managerial implications

Cluster	Cluster Characteristics	Managerial Implications
1. *The Efficients*	Particular focus on short online reviews that are timely and rated as helpful	Display recently published reviews that were rated as helpful at the top of the page Introduce character limits for online reviews Pay special attention to efficient website design
2. *The Meticulous*	Strong focus on all review characteristics, in particular to quality of content. Lowest focus on online review shortness	Introduce minimum length restrictions for online review texts Provide a large number of eWOM information cues on the website and enable readers to make their own selection of filters Close monitoring of eWOM activities, as it seems to be a crucial pre-purchase information source for this user
3. *The Quality-Evaluators*	Focus on author information, argument quality, and helpfulness	Introduce mandatory provision of author information for online review writers, such as real names or location Pay special attention to the quality appeal of the online review website, e.g. by giving reviewer authors tips for good review writing Implement additional quality signals, such as "verified purchase" of a product
4. *The Cautious Critics*	Focus on high-quality, negative content as well as structure and style of reviews	Stress adequate firm responses to negative online reviews Enhance structure and style of online reviews by providing structure templates to eWOM writers
5. *The Swift Pessimists*	Focus on short and negative online reviews	Providing personalized solutions for this cluster does not appear to be profitable, as this user type displays overall low focus on eWOM information cues and rate low on susceptibility to interpersonal influence At most, a light monitoring approach of negative eWOM seems feasible

Source:Gottschalk, & Mafael, (2017)

Comment areas should be unlocked on e-commerce sites to create a bridge between commenters and potential buyers. These areas should contain attention-grabbing discussion platforms, as well as sections specific to people to post their profiles. This will strengthen the bond and trust between individuals, thus strengthening e-WOM (Yan et al., 2018). In addition, consumers should be encouraged to comment via their social media profiles (Qiang et al., 2016). Thus, e-WOM will be strengthened thanks to the increased amount of social proof. However, controlling these comments and applying the necessary censorship is also inevitable. In particular, WOM comments that are virtual or visual in content (such as customer videos) can be introduced to potential or existing customers through different channels. On the other hand, pictures that customers share metaphorically can reflect their views about the brand, products, or services more accurately. Additionally, "ask a friend" features should be established on websites, and objective third-party sources such as Consumer Reports should also be included.

While facilitating e-WOM, precautions such as limiting users to one e-WOM should be considered to avoid misleading, manipulative, disingenuous e-WOM. In addition, limits such as word limit or video duration should also be established. Likewise, a reference-based system can also be set up for e-WOM. A certification structure related to credibility should be employed as well (for example, displaying the credibility ratings of e-WOM commentators). Free wi-fi should be offered to customers in offline channels to promote e-WOM.

Evidence from previous studies suggests that web care can stimulate positive responses in consumers after they have been faced with negative eWOM (Ismagilova et al., 2017). For this reason, customers who make negative e-WOM online should be contacted, and companies should try to eliminate their negative opinions about the company. It would be appropriate to decide the strategy to be applied in this context according to the value of e-WOM communications and the type of platform where these communications take place (İsmagilova et al., 2017). Additionally, the subconscious or root cause should be analyzed by performing metaphorical and in-depth interviews with negative commenters.

On the other hand, customers with high or low NPS scores are more likely to make positive or negative e-WOM communications; neutral customers do not exhibit a homogeneous behavior (Raassens & Haans, 2017). A strategy should be developed to transform negative and neutral comments into positive ones. Moreover, unlike the previous studies regarding this subject, customers are more likely to do negative e-WOM communications than positive ones, according to Raassens and Haans (2017).

Public relations should be established with online influencers so that companies can benefit from the positive e-WOM obtained from them. Companies should include influential or expert individuals in their e-WOM processes and cooperate with them, perhaps by sending free product samples. For product-based works, the focus should be on sharing entertaining information, while the production of information should be emphasized for service-based works (Rossmann et al., 2016). Since the credibility of e-WOM is higher for products with low financial risk, it is also particularly effective. For this reason, special attention should be paid to e-WOMs of low-priced and low-risk products, and resources should be allocated accordingly (Yan et al., 2018).

Finally, there exists a positive relationship between e-WOM and corporate sustainability projects (or corporate social responsibility projects) that provide well-designed information, protect personal data, provide effective customer services solutions and promote the proliferation of e-WOM's (Choi et al., 2019; Gerdt et al., 2019). In other words, people are more willing to do positive e-WOM communications (via Facebook) about companies engaging in such activities (Fatma et al., 2020). For this reason, it will be beneficial for companies to give life to sustainability projects that will increase e-WOM communications and positive PR. For instance, in the famous Oreo example (Writer, 2016), opportunities that may turn out to be real-time marketing opportunities should be capitalized on. Thus, unexpected positive e-WOM effects can be obtained. Moreover, consumers should be assured about information security and the protection of personal data.

FUTURE RESEARCH DIRECTIONS

In regard to e-WOM, the relationships between formats (i.e., verbal, written, and visual), the differences between channels (i.e., website, social media, platform), and the motivations to participate in e-WOM should be compared. Models should be developed to predict customer profiles and experiences with high e-WOM effects. Moreover, model studies should use personality traits to determine digital tools and e-WOM possibilities and preferences. Finally, the relationships between cultural levels and e-WOM behavior should also be investigated.

CONCLUSION

People or customers are social creatures. They are influenced by others both in determining and meeting their needs. That's why WOM is one of the oldest marketing tools. WOM has never disappeared and now it's improving in the digital world and replacing advertising and promotions. Customers trust their friends and other customers instead of the similar advertisements made by companies struggling in intense competition.

In this section, determinants of the traditional WOM like satisfaction, trust, commitment, and, outcomes of the traditional WOM like purchase and loyalty are handled. It will continue existing although it will be digitalized and turn into e-WOM for the most part. On top of that, e-WOM is faster and more effective. There are some differences between WOM and e-WOM: e-WOM reaches a larger audience, WOM has a definite source while e-WOM is generally anonymous, e-WOM's messages are conveyed more quickly among users at any time, WOM is only in spoken or written format, e-WOM is spread written, audio, and visual.

e-WOM has a primary upside and source: making (sender) and seeking (receiver). Some motivations for making e-WOM include altruism, self-enhancement, social benefits, receiving discounts, for seeking e-WOM include risk reduction, social approval, reduction of costs (time, effort, etc).

Clearly, e-WOM is a concept directly related to people's characteristics. The nature and amount of messages can affect people in different ways. However, it should be firmly stated that e-WOM's biggest issue is trust. For e-WOM to be successful, users (customers) first must trust the sender.

The main point of this section is e-WOM's quality to make customers feel confident. The core question managers should focus on is "How can we make customers feel confident in us?" For the managers who want to create a more efficient e-WOM, increase sales and gain the loyalty of customers, some of the suggestions given in the section are the following: to open more channels and use different formats, take care of negative e-WOMs, segment customers according to their e-WOM behavior, give intense and clear information, share fun messages, make the senders' identification accessible on social media, form honest relationships with influencers, organize social responsibility projects.

Today, e-WOM's influence on customers' purchasing decisions is inevitable. Managers who want to transform e-WOM, which can affect firms both positively or negatively, into something positive have to gain the trust of the customers because it is apparent that e-WOM will affect customers more easily and quickly in the future.

REFERENCES

Aydin, S. (2020). Dijital Çağda Pazarlama Anlayışının Dönüşümü. In G. Telli & S. Aydin (Eds.), Digital Transforming (pp.315-355). Kapital Medya.

Babić Rosario, A., Valck, K., & Francesca, S. (2019). Conceptualizing the electronic word-of-mouth process: What we know and need to know about eWOM creation, exposure, and evaluation. *Journal of the Academy of Marketing Science*, *48*(3), 422–448. doi:10.100711747-019-00706-1

Bai, X., Marsden, J., Roos, W. Jr, & Wang, G. (2017). How e-WOM and local competition drive local retailers' decisions about daily deal offerings. *Decision Support Systems*, *101*, 82–94. doi:10.1016/j.dss.2017.06.003

Bansal, H. S., & Voyer, P. A. (2000). Word-of-Mouth Processes within a Services Purchase Decision Context. *Journal of Service Research*, *3*(2), 166–177. doi:10.1177/109467050032005

Barnes, N. G., & Jacobsen, S. L. (2014). Missed eWOM opportunities: A cross-sector analysis of online monitoring behavior. *Journal of Marketing Communications*, *20*(1-2), 147–158. doi:10.1080/13527266.2013.797788

Belanche, D., Flavián, C., & Pérez-Rueda, A. (2019). Consumer empowerment in interactive advertising and eWOM consequences: The PITRE model. *Journal of Marketing Communications*, *26*(1), 1–20. doi:10.1080/13527266.2019.1610028

Belarmino, A. M., & Koh, Y. (2018). How E-WOM motivations vary by a hotel review website. *International Journal of Contemporary Hospitality Management*, *30*(8), 2730–2751. doi:10.1108/IJCHM-02-2017-0055

Bickart, B., & Schindler, R. M. (2001). Internet forums as influential sources of consumer information. *Journal of Interactive Marketing*, *15*(3), 31–40. doi:10.1002/dir.1014

Brackett, L. K., & Carr, B. N. Jr. (2001). Cyberspace advertising vs other media: Consumer vs. mature student attitudes. *Journal of Advertising Research*, *41*(5), 23–32. doi:10.2501/JAR-41-5-23-32

Bristor, J. M. (1990). Enhanced Explanations of Word of Mouth Communications: The Power of Relationships. *Research in Consumer Behavior*, *4*, 51–83.

Brown, J., Broderick, A. J., & Lee, N. (2007). Word of mouth communication within online communities: Conceptualizing the online social network. *Journal of Interactive Marketing*, *21*(3), 2–20. doi:10.1002/dir.20082

Brown, J. J., & Reingen, P. H. (1987). Social Ties and Word-of-Mouth Referral Behavior. *The Journal of Consumer Research*, *14*(3), 350–362. doi:10.1086/209118

Bu, Y., Parkinson, J., & Thaichon, P. (2020). Digital content marketing as a catalyst for e-WOM in food tourism. *Australasian Marketing Journal*, *13*(51). Advance online publication. doi:10.1016/j.ausmj.2020.01.001

Bulut, Z. A., & Karabulut, A. N. (2018). Examining the role of two aspects of eWOM in online repurchase intention: An integrated trust–loyalty perspective. *Journal of Consumer Behaviour*, *17*(4), 407–417. doi:10.1002/cb.1721

Cantallops, A. S., & Salvi, F. (2014). New consumer behavior: A review of research on eWOM and hotels. *International Journal of Hospitality Management*, *36*, 41–51. doi:10.1016/j.ijhm.2013.08.007

Cheung, C. M., & Thadani, D. R. (2012). The impact of electronic word-of-mouth communication: A literature analysis and integrative model. *Decision Support Systems*, *54*(1), 461–470. doi:10.1016/j.dss.2012.06.008

Choi, C. S., Cho, Y.-N., Ko, E., Kim, S. J., Kim, K. H., & Sarkees, M. E. (2019). Corporate sustainability efforts and e-WOM intentions in social platforms. *International Journal of Advertising*, *38*(8), 1224–1239. doi:10.1080/02650487.2019.1613858

Choi, J., Bell, D. R., & Lodish, L. M. (2012). Traditional and IS-enabled customer acquisition on the Internet. *Management Science*, *58*(4), 754–769. doi:10.1287/mnsc.1110.1447

Chu, S.-C., Lien, C.-H., & Cao, Y. (2018). Electronic word-of-mouth (eWOM) on WeChat: Examining the influence of sense of belonging, need for self-enhancement, and consumer engagement on Chinese travellers' eWOM. *International Journal of Advertising*, *38*(1), 26–49. doi:10.1080/02650487.2018.1470917

Dellarocas, C., Zhang, X. M., & Awad, N. F. (2007). Exploring the value of online product reviews in forecasting sales: The case of motion pictures. *Journal of Interactive Marketing*, *21*(4), 2–20. doi:10.1002/dir.20087

Duarte, P., Silva, S. C., & Ferreira, M. B. (2018). How convenient is it? Delivering online shopping convenience to enhance customer satisfaction and encourage e-WOM. *Journal of Retailing and Consumer Services*, *44*, 161–169. doi:10.1016/j.jretconser.2018.06.007

Ducoffe, R. H. (1996). Advertising value and advertising on the web. *Journal of Advertising Research*, *36*(5), 21–36.

Dutta, N., Verma, A., & Bhat, A. (2019). Analysis of Factors Influencing Negative e-Word of Mouth in Online Social Media Marketing. *ICSEB*, *2019*, 193–198. Advance online publication. doi:10.1145/3374549.3374556

Erkan, I., & Evans, C. (2018). Social media or shopping websites? The influence of eWOM on consumers' online purchase intentions. *Journal of Marketing Communications*, *24*(6), 617–632. doi:10.1080/13527266.2016.1184706

Fatma, M., Ruiz, A. P., Khan, I., & Rahman, Z. (2020). The effect of CSR engagement on eWOM on social media. *The International Journal of Organizational Analysis*, *28*(4), 941–956. doi:10.1108/IJOA-10-2019-1895

Forman, C., Ghose, A., & Wiesenfeld, B. (2008). Examining the relationship between reviews and sales: The role of reviewer identity disclosure in electronic markets. *Information Systems Research*, *19*(3), 291–313. doi:10.1287/isre.1080.0193

Gerdt, S.-O., Wagner, E., & Schewe, G. (2019). The relationship between sustainability and customer satisfaction in hospitality: An explorative investigation using eWOM as a data source. *Tourism Management*, *74*, 155–172. doi:10.1016/j.tourman.2019.02.010

Gottschalk, S. A., & Mafael, A. (2017). Cutting Through the Online Review Jungle— Investigating Selective eWOM Processing. *Journal of Interactive Marketing*, *37*, 89–104. doi:10.1016/j.intmar.2016.06.001

Gvili, Y., & Levy, S. (2016). Antecedents of attitudes toward eWOM communication: Differences across channels. *Internet Research*, *26*(5), 1030–1051. doi:10.1108/IntR-08-2014-0201

Gvili, Y., & Levy, S. (2018). Consumer engagement with eWOM on social media: The role of social capital. *Online Information Review*, *42*(4), 482–505. doi:10.1108/OIR-05-2017-0158

Hennig-Thurau, T., Gwinner, K. P., Walsh, G., & Gremler, D. D. (2004). Electronic word-of-mouth via consumer-opinion platforms: What motivates consumers to articulate themselves on the Internet? *Journal of Interactive Marketing*, *18*(1), 38–52. doi:10.1002/dir.10073

Hennig-Thurau, T., Hofacker, C. F., & Bloching, B. (2013). Marketing the Pinball Way: Understanding How Social Media Change the Generation of Value for Consumers and Companies. *Journal of Interactive Marketing, 27*(4), 237–241. doi:10.1016/j.intmar.2013.09.005

Hennig-Thurau, T., Malthouse, E. C., Friege, C., Gensler, S., Lobschat, L., Rangaswamy, A., & Skiera, B. (2010). The impact of new media on customer relationships. *Journal of Service Research, 13*(3), 311–330. doi:10.1177/1094670510375460

Huete-Alcocer, N. (2017). A Literature Review of Word of Mouth and Electronic Word of Mouth Implications for Consumer Behavior. *Frontiers in Psychology, 8*, 1256. doi:10.3389/fpsyg.2017.01256 PMID:28790950

Ismagilova, E., Dwivedi, Y. K., Slade, E., & Williams, M. D. (2017). *Electronic Word of Mouth (eWOM) in the Marketing Context: A State of the Art Analysis and Future Directions*. Springer. doi:10.1007/978-3-319-52459-7

Johnson, D., & Grayson, K. (2005). Cognitive and affective trust in service relationships. *Journal of Business Research, 58*(4), 500–507. doi:10.1016/S0148-2963(03)00140-1

Kaemingk, D. (2020, 30 October). *Online reviews statistics to know in 2021*. https://www.qualtrics.com/blog/online-review-stats/

Katz, E., & Lazarsfeld, P. F. (1955). *Personal Influence: The Part Played by People in the Flow of Mass Communications*. Free Press.

Kotler, P., Kartajaya, H., & Setiawan, I. (2017). *Marketing 4.0*. Optimist Publishers.

Kumar, V., Petersen, J. A., & Leone, R. P. (2010). Driving Profitability by Encouraging Customer Referrals: Who, When, and How. *Journal of Marketing, 74*(5), 1–17. doi:10.1509/jmkg.74.5.001

Liu, R. R., & Zhang, W. (2010). Informational influence of online customer feedback: An empirical study. *Journal of Database Marketing & Customer Strategy Management, 17*(2), 120–131. doi:10.1057/dbm.2010.11

McKnight, D. H., Kacmar, C. J., & Choudhury, V. (2004). Shifting Factors and the Ineffectiveness of Third Party Assurance Seals: A Two-Stage Model of Initial Trust in a Web Business. *Electronic Markets, 14*(3), 252–266. doi:10.1080/10196780420000245263

Murray, K. B. (1991). A Test of Service Marketing Theory: Consumer Information Acquisition Activities. *Journal of Marketing, 55*(01), 10–15. doi:10.1177/002224299105500102

Nabi, R. L., & Hendriks, A. (2003). The persuasive effect of host and audience reaction shots in television talk shows. *Journal of Communication, 53*(3), 527–543. doi:10.1111/j.1460-2466.2003.tb02606.x

Nieto, J., Hernández-Maestro, R. M., & Muñoz-Gallego, P. A. (2014). Marketing decisions, customer reviews, and business performance: The use of the Toprural website by Spanish rural lodging establishments. *Tourism Management, 45*, 115–123. doi:10.1016/j.tourman.2014.03.009

Nieto-García, M., Muñoz-Gallego, P. A., & González-Benito, Ó. (2017). Tourists' willingness to pay for an accommodation: The effect of eWOM and internal reference price. *International Journal of Hospitality Management, 62*, 67–77. doi:10.1016/j.ijhm.2016.12.006

Park, M.-S., Shin, J.-K., & Ju, Y. (2019). Attachment styles and electronic word of mouth (e-WOM) adoption on social networking sites. *Journal of Business Research, 99*(C), 398–404. doi:10.1016/j.jbusres.2017.09.020

Pihlaja, J., Saarijärvi, H., Spence, M. T., & Yrjölä, M. (2017). From Electronic WOM to Social eWOM: Bridging the Trust Deficit. *Journal of Marketing Theory and Practice, 25*(4), 340–356. doi:10.1080/10696679.2017.1345593

Pinch, T., & Kesler, F. (2011). How aunt Amy gets her free lunch: A study of the top-thousand customer reviewers at Amazon.com. In B. Czarniawska & O. Lofgren (Eds.), *Managing Overflow in Affluent Societies*. Routledge.

Qiang, Y., Shuang, W., Lingli, W., Pengfei, W., Hejie, C., & Guohong, W. (2016). E-WOM from e-commerce websites and social media: Which will consumers adopt? *Electronic Commerce Research and Applications, 17*(C), 62–73. doi:10.1016/j.elerap.2016.03.004

Raassens, N., & Haans, H. (2017). NPS and Online WOM: Investigating the Relationship Between Customers' Promoter Scores and eWOM Behavior. *Journal of Service Research, 20*(3), 322–334. doi:10.1177/1094670517696965 PMID:29046609

Reyes-Menendez, A., Saura, J. R., & Martinez-Navalon, J. G. (2019). The Impact of e-WOM on Hotels Management Reputation: Exploring TripAdvisor Review Credibility With the ELM Model. *IEEE Access: Practical Innovations, Open Solutions, 7*, 68868–68877. doi:10.1109/ACCESS.2019.2919030

Rossmann, A., Kumar, R., & Praveen, S. (2016). Drivers of user engagement in eWoM communication. *Journal of Services Marketing, 30*(5), 541–553. doi:10.1108/JSM-01-2015-0013

Schiffman, L. G., & Kanuk, L. L. (1997). *Consumer Behaviour*. Prentice Hall.

Sijoria, C., Mukherjee, S., & Datta, B. (2018). Impact of the antecedents of eWOM on CBBE. *Marketing Intelligence & Planning, 36*(5), 528–542. doi:10.1108/MIP-10-2017-0221

Steinbrück, U., Schaumburg, H., Duda, S., & Krüger, T. (2002). A picture says more than a thousand words–Photographs as trust builders in e-commerce websites. In *Proceedings of conference on human factors in computing systems CHI 2002, extended abstracts* (pp. 748–749). 10.1145/506443.506578

Sun, Y., Gonzalez-Jimenez, H., & Wang, S. (2021, June). Hector Gonzalez-Jimenez and Shenghui Wang. (In Press). Examining the relationships between e-WOM, consumer ethnocentrism and brand equity. *Journal of Business Research, 130*, 564–573. Advance online publication. doi:10.1016/j.jbusres.2019.09.040

Sundaram, D. S., Mitra, K., & Webster, C. (1998). Word of-Mouth Communications: A Motivational Analysis. *Advances in Consumer Research. Association for Consumer Research (U. S.), 25*, 527–531.

Utz, S. (2010). Show me your friends and I will tell you what type of person you are: How one's profile, number of friends, and type of friends influence impression formation on social network sites. *Journal of Computer-Mediated Communication, 15*(2), 314–335. doi:10.1111/j.1083-6101.2010.01522.x

Wilson, R. (2011). *A public relations disaster how saving $1,200 cost United Airlines 10,772,839 negative views on YouTube*. https://sentium.com/a-public-relations-disaster-how-saving1200-cost-united-airlines-10772839-negative-views-on-youtube/

Worldpay. (2017). *For each of the following circumstances, how important is it to read online reviews before purchasing a product or selecting a service provider?* http://www-statista-com.du.idm.oclc.org/statistics/713258/onlinereview-importance-circumstances-usa/

Writer, S. (2016). *2013: Oreo wins the Super Bowl with 'dunk in the dark' tweet*. https://www.thedrum.com/news/2016/07/10/marketing-moment-101-oreo-wins-super-bowl-dunk-dark-tweet

Xu, Q. (2014). Should I trust him? The effects of reviewer profile characteristics on eWOM credibility. *Computers in Human Behavior, 33*, 136–144. doi:10.1016/j.chb.2014.01.027

Yan, Q., Wu, S., Zhou, Y., & Zhang, L. (2018). How differences in eWOM platforms impact consumers' perceptions and decision-making. *Journal of Organizational Computing and Electronic Commerce, 28*(4), 315–333. doi:10.1080/10919392.2018.1517479

Zhao, P., Wu, J., Hua, Z., & Fang, S. (2019). Finding eWOM customers from customer reviews. *Industrial Management & Data Systems, 119*(1), 129–147. doi:10.1108/IMDS-09-2017-0418

ADDITIONAL READING

Ess, C. M. (2010). Trust and new communication technologies: Vicious circles, virtuous circles, possible futures. *Knowledge, Technology & Policy, 23*(3/4), 287–305. doi:10.100712130-010-9114-8

Hennig-Thurau, T., Malthouse, E. C., Friege, C., Gensler, S., Lobschat, L., Rangaswamy, A., & Skiera, B. (2010). The impact of new media on customer relationships. *Journal of Service Research, 13*(3), 311–330. doi:10.1177/1094670510375460

Huete-Alcocer, N. (2017). A Literature Review of Word of Mouth and Electronic Word of Mouth Implications for Consumer Behavior. *Frontiers in Psychology, 8*, 1256. doi:10.3389/fpsyg.2017.01256 PMID:28790950

Ismagilova, E., Dwivedi, Y. K., Slade, E., & Williams, M. D. (2017). *Electronic Word of Mouth (eWOM) in the Marketing Context: A State of the Art Analysis and Future Directions*. Springer. doi:10.1007/978-3-319-52459-7

Johnson, D., & Grayson, K. (2005). Cognitive and affective trust in service relationships. *Journal of Business Research, 58*(4), 500–507. doi:10.1016/S0148-2963(03)00140-1

Michelli, J. A. (2008). *The New Gold Standard: 5 Leadership Principles for Creating a Legendary Customer Experience Courtesy of the Ritz-Carlton Hotel*. McGraw-Hill Education.

Papadopoulou, P. (2007). Applying virtual reality for trust-building e-commerce environments. *Virtual Reality (Waltham Cross), 11*(2–3), 107–127. doi:10.100710055-006-0059-x

Taddeo, M. (2009). Defining trust and e-trust: Old theories and new problems. *International Journal of Technology and Human Interaction*, *5*(2), 23–35. doi:10.4018/jthi.2009040102

KEY TERMS AND DEFINITIONS

Altruism: A behaviour that is acting to help someone else. It is contrary to "self-interested" or "selfish" or "egoistic."

Credibility (Trust): A customer's belief in the reliability (truth) of a company.

Negative E-WOM: A word of mouth effect that is harming a company.

Positive E-WOM: A word of mouth effect that is supporting a company.

Receiver: A person who is seeking e-WOM to purchase some product or services.

Referral: An act of referring someone or something for consultation, review, or further action.

Sender: A person who is making e-WOM.

Compilation of References

Aaker, D. A. (1996). Measuring Brand Equity Across Products And Markets. *California Management Review*, *38*(3), 102–120. doi:10.2307/41165845

Absolute Reports. (2020). *Global Digital Retail Marketing Market Report 2020.* https://www.absolutereports.com/global-digital-retail-market-15595402

Abubakar, A. M., Ilkan, M., & Sahin, P. (2016). eWOM, eReferral and gender in the virtual community. *Marketing Intelligence & Planning*, *34*(5), 692–710. doi:10.1108/MIP-05-2015-0090

Adam, S., Mulye, R., & Deans, K. R. (2001). The evolution of relationships in e-marketing. In J. N. Sheth, A. Parvatiyar, & G. Shainesh (Eds.), *Customer Relationship Management: Emerging Concepts, Tools and Applications* (pp. 135–142). Tata McGraw-Hill.

Adam, S., Mulye, R., Deans, K. R., & Palihawadana, D. (2002). e-Marketing in perspective: A three country comparison of business use of the internet. *Marketing Intelligence & Planning*, *20*(4), 243–251. doi:10.1108/02634500210431649

Adivar, B., Hüseyinoglu, I. O. Y., & Christopher, M. (2019). A quantitative performance management framework for assessing omnichannel retail supply chains. *Journal of Retailing and Consumer Services*, *48*, 257–269. doi:10.1016/j.jretconser.2019.02.024

Advertising Association. (2020). *UK advertising trends, Advertising Matters.* Available from adassoc.org.uk

Agag, G. M., & El-Masry, A. A. (2017). Why do consumers trust online travel websites? Drivers and outcomes of consumer trust toward online travel websites. *Journal of Travel Research*, *56*(3), 347–369. doi:10.1177/0047287516643185

Agarwal, R., Gao, G., DesRoches, C., & Jha, A. K. (2010). Research commentary -The digital transformation of healthcare: Current status and the road ahead. *Information Systems Research*, *21*(4), 796–809. doi:10.1287/isre.1100.0327

Aguinis, H. (2011). Organizational responsibility: Doing good and doing well. In S. Zedeck (Ed.), *APA handbook of industrial and organizational psychology* (Vol. 3, pp. 855–879). American Psychological Association. doi:10.1037/12171-024

Aguinis, H., & Glavas, A. (2012). What we know and don't know about corporate social responsibility: A review and research agenda. *Journal of Management*, *38*(4), 932–968. doi:10.1177/0149206311436079

Agustin, C., & Singh, J. (2005). Curvilinear effects of consumer loyalty determinants in relational exchanges. *JMR, Journal of Marketing Research*, *42*(1), 96–108. doi:10.1509/jmkr.42.1.96.56961

Ahmad, S. Z., Ahmad, N., & Bakar, A. R. A. (2018). Reflections of entrepreneurs of small and medium-sized enterprises concerning the adoption of social media and its impact on performance outcomes: Evidence from the UAE. *Telematics and Informatics*, *35*(1), 6–17. doi:10.1016/j.tele.2017.09.006

Ahmad, S. Z., Bakar, A. R. A., & Ahmad, N. (2019). Social media adoption and its impact on firm performance: The case of the UAE. *International Journal of Entrepreneurial Behaviour & Research, 25*(1), 84–111. doi:10.1108/IJEBR-08-2017-0299

Ahrefs.com. (2021). https://ahrefs.com/blog/most-visited-websites/

Ajjan, H., & Hartshorne, R. (2008). Investigating faculty decisions to adopt Web 2.0 technologies: Theory and empirical tests. *The Internet and Higher Education, 11*(2), 71–80. doi:10.1016/j.iheduc.2008.05.002

Ajzen, I. (1991). The theory of planned behavior. *Organizational Behavior and Human Decision Processes, 50*(2), 179–211. doi:10.1016/0749-5978(91)90020-T

Akıncı, S., Atılgan-Inan, E., & Aksoy, S. (2010). Re-assessment of E-S-Qual and E-RecS-Qual in a Pure Service Setting. *Journal of Business Research, 63*(3), 232–240. doi:10.1016/j.jbusres.2009.02.018

Akkılıç, S. (2020). *Anlamlı Marka Olabilmek, Kalabalıkların Kültürü ve Anti-Prensesler...* http://serhatakkilic.com/2020/01/anlamli-marka-olabilmek-kalabaliklarin-kulturu-ve-anti-prensesler/

Alalwan, A. A., Rana, N. P., Dwivedi, Y. K., & Algharabat, R. (2017). Social Media In Marketing: A Review And Analysis Of The Existing Literature. *Telematics and Informatics, 34*(7), 1177–1190. doi:10.1016/j.tele.2017.05.008

Alden, D. L., Mukherjee, A., & Hoyer, W. D. (2000). The effects of incongruity, surprise and positive moderators on perceived humour in television advertising. *Journal of Advertising, 29*(2), 1–15. doi:10.1080/00913367.2000.10673605

Alexander, B., & Cano, M. B. (2020). Store of the future: Towards a (re)invention and (re)imagination of physical store space in an omnichannel context. *Journal of Retailing and Consumer Services, 55*, 101913. doi:10.1016/j.jretconser.2019.101913

Alloing, C. (2013). La médiation documentaire sur les réseaux socio-numériques comme vecteur de l'e-réputation. La Poste, Twitter et les agents-facilitateurs. *Communication et organisation, 43*, 73-84.

Alloing, C. (2016). *Réputation: Méditation, calcul, émotion*. CNRS Editions.

Alloing, C., & Pierre, J. (2012). *Construire un cadre d'analyse avec les SIC pour comprendre les pratiques et les enjeux de la réputation en ligne (des individus et des organisations)*. Academic Press.

Alonso-Almeida, Bernado, Llach, & Marimon. (2013). Building loyalty through functional and hedonic quality. *Industrial Management & Data Systems, 114*(3), 387–404.

Al-Qirim, N. (2007). A research trilogy into e-commerce adoption in small businesses in New Zealand. *Electronic Markets, 17*(4), 263–285. doi:10.1080/10196780701635872

Althonayan, A., & Sharif, A. M. (2010). Aligning business and technology strategy within the airline industry. *International Journal of Business Information Systems, 6*(1), 79–94. doi:10.1504/IJBIS.2010.034006

Amabile, T. M., Hil, K. G., Hennessey, B. A., & Tighe, E. M. (1995). The Work Preference Inventory: Assessing intrinsic and extrinsic motivational orientations. *Journal of Personality and Social Psychology, 66*(5), 950–967. doi:10.1037/0022-3514.66.5.950 PMID:8014837

Amazon Official Website-News. (2021). https://www.aboutamazon.com/news/transportation/amazons-custom-electric-delivery-vehicles-are-starting-to-hit-the-road

Anand, N. (2013). *Kotler adds a 5th P to his set of four – Purpose*. https://www.dnaindia.com/business/report-kotler-adds-a-5th-p-to-his-set-of-four-purpose-1812393

Anand, P., & Sternthal, B. (1990). Ease of message processing as a moderator of repetition effects in advertising. *JMR, Journal of Marketing Research, 27*(3), 345–353. doi:10.1177/002224379002700308

Anderl, E., Schumann, J. H., & Kunz, W. (2016). Helping firms reduce complexity in multichannel online data: A new taxonomy-based approach for customer journeys. *Journal of Retailing, 92*(2), 185–203. doi:10.1016/j.jretai.2015.10.001

Anderson, H., & Jacobsen, P. N. (2000). Creating loyalty: Its strategic importance in your customer strategy. *Customer Relationship Management, 55*, 67.

Anderson, E. W., Fornell, C., & Lehmann, D. R. (1994). Customer satisfaction, market share, and profitability: Findings from Sweden. *Journal of Marketing, 58*(3), 53–66. doi:10.1177/002224299405800304

Anderson, R. N. (2017). Petroleum Analytics Learning Machine for optimizing the Internet of Things of today's digital oil field-to-refinery petroleum system. In *2017 IEEE International Conference on Big Data (Big Data)* (pp. 4542-4545). IEEE. 10.1109/BigData.2017.8258496

Anghel, L. D. (2015). *The marketing of small and medium-sized enterprises.* Biblioteca Digitală ASE. http://www.biblioteca-digitala.ase.ro/biblioteca/

Ansari, A., Mela, C. F., & Neslin, S. A. (2008). Customer channel migration. *JMR, Journal of Marketing Research, XLV*(1), 60–76. doi:10.1509/jmkr.45.1.60

Antonopoulos, N., & Veglis, A. (2013). The evolution of the technological characteristics of media websites. *Proceedings of the 4th Annual Asian Conference on Media and Mass Communication (MediAsia 2013)*, 130-146.

Antonopoulos, N., Veglis, A., Gardikiotis, A., Kotsakis, R., & Kalliris, G. (2015). Web Third-person effect in structural aspects of the information on media websites. *Computers in Human Behavior, 44*, 45–58. doi:10.1016/j.chb.2014.11.022

Ardito, L., Scuotto, V., Del Giudice, M., & Petruzzelli, A. M. (2019). A bibliometric analysis of research on Big Data analytics for business and management. *Management Decision, 57*(8), 1993–2009. doi:10.1108/MD-07-2018-0754

Ardley, B., McIntosh, E., & McManus, J. (2020). From transactions to interactions: The value of co-creation processes within online brand consumer communities. *Business Process Management Journal, 26*(4), 825–838. doi:10.1108/BPMJ-10-2019-0444

Arens, W., Arens, C., Weigold, M., & Schaefer, D. (2011). *Advertising (M).* McGraw-Hill/Irwin.

Arnaboldi, M., Melisa, L. & Lema, D. (2021). The participatory turn in museums: The online facet. *Poetics*. doi:10.1016/j.poetic.2021.101536

Arrigo, E. (2018). Social Media Marketing In Luxury Brands. *Management Research Review, 41*(6), 657–679. doi:10.1108/MRR-04-2017-0134

Arzaghi, M., Berndt, E. R., Davis, J. C., & Silk, A. J. (2012). The unbundling of advertising agency services: An economic analysis. *Review of Marketing Science., 10*(1), 1546–5616. doi:10.1515/1546-5616.1164

Atzori, L., Iera, A., & Morabito, G. (2010). The internet of things: A survey. *Computer Networks, 54*(15), 2787–2805. doi:10.1016/j.comnet.2010.05.010

Aurier, P., Benavent, C., & N'goala, G. (2001). Validité discriminante et prédictive des composantes de la relation à la marque. *Cahiers de Recherche du CREGO*, (8), 51–70.

Autio, E. (2017). *Digitalisation, Ecosystems, Entrepreneurship and Policy. Perspectives into Topical Issues Is Society and Ways to Support Political Decision Making. Government's Analysis. Research and Assessment Activities Policy Brief 20/2017*. Prime Minister's Office.

Avouris, N. (2000). *Introduction to Communication Human – Computer* [Εισαγωγή στην Επικοινωνία Ανθρώπου – Υπολογιστή]. Diavlos.

Aydin, S. (2020). Dijital Çağda Pazarlama Anlayışının Dönüşümü. In G. Telli & S. Aydin (Eds.), Digital Transforming (pp.315-355). Kapital Medya.

Aziz, A. (2017). *Brand Purpose 101: Everything you wanted to know but were afraid to ask.* https://medium.com/@afdhelaziz/brand-purpose-101-everything-you-wanted-to-know-but-were-afraid-to-ask-21593fb37d33

Aziz, A., & Jones, B. (2016). *Good Is the New Cool: Market Like You Give a Damn.* Regan Arts.

Aziz, S., Shamin, M., Aziz, M. F., & Avais, P. (2013). *The Impact of Texting/ SMS Language on Academic Writing of Students-What do we need to panic about.* Elixir Languages and Translations.

Azuma, R., Baillot, Y., Behringer, R., Feiner, S., Julier, S., & MacIntyre, B. (2001). Recent advances in augmented reality. *IEEE Computer Graphics and Applications, 21*(6), 34–40. doi:10.1109/38.963459

Azwna, R. (1997). A survey of augmented reality. *Presence (Cambridge, Mass.), 6*(4), 355–385. doi:10.1162/pres.1997.6.4.355

Babić Rosario, A., Valck, K., & Francesca, S. (2019). Conceptualizing the electronic word-of-mouth process: What we know and need to know about eWOM creation, exposure, and evaluation. *Journal of the Academy of Marketing Science, 48*(3), 422–448. doi:10.100711747-019-00706-1

Bahri-Ammari, N. (2012). The effects of loyalty program quality on word-of-mouth recommendations intentions. *International Journal of Economics and Management Engineering, 6*(4), 619–628.

Bahri-Ammari, N., Van Niekerk, M., Khelil, H. B., & Chtioui, J. (2016). The effects of brand attachment on behavioral loyalty in the luxury restaurant sector. *International Journal of Contemporary Hospitality Management.*

Bai, H., McColl, J., & Moore, C. (2017). Luxury retailers' entry and expansion strategies in China. *International Journal of Retail & Distribution Management, 45*(11), 1181–1199. doi:10.1108/IJRDM-11-2016-0232

Bailey, A. A., Bonifield, C. M., & Elhai, J. D. (2021). Modeling consumer engagement on social networking sites: Roles of attitudinal and motivational factors. *Journal of Retailing and Consumer Services, 59*, 102348. doi:10.1016/j.jretconser.2020.102348

Bain & Company. (2020). *Eight Themes That Are Rewriting the Future of Luxury Goods.* https://www.bain.com/insights/eight-themes-that-are-rewriting-the-future-of-luxury-goods/

Bai, X., Marsden, J., Roos, W. Jr, & Wang, G. (2017). How e-WOM and local competition drive local retailers' decisions about daily deal offerings. *Decision Support Systems, 101*, 82–94. doi:10.1016/j.dss.2017.06.003

Baker, W., Hutchinson, J., Moore, D., & Nedungadi, P. (1986). *Brand familiarity and advertising: effects on the evoked set and brand preference.* ACR North American Advances.

Balasubramanian, S., Raghunathan, R., & Mahajan, V. (2005). Consumers in a multichannel environment:product utility, process utility, and channel choice. *Journal of Interactive Marketing, 19*(2), 12–30. doi:10.1002/dir.20032

Bansal, H. S., & Voyer, P. A. (2000). Word-of-Mouth Processes within a Services Purchase Decision Context. *Journal of Service Research, 3*(2), 166–177. doi:10.1177/109467050032005

Baptista, J. (2009). Institutionalisation as a process of interplay between technology and its organisational context of use. *Journal of Information Technology, 24*(4), 305–319. doi:10.1057/jit.2009.15

Bardhan, I., Krishnan, V., & Lin, S. (2013). Business Value of Information Technology: Testing the Interaction Effect of IT and R&D on Tobin's Q. *Information Systems Research*.

Barnes, N. G., & Jacobsen, S. (2013). Adoption of social media by fast-growing companies: Innovation among the Inc. 500. *Journal of Marketing Development and Competitiveness*, *7*(1), 11–17.

Barnes, N. G., & Jacobsen, S. L. (2014). Missed eWOM opportunities: A cross-sector analysis of online monitoring behavior. *Journal of Marketing Communications*, *20*(1-2), 147–158. doi:10.1080/13527266.2013.797788

Baron, N. (2008). *Always On*. Oxford University Press. doi:10.1093/acprof:oso/9780195313055.001.0001

Barry, J. M., & Graça, S. S. (2018). Humour Effectiveness in Social Video Engagement. *Journal of Marketing Theory and Practice*, *26*(1-2), 158–180. doi:10.1080/10696679.2017.1389247

Bashir, I., Naik, K., & Madhavaiah, C. (2013). Potential business applications of Quick Response (QR) codes. *Prajnan (Pune)*, *41*(4), 353–366.

Bastide, E. H. (2017). *L'influence de la réalité augmentée sur l'expérience de magasinage mobile: le cas de l'application Make-up Genius de L'Oréal, Mémoire en Science de Gestion*. Université du Québec à Montréal.

Batat, W. (2011). The coming out of the «new consumer»: Towards the theorisation of the concept in consumer research. *Advances in Consumer Research. Association for Consumer Research (U. S.)*, *9*, 304–312.

Batat, W. (2018). *Concevoir et améliorer l'expérience client digitale: Le Triangle de l'Expérience Digitale pour réussir la transformation digitale-Le Blue Sunflower Marketing pour innover efficacement-L'approche Physical 2030 pour performer*. Editions Eyrolles.

Batat, W. (2020). How can art museums develop new business opportunities? Exploring young visitors' experience. *Young Consumers*, *21*(1), 109–131. doi:10.1108/YC-09-2019-1049

Batat, W., & Frochot, I. (2014). *Le Marketing Expérientiel. Comment concevoir et stimuler l'éxpérience client*. Dunod.

Bathelot, B. (2016). *Définition: Réalité augmentée*. Récupéré sur Définitions marketing: http://www. definitions-marketing. com/definition/realite-augmentee

Batra, R., Ahuvia, A., & Bagozzi, R. P. (2012). Brand love. *Journal of Marketing*, *76*(March), 1–16. doi:10.1509/jm.09.0339

Bauer, H. H., Falk, T., & Hammerschmidt, M. (2006). A transaction process-based approach for capturing service quality in online shopping. *Journal of Business Research*, *59*(7), 866–875. doi:10.1016/j.jbusres.2006.01.021

Baumeister, R. F., & Leary, M. R. (1995). The need to belong: Desire for interpersonal attachments as a fundamental human motivation. *Psychological Bulletin*, *117*(3), 497–529. doi:10.1037/0033-2909.117.3.497 PMID:7777651

Beaconstac. (2019). *The Future of QR Codes: 2019 and Beyond*. https://blog.beaconstac.com/2019/07/what-they-think-of-qr-codes-in-2019/#The-Future-of-QR-Codes:-2019-and-beyond

Beall, G. (2017). *8 Key Differences between Gen Z and Millennials*. Retrieved May 8, 2020, from Huffington Post:https:// www.huffingtonpost.com/george-beall/8-key differencesbetweenb12814200.html?guccoun ter=1

Beard, F. K. (2008). *Humour in the advertising business: Theory, practice, and wit*. Rowman & Littlefield.

Beck, N., & Rygl, D. (2015). Categorization of multiple channel retailing in Multi-, Cross-, and Omni-Channel Retailing for retailers and retailing. *Journal of Retailing and Consumer Services*, *27*, 170–178. doi:10.1016/j.jretconser.2015.08.001

Belaid, S., & Behi, A. T. (2011). The role of attachment in building consumer-brand relationships: An empirical investigation in the utilitarian consumption context. *Journal of Product and Brand Management*, *20*(1), 37–47. doi:10.1108/10610421111108003

Belanche, D., Casaló, L. V., & Flavián, C. (2020). Frontline robots in tourism and hospitality: Service enhancement or cost reduction? *Electronic Markets*, 1–16.

Belanche, D., Flavián, C., & Pérez-Rueda, A. (2019). Consumer empowerment in interactive advertising and eWOM consequences: The PITRE model. *Journal of Marketing Communications*, *26*(1), 1–20. doi:10.1080/13527266.2019.1610028

Belarmino, A. M., & Koh, Y. (2018). How E-WOM motivations vary by a hotel review website. *International Journal of Contemporary Hospitality Management*, *30*(8), 2730–2751. doi:10.1108/IJCHM-02-2017-0055

Bellaaj-Gargouri, R., & Akrout, F. (2008). Nostalgie et fidélité du consommateur: le rôlemédiateur de l'attachement à la marque. *Proceedings of International Congress Marketing Trends*, 7.

Bell, D. R., Gallino, S., & Moreno, A. (2014). How to win in an omnichannel world. *MIT Sloan Management Review*, *56*(1), 45–53.

Bell, D. R., Gallino, S., & Moreno, A. (2018). Offline showrooms in omnichannel retail: Demand and operational benefits. *Management Science*, *64*(4), 1629–1651. doi:10.1287/mnsc.2016.2684

Ben Khelil, H., & Bahri-Ammari, N. (2015). Brand Attachment and its Effects on Proselytism and the Resistance to Change: Comparative Study between Two Categories of Products. *Nedra, Brand Attachment and its Effects on Proselytism and the Resistance to Change: Comparative Study between Two Categories of Products.*

Ben Khelil, H., & Bouslama, N. (2013). *L'impact de la perception de la qualité du service sur le prosélytisme: Cas des fournisseurs de service Internet en Tunisie* [The Impact of the Perception of the Quality of the Service on Proselytism: Case of Internet Service Suppliers in Tunisia]. Academic Press.

Ben Mimoun, M. S., & Ammar, O. (2013). Interactions between brands and strategies of self-presentation on Facebook. *Advances in Consumer Research. Association for Consumer Research (U. S.)*, *10*, 95–97.

Benghozi. (2003). De l'intermédiation à la prescription: le cas de la Télévision. Revue Française de Gestion, 29(402), 205-227.

Bennett, D. R., & El Azhari, J. (2015). *Omni-Channel Customer Experience: An Investigation Into The Use Of Digital Technology In Physical Stores And Its Impact On The Consumer's Decision-Making Process*. Academic Press.

Bennett, R., Härtel, C. E., & McColl-Kennedy, J. R. (2005). Experience as a moderator of involvement and satisfaction on brand loyalty in a business-to-business setting 02-314R. *Industrial Marketing Management*, *34*(1), 97–107. doi:10.1016/j.indmarman.2004.08.003

Benvenuto, M., Avram, A., Sambati, F. V., Avram, M., & Viola, C. (2020). The Impact of Internet Usage and Knowledge-Intensive Activities on Households' Healthcare Expenditures. *International Journal of Environmental Research and Public Health*, *17*(12), 4470. doi:10.3390/ijerph17124470 PMID:32580302

Berger, A. A. (2017). *An anatomy of humour*. Routledge. doi:10.4324/9781315082394

Berlyne, D. E., Margaret, M. A., Salapatek, P. H., & Judith, L. L. (1963). Novelty, complexity, incongruity, extrinsic motivation, and the GSR. *Journal of Experimental Psychology*, *66*(6), 550–567. doi:10.1037/h0045767 PMID:14087632

Berman, R., & Katona, Z. (2013). The role of search engine optimization in search marketing. *Marketing Science*, *32*(4), 644–651. doi:10.1287/mksc.2013.0783

Berman, S. J. (2012). Digital transformation: Opportunities to create new business models. *Strategy and Leadership, 40*(2), 16–24. doi:10.1108/10878571211209314

Berners-Lee, T. (1999). *Weaving the Web: The Past, Present and Future of the World. Wide Web by Its Inventor*. Orion Business Publishing.

Beuckels, E., & Hudders, L. (2016). An Experimental Study To Investigate The Impact Of Image Interactivity On The Perception Of Luxury In An Online Shopping Context. *Journal of Retailing and Consumer Services, 33*, 135–142. doi:10.1016/j.jretconser.2016.08.014

Bèzes, C. (2019). What kind of in-store smart retailing for an omnichannel real-life experience? [English Edition]. *Recherche et Applications en Marketing, 34*(1), 91–112. doi:10.1177/2051570718808132

Bhandari, R. S., & Bansal, A. (2018). Impact of Search Engine Optimization as a Marketing Tool. *Journal of Business Research, 7*(1), 24–36. doi:10.1177/2278682117754016

Bharadwaj, A., El Sawy, O. A., Pavlou, P. A., & Venkatraman, N. (2013). Visions and Voices on Emerging Challenges in Digital Business Strategy. *Management Information Systems Quarterly, 37*(2), 633–661. doi:10.25300/MISQ/2013/37.2.14

Bharadwaj, A., El Sawy, O., Pavlou, P., & Venkatraman, N. (2013). Digital business strategy: Toward a next generation of insights. *Management Information Systems Quarterly, 37*(2), 471–482. doi:10.25300/MISQ/2013/37:2.3

Bhattacharya, S., & Mishra, B. B. (2015). Evolution, growth and challenges in e-commerce industry: A case of india. *Sumedha Journal of Management, 4*(1), 45–58.

Bickart, B., & Schindler, R. M. (2001). Internet forums as influential sources of consumer information. *Journal of Interactive Marketing, 15*(3), 31–40. doi:10.1002/dir.1014

Bijmol, T. H., Leeflang, P. S., Block, F., Eisenbeiss, M., Hardie, B. G., Lemmens, A., & Saffert, P. (2010). Analytics for customer engagement. *Journal of Service Research, 13*(3), 341–356. doi:10.1177/1094670510375603

Bilgicer, T., Jedidi, K., Lehmann, D. R., & Neslin, S. A. (2015). Social Contagion and Customer Adoption of New Sales Channels. *Journal of Retailing, 91*(2), 254–271. doi:10.1016/j.jretai.2014.12.006

Bilolo, A., Boeck, H., Durif, F., & Levesque, N. (2015). *The impact of proximity marketing on consumer reactions and firm performance: A conceptual and integrative model*. Academic Press.

Blackburn, R., & Kovalainen, A. (2009). Researching small firms and entrepreneurship: Past, present and future. *International Journal of Management Reviews, 11*(2), 127–148. doi:10.1111/j.1468-2370.2008.00254.x

Blank, G., & Reisdorf, B. C. (2012). The Participatory Web: A user perspective on Web 2.0. *Information Communication and Society, 15*(4), 537–554. doi:10.1080/1369118X.2012.665935

Blazquez, M. (2014). Fashion Shopping in Multichannel Retail: The Role of Technology in Enhancing the Customer Experience. *International Journal of Electronic Commerce, 18*(4), 97–116. doi:10.2753/JEC1086-4415180404

Bloemer, J. M., & Kasper, H. D. (1995). The complex relationship between consumer satisfaction and brand loyalty. *Journal of Economic Psychology, 16*(2), 311–329. doi:10.1016/0167-4870(95)00007-B

Blom, A., Lange, F., & Hess, R. L. Jr. (2017). Omnichannel-based promotions' effects on purchase behavior and brand image. *Journal of Retailing and Consumer Services, 39*, 286–295. doi:10.1016/j.jretconser.2017.08.008

Blumer, J. G., & Katz, E. (1974). *The uses of Mass Communications Current. Perspectives on gratifications research.* Sage.

Blut, M., Chowdhry, N., Mittal, V., & Brock, C. (2015). E-Service Quality: A Meta-Analytic Review. *Journal of Retailing, 91*(4), 679–700. doi:10.1016/j.jretai.2015.05.004

Bonnemaizon, A., & Batat, W. (2011). How competent are consumers? The case of the energy sector in France. *International Journal of Consumer Studies, 35*(3), 348–358. doi:10.1111/j.1470-6431.2010.00937.x

Booker, C. (2004). The Seven Basic Plots: Why We Tell Stories. *Continuum.*

Booth Butterfield, S., & Booth-Butterfield, M. (1991). Individual differences in the communication of humorous messages. *Southern Journal of Communication, 56*(3), 205–218. doi:10.1080/10417949109372831

Boston Consulting Group (2020). *Challenging future for fuel retailers.* Academic Press.

Boston Consulting Group. (2019). *Is there a future for fuel stations? Boston Consulting Group.*

Boughzala, Garmaki, & Chourabi Tantan. (2020). *Understanding how Digital Intelligence Contributes to Digital Creativity and Digital Transformation: A Systematic Literature Review.* . doi:10.24251/HICSS.2020.040

Boughzala, I., Benhayoun-Sadafiyine, L. (2020). *Étude de cas. Le DMS (Digitalization Maturity System): Instrument d'évaluation de la maturité de la transformation digitale des entreprises.* Academic Press.

Boughzala, I. (2016). Social media and value creation: Exploring the perception of Generation Y toward corporate social networking applications use. *Journal of Organizational and End User Computing, 28*(2), 107–123. doi:10.4018/JOEUC.2016040107

Bourdieu, P. (1980). Le capital social. *Actes de la Recherche en Sciences Sociales, 31*(January), 2–3.

Bourgeois, L. III. (1984). Strategic Management and Determinism. *Academy of Management Review, 9*(4), 586–596. doi:10.5465/amr.1984.4277347

Bouwman, H. (1999). E-commerce: Cyber and physical environments. *Electronic Markets, 9*(1–2), 58–64. doi:10.1080/101967899359256

Bouwman, H., Nikou, S., & Reuver, M. (2019). Digitalization, business models, and SMEs: How do business model innovation practices improve performance of digitalising SMEs? *Telecommunications Policy, 43*(9), 101828. doi:10.1016/j.telpol.2019.101828

Boyd, D., & Crawford, K. (2012). Critical questions for big data: Provocations for a cultural, technological, and scholarly phenomenon. *Information Communication and Society, 15*(5), 662–679. doi:10.1080/1369118X.2012.678878

Boyd, M. D., & Ellison, B. N. (2007). *Social Network Sites: Definition, history and scholarship.* Michigan State University.

Boyer, A., & Nefzi, A. (2008). La relation entre la perception de la qualité et la fidélité. *La Revue des Sciences de Gestion, 234*(6), 37–48. doi:10.3917/rsg.234.0037

Brackett, L. K., & Carr, B. N. Jr. (2001). Cyberspace advertising vs other media: Consumer vs. mature student attitudes. *Journal of Advertising Research, 41*(5), 23–32. doi:10.2501/JAR-41-5-23-32

Bradshaw, H. K., Rodeheffer, C. D., & Hill, S. E. (2020). Scarcity, sex, and spending: Recession cues increase women's desire for men owning luxury products and men's desire to buy them. *Journal of Business Research, 120*, 561–568. doi:10.1016/j.jbusres.2019.07.021

Brakus, J. J., Schmitt, B. H., & Zarantonello, L. (2009). Brand experience: What is it? How is it measured? Does it affect loyalty? *Journal of Marketing, 73*(May), 52–68. doi:10.1509/jmkg.73.3.052

Brand Master Academy-How to Discover Your Brand Purpose. (2019) https://brandmasteracademy.com/brand-purpose/#discover

Brand New Purpose Official Website. (2013). http://brandnewpurpose.com

Bressolles, G. (2006). La qualité de service électronique: NetQu@l Proposition d'une échelle de mesure appliquée aux sites marchands et effets modérateurs. *Recherche et Applications en Marketing, 21*(3), 19–45. doi:10.1177/076737010602100302

Bristor, J. M. (1990). Enhanced Explanations of Word of Mouth Communications: The Power of Relationships. *Research in Consumer Behavior, 4*, 51–83.

Brodie, R. J., Ilic, A., Juric, B., & Hollebeek, L. (2013). Consumer engagement in a virtual brand community: An exploratory analysis. *Journal of Business Research, 66*(1), 105–114. doi:10.1016/j.jbusres.2011.07.029

Bronner, F., & de Hoog, R. (2014). Social media and consumer choice. *International Journal of Market Research, 56*(1), 51–71. doi:10.2501/IJMR-2013-053

Brown, J. J., & Reingen, P. H. (1987). Social Ties and Word-of-Mouth Referral Behavior. *The Journal of Consumer Research, 14*(3), 350–362. doi:10.1086/209118

Brown, J., Broderick, A. J., & Lee, N. (2007). Word of mouth communication within online communities: Conceptualizing the online social network. *Journal of Interactive Marketing, 21*(3), 2–20. doi:10.1002/dir.20082

Brown, S. (2001). Marketing-The retro revolution. *Sage (Atlanta, Ga.)*.

Brown, T. J., Barry, T. E., Dacin, P. A., & Gunst, R. F. (2005). Spreading the word: Investigating antecedents of consumers' positive word-of-mouth intentions and behaviors in a retailing context. *Journal of the Academy of Marketing Science, 33*(2), 123–138. doi:10.1177/0092070304268417

Bruggeman, H., Van Hiel, A., Van Hal, G., & Van Dongen, S. (2019). Does The Use Of Digital Media Affect Psychological Well-Being? An Empirical Test Among Children Aged 9 To 12. *Computers in Human Behavior, 101*, 104–113. doi:10.1016/j.chb.2019.07.015

Bruner, I. C., & Anand Kumar, A. (2005). Explaining Consumer Acceptance of Handheld Internet Devices. *Journal of Business Research, 58*(5), 553–558. doi:10.1016/j.jbusres.2003.08.002

Bruns, A. (2006). Towards Produsage: Futures for User-Led Content Production. In F. Sudweeks, H. Hrachovec, & C. Ess (Eds.), Proceedings Cultural Attitudes towards Communication and Technology (pp. 275–284). Academic Press.

Bruns, A. (2007). The Future is User-Led: The Path Towards Widespread Produsage. In A. Hutchinson (Ed.), *Proceedings of perthDAC 2007: The 7th International Digital Arts and Culture Conference* (pp. 68–77). Curtin University of Technology. https://eprints.qut.edu.au/12902/

Bryman, A., & Bell, E. (2019). Business Research Methods (5th ed.). Oxford University Press.

Brynjolfsson, E., Hu, Y. J., & Rahman, M. S. (2013). Competing in the age of omnichannel retailing. *MIT Sloan Management Review, 54*(4), 1–7.

Brynjolfsson, E., & Kahin, B. (Eds.). (2000). *Understanding the digital economy*. MIT Press. doi:10.7551/mitpress/6986.001.0001

Buhalis, D. (2003). eTourism: Information technology for strategic tourism management. Pearson Education.

Buhalis, D. (2000). Marketing the competitive destination of the future - Growth strategies for accommodation establishments in alpine regions. *Tourism Management, 21*(1), 91–116. doi:10.1016/S0261-5177(99)00095-3

Buhalis, D., Andreu, L., & Gnoth, J. (2020). The dark side of the sharing economy: Balancing value co-creation and value co-destruction. *Psychology and Marketing*, *37*(5), 689–704. doi:10.1002/mar.21344

Buhalis, D., & Law, R. (2008). Progress in information technology and tourism management: 20 years on and 10 years after the Internet—The state of eTourism research. *Tourism Management*, *29*(4), 609–623. doi:10.1016/j.tourman.2008.01.005

Buhalis, D., & Sinarta, Y. (2019). Real-time co-creation and nowness service: Lessons from tourism and hospitality. *Journal of Travel & Tourism Marketing*, *36*(5), 563–582. doi:10.1080/10548408.2019.1592059

Buijzen, M., & Valkenburg, P. M. (2004). Developing a typology of humour in audio-visual media. *Media Psychology*, *6*(2), 147–167. doi:10.12071532785xmep0602_2

Bulut, Z. A., & Karabulut, A. N. (2018). Examining the role of two aspects of eWOM in online repurchase intention: An integrated trust–loyalty perspective. *Journal of Consumer Behaviour*, *17*(4), 407–417. doi:10.1002/cb.1721

Burghardt, M., Heckner, M., & Wolff, C. (2012). The many ways of searching the web together: A comparison of social search engines. In D. Lewandowski (Ed.), *Social information research* (Vol. 4). Emerald Group Publishing Limited.

Busca, L., & Bertrandias, L. (2020). A Framework for Digital Marketing Research: Investigating the Four Cultural Eras of Digital Marketing. *Journal of Interactive Marketing*, *49*(1), 1–19. doi:10.1016/j.intmar.2019.08.002

Bu, Y., Parkinson, J., & Thaichon, P. (2020). Digital content marketing as a catalyst for e-WOM in food tourism. *Australasian Marketing Journal*, *13*(51). Advance online publication. doi:10.1016/j.ausmj.2020.01.001

Cadel, P. (2010). Le marché de l'e-réputation. *Les Cahiers du numérique*, *6*(4), 111-121.

Caluri, L., Jianu, M., Cerioli, P., & Silvestri, G. B. (2019, November). Open Innovation as Enabling Paradigm to Empower Digital Transformation in Oil & Gas Organizations. In *Abu Dhabi International Petroleum Exhibition & Conference*. Society of Petroleum Engineers.

Campos-Freire, F. (2008). Las redes sociales trastocan los modelos de los medios de comunicacióntradicionales. *Revista Latina de Comunicación Social*, *63*, 287–293.

Cantallops, A. S., & Salvi, F. (2014). New consumer behavior: A review of research on eWOM and hotels. *International Journal of Hospitality Management*, *36*, 41–51. doi:10.1016/j.ijhm.2013.08.007

Cao, L. (2014). Business Model Transformation in Moving to a Cross-Channel Retail Strategy: A Case Study. *International Journal of Electronic Commerce*, *18*(4), 69–96. doi:10.2753/JEC1086-4415180403

Cao, L., & Li, L. (2015). The impact of cross-channel integration on retailers' sales growth. *Journal of Retailing*, *91*(2), 198–216. doi:10.1016/j.jretai.2014.12.005

Capelli, S., Falchi, A., Hussler, C., & Sabadie, W. (2016). Co-innover avec ses consommateurs: oui, mais lesquels? De l'intérêt d'impliquer les consommateurs-membres dans le processus d'innovation des entreprises coopératives. *Gestion 2000*, *33*(4), 117-141.

Cappa, F., Oriani, R., Peruffo, E., & McCarthy, I. (2021). Big Data for Creating and Capturing Value in the Digitalized Environment: Unpacking the Effects of Volume, Variety, and Veracity on Firm Performance. *Journal of Product Innovation Management*, *38*(1), 49–67. doi:10.1111/jpim.12545

Carah, N., & Brodmerkel, S. (2021). Alcohol marketing in the era of digital media platforms. *Journal of Studies on Alcohol and Drugs*, *82*(1), 18–27. doi:10.15288/jsad.2021.82.18 PMID:33573719

Carlson, J., & O'Cass, A. (2011). Developing a framework for understanding e-service quality, its antecedents, consequences, and mediators. *Managing Service Quality*, *21*(3), 264–286. doi:10.1108/09604521111127965

Carlsson, C., & Walden, P. (2010). Supporting Tourists at the Bomarsund Fortress with a Mobile Value Service. *Journal of Information Technology Theory and Application*, *11*(1), 43–56.

Carrnigniani, J., Furht, B., Anietti, M., Ceravolo, P., Damiani, E., & Ivkovic, M. (2011). Augmented reality technologies, systems and applications. *Multimedia Tools and Applications*, *51*(1), 341–377. doi:10.100711042-010-0660-6

Carson, M., & Springer, P. (2012). *Pioneers of Digital: Success Stories from Leaders in Advertising, Marketing*. Kogan Page.

Carvajal, G., Maucec, M., & Cullick, S. (2017). *Intelligent digital oil and gas fields: concepts, collaboration, and right-time decisions*. Gulf Professional Publishing.

Carvalhosa, P., Portela, F., Santos, M. F., Abelha, A., & Machado, J. (2017). Pervasiveness in Digital Marketing—A Global Overview. In *Recent Advances in Information Systems and Technologies*. Springer International Publishing. doi:10.1007/978-3-319-56541-5_40

Casale, S., & Fioravanti, G. (2018). Why narcissists are at risk for developing Facebook addiction: The need to be admired and the need to belong. *Addictive Behaviors*, *76*, 312–318. doi:10.1016/j.addbeh.2017.08.038 PMID:28889060

Casaló, L. V., Flavián, C., & Ibáñez-Sánchez, S. (2020). Be creative, my friend! Engaging users on Instagram by promoting positive emotions. *Journal of Business Research*. Advance online publication. doi:10.1016/j.jbusres.2020.02.014

Casilli, A. A. (2010). *Les liaisons numériques, vers une nouvelle sociabilité?* Editions du Seuil.

Cassell, C., & Symon, G. (2012). Essential Guide To Qualitative Methods. In *Organizational Research*. SAGE Publications Ltd.

Castellano, S., & Dutot, V. (2013). Une analyse de l'e-réputation par analogie ou contraste avec la réputation: Une approche par les médias sociaux. *Revue française du Marketing*, (243).

Castellano, S., & Dutot, V. (2015). Designing a Measurement Scale for E-Reputation. *Corporate Reputation Review*, *18*(4), 294–313. doi:10.1057/crr.2015.15

Chandon, J. L., Laurent, G., & Valette-Florence, P. (2016). Pursuing The Concept Of Luxury: Introduction To The JBR Special Issue On Luxury Marketing From Tradition To Innovation. *Journal of Business Research*, *69*(1), 299–303. doi:10.1016/j.jbusres.2015.08.001

Chang, C.-W., & Heo, J. (2014). Visiting theories that predict college students' self-disclosure on Facebook. *Computers in Human Behavior*, *30*, 79–86. doi:10.1016/j.chb.2013.07.059

Chatman, J. A., & Spataro, S. E. (2005). Using Self-Categorization Theory to Understand Relational Demography-Based Variations in People's Responsiveness to Organizational Culture. *Academy of Management Journal*, *48*(2), 321–331. doi:10.5465/amj.2005.16928415

Chattopadhyay, A., & Basu, K. (1990). Humour in advertising: The moderating role of prior brand evaluation. *JMR, Journal of Marketing Research*, *27*(4), 466–476. doi:10.1177/002224379002700408

Chaudhuri, A., & Holbrook, M. B. (2001). The chain of effects from brand trust and brand affect to brand performance: The role of brand loyalty. *Journal of Marketing*, *65*(2), 81–93. doi:10.1509/jmkg.65.2.81.18255

Cheah, J.H., Lim, X. J., Ting, H., Liu, Y., & Quach, S. (2020). Are privacy concerns still relevant? Revisiting consumer behaviour in omnichannel retailing. *Journal of Retailing and Consumer Services*.

Cheema, U., Rizwan, M., Jalal, R., Durrani, F., & Sohail, N. (2013). The trend of online shopping in 21st century: Impact of enjoyment in TAM model. *Asian Journal of Empirical Research*, *3*, 131–141.

Cheikho, A. (2015). *L'adoption des innovations technologiques par les clients et son impact sur la relation client-Cas de la banque mobile* (Doctoral dissertation). Université Nice Sophia Antipolis.

Cheng, Y., Chen, Y.-R. R., & Hung-Baesecke, C.-J. F. (2021). Social Media Influencers in CSR Endorsement: The Effect of Consumer Mimicry on CSR Behaviors and Consumer Relationships. *Social Science Computer Review, 39*(4), 744–761. Advance online publication. doi:10.1177/0894439320987184

Chen, Y., Cheung, C., & Tan, C. (2018). Omnichannel business research: Opportunities and challenges. *Decision Support Systems, 109*, 1–4. doi:10.1016/j.dss.2018.03.007

Chesbrough. (2003). *Open Innovation: The New Imperative for Creating and Profiting from Technology*. HBS Press.

Chesher, C. (2020). How Computer Networks Became Social. In Second International Handbook of Internet Research (pp. 105-126). Springer. doi:10.1007/978-94-024-1555-1_4

Cheung, C. M., & Thadani, D. R. (2012). The impact of electronic word-of-mouth communication: A literature analysis and integrative model. *Decision Support Systems, 54*(1), 461–470. doi:10.1016/j.dss.2012.06.008

Child, J. (1972). Organization Structure, Environment and Performance: The Role of Strategic Choice. *Sociology, 6*(1), 1–22. doi:10.1177/003803857200600101

Cho, E. (2011). Development of a brand image scale and the impact of lovemarks on brand equity. *Graduate Theses and Dissertations*. 11962. Available at https://lib.dr.iastate.edu/etd/11962, doi:10.31274/etd-180810-4450

Choi, C. S., Cho, Y.-N., Ko, E., Kim, S. J., Kim, K. H., & Sarkees, M. E. (2019). Corporate sustainability efforts and e-WOM intentions in social platforms. *International Journal of Advertising, 38*(8), 1224–1239. doi:10.1080/02650487.2019.1613858

Choi, J., Bell, D. R., & Lodish, L. M. (2012). Traditional and IS-enabled customer acquisition on the Internet. *Management Science, 58*(4), 754–769. doi:10.1287/mnsc.1110.1447

Choi, Y., Hickerson, B., & Lee, J. (2018). Investigation of the technology effects of online travel media on virtual travel experience and behavioral intention. *Journal of Travel & Tourism Marketing, 35*(3), 320–335. doi:10.1080/10548408.2017.1340224

Christensen, C. M., & Bower, J. L. (1995). Disruptive Technologies: Catching the wave. *Harvard Business Review*.

Christodoulides, G. (2009). Branding in the post-internet era. *Marketing Theory, 9*(1), 141–144. doi:10.1177/1470593108100071

Chung, H., & Zhao, X. (2003). Humour effect on memory and attitude: Moderating role of product involvement. *International Journal of Advertising, 22*(1), 117–144.

Chu, S. C., Leung, L. C., Hui, Y. V., & Cheung, W. (2007). Evolution of e-commerce web sites: A conceptual framework and a longitudinal study. *Information & Management, 44*(2), 154–164. doi:10.1016/j.im.2006.11.003

Chu, S.-C., Lien, C.-H., & Cao, Y. (2018). Electronic word-of-mouth (eWOM) on WeChat: Examining the influence of sense of belonging, need for self-enhancement, and consumer engagement on Chinese travellers' eWOM. *International Journal of Advertising, 38*(1), 26–49. doi:10.1080/02650487.2018.1470917

Chylinski, M., Heller, J., Hilken, T., Keeling, D. I., Mahr, D., & De Ruyter, K. (2020). Augmented reality marketing: A technology-enabled approach to situated customer experience. *Australasian Marketing Journal, 28*(4), 374–384. doi:10.1016/j.ausmj.2020.04.004

Clemons, E. K., Barnett, S., & Appadurai, A. (2007). The Future of Advertising and the Value of Social Network Websites: Some Preliminary Examinations. *ACM International Conference Proceeding Series, Ninth International Conference on Electronic Commerce*, 267-76. 10.1145/1282100.1282153

Cline, T. W., & Kellaris, J. J. (2007). The influence of humour strength and humour—message relatedness on ad memorability: A dual process model. *Journal of Advertising*, *36*(1), 55–67.

Coates, A. E., Hardman, C. A., Halldord, J. C. G., Christiansen, P., & Boyland, E. J. (2020). "It's Just Addictive People That Make Addictive Videos": Children's Understanding of and Attitudes towards Influencer Marketing of Food and Beverages by YouTube Video Bloggers. *International Journal of Environmental Research and Public Health*, *17*(2), 449. doi:10.3390/ijerph17020449 PMID:31936672

Coelho, F. J., & Easingwoo, C. (2004). Multiple Channel Systems in Services: Pros, Cons and Issues. *Service Industries Journal*, *24*(5), 1–29. doi:10.1080/0264206042000276810

Coelho, F., Pereira, M. C., Cruz, L., Simões, P., & Barata, E. (2017). Affect and the adoption of pro-environmental behaviour: A structural model. *Journal of Environmental Psychology*, *54*, 127–138. doi:10.1016/j.jenvp.2017.10.008

Cohen, A. C. (2020). Seeing the market: Performative sensemaking and the case of advertising agencies and their clients. *Consumption Markets & Culture*, *23*(5), 481–505. doi:10.1080/10253866.2019.1625775

Cohen, J. E. (2007). Cyberspace as/and space. *Columbia Law Review*, *107*, 210–256.

Colella, G., Amatulli, C., & Martinez-Ruiz, M. P. (2019). Social Media Marketing and Luxury Consumption: A Literature Review. *International Journal of Marketing Studies*, *11*(4), 30–52. doi:10.5539/ijms.v11n4p30

Collins, J. C., & Porras, J. I. (2005). *Built to last: Successful habits of visionary companies*. Random House.

Constantinides, E., Lorenzo-Romero, C., & Gómez, M. A. (2010). Effects of web experience onconsumer choice: A multicultural approach. *Internet Research*, *20*(2), 188–209. doi:10.1108/10662241011032245

Corbin, J., & Strauss, A. (2015). *Basics of qualitative research: Techniques and procedures for developing grounded theory*. Sage publications.

Court, D., Elzinga, D., Mulder, S., & Vetvik, O. J. (2009). The consumer decision journey. *The McKinsey Quarterly*, *3*(3), 96–107.

Cox, K. (2015). *Hashtag or Crashtag: Should I use hashtags in my marketing campaign?* Retrieved September 28, 2019 from http://www.tmpmagnet.co.uk/blog/2015/03/hashtagor-crashtag-should-i-use-hashtags-in-my-marketingcampaign

Cox, J., & Dale, B. G. (2001). Service quality and e-commerce: An exploratory analysis. *Managing Service Quality*, *11*(2), 121–131. doi:10.1108/09604520110387257

Cramer, J., & Krueger, A. B. (2016). Disruptive change in the taxi business: The case of Uber. *The American Economic Review*, *106*(5), 177–182. doi:10.1257/aer.p20161002

Crayola Official Website-Brand Essence. (2021).https://www.crayola.com/about-us/company/brand-essence.aspx

Crayola Official Website-Company. (2021). https://www.crayola.com/about-us/company.aspx

Cristau, C. (2001). *Définition, mesure et modélisation de l'attachement à une marque comme la conjonction de deux dimensions distinctes et concomitantes(la dépendance et l'amitié vis-à-vis de la marque)*. Academic Press.

Cristobal, E., Flavian, C., & Guinaliu, M. (2007). Perceived e-service quality (PeSQ) Measurement validation and effects on consumer satisfaction and web site loyalty. *Managing Service Quality*, *17*(3), 317–340. doi:10.1108/09604520710744326

Croatian Bureau of Statistics. (n.d.). Retrieved May 15, 2020, from: https://www.dzs.hr/Hrv_Eng/publication/2019/SI-1639.pdf

Crosslin, M. (2011). When the Future Finally Arrives: Web 2.0 Becomes Web 3.0. In M. J. W. Lee & C. McLoughlin (Eds.), *Web 2.0-based e-learning: Applying social informatics for tertiary teaching* (pp. 380–393). IGI Global. doi:10.4018/978-1-60566-294-7.ch020

Crouch, G. I. (2011). Destination competitiveness: An analysis of determinant attributes. *Journal of Travel Research, 50*(1), 27–45. doi:10.1177/0047287510362776

Culbertson, H. M. (1991). Role Taking and Sensitivity: Keys to Playing and Making Public Relations Roles. *Journal of Public Relations Research, 3*(1-4), 37–65. doi:10.12071532754xjprr0301-4_2

Curbatov, O. (2003). *L'intégration du consommateur par le « Knowledge Marketing »: conception, production et consommation d'un produit personnel* (Doctoral dissertation). Université de Nice Sophia Antipolis.

Curbatov, O., & Louyot-Gallicher, M. (2011). *Le Knowledge Marketing et les compétences du consommateur au service de la co-création.* 32ème Congrès de l'Association Française de Marketing, Bruxelles, Belgique.

Curbatov, O. (2001). *La Construction et la Modélisation du Knowledge Marketing.* Document RODIGE.

D'Arpizio, C., Levato, F., Fenili, S., Colacchio, F., & Prete, F. (2020). *Luxury after Covid-19: Changed for (the) Good?* https://www.bain.com/insights/luxury-after-coronavirus/

Dabbagh, N., & Reo, R. (2011). Back to the future: Tracing the roots and learning affordances of social software. In M. J. W. Lee & C. McLoughlin (Eds.), *Web 2.0-based e-learning: Applying social informatics for tertiary teaching* (pp. 1–20). IGI Global. doi:10.4018/978-1-60566-294-7.ch001

Dabholkar, P. A., Shepherd, C. D., & Thorpe, D. I. (2000). AComprehensive Framework for Service Quality: An Investigation of Critical Conceptual and Measurement Issues through a Longitudinal Study. *Journal of Retailing, 76*(2), 139–173. doi:10.1016/S0022-4359(00)00029-4

Dacko, S. G. (2017). Enabling Smart Retail Settings via Mobile Augmented Reality Shopping Apps. *Technological Forecasting and Social Change, 124*, 243–256. doi:10.1016/j.techfore.2016.09.032

Dadzie, K. Q., Johnston, W. J., & Pels, J. (2008). Business-to-business marketing practices in West Africa, Argentina and the United States. *Journal of Business and Industrial Marketing, 23*(2), 115–123. doi:10.1108/08858620810850236

Dale, M. (2015). *How to uncover your brand purpose.* https://medium.com/@firebrand_design/how-to-uncover-your-brand-purpose-9dc420e550f1

Damanpour, F., & Damanpour, J. A. (2001). E-business e-commerce evolution: Perspective and strategy. *Managerial Finance, 27*(7), 16–33. doi:10.1108/03074350110767268

Datcu, D., Lukosch, S., & Brazier, F. (2015). On the Usability and Effectiveness of Different Interaction Types in Augrnented Reality. *International Journal of Human-Computer Interaction, 31*(3), 193–209. doi:10.1080/10447318.2014.994193

David, N. (2015). *Developing Strategic Business Models and Competitive Advantage in the Digital Sector.* IGI Global.

Davies, G., Chun, R., da Silva, R. V., & Roper, S. (2004). A corporate character scale to assess employee and customer views of organization reputation. *Corporate Reputation Review, 7*(2), 125–146. doi:10.1057/palgrave.crr.1540216

Davies, L. B., Shield, L., & Weininger, M. J. (1998). Godzilla can MOO, can you? MOOs for construction, collaboration & community and research. *Language Teaching, 22*(2), 16–21.

Davis, F. D., Bagozzi, R. P., & Warshaw, P. R. (1989). User acceptance of computer technology: A comparison of two theoretical models. *Management Science*, *35*(8), 982–1003. doi:10.1287/mnsc.35.8.982

Daymon, C., & Holloway, I. (2011). *Qualitative Research Methods in Public Relations and Marketing Communications* (2nd ed.). Routledge.

De Cremer, D., & Leonardelli, G. J. (2003). Cooperation in social dilemmas and the need to belong: The moderating effect of group size. *Group Dynamics*, *7*(2), 168–174. doi:10.1037/1089-2699.7.2.168

de Gregorio, F., Cheong, Y., & Kim, K. (2012). Intraorganizational Conflict within Advertising Agencies. *Journal of Advertising*, *41*(3), 19–34.

de Gregorio, F., & Windels, K. (2020). Are Advertising Agency Creatives More Creative Than Anyone Else? An Exploratory Test of Competing Predictions. *Journal of Advertising*, *1*(1), 1–10. doi:10.1080/00913367.2020.1799268

de Valck, K., van Briggen, G., & Wierengan, B. (2009). Virtual communities: A marketing perspective. *Decision Support Systems*, *47*(3), 185–203. doi:10.1016/j.dss.2009.02.008

Deephouse, D. L. (2000). Media reputation as a strategic resource: An integration of mass communication and resource-based theories. *Journal of Management*, *26*(6), 1091–1112. doi:10.1177/014920630002600602

Delgado-Ballester, E., & Munuera-Alemán, J. L. (2001). Brand trust in the context of consumer loyalty. *European Journal of Marketing*, *35*(11/12), 1238–1258. doi:10.1108/EUM0000000006475

Delgado-Ballester, E., Navarro, A., & Sicilia, M. (2012). Revitalising brands through communication messages: The role of brand familiarity. *European Journal of Marketing*, *46*(1/2), 31–51. doi:10.1108/03090561211189220

Dellarocas, C., Zhang, X. M., & Awad, N. F. (2007). Exploring the value of online product reviews in forecasting sales: The case of motion pictures. *Journal of Interactive Marketing*, *21*(4), 2–20. doi:10.1002/dir.20087

Deloitte. (2009). *A New Era Accelerating Toward 2020 – An Automotive Industry Transformed.* Deloitte.

Demangeot & Broderick. (2007). Conceptualising consumer behaviour in online shopping environments. *International Journal of Retail & Distribution Management*, *35*(11), 878-894.

Demirkan, H., & Spohrer, J. (2014). Developing a Framework to Improve Virtual Shopping in Digital Malls with Intelligent Self-Service Systems. *Journal of Retailing and Consumer Services*, *21*(5), 860–868. doi:10.1016/j.jretconser.2014.02.012

Dennison, L., Morrison, L., Conway, G., & Yardley, L. (2013). Opportunities and challenges for smartphone applications in supporting health behavior change: Qualitative study. *Journal of Medical Internet Research*, *15*(4), e86. Advance online publication. doi:10.2196/jmir.2583 PMID:23598614

Desai. (2013). *Innovation Engine Driving Execution for Breakthrough Result.* New Delhi: Wiley India Private Limited.

Desmichel, P., & Kocher, B. (2020). Luxury Single- versus Multi-Brand Stores: The Effect of Consumers' Hedonic Goals on Brand Comparisons. *Journal of Retailing*, *96*(2), 203–219. doi:10.1016/j.jretai.2019.09.002

Dey, I. (1993). *Qualitative Data Analysis: A User-Friendly Guide for Social Scientists*. Routledge.

Dholakia, U. M., Kahn, B. E., Reeves, R., Rindfleisch, A., Stewart, D., & Taylor, E. (2010). Consumer Behavior in a Multichannel, Multimedia Retailing Environment. *Journal of Interactive Marketing*, *24*(2), 86–95. doi:10.1016/j.intmar.2010.02.005

Dieck, T. (2017). Value of Augmented Reality at Cultural Heritage Sites: A Stakeholder Approach. *Journal of Destination Marketing & Management*, *6*(2), 110–117. doi:10.1016/j.jdmm.2017.03.002

Dieck, T. M. C., & Jung, T. (2016). Value of augmented reality to enhance the visitor experience: A case study of Manchester Jewish Museum. *Review of Tourism Research, 7*, 1–5.

Dimitriou, C. K., & AbouElgheit, E. (2019). Understanding generation Z's social decision-making in travel. *Tourism and Hospitality Management, 25*(2), 311–334. doi:10.20867/thm.25.2.4

Dimock, M. (2019). *Defining generations: Where Millennials end and Generation Z begins*. Pew Research Center. Retrieved May 11, 2020, from: https://www.pewresearch.org/fact-tank/2019/01/17/where-millennials-end-and-generation-z-begins/

Dimoulas, C. A., Veglis, A. A., & Kalliris, G. (2019). Semantically Enhanced Authoring of Shared Media. In Advanced Methodologies and Technologies in Media and Communications (pp. 277-289). IGI Global. Doi:10.4018/978-1-5225-7601-3.ch022

DiNucci, D. (1999). Fragmented future. *Print, 53*(4), 32–33.

DIPP–Discussion Paper on E-commerce In India 2013-14. (n.d.). Retrieved from https://indiafdiwatch.org/wp-content/uploads/2014/01/discussionpaper.pdf

Djambaska, A., Petrovska, I., & Bundaleska, E. (2015). Is Humour Advertising Always Effective? Parameters for Effective Use of Humour in Advertising. *Journal of Management Research, 8*(1), 18–36. doi:10.5296/jmr.v8i1.8419

Do, H.-N., Shih, W., & Ha, Q.-A. (2020, August). Effects of mobile augmented reality apps on impulse buying behavior: An investigation in the tourism field. *Heliyon, 6*(8), e04667. doi:10.1016/j.heliyon.2020.e04667 PMID:32923709

Dove Official Website. (2021). https://www.dove.com/us/en/home.html

Dove Official Website-About Dove. (2021). https://www.dove.com/us/en/stories/about-dove.html

Duarte, P., Silva, S. C., & Ferreira, M. B. (2018). How convenient is it? Delivering online shopping convenience to enhance customer satisfaction and encourage e-WOM. *Journal of Retailing and Consumer Services, 44*, 161–169. doi:10.1016/j.jretconser.2018.06.007

Dubey. (2009). Innovation with IT. Tata McGraw Hill Publishing Company Limited.

Ducoffe, R. H. (1996). Advertising value and advertising on the web. *Journal of Advertising Research, 36*(5), 21–36.

Duffett, R. G. (2015). Facebook advertising's influence on intention-to-purchase and purchase amongst Millennials. *Internet Research, 25*(4), 498–526. doi:10.1108/IntR-01-2014-0020

Duffett, R. G. (2017). Influence of social media marketing communications on young consumers' attitudes. *Young Consumers, 18*(1), 19–39. doi:10.1108/YC-07-2016-00622

Du, H. S., & Wagner, C. (2006). Weblog success: Exploring the role of technology. *International Journal of Human-Computer Studies, 64*(9), 789–798. doi:10.1016/j.ijhcs.2006.04.002

Du, S., Wang, L., & Hu, L. (2019). Omnichannel management with consumer disappointment aversion. *International Journal of Production Economics, 215*, 84–101. doi:10.1016/j.ijpe.2018.05.002

Dushlmann, Moorish, & Bhatnagar. (2016). Enterprise IoT Strategies and Best Practices Connected to Products and Services. O'Reilly.

Dutta, N., Verma, A., & Bhat, A. (2019). Analysis of Factors Influencing Negative e-Word of Mouth in Online Social Media Marketing. *ICSEB, 2019*, 193–198. Advance online publication. doi:10.1145/3374549.3374556

Eckler, P., & Bolls, P. (2011). Spreading the virus: Emotional tone of viral advertising and its effect on forwarding intentions and attitudes. *Journal of Interactive Advertising, 11*(2), 1–11. doi:10.1080/15252019.2011.10722180

E-commerce and Development Report. (2001). *UNCTAD Secretariat, United Nations*. Retrieved from https://unctad.org/en/docs/ecdr2001_en.pdf

E-Commerce in developing countries: Opportunities and Challenges for small and medium-sized enterprises. (2013). *World Trade Organization*. Retrieved from https://www.wto.org/english/r es_e/ books _e/eco m_brochure _e.pdf

E-commerce Industry in India. (2018). *India Brand Equity Foundation*. Retrieved from https://www.ibef.org/industry/ecommerce.aspx

E-Commerce, Government of India, Ministry of Statistics and Programme Implementation. (n.d.). Accessed January 2019, https://www.mospi.gov.in/1012-e-commerce

E-Commerce. (2019). *Statista*. Retrieved from https://www.statista.com/outlook/243/100/ecommerce/worldwide#market-revenue

Efanov, D., & Roschin, P. (2018). The all-pervasiveness of the blockchain technology. *Procedia Computer Science, 123*, 116–121. doi:10.1016/j.procs.2018.01.019

Eid, R., & El-Gohary, H. (2013). The impact of E-marketing use on small business enterprises' marketing success. *Service Industries Journal, 33*(1), 31–50. doi:10.1080/02642069.2011.594878

Eid, R., & El-Gohary, H. (2014). Testing and Validating Customer Relationship Management Implementation Constructs in Egyptian Tourism Organizations. *Journal of Travel & Tourism Marketing, 31*(3), 344–365. doi:10.1080/10548408.2014.883348

Eisend, M. (2009). A meta-analysis of humour in advertising. *Journal of the Academy of Marketing Science, 37*(2), 191–203. doi:10.100711747-008-0096-y

El-Gohary, H., Trueman, M., & Fukukawa, K. (2009). E-Marketing and Small Business Enterprises: A Meta Analytic Review. *Journal of International Business and Finance, 1*.

El-Gohary, H., Trueman, M., & Fukukawa, K. (2009). E-Marketing and Small Business Enterprises: A review of the literature from 1993 to 1997. *International Business & Technology Review*.

El-Gohary, H., Trueman, M., & Fukukawa, K. (2009). Understanding the factors affecting the adoption of E-Marketing by small business enterprises - Book Chapter. In E-Commerce Adoption and Small Business in the Global Marketplace (pp. 237–258). Academic Press.

El-Gohary, H. (2010). E-Marketing - A literature Review from a Small Businesses perspective. *International Journal of Business and Social Science, 1*(1), 214–244.

El-Gohary, H. (2010). Expanding TAM and IDT to understand the adoption of E-Marketing by small business enterprises. *International Journal of Customer Relationship Marketing and Management, 1*(3), 56–75. doi:10.4018/jcrmm.2010070105

El-Gohary, H. (2010, October). E-Marketing-A literature Review from a Small Businesses perspective. *International Journal of Business and Social Science, 1*(1), 214–244.

El-Gohary, H. (2010a). *E-Marketing: Towards a Conceptualization of a New Marketing Philosophy - Book Chapter. In E-Business Issues, Challenges and Opportunities for SMEs: Driving Competitiveness*. IGI Global.

El-Gohary, H. (2010b). *Exploring E-Marketing as a tool for globalisation: the case of Egyptian small business enterprises. In Electronic Globalized Business and Sustainable Development through IT Management: Strategies and Perspectives*. IGI Global.

El-Gohary, H. (2011). *Electronic Marketing Practises in Developing Countries: The case of Egyptian business enterprises*. VDM Verlag Dr Müller.

El-Gohary, H. (2012). Factors affecting E-Marketing adoption and implementation in tourism firms: An empirical investigation of Egyptian small tourism organizations. *Tourism Management, 33*(5), 1256–1269. doi:10.1016/j.tourman.2011.10.013

El-Gohary, H. (2012). *The impact of E-Marketing Practices on Marketing Performance: A Small Business Enterprises Context*. LAP Lambert Academic Publishing.

El-Gohary, H. (2012). *Transdisciplinary Marketing Concepts and Emergent Methods for Virtual Environments*. IGI Global.

El-Gohary, H. O. (2010). *The impact of E-marketing practices on market performance of small business enterprises. An empirical investigation*. University of Bradford.

El-Gohary, H., Edwards, D., & Huang, J. (2013). Customer Relationship Management (CRM) Practices by Small Businesses in Developing Economies: A Case Study of Egypt. *International Journal of Customer Relationship Marketing and Management, 4*(2), 1–20. doi:10.4018/jcrmm.2013040101

El-Gohary, H., & Eid, R. (2012). DMA Model: Understanding Digital Marketing Adoption and Implementation by Islamic Tourism Organizations. *Tourism Analysis, 17*(4), 523–532. doi:10.3727/108354212X13473157390885

El-Gohary, H., & Eid, R. (2013). *E-Marketing in Developed and Developing Countries: Emerging Practices*. IGI Global. doi:10.4018/978-1-4666-3954-6

El-Gohary, H., & El-Gohary, Z. (2016). An Attempt to Explore Electronic Marketing Adoption and Implementation Aspects in Developing Countries: The Case of Egypt. *International Journal of Customer Relationship Marketing and Management, 7*(4), 1–26. doi:10.4018/IJCRMM.2016100101

El-Gohary, H., O'Leary, S., & Radway, P. (2012). Investigating the Impact of Entrepreneurship Online Teaching on Science and Technology Degrees on Students attitudes in Developing Economies: The case of Egypt. *International Journal of Online Marketing, 2*(1), 29–45. doi:10.4018/ijom.2012010103

El-Gohary, H., Thayaseelan, A., Babatunde, S., & El-Gohary, S. (2021). An Exploratory Study on the Effect of Artificial Intelligent Enabled Technology on Customers Experience in Banking Sector. *Journal of Technological Advancements, 1*(1), 1–17. doi:10.4018/JTA.20210101.oa1

El-Gohary, H., Trueman, M., & Fukukawa, K. (2008). E-Marketing and Small Business Enterprises: A review of the methodologies. *Journal of Business and Public Policy, 2*(2), 64–93.

El-Gohary, H., Trueman, M., & Fukukawa, K. (2008). The Relationship between E-Marketing and Performance: Towards a Conceptual Framework in a Small Business Enterprises Context. *Journal of Business and Public Policy, 2*(2), 10–28.

Ellison, N., Steinfield, C., & Lampe, C. (2007). The benefits of Facebook "friends:" Social capital and college students' use of online social network sites. *Journal of Computer-Mediated Communication, 12*(4), 1143–1168. doi:10.1111/j.1083-6101.2007.00367.x

Elmer, S. (1999). Electronic Commerce - IDC. Definitions and Methodologies. In *OCDE Workshop "Defining and Measuring E-commerce"*. OECD.

Elo, S., & Kyngäs, H. (2008). The qualitative content analysis process. *Journal of Advanced Nursing, 62*(1), 107–115. doi:10.1111/j.1365-2648.2007.04569.x PMID:18352969

Emrich, O., Paul, M., & Rudolph, T. (2015). Shopping benefits of multichannel assortment integration and the moderating role of retailer type. *Journal of Retailing*, *91*(2), 326–342. doi:10.1016/j.jretai.2014.12.003

Eouzan, G., Michalon, C., Guissani, A., Bridier, K., & Dupuis, J. (2017). *Webmarketing: Définir, mettre en pratique et optimiser sa stratégie digitale*. Éditions Paris ENI.

Erkan, I., & Evans, C. (2018). Social media or shopping websites? The influence of eWOM on consumers' online purchase intentions. *Journal of Marketing Communications*, *24*(6), 617–632. doi:10.1080/13527266.2016.1184706

Eroglu, S. A., Machleit, K. A., & Davis, L. M. (2003). Empirical testing of a model of online store atmospherics and shopper responses. *Psychology and Marketing*, *20*(2), 139–150. doi:10.1002/mar.10064

Ershaghi, I., & Omoregie, Z. S. (2005, January). Continuing-education needs for the digital oil fields of the future. In *SPE Annual Technical Conference and Exhibition*. Society of Petroleum Engineers. 10.2118/97288-MS

Escalas, J. E., & Bettman, J. R. (2005). Self-construal, reference groups, and brand meaning. *The Journal of Consumer Research*, *32*(December), 378–389. doi:10.1086/497549

Eurostat, Digital Economy, and Society Index. (2020). *Country Profile, Romania*. https://ec.europa.eu/digital-single-market/en/digital-economy-and-society-index-desi

Eurostat. (2020). *Tourism statistics*. Retrieved April 20, 2020, from: https://ec.europa.eu/eurostat/statistics-explained/pdfscache/1171.pdf

Everett, C. (2019). *'Brand purpose' delivering ad impact but Nike dissent demonstrates its dangers*. https://www.mycustomer.com/marketing/strategy/brand-purpose-delivering-ad-impact-but-nike-dissent-demonstrates-its-dangers

Ewing, T. (2018). *10 Insights From Ad Ratings*. https://system1group.com/blog/ad-ratings-has-arrived-10-effectiveness-insights-from-system1s-new-service

Fan, X., Chai, Z., Deng, N., & Dong, X. (2020). Adoption of augmented reality in online retailing and consumers' product attitude: A cognitive perspective. *Journal of Retailing and Consumer Services*, *53*(March), 101986. doi:10.1016/j.jretconser.2019.101986

Fard, M. H., & Marvi, R. (2019, Aug.). Viral marketing and purchase intentions of mobile applications users. *International Journal of Emerging Markets*.

Fatma, M., Ruiz, A. P., Khan, I., & Rahman, Z. (2020). The effect of CSR engagement on eWOM on social media. *The International Journal of Organizational Analysis*, *28*(4), 941–956. doi:10.1108/IJOA-10-2019-1895

Faust, F., Roepke, G., Tiago, C., Fernanda, A., Marcelo, F., Gomes, G., & Deise, A. (2012). Use of augmented reality in the usability evaluation of products. *Work (Reading, Mass.)*, *41*(1), 1164–1170. doi:10.3233/WOR-2012-0298-1164 PMID:22316877

Felix, R., Rauschnabel, P. A., & Hinsch, C. (2017). Elements of Strategic Social Media Marketing: A Holistic Framework. *Journal of Business Research*, *70*, 118–126. doi:10.1016/j.jbusres.2016.05.001

Fernandes, V. (2012). En quoi l'approche PLS est-elle une méthode a (re)-découvrir pour les chercheurs en management?. *M@ n@ gement*, *15*(1), 102-123.

Fernie, J., Moore, C., Lawrie, A., & Hallsworth, A. (1997). The internationalization of the high fashion brand: The case of central London. *Journal of Product and Brand Management*, *6*(3), 151–162. doi:10.1108/10610429710175673

Field. (2009). *Discovering Statistics Using SPSS*. Sage Publications.

Figuera, G. (1999). *An analysis of international Internet diffusion* (PhD Thesis). Massachusetts Institute of Technology.

Fishbein, M., & Ajzen, I. (1975). *Belief. Attitude, Intention and Behavior: An Introduction to Theory and Research Reading*. Addison-Wesley.

Flagestad, A. (2002). *Strategic success and organizational structure in winter sports destinations. A multiple stakeholder approach to measuring organizational performance in Scandinavian and Swiss case studies*. ETOUR.

Flavian, C., Ibanez-Sanchez, S., & Orus, C. (2017). The influence of online product presentation videos on persuasion and purchase channel preference: The role of imagery fluency and need fortouc. *Telematics and Informatics*, *34*(8), 1544–1556. doi:10.1016/j.tele.2017.07.002

Flavian, C., Ibanez-Sanchez, S., & Orus, C. (2019a). The impact of virtual, augmented and mixed reality technologies on the customer experience. *Journal of Business Research*, *100*, 547–560. doi:10.1016/j.jbusres.2018.10.050

Flavián, C., Ibáñez-Sánchez, S., & Orús, C. (2019b). Feeling Confident and Smart with Webrooming: Understanding the Consumer's Path to Satisfaction. *Journal of Business Research*, *47*, 1–15.

Floreddu, B. P., & Cabiddu, F. (2014). Managing online reputation: the role of social media in insurance industry. In Academy of Management Proceedings (Vol. 2014, No. 1, p. 17040). Briarcliff Manor, NY: Academy of Management. doi:10.5465/ambpp.2014.17040abstract

Floreddu, P. B., & Cabiddu, F. (2013). Innovating distribution channels for competitive advantage. *XXV Convegno Annuale Di Sinergie, L'innovazione per La Competitività Delle Imprese*, 265–274. doi:10.7433/SRECP.2013.17

Forabosco, G. (1992). Cognitive aspects of the humour process: The concept of incongruity. *Humor: International Journal of Humor Research*, *5*(1-2), 45–68. doi:10.1515/humr.1992.5.1-2.45

Ford, T. E., Richardson, K., & Petit, W. E. (2015). Disparagement humour and prejudice: Contemporary theory and research. Humour. *International Journal of Humour Research*, *28*(2), 171–186.

Forman, C., Ghose, A., & Wiesenfeld, B. (2008). Examining the relationship between reviews and sales: The role of reviewer identity disclosure in electronic markets. *Information Systems Research*, *19*(3), 291–313. doi:10.1287/isre.1080.0193

Fornell, C., & Larcker, D. F. (1981). Evaluating structural equation models with unobservable variables and measurement error. *JMR, Journal of Marketing Research*, *18*(1), 39–50. doi:10.1177/002224378101800104

Franco, M., Haase, H., & Pereira, A. (2016). Empirical study about the role of social networks in SME performance. *Journal of Systems and Information Technology*, *18*(4), 383–403. doi:10.1108/JSIT-06-2016-0036

Frazier Gary, L. (1999). *Organizing and managing channels of distribution. Journal of the Academy of Marketing Science*, 27.

Frieman, E. (2020). *Cause marketing vs purpose-driven marketing*. https://keymedium.com/cause-marketing-vs-purpose-driven-marketing

Fuentes-Blasco, M., Moliner-Velázquez, B., Servera-Francés, D., & Gil-Saura, I. (2017). Role of marketing and technological innovation on store equity, satisfaction and word-of-mouth in retailing. *Journal of Product and Brand Management*, *26*(6), 650–666. doi:10.1108/JPBM-07-2016-1279

Füller, J. (2010). Refining virtual co-creation from a consumer perspective. *California Management Review*, *52*(2), 98–122. doi:10.1525/cmr.2010.52.2.98

Füller, J., Hutter, K., & Faullant, R. (2011). Why co-creation experience matters? Creative experience and its impact on the quantity and quality of creative contributions. *R & D Management*, *41*(3), 259–273. doi:10.1111/j.1467-9310.2011.00640.x

Gajjala, R. (2008). *Avatar research ethics*. Air-L Archive. http://listserv.aoir.org/pipermail/air-l-aoir.org/2008-March/016057.html

Galan, J. P., & Sabadie, W. (2001). *Les déterminants de la satisfaction de l'internaute: une étude exploratoire*. 17ème congrès international de l'Association Française de Marketing, Deauville.

Gallagher, D. (2016). Virtual reality is cool; this may be bigger; augmented reality devices like microsoft's HoloLens are still a work in progress, but they may bear more fruit for investors. *Wall Street Journal*.

Ganguly, B., Dash, S. B., & Cyr, D. (2009). Website characteristics, trust and purchase intention in online stores: An empirical study in the Indian context. *Journal of Information Science and Technology*, *6*(2), 22–44.

Gao, F., & Su, X. (2017). Online and offline information for omnichannel retailing. *Manufacturing & Service Operations Management*, *19*(1), 84–98. doi:10.1287/msom.2016.0593

Gao, F., & Su, X. (2018). Omnichannel service operations with online and offine self-order technologies. *Management Science*, *64*(8), 3595–3608. doi:10.1287/mnsc.2017.2787

Garbarino, E., & Johnson, M. S. (1999). The different roles of satisfaction, trust, and commitment in customer relationships. *Journal of Marketing*, *63*(2), 70–87. doi:10.1177/002224299906300205

García-Crespo, A., Chamizo, J., Rivera, I., Mencke, M., Colomo-Palacios, R., & Gómez-Berbís, J. M. (2009). SPETA: Social pervasive e-Tourism advisor. *Telematics and Informatics*, *26*(3), 306–315. doi:10.1016/j.tele.2008.11.008

Gartner Digital Business Transformation—Gartner IT Glossary. (n.d.). Available online: https://www.gartner.com/it-glossary/digital-business-transformation

Gauntlett, D. (2004). Web Studies: What's New. In D. Gauntlett & R. Horsley (Eds.), *Web.Studies* (2nd ed., pp. 3–23). Bloomsbury Academic.

Gazi, A., Cordeiro, P., Starkey, G., & Dimitrakopoulou, D. (2014). 'Generation C' and audio media: A cross-cultural analysis of differences in media consumption in four European countries. *Participations*, *11*(2), 239–257.

Gefen, D., & Straub, D. W. (2000). The relative importance of perceived ease-of-use in IS adoption: A study of e-commerce adoption. *Journal of the Association for Information Systems*, *1*(8), 1–31. doi:10.17705/1jais.00008

Gentina, E., Chen, R., & Yang, Z. (2021). Development of theory of mind on online social networks: Evidence from Facebook, Twitter, Instagram, and Snapchat. *Journal of Business Research*, *124*(C), 652–666. doi:10.1016/j.jbusres.2020.03.001

Gerdt, S.-O., Wagner, E., & Schewe, G. (2019). The relationship between sustainability and customer satisfaction in hospitality: An explorative investigation using eWOM as a data source. *Tourism Management*, *74*, 155–172. doi:10.1016/j.tourman.2019.02.010

Gervais, M., & Wilson, D. S. (2005). The evolution and functions of laughter and humour: A synthetic approach. *The Quarterly Review of Biology*, *80*(4), 395–430. doi:10.1086/498281 PMID:16519138

Gharbi, J. (1998). *Etude des facteurs qui influencent les processus décisionnels des consommateurs lors d'un achat sur Internet* (Thèse de doctorat). Ecole des Hautes Etudes Commerciales, Université de Montréal.

Ghilic-Micu B. (2002). Business in the Digital Economy. *Informatica Economica*, *3*(23).

Ghobakhloo, M. (2020). Industry 4.0, digitization, and opportunities for sustainability. *Journal of Cleaner Production*, *252*, 119869. doi:10.1016/j.jclepro.2019.119869

Giomelakis, D., & Veglis, A. (2021). Theory and Practice of Search Engine Optimization. In Encyclopedia of Organizational Knowledge, Administration, and Technology (pp. 1354-1367). IGI Global. doi:10.4018/978-1-7998-3473-1.ch093

Giomelakis, D., Karypidou, C., & Veglis, A. (2019). SEO inside Newsrooms: Reports from the Field. *Future Internet, 11*(12), 261. doi:10.3390/fi11120261

Giovannini, S., Xu, Y., & Thomas, J. (2015). Luxury fashion consumption and Generation Y consumers: Self, brand consciousness, and consumption motivations. *Journal of Fashion Marketing and Management, 19*(1), 22–40. doi:10.1108/JFMM-08-2013-0096

Glaeser, E. L., Kolko, J., & Saiz, A. (2001). Consumer city. *Journal of Economic Geography, 1*(1), 27–50. doi:10.1093/jeg/1.1.27

Global E-Commerce Trends and Statistics. (2017-2018). *Amasty Blog.* Retrieved from https://amasty.com/blog/global-e-commerce-trends-and-statistics-2017-2018/

Global Web Index. (2019). *The youth of the nations: Global Trends Among Gen Z.* Retrieved April 28, 2020, from: https://assets.ctfassets.net/inb32lme5009/7wDIuSsLOnSxTUqPmRb081/603b8ffb77757549d39034884a23743c/The_Youth_of_the_Nations__Global_Trends_Among_Gen_Z.pdf

Godey, B., Manthiou, A., Pederzoli, D., Rokka, J., Aiello, G., Donvito, R., & Singh, R. (2016). Social Media Marketing Efforts of Luxury Brands: Influence on Brand Equity and Consumer Behavior. *Journal of Business Research, 69*(12), 5833–5841. doi:10.1016/j.jbusres.2016.04.181

Goeldner, C. R., & Ritchie, J. R. B. (2003). *Tourism: principles, practices, philosophies.* Willey.

Golan, G. J., & Zaidner, L. (2008). Creative Strategies in Viral Advertising: An Application of Taylor's Six-Segment Message Strategy Wheel. *Journal of Computer-Mediated Communication, 13*(4), 959–972. doi:10.1111/j.1083-6101.2008.00426.x

Golden, B. (2012, June). How Cloud Computing can Transform Business Boston. *Harvard Business Review.*

Gonzales, A. L., & Hancock, J. T. (2011). Mirror, mirror on my Facebook wall: Effects of exposure to Facebook on self-esteem. *Cyberpsychology, Behavior, and Social Networking, 14*(1-2), 79–83. doi:10.1089/cyber.2009.0411 PMID:21329447

González-Rodríguez, M. R., Martínez-Torres, R., & Toral, S. (2016). Post-visit and pre-visit tourist destination image through eWOM sentiment analysis and perceived helpfulness. *International Journal of Contemporary Hospitality Management, 28*(11), 2609–2627. doi:10.1108/IJCHM-02-2015-0057

González-Tosat, C., & Sádaba-Chalezquer, C. (2021). Digital Intermediaries: More than New Actors on a Crowded Media Stage. *Journalism and Media, 2*(1), 77–99. doi:10.3390/journalmedia2010006

Gottschalk, S. A., & Mafael, A. (2017). Cutting Through the Online Review Jungle— Investigating Selective eWOM Processing. *Journal of Interactive Marketing, 37*, 89–104. doi:10.1016/j.intmar.2016.06.001

Gouldner, A. (1976). *The Dialectic of Ideology and Technology.* Seabury Press. doi:10.1007/978-1-349-15663-4

Grabher, G. (2001). Ecologies of creativity: The Village, the Group, and the heterarchic organisation of the British advertising industry. *Environment & Planning A, 33*(2), 351–374. doi:10.1068/a3314

Grabher, G. (2002). The Project Ecology of Advertising: Tasks, Talents and Teams. *Regional Studies, 36*(3), 245–262. doi:10.1080/00343400220122052

Granovetter, M. (1985). 'Economic Action and Social Structure: The Problem of Embeddedness'. *American Journal of Sociology, 91*(3), 481–510. doi:10.1086/228311

Granovetter, M. S. (2000). *Le marché autrement*. Desclée de Brouver.

Grant, I., McLeod, C., & Shaw, E. (2012). Conflict and advertising planning: Consequences of networking for advertising planning. *European Journal of Marketing*, *46*(1/2), 73–91. doi:10.1108/03090561211189248

Grégory, B., Francois, D., & Deans, K. R. (2015). An examination of the online service-profit chain. *International Journal of Retail & Distribution Management*, *43*(5), 727–751.

Gretzel, U., Werthner, H., Koo, C., & Lamsfus, C. (2015). Conceptual foundations for understanding smart tourism ecosystems. *Computers in Human Behavior*, *50*, 558–563. doi:10.1016/j.chb.2015.03.043

Griffin, G., Morrison, D. K., & Sheehan, K. B. (2009). Note from Guest Editors: Perspectives from Digital Creativity. Journal of Interactive Advertising, 9(2), 1-3. doi:10.1080/15252019.2009.10722150

Griffith, D. A., & Gray, C. C. (2002). The falacy of the level playing field. *Journal of Marketing Channels*, *9*(3-4), 87–102. doi:10.1300/J049v09n03_05

Guercini, S., & Runfola, A. (2015). Internationalization through e-commerce. the case of multibrand luxury retailers in the fashion industry. *Advances in International Marketing*, *26*, 15–31. doi:10.1108/S1474-797920150000026002

Gulas, C. S., & Weinberger, M. G. (2006). *Humour in advertising: A comprehensive analysis*. ME Sharpe.

Guo, H., Yang, Z., Huang, R., & Guo, A. (2020). The digitalisation and public crisis responses of small and medium enterprises: Implications from a COVID-19 survey. *Front. Bus. Res. China*, *14*(1), 19. doi:10.118611782-020-00087-1

Gupta, A., Su, B. C., & Walter, Z. (2004). An Empirical Study of Consumer Switching from Traditional to Electronic Channels: A Purchase-Decision Process Perspective. *International Journal of Electronic Commerce*, *8*(3), 131–161. do i:10.1080/10864415.2004.11044302

Gupta, N. (2011). Globalization does lead to change in consumer behavior: An empirical evidence of impact of globalization on changing materialistic values in Indian consumers and its aftereffects. *Asia Pacific Journal of Marketing and Logistics*, *23*(3), 251–269. doi:10.1108/13555851111143204

Gupta, S., Kar, A. K., Baabdullah, A., & Al-Khowaiter, W. A. (2018). Big data with cognitive computing: A review for the future. *International Journal of Information Management*, *42*, 78–89. doi:10.1016/j.ijinfomgt.2018.06.005

Gurău, C. (2008). Integrated online marketing communication: Implementation and management. *Journal of Communication Management (London)*, *12*(2), 169–184. doi:10.1108/13632540810881974

Gurviez, P., & Korchia, M. (2002). Proposition d'une échelle de mesure multidimensionnelle de la confiance dans la marque. *Recherche et Applications en Marketing*, *17*(3), 41–61. doi:10.1177/076737010201700304

Guttentag, D. A. (2010). Virtual reality: Applications and implications for tourism. *Tourism Management*, *31*(5), 637–651. doi:10.1016/j.tourman.2009.07.003

Gvili, Y., & Levy, S. (2016). Antecedents of attitudes toward eWOM communication: Differences across channels. *Internet Research*, *26*(5), 1030–1051. doi:10.1108/IntR-08-2014-0201

Gvili, Y., & Levy, S. (2018). Consumer engagement with eWOM on social media: The role of social capital. *Online Information Review*, *42*(4), 482–505. doi:10.1108/OIR-05-2017-0158

Haberly, D., MacDonald-Korth, D., Urban, M., & Wójcik, D. (2019). Asset Management as a Digital Platform Industry: A Global Financial Network Perspective. *Geoforum*, *106*, 167–181. doi:10.1016/j.geoforum.2019.08.009

Habermas, J. (1971). *Knowledge and Human Interests*. Beacon Press.

Hackley, C., & Hackley, A. R. (2019). Advertising at the threshold: Paratextual promotion in the era of media convergence. *Marketing Theory*, *19*(2), 195–215. doi:10.1177/1470593118787581

Hackley, C., & Tiwsakul, R. (2011). Advertising Management and Professional Identity in the Digital Age. In M. Deuze (Ed.), *Managing Media Work* (pp. 209–216). Sage.

Hada, T., Iuga, I., Deaconu, L., Vicol, D., & Căruţ, M. (2020). *Investment. Investment assessment. Theory. Case studies. Accounting monograph*. Pro Universitaria Publishing House.

Hadwich, K., Georgi, D., Tuzovic, S., Büttner, J., & Bruhn, M. (2010). Perceived quality of e-health services: A conceptual scale development of e-health service quality based on the C-OAR-SE approach. *International Journal of Pharmaceutical and Healthcare Marketing*, *4*(2), 112–136. doi:10.1108/17506121011059740

Haenlein, M., & Kaplan, A. M. (2009). Users of the world, unite! The challenges and opportunities of Social Media. *Business Horizons*, *53*, 59–68.

Hagberg, J., Jonsson, A., & Egels-Zandén, N. (2017). Retail digitalization: Implications for physical stores. *Journal of Retailing and Consumer Services*, *39*, 264–269. doi:10.1016/j.jretconser.2017.08.005

Haggerty, N., & Golden, B. (2002). Theorizing technological adaptation as a trigger for institutional change. In *ICIS 2002 Proceedings of the International Conference on Information System* (pp. 247–255). Academic Press.

Hagtvedt, H., & Patrick, V. M. (2016). Gilt and Guilt: Should Luxury and Charity Partner at the Point of Sale? *Journal of Retailing*, *92*(1), 56–64. doi:10.1016/j.jretai.2015.07.004

Hair, J. F., Black, B., Babin, B., Anderson, R. E., & Tatham, R. L. (2010). *Multivariate Data Analysis: A Global Perspective*. Pearson Education Inc.

Hair, J. F., Black, W. C., Babin, B. J., & Anderson, R. E. (2010). *Multivariate data analysis: A global perspective* (7th ed.). Pearson.

Hajdas, M., Radomska, J., & Silva, S. C. (2020). The omni-channel approach: A utopia for companies? *Journal of Retailing and Consumer Services*. doi:10.1016/j.jretconser.2020.102131

Haley, R. I. (1985). *Developing effective communication strategy: A benefit segmentation approach*. Wiley.

Hamad, H., Elbeltagi, I., & El-Gohary, H. (2018). An Empirical Investigation of Business-to-Business E-Commerce Adoption and its Impact on SMEs Competitive Advantage: The Case of Egyptian Manufacturing SMEs, Strategic Change. *Briefings in Entrepreneurial Finance*, *27*(3), 209–229.

Hamad, H., Elbeltagi, I., & El-Gohary, H. (2018). An Empirical Investigation of Business-to-Business E-Commerce Adoption and its Impact on SMEs Competitive Advantage: The Case of Egyptian Manufacturing SMEs. *Strategic Change: Briefings in Entrepreneurial Finance*, *27*(3), 209–229. doi:10.1002/jsc.2196

Hamad, H., Elbeltagi, I., Jones, P., & El-Gohary, H. (2015). Antecedents of B2B E-Commerce Adoption and its Effect on Competitive Advantage in Manufacturing SMEs. *Strategic Change*, *24*(5), 405–428. doi:10.1002/jsc.2019

Hameed, M. A., Counsell, S., & Swift, S. (2012). A Conceptual Model for the Process of IT Innovation Adoption in Organizations. *Journal of Engineering and Technology Management*, *29*(3), 358–390. doi:10.1016/j.jengtecman.2012.03.007

Hameed, M. A., Counsell, S., & Swift, S. (2012). A Conceptual Model for the Process of IT Innovation Adoption in Organizations. *Journal of Engineering and Technology Management*.

Han, D. I., Dieck, M. C., & Jung, T. (2018). User experience model for augmented reality applications in urban heritage tourism. *Journal of Heritage Tourism*, *13*(1), 46–61. doi:10.1080/1743873X.2016.1251931

Hänninen, M., Smedlund, A., & Mitronen, L. (2018). Digitalization in Retailing: Multi-Sided Platforms as Drivers of Industry Transformation. *Baltic Journal of Management*, *13*(2), 152–168. doi:10.1108/BJM-04-2017-0109

Han, S. L., & Kim, K. (2020). Role of consumption values in the luxury brand experience: Moderating effects of category and the generation gap. *Journal of Retailing and Consumer Services*, *57*, 102249. Advance online publication. doi:10.1016/j.jretconser.2020.102249

Hardey, M. (2011). Generation C: Content, Creation, Connections and Choice. *International Journal of Market Research*, *53*(6), 749–770. doi:10.2501/IJMR-53-6-749-770

Harms, B., Bijmolt, T. H., & Hoekstra, J. C. (2017). Digital native advertising: Practitioner perspectives and a research agenda. *Journal of Interactive Advertising*, *17*(2), 80–91. doi:10.1080/15252019.2017.1357513

Harris, L. C., & Goode, M. M. (2004). The four levels of loyalty and the pivotal role of trust: A study of online service dynamics. *Journal of Retailing*, *80*(2), 139–158. doi:10.1016/j.jretai.2004.04.002

Harris, L., Russell-Bennett, R., Plé, L., & Cáceres, R. C. (2010). Not always co-creation: Introducing interactional co-destruction of value in service-dominant logic. *Journal of Services Marketing*.

Hauben, R., & Hauben, M. (1997). *Netizens: On the History and Impact of Usenet and the Internet*. IEEE Computer Society Press.

Hearn, G., Foth, M., & Gray, H. (2009). Applications and Implementations of New Media in Corporate Communications. *Corporate Communications*, *14*(1), 49–61. doi:10.1108/13563280910931072

Heckle, S. E., & Childers, T. L. (1992). The role of expectancy and relevancy in memory for verbal and visual information: What is incongruency? *The Journal of Consumer Research*, *18*(4), 475–492. doi:10.1086/209275

Heilbrunn, B. (2001). *Les facteurs d'attachement du consommateur à la marque* (Doctoral dissertation). Paris 9.

Heine, K., & Berghaus, B. (2014). Luxury goes digital: How to tackle the digital luxury brand–consumer touchpoints. *Journal of Global Fashion Marketing*, *5*(3), 223–234. doi:10.1080/20932685.2014.907606

Heitz-Spahn, S. (2013). Cross-channel free-riding consumer behavior in a multichannel environment: An investigation of shopping motives, socidemographics and product categories. *Journal of Retailing and Consumer Services*, *20*(6), 570–578. doi:10.1016/j.jretconser.2013.07.006

Helfat, C. E., & Raubitschek, R. S. (2018). Dynamic and integrative capabilities for profiting from innovation in digital platform-based ecosystems. *Research Policy*, *47*(8), 1391–1399. doi:10.1016/j.respol.2018.01.019

Heller, J., Chylinski, M., De Ruyter, K., Mahr, D., & Keeling, D. L. (2019). Touchning the untouchable: Exploring multi sensory augmented reality in the of online retailing. *Journal of Retailing*, 1–16.

Hellwig, Z. (1968). Application of the taxonomic method to the typological division of countries due to the level of their development and the structure of qualified personnel. *Statistical Review*, *4*, 307–327.

Hennig-Thurau, T., Gwinner, K. P., Walsh, G., & Gremler, D. D. (2004). Electronic word-of-mouth via consumer-opinion platforms: What motivates consumers to articulate themselves on the Internet? *Journal of Interactive Marketing*, *18*(1), 38–52. doi:10.1002/dir.10073

Hennig-Thurau, T., Hofacker, C. F., & Bloching, B. (2013). Marketing the Pinball Way: Understanding How Social Media Change the Generation of Value for Consumers and Companies. *Journal of Interactive Marketing*, *27*(4), 237–241. doi:10.1016/j.intmar.2013.09.005

Hennig-Thurau, T., Malthouse, E. C., Friege, C., Gensler, S., Lobschat, L., Rangaswamy, A., & Skiera, B. (2010). The impact of new media on customer relationships. *Journal of Service Research, 13*(3), 311–330. doi:10.1177/1094670510375460

Henseler, J., Dijkstra, T. K., Sarstedt, M., Ringle, C. M., Diamantopoulos, A., Straub, D. W., & Calantone, R. J. (2014). Common beliefs and reality about PLS: Comments on Rönkkö and Evermann (2013). *Organizational Research Methods, 17*(2), 182–209. doi:10.1177/1094428114526928

Heravi, B. R., Boran, M., & Breslin, J. (2012). Towards social semantic journalism. In *Sixth International AAAI Conference on Weblogs and Social Media*. Dublin: AAAI Press.

Herhausen, D., Miočević, D., Morgan, R. E., & Kleijnen, M. H. (2020). The digital marketing capabilities gap. *Industrial Marketing Management, 90*, 276–290. doi:10.1016/j.indmarman.2020.07.022

He, W., Wang, F. K., & Zha, S. (2014). Enhancing social media competitiveness of small businesses: Insights from small pizzerias. *New Review of Hypermedia and Multimedia, 20*(3), 225–250. doi:10.1080/13614568.2014.889225

Hickman, E., Kharouf, H., & Sekhon, H. (2020). An omnichannel approach to retailing: Demystifying and identifying the factors influencing an omnichannel experience. *International Review of Retail, Distribution and Consumer Research, 30*(3), 266–288. doi:10.1080/09593969.2019.1694562

Hill, W. W., & Beatty, S. E. (2011). A model of adolescents' online consumer self-efficacy (OCSE). *Journal of Business Research, 64*(10), 1025–1033. doi:10.1016/j.jbusres.2010.11.008

Hirschman & Holbrook. (1982). Hedonic consumption: Emerging concepts, methods and propositions. *Journal of Marketing, 31*, 397-408.

Hofacker, C. F., & Murphy, J. (2009). Consumer web page search, clicking behavior and reaction time. *International Journal of Direct Marketing, 3*(2), 88–96. doi:10.1108/17505930910964759

Hoftman, D. L., & Novak, T. P. (1996). Marketing in Hypermedia Computer Mediated Environments: Conceptual Foundations. *Journal of Marketing, 60*(3), 50–68. doi:10.1177/002224299606000304

Holand, A., Svadberg, S., & Breunig, K. J. (2019). Beyond the Hype: A Bibliometric Analysis Deconstructing Research on Digitalization. *Technology Innovation Management Review, 9*(10), 38–50. doi:10.22215/timreview/1274

Hollebeek, L. (2011). Exploring customer brand engagement: Definition and themes. *Journal of Strategic Marketing, 19*(7), 555–573. doi:10.1080/0965254X.2011.599493

Hollebeek, L. D., Glynn, M. S., & Brodie, R. J. (2014). Consumer Brand Engagement in Social Media: Conceptualization, Scale Development and Validation. *Journal of Interactive Marketing, 28*(2), 149–165. doi:10.1016/j.intmar.2013.12.002

Hollenbaugh, E. E., & Ferris, A. L. (2014). Facebook self-disclosure: Examining the role of traits, social cohesion, and motives. *Computers in Human Behavior, 30*, 50–58. doi:10.1016/j.chb.2013.07.055

Holloway, B. B., & Beatty, S. E. (2008). Satisfiers and Dissatisfiers in the Online Environment: A Critical Incident Assessment. *Journal of Service Research, 10*(4), 347–364. doi:10.1177/1094670508314266

Holme, J., & Marra, M. (2002). Having a laugh at work: How humour contributes to workplace culture. *Journal of Pragmatics, 34*(12), 1683–1710. doi:10.1016/S0378-2166(02)00032-2

Holmqvist, J., Wirtz, J., & Fritze, M. P. (2020). Luxury in the digital age: A multi-actor service encounter perspective. *Journal of Business Research, 121*, 747–756. doi:10.1016/j.jbusres.2020.05.038

Holtzhausen, D. R., & Voto, R. (2002). Resistance From the Margins: The Postmodern Public Relations Practitioner as Organizational Activist. *Journal of Public Relations Research, 14*(1), 57–84. doi:10.1207/S1532754XJPRR1401_3

Homburg, C., Jozić, D., & Kuehnl, C. (2017). Customer experience management: Toward implementing an evolving marketing concept. *Journal of the Academy of Marketing Science*, *45*(3), 377–401. doi:10.100711747-015-0460-7

Hong, J. C., Lin, P. H., & Hsieha, P. C. (2017, February). The effect of consumer innovativeness on perceived value and continuance intention to use smartwatch. *Computers in Human Behavior*, *67*, 264–272. doi:10.1016/j.chb.2016.11.001

Honneth, A. (2013). La lutte pour la reconnaissance. Gallimard.

Hopkins, P. J., & Rees, M. J. (2007). Creating a Branded Information Environment with Social Media: positioning Bond University within Web 2.0. In *Library Services and IT Services papers*. Paper 16. http://epublications.bond.edu.au/library_pubs/16

Horsky, S. (2006). The changing architecture of advertising agencies. *Marketing Science*, *25*(4), 367–383. doi:10.1287/mksc.1060.0198

Hossain, S., Zhou, X., & Rahman, F. (2018). Examining the impact of QR codes on purchase intention and customer satisfaction on the basis of perceived flow. *International Journal of Engineering Business Management*, *10*, 1–11. doi:10.1177/1847979018812323

Houghton, Pressey, & Istanbulluoglu. (2021). Who needs social networking? An empirical enquiry into the capability of Facebook to meet human needs and satisfaction with life. *Computers in Human Behavior, 104*.

How Millennials Want to Work and Live. (2016). https://www.gallup.com/workplace/238073/millennials-work-live.aspx

Hsu, C. K. J. (2017). Selling products by selling brand purpose. *Journal of Brand Strategy*, *5*(4), 373–394.

Huang, H., Shen, H., Meng, Z., Chang, H., & He, H. (2019). Community-based influence maximization for viral marketing. *Applied Intelligence*, *49*(6), 2137–2150. doi:10.100710489-018-1387-8

Hudson, S., Huang, L., Roth, M. S., & Madden, T. J. (2016). The influence of social media interactions on consumer–brand relationships: A three-country study of brand perceptions and marketing behaviors. *International Journal of Research in Marketing*, *33*(1), 27–41. doi:10.1016/j.ijresmar.2015.06.004

Huete-Alcocer, N. (2017). A Literature Review of Word of Mouth and Electronic Word of Mouth Implications for Consumer Behavior. *Frontiers in Psychology*, *8*, 1256. doi:10.3389/fpsyg.2017.01256 PMID:28790950

Hughes, M. Ü., Bendoni, W. K., & Pehlivan, E. (2016). Storygiving as a co-creation tool for luxury brands in the age of the internet: A love story by Tiffany and thousands of lovers. *Journal of Product and Brand Management*, *25*(4), 357–364. doi:10.1108/JPBM-09-2015-0970

Huh, J., Kim, H., Rath, B., Lu, X., & Srivastava, J. (2020). You reap where you sow: A trust-based approach to initial seeding for viral advertising. *International Journal of Advertising*, *39*(7), 963–989. doi:10.1080/02650487.2020.1718823

Huikkola, T., & Kohtamäki, M. (2018). Business models in servitization. In *Practices and Tools for Servitization* (pp. 61–81). Palgrave Macmillan. doi:10.1007/978-3-319-76517-4_4

Hui, S., Inman, J., Huang, Y., & Suher, J. (2013). The effect of in-store travel distance on unplanned spending: Applications to mobile promotion strategies. *Journal of Marketing*, *77*(2), 1–16. doi:10.1509/jm.11.0436

Hu, J., & Zhang, Y. (2017). Discovering the interdisciplinary nature of Big Data research through social network analysis and visualization. *Scientometrics*, *112*(1), 91–109. doi:10.100711192-017-2383-1

Hu, L. T., & Bentler, P. M. (1999). Cutoff Criteria for Fit Indexes in Covariance Structure Analysis: Conventional Criteria versus New Alternatives. *Structural Equation Modeling*, *6*(1), 1–55. doi:10.1080/10705519909540118

Hung, Wong, & Cho. (2009). Ubiquitous Commerce for Creating the Personalized Market Place. IGI Global.

Huré, E., & Cliquet, G. (2011, September). Du multicanal au transcanal: le point de vue du consommateur. In *Actes du 14e Colloque Étienne Thil, Roubaix* (pp. 1-19). Academic Press.

Hurley, A. E., Scandura, T. A., Schriesheim, C. A., Brannick, M. T., Seers, A., Vandenberg, R. J., & Williams, L. J. (1997). Exploratory and confirmatory factor analysis: Guidelines, issues, and alternatives. *Journal of Organizational Behavior, 18*(6), 667–683. doi:10.1002/(SICI)1099-1379(199711)18:6<667::AID-JOB874>3.0.CO;2-T

Husein, K., Wiweka, K., Kurniawati, R., & Adnyana, I. N. (2017). *The profile and behavior of "SMART TOURIST' (Generation Z) in travel decision making*. 4th World Research Summit for Tourism and Hospitality, Orlando, FL.

Huuhka, A., Laaksonen, M., & Laaksonen, P. (2014). The Evolution Of New Systemic Forms In Retailing And Digital Business. *Contributions to International Business*, 239–249.

Ikea Official Website-Vision and Business Idea. (2021). https://www.ikea.com/gb/en/this-is-ikea/about-us/vision-and-business-idea-pub9cd02291

India's first e-commerce company Fabmart.com's founder k vaitheeswaran today said. (2017, July 11). *Business Standard*. https://www.business-standard.com/article/pti-stories/india-s-first-e-commerce-company-fabmart-com-s-founder-k-vaitheeswaran-today-said-117071100874_1.html

Informational Society Ministry. (n.d.). *National Strategy on Digital Agenda for Romania 2020*. https://ec.europa.eu/epale/sites/epale/files/strategia-nationala-agenda-digitala-pentru-romania-20202c-20-feb.2015.pdf

Inman, J. J., & Nikolova, H. (2017). Shopper-facing retail technology: A retailer adoption decision framework incorporating shopper attitudes and privacy concerns. *Journal of Retailing, 93*(1), 7–28. doi:10.1016/j.jretai.2016.12.006

Interactive Advertising Bureau. (2019). *2019 Full year digital ad spend results*. Author.

Ismagilova, E., Dwivedi, Y. K., Slade, E., & Williams, M. D. (2017). *Electronic Word of Mouth (eWOM) in the Marketing Context: A State of the Art Analysis and Future Directions*. Springer. doi:10.1007/978-3-319-52459-7

Israel, K., Zerres, C., & Tscheulin, D. K. (2019). Presenting hotels in virtual reality: Does it influence the booking intention? *Journal of Hospitality and Tourism Technology, 10*(3), 443–463. doi:10.1108/JHTT-03-2018-0020

Ištvanić, M., Milić, D. C., & Krpić, Z. (2017). Digital Marketing in the Business Environment. *International Journal of Electrical and Computer Engineering Systems, 8*(2), 67–75. doi:10.32985/ijeces.8.2.4

Iuga, I., & Mihalciuc, A. (2020). *Economic crises. Effects on banking systems and investment decision*. LAP Lambert Academic Publishing.

Jacobson, J., Gruzd, A., & Hernández-García, Á. (2020). Social media marketing: Who is watching the watchers? *Journal of Retailing and Consumer Services, 53*, 53. doi:10.1016/j.jretconser.2019.03.001

Jain, R., Aagja, J., & Bagdare, S. (2017). Customer experience–a review and research agenda. *Journal of Service Theory and Practice, 27*(3), 642–662. doi:10.1108/JSTP-03-2015-0064

Jain, S. (2016). Impact of Digitalization on Indian Luxury Market. *AIMA Journal of Management & Research, 10*(2/4), 1–10.

Jang, S., Farajallah, M., & So, K. K. F. (2021). The effect of quality cues on travelers' demand for peer-to-peer ridesharing: A neglected area of the sharing economy. *Journal of Travel Research, 60*(2), 446–461. doi:10.1177/0047287519897998

Jarvenpaa, S. L., & Todd, P. A. (1996). Consumer reactions to electronic shopping on the World Wide Web. *International Journal of Electronic Commerce, 1*(2), 59–88. doi:10.1080/10864415.1996.11518283

Javalgi, R. G., Todd, P. R., Johnston, W. J., & Granot, E. (2012). Entrepreneurship, muddling through, and Indian internet-enabled SMEs. *Journal of Business Research, 65*(6), 740–744. doi:10.1016/j.jbusres.2010.12.010

Javornik, A. (2014). Classifications of augmented reality uses in marketing. *Proceedings of the IEEE International Symposium on mixed and augmented realities.* 10.1109/ISMAR-AMH.2014.6935441

Javornik, A. (2016). Augmented reality: Research agenda for studying the impact of its media characteristics on consumer behavior. *Journal of Retailing and Consumer Services, 30*, 252–261. doi:10.1016/j.jretconser.2016.02.004

Javornik, A., Rogers, Y., Moutinho, A. M., & Freeman, R. (2016). Revealing the Shopper Experience of Using a" Magic Mirror" Augmented Reality Make-Up Application. *Conference on Designing Interactive Systems*, 871-882. 10.1145/2901790.2901881

Jepsen, A. (2006). Information Search in Virtual Communities: Is it Replacing Use of Off-Line Communication? *Journal of Marketing Communications, 12*(4), 247–261. doi:10.1080/13527260600694308

Jharotia, A. (2018). QR codes: Innovative technology for libraries in electronic environment. In Essential Technologies for Libraries in Digital Era. Lambert Academic Publishing.

Jiang, T., Li, H., & Hou, Y. (2019). Cultural differences in humour perception, usage, and implications. *Frontiers in Psychology*, 10.

Jocevski, M., Arvidsson, N., Miragliotta, G., Ghezzi, A., & Mangiaracina, R. (2019). Transitions towards omni-channel retailing strategies: A business model perspective. *International Journal of Retail & Distribution Management, 47*(2), 78–93. doi:10.1108/IJRDM-08-2018-0176

Joensuu-Salo, S., Sorama, K., Viljamaa, A., & Varamäki, E. (2018). Firm Performance among Internationalized SMEs: The Interplay of Market Orientation, Marketing Capability and Digitalization. *Administrative Sciences, 8*(3), 31. doi:10.3390/admsci8030031

Johnson, D., & Grayson, K. (2005). Cognitive and affective trust in service relationships. *Journal of Business Research, 58*(4), 500–507. doi:10.1016/S0148-2963(03)00140-1

Johnson, R. B., & Onwuegbuzie, A. J. (2004). Mixed methods research: A research paradigm whose time has come. *Educational Researcher, 33*(7), 14–26. doi:10.3102/0013189X033007014

Jones Christensen, L., Siemsen, E., & Balasubramanian, S. (2015). Consumer behavior change at the base of the pyramid: Bridging the gap between for-profit and social responsibility strategies. *Strategic Management Journal, 36*(2), 307–317. doi:10.1002mj.2249

Joo, Bong, & Choi. (2000). Self-efficacy for self-regulated learning, academic self-efficacy, and Internet self-efficacy in Web-based instruction. *Educational Technology Research and Development, 48*(2), 5 – 17.

Joreskog, K., & Sorbom, D. (1993). *LISREL 8: Structural Equation Modeling with the SIMPLIS Command Language.* Scientific Software International Inc.

Joyce, M., & Kirakowski, J. (2014). Measuring Confidence in Internet Use: The Development of an Internet Self-efficacy Scale. In A. Marcus (Ed.), Lecture Notes in Computer Science: Vol. 8517. *Design, User Experience, and Usability. Theories, Methods, and Tools for Designing the User Experience. DUXU 2014.* Springer. doi:10.1007/978-3-319-07668-3_25

Juckel, J., Bellman, S., & Varan, D. (2016). A humour typology to identify humour styles used in sitcoms. *HUMOUR, 29*(4), 583–603.

Jung, H., Kwon, K. M., & Yu, G. J. (2019). Fuels sales through retail chains and their store traffics and revenue. *Asia Pacific Journal of Marketing and Logistics, 31*(1), 2–13. doi:10.1108/APJML-04-2017-0058

Jurkowska, B. (2014). The Federal States of Germany – Analysis and Measurement of Development Using Taxonomic Methods. *Oeconomia Copernicana, 5*(3), 52. http://apcz.pl/czasopisma/index.php/OeC/article/view/OeC.2014.019/4316

Kádeková, Z., & Holienčinová, M. (2018). Influencer Marketing as a modern phenomenon creating a new frontier of virtual opportunities. *Communication Today, 9*(2), 90–106.

Kaemingk, D. (2020, 30 October). *Online reviews statistics to know in 2021.* https://www.qualtrics.com/blog/online-review-stats/

Kalia, P., Kaur, N., & Singh, T. (2017). E-Commerce in India: Evolution and Revolution of Online Retail. In M. Khosrow-Pour (Ed.), *Mobile Commerce: Concepts, Methodologies, Tools, and Applications* (pp. 736–758). IGI Global.

Kamal, S., Chu, S. C., & Pedram, M. (2013). Materialism, attitudes, and social media usage and their impact on purchase intention of luxury fashion goods among American and Arab young generations. *Journal of Interactive Advertising, 13*(1), 27–40. doi:10.1080/15252019.2013.768052

Kannan, P. K., & Alice, L. (2017). Digital marketing: A framework, review and research agenda. *International Journal of Research in Marketing, 34*(1), 22–45. doi:10.1016/j.ijresmar.2016.11.006

Kapferer, J. N. (2000). How the Internet impacts on brand management. *Journal of Brand Management, 7*(6), 389–391. doi:10.1057/bm.2000.30

Kapferer, J. N. (2015). The future of luxury: Challenges and opportunities. *Journal of Brand Management, 21*(9), 716–726. doi:10.1057/bm.2014.32

Kapferer, J. N., & Bastien, V. (2012). *The Luxury Strategy: Break The Rules of Marketing to Build Luxury Brands* (2nd ed.). Kogan Page Ltd.

Kaplan, A. M., & Haenlein, M. (2010). Users of the world, unite! The challenges and opportunities of Social Media. *Business Horizons, 53*(1), 59–68. doi:10.1016/j.bushor.2009.09.003

Katsikeas, C., Leonidou, L., & Zeriti, A. (2019). Revisiting international marketing strategy in a digital era: Opportunities, challenges, and research directions. *International Marketing Review, 37*(3), 405–424. doi:10.1108/IMR-02-2019-0080

Katz, E., & Lazarsfeld, P. F. (1955). *Personal Influence: The Part Played by People in the Flow of Mass Communications.* Free Press.

Kaye, B. K., & Medoff, N. J. (1999). *The World Wide Web: A Mass Communication Perspective.* Mayfield Publishing Company.

Kazecki, J. (2012). Laughter in the Trenches – Humour and the Front Experience in German First World War Narratives. Cambridge Scholar Publishing.

Kehoe, B. P. (2013). *Zen and the Art of the Internet.* Tredition Classics.

Kellmereit, D. (2013). *Daniel Obodovski (2013) the Silent Intelligence: Internet of Things.* DND Ventures.

Kennedy, G., Dlagarno, B., Gray, K., Judd, T., Waycott, J., Bennett, S., Maton, K., Kerri-Lee, K., Bishop, A., Rosemary, C., & Churchward, A. (2007). The net generation are not big users of Web 2.0 technologies: Preliminary findings. ASCILITE, 517-525.

Kenney, M., & Zysman, J. (2015). Choosing a future in the platform economy: the implications and consequences of digital platforms. In *Proceedings Kauffman Foundation New Entrepreneurial Growth Conference* (*Vol. 156160*). Academic Press.

Kent, R. J., & Allen, C. T. (1994). Competitive interference effects in consumer memory for advertising: The role of brand familiarity. *Journal of Marketing*, *58*(3), 97–105. doi:10.1177/002224299405800307

Keohane, K. (2016), *The Case For Purpose Driven Brands.* https://www.brandingstrategyinsider.com/the-case-for-purpose-driven-brands/#.YBl3oHczZn5

Key, T. M., & Czaplewski, A. J. (2017). Upstream social marketing strategy: An integrated marketing communications approach. *Business Horizons*, *60*(3), 325–333. doi:10.1016/j.bushor.2017.01.006

Khalifa, M., & Liu, V. (2007). Online consumer retention: Contingent effects of online shopping habit and online shopping experience. *European Journal of Information Systems*, *16*(6), 780–792. doi:10.1057/palgrave.ejis.3000711

Kilani, N. (2016). *Étude de l'expérience vécue sur trois canaux d'achat différents et son impact sur la relation marque-consommateur dans le cas des marques de luxe*. Academic Press.

Kilimis, P., Zou, W., Lehmann, M., & Berger, U. (2019). A Survey on Digitalization for SMEs in Brandenburg, Germany. *IFAC-PapersOnLine*, *52*(13), 2140–2145. doi:10.1016/j.ifacol.2019.11.522

Kim, A. J. Y., & Ko, E. J. (2010). The impact of design characteristics on brand attitude and purchase intention-focus on luxury fashion brands. *Journal of the Korean Society of Clothing and Textiles*, *34*(2), 252–265. doi:10.5850/JKSCT.2010.34.2.252

Kim, A. J. Y., & Ko, E. J. (2012). Do social media marketing activities enhance customer equity? An empirical study of luxury fashion brand. *Journal of Business Research*, *65*(10), 1480–1486. doi:10.1016/j.jbusres.2011.10.014

Kim, B.-K. (2005). *Internationalising the Internet: The Co-evolution of Influence and Technology (New Horizons in the Economics of Innovation)*. Edward Elgar Publishing Ltd. doi:10.4337/9781845426750

Kim, H. Y., Lee, J. Y., Mun, J. M., & Johnson, K. K. (2017). Consumer adoption of smart in-store technology: Assessing the predictive value of attitude versus beliefs in the technology acceptance model. *International Journal of Fashion Design, Technology and Education*, *10*(1), 26–36.

Kim, H., Choi, Y. J., & Lee, Y. (2015). Web atmospheric qualities in luxury fashion brand web sites. *Journal of Fashion Marketing and Management*, *19*(4), 384–401. doi:10.1108/JFMM-09-2013-0103

Kim, J. (2019). Luxury fashion goods ownership and collecting behavior in an omni-channel retail environment: Empirical findings from affluent consumers in the US. *Research Journal of Textile and Apparel*, *23*(3), 212–231. doi:10.1108/RJTA-01-2019-0001

Kim, J. H. (2019). Imperative challenge for luxury brands: Generation Y consumers' perceptions of luxury e-commerce sites. *International Journal of Retail & Distribution Management*, *47*(2), 220–244. doi:10.1108/IJRDM-06-2017-0128

Kim, J. H. (2020). Luxury brands in the digital age: Perceived quality and gender difference. *International Review of Retail, Distribution and Consumer Research*, *30*(1), 68–85. doi:10.1080/09593969.2019.1651379

Kim, J., & Joung, H.-M. (2016). Psychological underpinnings of luxury brand goods repurchase intentions: Brand-self congruity, emotional attachment, and perceived level of investment made. *Article in Journal of Global Scholars of Marketing Science, 26*(3), 284–299. doi:10.1080/21639159.2016.1174542

Kim, J., & Lee, J.-E. R. (2011). The Facebook paths to happiness: Effects of the number of Facebook friends and self-presentation on subjective well-being. *Cyberpsychology, Behavior, and Social Networking, 14*(6), 359–364. doi:10.1089/cyber.2010.0374 PMID:21117983

Kim, N., & Kim, W. (2018). Do your social media lead you to make social deal purchases? Consumer-generated social referrals for sales via social commerce. *International Journal of Information Management, 39*, 38–48. doi:10.1016/j.ijinfomgt.2017.10.006

Kincsei, A. (2008). Technology and society in the information age. In R. Pintér (Ed.), *Information Society: From Theory to Political Practice*. Gondolat - ÚjMandátum.

Kipper, G., & Rampolla, J. (2013). *Augmented reality: An emerging technologies guide to AR*. Elsevier.

Ko, E., Costello, J. P., & Taylor, C. R. (2019). What is a luxury brand? A new definition and review of the literature. *Journal of Business Research, 99*, 405–413. doi:10.1016/j.jbusres.2017.08.023

Ko, E., Phau, I., & Aiello, G. (2016). Luxury brand strategies and customer experiences: Contributions to theory and practice. *Journal of Business Research, 69*(12), 5749–5752. doi:10.1016/j.jbusres.2016.04.170

Kohli, A. (2017). Market orientation in a Digital World. *Global Business Review, 18*(3_suppl), 203S–205S. doi:10.1177/0972150917700769

Kohli, R., & Johnson, S. (2011). Digital Transformation in Latecomer Industries: CIO and CEO Leadership Lessons from Encana Oil & Gas (USA) Inc. *MIS Quarterly Executive, 10*(4).

Kohtamäki, M., Parida, V., Patel, P. C., & Gebauer, H. (2020). The relationship between digitalization and servitization: The role of servitization in capturing the financial potential of digitalization. *Technological Forecasting and Social Change, 151*, 119804. doi:10.1016/j.techfore.2019.119804

Kok, A. (2016). *Cultural, Behavioral and Social Considerations in Electronic Collaboration*. IGI Global. doi:10.4018/978-1-4666-9556-6

Konstantopoulou, A., Rizomyliotis, I., Konstantoulaki, K., & Badahdah, R. (2019). Improving SMEs' competitiveness with the use of Instagram influencer advertising and eWOM. *The International Journal of Organizational Analysis, 27*(2), 308–321. doi:10.1108/IJOA-04-2018-1406

Konus, U., Verhoef, P. C., & Neslin, S. A. (2008). Multichannel shopper segments and their covariates. *Journal of Retailing, 84*(4), 398–413. doi:10.1016/j.jretai.2008.09.002

Kopervas, G. (2019). *Cause Marketing vs. Purpose-Driven Brands*. https://www.20nine.com/cause-marketing-vs-purpose-driven-brands

Kotler, P. (2009). Marketing Moves. A new approach to profit, growth, and renewal. Meteor Press Publishing House.

Kotler, P. (2011). 'Reinventing marketing to manage the environmental imperative'. *Journal of Marketing, 75*(4), 132–135. doi:10.1509/jmkg.75.4.132

Kotler, P., Kartajaya, H., & Setawan, I. (2010). *Marketing 4.0: From Products to Customers to the Human Spirit*. John Wiley & Sons, Inc. doi:10.1002/9781118257883

Kotler, P., Kartajaya, H., & Setawan, I. (2017). *Marketing 4.0: Moving from Traditional to Digital*. John Wiley & Sons, Inc.

Kotler, P., Kartajaya, H., & Setiawan, I. (2016). *Marketing 4.0: Moving from traditional to digital*. John Wiley & Sons.

Kotler, P., Kartajaya, H., & Setiawan, I. (2017). *Marketing 4.0*. Optimist Publishers.

Kotler, P., Keller, K. L., & Martinovic, M. (2014). *Upravljanje marketingom*. Mate.

Kotler, P., Wong, V., Saunders, J., & Armstrong, G. (2009). *Principles of Marketing* (6th ed.). Pearson.

Koumartzis, N., & Veglis, A. (2014). Internet Regulation and Online Censorship. *International Journal of E-Politics*, *5*(4), 66–81. doi:10.4018/ijep.2014100104

Kramer, M. (2017). Brand purpose: The navigational code for growth. *Journal of Brand Strategy*, *6*(1), 46–54.

Krawford, K. (2011). *Digital Technologies Effect on Humans and Societies*. Academic Press.

Krey, N., Chuah, S. H.-W., Ramayah, T., & Rauschnabel, P. A. (2019). How functional and emotional ads drive smartwatch adoption: The moderating role of consumer innovativeness and extraversion. *Internet Research*, *29*(3), 578–602. doi:10.1108/IntR-12-2017-0534

Krishnan, H. S., & Chakravarti, D. (2003). A process analysis of the effects of humorous advertising executions on brand claims memory. *Journal of Consumer Psychology*, *13*(3), 230–245. doi:10.1207/S15327663JCP1303_05

Kujath, C. L. (2011). Facebook and MySpace: Complement or substitute for face-to-face interaction? *Cyberpsychology, Behavior, and Social Networking*, *14*(1-2), 75–78. doi:10.1089/cyber.2009.0311 PMID:21329446

Kullnig, C., Obermüller, A., & Aichhorn, K. (2020). Improving campaign performance using purpose marketing: Case study of Run For The Oceans. *Journal of Brand Strategy*, *9*(1), 7–17.

Kumar, N., Anusara, J., Sarkar, M. K., Chanthamith, B., Hossin, M. A., Shah, S., & Russel, M. I. H. (2018). Challenges and opportunities of E-Commerce in india: Pathway for sustainable E-Commerce. *International Journal of Engineering Business Management*, *2*(2). Advance online publication. doi:10.22161/ijebm.2.2.1

Kumar, V., Petersen, J. A., & Leone, R. P. (2010). Driving Profitability by Encouraging Customer Referrals: Who, When, and How. *Journal of Marketing*, *74*(5), 1–17. doi:10.1509/jmkg.74.5.001

Kumar, V., & Venkatesan, R. (2005). Who are the multichannel shoppers and how do they perform?: Correlates of multichannel shopping behavior. *Journal of Interactive Marketing*, *19*(2), 44–62. doi:10.1002/dir.20034

Kung, W.-S. (2020). Reconceptualizing the digital humanities in Asia: New representations of art, history and culture (vol. 2). Springer. doi:10.1007/978-981-15-4642-6

Kwabena, A. E., Li, K., Bonsu, O. A. M., Faamaa, O. B., & Alexander, B. (2020). Effects of Social Media on Firm Performance and Customer Relations-Evidence from Ghana. *Business and Economic Review*, *10*(1), 101–111.

Kwak, H., Lee, C., Park, H., & Moon, S. (2010), What is Twitter, a social network or a news media? *WWW '10: Proceedings of the 19th international conference on World wide web*, 591–600. 10.1145/1772690.1772751

Labrecque, L. I., vor dem Esche, J., Mathwick, C., Novak, T. P., & Hofacker, C. F. (2013). Consumer power: Evolution in the digital age. *Journal of Interactive Marketing*, *27*(4), 257–269. doi:10.1016/j.intmar.2013.09.002

Lacoeuilhe, J. (2000). L'attachement à la marque: proposition d'une échelle de mesure. Rechercheet Applications en Marketing, 15(4), 61-77.

Lacoeuilhe, J. (2000). L'attachement à la marque: Proposition d'une échelle de mesure. *Recherche et Applications en Marketing*, *15*(4), 61–77. doi:10.1177/076737010001500404

Ladhari, R. (2010). Developing e-service quality scales: A literature review. *Journal of Retailing and Consumer Services*, *17*(6), 464–477. doi:10.1016/j.jretconser.2010.06.003

Ladhari, R., Gonthier, J., & Lajante, M. (2019). Generation Y and online faschion shopping: Orientations and profiles. *Journal of Retailing and Consumer Services*, *48*, 113–121. doi:10.1016/j.jretconser.2019.02.003

Lafontaine, F., & Sivadasan, J. (2020). The Recent Evolution of Physical Retail Markets: Online Retailing, Big Box Stores, and the Rise of Restaurants. In *The Role of Innovation and Entrepreneurship in Economic Growth*. University of Chicago Press.

Lahiri, R., Ding, J., & Chinzara, Z. (2018). Technology adoption, adaptation and growth. *Economic Modelling*, *70*, 469–483. doi:10.1016/j.econmod.2017.08.026

Lam, L. (2012). An Innovative Research on the Usage of FaceBook in the Higher Education Context of Hong Kong. *The Electronic Journal of e-Learning*.

Lane, P., & Lubatkin, M. (1998). Relative Absorptive Capacity and Inter-Organizational Learning. *Strategic Management Journal*, *19*(5), 461–477. doi:10.1002/(SICI)1097-0266(199805)19:5<461::AID-SMJ953>3.0.CO;2-L

Lanzolla, G., & Giudici, A. (2017). Pioneering strategies in the digital world. Insights from the Axel Springer case. *Business History*, *59*(5), 744–777. doi:10.1080/00076791.2016.1269752

Lauria, R. M., & Ford-Morie, J. (2015). *Virtuality: AR as metamedia and herald of future realities. In Communication and Technology*. CPI Books.

Law, R., Buhalis, D., & Cobanoglu, C. (2014). Progress on information and communication technologies in hospitality and tourism. *International Journal of Contemporary Hospitality Management*, *26*(5), 727–750. doi:10.1108/IJCHM-08-2013-0367

Lawry, C. A., & Choi, L. (2013). The Omnichannel Luxury Retail Experience: Building Mobile Trust and Technology Acceptance of Quick Response (QR) Codes. *Marketing ZFP*, *35*(2), 144–154. doi:10.15358/0344-1369_2013_2_144

Lazaris, C., & Vrechopoulos, A. (2014). From Multichannel to "Omnichannel" Retailing: Review of the Literature and Calls for Research. *2nd International Conference on Contemporary Marketing Issues, (ICCMI)*. 10.13140/2.1.1802.4967

Leary, M. R., Kelly, K. M., Cottrell, C. A., & Schreindorfer, L. S. (2005). *Individual differences in the need to belong: Mapping the nomological network*. Working paper, Duke University.

Leeflang, P. S., Verhoef, P. C., Dahlström, P., & Freundt, T. (2014). Challenges and solutions for marketing in a digital era. *European Management Journal*, *32*(1), 1–12. doi:10.1016/j.emj.2013.12.001

Lee, H., Jung, T. H., Dieck, M. C. T., & Chung, N. (2020). Experiencing immersive virtual reality in museums. *Information & Management*, *57*(July).

Lee, I. (2015). *RFID Technology Integration for Business Performance Improvement*. IGI Global. doi:10.4018/978-1-4666-6308-4

Lee, J. H., Phaal, R., & Lee, S. H. (2013). An integrated service-device-technology roadmap for smart city development. *Technological Forecasting and Social Change*, *80*(2), 286–306. doi:10.1016/j.techfore.2012.09.020

Lee, K. C., & Chung, N. (2008). Empirical analysis of consumer reaction to the virtual reality shopping mall. *Computers in Human Behavior*, *24*(1), 88–104. doi:10.1016/j.chb.2007.01.018

Lee, K. M. (2004). Presence explicated. *Communication Theory*, *14*(1), 27–50. doi:10.1111/j.1468-2885.2004.tb00302.x

Lee, P. Y., & Lau, K. W. (2018). A new triadic creative role for advertising industry: A study of creatives' role identity in the rise of social media advertising. *Creative Industries Journal*, *11*(2), 137–157. doi:10.1080/17510694.2018.1434362

Lee, Y. H., & Lim, E. A. C. (2008). What's funny and what's not: The moderating role of cultural orientation in ad humour. *Journal of Advertising*, *37*(2), 71–84. doi:10.2753/JOA0091-3367370206

Lee, Z. W. Y., Chan, T. K. H., Chong, A. Y. L., & Thadani, D. R. (2019). Customer engagement through omnichannel retailing: The effects of channel integration quality. *Industrial Marketing Management*, *77*, 90–101. doi:10.1016/j.indmarman.2018.12.004

Leiner, B., Cerf, V., Clark, D., Kahn, R., Kleinrock, L., Lynch, D., Postel, J., Roberts, L., & Wolff, S. (2009). A brief history of the internet. *Computer Communication Review*, *39*(5), 22–31. doi:10.1145/1629607.1629613

Leite, A., & Oliveira, F. (2007). Empreendedorismo e novas tendências. *Estudo Edit Value Empresa Junior*, *5*, 1–35.

Lemke, F., Clark, M., & Wilson, H. (2011). Customer experience quality: An exploration in business and consumer contexts using repertory grid technique. *Journal of the Academy of Marketing Science*, *39*(6), 846–869. doi:10.100711747-010-0219-0

Lemoine, J. F., & Onnée, S. (2001). Vers une meilleure compréhension du statut" d'actionnaire individuel-client. *Gestion*, *2000*(4), 127–138.

Lemon, K. N., & Verhoef, P. C. (2016). Understanding customer experience throughout the customer journey. *Journal of Marketing*, *80*(6), 69–96. doi:10.1509/jm.15.0420

Lenderman, M. (2015). *Cause vs. Purpose: What's the Difference?* https://sustainablebrands.com/read/product-service-design-innovation/cause-vs-purpose-what-s-the-difference

Leroux, E. (2017). Cahier: Management du tourisme durable: conciliation, commercialisation et durabilité. *Revue Management & Avenir*, (96), 117–122.

Leția, A. (2014). Challenges of Business Digital Environment. *Calitatea – acces la success*, *15*(S4), 111. https://www.srac.ro/calitatea/en/arhiva/supliment/2014/Q-as_Vol.15_S4_Sept-2014.pdf

Levak, T., Baric Selmic, S. (2018). Escaping the "virtual promenade" – new trends in use of social networks by members of generation "Z". *Media, Culture and Public Relations*, *9*(1-2), 37-55.

Levy, D. (2013). My View of the Future. *WFoA Advertising 2020 Project*. https://wfoa.wharton.upenn.edu/perspective/douglevy/

Li, H., Daugherty, T., & Biocca, F. (2002). Impact of 3D advertising on product knowledge, brand attitude and purchase intention: The mediating role of presence. *Journal of Advertising*, *31*(3), 43–57. doi:10.1080/00913367.2002.10673675

Li, J., Konus, U., Langerak, F., & Weggeman, M. C. D. P. (2017). Customer Channel Migration and Firm Choice: The Effects of Cross-Channel Competition. *International Journal of Electronic Commerce*, *21*(1), 8–42. doi:10.1080/10864415.2016.1204186

Lin, C.-P., & Bhattacherjee, A. (2010). Extending technology usage models to interactive hedonic technologies: A theoretical model and empirical test. *Information Systems Journal*, *20*(2), 163–181. doi:10.1111/j.1365-2575.2007.00265.x

Lin, K.-Y., & Lu, H.-P. (2011). Intention to continue using Facebook fan pages from the perspective of social capital. *Cyberpsychology, Behavior, and Social Networking*, *14*(10), 565–570. doi:10.1089/cyber.2010.0472 PMID:21381968

Linowes, J., & Babilinski, K. (2017). *Augmented reality for developers: Build practical augmented reality applications with unity*. Packt publishing.

Lintula, J., Tuunanen, T., Salo, M., & Myers, M. D. (2018). When Value Co-Creation Turns to Co-Destruction: Users' Experiences of Augmented Reality Mobile Games. *International Conference on Information Systems. Association for Information Systems (AIS).*

Li, T., & Chen, Y. (2019). Will virtual reality be a double-edged sword? Exploring the moderation effects of the expected enjoyment of a destination on travel intention. *Journal of Destination Marketing & Management, 12*, 15–26. doi:10.1016/j.jdmm.2019.02.003

Liu, R. R., & Zhang, W. (2010). Informational influence of online customer feedback: An empirical study. *Journal of Database Marketing & Customer Strategy Management, 17*(2), 120–131. doi:10.1057/dbm.2010.11

Liu, S., Perry, P., & Gadzinski, G. (2019). The implications of digital marketing on WeChat for luxury fashion brands in China. *Journal of Brand Management, 26*(4), 395–409. doi:10.105741262-018-0140-2

Liu-Thompkins, Y. (2019). A Decade of Online Advertising Research: What We Learned and What We Need to Know. *Journal of Advertising, 48*(1), 1–13. doi:10.1080/00913367.2018.1556138

Liu, X., Burns, A. C., & Hou, Y. (2013). Comparing Online And In-Store Shopping Behavior Towards Luxury Goods'. *International Journal of Retail & Distribution Management, 41*(11/12), 885–900. doi:10.1108/IJRDM-01-2013-0018

Li, X., Jiang, P., Chen, T., Luo, X., & Wen, Q. (2020). A survey on the security of blockchain systems. *Future Generation Computer Systems, 107*, 841–853. doi:10.1016/j.future.2017.08.020

Li, Y. N., Tan, K. C., & Xie, M. (2002). Measuring web-based service quality. *Total Quality Management, 13*(5), 685–700. doi:10.1080/0954412022000002072

Li, Y., Liu, H., Lim, E. T. K., Goh, J. M., Yang, F., & Lee, M. K. O. (2018). Customer's reaction to cross-channel integration in omnichannel retailing: The mediating roles of retailer uncertainty, identity attractiveness, and switching costs. *Decision Support Systems, 109*, 50–60. doi:10.1016/j.dss.2017.12.010

Lodi, E. (2000). *Empreendedorismo – Ciência, Técnica e Arte*. Instituto Euvaldo Lodi.

Loebbecke, C., & Picot, A. (2015). Reflections on societal and business model transformation arising from digitization and big data analytics: A research agenda. *The Journal of Strategic Information Systems, 24*(3), 149–157. doi:10.1016/j.jsis.2015.08.002

Loiacono, E. T., Watson, R. T., & Goodhue, D. L. (2000). *Webqual: a web site quality instrument*. Working paper 2000-126-0, University of Georgia.

Lorenzo-Romero, C., Constantinides, E., & Brünink, L. A. (2014). Co-creation: Customer integration in social media based product and service development. *Procedia: Social and Behavioral Sciences, 148*, 383–396. doi:10.1016/j.sbspro.2014.07.057

Lucas, H. C. Jr, Agarwal, R., Clemons, E. K., El Sawy, O. A., & Weber, B. (2013). Impactful research on transformational information technology: An opportunity to inform new audiences. *Management Information Systems Quarterly, 37*(2), 371–382. doi:10.25300/MISQ/2013/37.2.03

Lule, J. (2001). *Daily News Eternal Stories: The Mythological Role of Journalism*. Guilford Press.

Luo, N., Wang, Y., Zhang, M., Tao, N., & Tu, J. (2020). Integrating community and e-commerce to build a trusted online second-hand platform: Based on the perspective of social capital. *Technological Forecasting and Social Change, 153*, 119913. doi:10.1016/j.techfore.2020.119913

MacCallum, R. C., Browne, M. W., & Sugawara, H. M. (1996). Power Analysis and Determination of Sample Size for Covariance Structure Modeling. *Psychological Methods*, *1*(2), 130–149. doi:10.1037/1082-989X.1.2.130

Madden, C. B. (2017). *Path to Purpose*. Sunday Lunch Pty Ltd.

Magne, S., & Lemoine, F. (2015). Essai de classification des pratiques de cocréation de produits et services. *6th Meeting of the AIMS Thematic Research Group on Innovation.*

Mahadin, B., Akroush, M. N., & Bata, H. (2020). The effects of tourism websites' attributes on e-satisfaction and e-loyalty: A case of American travellers' to Jordan. *International Journal of Web Based Communities*, *16*(1), 4–33. doi:10.1504/IJWBC.2020.105124

Mahad, M., Mohtar, S., & Othman, A. A. (2015). Disposition to trust, interpersonal trust and institutional trust of mobile banking in Malaysia. *Journal of Management Info*, *8*(1), 1–14. doi:10.31580/jmi.v8i1.45

Mahmoud, A. B., Fuxman, L., Mohr, I., Reisel, W. D., & Grigoriou, N. (2020). "We aren't your reincarnation!" workplace motivation across X, Y and Z generations. *International Journal of Manpower.*

Mahring, M., Wennberg, K., & Demir, R. (2018). Reaping Value From Digitalization in Swedish Manufactoring Firms: Untapped Opportunities? Managing Digital Transformation, 41–63.

Majchrzak, A., Markus, M. L., & Wareham, J. (2016). Designing for digital transformation: Lessons for information systems research from the study of ICT and societal challenges. *Management Information Systems Quarterly*, *40*(2), 267–277. doi:10.25300/MISQ/2016/40:2.03

Makrides, A., Vrontis, D., & Christofi, M. (2020). The gold rush of digital marketing: Assessing prospects of building brand awareness overseas. *Business Perspectives and Research*, *8*(1), 4–20. doi:10.1177/2278533719860016

Mallia, K. L., & Windels, K. (2011). Will changing media change the world? An exploratory investigation of the impact of digital advertising on opportunities for creative women. *Journal of Interactive Advertising*, *11*(2), 30–44. doi:10.1080/15252019.2011.10722183

Mandagi, D. W., & Aseng, A. C. (2021). *Millennials and Gen Z's perception of social media marketing effectiveness on the festival's branding: The mediating effect of brand gestalt. Asia Pacific Social Science Review.*

Mandelbaum, A. (2016). *What Should Your Hotel Know About Generation Z?* Retrieved April 27, 2020, from: https://lodgingmagazine.com/what-should-your-hotel-know-about-generation-z/

Manggiasih, S. S. D. P. (2019). Public relations campaign "Forever against animal testing" by the body shop. *International Journal of Humanities and Social Science Research.*, *5*(3), 39–44.

Marasco, A., Buonincontri, P., van Niekerk, M., Orlowski, M., & Okumus, F. (2018). Exploring the role of next-generation virtual technologies in destination marketing. *Journal of Destination Marketing & Management*, *9*, 138–148. doi:10.1016/j.jdmm.2017.12.002

MarchandA.Hennig-ThurauT.FlemmingJ. (2018). Social Media Resources as Strategic Determinants of Social Media Marketing Efectiveness. doi:10.2139srn.3112613

Mariutti, F. G., Giraldi, J. D. M. E., & Crescitelli, E. (2013). The image of Brazil as a tourism destination: An exploratory study of the American market. *International Journal of Business Administration*, *4*(1), 13–22.

Marketing Charts. (2012). *QR Codes most-used Mobile Channel for Engaging Customers*. https://www.marketingcharts.com/industries/retail-and-e-commerce-22519

Marques, M., Agostinho, C., & Zacharewicz, G. (2017). Decentralized decision support for intelligent manufacturing in Industry 4.0. Journal of Ambient Intelligence and Smart Environments, 9(3), 299–313.

Martínez-Cañas, R., Ruiz-Palomino, P., Linuesa-Langreo, J., & Blázquez-Resino, J. J. (2016). Consumer participation in co-creation: An enlightening model of causes and effects based on ethical values and transcendent motives. *Frontiers in Psychology*, *7*, 793. doi:10.3389/fpsyg.2016.00793 PMID:27303349

Mascarenhas, O. A., Kesavan, R., & Bernacchi, M. (2006). Lasting customer loyalty: A total customer experience approach. *Journal of Consumer Marketing*, *23*(7), 397–405. doi:10.1108/07363760610712939

Massetti, B. (1996). An empirical examination of the value of creativity support systems on idea generation. *Management Information Systems Quarterly*, *20*(1), 83–97. doi:10.2307/249543

Materne, S., & Charry, K. (2017). *Digitalisation des commerces traditionnels: une amélioration du parcours client pour les consommateurs?* Academic Press.

Matsiola, M., Dimoulas, C., Kalliris, G., & Veglis, A. A. (2015). Augmenting User Interaction Experience through Embedded Multimodal Media Agents in Social Networks. In Social Media and the Transformation of Interaction in Society (pp. 188-209). IGI Global. doi:10.4018/978-1-4666-8556-7.ch010

Matsiola, M., Dimoulas, C., Kalliris, G., & Veglis, A. A. (2018). Augmenting User Interaction Experience Through Embedded Multimodal Media Agents in Social Networks. In Information Retrieval and Management: Concepts, Methodologies, Tools, and Applications (pp. 1972-1993). IGI Global. doi:10.4018/978-1-5225-5191-1.ch088

Matsiola, M., Spiliopoulos, P., Kotsakis, R., Nicolaou, C., & Podara, A. (2019). Technology-Enhanced Learning in Audiovisual Education: The Case of Radio Journalism Course Design. *Education Sciences*, *9*(1), 62. doi:10.3390/educsci9010062

Maxham, J. G. III, & Netemeyer, R. G. (2002). A longitudinal study of complaining customers' evaluations of multiple service failures and recovery efforts. *Journal of Marketing*, *66*(4), 57–71. doi:10.1509/jmkg.66.4.57.18512

McAfee, A., & Brynjolfsson, E. (2012). Big Data: The management revolution. *Harvard Business Review*, *90*(10), 60–68. PMID:23074865

McGilvary, L. (2020). *How to avoid purpose-washing and create a more purposeful brand.* https://adage.com/article/industry-insights/how-avoid-purpose-washing-and-create-more-purposeful-brand/2270546

McKnight, D. H., Kacmar, C. J., & Choudhury, V. (2004). Shifting Factors and the Ineffectiveness of Third Party Assurance Seals: A Two-Stage Model of Initial Trust in a Web Business. *Electronic Markets*, *14*(3), 252–266. doi:10.1080/1019678042000245263

McLean, G., & Wilson, A. (2019). Shopping in the digital world: Examining customer engagement through augmented reality mobile applications. *Computers in Human Behavior*, *101*, 210–224. doi:10.1016/j.chb.2019.07.002

McLeod, C., O'Donohoe, S., & Townley, B. (2009). The elephant in the room? Class and creative careers in British advertising agencies. *Human Relations*, *62*(7), 1011–1039. doi:10.1177/0018726709335551

McLeod, C., O'Donohoe, S., & Townley, B. (2011). Pot noodles, placements and peer regard: Creative career trajectories and communities of practice in the British advertising industry. *British Journal of Management*, *22*(1), 114–131. doi:10.1111/j.1467-8551.2010.00705.x

McQuitty, S., Finn, A., & Wiley, J. B. (2000). Systematically varying consumer satisfaction and its implications for product choice. *Academy of Marketing Science Review*, *10*(1), 231–254.

Meaningful Brands Research Report. (2019). https://s3.amazonaws.com/media.mediapost.com/uploads/MeaningfulBrands2019.pdf

Mehra, Chawla, Sharma, & Dey. (2011). *New Paradigms in Business Management and Information Technology*. Kunal Books.

Mejri, E., & Gharbi, J. (2016). L'impact de la valeur perçue de la Co-création sur l'engagement des consommateurs. Université Tunis El Manar. *Proceedings of the Marketing Spring Colloquy (URAM)*, 6.

Melcrum. (2007). *How to use social media to engage employees*. Melcrum Publishing.

Melero, I., Javier Sese, F., & Verhoef, P. C. (2016). Recasting the Customer Experience in Today's Omni-channel Environment. *Universia Business Review*, *2016*(50), 18–37. doi:10.3232/UBR.2016.V13.N2.01

Melgarejo-Heredia, R., Carr, L., & Halford, S. (2016). The public web and the public good. In *Proceedings of the 8th ACM Conference on Web Science* (pp. 330-332). ACM. 10.1145/2908131.2908181

Melis, K., Campo, K., Breugelmans, E., & Lamey, L. (2015). The impact of the multichannel retail mix on online store choice: Does online experience matter? *Journal of Retailing*, *91*(2), 272–288. doi:10.1016/j.jretai.2014.12.004

Melović, B., Jocović, M., Dabić, M., Vulić, T. B., & Dudic, B. (2020). The impact of digital transformation and digital marketing on the brand promotion, positioning and electronic business in Montenegro. *Technology in Society*, *63*, 63. doi:10.1016/j.techsoc.2020.101425

Mercier, J., & Roux, E. (2017). L'attachement à la marque: mesure unidimensionnelle ou tridimensionnelle? *Centre d'étude et de recherché en gestion d'Aix-Marseille*, 1-38.

Mercklé, P. (2011). *Sociologie des réseaux sociaux*. La Découverte. doi:10.3917/dec.merck.2011.01

Meyer, C., & Schwager, A. (2007). Understanding Customer Experience. *Harvard Business Review*, *85*(2), 116. PMID:17345685

Michel, G. M., Feori, M., Damhorst, M. L., Lee, Y. A., & Niehm, L. S. (2019). Stories we wear: Promoting sustainability practices with the case of Patagonia. *Family and Consumer Sciences Research Journal*, *48*(2), 165–180. doi:10.1111/fcsr.12340

Miller. (2018). IOT Solutions Dummies. John Wiley & Sons Inc.

Miller, D. (1987). The Structural and Environmental Correlates of Business Strategy. *Strategic Management Journal*, *8*(1), 55–76. doi:10.1002mj.4250080106

Miller, D. (1988). Relating Porter's Business Strategies to Environment and Structure: Analysis and Performance Implications. *Academy of Management Journal*, *31*(2), 280–308.

Miller, D., & Friesen, P. (1983). Strategy-Making and Environment: The Third Link. *Strategic Management Journal*, *4*(3), 221–235. doi:10.1002mj.4250040304

Millman, C., & El-Gohary, H. (2011). New Digital Media Marketing and Micro Business: A UK perspective. *International Journal of Online Marketing*, *1*(1), 41–62. doi:10.4018/ijom.2011010104

Miloslavskaya, N., & Tolstoy, A. (2016). Big data, fast data and data lake concepts. *Procedia Computer Science*, *88*(300-305), 63. doi:10.1016/j.procs.2016.07.439

Miquel-Romero, M.-J., Frasquet, M., & Molla-Descals, A. (2020). The role of the store in managing postpurchase complaints for omnichannel shoppers. *Journal of Business Research*, *109*(3), 288–296. doi:10.1016/j.jbusres.2019.09.057

Mir-Bernal, P., Guercini, S., & Sádaba, T. (2018). The role of e-commerce in the internationalization of Spanish luxury fashion multi-brand retailers. *Journal of Global Fashion Marketing*, *9*(1), 59–72. doi:10.1080/20932685.2017.1399080

Mircea M. (2004). Dimensions and Characteristics of the Digital Economy. *Informatica Economică*, *4*(32).

Mirzaei, A., Webster, C. M., & Siuki, H. (2021). Exploring brand purpose dimensions for non-profit organizations. *Journal of Brand Management*, 1–13.

Mithas, S., Ramasubbu, N., Krishnan, M. S., & Fornell, C. (2007). Designing websites for customer loyalty across business domains: A multilevel analysis. *Journal of Management Information Systems*, *23*(3), 97–127. doi:10.2753/MIS0742-1222230305

Mollen, A., & Wilson, H. (2010). Engagement, telepresence, and interactivity in online consumer experience: Reconciling scholastic and managerial perspectives. *Journal of Business Research*, *63*(9-10), 919–925. doi:10.1016/j.jbusres.2009.05.014

Molnár, S., Kollányi, B., & Székely, L. (2008). Social networks and the network society. In R. Pintér (Ed.), *Information Society: From Theory to Political Practice*. Gondolat - ÚjMandátum.

Montecchi, M., & Nobbs, K. (2017). Let It Go: Consumer Empowerment and User-Generated Content—An Exploratory Study of Contemporary Fashion Marketing Practices in the Digital Age. In A. Vecchi (Ed.), *Advanced Fashion Technology and Operations Management* (pp. 294–317). IGI Global. doi:10.4018/978-1-5225-1865-5.ch013

Moorhouse, N., Tom-Dieck, C. & Jung, T. (2017). Augmented reality to enhance the learning experience in cultural heritage tourism: An experiential learning cycle perspective. *e-Review of Tourism Research*, *8*, 1–5.

Moretti, A., & Tuan, A. (2014). *Social media marketing and relationship marketing: revolution or evolution? A first step analysis. Sinergie Italian Journal of Management, 93.*

Morgan, R. M., & Hunt, S. D. (1994). The commitment-trust theory of relationship marketing. *Journal of Marketing*, *58*(3), 20–38. doi:10.1177/002224299405800302

Moroz, M. (2017). The level of development of the digital economy in Poland and selected European countries: a comparative analysis. *Foundations of Management*, *9*(1), 175–190.

Morrison, A. M. (2019). *Marketing and Managing Tourism Destinations*. Routledge.

Mosca, F., & Chiaudano, V. (2020). Digital channels and distribution in luxury market. *Marche et Organisations*, *37*(1), 147–163.

Mosca, F., & Giacosa, E. (2016). Old and new distribution channels in the luxury sector. IGI Global Publisher. doi:10.4018/978-1-4666-9958-8.ch010

Mosquera, A., Olarte-Pascual, C., Ayensa, E. J., & Murillo, Y. S. (2018). The role of technology in an omnichannel physical store: Assessing the moderating effect of gender. *Spanish Journal of Marketing-ESIC*.

Moubarak. (2016). Internet of Things for Home Automation. Media Engineering and Technology Faculty, German University in Cairo.

Muller, T. E., Tse, D. K., & Venkatasubramaniam, R. (1991). Post consumption emotions: Exploring their emergence and determinants. *Journal of Consumer Satisfaction, Dissatisfaction & Complaining Behavior*, *4*, 13–20.

Murray, K. B. (1991). A Test of Service Marketing Theory: Consumer Information Acquisition Activities. *Journal of Marketing*, *55*(01), 10–15. doi:10.1177/002224299105500102

Nabi, R. L., & Hendriks, A. (2003). The persuasive effect of host and audience reaction shots in television talk shows. *Journal of Communication, 53*(3), 527–543. doi:10.1111/j.1460-2466.2003.tb02606.x

Nadkarni, A., & Hofmann, S. G. (2012). Why do people use Facebook? *Personality and Individual Differences, 52*(3), 243–249. doi:10.1016/j.paid.2011.11.007 PMID:22544987

Nambisan, S., & Baron, R. A. (2009). Virtual customer environments: Testing a model of voluntary participation in value co-creation activities. *Journal of Product Innovation Management, 26*(4), 388–406. doi:10.1111/j.1540-5885.2009.00667.x

Nambisan, S., & Baron, R. A. (2010). Different roles, different strokes: Organizing virtual customer environments to promote two types of customer contributions. *Organization Science, 21*(2), 554–572. doi:10.1287/orsc.1090.0460

Neslin, S. A., Grewal, D., Leghorn, R., Shankar, V., Teerling, M. L., Thomas, J. S., & Verhoef, P. C. (2006). Challenges and opportunities in multichannel customer management. *Journal of Service Research, 9*(2), 95–112. doi:10.1177/1094670506293559

Neslin, S. A., & Shankar, V. (2009). Key Issues in Multichannel Customer Management: Current Knowledge and Future Directions. *Journal of Interactive Marketing, 23*(1), 70–81. doi:10.1016/j.intmar.2008.10.005

NeubertM. (2018). The Impact of Digitalization on the Speed of Internationalization of Lean Global. *Technology Innovation Management Review*, 8(5). Available at https://ssrn.com/abstract=3394507

Neuhofer, B., Buhalis, D., & Ladkin, A. (2014). A Typology of Technology-Enhanced Tourism Experiences. *International Journal of Tourism Research, 16*(4), 340–350. doi:10.1002/jtr.1958

Neuhofer, B., Buhalis, D., & Ladkin, A. (2015). Smart technologies for personalized experiences: A case study in the hospitality domain. *Electronic Markets, 25*(3), 243–254. doi:10.100712525-015-0182-1

Newby, T. J., Stepich, D. A., Lehman, J. D., Russell, J. D., & Leftwich, A. T. (2019). *Educational Technology for Teaching and Learning* (4th ed.). Pearson Education.

Nicolaou, C. (2011a). *Public Relations and New Technologies* [Unpublished CIPR Professional PR Diploma Thesis]. Chartered Institute of Public Relations, London, UK.

Nicolaou, C. (2020). Communication Skills through Audiovisual Media and Audiovisual Content. *ΣΚΕΨΥ, 7*(1), 166-174.

Nicolaou, C. (2021). Qualitative methods research through the Internet Applications and Services: The contribution of audiovisuals media technology as technology-enhanced research. *International Research in Higher Education, 6*(1). doi:10.5430/irhe.v6n1p1

Nicolaou, C. A. (2011b). *Public Relations: Future and New Technologies* [Δημόσιες Σχέσεις: Μέλλον και Νέες Τεχνολογίες of Greek language] [Unpublished Bachelor's Thesis]. University of Nicosia, Nicosia, Cyprus.

Nicolaou, C., & Kalliris, G. (2020). Audiovisual Media Communications in Adult Education: The case of Cyprus and Greece of Adults as Adult Learners. *European Journal of Investigation in Health, Psychology and Education, 10*(4), 967–994. doi:10.3390/ejihpe10040069

Nicolaou, C., & Karypidou, C. (2021). Generations and Social Media: The case of Cyprus and Greece. In *Proceedings of the 7th International Scientific Conference.*

Nicolaou, C., Matsiola, M., & Kalliris, G. (2019). Technology-Enhanced Learning and Teaching Methodologies through Audiovisual Media. *Education Sciences, 9*(3), 196. doi:10.3390/educsci9030196

Nicolaou, C., Matsiola, M., Karypidou, C., Podara, A., Kotsakis, R., & Kalliris, G. (2021b). Medias Studies, Audiovisual Media Communications, and Generations: The case of budding journalists in radio courses in Greece. *Journalism and Media*, *2*(2), 155–192. doi:10.3390/journalmedia2020010

Nicolaou, C., Podara, A., & Karypidou, C. (2021a). Audiovisual media in education and Generation Z: Application of audiovisual media theory in education with an emphasis on radio. In *Proceedings of the 6th International Scientific Conference on Communication, Information, Awareness and Education in Late Modernity* (pp. 294-302). Institute of Humanities and Social Sciences.

Nicoli, N., & Komodromos, M. (2013). *Principles of Public Relations*. University of Nicosia Press.

Nielsen, C., Lund, M., & Thomsen, P. (2017). From digital disruption to business model scalability. *ISPIM Innovations Conferencen i Wien 2017. ISPIM Conference.*

Nielsen, M. (2015). *The influence of product type, humour type, brand attitude, and gender on humour effectiveness in ads* (Doctoral dissertation).

Nieto-García, M., Muñoz-Gallego, P. A., & González-Benito, Ó. (2017). Tourists' willingness to pay for an accommodation: The effect of eWOM and internal reference price. *International Journal of Hospitality Management*, *62*, 67–77. doi:10.1016/j.ijhm.2016.12.006

Nieto, J., Hernández-Maestro, R. M., & Muñoz-Gallego, P. A. (2014). Marketing decisions, customer reviews, and business performance: The use of the Toprural website by Spanish rural lodging establishments. *Tourism Management*, *45*, 115–123. doi:10.1016/j.tourman.2014.03.009

Nike Official Website-About Nike. (2021). https://about.nike.com

Nike Official Website-Purpose. (2021). https://purpose.nike.com

Nikhashemi, S. R., Knight, H. H., Nusair, K., & Liat, C. B. (2021). Augmented reality in smart retailing: A (n)(A) Symmetric Approach to continuous intention to use retail brands' mobile AR apps. *Journal of Retailing and Consumer Services*, *60*, 102464. doi:10.1016/j.jretconser.2021.102464

Noble, S. (2010). *It's time to bury the marketing funnel*. Steven Noble's Blog.

North, K., Aramburu, N., & Lorenzo, O. J. (2020). Promoting digitally enabled growth in SMEs: A framework proposal. *Journal of Enterprise Information Management*, *33*(1), 238–262. doi:10.1108/JEIM-04-2019-0103

Novgorodtseva, A. N., Tomyuk, O. N., Dyachkova, M. A., & Piankova, M. P. (2020). Online marketplace: Student consumer strategies. *Economic Consultant*, *32*(4), 41–53. doi:10.46224/ecoc.2020.4.5

Nueno, J. L., & Quelch, J. A. (1998). The mass marketing of luxury. *Business Horizons*, *41*(6), 61–68. doi:10.1016/S0007-6813(98)90023-4

Nunes, J. C., Drèze, X., & Han, Y. J. (2011). Conspicuous consumption in a recession: Toning it down or turning it up? *Journal of Consumer Psychology*, *21*(2), 199–205. doi:10.1016/j.jcps.2010.11.002

Nunnally, J. C. (1978). *Psychometric Theory* (2nd ed.). McGraw-Hill.

O'Brien, H. L. (2010). The influence of hedonic and utilitarian motivations on user engagement: The case of online shopping experiences. *Interacting with Computers: Special Issue on User Experience*, *22*(4), 344–352. doi:10.1016/j.intcom.2010.04.001

O'Reilly T. (2007). What Is Web 2.0: Design Patterns and Business Models for the Next Generation of Software. *Communications & Strategies*, 17-37.

O'Reilly, T. (2005). *What is Web 2.0?* https://www.oreilly.com/pub/a/web2/archive/what-is-web-20.html

O'Reilly, T. (2009). Battelle John, Web Squared: Web 2.0 Five Years On. *Web 2.0 Summit*, 1-15.

OECD. (2007). *Participative Web and User-Created Content: Web 2.0, Wikis, and Social Networking*. OECD.

Oh, H. J., Ozkaya, E., & LaRose, R. (2014). How does online social networking enhance life satisfaction? The relationships among online supportive interaction, affect, perceived social support, sense of community, and life satisfaction. *Computers in Human Behavior*, *30*, 69–78. doi:10.1016/j.chb.2013.07.053

Okazaki, S., Katsukura, A., & Nishiyama, M. (2007). How mobile advertising works: The role of trust in improving attitudes and recall. *Journal of Advertising Research*, *47*(2), 165–178. doi:10.2501/S0021849907070195

Okonkwo, U. (2010). Luxury online: Styles, systems, strategies. Palgrave Macmillan UK. doi:10.1057/9780230248335

Okonkwo, U. (2009). Sustaining the luxury brand on the Internet. *Journal of Brand Management*, *16*(5–6), 302–310. doi:10.1057/bm.2009.2

Oktemgil, M., & Greenley, G. (1997). Consequences of high and low adaptive capability in UK companies. *European Journal of Marketing*, *31*(7), 445–466. doi:10.1108/03090569710176619

Oldenburg, R. (1991). *The Great Good Place*. Paragon House.

Ong, S. K., & Nee, A. Y. C. (2004). A brief introduction of VR and AR applications in manufacturing. In *Virtual and augmented reality applications in manufacturing* (pp. 1–14). Springer. doi:10.1007/978-1-4471-3873-0_1

Orlikowski, W. J. (2000). Using Technology and Constituting Structures: A Practice Lens for Studying Technology in Organizations. *Organization Science*, *11*(4), 404–428. doi:10.1287/orsc.11.4.404.14600

Orr, E. S., Sisic, M., Ross, C., Simmering, M. G., Arseneault, J. M., & Orr, R. R. (2009). The influence of shyness on the use of Facebook in an undergraduate sample. *Cyberpsychology & Behavior*, *12*(3), 337–340. doi:10.1089/cpb.2008.0214 PMID:19250019

Owen, M., Grant, L., Sayers, S., & Facer, K. (2006). *Social Software and Learning*. Futurelab. https://www.nfer.ac.uk/media/1820/futl57.pdf

Ozkaya, E., Ozkaya, H. E., Roxas, J., Bryant, F., & Whitson, D. (2015). Factors affecting consumer usage of QR codes. *Journal of Direct, Data and Digital Marketing Practice*, *16*(3), 209–224. doi:10.1057/dddmp.2015.18

Palacios-Marqués, D., Gallego-Nicholls, J. F., & Guijarro-García, M. (2021). A recipe for success: Crowdsourcing, online social networks, and their impact on organizational performance. *Technological Forecasting and Social Change*, *165*, 120566. doi:10.1016/j.techfore.2020.120566

Pal, S. K., & Jha, K. K. (2017). Personal marketing framework based on QR code. *Scholedge International Journal of Multidisciplinary & Allied Studies*, *4*(8), 65–87. doi:10.19085/journal.sijmas040801

Pantano, E. (2016). Engaging consumer through storefront: Evidences from integrating interactive technologies. *Journal of Retailing and Consumer Services*, *28*, 149–154. doi:10.1016/j.jretconser.2015.09.007

Pantano, E., & Di Pietro, L. (2012). Understanding consumer's acceptance of technology-based innovations in retailing. *Journal of Technology Management & Innovation*, *7*(4), 1–19. doi:10.4067/S0718-27242012000400001

Pantano, E., & Timmermans, H. (2014). What is smart for retailing? *Procedia Environmental Sciences*, *22*, 101–107. doi:10.1016/j.proenv.2014.11.010

Pantano, E., & Viassone, M. (2014). Demand pull and technology push perspective in technology-based innovations for the points of sale: The retailers evaluation. *Journal of Retailing and Consumer Services*, *21*(1), 43–47. doi:10.1016/j.jretconser.2013.06.007

Paquerot, M., Queffelec, A., Sueur, I., & Biot-Paquerot, G. (2011). L'e-réputation ou le renforcement de la gouvernance par le marché de l'hôtellerie. *Management Avenir*, (5), 280-296.

Parasuraman, Zeithaml, & Malhotra. (2005). E-S-QUALA Multiple-Item Scale for Assessing Electronic Service Quality. *Journal of Service Research*, *7*(3), 213–233. doi:10.1177/1094670504271156

Parasuraman, A., Zeithaml, V. A., & Berry, L. L. (1988). SERVQUAL: A multiple-item scale for measuring consumer perceptions of service quality. *Journal of Retailing*, *64*(1), 12–40.

Pardo, A. (2013). Digital Hollywood: How Internet and Social Media Are Changing the Movie Business. In *Handbook of Social Media Management* (pp. 327–347). Springer Heidelberg. doi:10.1007/978-3-642-28897-5_19

Parida, V., Sjödin, D., & Reim, W. (2019). Reviewing Literature on Digitalization, Business Model Innovation, and Sustainable Industry: Past Achievements and Future Promises. *Sustainability*, *11*(2), 391. doi:10.3390u11020391

Park, C. W., MacInnis, D. J., Eisinggerich, A. B., & Iacobucci, D. (2010). Brand attachment and brand attitude strength: Conceptual and empirical differentiation of two critical brand equity drivers. *Journal of Marketing*, *74*(November), 1–17. doi:10.1509/jmkg.74.6.1

Parker, P. (2006). *The Art and Science of Screenwriting* (2nd ed.). Intellect.

Park, J., Dayarian, I., & Montreuil, B. (2020). Showcasing optimization in omnichannel retailing. *European Journal of Operational Research*. Advance online publication. doi:10.1016/j.ejor.2020.03.081

Park, J., Song, H., & Ko, E. (2011). The Effect of the Lifestyles of Social Networking Service Users on Luxury Brand Loyalty. *Journal of Global Scholars of Marketing Science*, *21*(4), 182–192. doi:10.1080/21639159.2011.9726521

Park, M.-S., Shin, J.-K., & Ju, Y. (2019). Attachment styles and electronic word of mouth (e-WOM) adoption on social networking sites. *Journal of Business Research*, *99*(C), 398–404. doi:10.1016/j.jbusres.2017.09.020

Passavanti, R., Pantano, E., Priporas, C. V., & Verteramo, S. (2020). The use of new technologies for corporate marketing communication in luxury retailing: Preliminary findings. *Qualitative Market Research*, *23*(3), 503–521. doi:10.1108/QMR-11-2017-0144

Pasternack, B. A. (2008). Optimal pricing and return policies for perishable commodities. *Marketing Science*, *27*(1), 133–140. doi:10.1287/mksc.1070.0336

Patagonia Official Website. (2021). https://www.patagonia.com/home

Patagonia Official Website-Business Unusual. (2021). https://www.patagonia.com/business-unusual

Patagonia Official Website-One Percent For the Planet. (2021). https://www.patagonia.com/one-percent-for-the-planet.html

Patagonia Official Website-Worn Wear Recrafted. (2021). https://wornwear.patagonia.com/recrafted

Patagonia Official Website-Worn Wear Seconds. (2021). https://wornwear.patagonia.com/seconds

Patagonia Official Youtube Channel-Worn Wear. A Film About the Stories We Wear. (2021). https://youtu.be/z20CjCim8DM

Patterson, A. (2012). Social-networkers of the world, unite and take over: A meta-introspective perspective on the Facebook brand. *Journal of Business Research*, *65*(4), 527–534. doi:10.1016/j.jbusres.2011.02.032

Pauwels, K., & Neslin, S. A. (2015). Building With Bricks and Mortar: The Revenue Impact of Opening Physical Stores in a Multichannel Environment. *Journal of Retailing*, *91*(2), 182–197. doi:10.1016/j.jretai.2015.02.001

Pehlivan, E., Berthon, P. R., Pitt, L. F., & Chakrabarti, R. (2013). When outsourcing fragments: Customer creativity and technological transmutations. *Production Planning and Control*, *24*(4-5), 284–293. doi:10.1080/09537287.2011.648541

Penz, E., & Stöttinger, B. (2012). A comparison of the emotional and motivational aspects in the purchase of luxury products versus counterfeits. *Journal of Brand Management*, *19*(7), 581–594. doi:10.1057/bm.2012.7

Perry-Smith, J. E., & Shalley, C. E. (2003). The Social Side of Creativity: A Static and Dynamic Social Network Perspective. *Academy of Management Review*, *28*(1), 89–106. doi:10.5465/amr.2003.8925236

Persada, S. F., Ivanovski, J., Miraja, B. A., Nadlifatin, R., Mufidah, I., Chin, J., & Perwira Redi, A. A. N. (2020). Investigating Generation Z′ Intention to Use Learners' Generated Content for Learning Activity: A Theory of Planned Behavior Approach. *International Journal of Emerging Technologies in Learning*, *15*(4), 179–194. doi:10.3991/ijet.v15i04.11665

Pessoa, E. (2005). *Tipos de Empreendedorismo: Semelhanças e Diferenças*. https://www.administradores.com.br/informe-se/artigos/tipos-de-empreendedorismo-semelhancas-e-diferencas/10993

Pestek, A., & Sarvan, M. (2020). Virtual reality and modern tourism. *Journal of Tourism Futures*.

Petty, R. E., & Cacioppo, J. T. (1986). The elaboration likelihood model of persuasion. In *Communication and persuasion* (pp. 1–24). Springer.

Petty, R. E., Cacioppo, J. T., & Schumann, D. (1983). Central and peripheral routes to advertising effectiveness: The moderating role of involvement. *The Journal of Consumer Research*, *10*(2), 135–146. doi:10.1086/208954

Phillips, A. (2007). *Good writing for Journalists*. SAGE Publications, Inc.

Picot-Coupey, K., Ekaterina, V., & Cliquet, G. (2016, October). Coproduction de services enmagasin: impact des objets connectés sur la productivité du consommateur. *18ème colloque E. Thil.*

Picot-Coupey, K. (2013). Les voies d'avenir du magasin physique à l'heure du commerce connecté. *Gestion*, *38*(2), 51–61. doi:10.3917/riges.382.0051

Pierre, J. (2011). Génétique de l'identité numérique. *Les Cahiers du numérique*, *7*(1), 15-29.

Pihlaja, J., Saarijärvi, H., Spence, M. T., & Yrjölä, M. (2017). From Electronic WOM to Social eWOM: Bridging the Trust Deficit. *Journal of Marketing Theory and Practice*, *25*(4), 340–356. doi:10.1080/10696679.2017.1345593

Pinch, T., & Kesler, F. (2011). How aunt Amy gets her free lunch: A study of the top-thousand customer reviewers at Amazon.com. In B. Czarniawska & O. Lofgren (Eds.), *Managing Overflow in Affluent Societies*. Routledge.

Pine, B. J., & Gilmore, J. H. (1998). Welcome to the experience economy. *Harvard Business Review*, *76*(4), 97–105. PMID:10181589

Piñeiro-Otero, T., & Martínez-Rolán, X. (2016). Understading Digital Merketing – Basics and Actions. In MBA: Theory and Application of Business and Management Principles. Springer.

Pintér, R. (2008). *Information Society: From Theory to Political Practice*. Gondolat- ÚjMandátum.

Piotrowicz, W., & Cuthbertson, R. (2014). Retail: Toward Omnichannel Retailing. *International Journal of Electronic Commerce*, *18*(4), 5–15. doi:10.2753/JEC1086-4415180400

Pisani, F., & Piotet, D. (2009). La alquimia de las multitudes: cómo la web estácambiando el mundo (No. Sirsi). Barcelona: Paidós.

Plażyk, K. (2015). The democratization of luxury–a new form of luxury. Studia University of Economics in Katowice, 158–165.

Podara, A., Matsiola, M., Nicolaou, C., Maniou, T. A., & Kalliris, G. (2020). Transformation of television viewing practices in Greece: Generation Z and audio-visual content. *Journal of Digital Media & Policy*. doi:10.1386/jdmp_00034_1

Podara, A., Giomelakis, D., Nicolaou, C., Matsiola, M., & Kotsakis, R. (2021). Digital Storytelling in Cultural Heritage: Audience Engagement in the Interactive Documentary New Life. *Sustainability*, *13*(3), 1193. doi:10.3390u13031193

Podara, A., Matsiola, M., Nicolaou, C., Maniou, T. A., & Kalliris, G. (2019). Audiovisual consumption practices in post-crisis Greece: An empirical research approach to Generation Z. *Proceedings of the International Conference on Filmic and Media Narratives of the Crisis: Contemporary Representations.*

Poirel, C., & Bonet Fernandez, D. (2008). La stratégie de distribution multiple à la recherche de synergies entre canal physique et canal virtuel. *Revue Française de Gestion*, *34*(182), 155–170. doi:10.3166/rfg.182.155-170

Pollák, F., & Markovic, P. (2021). Economic Activity as a Determinant for Customer Adoption of Social Media Marketing. *Sustainability*, *2021*(13), 3999. doi:10.3390u13073999

Poncin I, (2008), Le comportement multicanal du consommateur est-il une simple évolution ou constitue-t-il une véritable révolution ? *Reflets et perspectives de la vie économique, 47*, 43-51.

Poncin, I., Garnier, M., Mimoun, M. S. B., & Leclercq, T. (2017). Smart technologies and shopping experience: Are gamification interfaces effective? The case of the Smart store. *Technological Forecasting and Social Change*, *124*, 320–331. doi:10.1016/j.techfore.2017.01.025

Poncin, I., & Mimoun, M. S. B. (2014). The impact of "e-atmospherics" on physical stores. *Journal of Retailing and Consumer Services*, *21*(5), 851–859. doi:10.1016/j.jretconser.2014.02.013

Pontefract, D. (2017). *Stop Confusing CSR With Purpose.* https://www.forbes.com/sites/danpontefract/2017/11/18/stop-confusing-csr-with-purpose/#377b8ed31904

Ponzi, L. J., Fombrun, C. J., & Gardberg, N. A. (2011). RepTrak™ pulse: Conceptualizing and validating a short-form measure of corporate reputation. *Corporate Reputation Review*, *14*(1), 15–35. doi:10.1057/crr.2011.5

Porter, L., & Golan, G. J. (2006). From subservient chickens to brawny men: A comparison of viral advertising to television advertising. *Journal of Interactive Advertising*, *69*(2), 30–38.

Porter, M. E., & Heppelmann, J. E. (2017, Nov.). *Why every organisation needs an augmented reality strategy. Havard Business Review.*

Poujol, F., & Siadou-Martin, B. (2010, October). De l'OC des vendeurs à la fidélité à l'entreprise: Le rôle modérateur de la propension relationnelle du client. In *Colloque Etienne Thil, La Rochelle* (pp. 7-8). Academic Press.

Powers, T., Advincula, D., Austin, M. S., Graiko, S., & Snyder, J. (2012). Digital and social media in the purchase decision process: A special report from the Advertising Research Foundation. *Journal of Advertising Research*, *52*(4), 479–489. doi:10.2501/JAR-52-4-479-489

Prahalad, C. K., & Ramaswamy, V. (2004). Co-creation experiences: The next practice in value creation. *Journal of Interactive Marketing*, *18*(3), 5–14. doi:10.1002/dir.20015

Prandini, M., & Ramilli, M. (2012). Raising Risk Awareness on the Adoption of Web 2.0 Technologies in Decision Making Processes. *Future Internet*, *4*(3), 700–718. doi:10.3390/fi4030700

Praveen, S. (2017). *Customer responses to failure of co-created products and services.* Academic Press.

Preece, J., Sharp, H., & Rogers, Y. (2015). Interaction design beyond human computer. Academic Press.

Priporas, C. V. (2020). Smart Consumers and Decision-making Process in the Smart Retailing Context through Generation Z Eyes. In *Retail Futures*. Emerald Publishing Limited. doi:10.1108/978-1-83867-663-620201017

Purani, K., Kumar, D. S., & Sahadev, S. (2019). e-Loyalty among millennials: Personal characteristics and social influences. *Journal of Retailing and Consumer Services*, *48*, 215–223. doi:10.1016/j.jretconser.2019.02.006

Pytkovska, J., & Korynski, P. (2017). *Digitalizing Microfinance in Europe*. Microfinance Centre. https://www.european-microfinance.org/sites/default/files/document/file/Digitalization-research-paper.pdf

Qazi, S. A. (2009). *Principles of Physical Geography*. APH Publishing Corporation.

Qiang, Y., Shuang, W., Lingli, W., Pengfei, W., Hejie, C., & Guohong, W. (2016). E-WOM from e-commerce websites and social media: Which will consumers adopt? *Electronic Commerce Research and Applications*, *17*(C), 62–73. doi:10.1016/j.elerap.2016.03.004

Quinn-Allan, D. (2010). Public relations, education, and social media: Issues for professionalism in the digital age. *Asia Pacific Public Relations Journal*, *11*(1), 41–55.

Raassens, N., & Haans, H. (2017). NPS and Online WOM: Investigating the Relationship Between Customers' Promoter Scores and eWOM Behavior. *Journal of Service Research*, *20*(3), 322–334. doi:10.1177/1094670517696965 PMID:29046609

Rachinger, M., Rauter, R., Müller, C., Vorraber, W., & Schirgi, E. (2018). Digitalization and its influence on business model innovation. *Journal of Manufacturing Technology Management*, *30*(8), 1143–1160. doi:10.1108/JMTM-01-2018-0020

Radón, A. (2012). Luxury brand exclusivity strategies-An illustration of a cultural collaboration. *Journal of Business Administration Research*, *1*(1), 106. doi:10.5430/jbar.v1n1p106

Raghubansie, A. D., & El-Gohary, H. O. A. S. (2021). Digital Advertising Creative Processes and Innovation in UK SME Advertising Agencies: An Empirical Investigation of Viral Advertising. *Scientific Journal for Financial and Commercial Studies and Research*, 2(1), 75-116.

Raghubansie, A. D., El-Gohary, H., & Lewis, C. (2014). Revising Extant Frameworks of Viral Marketing: Implications from Empirical Investigations of Digital Advertising Creative Managers' Practice in the UK. *ISBE 2014 Conference, The Future of Enterprise: The Innovation Revolution.*

Raghubansie, A., & El-Gohary, H. (2021). Digital Advertising Creative Processes and Innovation in UK SME Advertising Agencies: An Empirical Investigation of Viral Advertising. *Scientific Journal for Financial and Commercial Studies and Research, Faculty of Commerce*, 2(1), 75-116.

Raghubansie, A. D. (2014). Chasing ghosts: problems of participant recruitment from among innovators/practitioners in the UK advertising industry. *International Multidisciplinary Academic Conference*.

Raghubansie, A., El-Gohary, H., & Samaradivakara, C. (2013). An Evaluation of the Viral Marketing Research. *International Journal of Online Marketing*, *3*(4), 1–27. doi:10.4018/ijom.2013100101

Rajamannar, R. (2021). *What can marketers learn from 2020 to lead digital transformation in the new year?* https://www.mastercard.com/news/perspectives/2020/what-can-marketers-learn-from-2020-to-lead-digital-transformation-in-the-new-year

Raju, S., & Unnava, H. R. (2002). *The effects of brand commitment on the evaluation of competitive brands*. ACR North American Advances.

Ramadan, Z. (2019). The Democratization Of Intangible Luxury. *Marketing Intelligence & Planning*, *37*(6), 660–673. doi:10.1108/MIP-11-2018-0490

Ramaswamy, V. (2010). Competing through co-creation: Innovation at two companies. *Strategy and Leadership*, *38*(2), 22–29. doi:10.1108/10878571011029028

Ramli, N. A., Latan, H., & Nartea, G. V. (2018). Why should PLS-SEM be used rather than regression? Evidence from the capital structure perspective. In *Partial least squares structural equation modelling* (pp. 171–209). Springer. doi:10.1007/978-3-319-71691-6_6

Rathnayaka, U. (2018). Role of Digital Marketing in Retail Fashion Industry: A Synthesis of the Theory and the Practice. *Journal of Accounting & Marketing*, *7*(2), 1–7. doi:10.4172/2168-9601.1000279

Rauschnabel, P. A., Brem, A., & Ivens, B. S. (2015). Who will buy smart glasses? Empirical results of two pre-market entry studies on the role of personality in individual awareness and intended adoption of google glass wearables. *Computers in Human Behavior*, *49*, 635–647. doi:10.1016/j.chb.2015.03.003

Raven, V. P., Huang, X., & Kim, B. B. (2007). E-business in developing countries: A comparison of China and India. *International Journal of E-Business Research*, *3*(1), 91–108. doi:10.4018/jebr.2007010106

Rees-Rogers, P. (2019). *Greenwashing, purpose-washing, woke-washing and your brand.* https://www.linkedin.com/pulse/greenwashing-purpose-washing-woke-washing-your-brand-pia-rees-rogers

Reinartz, W., Wiegand, N., & Imschloss, M. (2019). The impact of digital transformation on the retailing value chain. *International Journal of Research in Marketing*, *36*(3), 350–366. doi:10.1016/j.ijresmar.2018.12.002

Renko, S., & Druzijanic, M. (2014). Perceived usefulness of innovative technology in retailing: Consumers′ and retailers′ point of view. *Journal of Retailing and Consumer Services*, *21*(5), 836–843. doi:10.1016/j.jretconser.2014.02.015

Rese, A., Baier, D., Geyer-Schulz, A., & Schreiber, S. (2017). How augmented reality apps are accepted by consumers: A comparative analysis using scales and opinions. *Technological Forecasting and Social Change*, *124*, 306–319. doi:10.1016/j.techfore.2016.10.010

Rese, A., Ganster, L., & Baier, D. (2020). Chatbots in retailers' customer communication: How to measure their acceptance? *Journal of Retailing and Consumer Services*, *56*, 102176. doi:10.1016/j.jretconser.2020.102176

Reyes-Menendez, A., Saura, J. R., & Martinez-Navalon, J. G. (2019). The Impact of e-WOM on Hotels Management Reputation: Exploring TripAdvisor Review Credibility With the ELM Model. *IEEE Access: Practical Innovations, Open Solutions*, *7*, 68868–68877. doi:10.1109/ACCESS.2019.2919030

Ries, A., & Trout, J. (1972). The positioning era cometh. *Advertising Age, 24*, 35-38. http://www.ries.com/wp-content/uploads/2015/09/Positioning-Articles002.pdf

Ries, A., & Trout, J. (2001). *Positioning*. McGraw-Hill.

Rigby, D. (2011). The future of shopping. *Harvard Business Review*, *89*(12), 65–76.

Rigby, D. (2011). The Future of Shopping. *Harvard Business Review*, *89*, 65–76.

Rindova, V. P., & Martins, L. L. (2012). Show me the money: A multidimensional perspective on reputation as an intangible asset. The Oxford handbook of corporate reputation, 16-33.

Ringberg, T., Reihlen, M., & Rydén, P. (2019). The technology-mindset interactions: Leading to incremental, radical or revolutionary innovations. *Industrial Marketing Management*, *79*, 102–113. doi:10.1016/j.indmarman.2018.06.009

Ritz, W., Wolf, M., & Mcquitty, S. (2019). Digital marketing adoption and success for small businesses: The application of the do-it-yourself and technology acceptance models. *Journal of Research in Interactive Marketing*, *13*(2), 179–203. doi:10.1108/JRIM-04-2018-0062

Rivza, B., Kruzmetra, M., Gudele, I., & Foris, D. (2019). Digitalization as an essential growth factor contributing in SME development (experience of Latvia and Romania). *Agronomy Research (Tartu)*, *17*(1), 261–270. doi:10.15159/AR.19.030

Roberts, K. (2005). *Lovemarks: The future beyond brands*. New York: Powerhouse Books.

Roberts, K. (2006). *The lovemarks effect: Winning in the consumer revolution*. Powerhouse Books.

Robinson, M. L. (2014). Building Brand Loyalty: Improving the Retail Fueling Experience. In Marketing Big Oil: Brand Lessons from the World's Largest Companies (pp. 130-135). Palgrave Macmillan.

Robinson, V. M., & Schänzel, H. A. (2019). A tourism inflex: Generation Z travel experiences. *Journal of Tourism Futures*, *5*(2), 127–141. doi:10.1108/JTF-01-2019-0014

Rodriguez-Torrico, P., Cabezudo, R. S. J., & San-Martin, S. (2017). Tell me what they are like and I will tell you where they buy. An analysis of omnichannel consumer behavior. *Computers in Human Behavior*, *68*, 465–471. doi:10.1016/j.chb.2016.11.064

Rogers, C. (2018). *Patagonia on why brands 'can't reverse into purpose' through marketing*. Marketing Week.

Roggeveen, A. L., & Sethuraman, R. (2020). How the COVID-19 Pandemic May Change the World of Retailing. In Journal of Retailing (Vol. 96, Issue 2, pp. 169–171). Elsevier Ltd. doi:10.1016/j.jretai.2020.04.002

Rohm, A., Kaltcheva, V. D., & Milne, G. R. (2013). A mixed-method approach to examining brand-consumer interactions driven by social media. *Journal of Research in Interactive Marketing*, *7*(4), 295–311. doi:10.1108/JRIM-01-2013-0009

Rolland, S., & Freeman, I. (2010). A new measure of e-service quality in France. *International Journal of Retail & Distribution Management*, *38*(7), 497–517. doi:10.1108/09590551011052106

Romeo, E. J., & Cruthirds, K. W. (2006). The Use of Humour in the Workplace. *The Academy of Management Perspectives*, *20*(2), 58–69. doi:10.5465/amp.2006.20591005

Roper, J. (2005). Symmetrical Communication: Excellent Public Relations or a Strategy for Hegemony? *Journal of Public Relations Research*, *17*(1), 69–86. doi:10.12071532754xjprr1701_6

Roscoe, J. T. (1975). *Fundamental research statistics for the behavioral sciences*. Academic Press.

Rose, S., Clark, M., Samouel, P., & Hair, N. (2012). Online customer experience in e-retailing: An empirical model of antecedents and outcomes. *Journal of Retailing*, *88*(2), 308–322. doi:10.1016/j.jretai.2012.03.001

Rossi, F., & Chintagunta, P. K. (2016). Price transparency and retail prices: Evidence from fuel price signs in the Italian highway system. *JMR, Journal of Marketing Research*, *53*(3), 407–423. doi:10.1509/jmr.14.0411

Rossmann, A., Kumar, R., & Praveen, S. (2016). Drivers of user engagement in eWoM communication. *Journal of Services Marketing*, *30*(5), 541–553. doi:10.1108/JSM-01-2015-0013

Rowland, Charier, Lui, Goodman, & Light. (2015). *Designing Connected Products: UX for the consumer Internet of Things*. O'Reilly.

Rowley, J. (2006). An analysis of the service literature: Towards a research agenda. *Internet Research*, *16*(3), 339–359. doi:10.1108/10662240610673736

Royle, J., & Laing, A. (2014). The digital marketing skills gap: Developing a Digital Marketer Model for the communication industries. *International Journal of Information Management*, *34*(2), 65–73. doi:10.1016/j.ijinfomgt.2013.11.008

Roy, P. A., Ponnam, A., & Mandal, S. (2017). Comprehending technology attachment in the case of smart phone-application: An empirical study. *Journal of Electronic Commerce in Organizations*, *15*(1), 23–43. doi:10.4018/JECO.2017010102

Roy, S. K., Balaji, M. S., Sadeque, S., Nguyen, B., & Melewar, T. C. (2017). Constituents and consequences of smart customer experience in retailing. *Technological Forecasting and Social Change*, *124*, 257–270. doi:10.1016/j.techfore.2016.09.022

Rozzani, N., Rahman, R. A., Mohamed, S. I., & Yusuf, S. N. S. (2013). Applying technology: Issues in microfinance operations. *Middle East Journal of Scientific Research*, *17*(3), 374–381.

Rutz, O. J., Bucklin, R. E., & Sonnier, G. P. (2012). A latent instrumental variables approach to modeling keyword conversion in paid search advertising. *JMR, Journal of Marketing Research*, *49*(3), 306–319. doi:10.1509/jmr.10.0354

Safko, L., & Brake, D. K. (2009). *The social media bible: tactics, tools and strategies for business success*. John Wiley & Sons.

Šafranić, P., Petljak, K., & Naletina, D. (2017, January). The growing importance of petrol stations as channels for expanding the retail services. Trade Perspectives 2017 Specialization and Customer Centered Retailing.

Samels, P. (2017). *Advice on Reliability Analysis with Small Samples - Revised Version. Technical Report*. ResearchGate.

San José-Cabezudo, R., & Camarero-Izquierdo, C. (2012). Determinants of opening-forwarding email messages. *Journal of Advertising*, *41*(2), 97–112. doi:10.2753/JOA0091-3367410207

Sancar, G. A. (2013). Political Public Relations 2.0 and the Use of Twitter of Political Leaders in Turkey. *Online Journal of Communication and Media Technologies*, *3*(1), 181–194. doi:10.29333/ojcmt/2417

Sands, S., Ferraro, C., Campbell, C., & Pallant, J. (2016). Segmenting multichannel consumers across search, purchase and after-sales. *Journal of Retailing and Consumer Services*, *33*, 62–71. doi:10.1016/j.jretconser.2016.08.001

San-Martín, S., Prodanova, J., & Jiménez, N. (2015). The impact of age in the generation of satisfaction and WOM in mobile shopping. *Journal of Retailing and Consumer Services*, *23*, 1–8. doi:10.1016/j.jretconser.2014.11.001

Saridou, T., Panagiotidis, K., Tsipas, N., & Veglis, A. (2019). Towards a semantic-oriented model of participatory journalism management: Perceptions of user-generated content. *Journal of Education, Innovation, and Communication*, *1*(1).

Sarridis, I., & Nicolaou, C. (2015, December). *Social Media: (Correct) Professional Use* [Μέσα Κοινωνικής Δικτύωσης: Η (σωστή) Επαγγελματική Χρήση τους of Greek language] [Paper presentation]. The 2nd Student Conference of the Department of Applied Informatics—University of Macedonia on Modern Entrepreneurship & Informatics Technologies, Thessaloniki, Greece.

Schiffman, L. G., & Kanuk, L. L. (1997). *Consumer Behaviour*. Prentice Hall.

Schivinski, B., & Dabrowski, D. (2016). The effect of social media communication on consumer perceptions of brands. *Journal of Marketing Communications*, *22*(2), 189–214. doi:10.1080/13527266.2013.871323

Schoenbachler, D. D., & Gordon, G. L. (2002). Multi-channel shopping: Understanding what drives channel choice. *Journal of Consumer Marketing*, *19*(1), 42–53. doi:10.1108/07363760210414943

Scholz, J., & Duffy, K. (2018). We ARe at home: How augmented reality reshapes mobile marketing and consumer-brand relationships. *Journal of Retailing and Consumer Services*, *44*, 11–23. doi:10.1016/j.jretconser.2018.05.004

Scholz, J., & Smith, A. N. (2016). Augmented reality: Designing immersive expenences that maximize consumer engagement. *Business Horizons, 59*(2), 149161. doi:10.1016/j.bushor.2015.10.003

Schröder, H., & Zaharia, S. (2008). Linking multi-channel customer behavior with shopping motives: An empirical investigation of a German retailer. *Journal of Retailing and Consumer Services, 15*(6), 452–478. doi:10.1016/j.jretconser.2008.01.001

Schwab, K. (2017). *The Fourth Industrial revolution.* Penguin Random House.

Schweer, D., & Sahl, J. C. (2017). *The digital transformation of industry–the benefit for Germany. In The drivers of digital transformation.* Springer.

Schweizer, R. (2012). The internationalization process of SMEs: A muddling-through process. *Journal of Business Research, 65*(6), 745–751. doi:10.1016/j.jbusres.2010.12.011

Scott, P. R., & Jacka, J. M. (2011). *Auditing Social Media: A Govermance and Risk Guide.* IIARF.

Scwarz, U., Hoffmann, S., & Hutter, K. (2015). Do men and women laugh about different types of humour? A comparison of satire, sentimental comedy, and comic wit in print ads. *Journal of Current Issues and Research in Advertising, 36*(1), 70–87. doi:10.1080/10641734.2014.912599

Sek, Y. W. (2016). *An Empirical Study of Learners' Acceptance of Open Learner Models in Malaysian Higher Education (Doctor of Philosophy).* RMIT University.

Sen, A. (1999). *Commodities and capabilities.* Oxford University Press.

Seyyedamiri, N., & Tajrobehkar, L. (2019). Social content marketing, social media and product development process effectiveness in high-tech companies. *International Journal of Emerging Markets.*

Shah, D., & Murthi, B. (2021). Marketing in a data-driven digital world: Implications for the role and scope of marketing. *Journal of Business Research, 125*, 772–779. doi:10.1016/j.jbusres.2020.06.062

Shamdasani, P., Mukherjee, A., & Malhotra, N. (2008). Antecedents and consequences of service quality in consumer evaluation of self-service internet technologies. *Service Industries Journal, 28*(1), 117–138. doi:10.1080/02642060701725669

Shane. (2008). Hand Book of Technology and Innovation Management England. John Wiley & Sons Limited.

Shankar, V., Inman, J. J., Mantrala, M., Kelley, E., & Rizley, R. (2011). Innovations in shopper marketing: Current insights and future research issues. *Journal of Retailing, 87*, S29–S42. doi:10.1016/j.jretai.2011.04.007

Shankar, V., Smith, A. K., & Rangaswamy, A. (2003). Customer satisfaction and loyalty in online and offline environments. *International Journal of Research in Marketing, 20*(2), 153–175. doi:10.1016/S0167-8116(03)00016-8

Sharma, A., Sharma, S., & Chaudhary, M. (2020). Are small travel agencies ready for digital marketing? Views of travel agency managers. *Tourism Management, 79*, 104078. doi:10.1016/j.tourman.2020.104078

Sharma, G., & Baoku, L. (2013). Customer satisfaction in Web 2.0 and information technology development. *Information Technology & People, 26*(4), 347–367. doi:10.1108/ITP-12-2012-0157

Sharma, S., & Gutierrez, J. A. (2010). An evaluation framework for viable business models for m-commerce in the information technology sector. *Electronic Markets, 20*(1), 33–52. doi:10.100712525-010-0028-9

Sharp, B., & Dawes, J. (2001). What is differentiation and how does it work? *Journal of Marketing Management, 17*(7-8), 739–759. doi:10.1362/026725701323366809

Sheel, T. (2017). Definitions, Theories, and Measurement of Humour. In *Humour at Work in Teams, Leadership, Negotiations, Learning and Health* (pp. 9–29). Springer. doi:10.1007/978-3-319-65691-5_2

Sherry, J. F. Jr. (1990). A Sociocultural Analysis of a Midwestern Flea Market. *The Journal of Consumer Research, 17*(June), 13–30. doi:10.1086/208533

Shin, D., Jung, J., & Chang, B. (2012). The psychology behind QR codes: User experience perspective. *Computers in Human Behavior, 28*(4), 1417–1426. doi:10.1016/j.chb.2012.03.004

Shuv-Ami, A. (2012). Brand commitment: A new four-dimensional (4 Es) conceptualization and scale. *Journal of Customer Behaviour, 11*(3), 281–305. doi:10.1362/147539212X13469450373155

Siano, A., Vollero, A., Confetto, M. G., & Siglioccolo, M. (2013). Corporate communication management: A framework based on decision-making with reference to communication resources. *Journal of Marketing Communications, 19*(3), 151–167. doi:10.1080/13527266.2011.581301

Siano, A., Vollero, A., & Palazzo, M. (2011). Exploring the role of online consumer empowerment in reputation building: Research questions and hypotheses. *Journal of Brand Management, 19*(1), 57–71. doi:10.1057/bm.2011.23

Sijoria, C., Mukherjee, S., & Datta, B. (2018). Impact of the antecedents of eWOM on CBBE. *Marketing Intelligence & Planning, 36*(5), 528–542. doi:10.1108/MIP-10-2017-0221

Silva, J. N. A., Southworth, M., Raptis, C., & Silva, J. (2018). Emerging applications of virtual reality in cardiovascular medicine, JACC. *Basic to Transitional Science, 3*(3), 420–430. doi:10.1016/j.jacbts.2017.11.009 PMID:30062228

Silva, S. C., Duarte, P., & Sundetova, A. (2020). Multichannel versus omnichannel: A price-segmented comparison from the fashion industry. *International Journal of Retail & Distribution Management, 48*(4), 417–430. doi:10.1108/IJRDM-07-2019-0232

Silverstein, M.J., Fiske, N., & Butman, J. (2003). *Trading up: The new American luxury*. Academic Press.

Silverstein, M. J., Fiske, N., & Butman, J. (2008). *Trading Up: why consumers want new luxury goods and how companies create them*. Portfolio.

Silvestri, L., Forcina, A., Introna, V., Santolamazza, A., & Cesarotti, V. (2020). Maintenance transformation through Industry 4.0 technologies: A systematic literature review. *Computers in Industry, 123*, 103335. doi:10.1016/j.compind.2020.103335

Simmons, G. (2008). Marketing to postmodern consumers: Introducing the internet chameleon. *European Journal of Marketing, 42*(3/4), 299–310. doi:10.1108/03090560810852940

Sinek, S. (2009). *Start with why: How great leaders inspire everyone to take action* (1st ed.). Penguin Group.

Sinek, S. (2011). *Start with why: how great leaders inspire everyone to take action* (Reprinted ed.). Penguin Group.

Sirgy, M. J., Grewal, D., Mangleburg, T. F., Park, J.-O., Chon, K.-S., Clairborne, C. B., Johar, J. S., & Berkman, H. (1997). Assessing the predictive validity of two methods of measuring self-image congruence. *Journal of the Academy of Marketing Science, 25*(3), 229–241. doi:10.1177/0092070397253004

Sirieix, L., & Dubois, P. L. (1999). Vers un modèle qualité-satisfaction intégrant la confiance? *Recherche et Applications en Marketing, 14*(3), 1–22. doi:10.1177/076737019901400301

Sjödin, H., & Törn, F. (2006). When communication challenges brand associations: A framework for understanding consumer responses to brand image incongruity. *Journal of Consumer Behaviour: An International Research Review, 5*(1), 32–42. doi:10.1002/cb.44

Slivar, I., Aleric, D., & Dolenec, S. (2019). Leisure travel behavior of generation Y & Z at the destination and post-purchase. *E-Journal of Tourism, 6*(2), 147–159. doi:10.24922/eot.v6i2.53470

Slot, M., & Frissen, V. (2007). Users in the 'Golden' age of the information society. *Observatório Journal, 1*(3), 201–224. doi:10.15847/obsOBS132007153

Smaoui, F. (2008, January). Les déterminants de l'attachement émotionnel à la marque: effet des variables relationnelles et des variables relatives au produit. In *Proceedings of the 2008 Marketing Trends Congress* (pp. 17-19). Academic Press.

Smith, A. (2020, April 10). *Evolution and growth of eCommerce in india.* Official Blog of Hidden Brains Infotech PVT LTD. https://www.hiddenbrains.com/blog/evolution-and-growth-of-ecommerce-in-india.html#:%7E:text=India%2C%20emerging%20economic%20superpower%20and,for%20the%20growth%20of%20eCommerce.&text=The%20rising%20literacy%20rate%20and,the%20growth%20of%20e%2DCommerce

Smith, A. (2013). *Smartphone ownership-2013 update* (Vol. 12). Pew Research Center.

Smith, A. D. (2008). Modernizing retail grocery business via knowledge management-based systems. *Journal of Knowledge Management, 12*(3), 114–126. doi:10.1108/13673270810875903

Smith, A. D. (2010). Retail-based loyalty card programs & CRM concepts: An empirical study. *International Journal of Innovation and Learning, 7*(3), 303–330. doi:10.1504/IJIL.2010.031949

Smith, K. T. (2011). Digital marketing strategies that Millennials find appealing, motivating, or just annoying. *Journal of Strategic Marketing, 19*(6), 489–499. doi:10.1080/0965254X.2011.581383

Smith, K. T. (2012). Longitudinal study of digital marketing strategies targeting millennials. *Journal of Consumer Marketing, 29*(2), 86–92. doi:10.1108/07363761211206339

Solima, L., Della Peruta, M. R., Maggioni, V., Al-Mashari, M., & Del Giudice, M. (2016). Managing adaptive orientation systems for museum visitors from an IoT perspective. *Business Process Management Journal, 22*(2), 10. doi:10.1108/BPMJ-08-2015-0115

Sommer, L. (2015). Industrial revolution - industry 4.0. Are German manufacturing SMEs the first victims of this revolution? Journal of Industrial Engineering and Management, 8(5).

Soon-hwa, C. (2009). Global Luxury Brands' Strategies to Fight Recession. *SERI Quarterly, 2*(4), 108–111.

Souiden, N., Chtourou, S., & Korai, B. (2017). Consumer attitudes toward online advertising: The moderating role of personality. *Journal of Promotion Management, 23*(2), 207–227. doi:10.1080/10496491.2016.1267676

Southgate, D., Westoby, N., & Page, G. (2010). Creative determinants of viral video viewing. *International Journal of Advertising, 29*(3), 349–368. doi:10.2501/S0265048710201221

Spary, S. (2015). *Unilever says 'brands with purpose' are growing at twice the speed of others in portfolio.* https://www.campaignlive.co.uk/article/unilever-says-brands-purpose-growing-twice-speed-others-portfolio/1345772

Special, W. P., & Li-Barber, K. T. (2012). Self-disclosure and student satisfaction with Facebook. *Computers in Human Behavior, 28*(2), 624–630. doi:10.1016/j.chb.2011.11.008

Speck, P. S. (1991). The humorous message taxonomy: A framework for the study of humorous ads. *Current Issues and Research in Advertising, 13*(1-2), 1-44.

Spence, R. (2009). *It's Not What You Sell, It's What You Stand for: Why Every Extraordinary Business Is Driven by Purpose.* Penguin Group.

Spielmann, N. (2014). How funny was that? Uncovering humour mechanisms. *European Journal of Marketing*, *48*(9/10), 1892–1910. doi:10.1108/EJM-07-2012-0393

Sproull, L. S., & Goodman, P. S. (1990). Technology and Organizations: Integration and Opportunities. In P. Goodman & L. Sproull (Eds.), *Technology and Organizations* (pp. 254–265). Jossey-Bass Inc.

Spyridou, L.-P., Matsiola, M., Veglis, A., Kalliris, G., & Dimoulas, C. (2013). Journalism in a state of flux: Journalists as agents of technology innovation and emerging news practices. *The International Communication Gazette*, *75*(1), 76–98. doi:10.1177/1748048512461763

Srinivasan, S. S., Anderson, R., & Ponnavolu, K. (2002). Customer loyalty in e-commerce: An exploration of its antecedents and consequences. *Journal of Retailing*, *78*(1), 41–50. doi:10.1016/S0022-4359(01)00065-3

Sriramesh, K., & Hornaman, L. B. (2006). Public Relations as a Profession: An Analysis of Curricular Content in the United States. *Journal of Creative Communications*, *1*(2), 155–172. doi:10.1177/097325860600100202

Sriram, G., & Kathiravan, C. (2014). Effect Of Social Media And Factors Influencing A Brand's Reputation. *International Journal of Innovative Research and Studies*, *3*(8), 366–378.

Stallkamp, M., & Schotter, A. P. J. (2019). Platforms without borders? The international strategies of digital platform firms. *Global Strategy Journal*, 1–23. doi:10.1002/gsj.1336

Standing, C., Tang-Taye, J.-P., & Boyer, M. (2014). The impact of the Internet in travel and tourism: A research review 2001–2010. *Journal of Travel & Tourism Marketing*, *31*(1), 82–113. doi:10.1080/10548408.2014.861724

Stark, J. (2020). Digital Transformation of a Retail Store. *Digital Transformation of Industry Decision Engineering*, 73–77.

Stathooulou, A., Borel, L., Christodoulides, G., & West, D. (2017). Consumer branded# hashtag engagement: Can creativity in TV advertising influence hashtag engagement? *Psychology and Marketing*, *34*(4), 448–462. doi:10.1002/mar.20999

Steinbrück, U., Schaumburg, H., Duda, S., & Krüger, T. (2002). A picture says more than a thousand words–Photographs as trust builders in e-commerce websites. In *Proceedings of conference on human factors in computing systems CHI 2002, extended abstracts* (pp. 748–749). 10.1145/506443.506578

Steinfield, C., Ellison, N. B., & Lampe, C. (2008). Social capital, self-esteem, and use of online social network sites: A longitudinal analysis. *Journal of Applied Developmental Psychology*, *29*(6), 434–445. doi:10.1016/j.appdev.2008.07.002

Stengel, J. (2011). *Grow: How ideals power growth and profit at the world's greatest companies*. The Crown Publishing Group.

Stentoft, J., Adsbøll Wickstrøm, K., Philipsen, K., & Haug, A. (2020). Drivers and barriers for Industry 4.0 readiness and practice: Empirical evidence from small and medium-sized manufacturers. *Production Planning and Control*, 1–18. doi:10.1080/09537287.2020.1768318

Sterntal, B., & Craig, C. S. (1973). Humour in Advertising. *Journal of Marketing*, *37*(4), 12–18. doi:10.1177/002224297303700403

Steuer, J. (1992). Defining virtual reality: Dimensions determining telepresence. *Journal of Communication*, *42*(4), 73–93. doi:10.1111/j.1460-2466.1992.tb00812.x

Stokes, D., & Bergin, R. (2006). Methodology or 'methodolatry'? An evaluation of focus groups and depth interviews. *Qualitative Market Research*, *9*(2), 26–36. doi:10.1108/13522750610640530

Stolterman, E., & Fors, A. C. (2004). Information Technology and the Good Life BT Information Systems Research: Relevant Theory and Informed Practice. Springer US.

Stone, M., Hobbs, M., & Khaleeli, M. (2002). Multichannel customer management: The benefits and challenges. *Journal of Database Marketing & Customer Strategy Management, 10*(1), 39–52. doi:10.1057/palgrave.jdm.3240093

Sundaram, D. S., Mitra, K., & Webster, C. (1998). Word of-Mouth Communications: A Motivational Analysis. *Advances in Consumer Research. Association for Consumer Research (U. S.), 25*, 527–531.

Sun, Y., Gonzalez-Jimenez, H., & Wang, S. (2021, June). Hector Gonzalez-Jimenez and Shenghui Wang. (In Press). Examining the relationships between e-WOM, consumer ethnocentrism and brand equity. *Journal of Business Research, 130*, 564–573. Advance online publication. doi:10.1016/j.jbusres.2019.09.040

Sun, Y., Yang, C., Shen, X. L., & Wang, N. (2020). When digitalized customers meet digitalized services: A digitalized social cognitive perspective of omnichannel service usage. *International Journal of Information Management, 54*, 102200. doi:10.1016/j.ijinfomgt.2020.102200

System1 Official Blog. (2018). https://system1group.com/blog/purpose-marketing-meet-the-brand-thats-quacked-it

Tabacnick, B. G., & Fidell, L. S. (2007). *Using Multivariate Statistics*. Pearson Education.

Tafheem, N., El-Gohary, H., & Sobh, R. (2022). Social Media User-Influencer Congruity: An Analysis of Social Media Platforms Parasocial Relationships. *International Journal of Customer Relationship Marketing and Management, 13*(1), 1–29.

Tafonao, T., Saputra, S., & Suryaningwidi, R. (2020). Learning Media and Technology: Generation Z and Alpha. *Indonesian Journal of Instructional Media and Model, 2*(2), 89–100. doi:10.32585/ijimm.v2i2.954

Taiminen, H. M., & Karjaluoto, H. (2015). The usage of digital marketing channels in SMEs. *Journal of Small Business and Enterprise Development, 22*(4), 633–651. doi:10.1108/JSBED-05-2013-0073

Tain, Y., & Stewart, C. (2007). History of e commerce. In A. Becker (Ed.), Electronic Commerce: Concepts, Methodologies, Tools and Applications (pp. 1–8). IGI Global. doi:10.4018/978-1-59904-943-4.ch001

Tajvidi, R., & Karami, A. (2017). The effect of social media on firm performance. *Computers in Human Behavior, 115*, 105174. doi:10.1016/j.chb.2017.09.026

Talwar, S., Talwar, M., Kaur, P., & Dhir, A. (2020). Consumers' resistance to digital innovations: A systematic review and framework development. *Australasian Marketing Journal, 28*(4), 286–299. doi:10.1016/j.ausmj.2020.06.014

Tao, Y. H., Cheng, C. J., & Sun, S. Y. (2009). What influences college students to continue using business simulation games? The Taiwan experience. *Computers & Education, 53*(3), 929–939. doi:10.1016/j.compedu.2009.05.009

Tarjan, L., Senk, I., Kovac, R., & Horvat, S. (2011). Automatic identification based on 2D barcodes. *Journal of Industrial Engineering and Management, 2*, 151–157.

Tarnaud, N. (2019). Le Luxe Dans Le Monde d'Aujourd'hui. *Les Echos*. https://www.lesechos.fr/idees-debats/cercle/le-luxe-dans-le-monde-daujourdhui-130583

Tate, C. (2016). *Purpose-washing. Is it the new green-washing?* https://carolyntate.co/purpose-washing-is-it-the-new-green-washing/

Taylor, M. (2020). *Energy subsidies: Evolution in the global energy transformation to 2050*. International Renewable Energy Agency.

TED Ads worth spreading report. (2012). https://wooshii.com/blog/author/wooshiiricardo/page/60/

Teece, D. (2018). Profiting from innovation in the digital economy: Enabling technologies, standards, and licensing models in the wireless world. *Research Policy*, *47*(8), 10. doi:10.1016/j.respol.2017.01.015

Teece, D. J. (2010). Business models, business strategy and innovation. *Long Range Planning*, *43*(2–3), 172–194. doi:10.1016/j.lrp.2009.07.003

Teece, D., Pisano, G., & Shuen, A. (1997). Dynamic Capabilities and Strategic Management. *Strategic Management Journal*, *18*(7), 509–533. doi:10.1002/(SICI)1097-0266(199708)18:7<509::AID-SMJ882>3.0.CO;2-Z

Terrance, A. R., Shrivastava, S., & Kumari, A. (2017). Importance of Search Engine Marketing is the Digital World. *ICITKM*, *14*, 155–158. doi:10.15439/2018KM24

Thackeray, R., Brad, L., Neiger, B. L., & Keller, H. (2012). Integrating Social Media and Social Marketing: A Four-Step Process. *Health Promotion Practice*, *13*(2), 165–168. doi:10.1177/1524839911432009 PMID:22382492

The Body Shop Official Website-Activism. (2021). https://www.thebodyshop.com/en-gb/about-us/activism/a/a00015

The Body Shop Official Website-Brand Purpose. (2021). https://www.thebodyshop.com/en-gb/about-us/our-story/brand-purpose/a/a00003

The Body Shop Official Website-Company. (2021). https://careers.thebodyshop.com/content/About-Us-The-Body-Shop/?locale=en_GB

The Body Shop Official Website-Forever Against Animal Testing. (2021). https://www.thebodyshop.com/en-gb/about-us/activism/faat/a/a00018

The Body Shop Official Website-Story. (2021). https://www.thebodyshop.com/en-gb/about-us/our-story/a/a00002

The Body Shop. (2018, December 21). *The Body Shop and Cruelty Free International Campaign to end cosmetic product and ingredient animal testing globally once and for all.* Cision Canada. https://www.newswire.ca/news-releases/the-body-shop-and-cruelty-free-international-campaign-to-end-cosmetic-product-and-ingredient-animal-testing-globally-once-and-for-all-625675423.html

The Deloitte Millennial Survey. (2016). https://www2.deloitte.com/us/en/pages/about-deloitte/articles/millennials-shifting-business-purpose.html

Theodoridis, P. K., & Gkikas, D. C. (2019). *How artificial intelligence affects digital marketing. In Strategic Innovative Marketing and Tourism.* Springer.

Thi Song, P., Le Monkhouse, L., & Barnes, B. R. (2017). The influence of relational capability and marketing capabilities on the export performance of emerging market firms. *International Marketing Review*, *34*(5), 606–628. doi:10.1108/IMR-07-2014-0235

Thomas, J., & Harden, A. (2008). Methods for the thematic synthesis of qualitative research in systematic reviews. *BMC Medical Research Methodology*, *8*(1), 45. https://www.biomedcentral.com/1471-2288/8/45/

Thomas, J. S., & Sullivan, U. Y. (2005). Managing Marketing Communications with Multichannel Customers. *Journal of Marketing*, *69*(4), 239–251. doi:10.1509/jmkg.2005.69.4.239

Thomson, M., MacInnis, D. J., & Park, C. W. (2005). The ties that bind: Measuring the strength of consumers' emotional attachments to brands. *Journal of Consumer Psychology*, *15*(1), 77–91. doi:10.120715327663jcp1501_10

Tiago, M. T. P. M. B., & Veríssimo, J. M. C. (2014). Digital marketing and social media: Why bother? *Business Horizons*, *57*(6), 703–708. doi:10.1016/j.bushor.2014.07.002

Tilson, D., Lyytinen, K., & Sørensen, C. (2010). Research commentary-digital infrastructures: The missing IS research agenda. *Information Systems Research*, *21*(4), 748–759. doi:10.1287/isre.1100.0318

Timperio, G., Tan, K. C., Fratocchi, L., & Pace, S. (2016). The impact of ethnicity on luxury perception: The case of Singapore's Generation Y. *Asia Pacific Journal of Marketing and Logistics*, *28*(2), 217–233. doi:10.1108/APJML-04-2015-0060

Tiwari, A. K. (2010). *Infrastructure for Sustainable Rural Development*. Regal Publications.

Tosun, L. P. (2012). Motives for Facebook use and expressing "true self" on the Internet. *Computers in Human Behavior*, *28*(4), 1510–1517. doi:10.1016/j.chb.2012.03.018

Trengove, A., Malczyk, A., & Beneke, J. (2011). *Internet Marketing*. GetSmarter.

Trevinal, A. M., & Stenger, T. (2014). Toward a conceptualization of the online shopping experience. *Journal of Retailing and Consumer Services*, *21*(3), 314–326. doi:10.1016/j.jretconser.2014.02.009

Trifecta Research. (2015). *Generation Z Media Consumption Habit*. Retrieved May 5, 2020, from: http://trifectaresearch.com/wp-content/uploads/2015/09/Generation-Z-Sample-Trifecta-Research-Deliverable.pdf

Truong, Y., McColl, R., & Kitchen, P. (2010). Practitioners' perceptions of advertising strategies for digital media. *International Journal of Advertising*, *29*(5), 709–725. doi:10.2501/S0265048710201439

Tscheu, F., & Buhalis, D. (2016). Augmented Reality at Cultural Heritage sites. In A. Inversini & R. Schegg (Eds.), *Information and Communication Technologies in Tourism 2016 ENTER* (pp. 607–619). Springer. doi:10.1007/978-3-319-28231-2_44

Turnbull, S., & Wheeler, C. (2017). The advertising creative process: A study of UK agencies. *Journal of Marketing Communications*, *23*(2), 176–194. doi:10.1080/13527266.2014.1000361

Tussyadiah, L. P. (2014). Toward a Theoretical Foundation for Experience Design in Tourism. *Journal of Travel Research*, *53*(5), 543–564. doi:10.1177/0047287513513172

Unneland, T., & Hauser, M. K. (2005). Real-time asset management: from vision to engagement-an operator's experience. In *SPE Annual Technical Conference and Exhibition*. Society of Petroleum Engineers. 10.2118/96390-MS

Ur Rahman, R., Ali Shah, S. M., El-Gohary, H., Abbas, M., Haider Khalil, S., Al Altheeb, S., & Sultan, F. (2020). Social Media Adoption and Financial Sustainability: Learned Lessons from Developing Countries. *Sustainability*, *12*(24), 10616. doi:10.3390u122410616

Utesheva, A., Simpson, J. R., & Cecez-Kecmanovic, D. (2016). Identity metamorphoses in digital disruption: A relational theory of identity. *European Journal of Information Systems*, *25*(4), 344–363. doi:10.1057/ejis.2015.19

Utz, S. (2010). Show me your friends and I will tell you what type of person you are: How one's profile, number of friends, and type of friends influence impression formation on social network sites. *Journal of Computer-Mediated Communication*, *15*(2), 314–335. doi:10.1111/j.1083-6101.2010.01522.x

Vahlne, J. E., & Bhatti, W. A. (2019). Relationship Development: A Micro-Foundation for the Internationalization Process of the Multinational Business Enterprise. *Management International Review*, *59*(2), 203–228. doi:10.100711575-018-0373-z

Vaithianathan, S. (2010). A review of e-commerce literature on India and research agenda for the future. *Electronic Commerce Research*, *10*(1), 83–97. doi:10.100710660-010-9046-0

Van de Vrande, V., De Jong, J. P., Vanhaverbeke, W., & De Rochemont, M. (2009). Open innovation in SMEs: Trends, motives and management challenges. *Technovation*, *29*(6), 423–437. doi:10.1016/j.technovation.2008.10.001

Van den Broeke, M., & Paparoidamis, N. (2021). Engaging in or escaping co-creation? An analytical model. *International Journal of Production Economics*, *231*, 107917. doi:10.1016/j.ijpe.2020.107917

Van der Heijden, H. (2004). User acceptance of hedonic information systems. *MIS Quarterly & The Society for Information Management*, *28*(4), 695–704.

Van Doorn, J., Lemon, K. N., Mittal, V., Nass, S., Pick, D., Pirner, P., & Verhoef, P. C. (2010). Customer engagement behavior: Theoretical foundations and research directions. *Journal of Service Research*, *13*(3), 253–266. doi:10.1177/1094670510375599

Van Krevelen, D. W. F., & Poelman, R. (2010). A survey of augmented reality technologies: Applications and limitations. *The International Journal of Virtual Reality: a Multimedia Publication for Professionals*, *9*(2), 1–20. doi:10.20870/IJVR.2010.9.2.2767

Van Laar, E., Van Deursen, A. J., Van Dijk, J. A., & De Haan, J. (2017). The relation between 21st-century skills and digital skills: A systematic literature review. *Computers in Human Behavior*, *72*, 577–588. doi:10.1016/j.chb.2017.03.010

Van Riel, A. C. R., Liljander, V., & Jurrie¨ns, P. (2001). Exploring consumer evaluations of e-services: A portal site. *International Journal of Service Industry Management*, *12*(4), 359–377. doi:10.1108/09564230110405280

Vanheems, R. (2009). Distribution multicanal- pourquoi les clients mixtes doivent faire l'objet d'une attention particulière? *Décisions Marketing*, *55*, 41–52. doi:10.7193/DM.055.41.52

Vargo, S. L., & Lusch, R. F. (2008). Service-dominant logic: Continuing the evolution. *Journal of the Academy of Marketing Science*, *36*(1), 1–10. doi:10.100711747-007-0069-6

Veglis, A. (2018). *Email. In The SAGE Encyclopedia of Surveillance, Security, and Privacy*. SAGE Publication, Inc.

Veglis, A., Abraham, E., & Pomportsis, A. (2004). *Research and Information Collection on the Internet* [Έρευνα και Συλλογή Πληροφοριών στο Διαδίκτυο of Greek language]. Tziolas Publications.

Venkatesan, R., Kumar, V., & Ravishanker, N. (2007). Multichannel shopping: Causes and consequences. *Journal of Marketing*, *71*(2), 114–132. doi:10.1509/jmkg.71.2.114

Verhoef, P. C., Kannan, P. K., & Inman, J. F. (2015). From Multi-Channel Retailing to Omni-Channel Retailing: Introduction to the special Issue on Multi-channel Retailing. Academic Press.

Verhoef, P. C., Kannan, P. K., & Inman, J. J. (2015). From Multi-Channel Retailing to Omni-Channel Retailing. Introduction to the Special Issue on Multi-Channel Retailing. *Journal of Retailing*, *91*(2), 174–181. doi:10.1016/j.jretai.2015.02.005

Verhoef, P. C., Neslin, S. A., & Vroomen, B. (2007). Multichannel customer management: Understanding the research-shopper phenomenon. *International Journal of Research in Marketing*, *24*(2), 129–148. doi:10.1016/j.ijresmar.2006.11.002

Vernuccio, M., & Ceccotti, F. (2015). Strategic and organisational challenges in the integrated marketing communication paradigm shift: A holistic vision. *European Management Journal*, *33*(6), 438–449. doi:10.1016/j.emj.2015.09.001

Vial, G. (2019). Understanding digital transformation: A review and a research agenda. *The Journal of Strategic Information Systems*, *28*(2), 118–144. doi:10.1016/j.jsis.2019.01.003

Viana, M. L. D., & dos Santos, M. C. L. (2020). Design Perspectives From Co-Creation Experiences in Brazilian Complex Social Contexts. In *3rd International Conference on Dwelling Form (IDWELL 2020)* (pp. 170-179). Atlantis Press. 10.2991/assehr.k.201009.018

Vieru, D., Bourdeau, S., & Bernier, A. (2015). Digital Competence. A Multi-dimensional Conceptualization and a Typology in an SME Context. In: *48th Hawaii International Conference on System Sciences (HICSS)* (pp. 4681–4690). IEEE. 10.1109/HICSS.2015.557

Vimali, S., & Khan, K. A. (2018). Impact of Digital Marketing on Consumers Purchase. *Journal of Management, 6*(1), 51–55.

Vivek, S. D., Beatty, S. E., & Morgan, R. M. (2012). Customer engagement: Exploring customer relationships beyond purchase. *Journal of Marketing Theory and Practice, 20*(2), 122–146. doi:10.2753/MTP1069-6679200201

Wadhwa & Harper. (2015). *Technology, Innovation and Enterprise Transformation*. IGI Global.

Wahsheh, H., & Luccio, F. (2020). Security and privacy of QR code applications: A comprehensive study, general guidelines and solutions. *Information (Basel), 11*(4), 1–23. doi:10.3390/info11040217

Wallace, D. W., Giese, J. L., & Johnson, J. L. (2004). Customer Retailer Loyalty in the Context of Multiple Channel Strategies. *Journal of Retailing, 80*(4), 249–263. doi:10.1016/j.jretai.2004.10.002

Walmart Official Website-Values. (2021). https://careers.walmart.com/values

Wang, A. (2006). Advertising engagement: A driver of message involvement on message effects. *Journal of Advertising Research, 46*(4), 355–368. doi:10.2501/S0021849906060429

Wang, T., Thai, T. D., Ly, P. T. M., & Chi, T. P. (2021). Turning social endorsement into brand passion. *Journal of Business Research, 126*, 429–439. doi:10.1016/j.jbusres.2021.01.011

Warby Parker Official Website-Buy A Pair GiveA Pair. (2021). https://www.warbyparker.com/buy-a-pair-give-a-pair

Warby Parker Official Website-History. (2021). https://www.warbyparker.com/history

Warby Parker. (2013, February 13). *Shiagi*. http://shiagi.com/warby-parker/

Warre, C., Barsky, A., Mcgraw, A. P., & MacInnis, D. (2018). Humour, Comedy, and Consumer Behaviour. *The Journal of Consumer Research*.

Watrick, S. (2002). Measuring Corporate Reputation: Defining and Data. Business and Society. *Journal of Marketing, 41*(4), 371–392.

We Are Social. (2020). *Digital 2020*. https://wearesocial.com/digital-2020

Weber, L. (2009). *Marketing To The Social Web: How Digital Customer Communities Build Your Business*. John Wiley & Sons. doi:10.1002/9781118258125

Weick, K. (1979). *The Social Psychology of Organizing* (2nd ed.). Addison-Wesley.

Weinberger, M. G., & Gulas, C. S. (1992). The impact of humour in advertising: A review. *Journal of Advertising, 21*(4), 35–59. doi:10.1080/00913367.1992.10673384

Wei, W., Qi, R., & Zhang, L. (2019). Effects of virtual reality on theme park visitors' experience and behaviors: A presence perspective. *Tourism Management, 71*, 282–293. doi:10.1016/j.tourman.2018.10.024

Wellman, B., & Berkowitz, S. D. (1988). Introduction: Studying Social Structures. In B. Wellman & S. D. Berkowitz (Eds.), *Social Structures: A Network Approach* (pp. 1–14). Cambridge University Press.

Westerman, G., Bonnet, D., & McAfee, A. (2018). *The Nine Elements of Digital Transformation/MITSloan Management Review*. Massachusetts Institute of Technology.

Whillans, A. V., & Chen, F. (2018). Facebook Undermines the Social Belonging of First Year Students. *Personality and Individual Differences, Vol., 133*(October), 13–16. doi:10.1016/j.paid.2017.03.043

White, R. (2015). *How Computers Work: The Evolution of Technology* (10th ed.). Que Publishing.

Wilcox, K., & Stephen, A. T. (2013). Are close friends the enemy? Online social networks, self-esteem, and self-control. *The Journal of Consumer Research, 40*(1), 90–103. doi:10.1086/668794

Willems, K., Smolders, A., Brengman, M., Luyten, K., & Schöning, J. (2017). The path-to-purchase is paved with digital opportunities: An inventory of shopper-oriented retail technologies. *Technological Forecasting and Social Change, 124*, 228–242. doi:10.1016/j.techfore.2016.10.066

Williams, B., Onsman, A., & Brown, T. (2010). Exploratory Factor Analysis: A Five Step Guide for Novices. *Journal of Emergency Primary Health Care, 8*(3), 1–13. doi:10.33151/ajp.8.3.93

Williams, K. C., & Page, R. A. (2011). Marketing to the Generations. *Journal of Behavioral Studies in Business, 3*(1), 1–18.

Wilson, R. (2011). *A public relations disaster how saving $1,200 cost United Airlines 10,772,839 negative views on YouTube.* https://sentium.com/a-public-relations-disaster-how-saving1200-cost-united-airlines-10772839-negative-views-on-youtube/

Wilson, P. F., Stott, J., Warnett, J. M., Attridge, A., Smith, M. P., & Williams, M. A. (2018). Museum visitor preference for the physical properties of 3D printed replicas. *Journal of Cultural Heritage, 32*(July–August), 176–185. doi:10.1016/j.culher.2018.02.002

Wind, Y. J., & Hays, C. F. (2016). *Beyond advertising: Creating value through all customer touchpoints.* John Wiley & Sons.

Wirtz, B. W. (2019). *Digital Business Models.* Springer International Publishing. doi:10.1007/978-3-030-13005-3

Wolfinbarger, M., & Gilly, M. C. (2003). Etailq: Dimensionalizing, measuring and predicting etail quality. *Journal of Retailing, 79*(3), 183–198. doi:10.1016/S0022-4359(03)00034-4

Wood, S. (2013). *Generation Z as consumers: Trends and innovation.* Institute for Emerging Issues: NC State University. Retrieved May 5, 2020, from: https://iei.ncsu.edu/wp-content/uploads/2013/01/GenZConsumers.pdf

Work Programme on Electronic Commerce, World Trade Organization. (n.d.). Retrieved from https://www.wto.org/english/tratop_e/ecom_e/ecom_e.htm

World Economic Forum. (2017). Digital Transformation Initiative Oil and Gas Industry. Author.

Worldpay. (2017). *For each of the following circumstances, how important is it to read online reviews before purchasing a product or selecting a service provider?* http://www-statista-com.du.idm.oclc.org/statistics/713258/onlinereview-importance-circumstances-usa/

Wright, L. T., & Crimp, M. (2000). *The Marketing Research process* (5th ed.). Pearson.

Writer, S. (2016). *2013: Oreo wins the Super Bowl with 'dunk in the dark' tweet.* https://www.thedrum.com/news/2016/07/10/marketing-moment-101-oreo-wins-super-bowl-dunk-dark-tweet

WTTC. (2020). *Economic Impact Reports.* https://wttc.org/Research/Economic-Impact

Xu, Q. (2014). Should I trust him? The effects of reviewer profile characteristics on eWOM credibility. *Computers in Human Behavior, 33*, 136–144. doi:10.1016/j.chb.2014.01.027

Yadav, G. P., & Rai, J. (2017). The Generation Z and their Social Media Usage: A Review and a Research Outline. *Global Journal of Enterprise Information System, 9*(2), 110–116. doi:10.18311/gjeis/2017/15748

Yang, H., & Lin, C. (2014). Why do people stick to Facebook web site? A value theory-based view. *Information Technology & People, 27*(1), 21–37. doi:10.1108/ITP-11-2012-0130

Yang, Z., Jun, M., & Peterson, R. T. (2004). Measuring customer perceived online service quality. *International Journal of Operations & Production Management, 24*(11), 1149–1174. doi:10.1108/01443570410563278

Yang, Z., Peterson, R. T., & Cai, S. (2003). Services quality dimensions of Internet retailing: An exploratory analysis. *Journal of Services Marketing, 17*(7), 685–701. doi:10.1108/08876040310501241

Yannopoylos, P. (2011). Impact of the Internet on Marketing Strategy Formulation. *International Journal of Business and Social Science, 2*(18).

Yan, Q., Wu, S., Zhou, Y., & Zhang, L. (2018). How differences in eWOM platforms impact consumers' perceptions and decision-making. *Journal of Organizational Computing and Electronic Commerce, 28*(4), 315–333. doi:10.1080/10919392.2018.1517479

Ye, J., & Kulathunga, K. M. M. C. B. (2019). How does financial literacy promote sustainability in SMEs? A developing country perspective. *Sustainability, 11*(10), 2990. doi:10.3390u11102990

Yim, M. Y., Chu, S. C., & Sauer, P. L. (2017). Is augmented reality technology an effective tool for e-commerce? An interactivity and vividness perspective. *Journal of Interactive Marketing, 39*, 89–103. doi:10.1016/j.intmar.2017.04.001

Yi, Y., & Gong, T. (2013). Customer value co-creation behavior: Scale development and validation. *Journal of Business Research, 66*(9), 1279–1284. doi:10.1016/j.jbusres.2012.02.026

Yoo, B., & Donthu, N. (2001). Developing a scale to measure the perceived quality of an internet shopping site (SITEQUAL). *Quarterly Journal of Electronic Commerce, 2*, 31–47.

Yoon, H. J. (2018). Creating the mood for humour: Arousal level priming in humour advertising. *Journal of Consumer Marketing, 35*(5), 491–501. doi:10.1108/JCM-01-2017-2074

Yousafzai, S. Y., Foxall, G. R., & Pallister, J. G. (2010). Explaining internet banking behavior: Theory of reasoned action, theory of planned behavior, or technology acceptance model? *Journal of Applied Social Psychology, 40*(5), 1172–1202. doi:10.1111/j.1559-1816.2010.00615.x

Yovchevam Z., Buhalism D., & Gatzidis, C. (2013). Engineering Augmented Tourism Experiences. In Information and Communication Technologies in Tourism 2013. Springer.

Yuce, A., Arasli, H., Ozturen, A., & Daskin, M. (2020). Feeling the Service Product Closer: Triggering Visit Intention via Virtual Reality. *Sustainability, 12*(16), 6632. doi:10.3390u12166632

Yurova, Y., Rippé, C. B., Weisfeld-Spolter, S., Sussan, F., & Arndt, A. (2016). Not all adaptive selling to omni-consumers is influential: The moderating effect of product type. *Journal of Retailing and Consumer Services*. Advance online publication. doi:10.1016/j.jretconser.2016.01.009

Yu, S., Hudders, L., & Cauberghe, V. (2017). Targeting the luxury consumer: A vice or virtue? A cross-cultural comparison of the effectiveness of behaviorally targeted ads. *Journal of Fashion Marketing and Management, 21*(2), 187–205. doi:10.1108/JFMM-07-2016-0058

Zachos, G., Paraskevopoulou-Kollia, E.-A., & Anagnostopoulos, I. (2018). Social Media Use in Higher Education: A Review. *Education Sciences, 8*(4), 194. doi:10.3390/educsci8040194

Zahiri, S., El-Gohary, H., & Hussain, J. (2018). Internet Marketing Adoption by Iranian Distribution Industry: An Attempt to Understand the Reality. *International Journal of Customer Relationship Marketing and Management, 9*(2), 33–61. doi:10.4018/IJCRMM.2018040103

Zaki, A. M., El-Gohary, H., & Edwards, D. (2021). Understanding Ethical and Other SMEs Internationalisation Determinants and Its Impact on Business Performance: A Primary Attempt to Understand Malaysian SMEs Internationalisation. *International Journal of Customer Relationship Marketing and Management, 12*(1), 1–27. doi:10.4018/IJCRMM.2021010101

Zaki, M. (2019). Digital transformation: Harnessing digital technologies for the next generation of services. *Journal of Services Marketing, 33*(4), 429–435. Advance online publication. doi:10.1108/JSM-01-2019-0034

Zarrella, D. (2009). *The Social Media Marketing Book*. O'Reilly Media.

Zeithaml, V. A., Berry, L. L., & Parasuraman, A. (1996). The behavioral consequences of service quality. *Journal of Marketing, 60*(2), 31–46. doi:10.1177/002224299606000203

Zemla, M. (2016). Tourism destination: The networking approach. *Moravian Geographical Reports, 24*(4), 2–14. doi:10.1515/mgr-2016-0018

Zhang, J. J., Lichtenstein, Y., & Gander, J. (2015). Designing Scalable Business Models. Advances in Strategic Management. In *Business Models and Modelling*. Emerald Press.

Zhang, H., Lu, Y., Wang, B., & Wu, S. (2015). The impacts of technological environments and co-creation experiences on customer participation. *Information & Management, 52*(4), 468–482. doi:10.1016/j.im.2015.01.008

Zhang, J., Farris, P. W., Irvin, J. W., Kushwaha, T., Steenburgh, T. J., & Weitz, B. A. (2010). Crafting Integrated Multichannel Retailing Strategies. *Journal of Interactive Marketing, 24*(2), 168–180. doi:10.1016/j.intmar.2010.02.002

Zhao, P., Wu, J., Hua, Z., & Fang, S. (2019). Finding eWOM customers from customer reviews. *Industrial Management & Data Systems, 119*(1), 129–147. doi:10.1108/IMDS-09-2017-0418

Zheng, X., Cheung, C. M. K., Lee, M. K. O., & Liang, L. (2015). Building brand loyalty through user engagement in online brand communities in social networking sites. *Information Technology & People, 28*(1), 90–106. doi:10.1108/ITP-08-2013-0144

Zhu, G. (2019). Precision retail marketing strategy based on digital marketing model. *Science Journal of Business and Management, 7*(1), 33–37. doi:10.11648/j.sjbm.20190701.15

Zhu, K., Kraemer, K., & Xu, S. (2003). Electronic business adoption by European firms: A cross-country assessment of the facilitators and inhibitors. *European Journal of Information Systems, 12*(4), 251–268. doi:10.1057/palgrave.ejis.3000475

Zollo, L., Rialti, R., Ciappei, C., & Boccardi, A. (2018). *Bricolage and Social Entrepreneurship to Address Emergent Social Needs: A 'Deconstructionist' Perspective*. Academic Press.

Zou, T., & Jiang, B. (2020). Integration of primary and resale platforms. *JMR, Journal of Marketing Research, 57*(4), 659–676. doi:10.1177/0022243720917352

Zu, X., Diao, X., & Meng, Z. (2019). The impact of social media input intensity on firm performance: Evidence from Sina Weibo. *Physica A, 536*, 122556. doi:10.1016/j.physa.2019.122556

About the Contributors

Hatem El-Gohary is the Editor-in-Chief of the IJOM, Associate Editor of IJCRMM and the UK Director for the Institute for Research on Global Business (UK). He has more than 26 years of experience in academia, worked as the marketing director of a multinational company as well as a marketing consultant for some national and multinational companies. His research interest includes Electronic Marketing, Electronic Business, Electronic Commerce, Internet Marketing and SMEs. He has published several books, articles and book chapters and presented several research papers in a various world leading well-established international conferences. He holds a PhD, MSc, MRes, PGDip, BSc as well as PGCHE. He is also a Certified E-Marketer (CeM), an AABPP Fellow, HEA Fellow, CMI Fellow, CIM member (MCIM) and has a significant record of experience in voluntary work in Egypt and the UK. Prof El-Gohary won The ISBE2014 Best Paper Award (Creative Industries Entrepreneurship Track), The American Academy of Business and Public Policy Best Paper Award 2009, Routledge Best Paper Award 2007 and the Ideal Student for Cairo University Award 1992.

David Edwards is a Professor of Plant and Machinery Management, Birmingham City University and Visiting Professor at the University of Johannesburg. His research interests focus mainly upon the management of plant and machinery in business throughout industry. His work has been funded through engineering councils, government bodies (e.g. Health and Safety Executive, UK Home Office and Defence Logistic Organisation, UK Ministry of Defence) and an extensive network of industrial collaborations. He has published over 300 scientific research papers in leading international journals and numerous conference contributions and textbooks. He is a peer referee for 60 scientific journals and editorial board member of various journals and conference events.

* * *

Vandana Ahuja is a Professor of Marketing at the Amity Business School. She has over 21 years of experience across the corporate sector and academia and is the author of the book on Digital Marketing – published by Oxford University Press. She is the proud recipient of the ILDC-AMP women excellence award for her exemplary contribution to the domain of Management teaching. She has published several manuscripts in international and national journals and also serves on the editorial board of several international journals as an Associate Editor, Guest Editor and Review board member. She has organised and chaired several National and International Conferences and is part of several committees for MBA Program Advisory and Review, NBA and AACSB accreditation at Amity Business School. Her teaching and research interests are Digital Marketing, Advanced Sales Management and Marketing Analytics and she has taught in several Management Development programs organised for the corporate sector. She has supervised 8 doctoral theses in the domain of management and is also the co-convenor of the Doctoral Research Conclave organised annually at Amity Business School.

Shirin Alavi has about 14 years of experience across the academia and corporate sector. She is currently working as an Assistant Professor with Jaypee Institute of Information Technology, Noida. She has earlier worked with the Standard Chartered Bank and has work experience in the domain of CRM operations and International Business and Marketing. She has conducted research in the domains of customer relationship management, online communities, marketing, social media and mobile apps and has several years of research experience. She has published several manuscripts in international and national journals and also serves on the editorial review board of international journals. She has completed one PhD guidance and is guiding PhD students in the domain of digital marketing, green marketing and consumer behaviour. She is member of NBA and NAAC accreditation committee of the institute.

Tooba Ali Akbar is a marketing scholar at the College of Business & Economics, Qatar University. She holds an MSc in Marketing. Her research interests include Marketing, Social Media, and Management.

Cesare Amatulli is Associate Professor of Marketing at the University of Bari, Italy. He has been Visiting Professor at LUISS University, Italy, and Visiting Researcher at the Ross School of Business, USA, and at the University of Hertfordshire, UK. He studies consumer behavior and most of his ongoing research projects investigate luxury consumption, sustainability and luxury tourism. He has published several articles in major international scholarly journals such as the Journal of Consumer Research, International Journal of Research in Marketing, Journal of Business Research and Psychology & Marketing.

Nedra Bahri-Ammari is an assistant professor of Marketing and Management at the IHEC of Carthage, Tunisia. She is member of the LARIME laboratory. She obtained her BS and Ph.D. Degrees from the Higher Institute of Management of Tunis. Dr. Bahri's researches include: business-to-customer and business-to-business marketing, customer relationships management (CRM), customer satisfaction, loyalty, retention, technology's implementation, firm profitability, enterprise Resource Planning (ERP) and Supply Chain Management. Her publications have appeared among, in Journal of Research in Marketing and Entrepreneurialship, International Journal of Engineering Science and Innovative Technology, Journal of Global Technology Management, Journal of Tourism Challenges and Trends Journal of Hospitality and Tourism Technology.

Roberson Bolzan graduated in Executive Secretariat, post graduated in Business Planning and Management and Master in Innovation Economics and Entrepreneurship.

Francesca Capo got a PhD in Management at Luiss Guido Carli University and has been visiting scholar at ESSEC Business School (France), Catolica Business School (Portugal) and Ross School of Business (Michigan, US). Among her main research interests are institutional change, institutional logics, hybrid organizations and social enterprises.

Giuseppe Colella is a PhD candidate of marketing and management at the University of Bari "Aldo Moro", Italy. He has been Ph.D Visiting Scholar at Universidad de Castilla-La Mancha, Spain, and Ph.D research fellow at the CRITEO, Italy. He has published several articles in any international scholarly journals such as Journal of Consumer Marketing, International Journal of Marketing Studies, and Journal of Management and Sustainability.

Sushmita Dhar is a postgraduate in Economics from University of Kashmir and an aspiring researcher.

Arzu Eren Şenaras is working as Associate Professor at Department of Econometrics in Bursa Uludağ University.

Silvia Fernandes is Assistant Professor at the Faculty of Economics of the University of Algarve. She holds a PhD from this university and is member of Cinturs (Research Centre for Tourism, Sustainability and Well-being). She lectures Information Technology and Innovation Economics in undergraduate and master courses. She has several publications in books and journals. Also, communications in national/international conferences in themes such as: information systems, innovation, emergent technologies, smart tourism, etc.

Emrah Gülmez graduated from Anadolu University, Department of Advertising and Public Relations, in 2008. In 2009, he started to work as a Research Assistant in Anadolu University, Department of Advertising and Public Relations, and is still working there as an Assistant Professor. He received his MS in 2011 and Ph.D. in 2017 in Public Relations and Advertising from Anadolu University. He writes and presents widely on issues of advertising strategies, creativity in advertising, and brand communication and teaches Creativity in Advertising, Designing Advertising Campaign, Advertising Copywriting Practices, Digital Advertising Copywriting, and Brand Communication Management.

Daniel Herman is a Lecturer at Polytechnic of Medjimurje in Cakovec, Croatia, and an experienced marketing enthusiast with an interest in Advertising, Strategic branding of innovative products and services, Tourism Marketing, Social Media Marketing, and Market Research.

Iulia Iuga holds a PhD in Finance (2002) from Babeş-Bolyai University from Cluj Napoca, Romania, and B.S. in Marketing (1997) from Bucharest Academy of Economic Studies, Romania. She has been working in the Finance-Accounting Department at "1 Decembrie 1918" University of Alba Iulia since 1999 and she is currently Assoc. professor PH.D. She teaches banking and investment disciplines, such as: Financial-banking management; Risk management and measuring bank performance; Banking techniques and operations; Investment evaluation and financing; Entity financing and investment management; Monetary economy and Financial-banking marketing. Her publications are found in the following fields of science: banking, investment and marketing and has written over 14 books and over 150 articles. She is member of editorial boards of specialized publications. She is ARACIS expert (The Romanian Agency for Quality Assurance in Higher Education) - Finance field.

Andrijana Kos Kavran holds a PhD in Marketing from January 2020. She is a Senior Lecturer at Polytechnic of Medjimurje in Cakovec and course holder of Basics of Marketing, Tourism Marketing, Sports Marketing, Market Research, Digital Marketing and Advertising and Tourism Destination Promotion. Her area of interest include the use of technology in marketing, as well as marketing in IT.

Paula Martins is Assistant Professor of the Electronics and Computers Engineering Department of Faculty of Sciences and Technology, University of Algarve, and is member of Cinturs (Research Centre for Tourism, Sustainability and Well-being). She has a PhD in Computer Science and Engineering from Instituto Superior Técnico da Universidade Técnica de Lisboa (IST/ULT). Her research interests are Software Process Improvement, Software Development Processes, Domain-Specific Languages, Modelling Languages and Business Process Modelling.

Volkan Polat is an Assistant Professor of Marketing at Business Administration Department, Yalova University, Turkey. He received his B.A. degree in economics from Ataturk University. He obtained his Master of Science degree in strategy science (technology and innovation management) from Gebze Institute of Technology, Turkey. He completed his Ph.D. degree in business administration from Gebze Technical University, Turkey. Previously, he served as marketing specialist and marketing manager in industry. He has published works in prestigious academic journals and conferences. His research interests include marketing strategies, brand management, technology and innovation management, new product development, and team management.

Antonius Raghubansie is Director of Learning Services which includes the digital student offer in India for the British Council. He has a background in UK HE having previously worked for over 12+ years in different academic and leadership roles in UK universities.

N. Raghavendra Rao is an Advisor to FINAIT Consultancy Services India. He has a doctorate in the area of Finance. He has a rare distinction of having experience in the combined areas of Information Technology and Finance.

Chandrani Samaradivakara is a UK university academic and completing her PhD at Lancaster, with special interest in services marketing.

Mustafa Şehirli graduated from Istanbul Technical University in 1994 as a Management Engineer. After working in different positions in the private sector for many years, he received the title of Ph.D. from Maltepe University in 2016. He works especially on marketing and human resources management. His specific issues are relationship-based issues such as customer experience, WOM, loyalty, and trust.

Hayrettin Kemal Sezen is working as Professor at Altınbaş University.

Emiliano Sola is an MBA & PhD with strong Engineering background and experience in multiple sectors: Avio & Aerospace, Automotive, Utilities. Passionate about strategic management, innovation and finance, he actively attended several international conferences on material sciences, construction and automotive and wrote several publictions with an overall of +150 citations. Emiliano participated and led many international projects on as professional. As well, he spent about 6 years in Germany and holds two international degrees.

Ali Yuce was born and grew up in Turkey. After working independently for his business, he changed his life dramatically and radically to follow his passion for academia. After receiving his Bachelor's degree from DePaul University, he obtained his Master's and Doctoral Degrees from Eastern Mediterranean

University. He has published two articles and several congress papers within the past several years. He also recently completed the book chapters about technology, tourism, and marketing. He is a lifelong learner who loves conveying every bit of knowledge that he learns for others.

Index

E

F

G

H

I

L

M

N

O

P

Q

R

S

T

U

V

Y

www.ingramcontent.com/pod-product-compliance
Lightning Source LLC
LaVergne TN
LVHW060353300926
849162LV00006B/1257